The Neoliberal Era

The Neoliberal Era

Alfonso Zurita Borbón

BLOOMSBURY ACADEMIC
NEW YORK • LONDON • OXFORD • NEW DELHI • SYDNEY

BLOOMSBURY ACADEMIC
Bloomsbury Publishing Inc, 1359 Broadway, New York, NY 10018, USA
Bloomsbury Publishing Plc, 50 Bedford Square, London, WC1B 3DP, UK
Bloomsbury Publishing Ireland, 29 Earlsfort Terrace, Dublin 2, D02 AY28, Ireland

First published in the United States of America 2026

Cover design by Adriana Brioso
Cover image: © Ed Bock/Getty

Library of Congress Cataloging-in-Publication Data

ISBN: HB: 979-8-216-38954-5
PB: 979-8-216-38955-2
ePDF: 979-8-216-38956-9
eBook: 979-8-216-38957-6

Typeset by Integra Software Services Pvt. Ltd.

Contents

Figure

Tables

Preface

Writing a book is always a hard process where the author confronts himself or herself to the unknown. At the start, the book is a sort of shaded idea the author has in his or her mind to comply with a kind of intellectual restlessness he or she is somehow forced to resolve. Frequently, the author sees the world in a particular manner based on the knowledge and experience she or he has accrued during her or his lifetime; and therefore, there is always something that moves her or his spirit to start working on a blank sheet. A painful process full of comings and goings that, during months, if not years, the author is constantly fighting to end his or her efforts in a bunch of written pages and perhaps, when done, he or she would say: Phew! I got it finally. Always doubting as to whether she or he should retrace her or his steps and redo much of the path followed.

When the subject relates to economics the problem is normally harder. Economics is an elusive science, sometimes close to fiction and some others to non-fiction. This is because the first issue in dealing with economics falls into its own definition. To this respect, avoiding beating around the bush, it would be worth to raise the definition of economics given by Lionel Robbins, who was very keen in connecting economics to human behaviour. '*Economics is the science that studies human behaviour as a relationship between limited resources and unlimited wants which have alternative uses*',[1] he said. Economics is thus concerned, on the one side, with the disposal of scarce goods; otherwise '*it would not be problems if resources were unlimited and, therefore, there would not be* «economic goods» *and there would hardly be any need for a study of economics or* «economizing»';[2] and on the other, '*economics cannot be dissociated from ethics*', as Robbins refers quoting Ralph Georges Hawtrey.[3]

Economics is a permanent matter of discussion, particularly because in our modern times it usually focuses on statistics, keeping it far from its fundamental sense, which should be, according to Lionel Robbins' opinion, the study of human behaviour in the frame of the scarcity of resources and its alternative uses in order to satisfy human necessities. Economics is undoubtedly a social science, '*whose final subject of study should not only be how to manage the GDP, deal with monetary policies, or keep inflation down, but also how to first create and then distribute wealth among people in the best*

1 ROBBINS, L. *An Essay on the Nature and Significance of Economic Science*, pg 15. Robbin's Essay can be reached freely from Misses Institute at: https://cdn.mises.org/Essay%20on%20the%20Nature%20and%20Significance%20of%20Economic%20Science_2.pdf

2 SAMUELSON, P. A. *Economics*, pg 16.

3 ROBBINS, L. *An Essay on the Nature and Significance of Economic Science*, pg 132.

way possible'.[4] Subsequently, people must be in the centre of the economy, either in the kernel of production and/or in the kernel of consumption. For the needs every person has are twofold: '*either she or he tries to increase her or his standard of leaving, or she or he looks to increase her or his level of comfort*.'[5] An idea concisely expressed by Arthur Cecil Pigou in his book on the economics of welfare when just at the beginning, in the first chapter, he includes a paragraph entitled '*The main motive of economic study is to help social improvement*.'[6] A synthesis of what should be the main objective of the political economy; that is, improving social wealth by keeping a wealthy state; because a poor state will sooner or later impoverish people. Something Pigou points out in the preface of his above-mentioned book: '*I would add one word for any student beginning economic study who may be discouraged by the severity of the effort which the study, as he will find it exemplified here, seems to require of him. The complicated analyses which economists endeavor to carry through are not mere gymnastic. They are instruments for the bettering of human life*.'[7] To conclude in the same paragraph: '*To search for it is the task, to find it, perhaps, the prize, which the* «dismal science of political economy» *offers to those who face its discipline*.'[8] Something Adam Smith pointed out many years before by saying: '*[P]olitical economy, considered as a branch of a statesman or legislator, proposes two distinct objects; first, to provide a plentiful revenue or subsistence for the people, or, more properly, to enable them to provide such a revenue or subsistence for themselves; and, secondly, to supply the state or commonwealth with a revenue sufficient for the public services. It proposes to enrich both the people and the sovereign*.'[9]

This is the context of Alfonso Zurita's new book, which we are about to sail: political economy and its influence over people and society. In '*The Neoliberal Era*', Zurita deeply discusses the two main economic philosophies of our time: '*Ordoliberalism*' and '*Neoliberalism*'. A discourse that helps to understand most of the issues that have occurred during the last century. For example: how economic crises arose or how those crises prompted major political changes at the beginning of the twenty-first century with the emergence of populism as a new political stance to divide society by putting the people against the so-called economic elites. In Zurita's own words: '*The book's main theoretical purpose is to shed new light onto when, why and how the new liberalism and its two main currents – ordoliberalism and neoliberalism – emerged and onto the key role they both played in the construct of the neoliberal thought collective*.'

4 OLIER, E. *Welfare Economics, Welfare State and the Real Economy.* AESTIMATIO, The IEB International Journal of Finance, pgs 160–83. https://www.ieb.es/ww2017/wp-content/uploads/2014/07/75.pdf
5 Ibid.
6 PIGOU, A. C. *The Economics of Welfare.* MACMILLAN & CO LIMITED. London. 1920. Analytical Table of Contents. pg IX.
7 Ibid. pg VII.
8 Ibid.
9 SIMTH, A. *La riqueza de las naciones. Libro IV. De los sistemas de economía política,* pg 539. (translated into English by E. Olier).

There is no need to go back hundreds of years to comment on how economic liberalism came into being. Liberalism, whether it is taken in its oldest fashion or in the way it is understood today, has always pitted private interests against public interests. It was, however, by the end of the eighteenth century, when Adam Smith connected liberalism to free trade, paving the way to Joseph Schumpeter at the beginning of the 1940s to discuss liberalism in the context of socialism, capitalism and democracy, which was nothing but discussing the inability of Marxism to generate economic wealth compared to the permanent continuity of capitalism, which, according to Schumpeter, enjoys a sort of '*creative destruction*' mechanism which helps it to rise from its ashes after an economic recession. For Schumpeter, '*free trade was one of the main planks in the platform of English liberalism*'.[10] Additionally: '*Marx was far too good an economist not to see what boon, in the circumstances of that time*'.[11] And finally: '*Had Marx been interested in those items for their own sake, he would have had no alternative but to coalesce with the radical wing of bourgeois liberalism*'.[12]

Coincidental with the Great Depression, Germany looked for harmonizing politics and economics from the top, and thus, ordoliberal theories were put into practice. It was a sort of state interventionism, in order to safeguard against and get rid of whatever economic disorders stemmed from private activities. Disorders, which could also influence social stability. It was still a decision to hamper any type of *laissez-faire* initiative. A kind of surveillance over markets' and people's activities to have them somehow under control. Meanwhile and at the same time, neoliberalism started emerging throughout Europe. However, although neoliberalism wanted likewise to intervene the economy by redefining the efficiency of markets, it also promoted people's freedom through the protection of their economic activities in the largest possible way.

Alfonso Zurita's seminal book on the above subjects provides a full compendium to understand the past, present and future of the theory and practice of those two economic currents since the end of the First World War. To do this, the author has divided his work into two large parts. The first theoretical one is devoted to discussing how the ordoliberal and neoliberal movements have constructed the economic thinking of our days. To overcome its difficulty, all school of economic thoughts are considered and its main economists are presented. Differences between the role of both economic movements are deeply discussed, including their role in shaping markets and regulatory structures. Contradictions and conflicts are investigated too. Part One provides a real demonstration of the lucid and deep knowledge Alfonso Zurita has on the political economy of our time.

Even though the first part could be a book in itself, the author moves away in Part Two to present a complete discussion on how ordoliberalism and neoliberalism

[10] SCHUMPETER, J. A. *Capitalism, Socialism & Democracy*, pg 317.
[11] Ibid.
[12] Ibid, pg 318.

have influenced the political economy of today's world. An impressive endeavour, undertaken in order to demonstrate how the political economy based on these two philosophies actually works in practice. The reader is then introduced to the actual processes and decisions taken by European and US governments that led to managing the economy based on free-market fundamentals, with special attention to some of the key people involved: Margaret Thatcher and Ronald Reagan in the 1980s, and Bill Clinton and Tony Blair in the 1990s. Additionally, he also reflects upon the influence both economic currents have always had across time in giving shape and form to the present European Union.

Likewise, and based on Zurita's profound knowledge on the Latin American phenomenon, he includes into his long journey three chapters on neoliberalism there, which provide a very relevant contribution to the understanding of the neoliberal reality of this important region.

The author equally delivers a deep reflection on how Europe has, through its post-crisis financial regulatory framework, revived ordoliberalism, thereby stabilizing its financial sector and making its banking sector more resilient. The 'ordoliberalisation of Europe', as it is called, is likewise witnsessing how ordoliberalism and neoliberalism are interacting once again extremely positively, just like they did during their early years together, invigorating the process of construction of neoliberal thought.

Lastly, Zurita offers a very innovative, deep evaluation and assessment of the present and future of the 'Neoliberal Era' that still prevails. Although neoliberalism remains deeply imbued in the institutional frameworks that promote its theory and practice, as well as in the multilateral economic structures that they support and assist, 'Neonationalism' has severely shifted and displaced the neoliberal world order, as well as badly weakening and debilitating its structure. The author subsequently produces a very interesting and profound critique of 'Neoliberal/Free-Market/Stakeholder Capitalism' and describes some of the underlying revised capitalist reformulations and financial models that are being pressed forward, like most particularly, Progressive Capitalism, Techno-Feudal Oligopolistic Capitalism and Modern Monetary Theory. Zurita concludes with a description of some of the inherent flaws of the present-day international financial-monetary system that are similarly making it drift towards a 'Global Liquidity Trap', which will, in turn, most probably lead the entire system to a new big financial crisis or as already denominated, 'Great Stagnation'.

Finally, in his Conclusion Zurita provides a very interesting glimpse into the on-going economic game-changing *'Industrial Revolution 4.0'* and the dawning of the *'Digital Age'*. As Zurita outlines and points out, there are many strong signals projecting that, paradoxically, our current era of Hayekian free markets and Friedmanian financial monetarism will be, in a very near future, entirely overshadowed by tomorrow's *'Digital Age'*, *'Decentralised Finance (DeFi)'*, *'Neobanks'* and *'Cryptocurrencies'*.

All in all, *The Neoliberal Era* by Alfonso Zurita represents a very important landmark in the study of the political economy, which we are still living in. A book that will undoubtedly represent a useful reference in the economic arena for the years to come.

Professor Eduardo Olier, PhD
President, Choiseul Institute, Spain and Latin American Countries
July 2025

Acknowledgements

The Neoliberal Era comes about at an extremely interesting point in time, where we find ourselves caught in the middle of a very delicate economic standstill, within which we are facing the biggest economic and financial turning point ever recorded in economic history. Regardless of the fact that our present economic and financial reality still prevails, for some time now a huge phenomenon has been manifesting itself in the form of yet another but highly critical historical economic crossroads or game-changing phase, which is altogether conveying a much vaster and limitless economic and financial virtual reality, as well as dawning a whole new 'Digital Age'.

Although we can still consider ourselves to be living in the 'neoliberal era' of Hayekian free markets, Friedmanian monetarism and stakeholder capitalism, it is nonetheless an era which is wading being progressively displaced by countering progressive thought, as well as fading, being gradually eclipsed by the dawning of the 'Digital Age'. Wedged in the middle of such a shifting economic reality and historical game-changing threshold, this book will prove very helpful for explaining and comprehending an economic era that still engulfs us, but which will soon unfortunately and inevitably become part of a very distant, irrelevant and obsolete past.

The overall elaboration of *The Neoliberal Era* has been made possible thanks to and in virtue of the many different institutions, scholars, academics and other associated peers and people, who at one stage or another have helped me immensely with it and to who I will be eternally grateful. *The Neoliberal Era* represents my seventh academic book and fourth book in economics, but notwithstanding, it is by far my most complete one as it includes and contains at the same time both my first scientific publications in the field of economics and parts of my latest publications, which have become increasingly more focused on neoliberalism, be they through either scientific publications or academic books.

The gradual intellectual build-up for the book has been possible thanks to the academic formation and professional training that I have received throughout my life from different institutions, which have formed me intellectually and trained me vocationally. Thus and therefore, I would like to, in the first place and most especially, thank the following: the University of Sussex, which induced my intellectual awakening; the Johns Hopkins University – School of Advanced International Studies (SAIS) – which induced my scientific awakening; the European Commission (EC); the Inter-American Development Bank (IDB); the United Nations – UNESCO Organization; the Spanish Ministry of Foreign Affairs and Cooperation; the BBVA Foundation and the Villarmir Group.

Correspondingly and in relation to the more specific groundwork for the book, I would like to above all express my deepest respect, admiration and gratefulness to the many related academics and their established scientific knowledge in the field, who have not just contributed immensely to my endeavour, but who have likewise greatly influenced the construct of my own individual economic thought.

As regards the actual writing of the book, I would like to most especially express my deepest appreciation and gratitude to various outstanding institutions, scholars and experts, without whose support I would not have been able to advance so much with the book, let alone complete it. I will be forever grateful to the following for their invaluable help, guidance, recommendations, contributions and inputs: Emeritus Chair in Latin American Studies and dear friend, Riordan Roett, for being my academic mentor in the United States, for having taught me so much about neoliberalism in Latin America and for motivating me to thrive forwards so much academically; Chair in International Law and Chair J. Monnet ad personam in EU Law and dear friend, Carlos Moreiro, for being my academic mentor in Spain and for helping me so much in channelling my academic potential in the right direction; the Elcano Royal Institute's Director Charles Powell and Senior Analyst Miguel Otero, for providing me with so much ever-patient assistance and succour in structuring the book, but most especially, for stimulating me so much in order to break through the mental barriers that ultimately allowed me to access both new frontiers of knowledge and higher states of economic consciousness. Lastly and most exceptionally, president of the Choiseul Institute and dear friend, Eduardo Olier, for counting with so many of my scientific contributions for so many interesting projects, but most particularly, for personally involving himself so kind-heartedly and profoundly in directing and reviewing the actual writing of the book.

In departure, I would like to extend my most profound and heartfelt gratitude to all my elder family relatives, who throughout my life have always shown me the way upwards and forwards, enlightening me so much with their universal minds, together with their balanced wisdom. From a very young age, they all imbued in me their extremely profound economic culture, based on a very rational revolving/collaborative (inter-family) economic thinking. Through those early beginnings, I gradually and progressively shaped and formed my present-day personal economic thinking, which is 'neo-ordoliberal' but with 'big eyes on the Digital Age'. I finally and most wholeheartedly thank my beloved parents, Margarita and Carlos, for the beautiful life and unconditional love they have gifted me with, for providing me with the countless possibilities and means to achieve in life what I have done so far and for enlightening me so much in order to perceive the world the way I do.

*****

Introduction

Neoliberal Orthodoxy at a Crossroads

Our economic epoch has unfortunately turned out to be extremely turbulent. We find ourselves cloaked by a very rarefied economic atmosphere, wherein both uncertainty and unpredictability have become the defining nuances of our time holding our economic future firmly still. The various economic crises, which have shaken the world in recent decades, have had disastrous results. Although the world had begun to recover after the 2007–15 Global Financial Crisis, it was once again bogged down and badly affected by the direct and indirect results of the COVID-19 Crisis or Coronavirus, which once again generated a massive slowdown in the world economic, productive and commercial activity. The whole world succumbed to the COVID-19 virus, which emerged as a new silent and aggressive global threat, fatally affecting millions of people and generating far worse socioeconomic consequences than those suffered by the Great Depression or the more recent Great Recession.[1] Besides the enormous distress caused by the global economic setback, it has, above all, reopened old wounds around the neoliberal paradigm and orthodoxy that have prevailed since the 1980s.

Although the economic recovery from the COVID-19 Crisis took place much quicker than the one from the two previous major global crises, the consequences suffered by the world economy have changed the economic landscape in such an irreversible way that nothing will ever be the same. With the transport, tourism, construction and education sectors, having been the most affected, dragging billions in losses, at the same time, innumerable large industries and companies, together with thousands of small and medium-sized enterprises (SMEs), micro-enterprises and entrepreneurs, have likewise perished.[2]

In the midst of such economic disarray and amongst many loud voices of a *'great financial re-tuning'*,[3] the managing director of the International Monetary Fund (IMF),

1 Ministerio de Defensa. Instituto Español de Estudios Estratégicos. Cuadernos de Estrategia 204. *La Dualidad Económica Estados Unidos y China en el Siglo XXI.* ZURITA, A. *Características Principales y Peculiaridades de la Economía China,* pgs 45–110.

2 Ibid.

3 Bitcoin.com. REDMAN, J. *The Great Financial Reset: IMF Managing Director Calls for a 'New Bretton Woods Moment'.* https://news.bitcoin.com/the-great-financial-reset-imf-managing-director-calls-for-a-new-bretton-woods-moment/

Kristalina Georgieva, foresees the advent of a *'huge change'*,[4] having even suggested that it would be a good time for a *'new Bretton Woods'*.[5] Similarly, the Deutsche Bank believes that the current *'Era of Disorder'* will in turn generate *'a new economic "super-cycle"'*.[6] With the first having stressed that *'today's economic difficulties are the same as the difficulties the world faced at the end of World War II'*,[7] the second has warned that the current phase that the world is going through has *'accelerated a change of stage in the economy, which will be characterized by a drastic revision in the main economic trends that have guided globalization in recent times'*.[8]

The Deutsche Bank has gone as far as observing that *'the most recent super-cycle, the second era of globalization (1980–2020) started slowly and has gradually worn off over the last half decade. However, the end of this era has been hastened by the COVID-19 and when we look in the rear-view mirror in the years to come, we may see 2020 as the beginning of a new era'*.[9]

The threshold of economic chaos and disorder equally revived in a very exacerbated way many thorny questions that were already under a lot of scrutiny. Since some years ago, some very prickly issues, such as the great loss of confidence in and the huge collective doubt surrounding the predominating neoliberal paradigm and orthodoxy, have been generating myriad fundamental changes across the economic landscape.

Since the 1980s, the 'Neoliberal World Order' (NLWO), established throughout the Western Hemisphere and many other parts of the world, has been and still is structured around the institutional frameworks that uphold and maintain the neoliberal paradigm and orthodoxy, such as international financial institutions and international and regional organizations, like the International Monetary Fund (IMF), the World Bank (WB), the Organization of American States (OAS), the Inter-American Development Bank (IADB) or the Central American Bank for Economic Integration (CABEI). Likewise and in turn, the NLWO's institutional frameworks represent and assist different economic multilateral structures, such as economic blocs like Latin America (LA) and the European Union (EU). The NLWO envelops two main neoliberal scenarios. The first scenario surrounds the globalized free market economy, and the second scenario covers the international financial monetary system (IFMS).

Although the NLWO is still-standing and continues to prevail, both the neoliberal paradigm and orthodoxy have, nonetheless, been fundamentally shifted and displaced

[4] Ibid.
[5] Ibid.
[6] Emprendedores. ADELANTADO, D.S. *La 'Era del Desorden': Así sera el nuevo 'super-ciclo económico' que se avecina.* https://www.emprendedores.es/la-solucion-post-covid/era-del-desorden/
[7] Bitcoin.com. REDMAN, J. *The Great Financial Reset: IMF Managing Director Calls for a 'New Bretton Woods Moment'.* https://news.bitcoin.com/the-great-financial-reset-imf-managing-director-calls-for-a-new-bretton-woods-moment/
[8] Emprendedores. ADELANTADO, D.S. *La 'Era del Desorden': Así sera el nuevo 'super-ciclo económico' que se avecina.* https://www.emprendedores.es/la-solucion-post-covid/era-del-desorden/
[9] Ibid.

by new progressive thought and practice, which fiercely opposes contemporary economic and financial models. The structure of the NLWO is being increasingly destabilized and weakened by both the clash between the old and new economic and financial models, as well as by flaws inherent to the financial monetary system. The two neoliberal scenarios clearly reflect that whereas the intellectual collapse of neoliberalism has produced an irreversible shift and displacement of neoliberal thought and practice, the IFMS is also on the verge of being monetarily overridden. It can be asserted that the direction both scenarios end up taking will largely determine the way in which our economic future will unfold.

The first neoliberal scenario shrouds the on-going intense and virulent clash between the old and still standing economic and financial models and the new countering models threatening to debunk them. On one hand, the free market economic model, which since the 1980s has been churning the machinery of the globalized free market economy, has been shifted and displaced by the revival of and growing preference for mercantilist, protectionist-isolationist economic models in key world neoliberal epicentres, such as North and South America and Europe. On the other hand, but to a lesser extent, the financial monetary model mechanizing the international financial system, has also experienced a displacement by new progressive financial models in Japan, with its influence likewise progressively growing in the United States and Europe. Similarly, at the underlying academic sector, stakeholder capitalism is equally being increasingly challenged and contested by new revised forms of capitalism. Most recently, President Trump's techno-feudal and oligopolistic capitalism has also burst into the scene with a lot of thrust.

Notwithstanding, ever since the 2007–15 global financial crisis exposed the regulation defects of neoliberalism, the model has undergone numerous international readjustments, most especially in the Eurozone, which however project continuity along the same neoliberal dynamics. Both neoliberal thought and practice are so deeply imbued within institutional frameworks and economic multilateral structures that the complete dismantling of the rigid neoliberal architecture, as well as of its dense infrastructure, would prove to be a very long-winding and complicated task.

However and despite the prevalence of the NLWO, during recent years, its structure has, nonetheless, been seriously destabilized and weakened by the growing expansion of mercantilist, protectionist-isolationist models, such as most significantly, 'Neo-Nationalism' or 'New Nationalism'. In the United States, where neonationalism is expressed in its freest and wildest form, President Trump's first Presidential mandate from 2017 to 2021 and its protectionist-isolationist stance produced very impressive internal results, with some surprisingly high economic indicators in numerous areas, although his 'Fair Trade vs. Free Trade' strategy also had very negative repercussions on many other political, economic and military issues. For example, the withdrawal of the United States from the global trading system and many other major trade pacts, such as the Trans-Pacific Partnership (TPP), the twelve-nation trade pact that accounts for 40 per cent of world trade, left the structure of the globalized free market economy severely dismembered. Since the beginning of his second Presidential mandate in January 2025, President Trump has reemerged but with a much more reinvigorated, twisted and aggressive, global neonationalist agenda, which includes and entails far more wide-spanning and deep-reaching, long-term neonational plans and objectives. Following the same trend generated by his first mandate, President Trump has so far and this time round continued dismembering the structure of the globalized free market economy much more by withdrawing from the Paris Climate Agreement; opting out of the World Health Organization and the UN Human Rights Council; discontinuing the funding of the UN Agency for Palestinian Refugees (UNRWA); as well as by reviewing US membership to all intergovernmental organizations, which could lead to the end of the country's participation in the WB and the IMF. Going even further, President Trump has also threatened with eliminating US contributions to the common funding of the UN and the North Atlantic Treaty Organization (NATO), as well as with shuttering dozens of American Embassies and Consulates all over the world.[10]

In a similar way but to a lesser degree, the financial monetary model has also been shifted and displaced by the up and rising, 'Modern Monetary Theory' (MMT), which is being promoted in many ways by President Trump, who has been hailed as the *'most MMT-like-President ever elected'*.[11] MMT has been yielding impressive results in Japan, as well as gaining more influencing ground across the international landscape. Correspondingly, at the underlying academic sector, the searing criticism surrounding stakeholder capitalism has equally spawned a strong outpour of revised capitalist counter-models, such as Joseph Stiglitz's 'Progressive Capitalism', as well as others, which are also acquiring more intellectual and practical weight and recognition, like President Trump's 'Techno-Feudal and Oligopolistic Capitalism'.

The second neoliberal scenario unfortunately veils more bad omens for the international financial-monetary system (IFMS). The IFMS is being increasingly constrained by deep-rooted defects, which are projecting very negative forecasts for the future of the global economy. The system has developed several deep flaws at its core, which could be leading the global economy into yet another major global financial crisis. The orthodoxy of monetary policy is being threatened by schisms within the system itself, which regrettably project risks of a 'Global Liquidity Trap', which would in turn generate an already denominated 'Great Stagnation'.

Such destabilizing events taking place around and within the NLWO have severely debilitated the structure of the globalized free market economy. However and regardless

[10] European Council on Foreign Relations (ECFR). *MAGA Goes Global: Trump's Plan for Europe*, pgs 15–16. https://ecfr.eu/publication/maga-goes-global-trumps-plan-for-europe/

[11] MEDIUM. *TRUMP: The First MMT President*. https://medium.com/@kevin_640/trump-the-first-mmt-president-9df44bd0784d

of such an ever-changing NLWO and its two neoliberal scenarios, it is paradoxically, altogether gradually becoming increasingly irrelevant vis-à-vis another huge historical economic turning point or game-changing phase, which has for some time now been manifesting itself. Our current economic situation is witnessing how much more so every day, the financial-monetary economy is being steadfastly overridden by the digital-virtual economy, with its ever-growing vast base of attractive crypto currencies, as well as progressively replaced by the new services and goods provided by a whole new virtual reality and metaverse. Such a massive turning point is conferring a totally different economic and financial digital-virtual nature, which is altogether dawning a whole new 'Digital Age'.

Economic history is repeating itself in much the same way as events have unfolded ever since the first industrial revolutions. Back then, the rural-agricultural economy was overtaken by the industrial-productive economy, and subsequently, during the 1980s, the latter industrial-productive economy was in turn replaced by the financial-monetary economy. Today, the on-going 'Fourth Industrial Revolution' or 'Industrial Revolution 4.0', which we are immersed in, is gradually and progressively leading to a total and complete substitution of the current type of financial-monetary economy, for another brand new, uncharted type of digital-virtual economy.[12]

Klaus Schwab, founder and executive president of the World Economic Forum, who in 2015 coined the term 'Industrial Revolution 4.0', has expressed that '*the First Industrial Revolution used water and steam power to mechanize production. The Second used electric power to create mass production. The Third used electronics and information technology to automate production. Now a Fourth Industrial Revolution is building on the Third, the digital revolution that has been occurring since the middle of the last century. It is characterized by a fusion of technologies that is blurring the lines between the physical, digital, and biological spheres*'.[13]

The Neoliberal Juggernaut

The intellectual origins and ideological roots of neoliberalism trace back to the 1920s–30s Europe, when the atmosphere of extreme discontent with the predominating economic ideology, – 'classical liberalism and laissez-faire' – generated an intense academic revolution beseeching its re-formulation, which eventually spawned two 'new liberal' economic currents, 'ordoliberalism' and 'neoliberalism'.

Following the First World War and throughout the 1920s and 1930s, Europe suffered a long period of acute socioeconomic depression, which induced a serious

[12] World Economic Forum. Agenda. SCHWAB, K. *The Fourth Industrial Revolution: What It Means, How to Respond*. https://www.weforum.org/agenda/2016/01/the-fourth-industrial-revolution-what-it-means-and-how-to-respond/

[13] Ibid.

reconsideration of the prevailing economic ideology, 'classical liberalism and laissez faire'. The generalized, post-First World War European economic and social hardship, together with the poverty and despair caused by, amongst other exacerbating factors, War Reparations, the Weimar Republic and the Great Depression, clearly exposed the imperfections and flaws of classical liberalism and laissez-faire. Thus, the decaying context triggered a profound academic revolution amongst leading liberal academics, which fervently searched for a new type of economic current, 'Third Way' or in-between, classical liberalism and laissez-faire.

The period's intellectual brainstorming saw the formation and evolution of a whole 'new liberal' way of thinking, which engendered and gave birth to two different 'new liberal' currents: 'Ordoliberalism' and 'Neoliberalism'. During the 1930s, whereas ordoliberalism appeared first in Germany as a socioeconomic response to the Weimar Republic, neoliberalism emerged soon after in Europe as the main theoretical counter-reaction to Keynesianism and collectivism. Especially throughout the post-Second World War period, the two currents inextricably connected West Germany's and West Europe's economic and social development and eventually provided the basis for the integration of the EU. While Ordoliberalism formed the economic basis of the post-Second World War, W. German social market economy, neoliberalism provided the economic bedrock for the European economic and monetary union.

Although from 1945 up to 1980 the Keynesian-designed Bretton Woods system of fixed exchange rates and embedded liberalism prevailed in practice, throughout the same decades, however, both ordoliberalism and neoliberalism shared a very intricate and contributory relationship towards the process of construction of neoliberal thought, which was carried out at the same time at the academic level. A process, which after many swerves from its original trajectory, eventually gave shape and form to the present-day neoliberal composition. During the same period, both currents also waged war together in the new liberal, ideological counter-revolution, which took place against Keynesianism, embedded liberalism and collectivism. By the early 1980s, Keynesian economics and the Bretton Woods system ultimately lost the battle against the neoliberal counter-revolution, which saw the establishment of the free market economy, as well as of the international financial-monetary system of flexible exchange rates. Since then, the Bretton Woods institutions – the International Monetary Fund (IMF) and the World Bank (WB) – which were created to uphold, supervise and maintain the Bretton Woods system of fixed exchange rates, ended likewise becoming the supervisors of the free-market economy of flexible exchange rates.

One of the most crucial aspects to bear in mind regarding the process of construction of neoliberal thought was that it was extremely complex, as well as continously riddled with huge swings and swerves from its original trajectory. While the contributory synergy created between ordoliberalism and neoliberalism towards the process is undeniable, during the decades that the process lasted, it however ended overshadowing, disregarding or even eliminating along the way, many of the early-day, new liberal joint-project's, intellectual actors, ideologies, ideas and inputs. Due to those reasons, neoliberal thought ultimately ended fractured, with the model's composition practically bereft of its early day, much more positive and balanced components and elements.

Initially, ordoliberalism and neoliberalism created and formed a very strong contributory synergy towards the construct of neoliberal thought. Ironically, however, throughout the same process, the two currents split and separated due to irreconcilable divergences between them in extremely crucial areas. During their early years, ordoliberalism and neoliberalism were very closely intertwined by one same common project, rotating around, among other issues, the axis of a 'major role for the state'. However, while the same 'major role for the state' common factor and others soon provoked big rifts and divisions amongst the ordoliberal and neoliberal academics involved, ordoliberalism ended likewise being shortly overshadowed by neoliberalism. In a similar way, neoliberalism was soon afterwards further split into two different factions, which ultimately embodied mainstream neoliberal thought in two separate and distinct schools of neoliberal thought: the European, or Austrian School of Thought (Austrian School) and the Anglo-American, or Chicago School of Thought (Chicago School). Since then, both schools have remained forever divided over issues related to their way of comprehending and analysing economics and economic phenomena, as well as with other monetarist issues. Whereas the Freiburg School's ordoliberalism led West Germany's social market economy, which produced its renowned German Economic Miracle, the Anglo-American or Chicago School's neoliberal prescriptions ended prevailing over the Austrian School's, being that way eventually chosen to run the globalized free-market economy, as well as regional development and integration processes into the international system. Those main differences between the two currents resulted in the extreme success of ordoliberalism in West Germany producing the economic miracle, and the disastrous worldwide results neoliberalism had on the entire economic-financial system, as well as in developing and integrating regions like Latin America (LA).

Through time, however, clear differentiation and distinction between the ordoliberal and neoliberal currents, as well as between the two neoliberal variants, have become somewhat blurred and distorted. The fact that the two economic currents share some related circumstances, such as the connected history between ordoliberalism and neoliberalism, plus ordoliberalism being often referred to as German neoliberalism, may have led to much confusion and mix-up of terms and ideas in the discourse about the currents. Additionally, since both currents actually share some common characteristics, such as free markets and customs unions, they may have sometimes been erroneously considered, associated or even perceived, as one same current or homogenous core-body of thought. Another possible cause for the confusion between the two currents is the fact that there is much literature on neoliberalism and very scarce knowledge on ordoliberalism and its founding institution, the Freiburg School, since most of the related Germanic literature was never actually translated, and following the German economic miracle, it did not travel far either. It thus never acquired the international diffusion neoliberalism did, most specially, the widely promoted Anglo-American variant.[14]

Originally and at first, neoliberal thought comprised a wide thesis of economic and social practices, which mainly proposed that within an institutional framework created and preserved by the state, characterized by strong private property rights, free markets and free trade, there would be a better advancement of human well-being, through the liberation of individual entrepreneurial freedoms and skills. However, with the rising influence of the Chicago School, neoliberalism mutated into geopolitically distinct hybrids, thereby acquiring a nature much more associated with the withdrawal of the state's supervision, removal of its social provisions in many areas, as well as with general widespread deregulation and privatizations.[15]

Ever since the 1980s, neoliberalism has evolved into something much greater than an exhilarating force in liberal economic thought and practice. Most of the globalized pluralist interdependent world has either voluntarily or coerced by internal or external pressures embraced some kind of neoliberal version or another or adjusted some sort of neoliberal policies and practices. Nowadays, hard-core believers and advocates of neoliberalism occupy high-level positions of immense influence in international financial institutions and organizations, corporations and multinationals, but most importantly, in the IMF and the WB, which supervise the globalized free-market economy and the IFMS, as well as international trade and development.[16]

While neoliberalism has become very deeply imbued within institutional frameworks and multilateral economic structures, it has likewise gone as far as defying traditional forms of state sovereignty. Moreover, it has equally changed welfare provisions, divisions of labour, attachments of the land, technological mixes, social relations, ways of life, as well as even our own '*habits of the heart*'[17] and reproductive activities.

Stretching out further, whereas neoliberalism has always been synonymous with economic and social development, integration and free markets, today, it has surpassed into many other political, economic, social and cultural realms. What is more, it has correspondingly structured many worldwide, academic and professional networks of history, economic history, economics and sociology, as well as been incorporated into numerous other interrelated areas of study and research, like health, education, science and technology, anthropology, demography and environmental issues.[18]

[14] BIEBRICHER, T. and VOGELMANN, F. (Eds). *The Birth of Austerity: German Ordoliberalism and Contemporary Neoliberalism*, pg 1.

[15] HARVEY, D. *A Brief History of Neoliberalism*, pgs 2–3.

[16] Ibid.

[17] Ibid, pg 3.

[18] Ibid, pgs 2–3.

Neoliberalism has, in short, become hegemonic as a mode of discourse. It has pervasive effects on ways of thought to the point where it has become incorporated into the common-sense way many of us interpret, live in, and understand the world.[19]

The neoliberal juggernaut has even managed to break through the boundaries of human ethics and beliefs. Whilst neoliberalism believes that market exchange is *'an ethic in itself, capable of acting as a guide to all human action, and substituting for all previously held ethical beliefs'*,[20] it also puts a very strong emphasis on contractual relations in the market place.[21] Whereas neoliberalism maintains that by stretching out the frequency and reach of market transactions, the social good will be maximized, at the same time, it also aims to include all human action into the realm of the market. Based on the requirement of creating and accumulating technologies of information, storage transfer, analyses and the utilization of huge databases to guide decisions in the global marketplace, neoliberalism procures an intense interest in the pursuit of information technologies for the information society. Additionally, the increase of such technologies has equally compressed the time and space of the rising density of market transactions, which have made the wider the geographical difference and the shorter the term of contracts, much more attractive.[22]

Against such a wide-arching neoliberal backdrop, after the 2007–15 global financial crisis revealed neoliberalism's intrinsic flaws, the model was subjected to several international readjustments, most especially in the EU. A sweeping EU Financial Reform, together with the establishment of a new EU Financial Regulatory Framework, engendered a huge ordoliberal revival, with the region re-tuning its financial-banking sector with an ordoliberal rules-based order, based on many new, strict regulating characteristics and traits. Paralleled with myriad monikers, such as the 'Ordo-Neoliberalization of Europe', the 'Ordoliberalization of Europe' or 'Europe's Ordoliberal Iron Cage', the reform has interestingly and once again witnessed the constructive interaction of the ordoliberal and neoliberal currents.

The new EU rules-based order has successfully improved market discipline, as well as stabilized the financial system and made the banking sector more resilient. Furthermore, the completion of both the Banking Union and the Capital Markets Union, which are under construction, together with the growing prospect of a European Monetary Fund, promises to reinforce the economic and monetary union much more.

The COVID-19 crisis further highlighted both the controversy that surrounds the neoliberal paradigm and orthodoxy, and the need to re-tighten the EU's financial

19 Ibid, pg 3.
20 Ibid.
21 Ibid.
22 Ibid, pgs 3–4.

sector's ordoliberal screws much more, with a lot of focus being placed on re-strengthening both the preventive and the corrective arms of the EU's Fiscal Pact's framework.[23]

Despite the bad karma and the many setbacks, the NLWO continues to prevail, with most international and regional readjustments clearly pointing to a continuation along the same neoliberal dynamics. Neoliberal thought and practice are so deeply imbued within institutional frameworks and multilateral economic structures that the whole dismantlement of the rigid neoliberal architecture, together with its deep-rooted infrastructure, would prove to be a very long-winding and complicated task.

However and regardless of the still-strong supremacy of the NLWO, it has, nonetheless, been severely destabilized, with the neoliberal paradigm and orthodoxy having been severely shifted and displaced by new progressive economic and financial models. In a similar fashion, stakeholder capitalism is also being increasingly challenged and contested by new revised forms of capitalism, and more recently, President Trump's techno-feudal and oligopolistic capitalism has equally burst into the scene with much vigour. Furthermore, the structure of the NLWO is being progressively further destabilized and weakened by flaws inherent to the financial monetary system.

At present, the NLWO's most powerful counter-force damaging its structure is represented by neonationalism, whose strong anti-globalization and anti-free market approach has critically weakened it and continues to further impair it. With neoliberalism having been displaced by neonationalism in key world epicentres, such as the United States, Italy and France, together with the UK's Brexit and China's hegemony in Asia, the 'neo-tribal' trend has boiled up very quickly and is increasingly closing more borders and restoring societies to a past homogeneity. What is more, such destabilizing effects have, in turn, also produced a huge geo-economic reconfiguration and geopolitical realignment, which are equally further debilitating the structure of the NLWO more than ever.

In much the same way, but to a lesser degree and with less intensity, MMT represents a new countering financial model, which is equally weakening the structure of the NLWO. MMT is gaining more and more traction, especially in the United States, where it has become in many ways adopted by President Trump. MMT policies are also present in Japan and New York, with Europe being likewise recommended to put MMT policies into practice.

23 Real Instituto Elcano. Elcano Policy Paper. December 2021. FEÁS, E., MARTÍNEZ MONGAY, C., OTERO-IGLESIAS, M., STEINBERG, F. and TAMAMES, J. *A Proposal to Reform the EU's Fiscal Rules*. https://www.realinstitutoelcano.org/en/policy-paper/a-proposal-to-reform-the-eus-fiscal-rules/

At the underlying academic sector, stakeholder capitalism is also being increasingly challenged and contested by new revised forms of capitalism, such as 'Progressive Capitalism', which are very rapidly gaining more credit and recognition in academia and international fora.

More recently, the newly generated US-Model designed by President Trump, 'Techno-Feudal and Oligopolistic Capitalism', has also appeared on the international landscape with a strong punch.

Such an ever-changing landscape of economic and financial models is further complicated by other threatening faultlines found within the IFMS. Ever since the 1980s switch to the financial-monetary economy, the IFMS has become increasingly vulnerable due to some deep flaws it has developed at its heart. As a direct result of the financialization process having conveyed too much market liquidity into the system, it has in turn caused many erratic stock market ups and downs, which are altogether shaking the foundations of the IFMS from within, projecting risks of a 'Global Liquidity Trap'. With the orthodoxy of monetary policy being jeopardized by schisms within the system itself, the global economy could be drifting towards yet another financial crisis. Ex-Governor of the Bank of England, Lord Melvyn King, has warned that while a 'financial Armageddon' would devastate the legitimacy of the democratic financial system, the fact remains that after having suffered from a Great Depression and having recently been hit hard by a Great Recession, *'the world could be sleepwalking into a new ... Great Stagnation'*.[24]

Notwithstanding, the biggest paradox about such an ever-changing NLWO and its destabilized scenarios is that, in a not-too-distant-future, it will have inevitably become part of an obsolete and irrelevant past. Since some years ago, the NLWO is being steadfastly overriden by a brand new technological and digital financial reality, which is dawning a whole new 'Digital Age'. Our current economic situation is witnessing how, much more so every day, the financial-monetary economy is being increasingly overshadowed by the digital-virtual economy and its ever-growing base of attractive crypto currencies, as well as progressively replaced by an endless array of financial instruments and services, provided by an entirely new virtual reality and metaverse.

In much the same way as economic history has unravelled since the first agrarian-industrial revolutions, we are currently experiencing another huge historical economic turning point or game-changing phase. We are bearing direct witnesses to the gradual eroding, de-phasing and ending of the time, epoch or age of Hayekian free markets, Friedmanian monetarism and physical currencies, through the newly evolving digital financial economy and its wide base of crypto currencies. In a very similar way to

[24] *The Guardian*. ELLIOT, L. *World Economy Is Sleepwalking into a New Financial Crisis, Warns Melvyn King*, pg 3. https://www.theguardian.com/business/2019/oct/20/world-sleepwalking-to-another-financial-crisis-says-mervyn-king

when in the 1980s the Keynesian Consensus and embedded liberalism were replaced by the current neoliberal paradigm, the latter paradigm is today being progressively overridden by the on-going 'Fourth Industrial Revolution' or 'Industrial Revolution 4.0'. It is widely expected that in a very near future, the neoliberal paradigm will be entirely replaced by the digital economy, decentralized finance (DeFi), neobanks and their broad base of crypto currencies, together with the infinite possibilities rendered by a timeless virtual reality and limitless metaverse.

In everyday life, many of those big changes and transformations brought about by such huge advancements in the technological-digital sectors have been very visible for a long time, with billions of people connected to mobile gadgets of all kinds, capable of unlimited processing, storage and access to information capabilities. Big technological advances in many other blossoming fields, such as artificial intelligence, robotics, nanotechnology, biotechnology and quantum computing, are equally announcing loud and clear the birth of a new technological-digital age.

The impact that the Industrial Revolution 4.0 is having on the economic, financial and business sectors is signalling very strongly that tomorrow's financial world will be based on decentralized finance (DeFi).[25] Since some years ago, decentralized and autonomous systems assisted by neobanks and down-rooted to a massive base of crypto currencies have been generating many second-order effects in the financial field.

DeFi is an emerging alternative financial system, which is built over a public blockchain that allows a much greater and more open accessibility, as anyone can connect to it. Blockchain technology shields the system with an infallible security mechanism, which makes transactions publicly visible, thus providing the system with much more transparency.[26]

'Neobanks' are equally reshaping the financial services industry, by way of an increased access to banking, as well as by driving innovation. 'Neobanks' have emerged as innovative digital-only financial institutions, which are seriously disrupting the banking sector by delivering services entirely online, which thus allows them to offer consumers accessibility benefits, as well as reduced fees, faster loan approvals and even early access to their paychecks.[27]

The cryptocurrency ecosystem has correspondingly been developing at a very accelerated pace, unlocking countless investment possibilities across the global

[25] Visual Capitalist. NEUFELD, D. *Cryptocurrency: Redefining the Future of Finance.* https://www.visualcapitalist.com/cryptocurrency-redefining-future-of-finance/

[26] Ibid.

[27] Plaid.com. ANTOSZ, D. *What Is a Neobank? How Fintech Is Transforming Banking.* https://plaid.com/resources/fintech/what-is-a-neobank/#:~:text=A%20neobank%20is%20a%20digital,challenger%20bank%2C%20or%20digital%20bank.

economy and redefining a whole new technological and digital financial age. Ever since crypto currencies burst into the scene, they have accommodated themselves onto the global stage, being progressively bolstered by new policies and rising adoption by worldwide public and private sector actors.[28] More and more so every day, new actors are engaging much more proactively in the evolving crypto currency ecosystem. In April 2020, China became the first country to launch and establish an official digital currency, the 'Digital Currency / Electronic Payment (DC/EP)', with the crypto currency becoming operative during the 2022 Winter Olympics in Beijing. Most other countries are following the same trend, having also broken into the new space with on-going, pilot, research or development programmes, for the establishment of official digital currencies.[29]

Book's Purpose

Under the light of such a convulsed economic hiatus, it will prove very useful to recapitulate on neoliberal thought and practice in order to comprehend much better our economic situation. Reviewing the past of neoliberal thought and practice will help assess and evaluate our neoliberal reality, as well as the degree to which it is being shifted and displaced by new countering models. The structure of the NLWO is being increasingly destabilized and weakened by both the clash between the old and new economic and financial models, as well as by flaws inherent to the financial monetary system. The two neoliberal scenarios clearly reflect that whereas the intellectual collapse of neoliberalism has produced an irreversible shift and displacement of neoliberal thought and practice, the IFMS is also on the verge of being monetarily overridden. However, and with such an increasingly unstable and weakened NLWO, at the same time, it is paradoxically becoming gradually de-phased by the on-going 'Industrial Revolution 4.0'. Eventually, in a not-too-distant future, it will be entirely eclipsed by the 'Digital Age'.

Following the 2007–15 global financial crisis, neoliberalism has been internationally reset to continue along the same dynamics. Furthermore, the fact that ordoliberalism has been resuscitated to re-strengthen the neoliberal bedrock of the EU and that it is once again interacting with neoliberalism reflects the positive synergy both currents create towards the provision of a more stable and equitable, rules-based economic and financial order. However and despite its prevalence, neoliberalism continues, nonetheless, being increasingly shifted and displaced by a much stronger and ever-expanding neonationalist movement, as well as by an up and rising MMT. Stakeholder capitalism is also being incessantly challenged and defied by a more humane and

[28] Visual Capitalist. NEUFELD, D. *Cryptocurrency: Redefining the Future of Finance.* https://www.visualcapitalist.com/cryptocurrency-redefining-future-of-finance/

[29] Mish Talk. MISH. *Central Bank Digital Currencies on the Way.* https://www.thestreet.com/mishtalk/economics/central-bank-digital-currencies-on-the-way

socially responsible, Progressive Capitalism, as well as other revised forms of capitalism, and more recently, President Trump's Techno-Feudal and Oligopolistic Capitalism has likewise begun ripping strongly through the international landscape. In addition, the IFMS is also on the verge of being monetarily overridden, with its monetary orthodoxy being threatened by schisms within the system itself.

The recent ordoliberal revival has been accompanied by an abundant production of both ordoliberal and neoliberal literature. Partly in response to a growing interest in governability studies and the European sovereign debt crisis, ordoliberalism and the Freiburg School have once again regained much traction, with many original Germanic texts being translated and more related literature materializing.[30] Since the financial crisis, neoliberalism has also seen a great deal more literature on it beginning to appear, with much more interest in it growing as a very prescient subject. The outflow of academic literature on ordoliberalism and neoliberalism has been supplemented by huge amounts of parallelisms and distinctions between the two, but most specially by a plethora of news pundits admiring ordoliberalism's traits and cussing neoliberalism's disastrous worldwide results, as well as its unfathomable instillment in many social and cultural areas and other non-related areas of life. Similarly, much literature has also begun to appear related to the new countering thought and practice displacing neoliberalism, such as neonationalism and MMT, as well as to the new revised forms of capitalism challenging and defying stakeholder capitalism.

As regards ordoliberalism, some of the most instructive literature mainly include Commun's '*L'Ordoliberalisme Allemand: Aux Sources de L'Economie Sociale de Marché*'; Biebricher's and Vogelmann's '*The Birth of Austerity: German Ordoliberalism and Contemporary Neoliberalism*'; Lechevalier's '*Eucken under The Pillow: The Ordoliberal Imprint in Europe*'; Biebricher's '*The Return of Ordoliberalism in Europe – Notes of a Research Agenda*'; Strassel's '*Le Modèle Allemand de L'Europe: L'Ordolibéralisme*' and Weisz's '*L'Intérêt pour une Approche Régulationniste du Detour par L'ordoliberalisme*'. Others also include Wren-Lewis's '*Ordoliberalism, Neoliberalism and Economics*' and Bonefeld's *Freedom and the Strong State: On German Ordoliberalism.*

In relation to neoliberalism, some of the most insightful books include Mirowski and Plehwe's '*The Road from Mont Pelerin: The Making of the Neoliberal Thought Collective*'; Audier's '*Le Colloque Walter Lippmann: Aux Origines du Neoliberalisme*'; Harvey's '*A Brief History of Neoliberalism*' and Steger and Roy's '*Neoliberalism: A Very Short Introduction*'. Springer, Birch and Macleavy's '*The Handbook on Neoliberalism*' represents a very good portrayal of the great variety of areas, contexts and ranges of neoliberal influence, and Eagleton-Pierce's '*Neoliberalism. The Key Concepts*' is extremely revealing as regards neoliberalism's main concepts and intricacies

[30] BIEBRICHER, T. and VOGELMANN, F. (Eds). *The Birth of Austerity: German Ordoliberalism and Contemporary Neoliberalism*, pg 1.

together with some of the generalized neoliberal lexicon; Crouch's '*The Strange Non-death of Neoliberalism*' is very enlightening in relation to the institutionalization of neoliberalism and the neo-corporatist character it has acquired within political and financial institutions; and Jones's '*Masters of the Universe. Hayek, Friedman and the Birth of Neoliberal Politics*' provides a very good account about the emergence of the 1940's neoliberal critique, through amongst others, Popper, Hayek and Mises, as well as on the spread and diffusion of neoliberalism during the post-Second World War period. Others also include Davies's '*The Limits of Neoliberalism*', which portrays neoliberalism's limitations regarding authority, sovereignty and the rationale behind competition, and Peck's '*Constructions of Neoliberal Reason*', which provides an interesting constructivist approach. Lastly, Cahill, Cooper, Koning and Primrose's '*The SAGE Handbook of Neoliberalism*' represents an incredibly vast compendium that explores the different ways in which neoliberalism has been comprehended and some of the key questions about its nature and areas of influence.

In connection with neonationalism, Gingrich and Banks's '*Neo-Nationalism in Europe and Beyond. Perspectives on Social Anthropology*' offers an excellent analysis of a phenomenon, which continues to spread out widely across the international landscape. In association with Modern Monetary Theory, Kelton's '*The Deficit Myth: Modern Monetary Economy and the Birth of the People's Economy*' presents a brilliant exposition on the basic tenets and benefits of the up and rising financial counter-model.

In correlation with Progressive Capitalism, Stiglitz's '*People, Power and Profits: Progressive Capitalism for an Age of Discontent*' rationalizes exceptionally well on the more humane and socially responsible form of alternative capitalism.

The elaboration of '*The Neoliberal Era*' has been made possible thanks to and in virtue of much of the past and more recent wide range of academic, professional and public press literature on the subject. With the book's research and findings being largely based on it, the book provides an updated succinct chronological account, review and analysis, of neoliberal thought and practice. However, it places a very special focus on some key innovative insights related to its construct of thought and readjusted practice, as well as to the current state of the NLWO vis-à-vis counter-models destabilizing it, which had been hitherto, either not too developed, very lightly touched upon or altogether excluded in other books. It will prove helpful to the fields of international relations, economic history, economics, political economy, economic and financial models, as well as economic development.

Recalling the intellectual history and the ideological roots of the new liberal currents, ordoliberalism and neoliberalism, as well as highlighting on the contributory role they both shared towards the complex process of construction of neoliberal thought, will help comprehend much better the ideological and conceptual vicissitudes that characterized the complex process. A process, which after several swerves from its original trajectory, finally produced a fractured neoliberal thought, which was then applied throughout multiple phases onto the global stage. Since then and after several crises, neoliberal thought has become swamped by abounding doubts and queries. For example, why were the intellectual pros of ordoliberalism so successful in Germany and the ideological flaws of neoliberalism so disastrous worldwide and in developing regions like Latin America? What were the main triggers of the anti-neoliberal turn in Latin America, and how successful has the substitution been in some countries of neoliberalism for other heterodox economic currents? What actions have been taken to fix and improve the fissures of neoliberal thought at the international and EU levels? How strong do neoliberal thought and practice stand today? How did they become so deeply imbued within the neoliberal world order's institutional frameworks that uphold and maintain it, as well as within the multilateral economic structures they represent and assist? Most importantly and focusing more directly on our immediate present, what are the main countering models, currently shifting and displacing neoliberal thought and practice? What new revised forms of capitalism are increasingly challenging and contesting stakeholder capitalism? How prominent are all those counter-forces becoming, how thick are they spreading-out across the international landscape and what levels of threat do they actually pose? Are neoliberal thought and practice holding or are they being gradually overridden by any of those alternative models, and if so, in what ways? Bearing in mind such an ever-changing economic landscape, to what extent are the neoliberal paradigm and orthodoxy relevant and pertinent vis-à-vis the game-changing 'Industrial Revolution 4.0' and the dawning of the 'Digital Age'? Will our current neoliberal era of Hayekian free markets and Friedmanian financial monetarism hold or is it being gradually overshadowed by the redefinition of a whole new, technological and digital financial age? Going even further and beyond, although we can still consider ourselves to be living in the '*Neoliberal Era*', it is paradoxically nonetheless an era which is wading, due to the displacement of neoliberal thought and practice by new progressive countering thought, as well as fading, being progressively eclipsed by the dawning of the '*Digital Age*', decentralized finance (DeFi), neobanks and crypto currencies.

The main reasons behind the title, '*The Neoliberal Era*', are quite simple and straightforward. If our previous economic time, age or epoch, saw the establishment and predomination of the Keynesian Consensus, our current economic period has likewise seen the establishment and predomination of the neoliberal paradigm and orthodoxy. If the years from 1945 until the 1980s represented the time or age of the Keynesian Consensus, characterized by the Bretton Woods system of fixed exchange rates and stimulated by socio-developmental capitalism, based on the same rationale, the years spanning from the 1980s until the present-day can equally be considered as the time, age, epoch or 'era', of Hayekian free markets and Friedmanian financial monetarism, spurred by stakeholder capitalism. Ever since the 1980s switch from the industrial-productive economy to the financial-monetary economy, the world's economy has been hinged to and rotated around free markets, widespread deregulation and privatizations. It has equally been structured around the international financial monetary system of floating exchange rates, as well as been goaded by stakeholder capitalism. Thus and therefore, it is an economic period of time, which for the sake and purpose of this book, just as the title defines and stipulates, can by analogous correlation also be perceived and considered as 'the neoliberal era'. It is an economic era, which still prevails, characterized by an orthodoxy that still predominates, rotating around maxims and dictums that are being continuously readjusted and re-tightened to carry on along the same dynamics. Notwithstanding, it is an economic era, which is at the same time being seriously shifted and displaced by new countering thought and practice, as well as being increasingly overshadowed by the dawning of the Digital Age.

The book has a theoretical objective and a practical objective, with the conclusion having an additional twofold objective of its own.

The chief objective of the theoretical part and its seven chapters is to highlight on the 1920s–30s academic revolution, beseeching the reformulation of classical liberalism and laissez-faire, which spawned two 'new liberal' currents, 'ordoliberalism' and 'neoliberalism'. It likewise provides a succinct chronological account of the role both currents played during the complex process of construction of neoliberal thought, which eventually produced the currently established neoliberal free market model and financial monetary model.

Some of the theoretical part's most innovative and insightful features include a description of the events, which triggered the 1920s–30s academic revolution seeking the reformation of classical liberalism and laissez-faire, which spurred both the emergence of ordoliberalism in Germany through the Freiburg School and the appearance of neoliberalism in Europe through the Colloque Walter Lippmann; an overview of the preceding late nineteenth- and early twentieth-century intellectual critique surrounding classical liberalism; an explanation of the ambiguous abstraction, which surrounds the concept of neoliberalism; a succinct chronological account of the intellectual and ideological brainstorming between the new liberal academics, through the Mont Pelerin Society, which gave shape and form to the very complex process of construction of neoliberal thought, to the conceptualization of neoliberalism, as well as to the neoliberal collective as a whole. Lastly, two in-depth analyses related to neoliberalism thought are also included. The first analysis concentrates on the differences between the two currents, ordoliberalism and neoliberalism, which formed the process of construction of neoliberal thought. The second analysis focuses on the divergences between the two most prominent schools of neoliberal thought, the Austrian School and the Chicago School.

The practice part is composed of five dimensions, with each dimension including different chapters related to ordoliberal and neoliberal practice. Each dimension has an individual objective of its own.

The first dimension (Chapters 8–13) has the main objective of reflecting on the impressive results obtained by ordoliberalism in guiding West Germany's social market economy, which produced the renowned German Economic Miracle.

The second dimension (Chapters 14–19) provides a historical chronology of the multiphased 'neoliberalization' of European Union (EU), as well as of the two successive waves of 'neoliberalization', which gradually set up the architecture of the globalized free market economy. It also reflects on how the flaws of neoliberalism eventually produced the 2007–15 global financial crisis, with a special focus on the EU's sovereign debt crisis and its effects in Spain.

The third dimension (Chapters 20 and 21) highlights the negative results the neoliberal basis of Latin American integration processes has had on the regional development and sub-development. The region has experienced a left-induced, radical anti-neoliberal swing, which has witnessed the abandonment of the neoliberal model in numerous countries, together with the experimentation with heterodox currents, such as Neo-Structuralism and Neo-Extractivism, together with the very successful, Bolivian, Social Communitarian Productive Economic Model. The latter has produced the Bolivian Economic Miracle.

The fourth dimension (Chapters 22 and 23) reflects on the post-crisis, EU Financial Reform and the EU Financial Regulatory Framework, which have seen the resuscitation of ordoliberalism at the EU level. The establishment of an innovative EU financial-banking rules-based-order, based on a strict set of regulating characteristics, has successfully stabilized the financial system and made the banking sector more resilient.

The fifth and last dimension (Chapters 24–26) provides an evaluation of the current state of the '*Neoliberal World Order*' *(NLWO).* Although the NLWO is still-standing and continues to prevail, with neoliberal thought and practice very deeply imbued within institutional frameworks and multilateral economic structures, it has nonetheless been severely destabilized. The neoliberal paradigm and orthodoxy have been fundamentally shifted and displaced by new progressive thought and practice, which fiercely opposes contemporary economic and financial models. The structure of the NLWO is being increasingly destabilized and weakened by both the clash between the old and new economic and financial models, as well as by flaws inherent to the financial monetary system. The two neoliberal scenarios clearly reflect that whereas the intellectual collapse of neoliberalism has produced a huge irreversible shift and displacement of neoliberal thought and practice, the IFMS is also on the verge of being monetarily overridden. On one hand, neoliberalism has been much shifted and displaced by 'Neo-nationalism' and 'Modern Monetary Theory' (MMT). 'Stakeholder Capitalism' is also being increasingly challenged and contested by new revised forms of capitalism, such as most particularly, 'Progressive Capitalism', and more recently, 'Techno-Feudal and Oligopolistic Capitalism' has also emerged with a lot of drive. On the other hand, the International Financial Monetary System (IFMS), likewise, reveals even more neoliberal fault-lines related to inherent flaws, which project risks of a 'Global Liquidity Trap', that would in turn consequentially generate a 'Great Stagnation'.

It can be asserted that the direction both scenarios end up taking will largely determine the manner in which our economic future unfurls.

The Conclusion has a two fold objective of its own. On one hand, it offers an evaluation on the on-going clash of economic models. On the other hand, and most importantly, it examines the on-going, economic game-changing '*Industrial Revolution 4.0*' and the dawning of the '*Digital Age*'. Since some years ago, the effects the Industrial Revolution 4.0 has been having in everyday life, but most especially on the economic, financial and business sectors, are very rapidly accelerating the overriding of the financial-monetary economy by the digital-virtual economy. Newer, much more advanced and sophisticated, decentralized and autonomous systems and neobanks, down-rooted to a huge base of crypto-currencies, have been generating myriad second-order effects in the financial world. '*Neobanks*' and the '*cryptocurrency ecosystem*' have been developing at an incredibly fast pace, unlocking countless investment possibilities across the global economy, as well as redefining a whole new, technological and digital financial age. There are many strong signs projecting that our current era of Hayekian free markets and Friedmanian financial monetarism will be entirely overshadowed by tomorrow's '*Digital Age*', '*decentralized finance (DeFi)*', '*neobanks*' and '*cryptocurrencies*'.

Part One

The Construct of Neoliberal Thought

1

Post-World War I Europe and the Reformulation of Classical Liberalism and Laissez-Faire

The post-First World War, 1920s decade onwards, generated many re-adjustments, variations and changes across the field of liberal economics, but most especially, within the plains of the predominating economic ideology – '*Classical Liberalism and Laissez-Faire*'.

'*Classical Liberalism*' emerged during the eighteenth century from the ideas developed by philosophers throughout the Enlightenment period and carried on evolving up until the late nineteenth and the early twentieth centuries. By the 1920s, most classical liberal societies were based on the economic principles of laissez-faire capitalism, with two main established diverging traditions of classical liberalism, namely the British tradition and the French tradition. British philosophers, such as Adam Smith, John Locke, David Ricardo, Bernard Mandeville, David Hume, Adam Ferguson, Josiah Tucker, William Paley and John Stuart Mill, represented a British tradition, which articulated beliefs in empiricism and common law, as well as in traditions and institutions, which had spontaneously evolved, but were imperfectly understood. The French tradition included philosophers, like Jean-Jacques Rousseau, Baron de Montesquieu, Marquis de Condorcet, the Encyclopaedists and the Physiocrats, who mainly based their beliefs in rationalism, although sometimes they also showed hostility towards tradition and religion.[1]

During the 1920s, the post-First World War European decaying socioeconomic situation, together with the way events unravelled throughout those years, put into outright manifestation the imperfections and flaws of classical liberalism and laissez-faire. The depressed context, together with a rising socialism and its deep probing into the economy, engendered and triggered a long-winding and profound academic revolution, beseeching the reformulation of classical liberalism and laissez-faire. Such academic revolution left a huge imprint in liberal economics, through the generation of a whole '*new liberal*' way of thinking, which today continues prevailing.

[1] Open Edition Journals. SLOMAN, P. *The Liberal Party and Economic Policy 1918–1964*. https://journals.openedition.org/mimmoc/695

The intellectual brainstorming mainly revolved around the notion that classical liberalism and laissez-faire had failed and that a renewed form of liberalism was needed, with a '*major role for the State*' and sought a half way, or '*Third Way*', between classical liberalism and laissez-faire. Eventually (as the ensuing chapters will further expand on), the academic revolution spawned two 'new liberal' economic currents, 'Ordoliberalism' and 'Neoliberalism'.

During the 1930s, Keynes's ideas rose to prominence, and from 1945 until 1980, the Bretton Woods system of fixed exchange rates predominated worldwide. However, at the academic level, the two new liberal currents began constituting the main theoretical counter-reaction to Keynesianism, embedded liberalism and collectivism, which would decades later completely debunk the Keynesian Consensus. The contributive synergy created between ordoliberalism and neoliberalism provided the framework for the process of construction of neoliberal thought, as well as set the stage for the neoliberal anti-Keynesian revolution that took place throughout the same decades. In the 1980s, the neoliberal counter-revolution completely displaced Keynesianism both in theory and in practice, hence producing the switch from the Keynesian Consensus and embedded liberalism to our currently established, neoliberal order of Hayekian free markets, Friedmanian monetarism and shareholder capitalism.

In broad terms, while the decades before 1913 are considered the time of the first globalization, the post-First World War years experienced a regression or '*globalization backlash*'. Instead of restoring the pre-war world economy, the post-war economic development made it actually disintegrate. '*The sciences, born in peace, went to war and made a gigantic scientific enterprise of it.*'[2] Although during the 1920s the gold standard, which was then considered as the solid foundation of the pre-war world economy, was restored in many countries in vain hope of reinstating the old international order, the consequential deflationary measures required in most of them actually hastened the world depression. The widespread global credit famine, which characterized the time, together with the even greater conflagration that ensued, would only be overcome years later, with the reflation of national economies due to rearmament for the Second World War.[3]

The post-First World War situation across Europe was most especially war-torn, with widespread economic misery, social despair and hopelessness, permeating the entire region. The badly affected environment was further impaired by the harshness of the Treaty of Versailles, the Dawes Plan and Young Plan, plus the ultimate collapse of the Weimar Republic. Such a decomposing socioeconomic and moral context produced much anger and resentment with the prevailing classical liberal economics and its failures, but above all, with its social disregards. With the decade's rampant

[2] International Encyclopedia of the First World War. DIETMAR, R. *Post-War Economies*, pg 1. https://encyclopedia.1914-1918-online.net/article/post-war_economies

[3] Ibid, pgs 1–2.

unemployment and poverty being aggravated even more by Europe's huge bouts of inflation and protectionist policies, the whole situation ultimately spiralled down into further chaos and disorder due to the vicious whiplashes of the Great Depression.

During the 1930s, however, Keynes's ideas rose to influence, most especially after the publication in 1936, of his *'General Theory of Employment, Interest and Money'*, which directly challenged and defied the conventional classical liberal economic orthodoxy, with its central argument pressing forward that the level of employment is determined by the level of aggregate demand, and not as classical liberals held by the price of labour. The publication gave way to the '*Keynesian Revolution*' in economic thinking. From 1945 to 1980, the Keynesian Consensus and embedded liberalism were established through the Bretton Woods system of fixed exchange rates, together with its emphasis on moderate interventionism and aggregate demand-led growth. The same period witnessed the substitution of the predominating economic ideology – classical liberalism and laissez-faire – for Keynes's social liberalism. At the same time, it also saw a big change in the form of capitalism – from the established, techno-bureaucratic capitalism, to Keynes's '*socio-developmental capitalism*'. Such positive changes likewise gave way to the '*Golden Age of Capitalism*', with historically unprecedented, sustained high industrial-led output levels and economic growth rates.[4]

Nonetheless, during the 1920s, at the theoretical level, much opposition and dissent equally bogged down classical liberalism and laissez-faire. Although the critique surrounding classical liberalism and laissez-faire had been brewing in academic circles since the nineteenth century, it began to increasingly boil up from the 1920s onwards. During the nineteenth century, many anti-interventionist doctrines apologizing free exchange had already been addressed by lots of French liberal economists and numerous English liberals, including the Manchester School, Herbert Spencer and his apology of the individual against the state, as well as Ernest Benn, the founder of *'The Society of Individualists'*. However, during the 1920s, the overall post-First World War European socioeconomic context, most particularly Weimar Germany's, created a very negative atmosphere of extreme disillusionment with classical liberalism and laissez-faire. Such a negative environment triggered an intense academic revolution, beseeching the reformulation of classical liberalism and laissez-faire, which eventually generated two 'new liberal' currents, 'ordoliberalism' and 'neoliberalism'.[5]

The events and circumstances that characterized the 1920s are where the intellectual origins and ideological roots of neoliberalism are most predominantly found. The decade represents the time during which, both socialism together with a new breed of new liberal academics, began pressing forward the main ingredients that would serve to redevelop classical liberalism and laissez-faire. Those years witnessed the

4 BRESSER-PEREIRA, L.C. *The Two Forms of Capitalism: Developmentalism and Economic Liberalism*, pgs 1–2. http://www.rep.org.br/PDF/149-2.PDF
5 AUDIER, S. *Aux Origines du Neo-Libéralisme: Le Colloque Walter Lippmann*, pgs 31–2.

sowing of the first 'new liberal' seeds, which eventually conceived and gave birth to ordoliberalism and neoliberalism, and eventually and in turn, to both neoliberal thought and the neoliberal collective. On one hand, the events that took place during the decade triggered the academic revolution seeking the reformulation of classical liberalism and laissez-faire. On the other hand, the academic brainstorming that was then spurred began providing some of the main inputs, ideas, notions and concepts, which would shape and form the new liberal, ordoliberal and neoliberal currents, that would through the years gradually configure the neoliberal collective.

As a direct result of the academic revolution, while in Germany, the Freiburg School advanced ordoliberalism as a neo-Kantian epistemology, socioeconomic response to the Weimar Republic, neoliberalism burst through Europe as the main theoretical counter-reaction to Keynesianism and collectivism. Ordoliberalism was considered an intermediate or '*Third Way*', between capitalism and communism (or extreme socialism). Neoliberalism was regarded as an in-between or '*Third Way*', between classical liberalism and laissez-faire, in deviation from Keynesianism and collectivism.[6] From then onwards, whereas both currents began to gradually configure the construct of neoliberal thought, at the same time, they also started constituting the main theoretical counter-reaction to Keynesianism, embedded liberalism and collectivism, which by the 1980s completely upturned the Keynesian Consensus and embedded liberalism, having prevailed ever since.

The rise of socialism (as the next chapter will delve into) also had a chief role in the reformulation of classical liberalism and laissez-faire. Many of its elements and components much influenced both the shaping of the new liberal currents, as well as in turn the forming of the neoliberal collective. During the 1920s, with the rapid spread of socialism across Europe and the socialist debate growing more popular, the academic revolution began to probe much deeper in its fervent search for a change of economic paradigm, seeking the '*socialization*' of the economy or a more socially conscious economic prototype.

[6] This book's references to the term, '*Third Way*', relate to both the ordoliberal search for a moderate stance or '*Third Way*', between capitalism and communism, and the neoliberal search for an in-between or '*Third Way*', between classical liberalism and laissez-faire, in deviation from Keynesianism, embedded liberalism and collectivism. The term '*Third Way*' is based on the exact same term that was chosen by the different academics who conceived the ordoliberal and neoliberal currents, as well as on the different connotations it carried for both currents. It should not be confused with the early 2000s, '*Third Way Social Democracy*', advocated in Great Britain by Prime Minister Blair's New Labour Government (discussed in detail in Chapter XVII), as there are fundamental differences that exist between them. For example, in relation to ordoliberalism, even though the ordoliberal idea of a social market is similar to that of the '*Third Way Social Democracy*', there are key differences between them that affect crucial areas. Whilst the '*Ordoliberal Social Market*' model combined government regulation to establish fair competition with private enterprise, the '*Third Way Social Democracy*' model promoted economic deregulation. While ordoliberalism was based on a social market economy open to the benefits of social welfare, the '*Third Way Social Democracy*' model has equally foreseen a clash of ideas regarding the establishment of the welfare state.International Encyclopedia of the First World War. DIETMAR, R. *Post-War Economies*, pgs 1–2. https://encyclopedia.1914-1918-online.net/article/post-war_economies

The Treaty of Versailles

The '*Treaty of Peace between the Allied and Associated Powers and Germany*', most commonly known as '*The Treaty of Versailles*' (the Treaty), was signed on 28 June 1919 in France at the Palace of Versailles and had a terrible impact on the German economy. Since then, Germany has always blamed the near-collapse of its economy on the Treaty, with some economists having gone as far as estimating that war reparations were the main cause of as much as one-third of the hyperinflation that the country endured.[7]

The Treaty's '*Article 231*', or the '*War Guilt Clause*', was the most punitive clause of all. In general, the Treaty forced Germany to disarm, make substantial territorial concessions, as well as pay reparations to certain countries that had formed the Entente powers. In 1921, the total cost of those reparations was estimated at 132 billion marks, which at the time was equivalent to $31.4 billion or £6.6 billion while in 2018 it was estimated to be more or less equivalent to US$442 billion or UK£284 billion. The Treaty also established an Allied '*Reparation Commission*' in order to determine the exact amount that Germany should pay, as well as the actual form the payment should take. While the commission was required to submit its conclusions by 1 May 1921, in the interlude, the Treaty required Germany to pay an equivalent of 20 billion gold marks (US$5 billion) in gold, commodities, ships, securities or other forms. The money was intended to help pay the Allied occupation costs and buy food and raw materials for Germany.[8]

The German economic system, however, was so deteriorated that only a small percentage of reparations was actually paid in hard currency. For Germany, even the payment of a small percentage of the original reparations (132 billion gold marks) burdened its economy significantly.[9] Exacerbating Germany much more, in March 1921, French and Belgian troops occupied part of the Ruhr industrial area, and a few years later, in January 1923, occupied the rest of it in reprisal for Germany failing to fulfil reparation payments. The German government reacted with passive resistance, with coal miners and railway workers refusing to obey any instructions by the occupation forces, which in turn provoked the disruption and coming to a standstill of both production and transportation. The subsequent financial consequences contributed much to German hyperinflation and totally ruined public finances. Subsequently, in late 1923, with the ending of passive resistance in the Ruhr area, Germany was allowed to undertake a currency reform and negotiate the Dawes Plan, which in 1925 eventually led to the withdrawal of French and Belgian troops from the Ruhr.[10]

7 THOMPSON, D. *Europe since Napoleon*, pgs 536–761.

8 Treaty of Versailles/Part VIII. Article 231. https://en.wikisource.org/wiki/Treaty_of_Versailles/Part_VIII#Article_232

9 THOMPSON, D. *Europe since Napoleon*, pgs 536–761.

10 International Encyclopedia of the First World War. DIETMAR, R. *Post-War Economies*, pgs 4–5.

With near-havoc breaking out in Germany, the newly formed Weimar Republic saw the country's democratic unity begin to drift apart with the appearance of extreme nationalist feelings, since most conservatives, nationalists and ex-military leaders condemned the Treaty. While politicians of the Weimar Republic who supported the Treaty along with socialists, communists and Jews were viewed suspiciously and of questionable loyalty, those who benefitted from a weakened Germany and the newly formed Weimar Republic were regarded as having betrayed their country.[11]

The Dawes Plan and Young Plan

During the European and German reparations process, the German hyperinflation bout gradually saw the value of its currency collapse, which provoked a standstill in the overall wrangle about reparations. Under much pressure from the United States, Europe refused to link reparations to inter-allied war debts, which hence caused much tension among its former co-belligerents. Consequently, in 1922, London emitted the '*Balfour Note*', communicating that it would seek reparations and wartime debt repayments from its European allies, equal to its debt with the United States. That same year, the US Congress created the '*United States War Debt Commission*', in order to negotiate repayment plans, which through further discussions about German reparations, produced the '*Dawes Plan*' and the '*Young Plan*'. However, although the Dawes Plan produced many changes in the German economy, the Young Plan was doomed to fail right from the start due to the advent of the Great Depression. Since up until 1928 loans from US banks had helped prop up the German economy, when those loans dried up, Germany's economy floundered.[12]

In late 1923, with the European powers bogged down over the German reparations issue, the Commission formed a committee to review the situation, headed by Charles G. Dawes (Chicago banker, former director of the Bureau of the Budget, and future US vice-president). In April 1924, the committee presented its Dawes Plan proposal. Within the Dawes Plan framework, Germany's annual reparation payments were reduced, increasing over time as its economy improved, although the full amount to be paid was, however, left undetermined. Economic policy-making in Berlin was reorganized under foreign supervision, with a new currency being adopted, – the '*Reichsmark*'. France and Belgium evacuated the Ruhr, and foreign banks loaned the German government US$200 million to help encourage economic stabilization. The banker, J.P. Morgan, floated the loan on the US market, and during the following four years, US banks continued to lend Germany sufficient funds in order to meet its reparation payments to countries like France and the UK.[13]

[11] Ibid.

[12] US Government. US Office of the Historian. *Milestones: 1921–1936. The Dawes Plan, the Young Plan, German Reparations, and Inter-Allied War Debts.* https://history.state.gov/milestones/1921-1936/dawes

[13] Ibid.

In the autumn of 1928, in a similar fashion to the Dawes Plan, another committee of experts was formed, intended to devise a final solution to and settlement of the German reparations problem: the Young Plan. '*In 1929, the committee, under the chairmanship of Owen D. Young, the head of General Electric and a member of the Dawes committee, proposed a plan that reduced the total amount of reparations demanded of Germany to 121 billion gold marks, almost $29 billion, payable over 58 years. Another loan would be floated in foreign markets, this one totalling $300 million. Foreign supervision of German finances would cease and the last of the occupying troops would leave German soil. The Young Plan also called for the establishment of a Bank for International Settlements, designed to facilitate the payment of reparations.*'[14]

Regardless of the established stipulations, in 1932, at the Lausanne Conference, European nations agreed to cancel their reparation claims against Germany, except for one last final payment. Paradoxically, by mid-1933, after several other attempts by European debtors to cancel their debts to the United States, all European debtor nations except for Finland had defaulted on their loans from the United States.[15]

The Weimar Republic

With the ending of the First World War, from 1919 to 1933, the '*Weimar Republic*' was established in Germany. 'Weimar Republic' was the unofficial historical denomination for the German state. The name derives from the city of Weimar, where the Weimar Republic's first constitutional assembly took place. Since 1871, the official name of the state, '*Deutsches Reich*' (German Realm), has remained unchanged, although in the English-speaking world, the country is simply referred to as Germany.

Due to Germany's very limited democratic traditions, together with a chaotic unstable democracy and severe economic problems, the Weimar Republic was, however, doomed to fail right from the beginning. Its flawed Constitution and other constitutional weaknesses even made it susceptible to the eventual establishment of a dictatorship. '*Article 48*' of the Constitution gave the president power to '*take all necessary steps*' if public order and security were seriously disturbed or endangered, and before 1933, it was often used to issue decrees without the support of parliament.

A crucial issue which affected the nervous system of the Weimar Republic most negatively was the extremely liberal economic policies, with radical cuts in social spending that were applied during those years, which generated many economic problems and, in turn, ultimately played a major role in its downfall.[16]

[14] Ibid.
[15] Ibid.
[16] PEUKERT, D.J.K. *The Weimar Republic: The Crisis of Classical Modernity*, pgs 35–42.

Soon after the end of the First World War, on 11 August 1919, a national assembly convened in Weimar produced a new constitution for the Deutsches Reich, which was henceforth adopted and established. During its fourteen years of existence, the Weimar Republic faced numerous problems, including contentious relationships with the First World War victors, political extremism with paramilitaries from both the Left and the Right, hyperinflation and bouts of extreme hyperinflation, together with continuous severe economic problems, poverty and hardship. The German people have in fact always blamed the Weimar Republic, rather than wartime leaders, for the country's defeat and the humiliating terms of the Treaty of Versailles. Although Weimar Germany fulfilled most of the requirements of the Treaty of Versailles, it never completely met its disarmament requirements and eventually only paid off a small portion of the war reparations, but only by twice restructuring its debt through the Dawes Plan and Young Plan.[17]

Although the Weimar Republic started off with difficulties and complications, due to, amongst other factors, Germany's defeat in the First World War, the harshness of the Treaty of Versailles and its war reparations, as well as the country's post-war moral and socioeconomic decay, it however enjoyed a mid-decade period of economic, social and cultural bonanza – '*The Swinging Twenties*'. Nevertheless, it was quite brief and its socioeconomic problems and others gradually led to its democratic collapse, and in a way even eased Hitler's rise to power.[18]

The Weimar Republic had some of the most serious economic problems ever experienced by any Western democracy in history, mainly related to its hyperinflation bouts, rampant unemployment and a large drop in living standards. Its first years of existence were very hard lived due to the Treaty of Versailles's punitive reparations, which caused much consternation and resentment. Although the actual economic damage resulting from the Treaty of Versailles is difficult to determine, it is clear that while official reparations were considerable, Germany, however, only ended up paying a fraction of them. Still, the reparations much damaged Germany's economy by discouraging market loans, which forced the Weimar government to finance its deficit by printing more currency, which thus caused huge hyperinflation. Although from 1923 to 1929 there was a short period of economic recovery, the Great Depression led to such a massive worldwide recession, with Germany being most particularly badly affected as it depended heavily on American loans. In 1926, there were two million Germans unemployed, and in 1932, the number rose to around six million. Whereas most of the German citizenship blamed the Weimar Republic for the socioeconomic downfall, the world economic stagnation exacerbated the whole context, leading to increased demands on Germany to repay the debts that it owed to the United States. Furthermore, the Great Depression not only had devastating effects on the fragile

[17] Ibid, pgs 42–7.
[18] Ibid.

existence of the Weimar Republic, but in fact also played a major role in the Nazi takeover, as some people blamed the economic decline for the citizenship's shift to extremist politics.[19]

The political and economic roles certain individuals played within the Weimar Republic, such as Paul von Hindenburg and Heinrich Brüning, have also been closely associated with the downfall of the Weimar Republic. In 1925, Paul von Hindenburg became '*Reichspräsident*' and was the person directly responsible for effectively ending the Republic by appointing Hitler as Chancellor. Heinrich Brüning is also much blamed for his 1930–2 liberal economic policy. Ultimately, whilst the end of the Weimar Republic came with the total collapse of democracy, the founding of a single-party state saw the rise to power of the Nazi party, with Adolf Hitler as '*Fuhrer*', which in turn and that way gave the birth of the Nazi Era.[20]

The Great Depression

From 1929 until more or less 1939, the world suffered one of its worst economic downturns – the '*Great Depression*' (the Depression) – which resulted in the longest and most severe socioeconomic depression ever experienced by the industrialized Western world. The Depression sparked off fundamental changes in economic theory and macroeconomic policy, as well as within economic institutions. Although the Depression originated in the United States, it affected almost every country of the world, causing drastic declines in output, acute deflation and severe unemployment. While Americans faced their worst economic adversity since the War of Independence, in Europe the already feeble socioeconomic base, especially in countries like Germany, Great Britain (GB) and France, was particularly further debilitated. The overall socioeconomic impact of the Depression was huge and included both extreme human suffering, as well as profound changes in economic policy. In a short period of time, world output and standards of living dropped precipitously. In the early 1930s, as much as one-fourth of the labour force in industrialized countries was unable to find work. Although by the mid-1930s conditions had begun to improve, complete recovery was not accomplished until the very end of the decade. With the international economic system being modified in many ways, gradual recovery from the Depression was finally only largely impelled by the abandonment of the gold standard, together with an ensuing monetary expansion.[21]

The '*1929 New York Stock Market Crash*' officially triggered the Depression. During the summer of 1929, there was an initial decline in US output, which is widely believed to have stemmed from a tight US monetary policy aimed at limiting stock market

[19] Ibid, pgs 107–25.
[20] Ibid.
[21] Encyclopedia Britannica. *The Great Depression.* https://www.britannica.com/event/Great-Depression

speculation. From the low in 1921 to the peak in 1929, stock prices had risen more than fourfold. By the fall of 1929, US stock prices had reached such levels that they could not be justified by reasonable anticipations of future earnings. As a direct result, in October 1929, when different minor events led to gradual price declines, investors lost confidence and the stock market bubble burst. On Thursday, 24 October 1929, or '*Black Thursday*', panic selling began. Since many stocks had been purchased on margin, the price declines forced some investors to liquidate their holdings, which thus exacerbated the fall in prices. Between their peak in September and their low in November, US stock prices declined 33 per cent. Because the decline in stock prices was so dramatic, the event is commonly often referred to as the '*Great Crash of 1929*' or '*1929 New York Stock Market Crash*'.

Amongst many other effects, the Great Crash of 1929 mainly made business investment and consumer purchases of durable goods fall sharply, which, in turn, reduced US aggregate demand substantially, making real output, which had been declining slowly up to that point, fall very rapidly. In the fall of 1930, there was another big blow to aggregate demand when the first of four waves of banking panics gripped the United States, which consequently caused severe contractions in the money supply.[22]

The Depression affected virtually every country in the world directly or indirectly, although the dates and magnitude of the downturn in economic activity and annual industrial production growth varied substantially across countries. Just to mention a few of the worst affected European countries, whereas since 1925 more or less, GB had been struggling with low growth and recession, during the early 1930, however, it slid into severe depression; in the early 1930s, France also experienced a relatively short downturn, with a short-lived recovery in 1932 and 1933, although once again, between 1933 and 1936, both production and prices fell substantially. Likewise, in early 1928, Germany's economy slipped into a downturn and then stabilized before turning down again in the third quarter of 1929, with a huge decline in industrial production.[23]

The Depression revealed many deep flaws within the international economic system, with the many consequential reactions that it generated changing the system in many crucial ways. Most importantly, the Depression hastened, if not caused, the end of the international gold standard. Although after the Second World War, the Bretton Woods system reinstated a system of fixed currency exchange rates, the world economies never actually embraced it with the same conviction as they had brought to the gold standard, and thus by 1973, fixed exchange rates were abandoned completely in favour of floating rates.[24]

Some other changes the Depression also produced included the '*1935 National Labor Relations Act*' or '*Wagner Act*', which encouraged collective bargaining; the '*1935 Social*

[22] Ibid.
[23] Ibid.
[24] Ibid.

Security Act', establishing unemployment compensation and old-age and survivors' insurance; the 1930s substantial increase in many countries of government regulation of the economy, especially of financial markets; the US establishment in 1934, of the '*Securities and Exchange Commission*' *(SEC),* in order to regulate new stock issues in stock market trading practices; and finally, the '*1933 Banking Act*' or '*Glass-Steagall Act*', which established deposit insurance in the United States and prohibited banks from underwriting or dealing in securities.[25] Macroeconomic policies were also developed for tempering economic downturns and upturns. During the Depression, the central role of reduced spending and monetary contraction also led Keynes to develop in 1936 his '*General Theory of Employment, Interest, and Money*'. Keynes's theories suggested that in order to counteract depressions, increases in government spending and tax cuts, together with monetary expansion, could be used.[26] While recovery from the Depression in the United States began in the spring of 1933, recovery in the rest of the world varied enormously, with some countries, like France, not being able to achieve full recovery phase until 1938.[27]

Following the many post-Depression modifications that were made to the international economic system and the new regulating measures implemented in the international financial sector, from 1945 until 1980 Keynesian economics and embedded liberalism began dominating the economic landscape.

Nonetheless, at the subjacent academic level, the damage was done, having triggered the academic revolution, which began reformulating classical liberalism and laissez-faire. With socialism having begun to plough deep into the socialization of the economy, soon after, the academic revolution spawned the two new liberal currents, ordoliberalism and neoliberalism, which would form the construct of neoliberal thought, as well as begin constituting the main theoretical counter-reaction to Keynesianism, embedded liberalism and collectivism.

That whole revisionist process eventually changed liberal economics forever both in theory and in practice, henceforth generating a completely 'new liberal' way of thinking, which still prevails encapsulated in the established neoliberal paradigm and orthodoxy.

25 Ibid.
26 Ibid.
27 Ibid.

2

The Role of Sociology in the Reformation of Classical Liberalism and Laissez-Faire: *The Socialist Calculation Debate*

Within the framework of the academic revolution beseeching the reformulation of classical liberalism and laissez-faire, 'sociology' played an extremely influencing role in the reformation of the economic ideology. Although, as ensuing chapters will reveal, there were other fields and areas, which equally gave shape and form to the 'new liberal' currents that the revolution spawned, 'Ordoliberalism' and 'Neoliberalism', sociology was one of the most influential of all. During the 1920s, some of the deepest and most transcendental probing, which was made into the modification of classical liberalism and laissez faire, was carried out by socialism.

By the early twentieth century, the socialist movement had already much contributed to the question of socialist-based economic coordination and calculation, although during the 1920s, a very heated academic debate began to be most pronouncedly staged in order to stimulate the '*socialization*' of the economic realm. With the heavy flow of contrasting new developing theories, with theories of past and contemporary economists, a rich and diverse discourse of opposing ideologies emerged, which altogether climaxed in the '*Socialist Calculation Debate*' (the Debate).

The Socialist Calculation Debate had a key role in the revision of classical liberalism and laissez-faire, since it began pressing forward many of the main actors, issues, ideas, notions and concepts, which would soon after serve to cast and mould the new liberal currents. On one hand, as the next chapter will explain further, sociology provided the bedrock for the ideological structure and composition of ordoliberalism's sociological variant. On the other hand, and most especially as regards neoliberalism, the Socialist Calculation Debate concentrated all at once: some of the main economists that were likewise involved in the consequent process of construction of neoliberal thought; some of the theories and arguments that became those economists' ideologically defining trademarks throughout their lifetimes; some of the notions and concepts, which became the main defining characteristics of the two schools of neoliberal thought, the Austrian School and the Chicago School. Many of the contributions delivered by the economists involved in the Socialist Calculation Debate influenced immensely, at one stage or another, both the shapingand the conceptualization of neoliberalism.

Ever since the end of the nineteenth century and the beginning of the twentieth century, socialism had begun building much momentum as a large-scale movement in the United States and Europe. In view of the Soviet Union's experimentation with communism, socialist proponents had high hopes for their ideas. Most especially after the success of the 1917 Bolshevik Revolution, socialism began to expand much more. Socialism had its economic foundations based on the legacies of intellectuals, like David Ricardo and Karl Marx, and hinged tightly on a central and vital role for government intervention in the economy. The socialist impetus was further bolstered by an increased influence of the working class in society, which put pressure for representation upon European parliaments and began securing concrete improvements in labour protection. While some proponents of decentralized economic planning and market socialism, such as Peter Kropotkin and Leon Trotsky, had presented earlier arguments against the utilization of central economic planning for a socialist economy, from the 1920s onwards, socialism began to probe much deeper into the renovation of classical liberalism and laissez-faire. Economists who favoured socialist-oriented changes in contemporary societies began to develop countless theories intended to address issues, like '*where, when and how the state should intervene in economic life*',[1] as well as how to reorganize societies based on such new precepts.

The wide array of past and new contrasting theories, together with the rich and diverse discourse of opposing ideologies that emerged henceforth, climaxed altogether in the Socialist Calculation Debate. The Debate served as a kind of precursor forum, which united some of the main economists, notions, concepts, theories and arguments that would influence, at one stage or another and in different ways, the conceptualization of the new liberal currents. Many of the notions and concepts pressed forward during the Debate for the modding of classical liberalism and laissez-faire served as some of the precursor elements and ingredients, which would later give shape and form to ordoliberalism, and most especially, to neoliberalism.

For example, socialism formed the basis of the sociological inclination of ordoliberalism and the social market economy, which produced the German Economic Miracle. Additionally, Ludwig von Mises's 'Anti-interventionism' theses, as well as Friedrich Hayek's 'Knowledge' and 'Price Mechanism' arguments, became both economists' defining trademarks, which likewise influenced immensely their contributions to the conception of neoliberalism.[2] Throughout Mises's life, 'Anti-interventionism' represented one of his and the Chicago School's main defining characteristics. Hayek likewise established his neoliberal stance, through his 'Knowledge Arguments'. What is more, the main concepts Hayek expressed in his 'Knowledge Arguments' have been extremely transcendental in different ways for different schools of economic thought,

[1] Gettysburg College. Gettysburg Economic Review. Volume 5. Article 6. ELLIOTT, C.A. *Friedrich von Hayek: The Socialist-Calculation Debate, Knowledge Arguments, and Modern Economic Development*, pg 78. https://pdfs.semanticscholar.org/8429/f1327b10c7c389c46f825a46dc52dc8b5a13.pdf

[2] Ibid, pg 79.

most especially for the Austrian School. Hayek's proposals on 'Price Mechanisms' are also particularly interesting as they equally greatly defined his own personal, as well as the Austrian School's frame of mind, regarding price theory.

The Socialist Calculation Debate

During the 1920s, in Austria, Vienna, Ludwig von Mises generated a series of '*Privatseminars*' in order to tackle the '*socialization of the economy*', which gave way to a very transcendental socialist forum of academic discussion – the '*Socialist Calculation Debate*'. From then onwards, an intense historical debate was cast between distinguished members of the Austrian School, such as Ludwig von Mises and Friedrich Hayek, who argued against the feasibility of socialism, and neoclassical and Marxian economists, like Cläre Tish, Oskar Lange, Abba Lerner, Fred M. Taylor, Henry Douglas Dickinson and Maurice Dobb, who were convinced that socialism was both feasible and superior to capitalism. The debates focused on subjects, such as the role of the competitive market, central planning boards, prices and entrepreneurial knowledge, and are considered very valuable not only in terms of their very often political motives, but most especially, in terms of the nature of the debates, which challenged economists and their theories relentlessly. Such intellectual hype both widened and deepened analyses, as well as comprehension of the new theories being developed and proposed by economists on both sides of the dispute.[3]

Although prior to the twentieth century many contributions to the question of economic coordination and calculation under socialism already existed within the socialist movement, in 1908, the Lausanne economist, Enrico Barone, was the first to discuss a formal '*socialist calculation*' argument. In his article, '*Ministry of Production in a Collectivist State*', Barone made the argument that at least in principle a socialist economy could perform just as well as a capitalist one, as within a Walrasian system, prices should be merely seen as the solution to a set of equations, which thus and therefore deemed irrelevant whether those equations were solved by the government or by the market.[4]

During the 1920s, Mises wrote an article published in '*Archiv für Sozialwissenschaften*', titled '*Economic Calculation in a Socialist Commonwealth*', which began to challenge socialist models much more seriously, by most especially rebuking the Soviet Union's practice of fully fledged socialism. The article coined for the first time the denominated term '*Socialist Calculation Debate*' or '*Economic Calculation Debate*'.[5]

[3] Ibid, pgs 78–9.

[4] History of Economic Thought. *The Socialist Calculation Debate,* pg 1. http://www.hetwebsite.net/het/essays/paretian/socialcalc.htm

[5] Gettysburg College. Gettysburg Economic Review. Volume 5. Article 6. ELLIOTT, C.A. *Friedrich von Hayek: The Socialist-Calculation Debate, Knowledge Arguments, and Modern Economic Development,* pg 81. https://pdfs.semanticscholar.org/8429/f1327b10c7c389c46f825a46dc52dc8b5a13.pdf

The Socialist Calculation Debate revolved around the entire discourse and literature, which appeared on the subject of how a socialist economy would perform economic calculation, given the inexistence of the law of value, money, financial prices for capital goods or private ownership of the means of production. More precisely, the debate focused specifically around the application of economic planning for the allocation of the means of production in the substitution of capital markets, as well as on whether in terms of efficiency and productivity, such an arrangement would perform better than a capitalist one.[6]

While the debate was popularly regarded as one between proponents of capitalism and advocates of socialism, a big part of it was, however, essentially perceived as a debate between socialists, with differing views regarding the utilization of markets and money in a socialist system, as well as the degree to which the law of value would continue to operate in a socialist economy. Socialists usually held one of the predominating positions in relation to the unit of calculation, which most ususally included that under a socialist system, money would continue to be the unit of calculation, that labour time would represent a unit of calculation or that socialism would be based on calculation '*in natura*' or on calculation performed '*in-kind*'.[7]

Caught in the middle of the socialist crossfire, Mises and Hayek joined ideological forces by pointing out that in freemarkets, 'prices' played a vital role informing producers and consumers what goods and services were in highest demand, as well as what raw materials were the most appropriate for the creation of those goods and services. Their rationale was based on the assertion that in the absence of free pricing and the possibilities of price discovery by entrepreneurs, rational economic production was therefore impossible. However, the 1920s economic crises made many supporters of capitalism begin to partly believe the socialist critique, which thus and in turn likewise made them begin promoting the reformation of capitalism, through a series of government-directed interventions in the economic system. Although interventionists hoped to preserve the productive powers of pure capitalism with the possibilities of more rational planning offered by socialism, from 1931 onwards, Mises generated his own '*Anti-interventionist*' crusade. Mises counter-argued that the interventionist's hope was false and impossible, as every 'intervention', in itself and as such, disrupts market operations by causing either surpluses or shortages. In turn and consequently, such interventions would require even further interventions, just to fix the problems caused by the first intervention, and so on and so forth, until practically a complete socialist system was achieved. For Mises, instead of fully fledged socialism, 'interventionism' was nothing more and nothing less than socialism introduced but in a slow and gradual way. Throughout Mises's life, 'anti-interventionism' represented one

[6] The History of Economic Thought. *The Socialist Calculation Debate,* pgs 1–3. http://www.hetwebsite.net/het/essays/paretian/socialcalc.htm

[7] Ibid, pgs 1–4.

of his personal, as well as the Chicago School's, main defining characteristics. In 1940, Mises wrote a book on the subject, titled '*Interventionism: An Economic Analysis*'.[8]

For Mises, '*interventionism does not want to abolish private ownership of the means of production but only to restrict it. It declares, on the one hand, that unlimited private ownership of the means of production is harmful to society; but it maintains, on the other hand, that public ownership of the means of production – socialism – is, either in general or at least for the time being, impractical. Thus it wants to create some third way: a state of society that is midway between private ownership of the means of production, on the one hand, and collective ownership of the means of production, on the other hand. In this way the 'excesses' and damages of capitalism are supposed to be prevented, while the advantages of free initiative and vitality, which socialism cannot provide, are preserved.*'[9]

Hayek was also very critical of socialism and likewise defined his neoliberal stance through his '*Knowledge Arguments*'. Through his 'Knowledge Arguments', Hayek underscored an issue for both mainstream and alternative school proponents, which challenged traditional equilibrium assumptions, as well as outlined a system wherein the applicability and efficiency of socialist models could not compare to competitive market processes that encouraged the best possible utilization of dispersed knowledge. In his 'Knowledge Arguments', Hayek conveyed several main concepts, such as dispersed knowledge among individuals; the discovery process surrounding such knowledge in a competitive market setting; the nature and role of tacit knowledge, together with the function of prices as conveyors of information about the market. Such concepts have been extremely transcendental in different ways for different schools of economic thought, most particularly, for the Austrian School. Mises's observation of the market being driven by profit-orientated entrepreneurs and Hayek's contribution to a better comprehension of the nature, role and continuous increase of knowledge in the market have influenced immensely the modern-day Austrian School's conceptualization of the market. Breaking away from standard neoclassical economics, and going even further, the Austrian school equally supports Hayek's function of competition, as '*for the modern Austrian approach, this perception of competition as the dynamic, driving force for discovery in the market process has become central*'.

Hayek's 'Knowledge Arguments' consisted of a series of research papers published from the late 1930s and throughout the 1940s, which explored the nature of equilibrium, and most especially, the process through which such state achieved. By doing so, Hayek challenged directly both traditional assumptions about static equilibrium and socialist theorists. The research presented by Hayek through his 'Knowledge Arguments' was seminal both for his own development of ideas and for the Socialist Calculation Debate. The above general set of ideas was first presented in Hayek's 1937

[8] Library of Liberty. *Mises on 'Interventionism' as a Third Way between the Free Market and Socialism (1930)*, pgs 1–2. http://oll.libertyfund.org/quotes/529

[9] Ibid, pg 1.

article '*Economics and Knowledge*', and it was further refined and improved in his 1945 article '*The Use of Knowledge in Society*'.[10]

Hayek's 1937 '*Economics and Knowledge*' was featured in a 1937 issue of '*Economica*' and sought to outline a more definite and clearer concept of equilibrium. Hayek's concept marked a total departure from pure theory of stationary equilibrium, which doesn't account for neither change nor time, and simply assumes that 'knowledge' amongst individuals is uniform and perfect, which therefore makes models based on such premises inapplicable to real-world situations. Hayek's research on 'knowledge', which he denotes as '*data*', distinguishes specifically between '*objective real facts, as the observing economist is supposed to know them*'[11] and '*subjective (data) as things known to the persons whose behaviour we try to explain*'.[12] According to his concept, a state of equilibrium can only truly last if the '*external data corresponds to the common experiences of all members of the society*'.[13]

Through that proposal of such new models of equilibrium, Hayek transcended the restraints of stationary models, allowing henceforth for equilibrium analyses to be applied to more realistic progressive societies. For Hayek, the correspondence of knowledge and intentions by entrepreneurs in the market '*is an evolutionary process with a consistent tendency towards equilibrium as economic actors come more and more into agreement … (or) become more and more correct*'.[14] As Hayek delved deeper, such tendency does not necessarily lead to an absolute state of equilibrium, due to the process through which individual knowledge is changed, or the '*nature of knowledge*'. For Hayek, the 'nature of knowledge' is based on how much and what kind of information different individuals actually possess. Interestingly, Hayek's '*Division of Knowledge*' framework is very similar in function to Smith's '*Division of Labour*', '*by assuming individually relevant knowledge*', which when put and taken together, allows for a '*spontaneous interaction of a number of people, each possessing only bits of knowledge, (to) bring about a state of affairs in which prices correspond to costs*'.[15] Hayek asserted that with individuals constantly learning new facts, 'knowledge' thus changes consistently over and over again, with individuals becoming progressively aware of new facts. Throughout his lifetime, Hayek always claimed that a greater refinement and better comprehension of his '*Division of Knowledge*' would allow for a much improved understanding of the '*equilibrating nature of the market*'.[16]

[10] Gettysburg College. Gettysburg Economic Review. Volume 5. Article 6. ELLIOTT, C.A. *Friedrich von Hayek: The Socialist-Calculation Debate, Knowledge Arguments, and Modern Economic Development*, pg 86. https://pdfs.semanticscholar.org/8429/f1327b10c7c389c46f825a46dc52dc8b5a13.pdf
[11] Ibid.
[12] Ibid.
[13] Ibid.
[14] Ibid, pg 87.
[15] Ibid.
[16] Ibid, pgs 87–8.

> *For Hayek, the 'Division of Knowledge' was the "central question of all social sciences, how the combination of fragments of knowledge existing in different minds can bring about results which, if they were to be brought about deliberately, would require a knowledge on the part of the directing mind which no single person can possess. To show that in this sense the spontaneous action of individuals will under conditions which we can define bring about a distribution of resources which can be understood as if it were made according to a single plan, although nobody has planned it, seems to me indeed an answer to the problem which has sometimes been metaphorically described as that of the 'social mind'".*[17]

In 1945, Hayek probed even deeper into the 1937 '*Economics and Knowledge*' proposals, through his '*Use of Knowledge in Society*', which likewise included his new suggestions related to '*Price Mechanisms*'. The publication included more profound 'knowledge' issues, such as the employment of systems of given preferences and perfect knowledge; proposed calculations applicable to a society; the concept of planning and decisions pertaining to the allocation of resources within a society; the planners making those decisions, and most importantly, the clear differentiation between '*scientific knowledge*' and '*tacit knowledge*'. On one hand, Hayek defined 'scientific knowledge' as that '*which we should with greater confidence expect to find in the possession of an authority made up of suitable chosen experts*'. On the other hand, he regarded 'tacit knowledge' as being '*more likely to be at the disposal of particular individuals ... the knowledge of the particular circumstances of time and place*'.[18] As Hayek reflected, although generally a greater emphasis is placed upon 'scientific knowledge', 'tacit knowledge' should however hold just as equal weight, since '*practically every individual has some advantage over all others in that he possesses unique information of which beneficial use might be made*'.[19]

The second half of Hayek's 1945 publication concentrated purely on '*Price Mechanisms*'. His new proposals on the subject are most particularly interesting, as they would also greatly cast and mould his and the Austrian School's frame of mind regarding 'price theory'. According to Hayek's predilection for the 'price mechanism', 'prices' have a very important role both as mediums of exchange and '*conveyors of information*'. For Hayek, 'prices' are a '*kind of machinery for registering change, or a system of telecommunications which enables individual producers to watch merely the movement of a few pointers ... in order to adjust their activities to changes of which they may never know more than is reflected in the price movement*'.[20] One of the most unique and distinguishable defining characteristics of the price mechanism is that it represents the complete anti-thesis of advocates of '*conscious direction*', like central planners and socialists, since due to its mere nature, it has '*evolved without design*'.[21]

[17] Ibid, pg 88.
[18] Ibid, pg 89.
[19] Ibid.
[20] Ibid, pg 90.
[21] Ibid.

3

Ordoliberalism

The academic revolution beseeching the reformulation of classical liberalism and laissez-faire, together with the intellectual brainstorming that it generated, soon saw the first 'new liberal' current – *'Ordoliberalism'* – emerge during the early 1930s in crisis-ridden Weimar Germany. The Freiburg School advanced ordoliberalism as a neo-Kantian epistemology, socioeconomic response to the Weimar Republic, promulgating a *'Third Way'* between capitalism and communism.

> *Taken as a package, German neoliberalism can be considered as an update and renewed version of the Scottish-English classical liberal tradition on German soil – with the significant exception of Müller-Armack's social democratic, redistributive notions of social market economy. Freiburg-style ordoliberalism does anticipate elements of the New Political Economy, such as public choice, constitutional economics and the new institutional economics. Nevertheless, it also harks back to the more rounded case for free markets in A. Smith, in which economic freedom forms part of the philosophical, legal and historical argument for a more encompassing, indivisible freedom. The liberal-conservative view of social market economy, allied to the legal-economic case for free markets and a limited state, is also largely compatible with the classical liberal tradition.*[1]

During the early 1930s, in the midst of crisis-ridden Weimar Germany, ordoliberalism emerged from the Freiburg School. Both its genesis and evolution must be comprehended within the temporal-spatial setting that characterized the period, as well as from the perspective of the critical perceptions its progenitors from the Freiburg School acknowledged from it.

From the very beginning, the newly founded Weimar Republic experienced numerous violent clashes between several political factions. Although they eventually subsided, war reparations made inflation upsurge, which left Germany facing severe economic difficulties, most often at the cost of a traumatized *'petit bourgeoise'*. In 1929, with the country only having begun to stabilize since the latter half of the decade, the Great Depression hit Germany hard, which caused even worse socioeconomic consequences.

1 COMMUN, P. (Dir.). *L'Ordoliberalisme Allemande. Aux Sources de l'Economie Sociale de Marché*, pg 36.

With the economic crisis quickly turning into a political crisis due to the fragile pluralist parliamentary democracy and the weak structures of its unstable political system, the German political and economic situation soon spiralled out of control. Within the context of very polarized party system, the untenable situation ultimately led to the collapse of the Weimar Republic, the Nazi takeover, as well as to the rapid transformation of the country into a totalitarian dictatorship.[2]

Academics from the Freiburg School perceived the overall situation, as one involving both political and economic problems clearly realizing that one could not be solved without the other. Freiburg School academics realized that since political, economic and social systems worked in synchronized coordination with one another, one system would therefore not work properly and harmoniously, without the other system's equal good functioning, for the instability of one system would affect the stability of the other system. For those academics, the political, legal, economic and social systems had to work in close harmonization with each other, since political stability needs economic stability, and likewise and in turn, economic stability needs a proper safeguarding legal framework, in order for economic activity to be carried out in a safe, equal and balanced way. Freiburg academics believed that otherwise and if not, the overall political-economical-social equilibrium would be altered by the instability of any one of the other spheres that it works in tandem with. Based on such a broadminded perception, the new breed of academics therefore advanced a view of society, which was self-consciously non-economical, beginning to henceforth tackle the various societal spheres and the individual problems occurring therein, as very closely interrelated. In view of the severe thrusts Germany had experienced through its various crises, together with its high levels of industrial concentration and the several hyperinflation bouts it had suffered, Freiburg academics thus developed a theory revolving around the concept of *'Ordnungstheorie'* or *'Theory of Orders'*, which was based on a very strict *'economic order'*.[3]

A select group of Freiburg School academics, formed by Walter Eucken, Franz Böhm and Hans Grobmann-Doerth, idealized and conceived *'Ordoliberalismus'* or *'Ordoliberalism'*, which promulgated a *'Third Way'*, between capitalism and communism. Through their new liberal current, ordoliberals established a very intelligent and rational, close working interdependent relationship, between the political, legal, economic and social realms. Ordoliberalism is considered a *'Metatheory'*, which defines a system, which is conceived through a cultural vision of society, based on philosophical and anthropological considerations, by integrating the methodological study of economic facts. Rotating around such a sophisticated transdisciplinary study of the economic field, through the mixing and blending of historical and cultural

2 BIEBRICHER, T. and VOGELMANN, F. (Eds). *The Birth of Austerity: German Ordoliberalism and Contemporary Neoliberalism*, pg 2–3.

3 Ibid.

dimensions, ordoliberalism simultaneously spawned an extremely innovative and refined, *'Kulturelle Ökonomik'* or *'Economic Culture'*.[4]

Ordoliberalism and the Freiburg School were officially given birth through the publication of the *'Ordo Manifesto of 1936'*. The term 'ordoliberalism' was, however, not invented nor claimed by those to whom it refers to. Following the ordoliberal publication, the label 'ordoliberalism' was curiously tagged onto the ordoliberal tradition, due to its adherents being nicknamed *'ordos'* or *'ordoliberals'* by other academics involved in the intellectual revolution.[5] Ordoliberalism has two main variants: one mostly based on economic orders, and another more sociologically slanted. 'Ordnungstheorie' or the 'Theory of Orders' is at the same time very deep-rooted in German economic, philosophical and religious thought.

When trying to comprehend ordoliberalism and breaking it down, one of its most clearly distinguishible and defining features is automatically conferred by its mere name. When divided, the word *'ordoliberal'*, through the separation of its two composing terms, *'ordo'* ('ordinem' in Latin, or 'order') and *'liberal'*, automatically implies *'ordered liberalism'* or *'liberal order'*. Most probably due to the ordoliberals' perception of the context of disorder that characterized Weimar Germany, their most paramount si-ne-qua-non chief precept, thus became *'order'*. In accordance with such precept, for ordoliberals, individual 'order' had to prevail within every single interrelated sphere of action, for them to function both individually and collectively in harmonious equilibrium. Ordoliberalism is deeply rooted in a social ontology, which views the totality of society, as an *'interdependence of orders'*. Therefore, for ordoliberals, a proper comprehension of any object of enquiry must be carried out by *'denken in ordnungen'* or *'thinking in terms of orders'*. For ordoliberals, every single sphere in question, whether it is the political, economic or legal spheres, is constituted by some kind of individual 'order' in itself, which will therefore and correspondingly make them either function, malfunction or otherwise be confined to a perpetual state of chaos and disorder. Based on such reasoning, ordoliberals thus made very distinct identifications and separations between the different structures and elements, which constitute the different functioning orders.[6]

The most wide-arching maxim of ordoliberalism is *'Ordnungspolitik'* or the *'Politics of Ordering'*. In accordance with that main dictum, it is the state who has the responsibility of generating the 'politics of ordering', as well as the obligation to put the 'politics of ordering' into practice in every single sphere, since every sphere must

[4] COMMUN, P. (Dir.). *L'Ordoliberalisme Allemande. Aux Sources de l'Economie Sociale de Marché*, pg 36.

[5] BIEBRICHER, T. and VOGELMANN, F. (Eds). *The Birth of Austerity: German Ordoliberalism and Contemporary Neoliberalism*, pg 3.

[6] Ibid, pgs 4–5.

be in good 'order' to function properly. In turn and correspondingly, all policies must be likewise based on that same dictum, if they are to be targeted properly.[7] In stark contrast to laissez-faire liberalism, for ordoliberals, the state has an essential role in defining and enforcing the *'Economic Constitution'* or *'legal-institutional framework'*, wherein markets operate. The market order itself is considered a *'legal-institutional order'* and not a *'natural event'*. As such a 'legal-institutional order', it therefore needs to be very closely and carefully cultivated, in order for it to be adequately maintained and kept functioning correctly. For ordoliberals, the way in which the market functions is a question of *'constitutional choice'*, with the choice of rules that are applied in the market, either providing the freedom or defining the constraints, with which the economic participants can pursue their personal objectives.[8]

While ordoliberalism strongly supports a state-supervising or semi-regulating interventionism, in order to assure and safeguard a legal and 'ordered' proper pattern of market behaviourism, at the same time, it also lets go of the reins of free and healthy competition. Ordoliberal state-interventionism is directed solely towards the *'Wirstschaftsverfassung'*, or *'Economic Constitution'* or *'Framework of Markets'*, and thus does not intervene directly in them or in any of their inner workings. It mainly focuses on generating proper patterns of free and healthy competitive market behaviour, and therefore does not interfere with any other modes of market conducts. In correlation with 'Ordnungspolitik' or the 'Politics of Ordering' maxim, it is the state who has the foremost responsibility of creating and establishing the legal framework, wherein free and healthy competition is to be carried out, with much respect towards the price mechanism. It is the state that must establish and enforce the respective regulations and rules of behaviour, so that competition and the price mechanism can function properly. By analogy, competition must also be based on good *'Leistungverfassung'* or *'Performance'*, so that it can render the desired *'performance'* competition.[9]

The ordoliberal emphasis on market 'order' demarcated itself very specifically from the *'laissez-faire and laissez-aller'* principle of allowing free markets and the interactions therein to develop by themselves that had led to collectivisms, as well as from other early 1930s rising Keynesian interventionist paradigms.[10] For ordoliberals, economic policy most especially must be based on a very sophisticated and refined comprehension of the functioning of markets. It should not subordinate the economy to the planning of a central administration or let alone confine it to *'mere stoic passivity in the face of social upheaval'*.[11] Within the ordoliberal economic sphere, the

[7] Ibid.

[8] VANBERG, V.J. *Ordoliberalism and Ordnugspolitik: A Brief Explanation,* pgs 9–10. https://www.eucken.de/wp-content/uploads/Ordoliberalism-and-Ordnungspolitik.pdf

[9] BIEBRICHER, T. and VOGELMANN, F. (Eds). *The Birth of Austerity: German Ordoliberalism and Contemporary Neoliberalism,* pgs 4–5.

[10] Ibid, pg 5.

[11] Ibid, pgs 4–5.

'*competitive order*' safeguards and ensures both proper competition, as well as the correct functioning of the price mechanism.[12]

Ordoliberalism is considered an interdisciplinary current, which juxtaposes the fields of law with political economy at its centre. It rotates around three main basic defining convictions. The first basic conviction is related to its view of society, which '*puts a particular emphasis on functioning markets as the necessary precondition for the material reproduction of society but is equally adamant that functioning markets in turn rely on certain societal preconditions*'.[13] The second conviction is related to the complexities inherent to such a broad-scoped approach, and therefore explicitly asserts that only scientific knowledge is capable '*of developing an accurate analysis of the multiple interdependencies between the economic and the non-economic spheres of society and thus of offering apt diagnoses as well as corresponding therapeutic recommendations*'.[14] Ordoliberalism firmly believes that social science should not be practised for its own sake, since, for it to be able to inform political decision-making properly, it has to strictly base itself on objective, '*scientific*' knowledge. The third and last conviction is related to the proper functioning of the price-mechanism. That conviction is based on the marginalist revolution led by the Austrian School's Carl Menger, and continued by its adherents, Friedrich Hayek and Ludwig Mises, and asserts that '*without a properly functioning price mechanism as the functional core of markets, allocation could not even remotely approximate efficiency*'.[15]

In clear deviation from the feud between planners and interventionists and laissez-faire and Manchester libertarians, ordoliberalism has three distinct levels of state interventionism. Above all else, ordoliberalism stresses on the indispensability of an appropriate state structure for the proper implementation of 'Ordnungspolitik', since an ad hoc political order should precede any subsequently applicable economic policy. For ordoliberalism, as far and as much, as the state has an indispensable role in its positive functions vis-à-vis the economy, clear definitions must be likewise developed regarding the kind of actions it should take, as well as the actual extent of those actions. At the same time, however, ordoliberalism also emphasizes that demarcations also have to be clearly delineated between what certain kinds of actions, societal spheres and contexts ought to be equivalently off-limits to the state.[16] For ordoliberals, the most crucial out-of-bounds area that the state should not interfere with surrounds Keynesian policies of economic stimulus, such as monetary and fiscal policies, as they would impede the workings of performance competition, as well as of the price mechanism. Keynesian instruments for stimulating the economy, like expansionary

12 Ibid.
13 BIEBRICHER, T. and VOGELMANN, F. (Eds). *The Birth of Austerity: German Ordoliberalism and Contemporary Neoliberalism*, pg 4.
14 Ibid.
15 Ibid.
16 Ibid, pg 6.

monetary policies, are most especially recommended against, as for Eucken, an intact monetary system is the most important feature for functioning markets. In much the same way, devaluations or the manipulation of the value of money are options that are also totally recommended against. *'Flushing markets with cheap money artificially boosts demand and thus leads to sales when, in actuality, goods would normally only sell at cheaper prices or increased quality. Consequently, this leads to a distortion of the price system, and the same goes for the inflationary effects that may be the result of an expansionist monetary policy.'*[17] For similar reasons, ordoliberalism equally totally rules out policies of fiscal stimulus, since *'its effects amount to a state subsidy to markets that are no longer competitive and competition only truly works if it creates winners and losers, with the latter ultimately being forced off the market'.*[18]

As regards crisis-management economic policy, ordoliberals also much diverge with Keynesian demand management. While the main ordoliberal emphasis on economic policy is placed upon the '*competitive order*', '*liberal interventionism*' should be aimed at hastening the respective transformations of the volatilities of capitalist reproduction, instead of at decreasing or moderating them.[19]

The scope of ordoliberal state-interventionism equally reaches into the realm of social policy, most particularly, as regards labour market policy. Once again, however, ordoliberalism stresses that within labour markets, the state should not interfere with proper competition or the price mechanism. The general maxim of 'Ordnungspolitik' regarding the safeguarding of competition and the price mechanism, holds for the labour market just as much as for any other market. For example, Eucken's critique of traditional labour policy is very interlaced with the ordoliberal 'proto-workfare' view. During the various economic glitches experienced by Weimar Germany, Eucken had always blamed union power for the rigidities that appeared in labour markets, alleging *'that the corporative structure of the labour market, together with the policy of full employment resulted in a marked tendency towards central control of the economy'.*[20] Accordingly, the politics of the '*competitive order*' remain static for both kinds of economic powers, which threaten proper competition and distort prices in check, as *'if cartels can artificially bolster prices for goods, and unions can do the same for the price of labour power, this amounts to a distortion of the price mechanism'.*[21] Ordoliberal labour policy is regarded as a sort of 'workfare' approach '*avant le lettre*', since, although it does accept a system of unemployment insurance and basic poor relief, it however considers minimum wages completely unacceptable. *'Since social policy must not interfere with the functioning of competitive markets, it must not de-commodify those unemployed yet able to work. Instead, it must activate them as potential participants in*

[17] Ibid.
[18] Ibid, pgs 6–7.
[19] Ibid, pg 7.
[20] Ibid.
[21] Ibid, pgs 7–8.

markets, first and foremost the labour market.'[22] By way of supporting the type of social policy, which turns participants into entrepreneurs and re-trains them for different kinds of jobs, ordoliberalism runs very close to what is termed as an '*activating*' welfare state.[23]

Within the framework of the ordoliberal 'Ordnungspolitik', the main objective of the state in 'ordering' all the different interrelated spheres of action is the generation of a proper functioning economic system or 'competitive order', so as to safeguard proper competition, as well as the functionality of the price mechanism. The economic realm constitutes the main point of focus of the state, with the 'competitive order' being the most important sphere of 'ordering', as well as of entrepreneurial interaction. The 'competitive order' is therefore, where the 'politics of ordering' finds its most direct, appropriate and suitable sphere of application.

> *The economic policy which underpins competitive ordering seeks to endow markets with a form of order that meaningfully integrates all parts of the economic process. The individual agriculturalist, industrialist, artisan and worker – i.e., each individual firm and household – should be free to plan and to act. Economic actors do not follow orders. Instead, they seek to deploy their own labour, productive capacity and capital in the manner that seems best to them. The result is not subordination, but rather co-ordination of households and firms. Firms are free to choose what they produce, which technologies they apply, which raw materials they use and which markets they sell to. By the same token, workers are not coerced to a specific function. They possess their own rights of free movement and free contract. But there is no freedom to dictate the rules of the game arbitrarily, or to determine the manner in which the economic process unfolds. And it is here that the policy of ordering Ordnungspolitik finds its realm of application.*[24]

Considering that the economy or 'competitive order' is where most economic policies are directly targeted at, the 'competitive order', thus and therefore, becomes that way, the epicentre of the rest of the spheres' interrelated attention. However, some questions do arise. For example, what is it exactly that defines the 'competitive order'? What are the specific characteristics and precise features, which define a well-balanced 'competitive order', wherein proper competition and the functionality of the price-mechanism would be appropriately safeguarded? Different national or regional situations and circumstances are always characterized by differing contexts, with different individual needs of economic steering and specifically orientated economic policies. Eucken, however, established six guiding principles, which define and delineate both an appropriate ordoliberal 'competitive order' and the kind of '*perfect*

[22] Ibid, pg 7.
[23] Ibid.
[24] BIEBRICHER, T. and VOGELMANN, F. (Eds). *The Birth of Austerity: German Ordoliberalism and Contemporary Neoliberalism*. EUCKEN, W. *What Is the Competitive Order*, pg 99.

competition' that should ideally take place therein. Some of the most important aspects of those six principles are:

"*1. Price-fixing and economic steering in textile provision, and also far beyond this sector, are shaped significantly by questions of whether the nation's wool mills are cartelised, whether the market is dominated by a few independent companies, or whether many mills compete with one another in order to supply an equally large number of dealers and weavers.*
2. The competitive order is ruled by the market model of 'perfect competition.' Ideally-speaking, perfect competition coordinates the planning and decision-making of individual firms and households.
3. What is perfect competition? It is a specific, exactly-defined market form that should not be confused with the laissez-faire model. It is also to be strictly distinguished from a 'monopoly conflict' market which is evident, for example, in the campaign waged by a partially-monopolistic syndicate against external parties who have emerged out of this shadow, or in the conflict between two oligopolistic shipping lines, railroads or petrol suppliers … Perfect competition is not constituted within the battle of man against man, but instead realised through parallel individual performances. It is neither an obstructive nor a destructive form of competition, but is instead founded within a 'performance competition' (Leistungswettbewerb) …
4. … Economic policy requires indicators, or symptoms, in order to implement competitive order … It needs rules of thumb.
5. Perfect competition does not merely serve within the competitive order as a means to increase production. Instead, it also steers the economic process through its pricing mechanism …
6. … Like the rule of law, the competitive order should also create parameters within which the free actions of an individual are limited by the sphere of freedom of other individuals such that a balance is attained between human rights to freedom. – In truth the desire for competitive order is closely related to the desire for freedom … ".[25]

The Ordo Manifesto of 1936

In 1936, with the publication of '*The Ordo Manifesto of 1936*' (the Manifesto), both ordoliberalism and the Freiburg School were simultaneously officially born.

While quintessential ordoliberal ideas had been written much before the Manifesto, the notions and concepts of the ordoliberal progenitors had likewise been flowing through Freiburg University and other places, years before the elaboration of the Manifesto. Notwithstanding, the Manifesto, projected for the first time, a common

[25] Ibid, pgs 101–3.

interdisciplinary agenda, based on an in-depth analysis of the totality of society, or of the 'interdependence' of the political, legal, economic and social orders. Within the context of Weimar Germany's chaotic political, economic and social spheres, the Manifesto can be perceived as both a critique of the Republic's practices and a wide-ranging recommendation for a political economy programme.

One of the main reasons for the interdisciplinary nature of ordoliberalism is closely associated with the intense political and intellectual struggles of Weimar Germany, together with the consequential countering ideological inclinations, which the Freiburg School academics adopted. Another explanation for the ordoliberal nature is also conferred by the different educational backgrounds of its ordoliberal progenitors, Walter Eucken, Franz Böhm and Hans Grobmann-Doerth. Alexander Rustow was an additional key academic, which although not-institutionally affiliated to Freiburg University, also influenced ordoliberal thought immensely with his ideas and theorems. Whereas Walter Eucken spent most of his academic career at Freiburg University as professor of political economy, Hans Grobmann-Doerth received his training in law. Similarly, Franz Böhm was a professor of law in Freiburg before moving to the University of Jena, and Alexander Rüstow had studied political economy and other social sciences, before receiving his doctorate in philosophy. Moreover, the University of Freiburg's Faculty of Law and Economics equally provided an extremely fertile environment for the integration of the legal and economic perspectives into the ordoliberal tradition, which became the defining trademarks of the Freiburg School.[26] Those four intellectuals are regarded as the ones who not only spurred the ordoliberal tradition, but also the ones who formed the main nucleus, of what would eventually be referred to as the Freiburg School.[27]

Originally, the Manifesto was titled '*Unsere Aufgabe*' or '*Our Task*'. However, the English translation of the Manifesto changed the title to 'The Ordo Manifesto of 1936'. The Manifesto was written by Walter Eucken, Franz Böhm and Hans Grobmann-Doerth, as a programmatic text for the editorial of a book series named '*Ordnung der Wirtschaft*' or '*Order of the Economy*'. It served as the main outlet for pressing forward ordoliberal ideas. At the same time, it likewise laid out the basic notions of what would later be named 'ordoliberalism', as well as the political ambitions of the three academics.[28]

In general terms, the Manifesto chided historicism severely for being incapable of producing objective knowledge on economic issues, as well as for making the sciences of law and political economy drift apart into general relativism. With the text insisting

[26] Ibid and VANBERG, V.J. *Ordoliberalism and Ordnugspolitik: A Brief Explanation,* pg 9. https://www.eucken.de/wp-content/uploads/Ordoliberalism-and-Ordnungspolitik.pdf

[27] BIEBRICHER, T. and VOGELMANN, F. (Eds). *The Birth of Austerity: German Ordoliberalism and Contemporary Neoliberalism,* pg 3.

[28] Ibid, pg 23.

explicitly on *'principled thinking that overcomes the arbitrariness of historicism'*,[29] its main focusing point is the '*Wirtschaftsverfassung*' or '*Economic Constitution*'. Another of its main premises also stresses that issues related to economic and social policy must be considered within the framework of the '*interdependence of different normative orders*', such as the political, legal, economic, social and moral orders. The rationale strongly holds that if not and if issues are treated in isolation, they will, in turn, entail undesired negative consequences. For those reasons and for such a complex task to be properly achieved, real ordoliberal faith relies solely on true and objective scientific knowledge, as it is considered the only kind of knowledge, which is inherently capable of providing correct methodological and theoretically based knowledge, for coherent and adequate policy recommendations. For ordoliberals, true scientific knowledge of the law and of political economy represents objective disinterested knowledge, with no direct or personal interest involved, which could in any sort of way blur, either the correct identification of true socioeconomic problems or of ad hoc recommendations for political or economic courses of action. *'What has happened as a consequence of the dethronement of the two disciplines, however, is that it is no longer scientifically-discovered truth, which informs policy making but rather interested parties and the ideologies they use to justify their particularistic demands.'*[30]

The Manifesto's format very clearly reflects a programmatic, scientific-based recommendation, for a wide-ranging national course of action, in order to tackle law and political economy issues, through the lens of the 'interdependence' of the political, legal, economic and social realms. The authors emphasize that '*the most urgent task for the representatives of law and political economy is to work together in an effort to ensure that both disciplines regain their proper place in the life of the nation. This is not only for the sake of science but, more important, in the interests of the economic life of the German nation*'.[31] Correspondingly, and in order to carry out such a complex task properly, the authors most strictly stress that only *'men of science, by virtue of their profession and position being independent of economic interests, are the only objective, independent advisers capable of providing true insight into the intricate interrelationships of economic activity and therefore also providing the basis upon which economic judgments can be made. They are also the only ones who, on the strength of their intimate knowledge of those interrelationships – a knowledge which is constantly being expanded and refined by the continuing penetration of new ideas – are capable of forming an objective judgment, independent of their own immediate economic interests, about economic measures appropriate in particular circumstances*'.[32]

The first part of the Manifesto rebukes both historical relativism and fatalism's influence, on the politico-legal attitude of many generations of German lawyers and

[29] Ibid, pg 24.
[30] Ibid.
[31] BÖHM, F., EUCKEN, W. and GROBMANN-DOERTH, H. *The Ordo Manifesto of 1936,* in BIEBRICHER, T. and VOGELMANN, F. (Eds). *The Birth of Austerity: German Ordoliberalism and Contemporary Neoliberalism*, pg 27.
[32] Ibid.

politicians, including Karl Marx and Gustav Schmoller, for having deeply influenced German political-economic and economic thought. The text also strongly highlights on the importance of the 'Economic Constitution', law and free competition, as well as on the importance of the linkage between the 'interdependent' sciences.[33]

The Manifesto likewise places key importance on the '*economic order*', with the text underlying that '*the economic constitution must be understood as a general political decision as to how the economic life of the nation is to be structured. Adherence to this idea alone provides the means of acquiring truly reliable and conclusive rules for interpreting many aspects of public or private law. This applies not only to the basic laws, but also particularly to special laws relating to economic matters*'.[34]

The '*interrelation*' between law and free competition is also very strongly emphasized upon by the Manifesto, with the text underlining that '*it is imperative, particularly in this instance, to reason out the problem in accordance with the provisions of the economic constitution, for free competition is an essential structural principle of the present-day German economy. Free competition, must not be stopped on the erroneous grounds of alleged unfair practice. On the other hand, it must not be allowed to degenerate into truly unfair competition either ... The collaboration of the two sciences, which in this respect still leaves much to be desired, is clearly essential*'.[35]

The Manifesto equally stresses on the fundamental '*interdependent*' relation between the individual sciences, by pointing out that '*it is the work being carried out on the problems themselves and not unhelpful methodological reflection, which is linking the individual sciences together again at a new level. Today physics, chemistry, mineralogy, physiology and other natural sciences no longer stand apart from one another. On the contrary, the physiologists are now compelled to employ the methods and results of chemistry, and the mineralogists and chemists those of physics. In the wide area of the humanities also a process of reconciliation on the part of the individual sciences is taking place everywhere ... The sciences of law and economics are also involved at various points in such a process of reconciliation*'.[36]

The Freiburg School

In 1497, Archduke Albert VI of Austria founded the Albert-Ludwigs-Universität, which is most commonly known as Freiburg University. Although Freiburg University specializes on a wide array of areas including history, law, economics, medicine and numerous other sciences, one of its most long-standing, traditional and specialized

[33] Ibid, pgs 29–36.
[34] Ibid, pgs 36–7.
[35] Ibid, pg 37.
[36] Ibid.

fields has been the *'Historical School of Economics'* (the Historical School), led by Gustav von Schmoller. The Historical School has always rejected the validity of economic theorems, by chiefly sustaining that history is the key source of knowledge as regards human actions and economic issues, and not economics, since economics is culture-specific, and cannot therefore hold through time and space.[37]

The ordoliberal progenitors, Walter Eucken, Franz Böhm and Hans Groebmann-Doerth, together with Alexander Rustow's intellectual inputs, developed '*Ordoliberalismus*', largely based on the beliefs of the Historical School, as well as on the socioeconomic aberrations generated by Weimar Germany. The conception of ordoliberalism, together with its official launching through the 'Ordo Manifesto of 1936', synchronously gave birth to the *'Freiburger Schule'* or *'Freiburg School'*. The Freiburg School places great importance on a lawful and legitimate role for the state in a democracy, as although some forms of competition are considered positive, others are viewed as requiring supervision. While the Freiburg School gave much more shape and form to the legal and political economy elements of ordoliberalism, the institution also ended constituting the economic core of post-Second World War Germany's social market economy, providing it with many leaders, advisors and technical experts.[38]

Walter Eucken, Franz Böhm and Hans Großmann-Doerth are considered the main nucleus of the Freiburg School, while other very influential members were also Edith Eucken-Erdsieck, Hans Gestrich, Friedrich A. Lutz, Karl Friedrich Maier, Fritz Meyer, Leonhard Miksch and Ludwig Erhard. Other non-affiliated members of the Freiburg School, who also contributed immensely to the foundations of ordoliberalism, were Alexander Rustow, Wilhelm Röpke and Alfred Müller-Armack.[39]

Throughout their lifetimes, Eucken and Böhm always insisted that their research programme was, above all, intended to develop and create a proper, desirable and maintainable economic order, and not simply meant as an academic enterprise. For the two of them, the juxtaposition of law and economics was an indispensable prerequisite, for the '*Wirtschaftsverfassungspolitik*' or '*Constitutional Economic Policy*', which aimed to improve the 'economic order' in an indirect way, by '*shaping the rules of the game*'. The 'Wirtschaftsverfassungspolitik' was counterbalanced by an economic policy targeted at improving outcomes through specific interventions in the economic process, by means of '*directly intervening*' in the '*playing of the game*' or by establishing the rules of play. According to both academics, the main objective of 'Ordnungspolitik' was to create and enforce a framework of rules, which would transform the self-interested efforts of market participants into socially beneficial ones.

[37] Freiburg. Albert-Ludwigs-Universität. http://www.uni-freiburg.de/ and Biografías y Vidas. *Gustav Schmoller.* https://www.biografiasyvidas.com/biografia/s/schmoller.htm

[38] VANBERG, V.J. *Ordoliberalism and Ordnugspolitik: A Brief Explanation,* pg 10. https://www.eucken.de/wp-content/uploads/Ordoliberalism-and-Ordnungspolitik.pdf

[39] COMMUN, P. (Dir.). *L'Ordolibéralisme Allemande. Aux Sources de l'Economie Sociale de Marché.* BILGER, F. *La pensée néolibérale française et l'ordolibéralisme allemand,* pgs 18–19.

In other words, the 'Wirtschaftsverfassungspolitik' had the main task of creating the conditions, wherein Adam Smith's *'invisible hand'* would carry out its beneficial work.[40] For them, whichever competitive process must be well protected by a set of unbiased rules of the game, in order to ensure *'Leistungswettbewerb'*, or the sort of competition, which achieves success through the provision of a better service to consumers. Basing themselves on such level of reasoning, they thus and therefore considered a primordial political task, or the task of 'Ordnungspolitik', to establish and maintain the environment and conditions, which would produce such 'Leistungswettbewerb' or *'beneficial competition'*.[41]

Freiburg School ordoliberals did not believe that any ordinary, *'unqualified state'*, could carry out such a task, and therefore, equally much emphasized on the need for a *'strong state'*, in order to protect against pressure from interest groups. It is for that main purpose that the ordoliberal state is assigned the role of 'watch-dog', or *'Hüter der Wettbewerbsord-nung'* or *'Guardian of the Competitive Order'*. At the same time, however, ordoliberalism does not favour an authoritarian state with over-extensive powers, but rather and instead favours a state constrained by a political constitution, which prevents it from becoming the target of self-interested rent seeking. For ordoliberals, the constraints placed upon the state are regarded as a safeguarding instrument in order to weaken any influence from special interests, which have the primary purpose of making ordinary politics more responsive to the common interests of citizens.[42]

Years later, Friedrich Hayek provided a very good synthesis of such ordoliberal characteristics by pointing out that *'the ordo-liberals espousal of the free economy does not entail a weak night-watchman state. The ordo-liberals declare for the strong state. They argue that economic freedom needs to be ordered so that freedom is not misused, as prices can be fixed, markets carved up, and competitive adjustment avoided by means of protectionism and manipulation of monetary policy; and workers can strike, the masses can revolt, and a proletarianised mass society can force the state to concede welfare. Just as the Hobbesian man requires the Leviathan to sustain her fundamental sociability, full competition requires strong state authority to assure the orderly conduct of self-interested entrepreneurs. Economic freedom is not unlimited. It is based on order, and exists only by means of order, and freedom is effective only as ordered freedom. Indeed, laissez-faire is "a highly ambiguous and misleading description of the principles on which a liberal policy is based"'*.[43]

Despite the fact that Freiburg School ordoliberals stressed strongly on providing constraints on both the state and legislators in order to prevent the granting of

[40] VANBERG, V.J. *Ordoliberalism and Ordnugspolitik: A Brief Explanation*, pgs 10–11. https://www.eucken.de/wp-content/uploads/Ordoliberalism-and-Ordnungspolitik.pdf

[41] Ibid, pg 11.

[42] Ibid, pgs 11–12.

[43] Ordoliberalism and the Austrian School. *Is Ordoliberalism Cyclical?*. https://ordoliberalism.wordpress.com/is-ordoliberalism-cyclical/

privileges to special interests, no recommendations were, however, ever provided by them regarding what exact constitutional safeguards should be installed, in order to effectively prevent any privilege-seeking or privilege-granting dynamics. The sole provision that was ever advanced by ordoliberals to that respect came through the strict limitation of the state's discretionary power, for *'its authority to intervene with special measures in the economic process'*.[44] They, nonetheless, always underlined instead that it is the wider framework of '*Ordnungspolitik*', which should confine the state's ambition to shape and structure the economy, so that it can govern in accordance with '*general rules*', rather than at its own discretion.[45]

Ordoliberal thought comprises two main intellectual inclinations, which are ab initio clearly discernible: a 'legal-economic' inclination, which was shared by the ordoliberal economists and lawyers, like Walter Eucken and Franz Böhm; and a more 'sociological inclination', that was held by ordoliberals like Alexander Rustow, Wilhelm Röpke and Alfred Müller-Armack. Despite all those academics, most especially Erhard, being very involved in the social market economy, there are, however, substantial conceptual differences, which separate ordoliberalism from the social market economy. Eucken and Böhm's concept of ordoliberalism and its economic orders was significantly different from other ordoliberal colleagues, who developed the sociological variant for the social market economy, along with its many other liberal sociological underpinnings. The true original, early Freiburg School economically orientated ordoliberalism differed immensely from the later developed, '*socio-logical-ordoliberalism*'.[46]

The Freiburg School Theory of Economic Orders

Although the main objective of Walter Eucken and his early contemporaries at the Freiburg School was to renew classical liberalism, the school's concerns for '*order*' are paradoxically, however, deemed somewhat classical liberal. As a matter of fact, the first-ever conceptualization of ordoliberalism is viewed as '*constructivist*' due to its institutional underpinning, plus the freedom factor beneath the law forming part of its research agenda. Whereas ordoliberalism casts faith upon human intelligence and knowledge in order to design and make a new, '*Ordo*' or '*Order*', it places equal faith on the state's ability to, in turn, regulate such an 'order'. The main objective of the role cast upon human design and state action is so as to modify the general features of the '*order*' or the '*framework of rules*', rather than to control specific processes and outcomes, like resource allocation in markets.[47] Although Eucken and Böhm's

[44] VANBERG, V.J. *Ordoliberalism and Ordnugspolitik: A Brief Explanation*, pg 12. https://www.eucken.de/wp-content/uploads/Ordoliberalism-and-Ordnungspolitik.pdf

[45] Ibid.

[46] COMMUN, P. (Dir.). *L'Ordolibéralisme Allemande. Aux Sources de l'Économie Sociale de Marché*. SALLY, R. *Ordoliberalism and the Social Market: Classical Political Economy from Germany*, pgs 31–2.

[47] Ibid, pg 33.

concept of ordoliberalism and its '*economic orders*' was substantially different from other latter colleagues who 'socialized' it, in some respects, Hayek always viewed early ordoliberalism as a kind of '*restraining liberalism*'.

The 'economic orders' approach strictly separates the spheres of '*process*' and '*order*'. It makes a very clear and specific distinction between the spontaneity of the economic process based on freely forming prices, and the '*rational-constructivist*' design and control features of the order. Eucken had very little faith in '*spontaneous orders*' and their self-generating properties, and thus, recommended the constructivist approach much more for the correction of endogenous degenerating tendencies of spontaneous orders, such as most especially, the rise of monopoly power.[48]

For Eucken, the founding economist of the Freiburg School, and just as he described in his posthumously published work on economic policy, '*Grundsätze der Wirtschaftspolitik*', within the economic sphere, freedom is intimately linked to the '*Rule of Law*', as well as to a society, which is formed from '*bottom-up*' and spontaneously, by families, local associations and the like. For Eucken, the objectives of a '*free economic order*' are twofold: to tackle the problem of scarcity as effectively as possible and hinging on the '*interdependent social and legal orders*', to enable participants '*to be ends in and of themselves*', and not mere and simple units, at the disposal of the achievement of other's self-interested ends.[49]

Most particularly for Eucken, the main conception of '*Ordo*' for the economy and what really forms the main essence of 'Ordnungspolitik' is the '*Rechtsstaat*' or '*Constitutional State*', which establishes a compatible 'Ordnungspolitik', and which in turn, also constitutes and regulates the '*Wettbewerbsordnung*' or '*Competitive Order*'. Although Eucken believed that the state should be bestowed the role of setting up and maintaining the '*institutional framework*' of the free economic order, he also held that the state should not, however, intervene in the price-signalling and resource allocation mechanisms of the '*competitive economic process*'.[50]

Eucken established eight '*constitutive*' and four '*regulative*' principles, which compose the '*policy of order*'. The main principles highlight on the following:

- *"The Constitution of the order requires the realisation of the basic principle of setting up a functioning price system. Anything that hinders the working of this first constitutive principle, such as anti-cyclical policy, monopoly formation, and exchange controls, should not figure in economic policy.*
- *The second principle concerns the 'primacy of currency policy' to safeguard the stability of the value of money.*

[48] Ibid.
[49] Ibid, pg 32.
[50] Ibid.

- *The third principle is that of open markets, excluding discriminatory intervention by the state and guaranteeing the freedom of trade.*
- *Private property is the fourth consecutive principle; an indispensable precondition to protect the private sphere of the individual in which he can act freely, remaining uncoerced by others.*
- *Then comes the principle of the freedom of contract that should not, however, extend to the freedom to prevent others from exercising their freedom of contract.*
- *Following this is the principle of liability to ensure that risk is tied to responsibility in economic transactions".*[51]

Eucken's concept of ordoliberalism was extremely influenced by his Freiburg legal colleague, Franz Böhm. Böhm considered the 'law' as a bulwark, which protected individual liberty from the tyranny of majorities and minority interests. For Böhm, the law, and private law especially, should actively form collective action, through the enforcement of general '*juristidictionary*' rules.[52]

Through his, '*Privatrechtsgesellschaft*', Böhm elaborated a concept for a '*Private Law Society*', which was based on a system of universally and impartially applied private (or civil) law, in order to protect the individual from interference from other individuals, groups and the state. The main emphasis of such concept was placed upon guaranteeing the individual's or the economic agent's civil liberties and autonomy. Clearly reflecting the ordoliberal free market economy's legal bedrock, within such a '*private law society*', the state exercises its political authority in order to establish and operate the basic '*rules of the game*'. In accordance with the concept, the state, therefore, has the role of neutral arbitrator, as well as the responsibility of establishing the free-market conditions, but should, however, not interfere any further with the economic process itself.[53]

In parallel to Eucken, Böhm also stressed the importance of the minimization of power formations in state and society. For Böhm, the deliberate limitation of the state's functions, together with its independence from the '*volontés particulières*' of private interests, allows for the qualitative exercise of its effective action where required, most especially, that of upholding the framework of general rules and the maintenance of order as a whole. '*The increasing dependence of the states on 'intermediary powers' in industrial societies (large industrial firms, banks, insurance firms, industry associations, trade unions) represents a weakening of the state's constitutional mandate in acting impartially and upholding a free order. The volonté générale is thus sacrificed on the altar of the volontés particulières; some actors are privileged over others, weakening the 'rules of the game' and undermining the order itself. Political intervention in the form of subsidies, tax breaks, the protection of monopolies, price fixing and trade protectionism, offends against the private law society.*

[51] Ibid.
[52] Ibid, pgs 33–4.
[53] Ibid, pg 34.

This kind of selective intervention favours particular interest groups and departs from the cardinal principle of the equality of all individuals before the law.'[54]

The Social Market Economy and the Sociological Underpinnings of Liberalism

In stark contrast to the Freiburg School's legal-economic constitutionalism, ordoliberalism also developed a *'sociological'* inclination. The 'sociological' variant was based on both philosophy of history and historical sociology, as well as on a piercing cultural critique, which all-combined, embodied the ordoliberal variant that gave shape and form to the '*Social Market Economy*'.

Alexander Rüstow and most other advocates of the social market economic tradition much diverged from the pragmatic empiricism of classical liberalism, through one major aspect. While Adam Smith and David Hume, as well as their ideological descendants, were firm embracers of the expansion of commercial society and its bourgeois urban values, the German social market tradition has a particular strain, which is extremely idealistic and romantic. Widely considered as an idealized version of Swiss cantonal life, such strain mostly chastises the urban values of mass society, while yearning for their return to communitarian life in small towns and villages, dominated by small enterprises and citizen-burghers.[55] The social market economy tackled at the same time sociological prerequisites for sustainable economic reform, as well as for the attainment of a '*free market economy-based society*'. As Wilhelm Röpke defined the economic model, what lies '"*beyond the supply and demand" is at least as important as the laws of supply and demand for the health and vigour of a society based on individual freedom*'.[56]

Within the social market economy tradition, there are two different conceptions of the '*social*' dimension: the first is the '*liberal conservative*' concept, and the second is the '*social democratic*' concept. The first 'liberal conservative' inclination is mostly associated with Röpke, and is encapsulated in his '*Jenseits von Angebot und Nachfrage*'. During his period in office, Ludwig Erhard clearly reflected through his written work and speeches that he shared the same liberal-conservative conception of the social market economy. Röpke's vision of society also merges with the societal views of Adam Smith, David Hume, Edmund Burke, Montesquieu, Alexis de Tocqueville and Michael Oakeshott. The vision's main assumption rests upon the belief that views society as a '*civic association*', comprised through the sporadic formations of small and overlapping groups, ranging from family, church, village and the workplace, to volunteer organizations. Such '*corps intermédiares*', which are wedged-in between the

[54] Ibid.
[55] Ibid, pgs 35–6.
[56] Ibid, pg 35.

state and individuals, are considered as the key binding elements of people in '*social microstructures*', which avoid any descents into '*social atomization*' and '*anomie*'.[57] It was such vision of society, which Röpke upheld for the social market economy, including a limited (but still important) role for the state. Otherwise and conversely, Röpke argued, an overactive state, busy with resource allocation and countless social policy objectives, would usurp and critically undermine civic society's traditional '*natural communities*'.[58]

The second 'social democratic' posture stems from Alfred Müller-Armack. Central to Müller-Armack's line of reasoning is the conception of '*social irenics*', which try to reconcile theoretical opposites like liberalism and socialism, and Catholic social ethics with Protestant equivalents. Müller-Armack had always envisioned an '*irenic*' order for post-war Germany, through the balancing of market freedom with social protection. Much like John Stuart Mill had done before him, Müller-Armack also strictly emphasized on distinguishing between production being organized on the basis of free competition and distribution. '*The state should have an active social policy to redistribute the fruits of a free market economy in the name of equal opportunity and social justice.*'[59]

The Ordoliberal Rooting in German Economic, Philosophical and Religious Thought

Within the vast fields of German economic thought, 'Ordnungstheorie' or the 'Theory of Orders' can be found very deep-rooted in its economic, philosophical and religious thought. Ordoliberalism has many neo-historicist aspects to its approach, as well as to the study of the interactions between the judicial, political and cultural spheres. Because of such features, ordoliberalism has always been perceived as both a heritage of Gustav Schmoller and Friedrich List, as well as a precursor of '*institutionalism*'.[60]

While ordoliberalism has much grounding in the Historical School of Economics, spearheaded by Gustav Schmoller, it has nonetheless also been very influenced by German '*cameralism*'. Similarly, the ordoliberal notion of 'order' can also be easily integrated into a 'Kulturelle Ökonomik' or 'Economic Culture' framework, which has provided many underlying influencing multidisciplinary elements to its approach. Whereas Walter Eucken included in his work plenty of vital philosophy inherited from his father, Rudolph Eucken, much of his philosophy also derives from Husserl's '*phenomenology*'. During the 1920s, a big portion of German intellectuals, and thus, a big part of 'Ordnungstheorie', were also very strongly influenced by 'phenomenology'.

[57] Ibid, pg 35.
[58] Ibid.
[59] Ibid, pgs 35–6.
[60] COMMUN, P. (Dir.). *L'Ordolibéralisme Allemande. Aux Sources de l'Économie Sociale de Marché*, pgs 13–14.

German Catholic social thought was similarly deeply ingrained in Wilhelm Röpke's conservative ordoliberal mind-frame, most especially, as regards the issue of the necessary authority of a strong state for the proper safeguarding of liberty, freedom and social justice.[61]

Pope Pius XI's cadre of propositions for the resolution of the social crisis is particularly interesting, as they provide an excellent indication of the profound influence, which religion, through Pope Pius XI, had in Röpke's interventionist thought:

- *"The state must first create a legal framework in which the activity of private economic intervention can be exercised for the benefit of the common good. The intervention of the State is indispensable to guarantee the institution of the property and to avoid abuses. Measures of nationalization or agrarian reform can be justified.*
- *Against Proletarianization, Pius XI calls for the support of workers 'savings, the formation of a capital by providing security for each family. In parallel, consumerism must be fought by respecting the moral law in business'.*
- *Beyond the fixation of a just salary, the pope envisions worker's participation in the life of the firm through the possession of part of the capital and a certain co-management"*.[62]

Lastly, Heinrich von Stackelberg's theories are also very clearly integrated in 'Ordnungstheorie', with ordoliberalism inheriting three key principles from him:

"1. *The economic system must realise the order of complete competition.*
2. *The key points for its realisation are found in the free formation of prices and atomized markets, assuming the abolition of price interventionism and legislation on the prohibition of cartels.*
3. *Unlike Paleoliberalism, which regarded the state as the only danger to free competition, private economic agents with some degree of market power threaten the survival of the free market order. From Ordnungstheorie itself, W. Eucken had deduced that the coordination of plans also depended on the monetary system. The free formation of prices therefore implies, in addition to the atomized forms of markets, a stable monetary system, guaranteeing an objective formation of individual plans. From his historical analysis, which has shown him that, in essence, an economic system has never been imposed, neither completely nor by his own strength, W. Eucken asserts that the order of competition is not a natural order of the economy"*.[63]

[61] Ibid.

[62] COMMUN, P. (Dir.). *L'Ordolibéralisme Allemande. Aux Sources de l'Économie Sociale de Marché.* YCRE, J-M. *Les Sources Catholiques de L'Ordolibéralisme Allemand: Röpke et la Pensée Catholique Sociale Allemand*, pg 166.

[63] COMMUN, P. (Dir.). *L'Ordolibéralisme Allemande. Aux Sources de l'Économie Sociale de Marché.* BROYER, S. *Ordnungstheorie et Ordolibéralisme: Les Leçons de la Tradition. Du Caméralisme à L'ordolibéralisme: Ruptures et Continuités?*, pg 97.

4

Neoliberalism

Within the framework of the academic revolution seeking the reformation of classical liberalism and laissez-faire, together with the intellectual turmoil that it spurred, the second 'new liberal' current – *'Neoliberalism'* – burst through Europe's academic scene during the late 1930s. Neoliberalism promulgated an intermediate, or *'Third Way'*, between classical liberalism and laissez-faire, and henceforth, began constituting the main theoretical counter-reaction to Keynesianism and collectivism.

The many political, economic and intellectual upheavals of the 1920s were further exacerbated by other complicated factors, such as the communist revolution and its fascist reaction, National Socialism, and most particularly, the world economic depression. The combination of all those events and issues induced the development in Germany, Austria, France and other industrialized countries, of a very strong intellectual movement, which sought vigorously the renewal of the old form of classical liberalism or economic liberalism.

The widespread intellectual brainstorming saw the advancement of a new economic concept, which was built upon three main fundamental pillars: (a) the consensus on the need to renovate traditional classical liberalism; (b) the common adhesion to the essential principles of classical liberalism and (c) the rejection of the new authoritarian and collectivist doctrines. Other axes of convergence, which academics also comprised for the new concept, included a differing theoretical approach for comprehending and analysing economic phenomena, a different philosophical and ethical option, as well as a divergent conceptualization of political action.[1]

The perception amongst mainly German, Austrian and French academics was that although the mere instauration of *'laissez-faire and laissez-passer'* did engender an extraordinary economic dynamism, it however simultaneously generated many risks related to the susceptibility of firms and businesses of abusing freedom, most particularly regarding restrictions to free competition. Academics believed that while such abuses would consequently create economic imbalances, which would

[1] COMMUN, P. (Dir.). *L'Ordolibéralisme Allemande. Aux Sources de l'Économie Sociale de Marché.* BILGER, F. *La pensée néolibérale française et l'ordolibéralisme allemand,* pgs 20–8.

entail other social distortions, they would in turn also cause the growth of extreme disharmony between particular interests and general interests. They alleged that the kind of public interventions the above motives required for their mere establishment only instigates the system to malfunction, which subsequently generates much negative public reaction that would ultimately require their complete abandonment. For those main reasons, academics perceived absolute liberalism or laissez-faire as having a genetic predisposition or extreme susceptibility to its own auto-destruction, as well as to inducing the re-establishment of previous forms of state organization, which were considered much inferior to the market economy.[2]

In order to avoid such a regression, new liberal academics therefore considered as absolutely imperative the fundamental substitution of the *'natural order'* of classical liberalism and its concept of freedom for a much more refined and carefully programmed form of liberty and freedom. They sought the establishment of a new liberal framework, which at the same time, assured the provision of economic liberties, satisfied collective needs and compensated social difficulties. Most specifically, academics pursued a redefinition of state economic and social interventionism, which was compatible with the proper functioning of the system, for the firm establishment of an efficient market economy that would ensure protected competition, monetary and credit emissions, a fiscal system, property, contracts, bankruptcy, as well as labour and social solidarity.[3]

In retrospect, however, the intellectual dissatisfaction and critique surrounding classical liberalism and laissez-faire had in fact been looming over Europe for a long time before the 1930s. Many anti-interventionist doctrines apologizing free exchange had already been addressed by many nineteenth-century French liberal economists and numerous English liberals, including the Manchester School, Herbert Spencer and his apology of the individual against the state, as well as Ernest Benn, the founder of *'The Society of Individualists'*. Frédérick Bastiat, the renowned publicist, became one of the favourite liberals of the American ultra-liberal and libertarian movement, with the influential *'Foundation for Economic Thought'*, even adopting his quasi-model and President Ronald Reagan venerating him. Gustave Molinari, in his *'Les Soirées de la Rue Saint-Lazare'*, also included numerous apologies to laissez-faire, as well as to the inviolability of individual rights and to the freedom of contracts. Other prominent figures of the same period that equally professed a vigorous antisocialism also included Yves Guyot and Eugène d'Eichthal, a partisan of progressive liberalism.[4]

Notwithstanding, during the 1920s–30s and greatly fuelled by the widespread apparition of countless academic monographs, articles, essays and treatises, condemning liberalism, the intellectual decline of the ideology in Europe began to be

[2] Ibid, pgs 21–2.
[3] Ibid, pg 22.
[4] AUDIER, S. *Aux Origines du Neo-Libéralisme: Le Colloque Walter Lippmann*, pgs 31–2.

most especially pronounced. What began with the 1926 text, written by John Maynard Keynes, '*The End of Laissez-Faire*', was further confirmed by the 1929 Wall Street Crash, which finally put into serious evidence the failure of liberalism, even giving way to many interventionist proposals stemming from the Unied States. Between 1930 and 1940, the book, '*La Fin du Libéralisme*', was published in France, and in 1938, the Nazi German, Herbert Backe, wrote *Das Ende des Liberalismus in der Wirstschaft* which also announced the end of liberalism. In 1932, the jurist Ernest Theil likewise postulated 'new foundations of the economy', while evoking the crisis of liberalism and denouncing the liberal doctrine and the 'economists' treason'. Following the peaking phase of liberal laissez-faire, the apparition of 'Progressivism' and 'Directed Economies' further demonstrated the strong flow of countering reactions towards it. Similarly, 'Communism', 'Fascism', 'Nazism', 'Planned Economies' and 'Fascist Anti-liberalism' all equally pointed to the end of classical liberalism.[5]

Within such an unbridled liberal atmosphere, libertarian intellectuals and new liberals reflected profoundly on the crisis by providing many views on how to renew, renovate or recast the doctrine. For such a reinvigorated breed of new liberals, the fact that capitalism had become increasingly more collectivist required the overtaking of the old form of economic individualism. Thus, a big portion of the directing economic elite, together with liberal theorists, found themselves progressively obliged to evolve, and henceforth, began to revise the established doctrine with myriad varying solutions. A very strong liberal revisionist tide was generated, most especially amongst French and German academic circles, which spurred a heavy flow of new liberal versions. From then onwards, heaps of varied proposals began to flow through Europe related to what sort of form the new liberalism should have and what kind of term should be applied to it. Nonetheless, most of the new proposals differed enormously, most particularly as regards the paths opened up for it, as well as in relation to the actual viability of the numerous types of political economies being thrust forward.[6]

For example, in 1927, Ludwig von Mises wrote, *Liberalismus* in which he referred to a '*new liberalism*', and Auguste Detoeuf also provided another of the countless outcries for the liberal revision. Detoeuf, in his 1936 article, '*La fin du Libéralisme*', bluntly stated that '*liberalism is dead; it has been killed, not by the will of men or caused by the free action of governments, but by an ineluctable internal evolution*'.[7] Detoeuf was years later also very involved in the neoliberal movement. In 1937, a university student named Denise Laroque likewise wrote a very interesting thesis which reflected the time's anti-liberal spirit, titled '*La Crise et les doctrines libérales françaises*'. Larocque pointed out that since it had been liberalism, which had prompted the world crisis, it was therefore being '*attacked from all sides*'. Amongst the array of critical responses and counter-proposals to Larocque's thesis that were generated, Jacques Rueff blamed

[5] Ibid, pgs 32–56.
[6] Ibid.
[7] Ibid, pg 57.

'interventionism', Henri Noyelle acquired a 'directionist' posture, and others, like Pierre Lucius, favoured a more 'corporatist' synthesis. Many other new prototypes of liberalism were also pressed forward including '*Ultra-Liberalism*', '*Orthodox Liberalism*', '*Moderated Liberalism*', '*Directed Liberalism*' and '*Corporatist Liberalism*'. Émile Labarthe, a theorist who had designed the concept of '*Neo-Statism*', proposed an intermediate '*Liberal Interventionism*', which was also supported by neoliberals like Henry Truchy and Alexander Rustow. In 1933, Daniel Villey, in his search for a new form of liberalism that steered away from classical liberalism, was inspired by a more interventionist and '*Statist*' archetype. His *Utopie Libérale, chimère socialiste, économie dirigée,* was an outright declaration of war on the '*social chimera*' and on '*atomised socialism*'. Additional fusions likewise ranged from '*Collectivist Socialism*' and '*Scientific-Optimist Liberalism*' to '*Mixed Economy*' and even to '*Orthodox Neoliberalism*'. During those years, other academics who would later also be very involved in the neoliberal nebula, such as Louis Marlio, Bernard Lavergne and Louis Rougier, began to participate very proactively in the revisionist crusade.[8] Louis Rougier, a French philosopher who would soon after spearhead the neoliberal offensive in France, diffused other new concepts as well, like '*Constructive Liberalism*' and '*Constructor Liberalism*'.[9]

Very curiously, since much before the 1930s, the actual word, term or concept – '*Neoliberalism*' – likewise already enjoyed a long prehistory, having been in constant international underground circulation, popping up intermittently. Harking back to the nineteenth century and early twentieth century, the word, 'neoliberalism', was very discernibly present in German, French and Italian economic thought. For example, one the first international tentatives at theorization and one of the first times the word 'neoliberalism' appeared in France was through a German moderate socialist named Karl Georg Winkelblech (1810–65), although he was known as Karl Marlo. Marlo, a chemist turned defender of the working class, had also theorized a '*Moderate Socialism*' between liberalism and communism. In his monumental book on work organization, published between 1848 and 1859, Marlo referred abundantly to a '*Neuliberalen Shulen*' or '*Neoliberal School*', when evoking a series of economists who without being socialists, had broken many classical liberal dogmas. Years later, in 1886, the French economist Maurice Block also wrote a critique of Marlo's book for the prestigious *Journal des Économistes* in which he also referred to Marlo's 'neoliberalism'. During the French Third Republic and amidst the turmoil of the Dreyfuss Affair, Mécislas Goldberg wrote an article for the journal *Tablette,* titled '*Le neo-liberalisme*'. In addition and much later, between 1910 and 1920, the historian Sebastien Charlety, in his contribution to the colossal compendium *Histoire de France Contemporaine depuis la Révolution jusqu'a la Paix de 1919* likewise wrote a whole chapter related to intellectual and political life from 1820 to 1830, which was exclusively dedicated to what he termed as '*Neo-liberalism*'. His 'new liberalism', or '*neo-liberalism*', was a sort of proclamation, which rinsed out the dissatisfactions felt by the young generations with the old dominant liberalism.[10]

[8] Ibid, pgs 56–9.
[9] Ibid, pg 63.
[10] Ibid, pgs 60–2.

However, from the 1920s onwards, the intellectual efforts that were put into the modification of classical liberalism got much more serious. Probably one of the first incursions into the twentieth-century reconsiderations on how to redefine both the role and the functions of the state in order to secure a free-market was contained in the 1921 book *Old and New Economic Liberalism*, written by the renowned Swedish economist, Eli F. Heckscher. Heckscher, who also became a member of the Mont Pelerin Society, together with his student Bertil Ohlin, eventually founded international trade theory, thus establishing the Heckscher-Ohlin factor proportion model. In 1925, and possibly one of the first times that the modern sense of the term '*Neoliberalism*' had ever appeared, was included in a book titled *Trends in Economic Ideas*, written by the Swiss economist, Hans Honegger. Honegger identified the concept '*Theoretical Neoliberalism*' as one which was based on the works of Alfred Marshall, Eugen von Böhm-Bawerk, Friedrich von Wieser, Karl Gustav Cassel and others. Honegger pointed out that '*neoliberalism propagated doctrines of competition and entrepreneurship, and posited the rejection of advancing socialist ideas and bolshevism in particular. However, the functions of the state were understood in a negative way, and therefore the heritage of classical liberalism loomed large*'.[11] In 1932, Bernard Lavergne, an activist of '*Cooperative Socialism*', who would be a future member of the Colloque Walter Lippman, wrote an article titled, '*L' Économie moderne et la doctrine libérale*', where in direct opposition to appellations like '*Neo-socialism*', '*Neo-radicalism*' and '*Neo-capitalism*', proposed '*Neo-liberalism*' instead. Lavergne even went as far as writing about Germany's '*Neo-liberal Principles*' when relating to the German author Julius Bonn and his work on German interventionism and cartels.[12]

Another very noteworthy and interesting fact about neoliberalism surrounds the question of when, why and how exactly was the prefix – '*Neo*' – attached to it? Why were not other prefixes, such as '*Quasi*' or '*Pseudo*' chosen instead? In that sense, the epoch's atmosphere of liberal revisionism provides one of the most plausible indicative explanations. When during the 1930s, the word and term 'neoliberalism' resurfaced, it had hitherto, already been curiously preceded by a flood of '*Neos*', which had been deployed during the climate of doctrinal revision in response to contemporary phenomena. Thus and accordingly, most of the new revisionist syntheses were therefore accompanied by an exigent advent of 'Neos'. The flourishing of 'Neos', was considered either a way of appeasing or reformulating doctrines, or a means of providing new deriving doctrines. For example, Charles Gide and Charles Rist, in contestation to the Marxist crisis, spoke of '*Neo-Marxism*'; a fraction of followers of Jules Guesde were considered as adherents of '*Neo-Guesdisme*'; and new forms of English, Italian and Spanish syndicalism were similarly labelled as pertaining to '*Neo-Syndicalism*'. In much the same revisionist spirit, other popular hybrids also included '*Neo-Romanticism*', '*Neo-Impressionism*', '*Neo-Saint-Simonisme*', '*Neo-Bavouvisme*', '*Neo-Radicalism*', '*Neo-Socialism*', '*Neo-Capitalism*' and '*Neo-Statism*'.[13]

[11] MIROWSKI, P. and PLEHWE, D. *The Road from Mont Pèlerin: The Making of the Neoliberal Thought Collective*, pgs 10–11.

[12] AUDIER, S. *Aux Origines du Neo-Libéralisme: Le Colloque Walter Lippmann*, pgs 66–7.

[13] Ibid, pgs 62–3.

Nevertheless, amidst the 1930s' intense intellectual hype, the term 'neoliberalism' began to progressively appear much more seriously in multiple contexts, becoming further established as the main designation of a new intellectual political-economic movement. While it started being diffused in the political arena with different senses in Switzerland and Belgium, it also quickly gained much consecration in France. Neoliberalism was likewise very present in Italy, with Luigi Einaudi becoming the most famous representative of the Italian neoliberal coterie. Interwar Austria equally began presaging neoliberal ideas, as well as *'proto-Mont Pelerin Society'* structures. In Vienna, Austrian School academics fostered a very strong *'extra-academic cosmopolitan intellectual formation'*. When during the 1920s, Ludwig von Mises began celebrating his *'Privatseminars'*, giving way to the Socialist Calculation Debate with the energetic participation of academics like Friedrich Hayek and Fritz Machlup, neoliberalism was then hoisted as the main intellectual foe of *'Scientific and Technocratic Socialism'*. Many other foreign academics who were equally involved, such as Lionel Robbins, Frank Knight and John van Sickle, would later likewise become key members of the Mont Pelerin Society.[14]

The year 1937 marked a whole new dawning for the history of neoliberalism. The publication of the book *'(An Inquiry into the Principles of) The Good Society'* by the American journalist Walter Lippman stressed the superiority of the market economy over state interventionism. The book brimmed with insights, which ended up constituting the main conventional wisdom within neoliberal circles. Most notably, it highlighted that *'in a free society the state does not administer the affairs of men. It administers justice among men who administer their own affairs. (Statemanship) is the ability to elucidate the confused and clamorous interests which converge upon the seat of government. It ... consists in giving the people not what they want but what they will learn to want'*.[15]

'The Good Society' included many anticipations of the New Deal and caused a huge sensation in Europe, most especially amongst French neoliberals. In France, the book was translated as *'La cité libre'* by the Librarie des Médicis Editions, a very popular French diffusion channel for publications on the renewal of liberalism. The book echoed many of the ideas, which were formulated by other new liberal authors who were also published by the Médicis Editions, like Jacques Rueff *(1935, 'La Crise du Liberalisme');* Ludwig von Mises *(1938, 'Le socialisme');* Lionel Robbins *(1938, 'L'économie planifiée et l'ordre internacional')*; Louis Rougier *(1938, 'Les mystiques économiques')* and Louis Marlio *(1938, 'Le sort du capitalisme').* Louis Rougier was so impressed by the book that he wrote the French edition's foreword, as well as organized the Colloque Walter Lippmann in Lippmann's honour. The Colloquium brought together the above

[14] MIROWSKI, P. and PLEHWE, D. *The Road from Mont Pèlerin: The Making of the Neoliberal Thought Collective*, pgs 11–12.

[15] Ibid, pg 13.

authors, along with other new liberal economists, sociologists and philosophers. Its main purpose was to critically revise capitalism in order to attempt to define a new genuine liberal doctrine, as well as its aims.[16]

The overall common determination beseeching the renovation of classical liberalism and laissez-faire ultimately materialized in 1938, with the organization of a major new liberal gathering in France, at the Colloque Walter Lippman. The Colloque Walter Lippman gave official birth to both the term *'Neoliberalism'* and to the neoliberal movement as a whole. The colloquium itself was named after Lippman's book *'The Good Society'* and united new liberals alike from both sides of the Atlantic. However, and despite the new liberal consensus, many rifts regarding interventionism and other issues soon emerged.[17] By the time the next new liberal meeting was held in 1947, in Switzerland, at the Mont Pelerin Society, those exact same rifts only widened and new fissures likewise opened up, which sadly began marking the decline of the original European neoliberal project, as well as the rise of the much more basic and aggressive, Anglo-American variant. Although the Freiburg School and the Austrian School influenced very much the original composition and early trajectory of neoliberal thought, the eventual rise of the Chicago School ended up totally overshadowing them. That way, while neoliberalism was left with a complete different set of components to the ones initially considered, its present-day conceptual definition is equally surrounded by much ambiguous abstraction.

The Colloque Walter Lippmann

From 26–30 August, 1938, the Paris-based Institut International de Coopération Intelectuelle hosted the Colloque Walter Lippmann, organized by Louis Rougier. The main objectives of the colloquium were to reflect, discuss and deliver on the pitiful and weak state of liberalism and the dangers of collectivism, as well as to designate a renewed form of liberalism.[18]

The prestigious conclave was formed by the following new liberal intellectuals: from France: Raymond Aron, Roger Auboin, Louis Baudin, Marcel Bourgeois, Auguste Detœuf, Bernard Lavergne, Étienne Mantoux, Robert Marjolin, Louis Marlio, Ernest Mercier, André Piatier, Jacques Rueff and Louis Rougier; from Austria: Friedrich August von Hayek, Ludwig von Mises, Stefan Thomas Possony and Alfred Schütz; from Great Britain: John Bell Condliffe and Michael Polanyi; from the United States:

[16] Ibid, pgs 12–14.

[17] COMMUN, P. (Dir.). *L'Ordolibéralisme Allemande. Aux Sources de l'Économie Sociale de Marché.* BILGER, F. *La pensée néolibérale française et l'ordolibéralisme allemand,* pgs 22–3.

[18] MIROWSKI, P. and PLEHWE, D. *The Road from Mont Pèlerin: The Making of the Neoliberal Thought Collective,* pgs 12–14.

Walter Lippmann and Bruce Hopper; from Germany: Alexander Rüstow and Wilhelm Röpke; from Spain, José Castillejo; and from Belgium, Marcel van Zeeland.[19]

Throughout the colloquium's five-day séances, many discussions and debates were developed, rotating around issues such as the reasons for the decline of liberalism; whether the decline of liberalism was due to endogenous causes; whether liberalism was capable of fulfilling its social tasks; the exploration of potential exogenous causes for the decline of liberalism, like psychological, sociological, political and ideological causes; and, considering that the decline of liberalism was inevitable and based on the preceding analyses, what would the most appropriate remedies be for the reprogramming of liberalism. The group also discussed what other actions should be taken by it in the future.[20]

However, from the beginning of the colloquium, some of the main conflicts that would later characterize the process of construction of neoliberal thought became very marked, growing to become very conflictive areas of discord. Some of the main conflictual areas were mostly related to the differences between ordoliberalism and radical libertarianism, to the divergences between the acceptance or rejection of interventionism, as well as to the discrepancies between partisans of a voluntarist liberal policy and those nostalgic for laissez-faire.[21]

During the colloquium, two separate, distinct groups were formed, which not only hugely divided opinions but also equally split the overall common objectives. One group, represented by Louis Rougier, August Detoeuf, Louis Marlio, Wilhelm Röpke and Alexander Rustow, believed that neoliberalism was fundamentally different from traditional liberalism in both its spirit and its program. Another group, formed by Louis Baudin, Jacques Rueff and the Austrian School's Ludwig Mises and Friedrich Hayek, defended the '*old liberalism*'. While the first group was much more pro-interventionist, the second group was much more defiant towards the state. In much the same way, the two groups also clashed heavily about other issues, such as the causes of the 1929 crisis, the role of the state, industrial concentration and social protection.[22]

The atmosphere of extreme disharmony, which prevailed within the Colloque Walter Lippmann, clearly reflected that from the very beginning, neoliberalism was a very disunified phenomenon. Even the name, which was to be given to the new liberal doctrine, became an issue of much disagreement. Whereas Louis Baudin preferred the term '*Individualism*', Louis Rougier proposed '*Positive Liberalism*' instead, and Jacques Rueff likewise favoured '*Left-Wing Liberalism*'. According to Louis Marlio, the term

[19] AUDIER, S. *Aux Origines du Neo-Libéralisme: Le Colloque Walter Lippmann*, pg 412.
[20] Ibid, pgs 411–12.
[21] MIROWSKI, P. and PLEHWE, D. *The Road from Mont Pèlerin: The Making of the Neoliberal Thought Collective*, pg 49.
[22] AUDIER, S. *Aux Origines du Neo-Libéralisme: Le Colloque Walter Lippmann*, pg 263.

itself only became prevalent after the colloquium and only due to strategic reasons: *'The words "neo" and "renovation", distinguish us from several authors of whom we did not accept all the practical theories and all objections (against) interventions which are accepted by most of us like perfectly normal things. For those who know it ... the word "neo" is perhaps not essential, but for those who do not know it, it is totally useful.'*[23] To be considered neoliberal was supposedly meant to imply the assumption that laissez-faire economics did not suffice and that *'in the name of liberalism a modern economic policy was needed'*.[24]

The 1938 Colloque Walter Lippmann plainly exposed that neoliberalism was nothing close to a *'pensée unique'*, stemming from different theoretical approaches that ranged from French neoliberalism, the Freiburg School, the Austrian School and the Chicago School. Notwithstanding, the colloquium gave official birth to the second new liberal current, 'Neoliberalism', and it is widely believed that it was thanks to the French initiative that neoliberalism officially emerged as an intellectual network. With the word and term 'neoliberalism' beginning to be officially used thereafter, neoliberalism was defined for the first time by an agenda with a clear set of postulates:

> *The use of the price mechanism as the best way to obtain the maximal satisfaction of human expectations, the responsibility of the state for instituting a juridical framework adjusted to the order defined by the market; the possibility for the state to follow goals other than short-term expedients and to further them by levying taxes; the acceptance of state intervention if it does not favour any particular group and seeks to act upon the causes of the economic difficulties.*[25]

In the words of Louis Rougier, *'to be (neo)liberal, doesn't mean to be a 'Manchesterian' who leaves the cars circulating in all directions, if such is their will, which can only result in traffic jams and incessant accidents; it doesn't mean to be a 'Planist' who gives every car its exit time and its route; it means to impose a highway code while admitting that it is not necessary to be the same at the time of the accelerated transports as at the time of diligences'*.[26]

At the end of the five-day colloquium and in order to provide proper continuum to those early beginnings, the participants launched a project agenda for neoliberalism, began printing a journal titled *'Cahiers du Libéralisme'* as well as created a think-tank named Centre International d'Études pour la Rénovation du Libéralisme.[27] However, with the outbreak of the war, the nascent effort to organize neoliberal forces was

[23] MIROWSKI, P. and PLEHWE, D. *The Road from Mont Pèlerin: The Making of the Neoliberal Thought Collective*, pg 48.
[24] Ibid.
[25] Ibid, pg 49.
[26] Ibid.
[27] Ibid, pg 14.

paused, and the participants and many other additional ones would only meet again a decade later, in 1947, at the Mont Pelerin Society.[28]

The Mont Pelerin Society

Following the Great Depression and throughout the 1930s, Keynes's interventionist theories rose to prominence. Most especially after the Second World War, Keynes's theories were chosen by the majority of policy-makers in order to guide them through the business cycle and keep control of recessions. From 1945 until 1980, more or less, the Keynesian Consensus and embedded liberalism prevailed worldwide. Notwithstanding, and during the same period, neoliberals also began fiercely opposing Keynes's theories, and much more so, the theories of intellectuals like Oscar Lange that were close to the Marxian tradition and related to centralized state planning. Neoliberals strongly believed that while state decisions were politically biased, they were also highly dependent on the strength of the interest groups involved (like unions, environmentalists and trade lobbies). Thus, and in turn, they therefore believed that state decisions related to issues of investment and capital accumulation were bound to be erroneous, since the information available to the state could not rival the information inherent to market signals.[29]

In clear displacement of the classical theories of Adam Smith, David Ricardo and Karl Marx, neoliberals developed a firm commitment to the ideals of personal freedom, adhering strongly to free-market principles of neoclassical economics, which had emerged during the second half of the nineteenth century, through Alfred Marshall, William Stanley Jevons and Leon Walras. Conversely, however, neoliberals also believed that Smith's '*hidden hand of the market*' was the best device for rallying the most basic of human instincts for everyone's benefit, like gluttony, greed and the desire for wealth and power.[30]

With the quick rise of state planning and socialism throughout Europe, fifteen of the neoliberals who attended the Colloque Walter Lippmann organized a second new liberal gathering, fundamentally basing themselves on the rationale of Hayek, Mises and others, that classical liberalism had failed due to crippling conceptual flaws. The book, written by Friedrich Hayek and published in 1944, '*The Road to Serfdom*', was a huge success and very transcendental in its powerful polemic against socialism. The book influenced the minds of new liberals profoundly, as well as further stimulated the renewal of classical liberalism. Hayek's book argued that fascism, National Socialism and socialism had common roots in central economic

[28] Ibid.
[29] HARVEY, D. *A Brief History of Neoliberalism*, pgs 20–1.
[30] Ibid, pg 20.

planning and empowered the state over the individual, which thus resulted in the total loss of individual freedom.[31]

From 1–10 April, 1947, organized and led by Friedrich Hayek and Albert Hunold, new liberals from Europe and the United States assembled in Switzerland, in a village near Lake Geneva, in Mont Pelerin, at the Hotel du Parc. Their main objective was to begin mobilizing the neoliberal movement. The elite contingent of participants included liberal economists, politicians, sociologists, philosophers, university professors, businessmen and journalists. Although Hayek had originally proposed naming the new liberal institution '*The Acton-Tocqueville Society*', ultimately, the name '*Mont Pelerin Society*' was decided upon. From then onwards, the Mont Pelerin Society (the Society) became a kind of international '*who's who*' of the classical liberal and neoliberal intellectuals, as well as the neoliberal collective's main representative institution.[32]

Since its birth in 1947, the Mont Pelerin Society was mainly characterized by two very distinct phases, throughout which different schools of neoliberal thought exerted their varying intellectual influence and ideological weight. The'first phase' of the Mont Pelerin Society was from 1947 until the 1960s, with the ideological issues discussed and the overall direction of the society's common project being primarily influenced by the European contingent's Austrian School, the Freiburg School, as well as other European neoliberals. The 'second phase' of the Mont Pelerin Society was from the 1960s onwards. Henceforth, both the ideological issues, together with the society's general direction, were much more heavily influenced by the American contingent, represented by the Chicago School and other American neoliberals.

From 1947 until the 1960s, during the '*first phase*' of the Mont Pelerin Society, Hayek, Mises, Polanyi, Robbins, Röpke, Aron, Baudin and Rüstow, who had helped launch the Mont Pelerin Society with others like Machlup, Haberler and Popper, were key instrumental members. Thus, during those years, the main influence within the Mont Pelerin Society came to a greater degree from the Austrian School and from the Freiburg School. However, and especially from the 1960s onwards, during the '*second phase*' of the Mont Pelerin Society, the US influence began to tilt the neoliberal balance of power much more towards the Chicago School neoliberal prescriptions, mostly stimulated by Milton Friedman, James Buchanan and George Stigler, who had ascended to leading positions within the Mont Pelerin Society, eventually becoming its Presidents.[33] Likewise and most significantly, during the 'second phase', ordoliberalism gradually became totally overshadowed by neoliberalism, and henceforth, neoliberal thought was forever narrowed down to its more basic, US aggressive monetarist composition.

[31] BUTLER, E. *A Short History of the Mont Pelerin Society*, pg 4. http://rybn.org/thegreatoffshore/THE%20GREAT%20OFFSHORE/1.ENCYCLOPEDIA/MONT%20PELERIN%20SOCIETY,%201947/DOCS/A%20SHORT%20HISTORY%20OF%20THE%20MONT%20PELERIN%20SOCIETY%20By%20Eamonn%20Butler.pdf

[32] MIROWSKI, P. and PLEHWE, D. *The Road from Mont Pèlerin: The Making of the Neoliberal Thought Collective*, pgs 15–16.

[33] Ibid, pg 21.

The Mont Pelerin Society established its still prevailing set of objectives through its 1947 Statement of Aims:

> *The central values of civilization are in danger ... the group holds that these developments have been fostered by the growth of a view of history which denies all absolute moral standards and by the growth of theories which question the desirability of the rule of law. It holds further that they have been fostered by a decline of belief in private property and the competitive market; for without the diffused power and initiative associated with these institutions it is difficult to imagine a society in which freedom may be effectively preserved. Believing that what is essentially an ideological movement must be met by intellectual argument and the reassertion of valid ideas, the group, having made a preliminary exploration of the ground, is of the opinion that further study is desirable inter alia in regard to the following matters:*

1. *The analysis and explanation of the nature of the present crisis so as to bring home to others its essential moral and economic origins.*
2. *The redefinition of the functions of the state so as to distinguish more clearly between the totalitarian and the liberal order.*
3. *Methods of re-establishing the rule of law and of assuring its development in such a manner that individuals and groups not in a position to encroach upon the freedom of others and private rights are not allowed to become a basis of predatory power.*
4. *The possibility of establishing minimum standards by means not inimical to initiative and the functioning of the market.*
5. *Methods of combating the misuse of history for the furtherance of creeds hostile to liberty.*
6. *The problem of the creation of an international order conducive to the safeguarding of peace and liberty and permitting the establishment of harmonious international economic relations.*[34]

While the Colloque Walter Lippmann gave official birth to neoliberalism, the Mont Pelerin Society both mobilized the neoliberal movement as well as officially gave way to the process of construction of neoliberal thought. The Mont Pelerin Society became a huge ecumenical undertaking, which saw the formation and coexistence of many different '*groups and clans*'. Although they much diverged in their orientations, they, however, all infused in one way or another their valuable ideological inputs into neoliberal thought. The Mont Pelerin Society joined and mixed ordoliberals and neoliberals with other purebred liberals of the classical tradition, who endorsed interventionist schemes to one degree or another. It included, at the same time, many anarchists, libertarians, methodological individualists and neo-classical marginalists with different conceptions on issues such as the size and role of the state, the gold standard and managed or floating exchange rates. Notwithstanding, although

[34] Ibid, pgs 24–5.

intellectuals at the Mont Pelerin Society were seeking to revitalize classical liberalism and laissez-faire, as well as to expose the damages of interventionism and socialism, despite some agreement permeating the new liberal atmosphere, paradoxically, there was also much prevailing disagreement. For example, on one hand, there was overall consensus on some topics related to how history had been used as an illiberal propaganda weapon, to the '*over-vaunted role*' and efficacy of government, as well as on the need for constitutional values and the rule of law as primary safeguards for liberty. However, on the other hand, there was equally much discordance in connection to issues like state control of the monetary system, the role of religion, minimum wages and the level of welfare provision that a free economy would be able to tolerate. For instance, whereas intellectuals such as Wilhelm Röpke and William Rappard believed liberalism had to be tempered by the contemporary human desire for security, others like Machlup and Mises, feared that such permits only represented the first steps down the '*road to serfdom*' and therefore kept a very rigid libertarian posture.[35]

Between 1947 and 1960, throughout the 'first phase' of the Mont Pelerin Society, many clashes prevailed between devout neoliberal interventionists like Albert Hunold and classical liberal anti-interventionists like Ludwig Mises, with numerous other conflicts emerging constantly as well between ordoliberals and neoliberals. From 1960 onwards, during the 'second phase' of the Mont Pelerin Society, Hayek's eventual siding with the United States during the Hunold Affair, over editorial and other issues, made the United States begin to bear more influence over neoliberal thought and the neoliberal collective as a whole. During both phases of the Mont Pelerin Society, financial matters also played a big role in the direction of the neoliberal collective. While during the 'first phase' European funding from the Volker Foundation biased their role and topics of discussion, during the 'second phase' the United States was able to mobilize many more funds, and thus, influence much more the ideological topics of discussion that ended prevailing within the Mont Pelerin Society, as well as the overall direction of the neoliberal collective.[36]

During the first phase of the Mont Pelerin Society, factors such as the support Alfred Hunold provided the Society with, as well as others, increased the size of the neoliberal group, although they did not, however, completely dominate the Society. By 1953 and the society's meeting in Seelisberg, the different groups were already very divided over ideological and language reasons, with many discussions and propositions regarding different interventionist schemes causing much discordance. For example, while

[35] BUTLER, E. *A Short History of the Mont Pelerin Society*, pg 4. http://rybn.org/thegreatoffshore/THE%20GREAT%20OFFSHORE/1.ENCYCLOPEDIA/MONT%20PELERIN%20SOCIETY,%201947/DOCS/A%20SHORT%20HISTORY%20OF%20THE%20MONT%20PELERIN%20SOCIETY%20By%20Eamonn%20Butler.pdf

[36] Ludwig von Mises Institute. HÜLSMANN, J.G. *Against the Neoliberals*, pgs 1–2. https://mises.org/library/against-neoliberals

John van Sickle proposed to tax rich heirs, Wilhelm Röpke favoured the charging of subsidies to homeowners, and Otto Veit counter-argued that heavy taxation would not deter entrepreneurs from working. However, after the ordoliberal German Minister of Economics, Ludwig Erhard, whose party had won the 1953 elections in Germany, gave a talk at the meeting, the ordoliberal ideas he expressed began gaining much influencing ground within the Mont Pelerin Society. For some years, the success of Erhard's ordoliberal German economic miracle changed relative weights significantly within the society.[37]

At the time of the 1953 Mont Pelerin Society's meeting in Seelisberg, the climate of mainstream economic opinion was mostly dominated by socialists and social democrats, who admired and considered truly miraculous the task Erhard had carried out in West Germany. In West Germany, Erhard's abolition of price controls, together with the transition from a centrally planned economy towards a market economy, yielded very impressive economic benefits. However, for classical liberals, such as Mises, who openly disliked German economists and ordoliberal interventionism even more, there was nothing 'miraculous' whatsoever to be found in the social market economy. Furthermore, Mises was much displeased by the fact that Freiburg School ordoliberals, like Erhard, his Undersecretary of State, Alfred Müller-Armack and others, like Walter Eucken, William Röpke and Alexander Rüstow, had become the '*champions of the social market economy*'. Nevertheless, Erhard was still able to vindicate themes, which Mises had always stressed should be excluded from discussion, such as antitrust laws and the possible virtues of credit expansion. However, and as regards both those issues, Mises also sided with German classical liberals, who equally opposed the interventionist excesses of the '*Ordo School*', like Volkmar Muthesius and Hans Hellwig. They all strongly argued that the best way to fight against monopolies was by abolishing the government institutions and policies, which had created them in the first place.[38] Mises even wrote openly about his dislike of ordoliberals, admitting that he had '*no illusions about the true character of the politics and politicians of the "social market economy"*'.[39]

Americans felt the same way as Mises regarding those issues, if not much more. Due to the '*near total ignorance of foreign languages, the American public had a very unrealistic notion about what the German 'social market' model stood for. The only issue of German politics included in the American debate was the monetary policy of the German central bank, which was much less inflationary than the policies of the US Federal Reserve. Thus the ruling class in Germany was perceived as devoted to classical-liberal principles such as sound money and international trade*'.[40]

From more or less 1953 until 1957, the Mont Pelerin Society struggled very much internally with such issues, as well as others, like the Hunold Affair. However, the final

37 Ibid, pgs 2–3.
38 Ibid, pgs 3–4.
39 Ibid, pg 4.
40 Ibid.

European showdown came in 1960, at the Kassel meeting. The 1960 Kassel meeting marked both the decline of European influence within the neoliberal collective as well as the beginning of the 'second phase' of the Mont Pelerin Society. With both Hayek and Hunold resigning from their positions after non-stop quarrelling about editorial issues and others, from 1961 onwards, ordoliberals were pushed deeper into the shadows, with Chicago School economists beginning to gradually take over the leadership of the Mont Pelerin Society. The stepping down of such influencing figures of the neoliberal '*old guard*' also marked the beginning of the narrowing down of neoliberal thought. Another key issue of discord, which hugely affected the tilting of the balance of power within the Mont Pelerin Society and that since then also began prevailing between Europeans and Americans, was the international financial system. With some members wanting to return to the gold standard, others, such as Friedman, much preferred flexible exchange rates. Although the number of members of the Mont Pelerin Society had hugely grown since its founding, having reached a total of 350 members in 1968, US membership had, accordingly, grown enormously as well. By 1971, when Friedman became president of the Mont Pelerin Society, the scope and range of the neoliberal collective was truly and foremost American, having practically left neoliberalism bereft of any of its original and 'early' European ordoliberal and neoliberal factors and elements. Other very prominent American members who succeeded Friedman as presidents of the Mont Pelerin Society, continuing his hardcore aggressive monetarist legacy, included, most notably, George Stigler, who presided in 1976; James Buchanan, who presided in 1984; and Gary Becker, who presided in 1990.[41]

The funding of the Mont Pelerin Society was another key issue, which, apart from the institution's internal quarrels, also played a key role in the tilting of the neoliberal collective's balance of power within the Mont Pelerin Society from Europe to the United States. Since during the 'first phase' of the Mont Pelerin Society most funding had come from the Wilhelm Volker Fund, a lot of European issues on the agenda were therefore very influenced by the ideologies of the fund's financiers. However, from the 'second phase' onwards, since much of its funding began to emanate from US institutions, like the Heritage Foundation, the Hoover Institute, the American Enterprise Institute, the John M. Olin Foundation and many others on US soil, the choices of, as well as the preferred, themes, which were developed in the Mont Pelerin Society, began to henceforth be very strongly influenced by them.[42]

At present, the Mont Pelerin Society is active and meets regularly, holding a General Meeting every two years, as well as Regional Meetings every year. The spirit and legacy of its founding ordoliberal and neoliberal members live on through the role both currents played in giving shape and form to neoliberal thought, as well as by having

[41] Ibid, pg 5.

[42] BUTLER, E. *A Short History of the Mont Pelerin Society,* pg 9. http://rybn.org/thegreatoffshore/THE%20GREAT%20OFFSHORE/1.ENCYCLOPEDIA/MONT%20PELERIN%20SOCIETY,%201947/DOCS/A%20SHORT%20HISTORY%20OF%20THE%20MONT%20PELERIN%20SOCIETY%20By%20Eamonn%20Butler.pdf

lately resuscitated ordoliberalism at the EU level. Many of its original members, like Ludwig Erhard, Luigi Einaudi and Jacques Rueff, went on to occupy high-ranking political positions. Others, like Friedrich Hayek, Milton Friedman, George Stigler, Maurice Allais, James M. Buchanan, Ronald Coase, Gary Becker and Vernon Smith, won the Nobel Memorial Prize in Economic Sciences. Likewise, the Mont Pelerin Society has many contemporary illustrious libertarian members, like Mario Vargas Llosa, who is also a Nobel Laureate. The Mont Pelerin Society is closely tied to the Atlas Economic Research Foundation, as well as to the network of think tanks that it sponsors.[43]

The Austrian School of Thought

The Austrian School is a *'heterodox'*, *'purist free-market'* school of thought, with *'laissez-faire'* policy recommendations. Paradoxically, the Austrian School is ideologically extremely divided. One part of the school is completely *'anti-governmental interventionism'* in the economy, and another part of the school is totally *'pro-interventionism'* in the economy. It is a heterodox school of thought which lies outside mainstream economics due to its different methodological approach to the study of economics and economic phenomena.

Its economic approach is mainly based on *'methodological individualism'*. Such approach stands in outright rejection of mathematical modelling, econometrics and macroeconomic analyses, as it pivots around a concept which views social phenomena as a direct result of the motivations and actions of individuals. The Austrian School strongly believes in pure logic and not in empirical reasoning for analysing the unpredictable course of human action.[44] With most of its work being mostly based on philosophy, logic and reasoning, the Austrian School's academics are very strong believers of the economy being based on the actions of individuals, strongly holding that no mathematical formulas can ever be utilized to predict human behaviour or let alone calculate why or how people act.[45]

The Austrian School originated in the late nineteenth and early twentieth centuries, in Vienna, through the work of, amongst others, Carl Menger, Eugen Böhm von Bawerk and Friedrich von Wieser. With its methodology approach fiercely opposing the Historical School of Economics (the Historical School), the Austrian School was born out of two main events. The first event was the publication in 1871 of Menger's book *'Principles of Economics'*, which is largely regarded as a key founding moment of

[43] Ibid, pgs 27–31.

[44] The Economic Review. *Chicago School vs Austrian School: Battle of Free-Marketeers,* pgs 1–2. https://theeconomicreview.wordpress.com/2011/09/24/chicago-school-vs-austrian-school-battle-of-the-free-marketeers/

[45] 71 Republic. *The Difference between Austrian and Chicago Economics,* pg 1. https://71republic.com/2018/10/21/difference-austrian-chicago-economics/

the Austrian School. The second event was the intense dispute that was held for years, known as '*Methodenstreit*' or the '*Methodology Struggle*'. The 'methodology struggle' began in 1883, when Menger defended the role of theory in economics as being totally different from the Historical School's study of historical circumstance. Menger's theory was very critically responded to by the leader of the Historical School, Gustav Schmoller, who, when referring to Menger and his followers and outcasting them as being too 'provincial', simultaneously coined the term 'Austrian School'. With the Austrian School's adherents adopting the label, henceforth, the term became thereby established.[46] Menger's book included one of the Austrian School's main economic areas of expertise and primary focus, which was the '*marginalist revolution in economic analysis*' or '*marginalism*'. The book also triggered the '*Marginalist Revolution*', which was spearheaded by the Austrian School. Menger strongly believed that '*economic analysis is universally applicable and that the appropriate unit of analysis is man and his choices. These choices are determined by individual subjective preferences and the margin on which decisions are made. The logic of choice is the essential building block to the development of a universally valid economic theory*'.[47]

The relationship between the Austrian School and what is today considered to be mainstream economics has been historically characterized by many tensions. On one hand, the first two generations of Austrian economists, like most particularly Carl Menger, Eugen Böhm von Bawerk and Friedrich von Wieser, fitted well into the neoclassical economics school by much contributing to its development with their contributions to 'methodological individualism', 'subjective value theory' and 'marginal utility'. On the other hand, the subsequent third- and fourth-generation economists, like Mises and Hayek, forever cast the Austrian School as heterodox and very far away from mainstream economics, through their work on the 'aggregation of knowledge' and 'monetary theory of the business cycle'.[48]

Among the early Austrian School's theoretical contributions to economics are the 'subjective theory of value', 'marginalism in price theory' and the 'formulation of the economic calculation problem'. Building upon Menger's work, both Mises and Hayek provided many incalculable contributions to, most particularly, the 'economic calculation problem' through their respective 'anti-interventionist theories', 'knowledge arguments' and 'price mechanism theories'. Especially after the 1940s, with the Austrian School becoming very divided about issues related to interventionism, Hayek ended up becoming a staunch believer of interventionism and Mises established himself as a devout enemy of interventionism. At present, whereas the Mises camp still regards

[46] Exploring Economics. *Austrian Economics,* pg 1. https://www.exploring-economics.org/en/orientation/austrian-economics/

[47] The Concise Encyclopedia of Economics. *Austrian School of Economics.* http://www.econlib.org/library/Enc/AustrianSchoolofEconomics.html

[48] Exploring Economics. *Austrian Economics,* pg 11. https://www.exploring-economics.org/en/orientation/austrian-economics/

neoclassical methodology as irredeemably flawed, the Hayek camp accepts a large part of neoclassical methodology while also being more tolerant of governmental economic interventionism.[49]

Through the work of, most particularly, Hayek, Mises and Machlup, the Austrian School gave shape, form, life and vigour to the Socialist Calculation Debate, the Colloque Walter Lippmann, as well as to the Mont Pelerin Society. Altogether, those academics, through the different new liberal gatherings, hugely influenced at the same time the conception of neoliberalism as well as the 'early' direction of the neoliberal collective. The Mont Pelerin Society, together with the mobilization of the neoliberal collective, was mostly Hayek's idea, and he fought incessantly to preserve its unity until the society's second phase, when the Hunold Affair and other issues made the tilting of US influence become too strong to hold. From 1931 to 1950, Hayek taught at the London School of Economics and from 1950 until 1961 at the Chicago School. From 1961 until 1973 (the year he retired), Hayek also taught at the universities of Freiburg and Salzburg. In 1974, Hayek was awarded the Nobel Memorial Prize in Economic Sciences for his work on 'individuals' acquisition' and the 'utilisation of knowledge in and through the market process'. Hayek passed away in 1992. Similarly, Mises also spent many years teaching in the United States, at Columbia University, until he passed away in 1973.[50] Other renowned Austrian School academics also include Murray Rothbard, Hans-Hermann Hope and Israel Kirzner.

By the 1980s, when the Reagan and Thatcher era began reviving neoliberal ideas, both Reagan and, most especially, Thatcher consulted very often with Hayek. Thatcher had avidly read Hayek's work while studying at Oxford University and truly admired his thinking. However, by that time, and unfortunately, Hayek's '*neoliberal dream*' had been shattered by the Chicago School and turned into a very different species, with very few features and components remaining from his original vision.

Today, the Austrian School's most distinctive areas of specialization revolve around 'Methodological Individualism'; 'Methodological Subjectivism'; 'Aversion and Mistrust against the use of Mathematical and Statistical Methods in economics'; 'Apriorism and Strong Deductivism'; 'Business Cycle Theory'; 'Monetary Crises Theory'; 'Fundamental Uncertainty'; 'Relevance of Prices and Free Competition'; 'Focus on the Entrepreneur'; 'Emphasis on Dynamics and Time in Economic Processes' and 'Opportunity Costs'.[51]

Some of the Austrian School's core defining areas of specialization, like 'Methodological Individualism' and ''Methodological Subjectivism', together with its 'Monetary Theory', are most especially interesting, rotating around the human axiom factor.

49 Ibid, pgs 1–4.
50 The Mont Pelerin Society. *F.A. Hayek*. https://www.montpelerin.org/how-to-join-mps-3/
51 Exploring Economics. *Austrian Economics*, pgs 1–4. https://www.exploring-economics.org/en/orientation/austrian-economics/ and HUERTA DE SOTO, J. *La Escuela Austriaca. Mercado y Creatividad Empresarial*, pgs 15–34.

The Austrian School's 'Theory of Methodological Individualism' seeks to comprehend economics and economic phenomena by way of examining the social ramifications of individual choice. The theory's main assumption is that the subjective choices of individuals, including individual knowledge, time, expectation and other subjective factors, are the main cause behind all economic phenomena. In 1949, the publication of Mises's book '*Human Action*' termed and established 'methodological individualism' as '*Praxeology*'. According to Mises, praxeology can be used to deduce a priori theoretical economic truths and experiments related to deductive economic thought and can produce conclusions, which follow irrefutably from their underlying assumptions. For Mises, 'conclusions' most especially cannot be inferred from empirical observation or statistical analysis. Mises also strongly advised against the use of probabilities in economic models. Praxeology is built around the '*human action axiom*', stressing emphatically that only individuals act purposefully, which confines the approach to questioning whether certain means satisfy the condition to achieve a given end. Within the praxeology framework, the origin of the actual end is absolutely irrelevant for the purpose of the analysis in question. For the Austrian School, an unalterable fact remains that although people can influence each other as to what their ends are, they still have to act in the first place in order to achieve those ends.[52]

The Austrian School likewise subscribes to a strong 'Methodological Subjectivism' or 'Ontological Individualism'. The approach strongly holds that the only existent world is the one perceived by individuals. It has ontological implications, since it stipulates that social specifics, like prices and costs, only exist within the individual. Additionally, even though the approach might consider aggregates or institutions, everything is ultimately reduced to individuals, as it is those individuals and their actions that form the starting point of such entities in the first place.[53]

The rationale asserts that, in general, the economic problems of individuals are mainly associated with the coordination of plans and the aggregation of knowledge, stressing that within the economic environment individuals can either perform as consumers or entrepreneurs. While, on one hand, consumers articulate their demands, that way determining the shape of the market, on the other hand, entrepreneurs also have the capability of detecting unexplored demand. The approach is very strongly associated with uncertainty and the dispersion of knowledge and information, as well as with the change of environmental conditions in historical time. However, some elder school members also favour the problem of allocation of scarce resources.[54]

Although the Austrian School's conception of human nature is very similar to the neoclassical economics concept of human nature, the Austrian School's image of

[52] Exploring Economics. *Austrian Economics,* pgs 6–7. https://www.exploring-economics.org/en/orientation/austrian-economics/
[53] Ibid, pgs 4–5.
[54] Ibid.

human nature is much more refined. Menger always defended the quite simplistic comprehension of the analytical construct of Mills's '*Homo Economicus*', with instrumental rationalism, perfect information and utility maximization. Other Austrian School academics have likewise integrated more social components, such as the social environment, institutions and power, into their interpretation of human nature. The approach and its acknowledgement of such contextual factors, however, do not imply that the focus on the individual as merely an acting subject is ignored. Instead, the approach infers that depending upon the historical context, the actions of the individual will change, with the individual receiving varying input.[55]

Another key aspect of the Austrian School's economic focus is placed upon its self-developed evolutionary perspective on the theory of money, through its 'Monetary Theory' and the economic dynamics associated with it. The Austrian School's theory of (commodity) money was advanced by Menger. It mainly highlights that the emergence of money is explained in terms of *'a spontaneous order of individual action and not in terms of deliberate government intervention'*.[56] Böhm-Bawerk, through his *'Agio Theory'* or 'theory of capital and interest', developed the thesis which holds that individuals consider and view goods in the present, as much more valuable than goods in the future. The same reasoning is often used in contemporary economics, which thus provides a justification for the existence of interest. Böhm-Bawerk also further elaborated on the 'process of value creation', which relates to the capacity of the producer to generate revenue that exceeds interest. His arguments emphasized on the fact that as the producer will utilize borrowed money to acquire capital goods, the latter can in turn be used to further expand the production process by adding more stages to it. The theory holds that, subsequently, those additional stages will make the whole production process much more successful, as the introduction of intermediary phases that increase both the time frame and the technological sophistication, will increase the quality and the quantity of the overall output.[57]

The Chicago School of Thought

During the 1940s, the Chicago School originated through the University of Chicago. It is a mainstream, *'orthodox neoclassical'*, school of thought. It is hardcore libertarian, as well as a strong believer in '*laissez-faire*', strongly rejecting Keynesian notions of governmental management of aggregate economic demand in order to promote growth. The Chicago School's economic bedrock rests on intense mathematical modelling to test hypotheses, with its main assumptions being strictly based on rational expectations. The school firmly believes that economics is a science, with rules that cannot be broken, and thus, relies very heavily on scientific truth, scientific

[55] Ibid.
[56] Ibid, pgs 3–4.
[57] Ibid.

logic, econometrics and mathematics, to base its theories on. The school's main tenets hold that free-markets are the best allocators of resources in the economy, and thus, place a very strong emphasis on reduced government interventionism in the economy. The school includes Milton Friedman's monetarist beliefs about the economy, which mainly stress that the money supply should be kept in equilibrium with the money demand. The school also rejects market regulation, except for the central bank's regulation of the money supply.[58]

Most especially after 1946, the Chicago School began to flourish when Friedman joined it and began promoting his currently established, '*Monetary Theory*' or '*Monetarism*'. From 1951 onwards, when Friedman initiated the Chicago School workshop on monetarism, the school's main nucleus of thought on monetary theory and policy began to stem from him. Henceforth, and as voiced in his 1953, *'Essays in Positive Economics'*, Friedman's main interests began rotating around the 'Neo-quantitative School', 'Monetarism', 'Explanations of the Relevance of Money' and the 'Limits of Monetary Policy'.[59] Friedman's '*Quantity Theory of Money*' holds that general price levels in the economy are determined by the amount of money in circulation. It mainly states that economic growth is better controlled through the management of general price levels, since individuals and groups make economic allocation decisions in a rational way.[60] In 1958, Friedman's close colleague, George J. Stigler, joined the school's faculty and revolutionized the field of microeconomics, with a very strong theory on '*Anti-government Regulation of Business*'. Friedman and most of the Chicago School established the school's allegiance to human liberty, free-markets and free trade. The school firmly believes that *'free-markets are the institutional guarantor of choice, opportunity, and limits on government control over people's lives.*[61] In 1962, Friedman's book *'Capitalism and Freedom'* (a corporate version of Hayek's *'The Road to Serfdom')* expressed his true allegiance to corporatism and market freedom. While it mainly stressed that *'economic freedom is an end in itself'*, it further claimed that *'monopoly, should it exist, is blamed on the government and is deemed to be relatively harmless. Patents are deemed not to be monopolies simply because they participate in the definition of property rights. There is no such thing as a social or political responsibility of corporations ... For advocacy of capitalism to mean anything, the proponents must be able to finance their cause ... Radical movements in capitalist societies ... have typically been supported by a few wealthy individuals ... a role of inequality in wealth in preserving political freedom that is seldom noted'.*[62] Friedman's book likewise proposed the abolition of the corporate income tax and the

58 Investopedia. *Chicago School.* https://www.investopedia.com/terms/c/chicago_school.asp

59 IESE Business School – Universidad de Navarra. ARGANDOÑA, A. *El Pensamiento Económico de Friedman,* pg 5. www.iese.edu/research/pdfs/di-0193.pdf

60 Investopedia. *Chicago School.* https://www.investopedia.com/terms/c/chicago_school.asp

61 Foundation for Economic Education. *Milton Friedman and the Chicago School of Economics,* pgs 1–2. https://fee.org/articles/milton-friedman-and-the-chicago-school-of-economics/

62 MIROWSKI, P. and PLEHWE, D. *The Road from Mont Pèlerin: The Making of the Neoliberal Thought Collective,* pgs 167–8.

privatization of state universities.[63] Furthermore, in 1980, Friedman's widely acclaimed book *'Free to Choose'* provided a crystal clear reflection of the economic mindset of the Chicago School by highlighting that *'economic freedom is an essential requisite for political freedom. By enabling people to cooperate with one another without coercion or central direction, it reduces the area over which political power is exercised. In addition, by dispersing power, the free market provides an offset to whatever concentration of political power may arise. The combination of economic and political power in the same hands is a sure recipe for tyranny'.*[64]

From the beginning of the revolution seeking the reformation of classical liberalism and laissez-faire, many Chicago School economists were actively involved in the neoliberal movement. While Frank Knight had represented the Chicago School at the Colloque Walter Lippmann, both Knight and Friedman were likewise present at the inaugural meeting of the Mont Pelerin Society. From the outset of the neoliberal mobilization, both formed an integral part of the neoliberal collective, and progressively, more and more of the Chicago School began to form part of it and influence it heavily. During the first phase of the Mont Pelerin Society, the Chicago School's mindframe was much more inclusive of the early neoliberal collective's issues, such as competition, monopoly and social proposals. However, once Milton Friedman took over the leadership of the school, and most especially during the second phase of the Mont Pelerin Society, the situation radically changed. With George Stigler, Aaron Director and Gary Becker, some of the school's long-running projects, like the '*Free Market Study Group*' and the '*Anti-Trust Project*', began to profoundly alter the school's mentality, with the most transfigured areas being the school's perception of competition and monopoly. However, other reasons for the Chicago School's transfiguration, were also rooted in the '*Business activism*' and in the radicalization of neoliberalism that the Cold War generated. From then onwards, neoliberal thought within the Mont Pelerin Society became more and more influenced by the United States, which thus and in turn, severely narrowed down the neoliberal collective's horizons. Since then, the Chicago School's basic neoliberal prescriptions of free-markets, deregulation and widespread privatizations have prevailed, with the international financial monetary system equally being mechanized by Friedman's aggressive monetarism.

Many of the Chicago School's members of the Mont Pelerin Society that formed part of the neoliberal collective, also received the Nobel Memorial Prize in Economic Sciences for their varying contributions to the field of economics. Milton Friedman received it in 1976, George Stigler in 1982 and Gary Becker in 1992. Others who were not so involved in the Mont Pelerin Society, but who also won the same Nobel Prize include Ronald Coase in 1991 and Robert Lucas in 1995. Likewise, in 2013, Peter Hansen, Eugene Fama and Robert Schiller also received the Nobel Prize for their work and contributions to 'Asset Pricing'. Eugene Fama's work on '*Efficient Market Hypothesis*

[63] Ibid.

[64] Foundation for Economic Education. *Milton Friedman and the Chicago School of Economics*, pg 3. https://fee.org/articles/milton-friedman-and-the-chicago-school-of-economics/

(EMH)' likewise represents one of the Chicago School's main economic pillars, having demonstrated that movements in stock prices are impossible to predict in the short term, with new information affecting prices almost immediately, which thus proves that the *'market is efficient'*. Fama's research has strongly influenced issues, such as the 'Development of Index Funds'.[65]

Especially from the 1970s onwards, the Chicago School gained much appraisal for applying its neoliberal model for the first time in LA, in Chile. The first-ever 'neoliberal experiment', subsequently generated a very powerful neoliberal wave, largely based on the Washington Consensus, which eventually splashed over the whole region. When in 1973, General Augusto Pinochet staged the Chilean coup d'état, he selected a close team of economists who had studied at the University of Chicago during the 1950s, having been taught by Friedman. Pinochet and his team of so-called *Chicago Boys,* spearheaded a sweeping neoliberal reform. The Chicago School carried out with great success the implementation of neoliberal objectives, such as economic liberalization, deregulation, privatization of state-owned companies and stabilization of inflation.[66]

Following that first-ever successful experimentation with neoliberalism at the national level, the Washington Consensus was subsequently applied to most development and integration processes in LA. A few years later, the Reagan and Thatcher and Clinton and Blair administrations likewise chose the Chicago School's neoliberal model in order to run the globalized free-market economy, as well as Friedman's monetarist policies to mechanize and churn the international financial monetary system.

However, following the 2007–15 global financial crisis, the Chicago School and its neoliberal prescriptions, were highly blamed for instigating the crisis. Since then, the prestige the school enjoyed before the crisis has been matched by much critique following the crisis. Much of such critique mainly revolves around the irony that if markets really were to behave efficiently, there would then not have been any major imbalances in the first place, let alone a crisis like the one that unfolded. Furthermore, while much debate has likewise arisen regarding the school's lack of regulation around the banking sector, another Nobel Laureate, Paul Krugman, has equally been extremely critical of the school's basic doctrines.

The fact that the *'Chicago School had suffered an "intellectual collapse"'*[67] is reflected by the displacement neoliberalism has experienced worldwide, most especially in the United States. Although President Biden has once again regenerated the US economy based on neoliberal principles, he has nonetheless done so by mixing and blending them with neonational characteristics.

[65] Investopedia. *Chicago School.* https://www.investopedia.com/terms/c/chicago_school.asp
[66] STEGER, M.B. and RAVI, K.R. *Neoliberalism: A Very Short Introduction,* pgs 99–101.
[67] Investopedia. *Chicago School.* https://www.investopedia.com/terms/c/chicago_school.asp

The Main Neoliberal Tenets

When during the second phase of the Mont Pelerin Society, the US contingent began to take over the control of the direction of the neoliberal movement, so began at the same time the final narrowing down of the neoliberal collective as a whole. Eventually, while the Chicago School's neoliberal formula emerged as quite basic and simple, the lack of neoliberal political and economic breadth has been clearly mirrored by neoliberalism's chaotic and disordered evolution, largely based on an uneven geographical development of its institutions, functions and powers.

Notwithstanding, neoliberalism is closely tied to several defining characteristics and distinguishing features, with some of the most important ones revolving around its conception of the role of the state, free-markets, deregulation, widespread privatizations, competition, personal freedom, the free flow of capital and goods, as well as around its aversion towards democratic rule.[68]

One of the main key defining neoliberal characteristics hinges around its conception of *'the role of the state'*. Neoliberalism strongly holds that the state should support *'strong individual private property rights, the rule of law and the institutions of freely functioning markets and free trade'*.[69] For neoliberalism, such an institutional framework, not only provides the main guarantor of individual freedoms, but also and at the same time, allows for a legal framework to be formed by freely negotiated contractual obligations between juridical individuals in the marketplace. The neoliberal state is at the same time meant to both protect those freedoms through its executive powers, as well as cover the sanctity of contracts and individual rights to freedom of action, expression and choice. Correspondingly, neoliberalism also holds that within such an institutional framework of free markets and free trade, the freedom of businesses and corporations (considered legal individuals) is regarded as a fundamental good. While issues such as private enterprise and entrepreneurial initiative are considered by neoliberalism as the keys to innovation and wealth creation, as well as to the proper protection of intellectual property rights through patents, it also believes that they will encourage further technological changes. Neoliberalism equally assumes that the increase in productivity will consequentially render higher living standards. One of the strongest neoliberal assumptions asserts that free-markets and free trade should eliminate poverty at all levels through the *'trickle-down effect'*.[70]

Three other very distinctive features of neoliberalism include, at the same time, *'deregulation'*, *'privatization'* and *'competition'*. Neoliberalism strongly believes that the combination of both 'deregulation' and 'privatization', together with 'competition', is meant to eliminate any potential bureaucratic slowdowns and long administrative

[68] HARVEY, D. *A Brief History of Neoliberalism*, pg 64.
[69] Ibid.
[70] Ibid, pgs 64–5.

procedures, *'increase efficiency and productivity, improve quality, and reduce costs, both directly to the consumer through cheaper commodities and services and indirectly through reduction of the tax burden'.*[71] The deregulation of state-run sectors and companies, as well as their handing over to the private sector, is a neoliberal must for the liberation of economic activity from any state interference. The privatization of other assets is also sought after diligently. Neoliberalism considers the lack of private property rights as one of the biggest institutional barriers to economic development and the improvement of human welfare, most especially in developing countries. For neoliberalism, the best and safest way to protect against the '*tragedy of the commons*' (the irresponsible tendency of individuals to super-exploit common property resources like land and water) is through the proper enclosure and assignment of private property rights. Competition, amongst and between regional groupings, nations, regions, cities, firms and individuals, is regarded by neoliberalism as a primary virtue, but one, which, however, has to be strictly based on the respect of ground rules for market competition. If such ground rules are not clearly laid out and property rights not clearly defined, the neoliberal state is then supposed to step in, in order to either impose or create market systems, like trading and pollution rights. Neoliberalism also stresses that the state should consistently seek internal reorganizations and new institutional arrangements, which improve its competitive position in regional and global markets.[72]

Another strong neoliberal belief surrounds the realm of *'personal freedom'*. Neoliberalism holds that although within the marketplace 'personal freedom' is guaranteed, every individual should, however, be held responsible and accountable for their own personal actions and well-being, a principle which is also extended to the realms of welfare, education, health care and pensions. Furthermore, the achievement of individual success or failure is interpreted by neoliberalism as very closely associated with either the entrepreneurial virtues of individuals or the lack of human capital invested in education.[73]

An additional key feature of neoliberalism is related to the *'free flow of capital and goods'*. Neoliberalism considers that free trade must be strictly based on the free movement of capital between sectors, countries and regions. Therefore, it deems the complete abolition of all tariffs, punitive taxation arrangements, planning and environmental controls, as well as other locational impediments, as sine qua non requirements for the generation of such trade. Neoliberalism likewise believes that state sovereignty over the movements of capital, commodities and goods should be voluntarily handed over to the global market. International competition is regarded by neoliberalism as very healthy as it improves efficiency and productivity and lowers prices, which in turn keep inflationary tendencies under control. Neoliberalism also strongly stresses that states should collectively seek the reduction of all barriers, for the opening up of markets to

71 Ibid, pg 65.
72 Ibid.
73 Ibid.

global exchange and the free flow of capital, commodities and goods across borders. At the same time, neoliberalism considers it of crucial importance for the establishment of the above at a global scale, the signing of international agreements between states, which guarantee the rule of law and freedoms of trade, such as the ones incorporated into the WTO.[74]

A last defining attribute of neoliberalism is related to its huge distrust and aversion towards *'democratic rule'*. Neoliberalism considers governance by majority rule, as a potential threat to individual rights and constitutional liberties and, thus, prefers governance through elites and experts. Although neoliberalism perceives democratic rule as only possible under conditions of relative affluence, it believes that such ruling has to be adequately counter-matched by the presence of a strong middle class for the assurance of political stability. Neoliberalism also prefers governance by 'executive order' and 'judicial decision-making', much more than governance by 'democratic' and 'parliamentary decision-making'. In a similar way, it also holds that key institutions like central banks should be kept isolated from democratic pressures. Neoliberalism hinges very tightly on both 'the rule of law' as well as on a strict interpretation of constitutionality. Therefore, it firmly relies on courts for the mediation of conflicts and opposition, as well as in the legal system for solving individual problems and finding solutions.[75]

Neoliberal Contradictions and Areas of Conflict

Although neoliberalism does possess several defining tenets and distinguishing features, it nonetheless finds itself very bogged down by several inherent contradictions, areas of conflict and shadow areas, which impede its fair and equitable practice. Some of the main neoliberal areas of conflict, which have proven to be intrinsically flawed, rendering unfair and uneven competition, market failure, asymmetric power and information, as well as creating glitches related to technological change, include the realms of 'competition', 'market and market failure', 'power relations and information' and 'technological change'.[76]

The first main neoliberal area of conflict surrounds the sphere of *'competition'*. The sphere is highly criticized due to the fact that the interaction between big and strong firms with much smaller and weaker firms ends up creating either monopolies or oligopolies. Although neoliberalism assumes that maximized efficiency is achieved if there are no barriers impeding the entry of more competitors, it is in practice difficult to expect the state to nurture that possibility, which thus and in turn only gives way to those kinds of market distortions. The issue of 'natural monopolies' is more

[74] Ibid, pg 66.
[75] Ibid, pgs 66–7.
[76] Ibid, pg 67.

problematic, since it is much harder to tackle and even more so to solve. Although neoliberalism does not see any sense in having multiple firms competing within the same areas where state regulation of provision, access and pricing is unavoidable, in some cases, it does give in to some sort of partial deregulation, although as many examples have demonstrated, the chances of profiteering and abuse under those circumstances are inevitable.[77]

A second very controversial neoliberal area surrounds the realm of '*market and market failure*', which is associated with dumping issues carried out by both firms and individuals of '*liabilities or externalities*' outside the market. One of the most typical cases of market failure is related to the issue of pollution. When in a neoliberal context, firms and individuals begin adopting certain illegal patterns of behaviour in order to avoid the costs incurred by the dumping of noxious residues in the environment, such actions mainly result in the degradation or destruction of many productive ecosystems, as well as of the environment. Furthermore, the exposure to dangerous substances in the workplace also affects human health. Although neoliberalism acknowledges such a setback and in some cases does give in allowing some kind of limited state interventionism, contradictorily, it also argues against it by pointing out that '*the cure will almost certainly be worse than the disease*'. The only type of interventionism that neoliberalism supports in such cases is the sort of interventionism that is carried out through market mechanisms, like, tax impositions or incentives, or trading rights of pollutants. The same kind of moderated interventionist approach is also used for competitive failures, as the costs of transactions increase with the proliferation of contractual and sub-contractual relations. However, further complications likewise arise, for instance, when all firms in the same region, employ the same technological machinery that ends up underutilized, which thus and in turn also drives up aggregate costs. Although state planning, regulation and forced coordination could help contain such costs, once again, neoliberalism does not support them either due to its mistrust of such interventions.[78]

Another very conflictive neoliberal area is related to '*power relations and information*'. Although within the neoliberal free market the market itself is meant to provide equal opportunities to all firms and individuals a very common drawback that emerges is related to the market's predisposition to the development of asymmetric power relations and information. Such tendency hinders the possibility of firms and individuals making rational choices in pursuit of their own interests. Many disadvantages arise when better-informed, and thus more powerful players have a much bigger advantage over the others, which in turn also leads to the reutilization of such information between the bigger players, who only become stronger and more powerful. Concurrently, the establishment of intellectual property rights like patents only encourages '*rent-seeking*' behaviour, as patent owners utilize their monopoly

[77] Ibid.

[78] Ibid, pg 68.

power to set monopoly prices for the prevention of technology transfers, or simply in order to carry out such technological transfers at very low costs. In such cases, the situation only gets worse, as unless the state intercedes to counter fight such practices, the amount of asymmetric power relations tends to increase rather than decrease. Due to such factors, neoliberalism is perceived by critics to cling to a *'false utopia'*, under the presumption of perfect information and an equal-level playing field, which in reality only ends up obfuscating processes that lead to the concentration of wealth, and thus once again to the restoration of class power.[79]

A last neoliberal shadow area surrounds *'technological change'*. Technological change relies very strongly on coercive powers of competition as the main driver for the search of new organizational forms, new production methods, as well as new products. The problem with such an imposed driver, however, arises when it becomes established as *'fetish belief'*, since it becomes so embedded in entrepreneurial common sense, that it makes-believe that there is some sort of technological solution for every problem. The trends of powerful independent technological change, which neoliberalism generates, can become very destabilizing and counterproductive. Furthermore, such technological developments can easily go amok when sectors dedicated exclusively to technological innovation, as well as to the creation of new products and new methods of functioning, find themselves without a suitable market for their end products. What is worse, the mobilization of technological innovations also allows expert hackers to hack into all sorts of systems, dangerously damaging or hindering institutions, as well as dominant social relations. One of the main reasons neoliberalism is considered to be intrinsically flawed is precisely due to the very short-circuited connection between *'technological dynamism, instability, dissolution of social solidarities, environmental degradation, deindustrialisation, rapid shifts in time-space relations, speculative bubbles, and the general tendency towards crisis formation within capitalism'*.[80]

The Ambiguous Abstraction Surrounding the Concept of Neoliberalism

When setting out trying to comprehend or define neoliberalism, one of the most baffling paradoxes that we first encounter is that despite the ideology having several distinguishing wide arching characteristics, like free-markets, deregulation and widespread privatizations, surprisingly however, there is no existing neoliberal theory, as such or in itself. There is no existing, official neoliberal theory, theoretical framework or governing theoretical core body of thought, which renders possible a proper definition of neither neoliberalism nor any sort of intrinsic analysis of it. What makes matters even more complicated is the fact that the concept of neoliberalism

[79] Ibid.
[80] Ibid, pg 69.

is also surrounded by much ambiguity and abstraction due to the many inexact and unclear definitions associated with it.

Although there are three broad utilizations of the term 'neoliberalism', there is not a single one of them which offers an acceptable exact definition of it. As an *'academic paradigm'*, neoliberalism is considered to be mostly based on the Chicago School's neoclassical economic theory; as a *'political ideology'*, neoliberalism denotes a conception of freedom as an overarching social value, associated with reducing state functions to those of a minimalist state; and as a *'developmental model'*, neoliberalism favours the rejection of structural economics in favour of the Washington Consensus.

> *Crisply unambiguous, essentialist definitions of neoliberalism have proved to be incredibly elusive. ... It would be [wrong] to reduce neoliberalism to some singular essence ... [because] it is contradictory and polymorphic.*[81]

Probably one of the most bizarre facts about neoliberalism is that since it was officially born in 1937, despite the masses of literature inked out about its defining tenets, distinguishing characteristics, pros and cons, as well as the dimensions and contexts it has been applied to, there is inexplicably, no existing governing neoliberal theoretical body, nor any conceptual or terminological, homogeneous definition of it either. When setting out in trying to comprehend neoliberalism, while the economic current is simply dichotomized and analysed in terms of its diverse peculiarities, effects and contextual applications, the concept of neoliberalism is likewise very enmeshed by much ambiguous abstraction. Although neoliberalism does possess several shifting amalgams of idiosyncratic postulates, which are very often described as either defining features or being constitutive of, there is, however, no contemporary academic work that can purport to be neoliberal theory as such. Neoliberalism is widely perceived as an artifice, willed into existence by critics and not theorists, which has been cut and shaped in order to fit its differing conceptual variants. The concept of neoliberalism is considered to be multipolar, with diverging identities coexisting within it.[82]

> *While there are many who give out and are given the title of neoliberal, there are none who will embrace this moniker of power and call themselves as such. There is no contemporary body of knowledge that calls itself neoliberalism, no self-described neoliberal theorists that elaborate it, nor policy makers or practitioners that implement it. There are no primers or advanced textbooks on the subject matter, no pedagogues, courses, or students of neoliberalism, no policies or election manifestoes that promise to implement it (although there are many that promise to dismantle*

[81] The London School of Economics and Political Science. LSE Research Online. VENUGOPAL, R. *Neoliberalism as Concept*, pg 6. Also see: Laruffa, F. *Making Sense of (Post) Neoliberalism*, pgs 586–629. https://journals.sagepub.com/doi/pdf/10.1177/00323292231193805; Magness, P. *The Pejorative Origins of the Term 'Neoliberalism'*. https://thedailyeconomy.org/article/the-pejorative-origins-of-the-term-neoliberalism/

[82] VENUGOPAL, R. *Neoliberalism as Concept*, pgs 13–15.

> *it). Pedantic as it may seem, this is a point that warrants repetition if only because there is a considerable body of critical literature that deploys neoliberalism under the mistaken assumption that in doing so, it is being transported into the front-lines of hand-to-hand combat with free market economics.*[83]

None of the various shifting components that form part of neoliberalism, or any advocates of market deregulation and private sector-led growth, consider or describe themselves or any of their policies as neoliberal. While neoliberalism is only defined, conceptualized and deployed exclusively by those who blatantly oppose it, in academic tracts, neoliberalism never features either as forming an elemental part of any deep analysis and deliberation, and when it does so, it only does so as part of rhetorical toolkits and general dismissal.[84]

Although since before the term 'neoliberalism' began having negative connotations, it had in fact only formed a small marginal part of the vocabulary of mainstream economics; nowadays, however, it has practically totally disappeared from the field of economics, gaining much more resonance, growing influence and usage instead in the field of social sciences. Today, the word or term 'neoliberalism' is only mostly used by self-conscious non-neoliberal critics and by non-economists, when referring to either economic phenomena or economic forms of reasoning.[85]

Going even further, the actual word/term – *'neoliberal'* – is totally non-existent in modern economics. Officially, the word/term, neoliberalism, does not appear in any of the established economic, macroeconomic or microeconomic textbooks, nor is it included in any of the economic scientific literature. The definition of neoliberalism as a '*macroeconomic doctrine*' is impossible to reconcile with the corpus of macroeconomic theory, since not even the word 'neoliberalism' appears in, for example, Mankiw's *'Principles of Macroeconomics'*, Blanchard's *'Macroeconomics'*, Obstfeld and Rogoff's *'Foundations of International Macroeconomics'*, Krugman, Obstfeld and Melitz's *'International Economics'*, nor in Agenor' and Montiel's *'Development Macroeconomics'*. The word or term 'neoliberalism' does not feature or is ever even mentioned in any of the field's widely read texts, like Debraj Ray's '*Development Economics*', Banerjee and Duflo's '*Poor Economics*' or Barr's '*Economics of the Welfare State*'. Across the spectrum of academic critique, even the most unorthodox and critical economists, like Paul Krugman and Joseph Stiglitz, do not utilize the concept at all. In Krugman's book '*End this Depression Now*', neoliberalism is only mentioned once in the preface as a passive footnote, and in Stiglitz's '*The Price of Inequality: The Avoidable Causes and the Invisible Costs of Inequality*', the term is totally absent. Moreover, since 1966, neoliberalism

[83] Ibid, pg 13.
[84] Ibid. Also see: Laruffa, F. *Making Sense of (Post) Neoliberalism*, pgs 586–629. https://journals.sagepub.com/doi/pdf/10.1177/00323292231193805; Magness, P. *The Pejorative Origins of the Term 'Neoliberalism'*. https://thedailyeconomy.org/article/the-pejorative-origins-of-the-term-neoliberalism/
[85] VENUGOPAL, R. *Neoliberalism as Concept*, pgs 13–14.

has only ever appeared fleetingly twice in the '*American Economic Review*'; since 1960, not appeared at all in the '*Quarterly Journal of Economics*'; and since 1956, not appeared either in the '*Journal of Political Economy*'. Furthermore, it has never been mentioned at all in the '*Journal of Development Economics*', and by comparison, it was only from 2012 onwards that the term ever appeared and only in ten articles in the '*Journal of Development Studies*'; in eight articles in '*World Development*'; in seventeen articles in '*Development and Change*' and in ten articles in the '*Journal of International Development*'.[86]

In order to try and comprehend neoliberalism better, as well as challenge it in different ways, the main nucleus of academic critique revolving around the concept of neoliberalism has developed a series of different approaches. On one hand, neoliberalism has been categorized as a given doctrine both by its key thinkers and as articulated in many '*canonical urtexts*'. On the other hand, neoliberalism can likewise be identified by the way in which the different types of neoliberalism that are active throughout the world describe the phenomenon from their own personal perspectives, by tracing its spheres of operation and explaining its dynamics. Another very effective approach views neoliberalism as a '*signifier*'. Such an approach explores its conceptual landscape by examining what the word or term has come to signify during different historical periods, the way in which it has and still is utilized, as well as the consequences it has had. In accordance with that approach, neoliberalism is broken down by the typology of the differing historical conceptual variants, which have contributed to its evolution. Most notably, and all chiefly associated with the Chicago School, neoliberalism can, at the same time, be regarded as part of an '*economic policy agenda*' as a project of '*authoritarian capital*' across the international landscape, as well as a '*global neo-colonialist project*' in developing regions.[87]

Beginning with the first 1930s and 1940s original conception of neoliberalism, and throughout the two different phases of the Mont Pelerin Society, both the utilization of the term neoliberalism, and the encapsulation of the concept have completely differed during three separate periods of time. During those three different time periods, the terminological usage of the term, which was originally conceived during the 1930s and 1940s, had by the 1980s totally changed. During the 1990s, it once again mutated dramatically in shape, form and content. From 1945 until the 1960s, neoliberal thought encapsulated the ideas that the Freiburg School, European neoliberals and the Austrian School pressed forward in the Mont Pelerin Society. However, between the 1960s and the early 1980s, neoliberalism metamorphosed yet again. Since then, it has been used in a very different way, mainly associated with the Chicago School's set of narrowed-down neoliberal prescriptions, based on free-markets, deregulation and widespread privatizations, which have gradually been applied to the first, second

[86] Ibid, pg 14.
[87] Ibid, pgs 1–17.

and third worlds. From the 1980s onwards, the concept hugely expanded to signify both a policy model, as well as a very broad '*political, ideological, cultural and spatial wunderkind*'. From the early 1990s until the present day, neoliberalism has been further elevated to the category of an '*epochal phenomenon*', being very often labelled as a '*prevailing dystopian zeitgeist*'. The original and early neoliberal collective's ideals and objectives were completely different to the current '*neoliberal present*', more defined by a radical and aggressive free-market project, which has come about through a series of haphazard contingent processes. With the transition to our present neoliberal '*new age*', having been described as *a 'revolutionary turning point in the world's social and economic history*', we continue to '*live in the age of neoliberalism*', under the banner of '*capitalism in its millennial manifestation*'.[88]

Although before 1980, neoliberalism was used very rarely, and '*only by economists*' as an esoteric term, it has since then become a widely used term across a broad range of disciplines of the social sciences – '*except in economics where it has disappeared*'. Whereas at present neoliberalism is considered to have climbed out of its '*conceptual crib*' in the realms of economic policy, political economy and the debate of state versus markets, it has, nevertheless, managed to crawl towards other domains, such as those of ideology and power. Neoliberalism has become a key feature in so many theoretical cadres and contexts that within the social sciences it has become a somewhat thwarted, descriptive and analytical burden. Coexisting ambiguous designations range from neoliberalism being in essence a macroeconomic doctrine to neoliberalism being about large corporations and corporatism, and even stretch out to neoliberalism being an unresolved and unengaged contradiction.[89] There are so many differing contexts where the term 'neoliberal' is deployed as an adjective that it includes at the same time:

> *states, spaces, logics, techniques, technologies, discourses, discursive framework, ideologies, ways of thinking, projects, agendas, programs, governmentality, measures, regimes, development, ethno-development, development imaginaries, global forms of control, social policies, multiculturalism, audit cultures, managerialism, restructuring, reform, privatization, regulatory frameworks, governance, good governance, NGOs, third sector, subjects, subjectivities, individualization, professionalization, normalization, market logics, market forms of calculation, the destatalization of government and the degovernmentalization of the state.*[90]

Today, neoliberalism finds itself surrounded by so much academic critique that the already heavily burdened signifier has been tagged with even more multiple, deeply nuanced, analytically dense identities. '*Neoliberalism is now an over-loaded and unwieldy*

[88] Ibid, pgs 3–4. Also see: Laruffa, F. *Making Sense of (Post) Neoliberalism*, pgs 586–629. https://journals.sagepub.com/doi/pdf/10.1177/00323292231193805; Magness, P. *The Pejorative Origins of the Term 'Neoliberalism'*. https://thedailyeconomy.org/article/the-pejorative-origins-of-the-term-neoliberalism/

[89] VENUGOPAL, R. *Neoliberalism as Concept*, pgs 13–14, pg 4.

[90] Ibid.

term that occupies a fluid and growing terrain that expands and contracts arbitrarily across several dimensions, but which increasingly lacks firm foundations in real world referents. The potential range of meanings has grown across numerous disciplines and theoretical enclaves, often in entirely unconnected settings and with different meanings. Nevertheless, the shared name continues to convey a misleading impression that they are all comparable and mutually compatible, anchored in some core, shared ontology, referring to the same sorts of phenomena, and connected together by some universalising impulse.'[91]

The concept of neoliberalism finds itself swamped by a dense, ambiguous abstraction. While neoliberalism is widely acknowledged in academic literature by its influential deployers as a puzzling and riddling term, at the same time, it finds itself profoundly enmeshed in much crisis-ridden controversy and incoherence. Although neoliberalism serves as a key dependent or independent variable in much empirical research, the term itself is left continuously undefined. Neoliberalism is very often regarded as '*an oft-invoked but ill-defined concept*', which is simultaneously '*omnipresent and promiscuous*', and whose meaning and definition '*seems to alter its shape from paper to paper*' in such a way that '*what it stands for and what it explains is both confused and confusing*'.[92] Whereas neoliberalism has '*a perplexing mix of overreach and underspecification*', it is frequently utilized as a '*constant master category that can be used both to understand and to explain all manner of political programs across a wide variety of settings*'.[93]

Although since the 1980s, neoliberalism has widely expanded into diverse theoretical and disciplinary contexts, being both adopted and adapted, there is a growing tide of academic critique, which probes deeply into the concept, questioning its usage and real significance. Neoliberalism, defined as a broad and catch-all term, simultaneously serves many different theoretical conceptualizations and phenomena, although it is also questioned whether it is an absolute state or being, or a relative category describing an exact means with a precise end. Neoliberalism implies synchronously a contraction of the state in relation to the market, a different sort of state that promotes and works at the behest of markets, a depoliticized and '*technocratic fetishization*' of the market, as well as a deep political agenda of class rule and neo-colonial domination. Does neoliberalism '*represent a radical, "paradigmatic" departure, or is it a far more modest recalibration of state-market relations with more continuities than discontinuities? Has the rise of "third-way" politics in the developed world and the rise of the poverty agenda in developing countries served to dethrone and moderate neoliberalism, or to extend and expand it more insidiously?*'.[94]

Owing to the dense conceptual abstraction surrounding neoliberalism, academics have developed several approaches in order to comprehend in a better way what has been termed '*deep*' neoliberalism. 'Deep' neoliberalism is considered to operate

[91] Ibid, pg 6.
[92] Ibid, pg 1.
[93] Ibid.
[94] Ibid.

'through a multiplicity of governing networks, nodes, and modes, that allow for far greater levels of contingency and context-specific variation'.[95] On one hand, one of the most influential versions of 'deep' neoliberalism is the *'governmentality approach'*, which places the main neoliberal emphasis on technologies of optimization and the *'formation of market-responsive subjectivities'*. On the other hand, one of the deepest approaches for comprehending neoliberalism stresses that it must be viewed as a *'radically decentred amorphous phenomenon'*, which involves at the same time *'a migratory set of practices ... (that) articulate diverse situations and participate in mutating configurations of possibility'.*[96] Another conceptualization of 'deep' neoliberalism, defines it as a *'decentralised and deeply contextualised force that produces very heterogenous outcomes and can only exist in messy hybrids'.*[97]

Throughout the conceptual evolution of neoliberalism, the term has come to portray a widespread assortment of real-life phenomena, which range from market deregulation policies to political agendas of class rule, as well as to *'technologies of the self'*. One part of the academic critique surrounding the conceptual multipolarity of neoliberalism considers that the developed theoretical frameworks have helped highlight many of the differing elements of what has turned out to be *'an extraordinarily vast, complex, nuanced, networked, and contradictory creature'.*[98] Another part of the critique chides neoliberalism's conceptual proliferation as it has only instigated the *'over-identification of different sets of otherwise unconnected phenomena under a single, and thus increasingly unstable and ambiguous label'.*[99]

Although such conceptual standpoints and approaches contain some sort of descriptive and explanatory lustre, they, however, do not suffice to acquire proper theoretical status. Moreover, the vast amount of neoliberal conceptual depictions has turned the ideology into an even more abstract and distorted being, which is impossible to properly define or let alone edge out. While on one hand, the academic sector deems neoliberalism as *'impossible to define theoretically'*, on the other hand, the ideology is widely held to be *'so contradictory, contingent and contextual, that it defies definition, and that to define it would inherently be to diminish this complexity'.*[100]

Despite the amount of neoliberal conceptual inconsistency and malfunctioning, within the comparative political economy of development literature, there are three main neoliberal conceptual variants that derive from the Chicago School, which serve

[95] Ibid, pg 5. Also see: Laruffa, F. *Making Sense of (Post) Neoliberalism*, pgs 586–629. https://journals.sagepub.com/doi/pdf/10.1177/00323292231193805; Magness, P. *The Pejorative Origins of the Term 'Neoliberalism'*. https://thedailyeconomy.org/article/the-pejorative-origins-of-the-term-neoliberalism/

[96] VENUGOPAL, R. *Neoliberalism as Concept*, pg 5.

[97] Ibid.

[98] Ibid.

[99] Ibid.

[100] Ibid, pgs 5–6.

as prime historical examples of its conceptual evolution. Whereas the first conceptual variant views neoliberalism as an '*economic policy agenda*', the second variant, identifies neoliberalism as a '*capitalist rule agenda*', and the third variant considers it to be a '*global neo-colonial project*'.

The first most established conceptual variant of neoliberalism included in development literature classifies it as an '*economic policy agenda*'. Such variant perceives '*the dominant economic doctrine of the last quarter of a century*' as a historical articulation in order to dismantle the Keynesian consensus and embedded liberalism, in favour of the goals of macro-economic policy (mainly full employment) and the diminishing of the welfare state. The variant considers neoliberalism to be a Chicago School-based radical laissez-faire economic policy experiment, drawn from the conclusions of orthodox neoclassical economics and the rational choice-based theories of human behaviour. It supports both a very tight delimited role for the state in regulating economic activity, as well as the establishment of market-friendly mechanisms and incentives, in order to organize wide ranging economic, social and economic activities. Its organizational logic rests almost entirely on the market, where economic rationality and individual incentives prevail.[101]

One of the best examples of the 'economic policy agenda' was provided by the Chicago School when it applied its neoliberal technocratic prescriptions in Chile. Chile served the Chicago School as the perfect '*neoliberal laboratory*', which put to test its textbook policies, that were later applied to most of LA, other developing regions and the globalized free-market economy. The case of Chile is widely regarded as a technocratic experiment carried out by the Chicago School, which, through the 'Chicago Boys', unfurled textbook models into real-world policies, insulated from political constrictions.[102] '*The new neoliberal economic team presented the technocratisation of decision-making as a guarantee that the government would pursue a rational economic model. From that moment on, government decisions were to be inspired by "technical and scientific" principles and not by political and ideological postulates as in the past.*'[103]

The 'economic policy agenda' variant also has a development premise, which is mainly associated with LA. Such variant denotes both a radical rupture between theory and practice, as well as a change of policy regime from state-led to market-based economies. Although between the 1950s and 1970s, mainstream development policy was aimed at accelerated state-led structural economic transformation of poor agricultural economies into wealthy industrialized ones, the neoliberal counter-revolution dismantled the project through the limitation of the state's economic regulation and the

[101] Ibid, pg 7.

[102] Ibid. Also see: Laruffa, F. *Making Sense of (Post) Neoliberalism,* pgs 586–629. https://journals.sagepub.com/doi/pdf/10.1177/00323292231193805; Magness, P. *The Pejorative Origins of the Term 'Neoliberalism'.* https://thedailyeconomy.org/article/the-pejorative-origins-of-the-term-neoliberalism/

[103] VENUGOPAL, R. *Neoliberalism as Concept*, pg 7.

liberalization of foreign trade, together with the abandonment of import substitution industrialization, as well as the imposition of tighter fiscal discipline.[104]

The neoliberal 'economic policy agenda' or 'depoliticized technocratic policy agenda' is surrounded by a double-edged critique, which rejects it on both technical grounds as well as for being too technocratic. The first rejection on technical grounds, blames both economic growth and development nurtured by structural transformations and industrialization for their *'failure in understanding economic structures within developing countries, in focusing on too narrow a set of objectives, and on too limited a set of instruments ... markets by themselves do not produce efficient outcomes when information is imperfect and markets are incomplete'*.[105] In contrast, the second technocratic critique finds neoliberal policies *'excessively technical, economistic, "cookie-cutter," context-blind, and politically naïve'*,[106] as the focus of economic growth is placed mostly on the '*means*' of development (economic growth), rather than on the '*ends*' of development like *'poverty alleviation, health, education, or other measures such as democracy, human rights, and gender equality'*.[107] Such market reforms have had extremely negative socioeconomic consequences and continue being extremely criticized.[108]

A second variant of neoliberalism is perceived by the development literature as a *'capitalist rule agenda'*. Such an archetype of neoliberal authoritarian capital provides an augmented and expanded version of the ideology, but one which is based much more on political power, involving at the same time, power, social actors and material interests. It provides an amplification of the neoliberal concept by incorporating and fusing together social actors, policies and material interests. While the concept still considers economic policy as important, it is, however, interlocked within a socio-political configuration, wherein market reforms are not an endgame in themselves, but a means to an end. Such concept defines neoliberalism as a very deep political phenomenon, within which the endgame is not just about the implementation of certain economic policies, but more about the achievement of the *'material interests of politically powerful economic elites'*. In scientific literature, the conceptual expansion of neoliberalism from economic policy to political power is termed as '*capital resurgent*' and denotes the *'reassertion of capitalist class power that seeks to dis-engineer the post-war compromises of tripartite corporatism and expanded social welfare'*.[109]

[104] Ibid, pgs 7–8.
[105] Ibid, pg 8.
[106] Ibid.
[107] Ibid.
[108] Ibid, pgs 8–9.
[109] Ibid, pg 9.

> *The extension of a political logic grafted over an economic policy-agenda has drawn neoliberalism smoothly into existing frameworks that explicitly reach across the political economic spheres such as regulation theory, within which it has been situated as a post-Fordist regime of accumulation.*[110]

However, in many cases when neoliberalism is drawn deeper into ideology, culture and power, such elements tend to be usually over-articulated at the expense of other under-articulated economic foundations. The ensuing problem that arises is the creation of a huge *'imbalance between an over-theorised ideo-political superstructure perched on an under-theorised economic base'*,[111] hinged to *'an absent interlocking rationale that connects them together into a congruent whole to demonstrate the desired direction of causality'*.[112]

The 'capitalist rule agenda' is based on the chief assumption that *'capitalists favour markets and markets benefit capitalists'*. Some critics argue against neoliberalism, since *'in its various guises, has always been about the capture and reuse of the state in the interests of shaping a pro-corporate, free-trading "market order"'*.[113] However, other critics recognize that *'the political and economic parts of the model connect successfully to produce the desired direction of causality only where market liberalization can be shown to favour identifiable politically powerful economic elites at the expense of non-elites; and conversely, where such economic elites actively identify and opt for market liberalization policies over a viable counter-factual'*.[114]

A third and last neoliberal conceptual premise established in development literature elevates neoliberalism to an international level as a *'global neo-colonial project'* in developing regions like LA. Bearing in mind that market reforms in LA came about at a time of economic crisis, the 'global neo-colonial project' framework is closely associated with the external imposition of neoliberal policies by powerful global actors, in order to reintegrate the region within a subservient dependency position into the global market economy.[115]

Within the 'global neo-colonial project' framework and across its hypothetical landscape, northern wealthy countries are perceived to coerce market reforms upon the southern poor countries, with their only true objectives being the realization of their own self-serving economic, political and military programs. A good example of

[110] Ibid.
[111] Ibid.
[112] Ibid.
[113] Ibid.
[114] Ibid, pgs 9–10. Also see: Laruffa, F. *Making Sense of (Post) Neoliberalism*, pgs 586–629. https://journals.sagepub.com/doi/pdf/10.1177/00323292231193805; Magness, P. *The Pejorative Origins of the Term 'Neoliberalism'*. https://thedailyeconomy.org/article/the-pejorative-origins-of-the-term-neoliberalism/
[115] VENUGOPAL, R. *Neoliberalism as Concept*, pg 10.

such a framework being applied was provided by the establishment of the Washington Consensus throughout LA, together with the actions of the WB, the IMF and the US Treasury, conveying the idea of a neo-colonial agenda being imposed onto an unwilling and vulnerable third world.[116]

The 'global neo-colonial project' framework is very similar to dependency theory and its associated logic of unequal power relations, blocked development and adverse incorporation into the global economy. Within such framework, the unequal coercive relationship between rich and poor countries is reflected by the nature and dynamics of structural adjustment and conditionality-based development aid, which also *'requires poor countries to implement self-destructive economic policies, including open-door trade and investment regimes that result in de-industrialisation and vulnerability to speculative financial flows'*.[117] Likewise, the approach also *'pushes developing countries backwards in development to a colonial-era structure of primary commodity exports, locking them into a vulnerable and dependent position of enduring weakness'*.[118]

The global neocolonial analytical framework perceives rich industrialized countries as imposing liberal economic policy regimes and neoliberal policies onto poor rural countries, ranging *'from trade liberalisation and carbon emissions restrictions to "good governance" and democratisation'*. The sole objective behind the mask of technocratic policy advice is the assurance of their own vested interests and venality, as well as their wider agenda of preserving their northern position of power and influence over the south.[119]

Ironically, as far and as much as neoliberal theory is totally non-existent, the concept of neoliberalism is defected and clearly malfunctions, and by doing so, it does so in a very peculiar way. The concept merely *'serves as a rhetorical device through which those outside mainstream economics grasp, label and attach moral sensibility to a range of contemporary economic, social, political, spatial, and cultural phenomena'*.[120] It works much *'more as a socially constructed term of struggle that frames criticism and resistance than as a rigorously defined concept that can guide research in anthropology and other social sciences'*.[121]

Although neoliberalism has managed to climb out of its *'political economy conceptual crib'*, many critical concerns still lurk around its present-day relevance, viability and practicality. Regardless of the many attempts that have been made in order to distil or purify neoliberalism by either inter-linking it to its original ideological essence or by

116 Ibid.
117 Ibid.
118 Ibid.
119 Ibid.
120 Ibid, pg 16.
121 Ibid, pg 17.

reconceptualizing it as a complex ontological species, the concept's incoherence has gone far beyond its ambiguous abstraction, coming to be utilized in very opposing and contradicting ways. The conflation of significantly differing phenomena under the same common term has created many analytical blind spots, which in turn and at the same time, have caused much terminological dysfunction.[122]

At present, although the neoliberal concept continues to pivot around much ambiguous and abstract dysfunctionality, it nonetheless lives on. However, it only does so, mostly *'as a problematic rhetorical device that bundles together a proliferation of eclectic and contradictory concepts; a tableau of critical explorations of the material world by non-economists, clustered together by a shared signifier that thematically links them to a broader set of morally devolved referents about markets, economics, subjectivities, state authority, globalization or neo-colonialism'*.[123]

[122] Ibid.

[123] Ibid. Also see: Laruffa, F. *Making Sense of (Post) Neoliberalism,* pgs 586–629. https://journals.sagepub.com/doi/pdf/10.1177/00323292231193805; Magness, P. *The Pejorative Origins of the Term 'Neoliberalism'.* https://thedailyeconomy.org/article/the-pejorative-origins-of-the-term-neoliberalism/

5

The Process of the Construction of Neoliberal Thought

Although the academic revolution and its search for an in-between classical liberalism and laissez-faire spawned two very conceptually divergent 'new liberal' currents – 'ordoliberalism' and 'neoliberalism' – the two offshoots, however, shared a very intricate relationship throughout the liberal revisionist crusade that swept through Europe. In fact, the synergy created between both currents contributed immensely to the whole 'new liberal' movement by providing the framework within which the process of construction of neoliberal thought was developed.

While the Colloque Walter Lippmann gave official birth to neoliberalism, the Mont Pelerin Society both mobilized the neoliberal movement and sparked off the process of construction of neoliberal thought. Notwithstanding, one of the most crucial aspects to bear in mind regarding the process of construction of neoliberal thought is that it was extremely complex, being continuously puzzled and riddled with huge swings and swerves from its original trajectory, as well as by many other further ensuing changes and transformations.

The common determination beseeching the modification of classical liberalism and laissez-faire, bore witness to how the Colloque Walter Lippmann and the Mont Pelerin Society gave way to the formation of a massive ecumenical undertaking, through the mixing and blending of a huge array of *'groups and clans'* of diverging intellectual orientations and ideological inclinations, in order to revitalize classical liberalism and laissez-faire, as well as to expose the damages of interventionism and socialism. Nonetheless, although the potpourri of ordoliberals, neoliberals, purebred liberals of the classical tradition, libertarians, methodological individualists, neo-classical marginalists and anarchists, infused in one way or another, their valuable contributions and inputs into the overall process of construction of neoliberal thought, eventually and throughout the same process, the emergence of ideological rifts and fissures over key issues between the intellectual formations, changed the direction of the neoliberal movement forever. Such a change of direction gradually both narrowed down the horizons of the neoliberal collective, as well as ultimately and in turn produced a fractured neoliberal thought.

From the beginning of the process of construction of neoliberal thought, the contributory synergy created between ordoliberalism and neoliberalism towards the whole process is undeniable. However, over the decades that the process lasted, it ended up overshadowing, disregarding and even eliminating along the way many of the early joint project's schools of thought, intellectual actors, ideologies, concepts and notions. With ordoliberalism being eventually completely eclipsed by neoliberalism, neoliberal thought was likewise forever narrowed down to its more basic and aggressive US monetarist mind frame, which in turn finally produced a fractured neoliberal thought, practically bereft of its much more positive and balanced, original components and elements. Throughout the whole process and within the collective of the Mont Pelerin Society, the evolution of neoliberalism never really projected a homogeneous set of ideas, embodying a minimal state or an anarcho-capitalist caricature, being replete with riddling mutations.

The process of construction of neoliberal thought was characterized by two very different phases of intellectual and ideological influence, which ran in very close parallel to the two phases that typified the Mont Pelerin Society. The *'first phase'* of the process of construction of neoliberal thought can be considered to have begun during the 1930s and lasted until 1960, more or less. Throughout that period, both the overall direction of the collective's common project, together with the intellectual and ideological issues considered and discussed, were mainly influenced by the European contingent's Austrian School, the Freiburg School and other European neoliberals. The *'second phase'* of the process of construction of neoliberal thought took place from the 1960s onwards, with both the general direction of the collective and the intellectual and ideological issues deliberated being much more heavily influenced by the American contingent, mainly represented by the Chicago School and other American neoliberals.

During the 'first phase' of the process of construction of neoliberal thought, many clashes prevailed between staunch neoliberal interventionists, such as Hunold, and classical liberal anti-interventionists, like Mises. There were likewise numerous other clashes between ordoliberals and neoliberals. Throughout that same period, European academics, such as Hayek, Mises, Polanyi, Robbins, Röpke, Aron, Baudin and Rüstow, exerted most of the influence within the neoliberal movement. During the 'second phase' of the process of construction of neoliberal thought, some issues of extreme dispute, such as the Hunold Affair, over editorial issues and other concerns, made the US influence begin to bear more influence over the neoliberal movement. From then onwards, the Chicago School's neoliberal prescriptions, strongly stimulated by the rising influence of Milton Friedman, James Buchanan and George Stigler (who eventually became presidents of the Mont Pelerin Society), sadly began both narrowing down the horizons of the neoliberal collective and producing a fractured neoliberal thought. Other quarrels over financial issues, which prevailed throughout the whole process, likewise instigated the final transatlantic split within the neoliberal movement. For example, whereas during the 'first phase' of the process of construction of neoliberal thought, the Volker Foundation, which funded the Europeans, biased their role and topics of discussion, during the 'second phase' of the process, the United States was able to mobilize many more funds and thus influence much more the intellectual and ideological direction of the neoliberal movement.[1]

Originally and during their early years of coexistence, ordoliberalism and neoliberalism were very closely intertwined by one same common interventionist joint venture. Paradoxically, however, their dual progression along the same parallel ideals of an economy with a strong role for the state soon diverged. While right from the start the same issue of a 'major role for the state' provoked serious rifts and fissures amongst the *'old-school liberals'*, ordoliberals and *'true Third-Way neoliberals'*. Ordoliberalism soon ended up likewise overshadowed by neoliberalism. In a similar way and throughout the years that followed, neoliberalism morphed once again, being split into two different variants. Those last two variants ultimately embodied mainstream neoliberal thought in its two main neoliberal schools: the European (Austrian School), represented mainly by Friedrich Hayek and Ludwig von Mises, and the Anglo-American (Chicago School), with Milton Friedman as one of its most outstanding contributors. Since then, both schools have remained divided, amongst other issues, over questions to do with their comprehension and analysis of economics and economic phenomena, the role of the state, regulation, as well as monetarist matters.

'First Phase' of the Process of Construction of Neoliberal Thought – 1930s–60s

Throughout the 'first phase' of the process of construction of neoliberal thought, most especially during the 1930s and 1940s, the Freiburg School's ordoliberal academics were the most influential in the overall direction of the process. At the 1938 Colloque Walter Lippmann, the Freiburg circle held the strongest views on interventionist actions in economic matters and later also had a huge success in generating the West German social market economy and producing the German economic miracle. One of the Freiburg School academics, Wilhelm Röpke, officially sparked the neoliberal counter-revolution against Keynesianism with the launching of an attack on Keynesianism and collectivism through the unsuccessful publication of an international journal, '*Occident*'. Ironically, however, the same colloquium soon also witnessed the apparition of rifts over the exact same interventionist question, between '*old-school liberals*', such as Ludwig von Mises and Friedrich Hayek, and '*true Third Way neoliberals*', like Alexander Rustow and Walter Lippman.[2]

In much the same way, during the 1930s and 1940s, neoliberalism was much broader and more moderate, as well as a lot more tolerant of interventionism than its latter

1 Ludwig von Mises Institute. HÜLSMANN, J.G. *Against the Neoliberals*, pgs 1–2. https://mises.org/library/against-neoliberals

2 Ibid, pgs 1–2.

version. Although both the Freiburg School and ordoliberalism were very influential in the early construct of neoliberal thought, by the time of the next new liberal meeting – the founding moment of the main neoliberal institution, the Mont Pelerin Society – they began to gradually lose influence. Eventually, ordoliberalism would end totally overshadowed by neoliberalism. Similarly, during the same neoliberal congregation, the neoliberal collective was split even further due to differences on issues like market behaviourism, price-controlling mechanisms and monetarism. Thus and once again, neoliberalism ended up being divided into two extremely opposing schools of neoliberal thought: the Austrian School and the Chicago School. Between then and the early 1960s, when Röpke and others resigned from the Mont Pelerin Society, the neoliberal collective's balance of power and general ideas began to seriously shift within the society. Since then, both schools have remained divided over those exact same issues. The rise of the Chicago School, together with other collectivist differences, gradually led to the eventual breakdown of the unity of the Mont Pelerin Society and, hence, of the true original neoliberal project.[3]

During the 1930s and 1940s, early neoliberals advocated state regulation for the breaking up of large corporations, although it soon clashed quite markedly with later neoliberal thought, which privileged the sovereignty of the individual over the wider community. Likewise, during the 1950s, the ideas of German ordoliberalism, together with those of its continental counterparts, lost much influence as the Chicago School, spearheaded by Milton Friedman, rose to prominence. What is more, during the late 1950s and early 1960s, the Hunold Affair divided the neoliberal collective further, which determined to a great extent the changing of direction of the process of construction of neoliberal thought. During the Hunold Affair, Friedrich Hayek, the Mont Pelerin Society's pivotal arbiter, aligned himself with the Americans, which led Wilhelm Röpke, one of the key ordoliberals and then president of the Mont Pelerin Society, to leave the society. By siding with the Chicagoans, Hayek thus turned his back on his long-time friend and companion, with whose thinking on the original neoliberal project he had much more in common.[4]

Within the framework of the process of construction of neoliberal thought, the breakdown of the unity of the Mont Pelerin Society was imperative in the subsequent development and evolution of neoliberal thought, as well as in its final version portrayal as a homogenous set of ideas, often as a tool of US-led imperialism, *'market fundamentalism'* or a conspiracy of financial capital. The early, original neoliberal strategy was much wider and deeper. However, the loss of influence within the Mont Pelerin Society of a set of uniform ordoliberal ideas, together with the rise of the Chicago School and Milton Friedman's opposition to collectivism, plus the role Hayek played during the Hunold Affair, all made the neoliberal pendulum begin to tilt heavily from Europe to the United States.

[3] Ibid.
[4] Ibid.

Ironically, the Chicago School equally subjected neoliberalism to even further conversions. While at first the Chicago School's neoliberalism combined more ordoliberal '*social*' characteristics, from 1946 onwards, it began adopting many more of its increasingly radical, economics driven, Friedmanite monetarist features. Since neoliberalism's inception, and most especially its '*transatlantic conversion*', neoliberalism has adapted, settled and tried to fix markets, but has likewise required continuous reconstruction. At first, the Mont Pelerin Society's neoliberal collective represented a *'free company of people who think together'*.[5] However, eventually, it regretably turned and changed into a '*team of fighters*', which raped and narrowed the neoliberal horizons from their original confines, sadly paving the way for its much-maligned, Anglo-American version.[6]

During the 'first phase' of the process of construction of neoliberal thought, the original '*early*' ordoliberal and neoliberal agendas were very closely interrelated by their mutual quest for an in-between classical liberalism and laissez-faire, involving a 'strong role for the state' in the economy. The early neoliberal agenda, in fact, supported state interventionism in the economy much more than its radical Anglo-American version. Throughout the revisionist crusade, economic liberals swam against the popular tide of the 1930s totalitarian regimes, populist politics, economic planning and protectionism, trying to attenuate the excesses of laissez-faire. Although academics and intellectuals in Europe and the United States retained their faith in free markets, they all, nevertheless, acknowledged that something beyond 'laissez-faire' had to be done. During the 1930s and 1940s, neoliberal thought enjoyed a lot more similarities, which are not usually included in the recent projections of the movement as being closer to a renewal of laissez-faire or market fundamentalism. During the early years of the process of thought construction, European and American neoliberalism converged in many areas, such as competition and monopoly, with similar ideas also being put forward in relation to stable monetary conditions. For instance, the viewpoints of the Chicago School's Henry Simons (Friedman's mentor) and the Freiburg School's Walter Eucken, Franz Böhm, Alexander Rustow, Alfred Muller-Armack and Wilhelm Röpke clearly identified and recognized the concentration of power, in the form of monopolies and cartels, as the biggest threat to economic and political liberty. For those neoliberals, regulation was both crucialand a key objective in order to prevent such concentrations of power. During those same years, the Austrian School's Friedrich Hayek, who spent most of the 1930s at the London School of Economics, also showed some sympathy towards such postures. Another crucial area, wherein their ideas and interests also converged, was related to stable monetary conditions, proffering from fiat money manipulation, to the gold standard and even to Hayek's later proposal of *'choice of currency'*.[7]

5 Ibid.
6 Ibid.
7 Ibid, pg 3.

A couple of very interesting facts about the 'first phase' of the process of construction of neoliberal thought are linked to the official definitions and terms that the two new liberal currents were given. During the 'first phase' of the process and the 'early' interventionist period, both ordoliberalism and neoliberalism were provided with their currently established and known definitions, names and terms. On one hand, during Weimar Germany's economic threshold, Walter Eucken and Franz Böhm elaborated their agenda of employing the law to enforce economic competition and preserve freedom, which they both perceived as undermined at the time by political decisions '*in hoc*' to vested interests.[8] Due to the German contingent's and Ludwig Erhard's persistence on '*order*', in '*ordering*' and on '*order in every single individual sphere of action*', they therefore ended up being nicknamed '*Ordo-liberals*'. Both the definition and term have since prevailed. On the other hand, during the 1938 Colloque Walter Lippmann, amidst the brainstorming of terms and definitions, which took place in order to find an appropriate term for the second new liberal current, Alexander Rustow was the intellectual who first coined the term '*Neoliberalism*', as well as the one who came up with the principle of '*free economy-free state*'. Moreover, one of those first-batch, most extreme ordoliberal interventionists, Wilhelm Röpke, is widely considered as one of the most eloquent '*founding fathers*' of the neoliberal collective.[9] Röpke and Hayek were very close friends and both had central roles in the early direction of the Mont Pelerin Society. Together, they formed the strongest neoliberal synergy, which unleashed its new liberal ideas in a non-stop counter-fight against the strong tide of Keynesianism and collectivism.[10]

Wilhelm Röpke was born in 1899 and, like most of his fellow ordoliberals, was a veteran of the Great War. After the war, Röpke studied cartels of the potash mining industry and consequently took a professorship at the University of Marburg. Due to his educational background and being a staunch liberal, Röpke was very '*weary of coercion*' by those in power. Throughout his life, Röpke wrote numerous books, with his main intellectual area of focus becoming '*preventing the formation of vested interests and monopolies*'.[11] Röpke, just like his fellow contemporaries at the University of Freiburg, Eucken and Böhm, had very similar ideas of a '*Third Way*', or '*of the prevention of what he dubbed "proletarianisation" and the curbing of laissez-faire's excesses – while retaining economic freedom*'.[12] Unlike most other schools of neoliberalism, German ordoliberals

[8] BIEBRICHER, T. and VOGELMANN, F. (Eds). *The Birth of Austerity: German Ordoliberalism and Contemporary Neoliberalism*, pgs 4–5.

[9] Ordoliberalism and the Austrian School. KEMENY, P.J. *The Decline of Ordoliberal Influence in the Mont Pelerin Collective. Röpke's Occident, the 'Hunold Affair' and the Rise of the Chicago School*, pg 3. https://ordoliberalism.wordpress.com/ Also see: MIROWSKI, P. and PLEHWE, D. (Eds). *The Road from Mont Pelerin: The Making of the Neoliberal Thought Collective* and BIEBRICHER, T. and VOGELMANN, F. (Eds). *The Birth of Austerity: German Ordoliberalism and Contemporary Neoliberalism.*

[10] Ordoliberalism and the Austrian School. KEMENY, P.J. *The Decline of Ordoliberal Influence in the Mont Pelerin Collective. Röpke's Occident, the 'Hunold Affair' and the Rise of the Chicago School*, pg 3.

[11] Ibid.

[12] Ibid.

viewed and regarded markets as a means or as a '*social instrument*' – not as an end. Due to Röpke's strong religious convictions, which greatly influenced his later work, he is very often also strongly associated with the fusion between 'economic liberalism' and 'social conservatism'. In fact, his profound and insightful work on 'interventionism' established an official scale for classifying different types of interventionism, or what he referred to as '*market compatible*' and market '*incompatible*' interventions.[13]

Röpke, unlike most German ordoliberals, was extremely anti-Nazi and when the Nazis rose to power, he went into exile to, amongst other places, Switzerland, Geneva. During his time in exile, Röpke remained in close contact with Hayek, and in 1938, they both attended the Colloque Walter Lippmann in Paris. Although Röpke and other German ordoliberals, together with Hayek, had much influence in the direction of the neoliberal collective, the Colloque Walter Lippmann, however, soon revealed many splits within the hard-core neoliberal nucleus, concerning the actual levels of interventionism an economy should be subjected to.[14]

Following the Colloque Walter Lippmann, Röpke and Hayek played a key role in prompting the next 1947 neoliberal foundational gathering at the Mont Pelerin Society. However, the two of them had very divergent personal interests and objectives. For example, during the 1940s, while Röpke wanted to organize a liberal international journal named '*Occident*', Hayek pursued instead a similar format to the Paris-held colloquium, which he believed represented better an '*academy of intellectual discussion*'. Nevertheless, it was Röpke's objectives for '*Occident*' – '*that it must appeal to the upper intellectual class*'[15] and '*thus obviate vulgarisation and all concessions to the tastes of the multitude*',[16] which ended up attracting the interests of several Swiss financiers, such as most particularly, businessman Albert Hunold. During the summer of 1946, after several heated disputes over issues related to editorial control and rights of ownership, Hunold gave up the idea of funding the journal. Nonetheless, Hayek took up the neoliberal flame and carried on pressing forward Röpke's plan for '*Occident*', but instead, based much more on a conference format. Notwithstanding the change of formats, both Röpke's and Hayek's principles converged, and together they established the basis for the neoliberal counter-revolution against Keynesianism and central planning. They were convinced that '*liberalism needed a truly radical revision, that a collective should be a grand coalition of individuals that shared broad principles, and a faith in the potential for abstract intellectual discourse to inspire political change*'.[17]

[13] Ibid.
[14] Ibid, pgs 3–4.
[15] Ibid, pg 4.
[16] Ibid.
[17] Ibid. Also see: MIROWSKI, P. and PLEHWE, D. (Eds). *The Road from Mont Pelerin: The Making of the Neoliberal Thought Collective* and BIEBRICHER, T. and VOGELMANN, F. (Eds). *The Birth of Austerity: German Ordoliberalism and Contemporary Neoliberalism.*

Hunold and Hayek were also acquainted, as in late 1945 Hunold had invited Hayek to speak to a group of businessmen in Zurich about his proposed conference. Thus, after Hayek managed to persuade Hunold to redirect his funding from the *'Occident'* journal format to the Mont Pelerin Society conference format, the Mont Pelerin Society met in Switzerland for the first time in 1947. Henceforth, after Hayek assumed leadership of the neoliberal movement,[18] bearing in mind how much he battled restlessly for the unity of both the Mont Pelerin Society and the neoliberal movement as a whole, he can be regarded as the '*Grandfather*' of neoliberalism. However, from the beginning of the neoliberal mobilization at the Mont Pelerin Society, it became evident that *'there was no collective view and ... no one voice represented it'*.[19] James Buchanan, one of the Mont Pelerin Society's members and Public Choice theorists, pointed out that '*Hayek dominated the group, was treated with respect that approached awe and was accorded too much deference*'.[20]

Although Röpke had much more of an ordoliberal interventionist-consistent mind frame than Hayek and his associated contingency of the Austrian School, Hayek's sympathies and positions vis-à-vis the early direction taken by the process of construction of neoliberal thought, as well as by the collective of the Mont Pelerin Society, were very transcendental. Despite Röpke and Hayek having many ideological differences between them, they were nonetheless very close. As much as *'Hayek was always more moderate than the subsequent cliché of a "market fundamentalist"'*,[21] the ordoliberals were also very prominent in the early years of the Mont Pelerin Society. Spearheaded by the Freiburg School and especially Röpke, the ordoliberals never ceased to press forward *'many familiar neoliberal models of monetary control by an independent central bank, as well as a number of state functions such as anti-trust and competition enforcement embedded in law. In addition to his ordoliberal focus on the curtailment of concentration of power, Röpke identified the need to prevent "proletarianization", and therefore the class resentment that had led to social upheaval and revolution earlier in the century'*.[22] While the latter theme rang many familiar bells with conservative ideas, such as '*property-owning democracy*', the book written by Röpke in 1946, '*The German Question*', had the same impact, albeit almost exclusively in the German-speaking world. Röpke always strongly believed that his economic thought truly represented a *'"Third Way" between laissez-faire and planning'*.[23]

The two main opposing wings of the originally projected neoliberal flight – ordoliberalism and neoliberalism – were at first very closely interlaced. For example, during the first 1947 Mont Pelerin Society meeting, in the middle of a discussion

[18] Ordoliberalism and the Austrian School. KEMENY, P.J. *The Decline of Ordoliberal Influence in the Mont Pelerin Collective. Röpke's Occident, the 'Hunold Affair' and the Rise of the Chicago School*, pg 4.
[19] Ibid.
[20] Ibid.
[21] Ibid, pg 5.
[22] Ibid.
[23] Ibid.

regarding the issue of '*competitive order*', Eucken, one of the ordoliberal progenitors, clashed quite markedly over the intervention issue with the much more classical liberal Mises, although Hayek attempted to bridge the divide by stating that '*that we shall strongly disagree on these topics, the more the better*'.[24] Following another initial steamy session in 1949, Mises notoriously likewise so-called his colleagues '*socialists*' and later on described the '*ordo-interventionists*' as '*not much better than "totalitarian socialists"*'.[25] Although Hayek defined the '*Ordo circle*' more diplomatically as a kind of '*restraining liberalism*', the ordoliberals, however, reacted with reproach by henceforth branding classical liberals, such as Mises, as '*Paleoliberals*'. In an interchange of correspondence between Rüstow and Röpke, the former wrote that Hayek '*and his master Mises deserved to be put in spirits and placed in a museum as one of the last surviving specimens of the extinct species of liberals which caused the current catastrophe*'.[26]

Within the context of the 'first phase' of the process of construction of neoliberal thought, the 1940s and 1950s were the highest peaking point of German ordoliberalism. The influential position held by ordoliberalism was most especially dominant during the first meetings of the Mont Pelerin Society. Likewise, the extreme success in West Germany of the social market economy producing the German Economic Miracle clearly reflected the sophisticated and refined nature of ordoliberalism. While the ordoliberal at heart, Ludwig Erhard, acted as finance minister of the social market economy, he helmed it together with a lot of other ordoliberals, who likewise became ministers and associated economists. Furthermore, during the second Mont Pelerin Society meeting in 1949, Röpke lectured about '*The Proletarianized Society*'; in 1953, Erhard and Muller-Armack gave a joint lecture titled '*The Recovery of Germany*'; and in 1956, at the seventh societal meeting, Böhm and Rüstow equally imparted additional lectures on ordoliberalism. In 1948, Eucken and Böhm also set up a journal titled '*ORDO*', which represented ordoliberal thinkers. While Röpke was a founding member of the advisory board of '*ORDO*', Hayek formed part of it as well. However, and although '*ORDO*' did exert some influence, it never achieved the methodological breadth or cosmopolitan reach that Röpke had envisioned for '*Occident*'.[27]

During the 1950s and 1960s, a succession of events took place, which gave way to the 'second phase' of the process of construction of neoliberal thought. Those events provoked both the beginning of the narrowing down of the original neoliberal collective's width and breadth, as well as the final fracturing of neoliberal thought. Sadly, they condemned neoliberalism to its much vilified and maligned variant. All combined, they changed the direction of the neoliberal movement forever, as well

24 Ibid.

25 Ibid, pgs 5–6.

26 Ibid. Also see: MIROWSKI, P. and PLEHWE, D. (Eds). *The Road from Mont Pelerin: The Making of the Neoliberal Thought Collective* and BIEBRICHER, T. and VOGELMANN, F. (Eds). *The Birth of Austerity: German Ordoliberalism and Contemporary Neoliberalism.*

27 Ordoliberalism and the Austrian School. KEMENY, P.J. *The Decline of Ordoliberal Influence in the Mont Pelerin Collective. Röpke's Occident, the 'Hunold Affair' and the Rise of the Chicago School*, pg 6.

as produced its final, definite and disruptive split into the two European and Anglo-American schools of neoliberal thought. The most significant of those events were: the uprising of the Chicago School's prominence under the leadership of Milton Friedman; the shifting of positions within the Chicagoan circle due to differences on monopoly issues, which ranged from more moderate interventionist ordoliberal approaches to increasingly more radical pro-market ones; and, in the late 1950s and early 1960s, the loss of influence within the Mont Pelerin Society of Europeans, like Röpke. Furthermore, after the American-staged coup – the Hunold Affair – European influence within the neoliberal collective also began to decrease significantly. Another very important factor, which ultimately tilted the pendulum of intellectual and ideological influence within the neoliberal collective forever, was the fact that Hayek joined and sided with the American side during the Hunold Affair, which in turn likewise purged the Mont Pelerin Society from its original Swiss benefactor.[28]

Probably one of the most decisive factors which induced the final neoliberal transatlantic conversion was another last ideological transformation that occurred during those years within the Chicago School's neoliberal core, which ended up producing the deepest splits within neoliberal thought. The subjection of neoliberalism to that last mutation ultimately gave way to and established the present-day fractured neoliberal thought. During the 'early' years of the Chicago School, Henry Simons had always represented its most important figure until he passed away in 1946. Simons, together with other German ordoliberals, like Eucken, Böhm and Röpke, had shared the most equal postures towards issues, such as competition. However, when in 1946 Milton Friedman took over the leadership of the Chicago School, the situation changed radically. The newly nicknamed '*second Chicago School*' included much more aggressive economists, like George Stigler, Aaron Director and Gary Becker. During the 1950s, the 'second Chicago School' put into practice some of its long-running projects, which, in general, completely changed the school's economic mind frame, outlook and approaches. Projects such as the '*Free Market Study Group*' and the '*Anti-Trust Project*' subjected the school's mindset to a profound conversion, particularly transfiguring the school's perception of competition and other monopoly issues. The new, hardcore structure of the 'second Chicago School', led by Stigler, came to believe that although governments sustained monopolies, the exact same sustaining function could also be carried out by large companies. Most especially after 1951, Friedman relaxed his attitude even more towards '*any imposition of competition*', proclaiming that most markets had '*giants and pigmies side by side*' and that there was an inclination to '*overemphasize monopoly*'. Furthermore, the '*social*' proposals put forward by the early neoliberals also began to slowly and gradually fade due to other uprising factors, such as the many changes undergone by Western societies, the Cold War having '*radicalized*' neoliberalism, as well as the flow of new beliefs related to '*business activism*'. In 1962, Friedman provided yet

[28] Ibid.

another plausible explanation for the Chicago School's change of economic mindset when he pointed out that a relatively active role for the state was only sought at a time when governments were small in relation to present-day standards.[29]

What is regarded as one of the main causes behind both the final dismemberment of the Mont Pelerin Society and the definite breakup of the unity of the neoliberal collective was the upsetting key role Hayek played during the Hunold Affair. During the 1950s and 1960s, Hayek had relentlessly fought to preserve the unity of the collective, remove disruptive elements and steer the group in the best possible direction. Although at first Hayek had approved a secretary role for the Mont Pelerin Society's chief financier, Albert Hunold, Hayek had, however, become increasingly concerned about Hunold's behaviour. Hunold sought much change within the society and wanted to provide it with a higher profile, which ran in direct contrast to Hayek, who preferred to stay above the fray and detached from political concerns. Furthermore, Hunold clashed with the collective even more by creating much ill will at several of the society's meetings, most markedly in 1958 at Princeton University and in 1959 at Oxford University. Additionally, Hunold also wanted to publish a *'Mont Pelerin Society Quarterly'*, which once again collided with Hayek's wishes. Within such a tense atmosphere and with other members also trying to remove Hunold from office, Röpke sided with Hunold by supporting him the most, since he considered the society to be indebted to him for his initial funding. With Europeans, like Röpke and Böhm, standing by Hunold, the strongest opposition came from Americans, like Friedman and Stigler. While Erhard likewise tried to intervene in order to appease the impasse, Hayek ended up caught in the middle of the dispute with the role of arbitrator. Friedman believed the conference format was much more useful in Europe than in the United States, where there were many more *'partisans of free markets and free enterprise than in most other countries'*.[30] Throughout the heated affair, Friedman supported Hayek very strongly, with his interventions being of '*extraordinary intensity*', compared to the *'reactionary'* intercessions of Hunold and the '*agrarian*' intercessions of Röpke. When, in 1971, Friedman became president of the Mont Pelerin Society, he even tried to (unsuccessfully) terminate the group, since he believed that *'Hayek's original objectives had been achieved and that the society had become too large and unwieldy'*. Although Friedman did not necessarily agree about the centrality of the Mont Pelerin Society as regards the neoliberal movement, he nevertheless always represented a key-influencing figure in the composition of the Mont Pelerin Society. Most especially, Friedman played a chief role in the direction of the more abstract Anglo-American neoliberal movement.[31]

[29] Ibid, pgs 6–7. Also see: MIROWSKI, P. and PLEHWE, D. (Eds). *The Road from Mont Pelerin: The Making of the Neoliberal Thought Collective* and BIEBRICHER, T. and VOGELMANN, F. (Eds). *The Birth of Austerity: German Ordoliberalism and Contemporary Neoliberalism.*

[30] Ordoliberalism and the Austrian School. KEMENY, P.J. *The Decline of Ordoliberal Influence in the Mont Pelerin Collective. Röpke's Occident, the 'Hunold Affair' and the Rise of the Chicago School,* pg 7.

[31] Ibid.

'Second Phase' of the Process of Construction of Neoliberal Thought – 1960s Onwards

Following such a succession of events, the 'second phase' of the process of construction of neoliberal thought began from the 1960s onwards. That period witnessed the last transatlantic split within the neoliberal movement, the definite narrowing down of the neoliberal collective and ultimately, the final fracturing of neoliberal thought.

In 1961, after a frenzied meeting in Turin, Italy, both Hunold and Röpke resigned, with the latter sadly perceiving *'a split between America and Europe within our Society'*.[32] Those years marked a true *'narrowing of the Mont Pelerin Society's horizons'*,[33] and in general, demonstrated that *'the Society's members had moved to the opinion that the state can do no right, and private enterprise no wrong'*.[34] After the establishment of such differing and opposing points of view vis-à-vis the *'role of the state'*, between Hayek and Friedman, Hayek observed that *'Milton's monetarism and Keynesianism have more in common with each other than I have with either'*.[35] Henceforth, while Hayek tried to preserve the unity of the society's collective, as well as play down its ideological splits, at the same time, he continued waging war against 'collectivism'. Maybe due to the fact that Hayek had always been very conscious of not allowing the group to splinter into Hayekian and Friedmanite factions, he might have erroneously led people to perceive neoliberalism as one single homogenous set of ideas, with all its protagonists interacting in broad agreement as one single bunch of *'happy people'*.[36]

Although the neoliberal collective was indeed established and generated by a group of individuals who at first shared the same ideas, it gradually evolved into a group of people with mixed ideas, who were strongly influenced by many of the events that took place during the time. After the 1962 resignations of Hunold and Röpke, the Mont Pelerin Society's collective breadth of views was seriously narrowed down, with the significance and influence of German ordoliberalism within neoliberal thought also declining and fading. Once again and as reflected, such changes were mainly caused by the 1940s failure of *'Occident'*, the shift of gravity within the Mont Pelerin Society from Europe to the United States during the Hunold Affair, as well as by Hayek's allegiance to the American side during the affair. The Hunold Affair also clearly reflected, for the first time, the scale of influence that Friedman bore over his neoliberal contemporaries, which in a way also pointed to the decline of European neoliberalism and the ascendance of Anglo-American neoliberalism.[37]

[32] Ibid. Also see: MIROWSKI, P. and PLEHWE, D. (Eds). *The Road from Mont Pelerin: The Making of the Neoliberal Thought Collective* and BIEBRICHER, T. and VOGELMANN, F. (Eds). *The Birth of Austerity: German Ordoliberalism and Contemporary Neoliberalism.*

[33] Ordoliberalism and the Austrian School. KEMENY, P.J. *The Decline of Ordoliberal Influence in the Mont Pelerin Collective. Röpke's Occident, the 'Hunold Affair' and the Rise of the Chicago School,* pg 7.

[34] Ibid.

[35] Ibid.

[36] Ibid.

[37] Ibid.

The early new liberal, ordoliberal and neoliberal '*marriage of convenience*' shared a common interventionist joint project, with some suggestions even forwarding that '*ordoliberalism is substantially less different than other streams of neoliberal thought than many have thought, due to a limited, primarily economic understanding of freedom and a strong authoritarian element, which is displayed in a fundamental scepticism toward democracy*'.[38] However, since the beginning of the process of construction of neoliberal thought, there were always very marked differences between the two currents, as well as within the collective of coalitions and intellectuals, which were formed in the Mont Pelerin Society. While Europeans and Chicagoans always had irreconcilable differing views regarding the role of the state and monetary control, in a similar way, the views of ordoliberals, Austrians and Chicagoans equally very strongly diverged in relation to competition and monopoly, as well as in connection to the role of law in a market economy.[39]

During the 'second phase' of the process of construction, and most especially from the 1960s onwards, the resurgence of liberal thought became much more closely associated with Milton Friedman and his ideas on monetarism, and in a much less defined way, with Friedrich Hayek. From then onwards, the Mont Pelerin Society, neoliberal thought and the neoliberal collective as a whole became much narrower and largely based on, motivated and guided by the Chicago School's technocratic views and policies and, to a much lesser extent, by the more libertarian Austrian School.[40]

Although, in general, Friedman's wider narrative promoted free markets and deregulation, he nevertheless always admired and applauded ordoliberalism and the prosperity it had generated in West Germany. He even took selective advantage of it, since it fit well into the framework of his narrative. For example, in 1948, Friedman lauded both Erhard's currency reform as a precursor to an economic miracle and elevated West Germany's case as an excellent example of successfully applied '*shock therapy*'. Friedman actually somewhat invoked ordoliberalism for the first implementation of neoliberalism in Chile when he wrote to Dictator General Augusto Pinochet, '*stressing the importance of implementing a "social market economy"*'.[41] Nonetheless, while Friedman's ideas on regulation and monopoly always completely diverged from ordoliberalism, he never really emphasized so much the '*social*' element of the German model. Likewise, the 'second' Chicago School's programme was equally totally devoid of other key ordoliberal tenets related to legally enforcing competition, monopoly prevention, social protection and limiting proletarianization.[42]

38 Ibid, pg 8.
39 Ibid. Also see: MIROWSKI, P. and PLEHWE, D. (Eds). *The Road from Mont Pelerin: The Making of the Neoliberal Thought Collective* and BIEBRICHER, T. and VOGELMANN, F. (Eds). *The Birth of Austerity: German Ordoliberalism and Contemporary Neoliberalism.*
40 Ordoliberalism and the Austrian School. KEMENY, P.J. *The Decline of Ordoliberal Influence in the Mont Pelerin Collective. Röpke's Occident, the 'Hunold Affair' and the Rise of the Chicago School,* pg 8.
41 Ibid.
42 Ibid.

From the 1960s onwards, the split within the Mont Pelerin collective clearly mirrored that a big faction of it was already strongly clinging to libertarian positions, which were extremely hostile towards government and whose thought was in complete conflict with ordoliberalism. Such ideological barriers likewise impeded ordoliberalism from gaining much ground in the English-speaking world. With the ideas of ordoliberalism becoming lost in German history books and European neoliberalism waning, the Anglo-American Chicago School literature related to twentieth-century economic liberalism began to flourish, being promoted worldwide. By 1979, when Anglo-Saxon governments, such as Margaret Thatcher's and Geoffrey Howe's, undertook their supposed neoliberal agendas, ordoliberalism had been practically lost and forgotten about in German history books. Likewise, other conservative '*free marketeers*', like Nigel Lawson, opted much more instead for conflating the ideas of Hayek and Friedman with British economists like Adam Smith and David Hume.[43]

Since then, the events that followed, more related to our more recent history, suffice to explain the rest of the neoliberal chronicle. From the 1990s and the beginning of the twenty-first century onwards, most of the literature that began to abundantly blossom included mostly Anglo-American neoliberal rhetoric, linked to governments, like Reagan's and Thatcher's and Clinton's and Blair's, as well as to phenomena like globalization and free markets. Moreover, the vast majority of the literature simply and merely reflected on the most basic of the neoliberal tenets, such as free markets, widespread deregulation and privatizations.

[43] Ibid.

6

Main Differences between Ordoliberalism and Neoliberalism Related to the Role of the State, Regulation, Market Behaviourism and Price-Controlling Mechanisms

As far and as much as ordoliberalism and neoliberalism formed an integral part of the early process of construction of neoliberal thought, there were always very marked differences between the two currents, which prevailed throughout the course of the process. Paradoxically, while most of their diverging issues are related to the original ones that had in fact stimulated and influenced their early common project in the first place, at the same time, they are elements, which have left ordoliberalism and neoliberalism ideologically and conceptually worlds apart. The most salient of such differing issues are related to their conceptions on the role of the state, interventionism, regulation, anti-monopoly, anti-cartels and anti-trust laws, as well as the social contract.[1]

> *The main difference between the German Ordoliberals and the 'Austrians' was their view of the state. The Austrians saw government as the greatest potential threat to freedom, and therefore wanted to keep it out of the economy. Power formations in the private sector, such as cartels, would eventually break down 'spontaneously', they thought. In that sense, they have been called 'market fundamentalists'. The Germans, by contrast, wanted a 'strong' state (though not a large one) that would step in as referee and break up cartels.*[2]

Since the beginning of their interventionist joint venture, there were clearly many discernible ideological and conceptual contrasts between ordoliberals and some of the most luminary neoliberals, like Hayek and Friedman. Both currents also ended extremely opposed in key areas related to some of the economic system's structural issues. Most particularly, as regards the areas connected with the role of the state, regulation, market behaviourism and price-controlling mechanisms. On the one hand,

1 Social Europe. WREN-LEWIS, S. *Ordoliberalism, Neoliberalism and Economics,* pgs 1–2. https://www.socialeurope.eu/ordoliberalism-neoliberalism-economics
2 HANDELSBLATT, *Ordoliberalism and the Alleged Aberration of German Economics,* pg 2.

ordoliberalism considers as indispensable the existence of a supervising state-locus overarching the legal-economic system, ensuring the prevalence of order and fairness within the economic sphere, the market and its price-controlling mechanisms. On the other hand, and in stark contrast, neoliberalism totally divorces the state and any sort of interventionism from the market. For neoliberalism, the state-less deregulated free market is left to freely run on 'laissez-faire' principles, which allows its supply and demand – Smith's '*invisible hand of the market*' – to determine by itself the programming and establishment of prices. Whereas ordoliberalism does not consider markets to be a natural phenomenon, which should thus and therefore be properly sustained and supported and not left to their own devices – neoliberalism perceives markets as a natural order, based on pure unregulated free will.[3]

Such conceptual and ideological differences between the two currents resulted in the Freiburg School's ordoliberalism leading West Germany's social market economy, which produced its famous German Economic Miracle, and the Anglo-American or Chicago School's neoliberal prescriptions prevailing over the Austrian School's. Eventually, the Chicagoan neoliberal formula was chosen to run the globalized free-market economy, as well as many regional development and integration processes into the international system. Their differing approaches are particularly interesting and relevant, since they fundamentally determined both the extreme success of ordoliberalism in West Germany, producing the German economic miracle, and the disastrous worldwide effects neoliberalism had on the entire international economic-financial system, as well as on developing and integrating regions like Latin America.

Despite their differences, since the birth of both ordoliberalism and neoliberalism, the symbiotic relationship forged between them throughout the Colloque Walter Lippmann and the Mont Pelerin Society during the early days of the process of construction of neoliberal thought was very dynamic. From the 1930s through to the mid-1950s, the ordoliberals were the most influential members of the broader family of neoliberal scholars. Even Milton Friedman, in his 1951 article, '*Neoliberalism and Its Prospects*', wrote very positively about the doctrine by making use of optimistic ordoliberal rhetoric. However, from the late 1950s and 1960s onwards, while the ordoliberal hold on neoliberal thought loosened drastically, Chicago School neoliberalism continued its solitary progressive evolution down its aggressive monetarist path. Henceforth, ordoliberalism and neoliberalism were left forever divergent and conflictual, as regards their individual conceptions of some vital areas of the economy.[4]

In a very similar way, although some of Hayek's ideas and theories were quite germane with those of ordoliberals, especially regarding forms of interventionism and price-controlling mechanisms, and despite the fact that Hayek ended his career teaching

[3] Near Futures. BIEBRICHER, T. *Return or Revival: The Ordoliberal Legacy*, pg 3. http://nearfuturesonline.org/return-or-revival-the-ordoliberal-legacy/

[4] Social Europe. WREN-LEWIS, S. *Ordoliberalism, Neoliberalism and Economics*, pgs 1–2. https://www.socialeurope.eu/ordoliberalism-neoliberalism-economics

at the Freiburg School – the alma mater of ordoliberal thought – there existed, however, crucial differences between them concerning market order. On the one hand, ordoliberals strongly believed that a properly functioning market order, based on free and fair competition, required a framework of norms and rules, with the formulation of the latter being an exercise of economic and political imagination. On the other hand, and especially during the last part of his career, Hayek was very sceptical of such a vision, since he believed it bordered on '*rational constructivism*', as well as the notion of utilizing political and economic reasoning to draw up such rules and regulations, expecting them to work. Hayek held that the market order could only be the result of a spontaneous evolutionary process, for which rules serve to assist such an evolution and not hamper it. In that sense, some constitutional economists, like James Buchanan, shared the same ordoliberal belief and not Hayek's cultural evolution notion and his persistence on the impossibility of norms just being simply invented.[5]

Similarly, during his early career, Friedman was also influenced by ordoliberal thought, although his ideas eventually changed very radically. In fact, and to a great extent, Friedman's monetary theory ran very much in parallel to ordoliberal thought in relation to '*sound money*'. However, in more general terms, Friedman's neoliberal ideas mainly revolved around a strict non-interventionist role for the state in making markets thrive, together with the combination of monetarist ideas with supply-side economics, which ran in complete divergence with the ordoliberal belief that a wide set of public policies is necessary to maintain the necessary market order. Friedman believed that the only role public authorities should have regarding economic policy, is to provide a continuous and gradual expansion of circulating money. Contrary to Keynesianism, Friedman did not believe in trying to engage in anti-cyclical economic policy through the utilization of monetary or fiscal policy. For Friedman, both a proactive fiscal policy and the tinkering with interest rates only attain exact opposite results, such as inflation and stagnation.[6]

In broad terms, one of the foremost differing peculiarities between ordoliberalism and neoliberalism revolves around the ordoliberal interdependent relationship between the political, legal-economic and social orders and the neoliberal separation of the political, economic and social spheres of action. While for ordoliberalism, the political and economic spheres are innately connected and need to operate interdependently of each other in order to preserve market liberty, for neoliberalism, the political, economic and social spheres are intrinsically separate. In direct contrast to ordoliberalism, neoliberalism keeps the political, economic and social spheres free from any state interventions, regulations or rules, as well as without the interference of any one of those spheres in the other sphere's individual freedom, or let alone their individual functioning. However, for ordoliberalism, the state represents the political form of economic liberty, and thus, and therefore, strongly insists on the control and restraint of economic agents, not because their '*greed oils the wheels of competition*', but because

[5] Ibid, pg 5.
[6] Ibid.

their political influence and assertion are believed to undermine the market's perfect liberty. Neoliberalism is very clear about non-state interference in the different spheres of action. While for neoliberals the state takes care of political issues, the economic sphere takes care of market and competition issues, and accordingly, the social realm takes care of social issues, for ordoliberals, the state must monopolize the political sphere, depoliticize socioeconomic relations and imbue into society the necessary moral values and norms of market liberty, in order to embed austerity and transform '*querulous proletarians into individualised and willing participants in the market price mechanism*'. [7] The ordoliberal strong state acts as a security state, which, whenever necessary, becomes a state of emergency, as there is a tight connection between economic freedom and the constraint of that freedom. For ordoliberals, '*freedom is ordered freedom*' and the state is thus central and chief in forming the locus of the interdependent economic, social and moral order.[8]

The fundamental objective of ordoliberalism, in clear contrast with the neoliberal '*laissez-faire*' market, is to promote '*enterprise and secure the role of the entrepreneur in the face of powerful demands for employment and welfare, and protection from competitive pressures*'.[9] For ordoliberalism, it is a political responsibility to solve the social deficiencies of capitalism, and in that sense, '*Vitalpolitik*' or the '*Politics of Life*', must comprise a social policy to change '*recalcitrant workers into willing entrepreneurs of their own labour power*'.[10] The ordoliberal free economy is considered a governmental practice, wherein the strong state assures both the safe conduct of market liberty and the provision of '*requisite social and ethical frameworks to embed entrepreneurialism as a character trait into society at large*'.[11]

Besides such broad differentiations between ordoliberalism and neoliberalism, there are much deeper differences between the two currents, which will be subsequently analysed, mainly linked to the role of the state, regulation, market behaviourism and price-controlling mechanisms.

The Ordoliberal Strong State versus the Neoliberal Minimalist State

One of the main differing premises between ordoliberalism and neoliberalism is related to the ordoliberal interdependence of orders and the neoliberal disconnection of the spheres of action. While ordoliberalism considers a strong role for the state

[7] BONEFELD, W. *Freedom and the Strong State: On German Ordoliberalism*, pgs 34–5. https://www.tandfonline.com/doi/abs/10.1080/13563467.2012.656082
[8] Ibid, pg 35.
[9] Ibid, pg 4.
[10] Ibid.
[11] Ibid.

as indispensable in the economic realm, neoliberalism totally disconnects the state and any of the state's actions from the economic sphere. One of the main pillars of the theory of the social market economy is, in fact, Rüstow's enunciation of the strong state. Whereas for ordoliberalism, a strong state resists '*statism*', which is defined as a form of collectivist tyranny that smothers individuals as entrepreneurs of economic value, the minimalist and weak neoliberal state is incapable of limiting itself to ordered freedom, as it is instead '*pulled apart by greedy self-seekers. Each of them terms out a piece of the state's power for himself and exploits it for its own purposes*'.[12]

Ordoliberalism, in divergence with neoliberalism, '*needs a state that governs, that is, a strong state, a state standing where it belonged, above the economy and above the interest groups*'.[13] On the one hand, ordoliberalism strongly believes that only within the framework of state authority can economic freedom exist through order and proper '*ordered freedom*' take place, since '*the stateless sphere of economic conduct rests on the complete eradication of all orderlessness from markets and the elimination of private power from the economy*'.[14] On the other hand, the neoliberal context of unregulated market dynamics only gives way to patterns of behaviour based on the law of the jungle, with very disparately unequal and distorted results. Ordoliberalism demands the exact opposite of neoliberalism and its minimalist, weak and unvigilant state, since it seeks '*freedom for economic development under state protection*' for the prevention of '*coercion and violence*'. Within the ordoliberal framework, the state must remain a '*strong and neutral guardian of the public interest, of the bonum commune of capitalist social relations, asserting its authority vis-à-vis the interest groups that press upon the government and clamor for recognition of their particular needs and wants*'.[15] For ordoliberalism, the strong state protects the state-less sphere of the free market – a sphere that is itself a political creation belonging to the state, '*whose right to determine the character of freedom, and to set and enforce the rules of freedom, is derived from its responsibility for the whole of society*'.[16]

Staunch ordoliberals, such as Rüstow and Röpke, were amongst the most insistent on a strong state, while other neoliberals, like most particularly Mises, were amongst the most anti-state interventionist in the economic realm. Mises clearly reflected that in the Socialist Calculation Debate through his '*anti-interventionist*' theses, as well as throughout the rest of his career. On the one hand, Rüstow believed that the '*economic system requires a market police with strong state authority for its protection and maintenance*'[17] and that effective '*policing*' requires '*a strong state, a state where it*

[12] Ibid, pg 26.
[13] Ibid.
[14] Ibid, pg 27.
[15] Ibid, pg 28.
[16] Ibid.
[17] Ibid, pg 28.

belongs: over and above the economy, over and above the interested parties'.[18] On the other hand, Röpke stressed that '*freedom … of economic life from political infection presupposes the strong state as the means of that freedom*'.[19] Within the ordoliberal framework, a strong state is fundamentally required for the depoliticization of socio-economic relations and the prevention of private power assertion in order to, that way, guarantee both proper undistorted competition and the regulation of private decision-making through the free price mechanism.[20]

At one level, ordoliberalism believes that an unchecked and non-supervised '*proletarianization*' tendency, intrinsic to capitalist social relations, is the root cause of '*social crisis, turmoil and disorder*', and at another level, neoliberalism holds that the state must limit itself to the political sphere, should not interfere whatsoever around or within the economic sphere and should allow market competitiveness to develop through its own natural laws. For ordoliberalism, the containment of proletarianization belongs to the state, and containment is thus and therefore a political responsibility, which can be carried out in different ways. In accordance with Müller-Armack, such variations can either include the '*internalisation of competitiveness*'[21] or, in accordance with Röpke, '*the creation of a stake-holder society and transformation of mass society into a property owning democracy*'.[22] The strong ordoliberal state has to be permanently vigilant and be ready to act whenever necessary '*if liberty is to have a chance of survival and if rules are to be maintained which secure free individual decisions*'. Furthermore, if and when the ordoliberal state is obliged to act, '*the most fundamental principles of a free society … may have to be temporarily sacrificed … [to preserve] liberty in the long run. The prize is freedom*'.[23]

While for ordoliberalism a strong state is an absolute sine qua non prerequisite in the economic realm, for neoliberalism, the state and any of its actions are totally non-existent in the economic sphere or any other domains, as they are all, most especially the economic sphere, ungoverned spheres of natural free action. For ordoliberalism, the state is responsible for the economic freedom, which is freed within the legal, social and moral frameworks. The ordoliberal theme of a strong state in the economy entails a much wider and deeper encompassing role than just '*policing the market order, by means of a central authority strong enough to maintain formal exchange equality between all economic agents*'.[24] The ordoliberal state must also, and most fundamentally, '*police*' the social order, which also includes the '*ethical, moral and normative frameworks of individual behaviour*'.[25] In correlation with Röpke and Rüstow's '*construction of a*

18 Ibid.
19 Ibid, pg 29.
20 Ibid.
21 Ibid, pg 32.
22 Ibid.
23 Ibid.
24 Ibid, pg 33.
25 Ibid.

human economy', the ordoliberal conception of a strong state lies in the creation of a social-moral order, which neatly aligns '*citizenship to entrepreneurship, private property and the market price mechanism*'.[26] In that sense and based on the ordoliberal principle of '*Vitalpolitik*', the ordoliberal state does not govern over society but rather governs through society in order to secure the '*transformation and multiplication of the social fabric into competitive enterprises*'.[27] Unlike the neoliberal government, the ordoliberal government does not yield to demands that '*seek freedom from want or value for nothing*' but instead facilitates enterprise and ingrains competitiveness into a social lifestyle. Ordoliberal freedom is not only dependent on political authority but is, at the same time and by itself, a reflection of authority. For ordoliberalism, whereas freedom cannot exist without social order, social order can only come about through the construction of a moral order. In general and broader terms, ordoliberalism demands the '*etatisation of society*', which assures '*that individuals react to economic shocks in a spirited and entirely self-responsible manner*'.[28]

Ordoliberal Interventionism versus Neoliberal Deregulation

Another key issue of extreme discrepancy between ordoliberalism and neoliberalism is connected to state interventionism and regulation. Ordoliberalism very strongly depends on the state's interventionist actions and regulating measures in the economic sphere in order to assure healthy, safe, equal and undistorted market behaviourism and competition. Neoliberalism, however, totally opposes such actions and measures, preferring instead to deregulate markets and allow '*laissez-faire*' market behaviourism and competition to develop according to their own supposedly innate, natural patterns of behaviour, mostly based on lawless free will.

For ordoliberalism, the question is not about whether the state should or should not intervene, but rather, and conversely, it is about '*the objective, aim, purpose and method*'[29] of state interventionism. The ordoliberal strong state intervenes for the assurance of proper, undistorted competitive relations and interactions, and not for specific social ends. Whereas for Müller-Armack state interventions in the economic and non-economic spheres are meant to '*secure the social and ethical conditions upon which efficiency competition rests*',[30] for Eucken, '*economic power can never be solved by further concentration of power, in the form of cartels and monopolies*'.[31] In that sense, ordoliberalism is also extremely different to neoliberal laissez-faire policies, which allow the '*misuse of the freedom of contract to destroy freedom*'.[32] Eucken always stressed

26 Ibid.
27 Ibid.
28 Ibid.
29 Ibid, pg 11.
30 Ibid.
31 Ibid.
32 Ibid.

that the *'problem of economic power can only be solved by an intelligent co-ordination of all economic and legal policy … Any single measure of economic policy should, if it is to be successful, be regarded as part of a policy designed to establish and maintain economic order as a whole.'*[33] Ordoliberal interventionism is meant for the proper safeguarding of the economic system and of the interactions therein, which are in constant need of supervision and protection. It is extremely against neoliberal free markets, where the law of the jungle is most times the main reason behind their major downfalls. *'Free markets do not by themselves produce and maintain an effective economic system. On the contrary, they destroy the economic system based on freedom. They thus require the authority of the state to facilitate that very economic freedom upon which the free economy rests. Economic freedom needs to be restrained to sustain that same freedom.'*[34] For ordoliberals, it is the responsibility and obligation of the political authority to consciously shape, supervise and sustain the economic system.[35]

The ordoliberal principles of regulation must be comprehended against the backdrop of the ordoliberal search for a '*Third Way*', between '*laissez-faire*' liberalism and collectivism, as well as of the conceptualization of the current, as '*a new liberalism that commits itself to battle and secure liberty in the face of selfish interest groups and the proletarian society*'.[36] On the basis of that principle, ordoliberals stress that neoliberal free market '*laissez-faire*' policies cannot be the answer, or let alone the solution, '*to the hungry hordes of vested interests*'.[37] For Röpke, while '*the crisis of liberal capitalism was the necessary outcome of a socially and psychologically unbalanced mass society in revolt*',[38] he always likewise rebuked '*laissez-faire liberalism for turning a blind eye to the sociological effect of industrialisation and market competition on workers*',[39] and not being able to '*defend what it cherished the most – Liberty*'.[40] Rüstow also shared the same rationale by reproaching that '*traditional liberalism was blind to the problems lying in the obscurity of sociology*'[41] and that '*laissez-faire conceptions of the invisible hand amounted to deist providentialism*',[42] which he believed defined '*the theological-metaphysical character of liberal economics*'.[43] For Rüstow, while traditional liberalism naturally assumes the '*unconditional validity of economic laws*', it however does so, but without carrying out a proper enquiry into their '*social, ethical, and political preconditions*'.[44]

[33] Ibid.
[34] Ibid, pgs 11–12.
[35] Ibid, pg 12.
[36] Ibid.
[37] Ibid.
[38] Ibid.
[39] Ibid.
[40] Ibid.
[41] Ibid.
[42] Ibid.
[43] Ibid.
[44] Ibid.

While, on the one hand, the ordoliberal, non-natural and consciously established interdependence of orders is able to achieve an overall harmonious equilibrium, on the other hand, the neoliberal unregulated spheres cannot ever achieve such perfect forms of equilibrium due to their own natural laws. For ordoliberals, '*the invisible hand does not create harmony just like that*' and it must therefore be consciously applied by a strong state, which, whenever necessary, should intervene and regulate any dysfunctionalities in any of the orders, so as to avoid the emergence of anarchy and disorder. One of the main reasons behind market distortions, inequality and the widening breaches between strong and weak participants in neoliberal free markets is precisely linked to the total lack of neoliberal state interventionism, regulations and rules of the game. The fact that the neoliberal '*free market order is invisible and not brought about by a conscious effort of individuals, is one of the reasons for the tremendous advantage it has over other economic systems as far as the production of material wealth is concerned*'. The ordoliberal strong state has the obligation to provide, deliver and look after the '*robust political-legal-ethical institutional framework*', which competitive markets are highly dependent on.[45] For ordoliberals, '*thus, competition, and therewith, economic regulation by the invisible hand, is indispensable – in the economic sphere*'.[46] Notwithstanding, they likewise hold that a social-ethical-moral framework must equally accompany competition, since it '*does not breed social integration. Nor does it provide for the general framework of society ... it is unable to integrate society as a whole, to define those common attitudes and beliefs or those common value standards without which a society cannot exist*'.[47] The ordoliberal strong emphasis on the interventions and regulations of a strong state assures the proper maintenance of the interdependence of orders, as well as the full enjoyment of a harmonious equilibrium. Competition '*appeals ... solely to selfishness*' and is therefore '*dependent upon ethical and social forces of coherence*'. Ordoliberals strongly believe that '*in order to sustain liberty one has to look outside the market for that integration which was lacking within it*'.[48]

While ordoliberalism views the authority of the state as the sole political master and defender of the free economy, the neoliberal '*laissez-faire*' doctrine is regarded as extremely susceptible to conceding '*to illiberal demands for welfare and is thus incapable of defending liberty*'.[49] Ordoliberal freedom '*is freedom within the framework of order, and order, is a matter of political authority*'.[50] Freedom can only truly flourish over a proper and solid bedrock of order, and only that way can free participants be truly trusted to adjust to the price mechanism willingly and responsibly. For ordoliberals, the '*maintenance of order depends on a strong state that governs over the social interests*'.[51]

45 Ibid, pg 13.
46 Ibid, pg 12.
47 Ibid, pgs 12–13.
48 Ibid, pg 13.
49 Ibid, pg 15.
50 Ibid.
51 Ibid.

The ordoliberal strong state is required to remove all '*orderlessness*' from markets, depoliticize market relations as apolitical exchange relations, and monopolize the political. For them, the '*depoliticization of socio-economic relations and politicisation of the state belong together as interdependent forms of social organisation*'.[52] Ordoliberalism likewise firmly believes that '*the political task of sustaining market liberty on the basis of the rule of law is not enough. Fundamentally, market behaviour needs to be embedded into the "psycho-moral forces" at the disposal of a competitive society.*'[53]

Ordoliberal Market Order versus Neoliberal Laissez-Faire

Another fundamental area of extreme discord between ordoliberalism and neoliberalism is linked to economic freedom and market freedom or market behaviourism. On the one hand, ordoliberalism strictly believes in ordered freedom within the market so that freedom is not in any way misused, as well as for the sound development of regulated, fair and equal competition based on a properly functioning price mechanism. On the other hand, while neoliberalism deregulates markets, its '*laissez-faire*' principles set free the reins of anarchic behaviour, which in turn only gives way to both unequal distorted competition and the tampering of prices.

Within ordoliberal markets, '*full competition requires strong state authority to assure the orderly conduct of self-interested entrepreneurs. Economic freedom is not unlimited. It is based on order, and exists only by means of order, and freedom is effective only as ordered freedom.*'[54] Within neoliberal free markets, '*prices can be fixed, markets carved up, and competitive adjustment avoided by means of protectionism and manipulation of monetary policy, and workers can strike, the masses can revolt, and a proletarianized mass society can force the state to concede welfare*'.[55] Neoliberal '*laissez-faire*' is a '*highly ambiguous and misleading description of the principles on which a liberal policy is based*'.[56] For ordoliberalism, the '*sacrosanct*' purity of individual freedom is highly dependent on the strong state as the '*coercive force of that freedom*'. The ordoliberal free economy and political authority share a very symbiotic coexistence with the ordoliberal interdependence of orders, with its tight connection between the political sphere and the economic sphere. Without such a connection, ordoliberalism holds that one sphere will not function harmoniously without the other sphere's equal proper functioning and vice versa. Each and every single sphere is interdependent on all other spheres in such a way that any dysfunction in one sphere will cause a disruption in the other sphere, which will thus and therefore ultimately affect the system's overall harmonious equilibrium. '*All spheres have to be treated together interdependently and have to operate*

52 Ibid.
53 Ibid.
54 Ibid, pg 10.
55 Ibid.
56 Ibid.

interdependently for each other to maintain the system as a whole.'[57] For ordoliberals, the establishment and maintenance of a sound and proper cohesive system require the close coordination of the political, economic, social and moral spheres. Within the ordoliberal framework, the strong state represents both the organizational epicentre and the main source of the power of interdependence, which, thus, makes the state '*fundamental as the premise of market freedom*'. In accordance with Eucken, '*the economic has no independent existence. Economic constitution is a political matter*'.[58]

The ordoliberal idea of economic freedom is based on distrust, which represents the complete opposite of the neoliberal arbitrary-less free market, with no rules to rationally guide the actions of individuals or their interactions. For ordoliberalism, there is no freedom without surveillance to assure that the orderly conduct of self-interested entrepreneurs does not lead to proletarianization. '*The free market presupposes vitally satisfied individuals, who in the face of natural tendency towards proletarianization, perceive poverty as an incentive to do better, see unemployment as an opportunity for employment, price themselves into jobs willingly and on their own initiative, meet a part of their subsistence needs by working for themselves, and who enter the realm of coined freedom as stock market investors. Vitally satisfied workers are those who take their life into their own hands, get on with things, live courageously put up with life's insecurities and risks, fit in extra hours of independent work to meet subsistence needs and help others, and who see unemployment as an opportunity for employment.*'[59] Ordoliberal market freedom, unlike the neoliberal unfettered freedom, is not an economic product but the political practice of '*Vitalpolitik*' or the '*Politics of Life*'. For ordoliberals, '*freedom is a constantly empowered freedom*',[60] which has to be properly sustained, and in accordance with Eucken, '*requires a market police with strong state authority*'.[61] The ordoliberal free economy is a sphere, which is defined as a state-less sphere of economic freedom, but with strong state control of it at the same time.

On the other hand, while ordoliberalism strongly believes in markets being equally sustained and strengthened by social policies, neoliberal free markets, totally undermine social policies, rights, cohesion and protection, with their separation of the economic from the social. Ordoliberalism deems free markets as incapable of integrating society as a whole, requiring constant maintenance through social policies, which assure social cohesion and integration, as well as the preservation of the entrepreneur's vitality, that way '*restraining the natural tendency towards proletarianization by a political effort at formatting entrepreneurial personalities. The masses benefit from this development but lack insight and understanding.*'[62] One of the most special and

57 Ibid, pg 11.
58 Ibid.
59 Ibid, pgs 25–6.
60 Ibid, pg 26.
61 Ibid.
62 Ibid, pg 24.

Table 1 Differing Characteristics between Ordoliberalism and Neoliberalism Regarding Issues on Competition Policy

Issues Relevant for Competition Policy	Ordoliberalism	Neoliberalism
a) The State	Should be strong.	Should be less strong. (Hayek's formulations about a strong state are different from Eucken's concept of a strong state).
b) Economic Freedom	Restrictions are necessary in order to take care of consumers.	Unrestricted freedom of contract.
c) Market Forces	Should be properly and carefully *cultivated.*	Should be left untouched.
d) The Role of Consumers	Consumer interests should be sanctioned both through consumer protection legislation and through market forces.	Business profit-maximizing activities are, *per definition,* in the interest of consumers.
e) Mergers	Should be banned if they harm the consumer interest.	Should not be banned.

Source: NEDERGAARD, P. *The Influence of Ordoliberalism in European Integration Processes – A Framework for Ideational Influence with Competition Policy and the Economic and Monetary Policy as Examples,* pgs 7–8.https://mpra.ub.uni-muenchen.de/52331/1/MPRA_paper_52331.pdf

characteristic interrelating features of the social market economy was that the social factor connected market freedom with individual responsibility, reconciled workers with the law of private property and promoted enterprise, and delivered society from proletarianized social structures. '*The significance of the term "social" in the conception of the social market economy does thus not refer to a policy of social justice associated with a welfare state. Social policy is meant to "enable" individuals as self-responsible entrepreneurs.*'[63] For ordoliberals, the strong state represents the absolute '*guardian of enterprise*' and of entrepreneurs.[64]

The Ordoliberal Price-Controlling Mechanism versus the Neoliberal Free Price Mechanism

One additional, very conflictive area between ordoliberalism and neoliberalism, concerns price-controlling mechanisms. While ordoliberalism makes a very intelligent utilization of the price-controlling mechanism as a signalling instrument that allows for

[63] Ibid, pg 25.
[64] Ibid.

social cooperation between participants, neoliberalism sets free its price mechanism, thus allowing the free market's supply and demand to self-determine and set prices accordingly, which inevitably leads to price distortions.

Whereas ordoliberalism conceives individual freedom as the freedom of the entrepreneur to engage in competition and seek gratification through voluntary exchanges in free markets, '*free markets are governed by the principles of scarcity, private property, freedom of contract, and exchange between equal legal subjects, each pursuing their own self-interested ends*'.[65] Within the ordoliberal market, the price mechanism represents a very useful and indicative contraption of market scarceness. '*The free market allows social cooperation between autonomous individuals by means of a "signalling system," the price mechanism. It thus requires monetary stability to permit its effective operation as a "calculating machine" that informs consumers and producers of the degree of scarcity in the whole economy.*'[66] Such a '*scarcity gauge*' is crucial for ordoliberals, as it has the double function of both withstanding the '*non-coerced coordination*' and balancing the interests of huge amounts of participants who are each involved in a '*continuous consumer plebiscite*'. Röpke considered prices as extremely important indicators, which he perceived as '*orders by the market to producers and consumers to expand or to restrict*'.[67] For ordoliberalism, the free market is a very particular '*social instrument*', which allows '*the spontaneous communication between self-interested individuals*'.[68]

[65] Ibid, pg 9.
[66] Ibid.
[67] Ibid.
[68] Ibid.

7

Main Divergences between the Austrian and the Chicago Schools Connected with the Conception of Economic Science, Methodological Stereotypes and Monetary Theory

Within the framework of the process of construction of neoliberal thought, the Austrian School, the Freiburg School and the Chicago School developed from the very beginning an extremely contributing relationship towards the whole process through their collective brainstorming, as well as via the infusion by the wide variety of 'new liberal' academics involved with their differing ideas and inputs.

The Austrian School originated during the late nineteenth and early twentieth centuries, which was much earlier than the other two schools. It was followed by the Freiburg School, which emerged during the 1930s, and finally, by the Chicago School, that apperared during the 1940s. However, the eventual fusion of the three schools, through their same common determination beseeching the reformulation of classical liberalism and laissez-faire, proved to be invaluable as regards the generation of the 'new liberalism', which emerged henceforth. Together, they induced the conception and generation of ordoliberalism and neoliberalism, as well as the ensuing process of construction of neoliberal thought that took place. Such a triple alliance or triad, which the three schools formed, together with the 'new liberalism' that was conceived through their interactions at the Colloque Walter Lippmann and the Mont Pelerin Society intricate lobbying machine, has indeed proven extremely prolific.

Notwithstanding, despite the fact that the three schools shared the same common opposition to Manchesterism and socialism, the three were extremely divergent, most especially, as regards Euckenasian and Röpkesian ordoliberalism, as well as Hayekian neoliberalism and Friedmanian neoliberalism. Clear separations must be made and distinctions be discerned between ordoliberalism and neoliberalism, between neoliberalism and libertarianism, and even more so, between the Austrian School's heterodoxy and the Chicago School's neoclassicism. Such separations are absolutely paramount, most especially considering that it was the Chicago School's neoliberal prescriptions, which ended triumphing within the Mont Pelerin Society, and which today embody the contemporary neoliberal orthodoxy and thought, established since the 1980s.[1]

Although the Austrian and the Chicago Schools share a common predilection for free markets, the two schools are, however, completely skewed as regards philosophy, ideology and methodology. Maybe due to the fact that the Austrian School was born many years before the Chicago School, it was thus and therefore able to gain much more ground in terms of recognition and status, as well as establish much earlier its immutable purist approach to the study of economics and analysis of economic phenomena. In stark contrast, when the Chicago School arose during the 1940s, the time's scientific rigour of the physical sciences, together with the irrefutable conclusions they produced, became extremely attractive for the school's economists. Therefore, neoclassical economists began imitating the methodology, as well as the models provided by the physical sciences, in order to test and validate their own economic empirical research and hypotheses. For that main reason, Chicago School neoclassical economists henceforth adopted and established the same mathematical approach utilized in the physical sciences, which since then became the school's defining trademark.[2] The differing monetary theories of the two schools are also extremely interesting, most especially the Chicagoan thesis, as it is the monetary thesis, which provides the international financial-monetary system with the mechanics that make it function.

Although both the Austrian and the Chicago Schools are totally pro-free-markets, most especially in relation to typical issues, such as government stimulus spending, tariffs and wages, they, nevertheless, differ drastically in relation to their scientific and methodological approach to the study of economics and economic phenomena. While the first relies very heavily on unorthodox non-scientific approaches and methodologies, the second bases itself much more on orthodox scientific models and methods. Because of that main difference, while the Austrian School is considered to lie outside the economic mainstream as a purist heterodox school of thought, the Chicago School is seen as standing inside mainstream economics as an orthodox neoclassical school of thought. Whereas the Austrian School primarily bases its economic approach on methodological individualism, pivoting around the concept of social phenomena being a direct result of the motivations and actions of individuals, the Chicago School grounds itself on a solid bedrock of intense mathematical modelling to test hypotheses, with its main assumptions strictly based on rational expectations. Whilst the Austrian School believes strongly in pure logic and not in empirical reasoning for analysing the very unpredictable course of human action,[3] the Chicago School

1 Ludwig von Mises Institute. BAGUS, P. *Why Austrians Are Not Neoliberals*, pg 3. https://mises.org/library/why-austrians-are-not-neoliberals

2 Ibid, pg 2.

3 The Economic Review. *Chicago School vs Austrian School: Battle of Free-Marketeers*, pgs 1–2. https://theeconomicreview.wordpress.com/2011/09/24/chicago-school-vs-austrian-school-battle-of-the-free-marketeers/

strongly believes that economics is a science, with rules that cannot be broken, relying heavily on scientific truth, scientific logic, mathematical modelling, econometrics and macroeconomic analysis, to base its theories on. '*The Chicagoans like to don the white robe of scientists whenever they deal with economic phenomena*'.[4] The Austrian School believes that since the economy is based on the actions of individuals, no mathematical formulas can therefore predict why or how people act, and thus, in divergence with the Chicago School, its work is mostly based on philosophy, logic and reasoning.[5] While the Austrian School's axiom is '*logic doesn't lie, but numbers can deceive*', the Chicago School's motto is considered to be '*numbers don't lie, but con-colluded assumptions can deceive*'.[6] As a matter of fact, the difference between the methodological approaches of both schools is so abysmal that it is often questioned whether their agreement on the superiority of the free-market is not simply coincidental. '*The empirical data of the Chicago School merely validates in practice what the Austrians believe in theory. Either the Chicago school utilizes incorrect numbers or misinterprets models, or the Austrian school makes illogical claims. This conflict point is what makes the Austrian and Chicago schools two different schools, rather than two methodological heads of the same beast.*'[7]

On one hand, Austrians based on the Misean tradition derive logically *a priori* economic laws from the axiom of human action, aided by some general presuppositions, although they do not investigate the outside world to make experiments, exploring instead the inside of humans by utilizing introspection to find truth. On the other hand, Chicagoans based on Friedmanian thought utilize a positivist methodology. Austrian scholars hold that in order to comprehend history, what is needed in the first place is a 'theory', while Chicagoan academics derive economic laws from history, occasionally through the application of econometric analyses. Whereas Viennese theorists perceive reality as a '*dynamic process of human interaction*', Chicagoan economists base themselves much more on equilibrium models, wherein entrepreneurship and creativity are absent, and '*the market process is frozen*'.[8] Heterodox analysts aim to comprehend and explain the laws that govern the dynamic market process, whereas neoclassical experts aim to make correct predictions. In a similar way, while the Austrians aim to provide realistic explanations of the market process, the Chicagoans assert that the realism of assumptions is irrelevant, strictly stressing that '*only the predictive power of a theory counts*'.[9]

[4] Reason.com. SENNHOLZ, H. *Chicago Monetary Tradition in the Light of Austrian Theory*, pg 11. https://reason.com/1971/10/01/chicago-monetary-tradition-in

[5] 71 Republic. *The Difference between Austrian and Chicago Economics*, pg 1. https://71republic.com/2018/10/21/difference-austrian-chicago-economics/

[6] The Economic review. *Chicago School vs Austrian School: Battle of Free-Marketeers*, pg 3. https://theeconomicreview.wordpress.com/2011/09/24/chicago-school-vs-austrian-school-battle-of-the-free-marketeers/

[7] Ibid.

[8] Ludwig von Mises Institute. BAGUS, P. *Why Austrians Are Not Neoliberals*, pgs 4–5. https://mises.org/library/why-austrians-are-not-neoliberals

[9] Ibid, pg 5.

Some of the main differing features between the two schools' diverging methodological foundations are very interesting, as, in turn, they produce even further variations between the two, as regards competition and capital, as well as in relation to their explanations of booms and busts.

In relation to competition, whereas Viennese scholars oppose governmental intervention into the dynamic market process in the form of antitrust laws, Chicagoan academics diversely support and devise antitrust laws, in order to make reality adapt more to their model of perfect competition.[10]

The high aggregation required by model building and mathematization has also led the Austrian and Chicago Schools to have very fundamentally opposing views on capital, with a very intense debate existing between them-regarding the issue. Whilst Viennese capital theory and its view of production as a time consuming process allowed its economists to develop '*a theory of intertemporal distortions in the structure of production induced by credit expansion unbacked by real savings*',[11] Chicagoan capital theory (with the letter *K* denoting capital in its models) considers capital as '*a homogenous, permanent fund that synchronously and automatically produces income*'.[12] Friedrich Hayek and Fritz Machlup severely criticized Frank Knight for the '*meaningless concept of capital as a homogenous, automatically self-maintaining fund*'.[13] In general, neoclassical economists do not commonly comprehend the heterodox business cycle theory, as they lack the necessary theoretical instruments, and are thus unable to develop them with their own methodological approach. However, the neoclassical framework for mathematization and formalization directly influences and affects their view both on capital as a homogenous fund and on production as instantaneous.[14]

Lastly, the Austrian and Chicago schools' varying interpretations of the Great Depression are also very indicative and explicative of their differing explanations of booms and busts. From one angle, the Austrian business cycle theory's explanation of the Great Depression bases itself on the extraordinary credit expansion of the 1920s and the concomitant mal-investments, as well as on the governmental interventions of the 1930s, like the Smoot-Hawley Tariff Act or the New Deal. The Austrians, however, believe that the re-inflation of the money supply '*disturbs the necessary readjustment as it stabilizes artificially old malinvestments and stimulates additional ones*'.[15] From another angle, the Chicagoans base themselves on the theory of Milton Friedman and Ana Schwartz, strictly holding that the Great Depression happened due to errors committed by the Federal Reserve, since it did not expand the monetary base quickly enough during the 1930s.[16]

10 Ibid.
11 Ibid.
12 Ibid.
13 Ibid.
14 Ibid.
15 Ibid, pg 6.
16 Ibid, pg 5.

Asides from those broad differences between the Austrian and the Chicago Schools, the philosophical, ideological and, most especially, scientific and methodological divergences between the two schools are most especially relevant and transcendental, as they affect all other economic areas and phenomena that they touch upon. While all their assumptions depart from the same individual rationale and premise, the ensuing assumptions that are generated are thus and likewise equally deep-rooted therein.

The following analysis will probe deeply into the Austrian and the Chicago Schools' diverging conceptions of economic science, their different ways of approaching economic science and analysing economic phenomena, their different methodological stereotypes, as well as their differing monetary theories.

The Austrian School's Theory of Action versus the Chicago School's Theory of Decision

The Austrian and Chicago schools' frameworks of divergent philosophical, ideological and most especially, scientific and methodological differences overarch all other areas of economic study and analysis of phenomena. One of their most transcending differing principles is related to both schools' economic viewpoints and the way they approach, conceive and analyse economic science. On one hand, the Austrian School's concept of economic science is based on the '*Theory of (human) Action*' or '*Methodological Individualism*', or in Misean terminology, on '*Scientific Praxeology*', which perceives economic science as a dynamic process. On the other hand, the Chicago School's notion of economic science is based on the '*Theory of Decision*', wherein economic science is perceived as '*rational*' and strictly based on constraint maximization.[17]

The Viennese theory of human action, methodological individualism or '*praxeology*' comprises the Chicagoan concept of individual decision and much more. The heterodox concept of action includes, at the same time, the neoclassical hypothetical process of decision in an environment of '*given knowledge*' of the ends and means, but much more importantly and above all else, '*the very perception of the ends-means framework within which allocation and economizing is to take place*'.[18] The Austrians strongly believe that economics and the study and analysis of it are directly connected to a theoretical corpus of social interaction processes, within which, depending on the projected awareness of the different actors involved in every entrepreneurial action, can, to a greater or lesser extent, be coordinated. Because of such a wide arching approach, the Austrian theory of action is considered to reach much further and beyond, as well as cover much more, than the Chicagoan theory of choice or theory of decision. While heterodox praxeology can be utilized to deduce *a priori* theoretical economic truths, with its deductive economic thought experiments capable of producing conclusions

[17] HUERTA DE SOTO, J. *La Escuela Austriaca. Mercado y Creatividad Empresarial*, pg 19.

[18] Ibid.

that follow irrefutably from their underlying assumptions, the neoclassical theory of decision cannot infer conclusions simply based on empirical observation or statistical analysis.[19]

Whereas the Austrian scholars' conception of economics integrates it into a much wider framework, thus converting it into a broader science through its general theory of human action, the notion of Chicagoan academics reduces its concept of economics to a much narrower framework, which is mainly based on its theory of human decision.[20] In other words, Viennese thought is strictly opposed to the limited conception of economics of Lionel Robbins, which in direct correlation with the Chicagoan paradigm is grounded on his renowned definition of economics as a science, which studies the utilization of scarce resources that could be used in alternative ways in order to satisfy human needs.[21] For Robbins, the *'economic problem is reduced to a mere technical problem of allocation, maximization or optimization, subject to known constraints'*, and implies *'given knowledge on ends and means'*.[22] While from one angle heterodox theorists believe that *'what man really does, rather than allocating given means to given ends, is to constantly seek new ends and means, learning from the past and using his imagination to discover and create (by action) the future'*, from another angle, for neoclassical economists, *'the Robbinsian man is an automaton or caricature of the human being, who merely reacts passively to events'*.[23]

The Austrian School's Subjectivism versus the Chicago School's Objectivism

A second central diverging aspect between the Austrian and the Chicago schools is associated with the Austrian *'Methodological Subjectivism'* or *'Ontological Individualism'*, and the Chicagoan, *'Objectivism'*. While, on one hand, Viennese methodological subjectivism or 'ontological individualism' views economic science as rooted in the human being as he is the creative and leading actor in social processes, on the other hand, Chicagoan objectivism perceives economic science as based on aggregates or *'tangible material objects'*. For heterodox economists, economic science has profound ontological implications, which hold that social specifics, like prices and costs, only exist within the realm of the individual human being. For Mises, in blatant opposition to neoclassical analysts, economics *'is about men, their meanings and actions. Goods, commodities and wealth and all other elements of conduct are not*

19 Ibid.
20 Ibid, pg 20.
21 Ibid, pg 19.
22 Ibid.
23 Ibid, pg 20.

elements of nature; they are elements of human meaning and conduct. He who wants to deal with them must look at the external world. He must search for them in the meaning of acting men'.[24] Whereas for Austrian experts, economic constraints are imposed by human entrepreneurial subjective knowledge, for Chicagoan researchers, economic constraints are foisted by either objective phenomena or material factors of the external world.[25]

The Austrian School's Entrepreneur versus the Chicago School's Homo Oeconomicus

A very poignant force of the Austrian School, which plays a chief role in its economic theory, is '*Entrepreneurship*'. Notwithstanding, it is a field which is conspicuously absent from the Chicago School's economic science. Although entrepreneurship represents a most typical phenomenon in the real world that is in constant disequilibrium, paradoxically, it does not and cannot play any sort of role in the neoclassical models of equilibrium.

In complete demarcation from Viennese theory, in Chicagoan theory, entrepreneurship is simply considered as one more production factor, which in accordance with its costs and benefits may be allocated. However, such action is carried out without realizing that when analysing the entrepreneur that way, the analysis itself falls prey to an irredeemable logical contradiction: '*to demand entrepreneurial resources in accordance with their expected benefits and costs implies the belief that some information is available today (the probable value of the future costs and benefits) before it has been created by entrepreneurship itself*'.[26] Because of such feature, neoclassical models of equilibrium are considered to have intrinsic flaws due to the fact that '*the main function of the entrepreneur consists of creating and discovering new information that did not previously exist and cannot be known, meaning that it is humanly impossible to make any neoclassical prior decision on allocation on the basis of expected costs and benefits*'.[27]

Furthermore, while heterodox scholars also share the common belief that '*entrepreneurial profit arises from the simple assumption of risks as a fallacy*',[28] contrariwise, risk itself, only gives way to yet another cost in the production process, which has no relationship whatsoever with pure entrepreneurial profit.[29]

24 Ibid.
25 Ibid, pg 21.
26 Ibid.
27 Ibid.
28 Ibid, pgs 21–2.
29 Ibid, pg 22.

The Austrian School's Entrepreneurial Coordination versus the Chicago School's General and/or Partial Equilibrium

Through a much broader contextual association with the above, while in Austrian School equilibrium models, '*Entrepreneurship*' represents a very '*strong coordinating force*', in Chicago School equilibrium models, entrepreneurial coordination is usually ignored if not totally non-existent. Furthermore, for the Austrians and in empirical terms, the '*coordinating nature of entrepreneurship is the only factor which makes it possible for economic theory to exist as a science, understood as a theoretical corpus of laws of coordination which explain the social processes*'.[30] For that reason, whereas Viennese academics are mostly interested in studying the dynamic concept of competition (as a process of rivalry), Chicagoan theorists concentrate solely on equilibrium models, which are typical of comparative statistics, such as perfect competition, monopoly and imperfect or monopolistic competition.[31]

Neoclassical academics have turned the model of equilibrium into the central aspect of their research. Within such model, all information is assumed to be '*given*' (whether in dependent or absolute terms), and the different variables involved are perfectly adjusted. Conversely, for heterodox academics, the utilization of that methodology has an inherent flaw, rooted in its given assumption that all variables and parameters involved are perfectly adjusted, which in turn gives way to erroneous conclusions being easily drawn over the cause-effect relationships between different economic concepts and phenomena. That way, 'equilibrium' acts as a sort of '*veil*', which does not allow the theorist to discover the true existing direction between the cause-effect relationships in economic laws. The Chicago School holds that laws of tendency do not go in one single direction, and that what instead actually exists '*is a mutual (circular) determination between the different phenomena, the initial origin of which (human action) remain concealed or is considered of no interest*'.[32]

Seen through the prism of the Austrian School, the entrepreneurial force creates and transmits information, but above all and more importantly, '*drives the coordination between the unadjusted behaviours of agents in society*'.[33] In reality, all social discoordination becomes an opportunity for gaining, which remains latent until entrepreneurs discover it. Once an entrepreneur perceives that there is an opportunity of making profit and acts to take advantage of it, the opportunity then disappears, thus provoking a '*spontaneous process of coordination*', which explains the tendency within market economies of attaining equilibrium.[34]

30 Ibid, pgs 23–4.
31 Ibid, pg 24.
32 Ibid, pg 27.
33 Ibid, pg 24.
34 Ibid.

Mises strongly held that it is pointless to construct science based on the model of equilibrium, which assumes that all relevant information for defining the corresponding functions of supply and demand is considered as '*given*'. His unwavering thesis emphasized that economics is based on studying '*the dynamic process of social coordination in which the different individuals are continually generating new information (which is never "given") when they seek the ends and means that they consider relevant in the context of each action in which they are involved, thus establishing, without realising it, a spontaneous process of coordination*'.[35] While within the Viennese paradigm the basic economic problem is not about the maximization of a known target function, subject to constraints that are also known, within the Chicagoan model, economic problems are conceived as technical or technological, '*when they assume that the ends and means are "given" and pose the economic problem as if it were a mere technical problem of maximization*'.[36] For heterodox scholars, everything is strictly economic. In other words, '*it emerges when there are many ends and means competing among themselves, when knowledge of them is neither given nor constant, but is dispersed over the minds of innumerable human beings who are continually creating and generating it ex novo and, therefore, all the possible alternatives which exist, all those which will be created in the future, and the relative intensity with which each of them will be pursued cannot even be known*'.[37]

In general, the Austrian entrepreneurial coordination model is regarded as much wider, deeper, richer and more explicative of real-life economic interactions and phenomena than the Chicagoan equilibrium model, wherein the social reality is merely a specific case of relative minor importance. Viennese academics reflect that '*it is necessary to realize that even what appear to be merely maximizing or optimizing human actions always have an entrepreneurial component, since the actor involved in them must have realized previously that this course of action, which is so automatic, mechanical and reactive, is the most advisable in the specific circumstances in which he has found himself*'.[38]

In that sense, a last and very transcending diverging aspect between the Austrian and Chicago Schools is related to microeconomics and macroeconomics. While the Viennese dimension juxtaposes and interrelates the two areas, treating them as one single homogenous field, the Chicagoan dimension separates microeconomics and macroeconomics, positing them in two different, hermetically sealed compartments. Due to such reasons, while the heterodox methodology is considered much more comprehensive, all-inclusive, accurate and technical, the neoclassical methodology is viewed as much more superficial, vague and unprecise. For the heterodox school, '*economic problems should be studied together on an inter-related basis, without distinguishing between their micro and macro components. The radical separation*

[35] Ibid, pg 25.
[36] Ibid.
[37] Ibid.
[38] Ibid.

between the "micro" and "macro" aspects of economic science is one of the most characteristic insufficiencies of modern introductory manuals and textbooks on political economy'.[39] Whereas heterodox theorists provide a wholly and unified approach and treatment of economic problems, neoclassical economists always tackle and present economic science as divided into two very differing and unconnected disciplines – microeconomics and macroeconomics – which are disassociated between them, and therefore, studied as individually and unrelatedly. In accordance with Mises, *'this separation originates from the use of concepts which, like the general price level, ignore the application of the subjective and marginalist theory of value to money and continue anchored in the pre-scientific stage of economics, when it was still attempted to make analyses in terms of global classes or aggregates of goods, rather than in terms of incremental or marginal units of them'.*[40]

The Austrian and the Chicago School's Differing Monetary Theories

A last key area of extreme divergence between the Austrian and the Chicago Schools is related to '*Monetary Theory*' or '*Monetarism*'. Ever since Friedman provided the Chicago School with its main defining monetary characteristic, the school has become to be known as the 'monetarist school', with its Friedmanite aggressive monetarist thought and policies, distinguishing it very predominantly. For Friedman, *'economics is pure macroeconomics, with the national government as the one unit, the one dynamic force, controlling the economy through the money supply. Friedman's economics are completely demand-focused. Money and credit are the pervasive, and indeed the only, economic reality. That Friedman sees money supply as original and interest rates as derivative, is not much more than minor gloss on the Keynesian scriptures'.*[41]

While Austrian analysts firmly believe in the connection between monetary effects and social phenomena, Chicagoan experts claim that such link is not absolute, strongly sustaining that the money supply should be kept in equilibrium with the money demand.[42] Whereas, in general, most Viennese researchers are in favour of the complete abolition of central banks and the creation of a specific currency for free markets, like a 100 per cent gold standard, Chicagoan scholars are against the entrustment of the money supply to the market, although they, however, favour central banks issuing fiat money. For Chicago school's academics, central planning money is not considered as a problem, but rather as a solution to banking sector crises.[43] Whilst

39 Ibid, pg 26.

40 Ibid.

41 Ludwig von Mises Institute. HUERTA DE SOTO, J. *The Difference between Austrians and Everyone Else – In One Easy Chart,* pg 2. https://mises.org/wire/difference-between-austrians-and-everyone-else-%E2%80%94-one-easy-chart

42 Ibid, pg 4.

43 Ludwig von Mises Institute. BAGUS, P. *Why Austrians Are Not Neoliberals,* pg 6. https://mises.org/library/why-austrians-are-not-neoliberals

for heterodox theorists, money affects production processes through the modification of the structure of relative prices, for neoclassical economists, money affects the general level of prices.[44]

Although both the Austrian and the Chicago Schools apply the same type of macroeconomic methodology to the economy, Chicagoan analysts lack a general theory of capital or capital theory. For Viennese experts, '*monetary assaults*' on the economy, like credit expansion, explain the system's endogenous tendency to move away from equilibrium and drift '*towards an unsustainable path*'. Whereas for Austrians, '*the capital supply structure tends to be incompatible with economic agents' demand for consumer goods and services*',[45] they nonetheless also hold that '*certain inexorable, microeconomic forces, driven by entrepreneurship, the desire for profit, and variations in relative prices, tend to reverse the unbalancing effects of expansionary processes and return coordination to the economy*'.[46]

In other words, heterodox researchers believe that money, whether in the short, middle or long run, is never neutral, and that institutions that deal with it, like most particularly, banks, '*must be founded on universal legal principles which prevent a "falsification" of relative prices due to strictly monetary factors*',[47] as '*such falsifications lead to the widespread malinvestment of resources, and inevitably, to crisis and recession*'.[48] In direct opposition to neoclassical academics, heterodox academics consider that a sound macroeconomic policy must adhere to the three following fundamental principles: '*a) the quantity of money must remain as constant as possible (i.e., as in a pure gold standard), and credit expansion must be particularly avoided; b) every attempt should be made to insure that the relative prices of different goods, services, resources, and factors of production remain flexible. In general the greater the credit and monetary expansion, the more rigid relative prices will tend to be, the more people will fail to recognize the true cost of a lack of flexibility, and the more corrupt the habits of economic agents will become*';[49] and lastly, that '*c) when economic agents enter into long-term contracts negotiated in monetary units, they must be able to adequately predict changes in the purchasing power of money*'.[50]

For Austrian theorists, while money represents the most marketable good people can acquire, for Chicagoan economists, the principal '*function of money is the measure of values*'. Viennese analysts strongly reject the Chicagoan quantity theory or monetary

44 Ludwig von Mises Institute. HUERTA DE SOTO, J. *The Difference between Austrians and Everyone Else – In One Easy Chart*, pg 3. https://mises.org/wire/difference-between-austrians-and-everyone-else-%E2%80%94-one-easy-chart
45 Ibid.
46 Ibid, pgs 3–4.
47 Ibid.
48 Ibid.
49 Ibid, pg 4.
50 Ibid.

Table 2 The Austrian and the Chicago School's Contrasting Approaches to Economics

The Austrian School (Heterodox)	***The Chicago School (Neoclassical/Orthodox and Monetarist)***
1. Time plays an essential role.	1. The influence of time is ignored.
2. 'Capital' is viewed as a *heterogenous* set of capital goods which receive constant wear and must be replaced.	2. Capital is viewed as a *homogenous* set which *reproduces* on its own.
3. The production process is *dynamic* and is divided into *multiple vertical* stages.	3. There is a notion of a one-dimensional, *horizontal* productive structure in *equilibrium* (circular flow of income).
4. Money affects the process by modifying the structure of *relative* prices.	4. Money affects the *general* level of prices. Changes in relative prices are not considered.
5. Macroeconomic phenomena are explained in *microeconomic* terms (variations in relative prices).	5. *Macroeconomic aggregates* prevent the analysis of underlying microeconomic factions (malinvestments).
6. Austrians hold a theory of on the *endogenous* causes of economic crises which explain their *recurrent* nature (corrupt institutions: fractional-reserve banking and artificial credit expansion).	6. An endogenous theory of cycles is lacking. Crises have *exogenous* causes (psychological, technological and/or errors in monetary policy).
7. Austrians hold an elaborate *capital theory* (structure of production).	7. A theory of capital is lacking.
8. *Saving* plays a decisive role. It causes a *longitudinal* change in the productive structure and determines the sort of technology to be used.	8. Saving is not important. Capital reproduces *laterally* (more of the same), and the *production function* is fixed and is determined by the state of technology.
9. There is an *inverse* relationship between the demand for capital goods and the demand for consumer goods. All investment requires saving and thus a temporary relative drop in consumption.	9. The demand for capital goods is *directly* related to the demand for consumer goods.
10. It is assumed that production costs are *subjective* and not predetermined.	10. Production costs are *objective*, real and predetermined.
11. Market prices tend to determine production costs, not *vice versa*.	11. Historical costs of production tend to determine market prices.
12. The interest rate is a market price determined by subjective valuations of time preference. The interest rate is used to arrive at the present value (toward which the market price of each capital good tends) by discounting its expected future flow of returns.	12. The interest rate tends to be determined by marginal productivity or efficiency of capital, understood as the internal rate discount at which the expected flow returns is equal to the historical cost of producing each capital good (which is considered invariable and predetermined). The short-term interest rate is believed to have a predominantly monetary origin.

Source: Ludwig von Mises Institute. HUERTA DE SOTO, J. *The Difference between Austrians and Everyone Else – In One Easy Chart*, pg 4.https://mises.org/wire/difference-between-austrians-and-everyone-else-%E2%80%94-one-easy-chart

supply and demand equilibrium model, as they consider it both a '*manifestation of holistic thought*' and a mere instrument for government intervention. Whereas for heterodox experts money is never either '*idle*' nor '*in circulation*', with someone always in possession of it or in control of it, for neoclassical researchers, money has always been criticized for its '*lack of stability, which frustrates accurate measurement and thereby precipitated grievous economic and social evils*'.[51] From one perspective, the Austrian School considers the demand for money under the same terms as all other goods and services, and in order to acquire money, people expend labour and give up the enjoyment of goods and services. By doing so, '*individual demand and supply ultimately determine the purchasing power of money in the same way as they determine the mutual exchange ratios of all other goods*'.[52] For the Austrians, the quantity theory of money is basically another example of the general theory of demand and supply. From another perspective, the Chicago School holds monetary instability responsible for the business cycles, which have repeatedly caused havoc on market economies. Neoclassical scholars strongly believe that '*if only the price level could be stabilized and thus money be permitted to serve its true function*'.[53]

Whereas for Austrian School academics money is a marketable commodity just like silver or gold, having become a widely accepted medium of exchange, for Chicago School theorists, money is a governmental product, created and managed in accordance with some rule of the game, decided upon by way of political process. From one standpoint, for Austrian economists, money is just a product of trade entered upon voluntarily by individuals, with banknotes and demand deposits merely representing substitutes that only become valuable through money itself. Heterodox analysts abhor governmental seizures of commodity money and its substitution with fiat money, which are always '*characterized by rapid inflation and depreciation*'.[54] In fact, one of the main reasons behind their advocacy of the orthodox gold standard is that it actually makes the value of money independent from government, since the quantity of existing gold is autonomous of the wishes and manipulations of government officials, politicians, parties and pressure groups.[55] From another standpoint, although neoclassical experts condemn the gold standard unanimously, they, however, favour government fiat money '*on purely scientific grounds*', and at the same time also '*pay lip service*' to monetary freedom. Ironically, while Friedman would equally support buying gold and utilizing it in all economic exchanges, he would conversely also levy a fiat standard.[56]

51 Reason.com. SENNHOLZ, H. *Chicago Monetary Tradition in the Light of Austrian Theory*, pg 12. https://reason.com/1971/10/01/chicago-monetary-tradition-in
52 Ibid.
53 Ibid.
54 Ibid, pgs 14–15.
55 Ibid, pg 15.
56 Ibid.

Part Two

Dimensions of Ordoliberal and Neoliberal Practice

Dimension One

The German Wirtschaftswunder: *Ordoliberalism and the West German Social Market Economy*

8

The Role of the Freiburg School and Ordoliberalism in West Germany's Reconstruction

Throughout the years 1933 to 1945, although there were many differing strands of economic thought flowing through Germany, ordoliberalism gradually gained more and more admiration and status, most especially regarding the diverging ideas of the members of the Freiburg School related to how to transition from a wartime economy to a peacetime economy.[1]

One issue all members of the Freiburg School however agreed on was the need of a (permanent) order – the market economy – having to be introduced in a gradual way (a transitional order), rather than in an abrupt manner. During the 1940s–50s, the *'Freiburg Imperative'* was therefore chosen to achieve and establish in West Germany, a lasting, free and humane economic and social order. The main key feature, behind the success of West Germany's social market economy and the German Economic Miracle, was the Freiburg School and its team of ordoliberal economists, many of who occupied very influential positions during the years of the country's post-war re-construction.[2]

> *The modern market economy which we seek to build should have a decidedly social constitution. Its social character is based primarily on the fact that it is able to offer a greater and more varied quantity of goods at prices determined by the demands of the consumer, the resulting low prices raising the real value of wages and thereby permitting a greater and more extensive satisfaction of human needs.*[3]

Out of the two ordoliberal variants of the Freiburg School – the early concept of ordoliberalism and its theory of economic orders, and the later developed concept of sociological ordoliberalism – it was the latter, sociological type, which finally gave shape and form to the social market economy that produced the much acclaimed *'Wirtschaftswunder'* or *'Economic Miracle'*. In contrast to the Freiburg School's legal-economic constitutionalism, the sociological slant, largely based on philosophy of

[1] Between 1920 and 1950, amongst others, *'Paleoliberalism'* (extreme political liberalism) was another heterodox current that flowed vigorously through Germany.

[2] The European Journal of the History of Economic Thought. Volume 1. 1993 – Issue 1. RIETER, H. and SHMOLTZ, M. *The Ideas of German Ordoliberalism 1938–45: Pointing the Way to a New Economic Order.*

[3] TRIBE, K. *Ordoliberalism and the Social Market Economy*, pg 1.

history, historical sociology and a piercing cultural critique, moulded and outlined the social market economy. Likewise, both of the social market economy's differing conceptions of the *'social'* dimension, embodied by the liberal conservative version and the social democratic variant, also played a key role in the whole process. On one hand, the influence of Röpke's first liberal conservative version is clearly reflected in Ludwig Erdhard's written work and speeches. On the other hand, Müller-Armack's second social democratic stance and its conception of *'Social Irenics'*, reconciling theoretical opposites like liberalism and socialism and Catholic social ethics with Protestant equivalents, are clearly mirrored in post-Second World War Germany's *'irenic order'*, which perfectly balanced market freedom with social protection.[4]

Although in late 1947 Müller-Armack is credited with having minted the term *'Social Market Economy'* by the late 1940s, the idea that such an order should have a social framework was not novel at all. By May 1948, Müller-Armack *'had elaborated the term to cover a range of measures involving worker participation, competition policy, macroeconomic policy and social policy which, taken together, can be recognised today as a blueprint for the economic order constructed in post-war Germany'*.[5] While the majority of the Freiburg School's ordoliberal literature, such as books and articles, were published during the Nazi period, much of its remaining unpublished works, like discussion papers, were produced mostly during the war, although a certain amount of myth surrounds the latter assertions.[6]

Due to the time's German bellicose atmosphere, the production of some of the Freiburg School's work is associated with the wartime resistance to Nazism, although such assumptions have been proven to be inexact for a number of reasons. In general, most of the Freiburg Circle's deliberations were not considered subversive towards the regime, and in fact, many of the ideas forwarded by it were included in official discussions about Germany's post-war order. In addition, Eucken's *'Grundlagen der Natinalökonomie'* was first published in 1940, being praised at the time for pressing forward concepts for a *'new German economics'*, with even a third edition being published in 1943. What is more, one of Eucken's students, Leonhard Miksch, author of works, like *'Wettbewerb als Aufgabe'*, Heft 4 in the *'Schriftenreihe Ordnung der Wirtschaft'*, also wrote many articles during the war for the journal, *'Wirtschaftskurve'*, with the main objective of such publications focused on improving of the *'understanding, formulation, and implementation of official policy'*. Furthermore, and on one hand, Müller-Armack was actually a member of the NSDAP and provided advice on the economic reorganization of the Eastern *'economic space'*, created by the elimination of Poland and the invasion of the Soviet Union. On the other hand, in 1943 and 1944, people like Ludwig Erhard contributed to the discussion of the post-war economic order, organized through the

[4] COMMUN, P. (Dir). *L'Ordolibéralisme Allemande. Aux Sources de l'Économie Sociale de Marché.* SALLY, R. *Ordoliberalism and the Social Market: Classical Political Economy from Germany,* pgs 31–6.

[5] TRIBE, K. *Ordoliberalism and the Social Market Economy,* pg 1. https://jshet.net/old/annals/het47-50/4901/tribe4901.pdf

[6] Ibid, pg 2.

'*Reichswirtschaftsministerium*' and '*openly articulated arguments very similar to those that can be found in the Freiburg discussion papers of the time*'.[7]

Notwithstanding, it is evident that before 1945, although Müller-Armack's conception of welfare and economic efficiency became a routine post-war statement of social market principles, it was not one to have as such been hitherto unequivocally expressed before then. However, one factor that did express continuity from a pre- to a post-war economy was that the instrumental conception of the economy conveyed by Müller-Armack was actually underscored in 1937 by two features of the joint statement of intent, elaborated by the editors of the '*Schriftenreihe*'. The first of those features rotated around the idea that academics were '*independent of economic interests*' and that their recommendations were purely '*objective judgements offered to a strong State*'. Very similarly, economists were also considered as capable experts of providing government with unbiased advice on the formulation and execution of policy. The second feature revolved around the fact that such advisors favoured a strong government capable of producing clear policy, as well as of implementing it effectively and '*if necessary against the immediate wishes of a population who did not necessarily understand the wisdom of any given measure*'.[8] In such a context and in that pertaining sense,'*understanding*' had two different plains. Whereas the first plain involved that '*policy-makers should understand the impartiality and technical propriety of the advice they were given*',[9] the second plain included that '*subject populations should understand that any given policy was impartial and accept it without argument*'.[10]

In stark contrast to the neoliberal faction, who, in accordance to Hayek's '*Road to Serfdom*' mould, invoked the classical nineteenth-century vision of a '*minimal state and free economy*', ordoliberals favoured a strong state instead, since it was able to implement, sustain and withhold the type of regulatory framework that free-market competition required for the subjugation of monopolistic tendencies. Ordoliberals strongly believed in and thus implemented, a much more '*modern conception of twentieth century polity*'.[11] Whereas the Mont Pelerin Society was very successful in the creation of an international forum of '*liberal ideologues*', it was, however, regrettably unsuccessful in the pavement of '*common ground on the nature of state and economy in the second half of the twentieth century*'.[12]

Indubitably, the Freiburg School and its team of ordoliberal economists conceived and gave birth to a very individual and unique brainchild – the '*Social Market Economy*'. Thanks to the extremely rational, ordoliberal interdependence between a strong state and the legal-economic and social realms, West Germany was able to produce in just a few years the world-famous '*German Economic Miracle*'.

[7] Ibid.
[8] Ibid, pg 4.
[9] Ibid.
[10] Ibid.
[11] Ibid.
[12] Ibid.

9

The Americanization of the German Economy

Considering the destruction of nations, disintegration of cities, the overall loss of lives and property and the breakdown of economic systems, the Second World War was the most destructive conflict in history. Europe was the core of destruction, with people having no homes, shelters and barely enough food to subsist. The bombing of roads, roadbeds, bridges, plugged-up canals and blocked bridges further exacerbated the situation by making transportation and shipping seem hopeless.[1] The state in Germany was even more chronic, with allied strategic air raids having bombed cities into oblivion, which heavily impacted on the Rhineland-Westphalian or Ruhr industrial area.[2] Its drained national resources badly affected industrial system and the non-existent capital funds for generating income from foreign investment, characterized its quasi-paralysed economic nervous system. Germany seemed to be on the verge of a total and complete, mind, body and soul breakdown.[3]

On one hand, at the European level, the collapsed inter-European trade system, an acute shortage of raw materials and the emergence of the US-Europe dollar gap, made rehabilitation, rebuilding and reconstruction in general appear inconceivable.[4] On the other hand, at the German level, '*after World War II the German Economy lay in shambles. The War, along with Hitler's scorched-earth policy, had destroyed 20 per cent of all housing. Food production per capita in 1947 was only 51 per cent of its level in 1938, and the official food ration set by the occupying powers varied between 1,040 and 1,550 calories per day. Industrial output in 1947 was only one-third of its 1938 level. Moreover, a large percentage of Germany's working-age men were dead*'.[5]

The multi-dimensional and manifold investments carried out by the United States, however, soon turned the situation around. The fact that the European economic system was quasi-paralysed meant that one of the main international economic-

1 MAYER, H.C. *German Recovery and the Marshall Plan, 1948–1952*, pg 7.

2 NICHOLLS, A.J. *Freedom with Responsibility: The Social Market Economy in Germany, 1918–1963*, pg 122.

3 MAYER, H.C. *German Recovery and the Marshall Plan, 1948–1952*, pg 80.

4 NICHOLLS, A.J. *Freedom with Responsibility: The Social Market Economy in Germany, 1918–1963*, pg 160.

5 The Concise Encyclopedia of Economics. HENDERSON, D.R. *German Economic Miracle*, pg 1. http://www.econlib.org/library/Enc1/GermanEconomicMiracle.html

financial epicentres was missing, which in turn affected very negatively the United States' interests not only in Europe, but also across the whole world. The initial efforts that the United States put into West Germany represented a necessary pre-condition, for the generation via West Germany of a new united European economic system, as well as its subsequent super-imposition, onto the global liberal-capitalist economic order, the United States had envisioned.

Secretary of State George C. Marshalls' dual-perception of the Europeans' acute starving conditions, plus the emergence of the Communist bloc, led to his be-brothering demise and initiation of the, European integration '*Plan*', on 5 June 1948.[6] Economic reasons were also a key issue in the American venture, as the United States needed an economically strong and prosperous Europe, in order to sell to and trade with. The fact that an inter-European trade system did not exist, together with the inflation-threat imposed on the American economy, meant that her exports would fall from 13 billion to about 4 or 5 billion.[7] However, at a higher level than moral and economic reasoning and as Secretary of State Marshall affirmed, the plan's wider perspective was to synchronize and generate through West Germany, a European economic system of close co-ordination.[8]

While time, effort and money, infused into the W. German political, economic and social realms, rehabilitated and stabilized them for the realization of the American idea, the German nation's collective effort developed and continued those intrinsic changes. Very impressively, and arising like a phoenix from its post-war infra-human conditions, Germany's political, economic and social spheres experienced a gradual and complete infra-structural, structural and essential transformation.

The Marshall Plan

The first biggest step taken by the Americans and the Allied forces in West Germany was directly targeted towards getting the country physically back in order through the generation of the '*European Recovery Program (ERP)*', or most commonly known as the '*Marshall Plan*'. The three main objectives of the Marshall Plan focused on the promotion of industrial, agricultural and cultural production; the restoration of the consistency of European currencies, budgets and finances; the facilitation and stimulation of international trade growth; as well as the reduction of trade barriers amongst member countries and others.[9]

Thus and in accordance with those three objectives, the US and British military governments first began closely co-ordinating efforts in order to re-generate West

6 Ibid.
7 MAYER, H.C. *German Recovery and the Marshall Plan, 1948–1952*, pg 18.
8 Ibid, pg 96.
9 Ibid, pg 27.

Germany's economic life. Such a task was mainly achieved through the creation of three '*Landër*' (State) governments, as well as the set-up of a Bi-zonal Economic Council, under the economic directorate of the ordoliberal economist, Professor Ludwig Erhard.[10]

At the same time, Europe was also prospering quite rapidly. From 9 April to 30 June 1948, while the United States provided the region with 72 per cent of its agricultural products and 63 per cent of its industrial goods,[11] coal and steel industrial co-operation also gave much impetus to European industrial recovery.[12] Furthermore, from 31 December 1948 to 31 March 1949, the Economic Co-operation Administration (ECA) provided an increased and steady supply of raw materials, good harvests and an augmented labour output, which very quickly made ECA members reach their pre-war levels.[13]

From 1946 to 1948 and administered by the US Army, the Marshall Plan had already provided West Germany with US$478,000,000 ECA aid and US$135,500,000 GARIOA funds.[14]

One of the Marshall Plan's star reforms was the 'Currency Reform'. As a pre-condition for European economic recovery, the principle of restoring and equilibrating monetary stability was enacted on 20 June 1948, with a Bi-zonal Currency Reform imposed by the Allies. By mainly substituting the depreciated Reichsmark (RM) for a new Deutsche Mark (DM), the reform allowed DM6.5 for each RM100, with the six being meant for free use and the other half for blocked accounts or medium- and long-term credits. The reform caused a huge psychological effect on the post-war German people, since it gave them economic freedom to thrive and prosper, providing them with the essential currency base for a confident and constructive economic system to build upon.[15]

Although in September 1949, Europe was badly affected by G. Britain's 30.5 per cent devaluation, the economic epidemic did not cause a strong impact on the recovering economies. The US objective of an integrated economic system in Western Europe, without monetary barriers and tariffs restricting the movements of goods, was beginning to materialize.[16] In West Germany, an especially improved expansion in the consumer goods industries kept up the Bi-zones' developing pace, and the dismantling interruption of the 914 listed industrial units, when only 381 had been dissected, was even more positive.[17]

10 Ibid, pg 13.
11 Ibid, pg 29.
12 Ibid, pg 30.
13 Ibid, pg 31.
14 Ibid, pg 34.
15 Ibid, pg 35.
16 Ibid, pg 43.
17 Ibid, pg 36.

In the second year of the Marshall Plan, Europe had already managed to achieve a stable condition. From 1 October to 31 December 1949, Germany had received US $848,700,000[18] and its internal financial stability was good, despite Berlin's 25 per cent high-level unemployment.[19]

By 1950, Europe was permeated by an enhanced sense of community and unity against Communist imperialism.[20] With an increased French, Italian and W. German automobile development, the Organisation for European Economic Co-operation (OEEC), inspired by the Schuman Plan, began a series of unification efforts for merging Europe's Coal and Steel industries.[21]

During the third year of the Marshall Plan, from 1 July to 30 September 1950, an oil refinery project was drawn up for West Germany to be erected at Lingen, with a projected output of 600,000 metric tonnes of gasoline, diesel, oil and coke.[22] Between 1 October and 31 December 1950, Germany's industrial production level rose substantially to 110 per cent, reflecting a 37 per cent increase since the same 1949 period.[23]

From 1 January to 31 March 1951, Germany boasted a 34 per cent production index above its pre-war level, which was the largest in W. Europe. Although unemployment slowed down agricultural progress, its automobile output was up by 50–60 per cent, with foreign trade also increasing steadily.[24] During the period from 1 April to 30 June 1951, W. German industrial production rose another 21 per cent above its 1950 level, having the largest coal production figure at 13 per cent above the 1950 level. Due to the demographic increase, although consumption also rose 40 per cent above the pre-war level, agriculture, however, still advanced slowly.[25]

Counterpart Funds

Another crucial element of the ERP was the total Marshall Plan Counter Part funds, amounting to US$10,826,000,000, which were infused into sixteen countries for rebuilding their economic systems.[26]

18 Ibid, pg 46.
19 Ibid, pg 51.
20 Ibid, pg 52.
21 Ibid, pg 55. The French Foreign Minister, Robert Schuman's plan, provided Germany with equality vis-à-vis European unity. NICHOLLS, A.J. *Freedom with Responsibility: The Social Market Economy in Germany, 1918–1963*, pg 334.
22 MAYER, H.C. *German Recovery and the Marshall Plan, 1948–1952*, pg 60.
23 Ibid, pg 61.
24 Ibid, pg 65.
25 Ibid, pg 68. In 1950–1, ECA was forced to deviate from its original mission, adopting a more military-orientated economic joint-mission, with the Mutual Security Agency (MSA-1951-52). For 1950–51, West Germany was allotted US$91,700,000, although as the *'fourth year of the Marshall Plan was completely altered to divert the resources of European Nations to the needs and demands of NATO as an active defense operation'*, US foreign policy also deflected from West Germany. Ibid, pg 70.
26 Ibid, pg 85.

In West Germany, the creation of a cabinet ministerial position for the administration of funds reflected an expanded freedom in the fields of finance, with five banks and seven government departments administering those funds.[27] Whereas they were especially reserved for physical capital investment, they soon revived work spirit and ability, with the total amount of US$1,346,200,000 German funds being channelled in different directions.[28] The largest funds went into physical rebuilding of power plants, industrial plants, railways and agriculture.[29] For example, from July to September 1950, the designated allotment of US$84,400,000 mainly financed manufacture, farming, power plants and production stimulating projects. The rest was infused into workers' housing and tourism promotion,[30] with ECA also providing business firms with an additional US$38,000,000.[31]

European Trade Liberalization

The European Payments Union (EPU) created a multilateral compensations system for clearing and balancing all international trade between its members, which paved the way for economic integration, by developing a single competitive market, the convertibility of currencies and the reduction of trade barriers. In connection with OEEC measures, it all enhanced and intensified its members' sense of unity.[32]

Such bond was further strengthened on 18 April 1951, with the signing of the Schuman-devised, Coal and Steel Authority, between Belgium, France, Italy, Luxemburg, the Netherlands and West Germany. With its Executive Body being composed of a High Authority of nine member-states, the Court of Justice provided for the elimination of trade barriers (tariffs, subsidies and double-pricings), competition-reducing measures, regulation of prices, as well as sound employment practices.[33]

Technology

The infusion of American technology, together with a counter-balanced, open-minded absorbtion by the W. Germans, also contributed immensely to the modernization of developments and to the continuation of growth.[34] In September 1950, for example, Germany received US$17,400,000 for technical assistance, out of

[27] Ibid, pg 83.
[28] Ibid, pg 90.
[29] Ibid, pg 51.
[30] Ibid, pg 90. For example, out of West Germany's total amount of funds, 726,000,000DM financed housing projects around the country, erecting 600–800 units with the right to ownership. Ibid.
[31] Ibid, pg 60.
[32] Ibid, pg 37. Another OEEC objective was to reduce restricting private business practices, for stabilizing currencies and trade. Ibid, pg 49.
[33] Ibid, pg 66.
[34] Ibid, pg 95.

which 42 per cent was channelled into industrial areas and 15 per cent was steered towards agricultural areas.[35]

The ERP or Marshall Plan not only provided the basic ground-base for West Germany's physical rehabilitation, by providing gastronomy, commodity and service needs, but at the same time equally supervised and controlled the proper re-generation of individual currencies, as well as developed the necessary infrastructure, for a structured, proper and firm functioning of the European Trade System.[36]

35 Ibid, pg 60.
36 Ibid, pg 98. Total US quantitative infusion into Europe was US $13,365,400,000. Ibid.

10

Germany's Physical Reality: *An Economy of Bottlenecks*

Following Germany's unconditional surrender on 8 May 1945 and as a direct result of the Potsdam Agreement, on 5 June, five allies – the United States, G. Britain, France, and the Soviet and Polish – institutionalized the Allied Control Council in Berlin, in order to begin exercising absolute legislative, judicial and executive authority over West Germany.[1] While East Germany was put under the satellite control of the Soviet Union, the West was split into three United States, British and French, military control zones.[2]

From the perspective of its industrial structure, post-war West Germany was not that hampered, considering that 67 per cent of basic materials industries, as well as 60 per cent of basic goods industries, were still standing.[3] Likewise, capital goods industries had only suffered a 6.5 per cent loss[4] and machine tools were also abundant.[5] In 1945, adding extra strength to the robust industrial base, the Allies mechanized the iron and steel industries.[6] Additionally, the basic infrastructure of a capitalist economy, like banks, joint-stock companies, insurance firms, wholesalers and retailers, still existed, as the irrational war economy had not used its full industrial potential.[7] Furthermore, Germany's 1946, post-war capital stock, was at the considerable level of 8.6 billion Reichsmarks above the 1938 pre-war levels.[8]

However, and from a higher viewpoint, the image was quite different. In 1946, despite the seemingly healthy industrial structure, industrial production was at a low one-fifth of its pre-war level. Furthermore, many economic bottlenecks were also created,

[1] HARDACH, K. *The Political Economy of Germany in the Twentieth Century*, pg 90.
[2] MAYER, H.C. *German Recovery and the Marshall Plan, 1948–1952*, pg 13.
[3] HARDACH, K. *The Political Economy of Germany in the Twentieth Century*, pg 172.
[4] NICHOLLS, A.J. *Freedom with Responsibility: The Social Market Economy in Germany, 1918–1963*, pg 124.
[5] Ibid, pg 166.
[6] BERGHAHN, V.P. *The Americanisation of West German Industry, 1945–1973*, pg 64.
[7] NICHOLLS, A.J. *Freedom with Responsibility: The Social Market Economy in Germany, 1918–1963*, pg 2.
[8] DORNBUSCH, R., NÖLLING, W. and LAYARD, R. (Eds). *Post-War Economic Reconstruction and Lessons for the East Today*, pg 32.

due to its collapsed technological-financial infrastructure, an obstructed transport system, damaged power stations and an inactive communications network.[9] Post-War West Germany was thus unable to produce satisfactorily, with a low raw materials exporting capital influx of US$52 million from August to December 1945, $201 million in 1946, US$315 million in 1947 and US$642 million in 1948.[10] Exacerbating the situation even more, although by June 1946, 93 per cent of railway tracks and 800 bridges had been re-planted, the vicious winter of 1946–7 re-tightened bottlenecks, which impeded transportation and restricted food and fuel supplies.[11]

In addition, through the dismantling of about 914 plants and sub-plants,[12] the March 1946 '*Level of Industry Plan*' reduced the German living standard to its 1932 level, by reducing its absolute industrial capacity within 50–55 per cent of its 1938 level.[13] What is more, from 1945 to 1950, and further magnifying those restrictive post-war conditions, as well as the homeless problem, a demographic increase caused by the influx of 10 million Czecho-Slovaks, East Prussians, Pomeranians, Upper Silesians and East Germans[14] overcrowded the poor housing conditions of the Western Zone, which consequently affected labour performance negatively, which was at 40–50 per cent of its pre-war level.[15] Notwithstanding and in contrast, the industrial Ruhr area's coal production, with its skilled labour, was, however, allowed to expand for an external low-price enjoyment.[16]

At ground level, the Government Aid Relief in Occupied Areas (GARIOA) (administered by the American Army) had begun urgent physical rehabilitation of the Germans. Between 1945 and 1948, it shipped US$1,010,000,000 worth of food and agricultural inputs, like fertilizers, seeds, grain and flower.[17] However, and until 1948,

9 Ibid, pg 33.
10 Ibid, pg 97.
11 NICHOLLS, A.J. *Freedom with Responsibility: The Social Market Economy in Germany, 1918–1963*, pg 165.
12 MAYER, H.C. *German Recovery and the Marshall Plan, 1948–1952*, pg 44.
13 HARDACH, K. *The Political Economy of Germany in the Twentieth Century*, pg 93. In the Capital Goods sector relative to 1938: ¼ of the Steel industry, 1/3 of the Basic Chemicals and Engineering industries, ½ of the Cement industries, and 1/10 of the Machine Tools industries' capacities were allowed. In the Consumer Goods sector: ½ of the Textile-Shoe and 1/5 of the Automobile industry was allowed. Predetermined outputs were also established in: Car industry – 40,000, Truck industry – 40,000, Motorcycle industry – 10,000, Steel industry – 5.8 million tons being allowed. Furthermore, the production of oceangoing-ships, aircraft, synthetic gasoline and rubber, ammonia, aluminium and other light metals, as well as heavy machine tools was prohibited. Ibid.
14 MAYER, H.C. *German Recovery and the Marshall Plan, 1948–1952*, pg 99. Immigrants were gradually adopted into the W. German life and soul and began representing the human factors of Industrial production. Ibid.
15 HARDACH, K. *The Political Economy of Germany in the Twentieth Century*, pg 99. In the US and British zones, there was about 29 per cent of total housing damaged, with 18 per cent of approximately 9.3 million apartments destroyed. Ibid.
16 Ibid, pg 93.
17 MAYER, H.C. *German Recovery and the Marshall Plan, 1948–1952*, pg 25.

food rations remained low with an average daily fluctuating ration of food equivalent to between 1,080 and 1,550 calories.[18]

On 1 January 1947, the United States and G. Britain merged their zones into a Bi-zone in order to enhance economic development.[19] Notwithstanding, the state of the economy was deteriorating with a practically in-existent value of the Reichsmark, sustained growth, low industrial investments and authority-failure to maintain ration levels.[20] Furthermore, the overall widespread atmosphere of low morale and confidence also gave rise to black markets and barter deals.[21]

Nevertheless, and departing from such paralysis of life and economic inertia, West Germany gained impetus soon after, with the Allies clearly realizing that only political change would cause a complete reversal in the economic field, which made them place more emphasis on German economic reconstruction and integration.

Within the framework of European recovery, it became very clear that *'if Germany was to remain in economic chains, Europe would remain in drags'*. Germany's military occupation, divided territory and the disruption of its traditional industrial and commercial system, merely represented a necessary infra-structural rehabilitation phase for a subsequential rapid expansion capacity.[22]

18 HARDACH, K. *The Political Economy of Germany in the Twentieth Century*, pg 98.

19 BERGHAHN, V.P. *The Americanisation of West German Industry, 1945–1973*, pg 65.

20 HARDACH, K. *The Political Economy of Germany in the Twentieth Century*, pg 104. Its minimal legal value merely served to pay rent, taxes, utilities and fares. 'Cigarettes' for example, became a preferred form of currency. Ibid.

21 NICHOLLS, A.J. *Freedom with Responsibility: The Social Market Economy in Germany, 1918–1963*, pg 167.

22 HARDACH, K. *The Political Economy of Germany in the Twentieth Century*, pg 95.

11

Germany's Rationalization

On 20 June 1948, the Allied Bi-zone introduced a three-fold '*Reform*', which consisted of a Currency Reform, a Tax Reform, together with the Liberalization of the Bi-zone's Market.[1]

The Currency Reform

The Currency Reform is considered one of the chief stimulants, which eventually produced the German Economic Miracle. Through the contraction of the money supply, the Deutsche Mark (DM) substituted the devalued Reichsmark (RM). The new ratio of the DM, depending on its debt size, was scaled from 0 (public debts), to 6.5 per cent (bank-deposits and cash), to 10 per cent (mortgages and other public debts) and up to 100 per cent (rents, wages and prices). While at the individual level, people got DM40, in addition to DM20 two months later, at the firm level, shopkeepers, employees and the self-employed were given DM60. Between October 1947 and March 1948, the different public sector levels received allowances for their RM receipts of about DM2.4 billion for the states and communities, DM300 million for the postal service and the railroad and almost DM800 million for the occupying powers. Reflecting the market's real state, the devaluation of the old coins' former value to 10 per cent removed the '*veil of money*', thereby establishing the basis for price formation through firm accounting.[2]

The tax reform also much stimulated capital growth. The top 95 per cent income tax rate was reduced by about 1/3, and the corporate income tax rate lowered from 65 to 50 per cent. In contrast, although local tax rates were increased, tax conversion premiums were also given as compensation for saved and invested income.[3]

On 8 June 1948, the third reform liberalized a great section of the market, when the Bi-zonal government empowered Ludwig Erhard to abolish the system of price controls in manufactured goods and some foodstuffs.[4]

1 DORNBUSCH, R., NÖLLING, W. and LAYARD, R. (Eds). *Post-War Economic Reconstruction and Lessons for the East Today*, pg 2.
2 HARDACH, K. *The Political Economy of Germany in the Twentieth Century*, pg 107.
3 DORNBUSCH, R., NÖLLING, W. and LAYARD, R. (Eds). *Post-War Economic Reconstruction and Lessons for the East Today*, pg 3.
4 Ibid.

'On 21st June, 1948, goods reappeared in the stores, money resumed its normal function, black and grey markets reverted to a minor role, foraging trips to the country ceased, labour productivity increased, and output took off on its great upward surge.'[5]

The stable monetary system, created and imposed by the currency reform, was reflected by the June–27 December production increase (1936 as base year), the practical disappearance of parallel black and grey markets, together with the abundance of consumer goods.[6] The stable and anti-cyclical pre-condition for a subsequenvt production expansion was provided by replenishing the capital stock and infusing it into industrial repairs, the stabilization of working hours and the full mechanization of equipment and machinery. In the long run, the steep capital stock annual growth rate of 5.6 per cent increased investment through business profits, foreign aid and the public sector's fiscal surplus financing.[7]

The Solow Economic Growth Concept

Besides the Marshall Plan, the main underlying economic reasoning behind West Germany's economic recovery was provided by Robert Solow's economic development and growth theory. The theory holds that when wars or armed conflicts destroy a steady-state economy's capital stock, the level of output will undoubtedly immediately fall. However, if the saving rate (the fraction of output devoted to saving and investing) is unchanged, the economy will then experience a period of high growth. Output grows because at the lower capital stock, more capital is added by investment than is removed by depreciation. Such high growth will continue until the economy reaches its former steady state. Thus, although destroying part of the capital stock immediately reduces output, the subsequent growth that is generated will be higher than normal.[8]

For an increase in the saving rate, the Solow model provides the assumption that the saving rate is a key determinant of the steady state capital stock.[9] Such assumption rests upon the primordial belief that the relationship between saving and investment is only positive in the short-run, as a higher saving will enhance faster growth, until the economy reaches its newly desired steady state. The maintenance of a high saving rate in the economy will also support a large capital stock and a high level of output. However, while on one hand, such a high saving rate will not maintain a continuous process of high growth rate, on the other hand, population growth, technology and productivity will.[10]

5 Ibid, pg 38.
6 Ibid, pg 4.
7 Ibid, pg 7. Between July 1948 and March 1949, that was 1.5 per cent of GNP. Ibid.
8 MANKIW, N.G. *Macroeconomics*, pg 85.
9 Ibid. The logical contrast of such function also determines that if the steady state is low, the economy will have a small capital stock and a low level of output. Ibid.
10 Ibid, pg 86.

Table 3 Growth in Output per Person (% per annum)

Country	1948–72
Japan	8.2
West Germany	5.7
Italy	4.9
France	4.3
Canada	2.9
UK	2.4
United States	2.2

Source: GREGORY MANKIW, N. *'Macroeconomics'*.

Through Marshall Plan aid and the proper channelling of funds, West Germany was provided with the necessary savings and investing time and space, for a proper application of the short-run Solow Model economic growth predictions for countries whose capital stocks have been greatly reduced by war. The model's long-run predictions were in turn strongly supported by the demographic increase and pre-reform technical production.

From a global perspective, Table 3 reflects the success West Germany had in materializing such a theorem, based on the real GDP growth-percentage per person of the world's seven major economies, which even ranked much higher than its US benefactor.

The Political Economy of West Germany

On 7 October 1949, the German Democratic Republic was established in the West. The Occupation Statute of 8 April gave Germany more self-governing freedom, and on 8 May the Constitution was ratified. On 24 May, the Constitution came into force as the '*Basic Law of the Federal Republic of Germany*', comprising Berlin, plus ten other states. On 14 August, and following the '*Bundestag*' elections, the Conservative Konrad Adenauer was elected as Chancellor.[11] The Freiburg School's ordoliberal economist Professor Ludwig Erhard continued directing the economic administration,[12] thereby creating and establishing a new political and mixed-economic network-order,[13] wherein

[11] HARDACH, K. *The Political Economy of Germany in the Twentieth Century*, pg 106.

[12] Ibid, pg 143. Having been elected for this position in March 1948. Ibid.

[13] In emancipation from the Germans' absolutist Nazi regime, which had juxtaposed the political and economic realms in order to merely subject the public sphere to Cartel monopolists' private forces. MAIER, C.S. *In Search of Stability. Explorations in Political Science*, pg 182).

the national and local governments,[14] public entities, co-operative associations and the employed workforce, all shared equal ownership.[15] With the economic arena being vitalized by free entrepreneurial activity,[16] Erhard very successfully led the '*Soziale Marktwirtschaft*' or '*Socially Conscious Free Market Economy*', with the Freiburg School's ordoliberalism, forming its ideological basis, substance and rationale.[17]

In broad terms, the '*Social Market Economy*' was considered to have inherent free-market fundamentals and adherence to market principles, with the underlying ordoliberal interdependent basis, assuring a competitive economy, whose private benefits, anti-trust policy and social protection measures, provided for the evolution of a healthy, equal and spiritual society.[18] Despite its utopian aspirations, and at a lower level than economic reasoning, the '*Soziale Marktwirtschaft*' was forward looking, as well as comprehensive to West Germany's future. Instead of re-distributing wealth, the ordoliberal social policy enhanced the competitive system, which consequently increased the gross national product.[19]

In 1948, Erhard advocated the elimination of power-concentration and economic division, through the stratification of the '*craft industries and small businesses*'.[20] The basis of his policy was formed by the ordoliberal objective of allowing market-forces to regulate price-adjustments.[21] The by then complete W. German economic and socio-political transformation promised prosperous continuity.

The extremely economically sophisticated and refined contingency, formed by the Freiburg School ordoliberal academics and advisors, which conceptualized the '*Sociale Marktwirtschaft*' school of thought, had a very lasting impact on West Germany's political economy. Nonetheless, the new order, however, was not exempt from disapproval, and likewise faced much critique. While many Left-wing socialists claimed that the model's '*social*' epithet merely served as a cover-up for a Darwinian

[14] HARDACH, K. *The Political Economy of Germany in the Twentieth Century,* pg 106. The Federal Governments' big scope of influence had two levels for exerting its administrative control of the economy: a) state (subdivided into districts and municipalities) governments administrated domestic areas of police, justice, public health, education, cultural affairs, radio and television, as well as collected general property taxes on personal and corporate income; b) local governments collected trade taxes, landed property taxes and state budget contributions. The Federal Treasury took care of the rest. Ibid, pg 156.

[15] Ibid. In direct contrast with the 1930's National Socialism sole objective of National Power, and not worker-welfare. TEMIN, P. *Soviet and Nazi Economic Planning in the 1930s,* pg 592.

[16] HARDACH, K. *The Political Economy of Germany in the Twentieth Century,* pg 143.

[17] Ibid, pg 144. Other collectivist solutions for Germany's economic imbalances were provided by the Social Democrats, who advocated planning and the nationalization of major entities, the Christian Democrats, who preferred curbing capitalist excesses, as well as the Roman Catholic Centre Party, who were against free trade. NICHOLLS, A.J. *Freedom with Responsibility: The Social Market Economy in Germany, 1918–1963,* pg 131.

[18] Ibid, pg 145.

[19] Ibid, pg 394.

[20] Ibid, pg 158.

[21] Ibid, pg 196.

capitalist revival, many other Right-wing Paleo-Liberalists believed that the social tag was merely a sidetracking device for a state-directed economy.[22]

Regardless of such negative criticism, Erhard's free-price mechanisms, trade liberalization policies and consumer choice were a huge success. In 1950–1, the Federal Republic entered the General Agreement on Tariffs and Trade (GATT),[23] and in 1959 the Deutsche Mark became fully convertible.[24] The mid-1950s below 4 per cent unemployment rate also pointed to very much improved, standards of living. However, that objective as such had not been government policy per se, since the Conservatives' true and main ordoliberal economic objective was to maintain the DMs domestic and foreign trade purchasing power through a tight and balanced monetary and fiscal management, which rejected full employment policies. In fact, the 1948 resolution to allow the growth of the private sector in order to improve general living standards actually led to abysmal private wealth differences that polarized society. The little and slow distribution of income, the lack of economic diffusion and the undisciplined influence of interest groups have, in parallel with the Left/Right's fears, shed some ambiguity on the social element of '*Soziale Marktwirtschaft*'. Despite the impressive economic results, it is in many ways avowed that W. German economic progress more than out-balanced social equality.[25]

From 1962 onwards, the situation in West Germany began to really go downhill. While the Federal Government's capabilities were reduced by the development of permanent budget deficits,[26] by the 1965 election year, federal expenditure and revenue had become so unequal that Erhard was unable to correct it. Consequentially and ultimately, while in 1966 Erhard's cabinet fell, in 1969, the new Social-Liberal coalition was formed, thereby forever ousting the last elements and remnants of the 'Soziale Marktwirtschaft'.[27]

22 HARDACH, K. *The Political Economy of Germany in the Twentieth Century*, pg 144.
23 NICHOLLS, A.J. *Freedom with Responsibility: The Social Market Economy in Germany, 1918–1963*, pg 355.
24 Ibid, pg 322.
25 HARDACH, K. *The Political Economy of Germany in the Twentieth Century*, pg 178.
26 Ibid, pg 175.
27 Ibid.

12

The German Banking System

Since most especially, 1870 and 1890, the German banking system has always played an eminent and exemplary role within the German economy. After the Second World War and during the years of West Germany's economic reconstruction, such prominent role was further enhanced with the banking system and industry being closer juxtaposed, due to industry's growing concentration and the forming of trusts and cartels.[1]

In May 1945, after Germany's unconditional surrender, the branches of '*Big Banks*' continued operating through '*directing centres*' in Hamburg, despite the network's only weak basis of activity being the collection of deposits for boosting up their high cash liquidity.[2] In 1947, Law nº 57 of the US military government broke its Bavaria, Hesse, Würtemberg and Länder ramifications, on discovering that Big Banks had directly financed Nazis, like Heinrich Himmler, had contributed to re-armaments, had taken banking control of Aryanized property, as well as exploited occupied countries during the war.[3]

The re-designed and much more sophisticated W. German banking system's infrastructure (based on the American model) created and articulated a brand new independent and hierarchical system, for the control of monetary policy.[4]

Creation of the New Banking Network

In March 1948, the '*Bank Deutscher Länder*' or '*Central Bank*' was created as head of the new de-centralized banking network.[5] Ranking below it, the network's structure was composed of ten '*Deutsche Banks*', eleven '*Dresdner Banks*' and for the first time in the history of banking, – the innovative creation and establishment of nine '*Commerz*

1 EINAUDI, G. (Ed). *Rivista di Storia Economica*, pg 94.
2 Ibid, pg 96.
3 Ibid, pg 97.
4 Ibid, pg 98. Although the previous activities of Big Banks were suspended, they were not liquidated. Ibid, pg 106.
5 DORNBUSCH, R., NÖLLING, W. and LAYARD, R. (Eds). *Post-War Economic Reconstruction and Lessons for the East Today*, pg 3.

Banks'. Although Big Banks and successor banks were not connected by the system's structure, they were however inter-linked, for a very close and co-ordinated inter-relationship.[6]

Notwithstanding, in 1957, the '*Deutscher Länder*' became the '*Deutsche Bundesbank*', with the de-centralized system being re-centralized once again.[7] The new infrastructure's organizational set-up was much more subservient to Federal Government influence. In accordance with the ordoliberal necessary objective of maintaining monetary stability for a competitive market, while on one hand, Adenauer's government emphasized on stable prices, on the other hand, the '*Bundesbank*' prevented alterations on the DM's purchasing power from domestic and foreign trade inflation.[8]

Mechanization of the New Banking System

Following the currency reform, commercial banks received low-interest '*Equalization Claims*', which solved about 4 per cent of their Reichsmarks (RM) balances, as well as government bonds. Banks were given deposits in the Central Banking System, which amounted to 15 per cent of their demand deposits and 7.5 per cent of their time and savings deposits. A further 50 per cent increase in their new minimum reserve deposits was likewise scoped for credit expansion.[9]

The applied technique was based on channelling the supply and utilization of money, through the standard instruments of monetary policy (like open market operations, minimum reserve requirements and discount rates), so that the consequent alteration in the total flow of consumer and investment expenditures affected prices, employment and production.[10]

The new, post-reform banking system had three different levels for controlling economic branches and policies.

By the mid-1960s, and representing the top level of the new hierarchical system, the Big Three Banks (Deutsche, Dresdner and Commerz) managed nearly 1/7 of total

6 EINAUDI, G. (Ed). *Rivista di Storia Economica*, pg 106. Its inherent board of managers, additional consultative board and balance sheet drawing, reflected the independence of the successor network. Ibid.

7 HARDACH, K. *The Political Economy of Germany in the Twentieth Century*, pg 153.

8 Ibid, pg 175.

9 DORNBUSCH, R., NÖLLING, W. and LAYARD, R. (Eds). *Post-War Economic Reconstruction and Lessons for the East Today*, pg 3. On 6 March 1961, the threat of Germany's incredible export gains importing inflation due to the increased domestic supply of money, plus the fear that her external imbalance would disrupt the whole European payments system, caused a revaluation of the DM by 5 per cent, setting the new parity at DM4 to the $. HARDACH, K. *The Political Economy of Germany in the Twentieth Century*, pg 193.

10 Ibid, pg 153.

bank businesses, by controlling 1/5 of all deposits and loans and 1/3 of all sight and time deposits. During that period, they also owned about 2/3 of all bank holdings in other companies, as well as controlled about 70 per cent of stockholders' shares in about 400 companies.[11]

At a second level, agricultural and industrial co-operatives managed about 15 per cent of total banking business, providing credit to farmers and small businesses.[12]

At the bottom level, the '*Girozentralen*' or '*Central Giro Institutions*' operated as a clearing system for local savings banks, supplying loans to local authorities. The efficiency of the twelve Central Institutions, together with their competitive posture vis-à-vis Big Banks, made them gradually become full-service banks.[13]

Other banking institutions, such as the state-owned '*Industry Credit Bank*', the '*Equalisation of Burdens Bank*' and the '*Berlin Industry Bank*', provided loans to industrial and trading enterprises, as well as financed economic development in problem areas.[14]

The banking system's infra-structural changes, together with its concentration, were crucial for the achievement of monetary stability and equally further stimulated industrial concentration. With the Central Bank acting as '*guardian*' of the whole system, the scale of influence of the '*Big Three Banks*' on large businesses via voting or direct holdings, credit relations, stock and bond issues and representation on supervisory boards made them quickly become the '*prefects*' of the W. German industry and the '*helmsmen*' of the W. German economy. Today and at present, the Bundesbank's world personality still reflects the successful evolution of the new banking system.[15]

[11] Ibid.
[12] Ibid.
[13] EINAUDI, G. (ED). *Rivista di Storia Economica*, pg 108.
[14] HARDACH, K. *The Political Economy of Germany in the Twentieth Century*, pg 154.
[15] Ibid, pg 153.

13

The Industrial Sphere

The American objective of generating the industrial potential of West Germany to act as dynamo for restructuring Western Europe's industrial economy subjugated the German industrial sphere to a dosaged, present and future, material-structural reorganization. A structural and moral-political transformation also transcended its inherent lower level Labour realm.[1]

Industry

The July to August 1945 Potsdam Agreement results extinguished the Nazi material and psychological principle of order, so as to condition the ordoliberal economic arena, for the successful pro-creation of the leaders of European reconstruction, through *'economic de-concentration, industrial disarmament, de-Nazification and de-cartelisation'*.[2] Similarly and for the proper evolution of an ordoliberal democratic system, through a free and *'pluralist'* network of operating associations,[3] trusts and monopolistic and quasi-monopolistic enterprises,[4] all existing cartels and syndicates were totally eliminated.[5]

Whilst the total '*Level of Industry*' reparations only reduced the Western Zones' industrial capacity by 4.4 per cent,[6] the Rhur industrial area was *'de-concentrated'*

1 BERGHAHN, V.P. *The Americanisation of West German Industry, 1945–1973,* pg 103. Such alterations emancipated German Industry from its history. The Industrial development economic principles were completely new, and the German mentality and behaviour totally diverged from the American-incepted system. Ibid.

2 HARDACH, K. *The Political Economy of Germany in the Twentieth Century*, pg 91.

3 BERGHAHN, V.P. *The Americanisation of West German Industry, 1945–1973,* pg 41.

4 Ibid, pgs 94–5. '*IG Farben*' chemical industry's quasi-monopolistic character, was the first to be broken up. In May 1952, and as substitutes, '*Farbwerke*', '*Hoechst*', *'Bayer'*, '*Badische Anilin-und Sodafabriken (BASF)*' and '*Casella*' were created *'for the continuation and development of West Germany's chemical industry'*. Ibid.

5 HARDACH, K. *The Political Economy of Germany in the Twentieth Century*, pg 96. Power groups, big businesses, Junkers and the army had inspired Germany's power-based aggressive foreign policy. Ibid.

6 BERGHAHN, V.P. *The Americanisation of West German Industry, 1945–1973,* pg 77.

by decreasing the high production level of heavy industry in companies, like the '*Vereignigte Stahlwerke*' (which in 1938 produced 38.7 per cent of German steel), '*Friedr. Krupp AG*', '*Hoesch AG*', '*GHH*' and the '*Hannesmann Röhrenwerke AG*' iron and steel industries. The '*VSt*' was further fragmented into thirteen independent units, which together with the reduction of steel's control of coal by 11 per cent also eliminated linkages between steel and coal.[7]

On 24 February 1947, the Bi-zone created the peak industrial conservative association, '*Arbeitsgeneinschaft Eisen und Metall*', for the juxtaposition and subsequent elevation of the zonal network of the industrial organization branches to a supra-regional level.[8] In 1949, and as further connections, the liberal capitalist '*Deutsche Industrie- und Handelstag (DIHT)*' and the conservative '*Arbeitgeberverbände (BDA)*' were also created.[9]

With West Germany's total industrial production, being supplied by 7,000 large entities with a 200 work force, 35,000 medium-sized units with 20–199 employees and 60,000 small enterprises with fewer than twenty employees,[10] it was thus able to acquire a much more superior and progressive industrial development within Europe.

West Germany's Return to the World Market

The 1950s and 1960s were very clearly marked periods of German unparalleled growth and capital formation, with militant production reflecting much solidarity and working-class power. The United Economic Region of West Germany (member of the Organisation of European Economic Cooperation), together with the framework of the European Payments Union's (EPU), which removed trade restrictions and created an effective inter-European payments system, paved the way for the liberalization of trade. By 1950, Germany had removed 60 per cent of her imports' trade barriers and had an inflow of 45 per cent foodstuffs and 30 per cent raw materials.[11]

However, in 1951, with the outbreak of the Korean War, along with the 1951 payments-crisis, West Germany's economic bottlenecks were once again re-tightened, due to a raw materials shortage. Nonetheless, a crisis-induced Keynesian-like stimulus, owing to a reduction of foreign competition and an increased international demand,

[7] Ibid, pg 110.
[8] Ibid, pg 65. Including the organizations of iron, sheet metal, as well as metal and manufacturing industries. Ibid.
[9] Ibid, pg 68.
[10] HARDACH, K. *The Political Economy of Germany in the Twentieth Century*, pg 146. In addition, spreading-out the Rhine and Ruhr regions' industries even more, new industrial centres also flourished in Munich, Stuttgart and Frankfurt. Ibid.
[11] Ibid, pg 172. By August 1952, 81 per cent of trade was liberalized and by April 1953, 90 per cent was free. Ibid.

re-generated its armaments industry and uplifted its steel and machinery exports.[12] By mid-1951, Germany showed her first export surpluses.[13]

During the *'golden fifties'*, Germany's largest companies with internationally established positions, such as AEG and Siemens, together with Daimler-Benz's production of Mercedes, made her exports develop very impressively. The 1952 to 58 120 per cent rise represented Germany's first equilibrated trade-balance, with the Volkswagen company's '*Beatle*'[14] reflecting the huge success of the automobile industry, which enjoyed an increasing daily production of 30 units in 1946–7, to over 300 units in 1950, beyond 1000 units in 1955 and up to about 4000 units by the end of 1960.[15]

The State as Entrepreneur

Despite Germany's transition from an agrarian-based society to an industrially led society, the state's agricultural regulations reflect that there was a will to improve general welfare through that sector.[16] The main objective of the 1955 Agricultural Law was to provide a reasonably priced food supply, as well as to increase agricultural and non-agricultural income parity. Subsequently, prices and inputs were directly subsidized, the agricultural structure was improved through '*consolidation projects*', product marketing was mechanized, and retirement plans for farmers were likewise improved.[17]

The housing industry was also subject to regulations. However, the objectives to promote private building projects by providing tax and interest concessions, as well as to designate important budget funds for public housing constructions, induced the passing of the Construction Laws in 1950 and 1956. With deregulation beginning in 1960, a free housing market began to spread through Germany, although it remained narrow and required protective laws against overpricing landlords.[18]

[12] BERGHAHN, V.P. *The Americanisation of West German Industry, 1945–1973*, pg 262.

[13] DORNBUSCH, R., NÖLLING, W. and LAYARD, R. (Eds). *Post-War Economic Reconstruction and Lessons for the East Today*, pg 14. By the mid-1950s, Germany's export trade surpluses were so excessive that it caused huge complaints from international organizations. Ibid.However, internal imbalances were created by a limited production capacity in the clothing, glass, precision and optical equipment and electrical industries, together with a quasi-total lack of production in hosiery and gloves, as well as some textile and office machinery industries. HARDACH, K. *The Political Economy of Germany in the Twentieth Century*, pg 175.

[14] HARDACH, K. *The Political Economy of Germany in the Twentieth Century*, pg 189. Paradoxically, the '*KdF-Wagen (Strength-through-Joy-Car)*' was designed in 1934, by Ferdinand Porsche, under Hitler's orders. Ironically, it was Hitler who idealized the 1970's most renowned and popular car, – the '*Love Bug*,' – which also became the symbol of the '*Peace and Love*' counter-culture, as well as of the '*Make Love, Not War*' generation and hippie movement. Ibid.

[15] Ibid, pg 190. Which also reflected, an increased internal welfare. Ibid.

[16] BERGHAHN, V.P. *The Americanisation of West German Industry, 1945–1973*, pg 41.

[17] HARDACH, K. *The Political Economy of Germany in the Twentieth Century*, pg 150.

[18] Ibid, pg 151.

Likewise, the transport industry was equally put under state control for the prevention of an overburdened road network, as well as to *'secure an apt inland navigation transport volume'*.[19]

The state, nonetheless, continued with its traditional, pre-war parallel entrepreneurial functions, in the areas of railroads, inland motorways, airlines, most local transportation systems, telegraphs, telephones, postal communications and television and radio networks. Both Lufthansa Airlines (founded in 1953) and Volkswagen Works were completely owned by the state. Furthermore, through the indirect ownership of the '*Vereinigte Electrizitäts-und Bergwerks AG*' (United Electrical and Mining Co. Inc.-VEBA), the state controlled subsidiaries and produced coal, coke, lignite and electricity. With the '*Vereinigte Industrie-Unternehmungen AG*' (United Industrial Enterprises Co. Inc.-VIAG), the Federal Government's interests in the steel, aluminium and chemical industrial firms were also firmly held.[20]

The Labour Realm

In November 1948, the labour market was also liberalized, through the elimination of wage freezes and the restoration of collective bargaining.[21] For a progressive counter-balance between economic democracy and economic liberalism, the 1947 Allied De-cartelization Laws abolished the closed-space German '*Verbundwirtschaft*' (cartels) system, of horizontal, competition-limiting agreements. However, and in essence, cartel agreements exceptions were permitted for trade conditions, rebate rationalization programmes, foreign trade and structural crisis adjustments. Syndicates and quota arrangements also became extinct.[22] Although the agricultural, housing, transportation, banking and insurance sectors were not affected, a clear reflection of the anti-trust spirit that prevailed was provided by the fact that while in 1930 there were about 3000 existing cartels, by the mid-1960s, only 130 cartels were left.[23]

The ordoliberal political-economic-social strategy of inter-linking the Chancellorship and the labour spheres was realized by the co-determination principle, which saw the evolution of a socio-economic progressive state, through a consultation and

[19] Ibid.

[20] Ibid, pg 154. In addition, during the 1950s, the state owned and distributed 60 per cent of electricity and 90 per cent of gas industries, 20 per cent of national production of coal, coke, crude oil, pig iron and steel, 50 per cent of automobile construction, iron ore, lead and zinc production, as well as 70 per cent of aluminium smelting. It also had high interests in shipbuilding, housing and chemical industries. Ibid.

[21] HARDACH, K. *The Political Economy of Germany in the Twentieth Century*, pg 144.

[22] Ibid, pg 148. In German industrial history, 'Cartels' had always been regarded by both the governmental and academic realms as an '*element of order*'. Despite its authoritarianism, while special interest groups supported them, they also provided Labour job-security, as well as safeguarded small producers against market-extinction. Ibid.

[23] Ibid, pg 150.

interest representation system, which protected the social community against asocial un-democratic forces. Altogether and in general, a very closely coordinated market economy was put into extremely effective practice.[24]

The scope of Organized Labour's participatory economic decision-making was also further amplified.[25] Between 1947 and 1950, and extending Labours' social-influencing fields,[26] the eight '*Länder*' governments passed legislations extending co-decision and joint-consultation representation, as '*a co-operative economic order shall obtain an economic and social constitution which is commensurate with the rights and dignity of man, serves the spiritual and material reconstruction of our nation and secures peace at home and abroad*'.[27] The 1951 '*Iron and Steel Industry Co-determination Law*' provided parity in selecting supervisory boards, and likewise, the 1952 Works Constitution Act also extended social issues co-determination, although it restricted personnel and economic issues jurisdictions.[28]

In 1949, the '*Deutsche Gewerkschaftsbund, DGB*' (German Trade Union Federation) political organization, which was formed by sixteen '*umbrella*' constitutive units, covering a major industrial union system, was created as a medium for consumer interests.[29] The BDI, DIHT and BDA helped tremendously in filtering the structural and mental adjustment-evolution between labour and management.[30]

Whereas some public-law entities, like the Chambers of Industry and Commerce, Handicrafts and Agriculture, had governmental functions, other, private law, collective '*Verbände*' or economic associations, represented community interests vis-à-vis the government.[31]

Labour's hard and long industrious working hours, plus the fact that they did not pursue aggressive wage policies, proved to be key factors of reconstruction. Despite the 10 million-immigrant influx altering the state of housing, hospital, production

[24] Ibid. Thus ensuring peace in the Labour realm and refuting Paleo-Liberalist's claims. Ibid.

[25] BERGHAHN, V.P. *The Americanisation of West German Industry, 1945–1973*, pg 213. Co-determination's final structure was: In the Boards of Directors, out of three directors with equal responsibilities, 1 was a worker director approved by the Workers and Unions' Council. In the steel company supervisory boards, five out of eleven members represented entrepreneurial interests, five represented labour interests and one was neutral. On the employers' side, there were three trust representatives, one new-company representative and one public sector representative. On the employees' side, there were two Works council representatives (one white-collar, two blue-collar), two '*DGB*' and '*IG Metall*' union representatives and one public service sector representative. Ibid.

[26] LOCKE, R.R. *The Collapse of the American Management Mystique*, pg 61.

[27] BERGHAHN, V.P. *The Americanisation of West German Industry, 1945–1973*, pg 207.

[28] LOCKE, R.R. *The Collapse of the American Management Mystique*, pg 65.

[29] DORNBUSCH, R., NÖLLING, W. and LAYARD, R. (Eds). *Post-War Economic Reconstruction and Lessons for the East Today*, pg 11.

[30] BERGHAHN, V.P. *The Americanisation of West German Industry, 1945–1973*, pg 234.

[31] HARDACH, K. *The Political Economy of Germany in the Twentieth Century*, pg 157.

and hyper-unemployment, industry's workforce was increased, reaching in 1950 its weekly 48-hour level.[32]

After mid-1948, the job gains from the 600,000 expanding sectors much out-balanced the job losses from the 370,000 contracting economic sectors. In 1949, with 140,000 jobs being lost nationwide, the low-productive agriculture and forestry sectors lost an outstanding 350,000 jobs. However, the 26.3 and 17.3 per cent unemployment rates in the respective northern rural, Schleswig-Holstein and Lower Saxony States, contrasted with the urban-industrial North Rhine-Westphalia region's 4.5 per cent and the Baden-Würtemburg quasi-states' 4.6 per cent. Such factors clearly indicated that construction, high-productivity manufacturing and investment goods industries sponged the employment surge well.[33] Medium and small enterprises (SMEs), considering their strategic position within the private sector structure and their individual capabilities, also played a very important and relevant role during the whole process.

The post-war, labour market's re-structured organization provided, at the same time, a more ample field of action, as well as a wider scope of influencing participation.[34] Although from 1948 to mid-1953, real weekly incomes had substantially risen by 80 per cent, labours' share of national income did not increase that much, remaining at 59.4 per cent in 1954. However, through the 1951 Co-determination Law, the coordinated market economy interlinked German Trade Unions, employers and management associations, thus and therefore, making them '*social partners*'. Wage restraint and high-productivity likewise established a necessary calm and peaceful environment for Germany's recovery and transformation.[35]

Management and Technology

The strong interconnection between management and labour counter-balanced the market economy.[36] For a much improved, employee mental and spiritual attitude in the work and task of deliberating industrial growth, a sound understanding of the '*psyche of the masses*' was also developed, which thereby created a new management and labour co-operation system of industrial relations.[37]

[32] Ibid, pg 170.

[33] DORNBUSCH, R., NÖLLING, W. and LAYARD, R. (Eds). *Post-War Economic Reconstruction and Lessons for the East Today*, pg 8. The '*Baden-Würtemburg*' quasi-states were mostly rural before the war, although afterwards, they gradually became strong industrial ones.

[34] HARDACH, K. *The Political Economy of Germany in the Twentieth Century*, pg 157.

[35] Ibid, pg 170.

[36] BERGHAHN, V.P. *The Americanisation of West German Industry, 1945–1973*, pg 236.

[37] Ibid, pg 238.

Accorddingly, works Councils received scientific knowledge on work and organizational psychology,[38] and week-long seminars on *'Psychology for Working Unions'* were also given to work and personnel councillors, as well as to supervisory boards' members for lessons on role-playing and negotiation techniques.[39]

The Taylorist managerial control system's, *'will to work and to be led'*,[40] was clearly reflected by the static fusion created between the German army's inherent militant leadership training and American managerialism – *'Action through people'*.[41]

Whereas on one hand, Europe's *'mental revolution'* was transcended by American management ethics, methods and techniques,[42] on the other hand, the Marshall Plan infused organization, knowledge and methodology, for Germany's recovery and growth.[43]

Technology equally played a very central role throughout the whole endevour. The *'technical intelligentsia's'* economic-political socialization was also boosted, as it was foreseen that *'technology and economy will decisively contribute to shaping the future conditions of life and humanity'*.[44]

With the main objective in mind to *'transform distributive battles into the search for a shared abundance, and political problems into technical ones that were solvable ... by adopting American engineering production and marketing techniques'*,[45] West Germany spent $1.3 million on technical assistant programme trips. Consequently, it also spread their knowledge to the government, management and labour realms.

While the Freiburg School's ordoliberal social market economy managed to apply and maintain with clinical precision, the interdependence of orders, it likewise managed to generate extremely successfully, concerted actions' integrating measures, wealth creation, co-determination and social partnership, which altogether helped restructure the W. German economic system.

In virtue of such motivating efforts, together with the German nation's symbiotic mental and behavioural emancipation from its pre-war state and condition, as well

[38] LOCKE, R.R. *The Collapse of the American Management Mystique*, pg 86.
[39] Ibid, pg 91.
[40] Ibid, pg 83.
[41] Ibid, pg 1.
[42] Ibid, pg 17.
[43] Ibid, pg 10. Industry and Unions' pedagogical objective also induced W. German businessmen to travel to the United States, in order to study the American industrial system and the *'human-psychological'* aspects of industrial relations. Ibid.
[44] BERGHAHN, V.P. *The Americanisation of West German Industry, 1945–1973*, pg 301.
[45] LOCKE, R.R. *The Collapse of the American Management Mystique*, pg 51.

as industry's transformation from autarky to oligopoly, West Germany was able to experience a complete transformation. If the political realm represents the mind of a nation, with the body of the nation characterized by the economic realm and the soul reflected by the social realm, West Germany truly experienced an ordoliberal, mind, body and soul, metamorphosis. The very sophisticated and refined motorization of the United States' idea both created and very successfully generated the currently established, European multilateral liberal-capitalist trading system.

Dimension Two

Neoliberalism and the *Globalized Free Market Economy*

14

The Keynesian Revolution and the Neoliberal Counter-Revolution

After having suffered from both the Great Depression and the Second World War, a generalized state of extreme socioeconomic hardship, characterized by widespread depression and rampant unemployment, prevailed throughout most of Europe. What is more, the international economic system was lacking one of its main economic-financial epicentres, due to the quasi-paralysed European economic system, without which neither the United States nor Europe would have been able to survive for very long.

The United States, however, soon turned the situation completely around, while at the same time, enjoying seeing the rise of its military, political-democratic, economic and cultural hegemony, begin to flourish across the international landscape. The immediate post-war environment of chaos and disorder was very quickly replaced by a long period of very strong economic growth and stability, rising living standards and increased opportunities.[1]

The post-the Second World War period of economic growth and expansion, '*post-war economic boom*', or simply the '*long boom*', began in 1945 and it lasted more or less until the early 1970s oil crisis or 1973–5 recession. In view of the period's economic bonanza, it is also referred to as the '*Golden Age of Capitalism*'. Most particularly the United States, as well as some countries in Western Europe, the Soviet Union and East Asia, experienced extremely high and sustained growth levels, paralleled by full employment levels. Paradoxically, the world's economic upsurge was most especially led by some of the countries that had been devastated by the war, but who contradictory-wise to normal expectations, subsequently experienced economic miracles, such as West Germany, Japan, Italy and Greece.[2]

The revitalization of West Germany's economic prowess was very successful in the regeneration of the European economic system, which subsequently and in turn

1 George Mason University. Mercatus Center. *Economic Recovery: Lessons from the Post-World War II Period,* pg 1. https://www.mercatus.org/publication/economic-recovery-lessons-post-world-war-ii-period

2 Ibid, pgs 1–2.

likewise gave much life and vigour to the new international multilateral liberal-capitalist system. Whereas from 1945 up until the 1970s the recipes of British economist John Maynard Keynes were applied across the globe, Keynesian economics gradually became the leading theoretical influence on economic life in most of the developed world.

The *'Keynesian Revolution'* in economic thought was in a way intellectually automatically triggered in 1936, with the publication of Keynes's book *'The General Theory of Employment, Interest and Money'* (or Keynes's General Theory). By the end of the 1940s, Keynes's theories had been elevated to an ascendant position in mainstream economics. Keynesianism conquered the Western academic and political-economic world, probably as much as Marxism conquered Russia and China. In 1944, Lord Keynes was one of main architects of the practical and technical details of the Bretton Woods Conference, which helped create and establish the 'Bretton Woods System', which in turn provided the framework for the post-Second World War international monetary and trading system.

During the 1950s and 1960s, the 'Keynesian Consensus' and 'embedded liberalism' prevailed throughout the world. Most of the industrialized countries adopted Keynesian principles, mainly based on moderate governmental intervention in their domestic economies and aggregate demand-based policies. The period yielded high average global growth, high levels of employment, a huge reduction of inequality, the lowering of public debt, as well as much prosperity.[3]

Notwithstanding, from more or less the mid-1940s up until the 1970s, at the academic level Keynesianism was very influential, but, however, not entirely central. During the same period, but most especially from the 1960s onwards, the Chicago School and neoclassical economics, together with its neoliberal prescriptions, began brewing as a major theoretical force, which by the mid-1980s completely debunked Keynesianism. While some experts blamed Keynes for the poor economic performance which led to the 'stagflation' period of the 1970s, the incapability of his economic policies of stopping it gave more and more credibility to both academic and popular attacks on his ideas. Such a swift displacement of Keynesian thought was primarily driven by those who leaned more towards free-market ideals and principles, rather than by mixed economy policies that required a significant role for government intervention. The motivations of Keynes's opponents were mainly driven by an extreme dislike for big government, which was considered susceptible to excessive interference in the lives of citizens, by an intellectual preference for neoclassical economics, as well as in some cases, by the belief that the promotion of a limited role for the government would best serve their interests.[4]

3 HALL, P. *The Political Power of Economic Ideas: Keynesianism across Nations.*

4 PILLING, J. *Reactions to the Crisis of Keynesianism*, pgs 1–24. https://www.marxists.org/archive/pilling/works/keynes/ch01.htm

Ultimately, the Keynesian consensus and embedded liberalism were displaced by the neoliberal counter-revolution, which had grown very strong, comprising the efforts begun at the Mont Pelerin Society (MPS), together with the rising influence of the Chicago School's neoliberal prescriptions and Milton Friedman's monetarist formulae.

1945–80: The Keynesian Consensus and Embedded Liberalism

The 1920s–30s academic critique tackled hard the reprogramming of the classical-liberal creed on a pragmatic basis. The growing need for a solution to the spreading crisis of the capitalist system, together with its compatibility with the continued survival of the system, fuelled most of the groundwork developed by Keynes for his General Theory.

The '*new wave*' of international critics involved political leaders and economists from many differing economic backgrounds and currents, such as '*enlightened bourgeois thinkers*', '*socialists*' and '*Marxists*'. Within the prevailing context of depression and mass unemployment, a wide variety of sources pressed forward many proposals for major public works, anti-cyclical injections of public money and even for bank expropriations. Some of those included *"Germany's Doctor Schacht; the Belgian socialist Deman; the founders of the Stockholm School, backed by the Swedish social democrats; Fabian socialists and John Maynard Keynes in Britain; J. Tinbergen in the Netherlands; Frisch in Norway; the Groupe X-crise in France; Mexican president Lazaro Cardenas (1935–1940); adepts of Peronism in the Argentina of the 1930s and US president Roosevelt (elected in November 1932) and his New Deal"*.[5]

The entire range of proposals and pragmatic policies was partially included in Keynes's General Theory. Keynes had been involved in politics since the First World War, when he had been employed by the British Exchequer and had participated actively in the negotiations of the Treaty of Versailles, although he ended up resigning due to his extreme displeasure with the harshness of the impositions set on Germany. In 1919, Keynes wrote '*The Consequences of the Peace*', and in 1929, with the Wall Street crash deepening the economic crisis, he produced a profound analysis of employment, interest and money, which reinforced his conviction that there should be more state interventionism. Keynes very strongly believed that '*to compensate for the shortfall in demand, the state should increase spending in order to give a boost to the economy and employment*'.[6]

Although Keynes and his followers were convinced that the root cause of the Great Depression had been the breakdown of investment, in broad terms, Keynes actually

[5] TOUSSAINT, E. *The Keynesian Revolution and the Neo-Liberal Counter-Revolution*, pg 1. https://www.globalresearch.ca/the-keynesian-revolution-and-the-neo-liberal-counter-revolution/14376

[6] Ibid.

viewed the consequences of his policies as '*moderately liberal*'. Keynesian economics mainly rotated around an active role for government interventions in times of depressions and recessions, as well as advocated a managed market economy, predominantly based on the private sector. For Keynes, economics thus revolved around aggregate demand being volatile and unstable, strongly believing that economic policy responses, which can help stabilize output over the business cycle, can mitigate the market economy's often experienced inefficient macroeconomic outcomes in the form of economic recessions when demand is low and inflation when demand is high – most particularly, responses such as governmental fiscal policy actions and central bank monetary policy actions.[7] Keynes stressed that '*consumption and investment had to be sparked by strong state interventionism*'[8] and that wages should be increased to '*stimulate consumption*'. He held that if governments did not pursue objectives of full employment and greater equality, there was a big risk of either fascism or Bolshevik communism taking over. '*Economic policy should be geared towards reducing the high unemployment rate and distributing revenues in a more egalitarian manner*'.[9] For Keynes, economic policy should be directed towards the reduction of the high unemployment rate and the distribution of revenues in a more egalitarian manner. On the other hand, however, he likewise believed that government policy should be aimed towards the reduction of high interest rates, which channel vital resources into the financial sector. The main objective of lowering of interest rates was in order to favour the destruction of the '*scourge of the capitalist system*' – the '*rentier class*' living on unearned income. Keynes's recipes strongly highlighted '*the vital importance of establishing certain central controls in fields that today remain completely in the hands of private initiative, it also leaves a great many fields of activity in private hands ... It does not actually call for a system of state socialism that would subject most of the community's economic life to its control*'.[10]

From 1945 until 1980 more or less, the '*Bretton Woods system*', structured around the '*Keynesian Consensus*' and *embedded liberalism*', prevailed worldwide. While Lord Keynes is widely perceived as the most influential economist of the twentieth century, the Keynesian consensus is likewise considered as one of the greatest modern accomplishments in '*social design*'. Lord Keynes also triggered the switch from the established '*technobureaucratic capitalism*' to the '*socio-developmental capitalism*', which ushered in the '*Golden Age of Capitalism*'. The Bretton Woods system Keynes had helped design and construct, together with the 'embedded liberalism' it established, put into practice the first-ever international financial-monetary order in history. Following the 1944 Bretton Woods Conference and in accordance with the '*Bretton Woods Agreement*', the Bretton Woods system of monetary management established the rules

7 PILLING, J. *Reactions to the Crisis of Keynesianism*, pgs 2–7. https://www.marxists.org/archive/pilling/works/keynes/ch01.htm

8 TOUSSAINT, E. *The Keynesian Revolution and the Neo-Liberal Counter-Revolution*, pg 2. https://www.globalresearch.ca/the-keynesian-revolution-and-the-neo-liberal-counter-revolution/14376

9 Ibid.

10 Ibid.

for financial and commercial relations between the United States, Canada, Western European countries, Australia and Japan. The Bretton Woods system represented the world's first example of a fully negotiated international monetary order, based on fixed exchange rates, which was created and intended in order to govern monetary relations among independent states.[11]

The Bretton Woods system also produced a set of institutions in order to regulate its international monetary system, supervise rules and assist with procedures. It created and established the International Monetary Fund (IMF) and the International Bank for Reconstruction and Development (IBRD), or the World Bank (WB). At the time, and due to the United States controlling two-thirds of the world's gold, it therefore insisted that the Bretton Woods system be based on both gold and the US dollar.[12]

The system's key characteristics revolved around the obligation for each country to adopt a monetary policy that maintained its external exchange rates within 1 per cent, by tying its currency to gold and the ability of the IMF to bridge temporary imbalances of payments. There was also a need to address the lack of cooperation among other countries, as well as the prevention of competitive devaluation of their currencies.[13]

Until the 1980s, Keynesian fiscal and monetary policies were widely deployed in order to dampen business cycles and to assure reasonably full employment. The advocation of a '*class compromise*' guaranteed domestic peace and tranquillity, with states intervening actively in industrial policy and setting new standards for social wages, by creating diverse welfare systems such as health care, education and the like.[14] The new form of political-economic organization, or '*embedded liberalism*', signalled '*how market processes and entrepreneurial and corporate activities were surrounded by a web of social and political constraints and a regulatory environment that sometimes restrained but in other instances led the way in economic and industrial strategy. State-led planning and in some instances state ownership of key sectors (coal, steel, automobiles) were not uncommon (for example in Britain, France, and Italy)*'.[15]

Both Keynesianism and embedded liberalism made the state become a kind of '*force field*', which internalized class relations and allowed Left-winged political parties and working-class institutions, like labour unions, to have much influence within the state apparatus.[16] While, on one hand, the appliance of Keynes's fiscal and monetary policies successfully controlled the business cycle, on the other hand the activities of an interventionist state fostered a social and moral economy, which

[11] The Bretton Woods Project. *What Are the Bretton Woods Institutions?*. https://www.brettonwoodsproject.org/2019/01/art-320747/
[12] Ibid.
[13] Ibid.
[14] HARVEY, D. *A Brief History of Neoliberalism*, pgs 10–11.
[15] Ibid, pg 11.
[16] Ibid, pgs 11–12.

was sometimes further supported by a strong sense of national identity. During the 1950s and 1960s, 'embedded liberalism' in advanced capitalist countries delivered high economic growth rates, partly due to the United States' largesse in being prepared to run high deficits with the rest of the world and to absorb excess product within its borders. The *'system conferred benefits such as expanding export markets (most obviously for Japan but also unevenly across South America and to some other countries of South-East Asia), but attempts to export "development" to much of the rest of the world largely stalled. For much of the Third World, particularly Africa, embedded liberalism remained a pipe dream'.*[17] In general, active state interventions in the economy and some degree of development planning worked extremely well. *'Redistributive politics (including some degree of political integration of working-class trade union power and support for collective bargaining), controls over the free mobility of capital (some degree of financial repression through capital controls in particular), expanded public expenditures and welfare state-building',*[18] brought about relatively high growth rates.[19]

Notwithstanding, since before the Arab-Israeli War and the OPEC oil embargo of 1973, the Bretton Woods system of fixed exchange rates, backed by gold reserves, already found itself in complete disarray. *'The porosity of state boundaries with respect to capital flows put stress on the system of fixed exchange rates. US dollars had flooded the world and escaped US controls by being deposited in European banks. Fixed exchange rates were therefore abandoned in 1971.'*[20] Ultimately, with gold no longer being able to function as the international base of the global monetary system, exchange rates were finally freed and allowed to float, and soon after, attempts to control the floating were also abandoned.[21]

By the end of the 1960s, Keynesian policies were no longer working and embedded liberalism was breaking down internationally, as well as within national economies. At the same time, a serious worldwide crisis of capital accumulation was also becoming very evident. With the huge upsurge of inflation and unemployment, a global phase of *'stagflation'* (the simultaneous increase of both inflation and unemployment) was ushered in, which persisted throughout most of the 1970s. With the plunging of tax revenues, together with the soaring of social expenditures, the stagflation phase caused massive fiscal crises in various countries, with Britain having to be bailed out in 1975–6. It became clear that embedded liberalism was exhausted and no longer working and that different alternatives had to be found to overcome the crisis.[22]

[17] Ibid, pg 11.
[18] Ibid.
[19] Ibid.
[20] Ibid, pg 12.
[21] Ibid.
[22] Ibid.

The most widespread answer in the United States and throughout Europe was found in both the deepening of state control and the increasing of economic regulation through '*corporatist strategies*', which most especially in Europe, included '*curbing the aspirations of labour and popular movements through austerity measures, incomes policies, and even wage and price controls*'.[23] In the early 1970s, the United States, with Congress dominated by the Democratic Party, legislated a massive wave of regulatory reforms signed by Republican President Richard Nixon, which governed everything from environmental protection to occupational safety and health, civil rights and consumer protection.[24] Across Europe and in various countries, socialist and communist parties likewise put into practice innovative governance experiments: in Italy and in communist-controlled '*Red Bologna*'; '*on the revolutionary transformation of Portugal in the wake of the collapse of fascism, on the turn towards a more open market socialism and ideas of Eurocommunism, particularly in Italy (under the leadership of Berlinguer) and in Spain (under the influence of Carrillo), or on the expansion of the strong social democratic welfare state tradition in Scandinavia.*'[25] With the Left beginning to assemble more popular power behind such programmes, it came close to power in Italy, acquired state power in Britain, France, Portugal and Spain, and retained power in Scandinavia.[26]

By the mid-1970s, the Left had failed to go much beyond '*traditional social democratic and corporatist solutions*', having proved inconsistent with the requirements of capital accumulation. The overall effect polarized the debate between, on one hand, those ranging behind social democracy and central planning, and on the other hand, the interests of those concerned with the liberation of corporate and business power and the re-establishment of market freedoms. Nonetheless and from then onwards, the common interest of the latter group began to progressively predominate, and eventually, by around 1980, completely took over the running of international economics.[27]

The Neoliberal Counter-Revolution

Ever since the 1930s, when Keynesian policies had begun to be applied at the underlying academic level, the intense debate between Friedrich Hayek, Ludwig von Mises and many others had, at the same time, begun to swell much more. The 'new liberal' contingency thrust forward their set of ultraliberal ideas in fierce opposition to classical liberalism and laissez-faire, representing the main theoretical counter-reaction to Keynesianism, embedded liberalism and collectivism. Hayek and his followers were very against Keynes's state interventionism, also strongly believing that the main cause

[23] Ibid.
[24] Ibid, pg 13.
[25] Ibid, pg 12.
[26] Ibid, pgs 12–13.
[27] Ibid, pg 13.

of over-investment was rooted in slack monetary policies, and that both consumption and investment had to be lowered for the insurance of renewed full employment.[28]

Beginning in the 1930s–40s, Hayek and Mises spearheaded the neoliberal counter-revolution, which set out to demolish Keynes's state-interventionist proposals, as well as socialism.[29] '*Since 1945, in various academic and business circles, different projects have emerged simultaneously to bring together the qualified defenders of liberalism (neo-classical economics) with the aim of organising a joint response to the advocates of state intervention and socialism. Three centres where this post-War resistance was organised were: the Institut universitaire de hautes études internationales (IUHEI) in Geneva, the London School of Economics (LSE) and the University of Chicago.*'[30]

In April 1947, during the time Hayek was teaching at the London School of Economics (LSE), the Mont Pelerin Society was founded, very soon becoming established as the leading think-tank for the neoliberal counter-offensive.[31] Since its genesis, the Mont Pelerin Society was always perceived as a '*a kind of neo-liberal Freemasonry, very well organised and devoted to the dissemination of the neo-liberal creed, with regular international gatherings*'.[32]

Although initially the Mont Pelerin Society had little impact outside academic circles and on the wider world, during the decades following its establishment, it gradually acquired a very central role within an expanding network of over 100 pro-free-market think tanks located all around the world. With an increasing number of think tanks enjoying more and more financial support from a growing array of commercial interests, they collectively won increased acceptance for free-market thinking within academia and public opinion, but much more significantly so, amongst governments. While in the United States, two of the most influential free-market think tanks were the Foundation for Economic Education and the Heritage Foundation, in the UK, the most influential ones were the Institute of Economic Affairs and the Adam Smith Institute. After the 1950s, whereas Hayek left mainstream economics and went to work mainly on political philosophy, Friedman and other allies continued their work as economists, although at first only with marginal influence on the discipline as a whole.[33]

In 1956, the publication of Friedman's '*Studies in the Quantity Theory of Money: A Restatement*' marked an important milestone in Friedman's campaign against Keynesianism. Friedman's work both restated the '*Quantity Theory of Money*' and caught the attention of several Keynesian economists. Although Friedman admitted

[28] TOUSSAINT, E. *The Keynesian Revolution and the Neo-Liberal Counter-Revolution*, pg 2. https://www.globalresearch.ca/the-keynesian-revolution-and-the-neo-liberal-counter-revolution/14376
[29] Ibid.
[30] Ibid.
[31] Ibid.
[32] Ibid.
[33] Ibid.

that Keynes was right in stating that the velocity of the circulation of money in the '*Equation of Exchange*' can vary instead of being a constant, as assumed by classical economists, his restatement was, however, much closer to the classical view, which reduced the scope for beneficial government intervention in the economy. In 1963, Friedman published yet another even more influential publication, titled '*A Monetary History of the United States*'. Based on empirical data, Friedman's book further strengthened his previous work on the Quantity Theory of Money, by stressing that inflation was, at all times and everywhere, a monetary phenomenon, while conceding that it could take one or two years for an increase in the money supply to lead to inflation. With such publications, Friedman directly contested the prevailing orthodox Keynesian interpretation. His natural-rate-of-unemployment doctrine denied any long-run trade-off between inflation and unemployment, as modelled in Irving Fisher's '*Phillips curve*', which predicted an inverse relationship between the two variables. During that time, most governments based their models on the Phillips curve, in order to calculate the expected cost in terms of inflation for a stimulus designed for the restoration of full employment. Going even further, in 1968 Friedman published another very transcendental paper, challenging that the fixed relationship implied by the Phillips curve did not exist and that it was possible to have inflation and unemployment rise at the same time. Eventually, just as Friedman predicted in that latter publication, during the early 1970s, the simultaneous rise of inflation and unemployment led to the 'stagflation' period, which saw the definite refutation by Friedman of one of Keynes's main theoretical assumptions. Friedman had also argued that the expectations of workers of future high inflation could lead to an inflationary spiral, as they would press in advance for increased wages to try and compensate future expected inflation.[34]

Most especially after 1973, in the wake of stagflation, the Chicago School began to progressively rise with Friedman's challenging work gaining increased acceptance and recognition among academics. While in 1973 the global economy suffered from the inflationary shock caused by Oil Crisis, Friedman argued convincingly that inflation was much higher than it would have been due to the 1971 governments' rapid expansion of the money supply. By the late 1970s, mainstream economists accepted Friedman's hypotheses much more, when empirical data suggested that Friedman was correct to emphasize the role of expectations on inflation. Soon after, Friedmanian economics superimposed themselves over Keynesian economics. In a way, part of the reason for the intellectual victory of Friedman over Keynes was found in the fact that most mainstream economists of the time, or '*Neo-Keynesians*', completely miscomprehended Keynes's ideas, and thus, did not have any proper solid or consistent framework to rebut attacks on them.[35]

[34] Elsevier. Investigaci6n Econ6mica. PALLEY, T.I. *Economía y Economía Política de Friedman: Una Critica desde el Viejo Keynesianismo*, pgs 12–30. https://www.elsevier.es/es-revista-investigacion-economica-122-pdf-S0185166714709178

[35] Ibid.

The neoliberal counter-revolution, together with its strong emphasis on Friedman's monetary theory, had a key role in overturning the Keynesian consensus, although there were other factors that were likewise very influential. For example, during the 1970s, the Austrian School and Hayek enjoyed a parallel resurgence, with Hayek's thinking influencing key figures, like Margaret Thatcher, who later applied it to her policies. Other additional proposals which further reflected the contemporary anti-Keynesian thinking ranged from the '*Policy Ineffectiveness Proposition*' to '*Game Theory*', together with other arising ideas from the Cold War. All combined, they provided an increasingly stronger support for the theories Hayek had articulated during the 1940s, which thus helped them progressively spread out and gain more and more acceptance.[36]

By the early 1980s, the Keynesian-designed Bretton Woods system of fixed exchange rates and embedded liberalism had been completely switched, for the currently established, Hayekian free market economy and Friedmanian financial monetary system of flexible exchange rates. Correspondingly and in much the same way, the swing from the Keynesian Consensus to the Hayekian free market economic order and Friedmanian financial monetarist system, induced the mutation of 'socio-developmental capitalism' into its present-day, capitalist hybrid form of '*free market neoliberalism*' or '*stakeholder capitalism*'.

[36] Ibid.

15

The Multiphased Neoliberalization of the European Union

From the very beginning, neoliberalism had always and above all represented an ideological and theoretical agenda for a restructured capitalist economy and social system. The project was equally highly dependent on material forces and institutions, in order to shape expectations and norms so that they would be responsive to market incentives. Since it emerged, neoliberalism has been mostly considered a transnational project. Although from 1945 to 1980 the Keynesian revolution churned the world's economic machinery, it was, however, extremely antagonized by the neoliberal counter-revolution. The neoliberal uprise eventually generated both the gradual and multi-phased '*neoliberalization*' of the European Union (EU), and ultimately, the process of '*global neoliberalization*', which ended completely taking over the running of international economics.[1]

The '*neoliberal agenda's*' first objective was Europe. The European process of '*neoliberalization*' primarily rotated around different key planks, such as '*free*' trade, '*free*' capital mobility, monetary restraint and budgetary austerity.[2]

In broad terms, the European process of '*neoliberalization*' began with the creation of the EU, as well as the application of many subsequent multi-levelled European policies. The most predominant of those policies included the Single Market Project, Competition Policy, Economic and Monetary Union, together with the European Employment Strategy. All those policies had different institutional arrangements underpinning them, as well as broader implications.[3]

However, the idea of a 'single market' preceded both the foundation of the European Economic Community (EEC) and that of its successor, the EU. Throughout the Second World War, and henceforth, the idea of a single market already represented a very prominent issue discussed in many liberal spheres, most especially in the chief neoliberal think-tank, the Mont Pelerin Society. Nonetheless, during the immediate

[1] FORBA. FORBA Discussion Paper 3/2007. HERMANN, C. *Neoliberalism in the European Union,* pgs 1–2. http://www.forschungsnetzwerk.at/downloadpub/neoliberalism_eu_SR%2003-07.pdf
[2] Ibid.
[3] Ibid, pg 1.

post-Second World War years, economic planning and coordination prevailed, with neoliberal visions of unbridled capitalism continuing to be largely discredited by the still vivid memories of the disastrous consequences of the Great Depression. The huge success in West Germany of ordoliberalism running the social market economy and producing the German Economic Miracle served as an excellent prime example of the unique traits of economic planning and coordination. Likewise, the United States also went to great lengths in order to administer closely the European economic reconstruction, through the European Recovery Plan (ERP) or Marshall Plan. ERP funds were utilized to direct investment flows to the newly created Fordist industries, some of which were owned by US capital. Thus, while the gold standard was abandoned, the Bretton Woods system of fixed currency exchange rates was established, with Keynesianism providing the theoretical basis and practical instruments for national macro-economic coordination.[4]

Notwithstanding, despite the prevalence of the Keynesian Consensus, the neoliberal counter-revolution was at the same time, beginning to equally influence the minds of policy-makers, with its diverging ideas and notions. In fact, the neoliberalization of the EU, together with the policies delivered to achieve it, ran in very tight parallel to the mainstream neoliberal thought. Major policy issues, such as the Single Market Strategy, European Competition Policy, Economic and Monetary Integration, together with the European Employment Strategy, altogether enhanced '*free trade*' and '*free capital mobility*', monetary restraint and budgetary austerity, the flexibilization of labour markets, as well as the erosion of employment security. Since then, Eurozone member states have even gone further than the neoliberal front-runners, the United States and the UK, in enacting the neoliberal agenda in other different key areas, like monetary and fiscal policies.[5]

The European Union's Single Market Strategy

Initially, the huge success of ordoliberalism in West Germany greatly influenced both the Schuman Plan and the foundation of the European Coal and Steel Community (ECSC). The two of them were actually inspired by the notion of coordination and cooperation, rather than by market-mediated competition. The 1957 signature of the Treaties of Rome, together with the establishment of the EEC, consummated that first impulse. The Treaty of Rome created an institutional framework and paved the way for the establishment of the Single European Market, with its Article 3, affirming the commitment of member states to the creation of a '*common market free from distortions to competition*', such as tariffs and quotas. The free movement of capital, individuals and services, was left subjected to various restrictions. Despite that by the

[4] Ibid, pg 8.
[5] Ibid, pg 23.

late 1960s, the European Customs Union had been finalized, '*nothing like a common market, in which complete factor mobility exists, came into being during the early years of the Community. An economic union, with unified monetary and fiscal policies, was not even on the radar screen*'.[6]

Although by 1965, the ECSC, the EEC and the Euratom were merged into the European Communities (EC), the deepening of the common market was still quite limited, with the integration process being constinously hampered by the reluctance of member states to cede more competencies to the increasingly powerful European Commission (EC, or the Commission). Only after 1986, with the adoption of the Single European Act (SEA), did the single market issue begin to be seriously included in the European agenda. Many have in fact pointed to the '*re-launch of the single market project as the decisive moment turning the European Integration process towards neoliberalism ... Scientists, journalists and politicians succeeded in presenting the Single Market as the breaking-up of incrusted and rigid structures of European labour and social regulations*'.[7]

The re-launching of the single market coincided with the birth of the European Round Table of Industrialists (ERT) – an organization representing Europe's most powerful corporations, which lobbied vigorously in Brussels and national capitals, for the creation of a common market. '*This pressure from industrial leaders for the unification of European markets was precisely the momentum towards further integration that the Commission had been seeking.*'[8] The ERT propositions, as formulated in their '*Europe 1990: An Agenda for Action*' proposal, were adopted almost literally in the Commission's '*White Paper on Completing the Internal Market*'. The ERT's strategy for a common market, however, was not from the offset completely neoliberal. Proponents of free trade were strongly opposed by supporters of a neo-mercantilist approach, who instead favoured a common but closed market, in order to facilitate the creation of '*European champions*' capable of competing in the world market.[9]

Although such struggles were important, the writing of the European Constitution further ensured the continuation of the European economy's openness to non-European competitors, with the key to the process being the principle of mutual recognition. '*The principle stated that those areas and products for which the European Union had not introduced specific European- wide regulations, member states were obliged to accept products and services which are legally produced and marketed in one of the other member states ... The tactical brilliance of the market completion programme, is to bypass wherever possible the need for common supervisory procedures and harmonised standards to replace the inconsistent systems of the nation states. Complex*

[6] Ibid, pg 9.
[7] Ibid.
[8] Ibid.
[9] Ibid.

negotiations towards a European system can thus be dispensed.'[10] Mutual recognition, beyond the creation of a '*common level playing field*', also had a liberalizing tendency within the EU, with half the product standards for goods traded within the EU still being based on the same principle. That way, the common market therefore became a neoliberal market, characterized by very weak regulations and much deregulation. The principle of mutual recognition not only eroded higher national product standards, but also amounted to a '*de facto liberalisation of the "external" trade policies of EU states*'. In parallel to the weakening of national regulations, entry barriers for non-European corporations were also minimized, which likewise much contributed to the development of EU trade policy and trade liberalization. The Single Act also introduced the need for qualified-majority voting, '*which gave "free trade" advocates like Germany and the UK a strong bargaining position in trade negotiations. They could easily veto any proposals by protectionists (already in the 1950s the German government position was that the customs union be compatible with the General Agreement on Tariffs and Trade)*'.[11]

The overall result proved very positive. Between 1992 and 2000, while extra-EU imports of goods as a percentage of GDP increased by 55 per cent, intra-EU imports grew by 30 per cent. Since then, the EU's markets have remained very open, except for a few politically sensitive agricultural products, with the EU also pressing forward for free trade in bi- and multilateral agreements with non-European countries.[12]

European Competition Policy

The Single Market Strategy shared very strong links with the development of a European Competition Policy. The neoliberalization process, through the creation of the Single Market, much helped and assisted with the advancement of intra-European competition, which in accordance with the beliefs of liberalization advocates would strengthen European businesses and benefit consumers, as monopolistic firms or oligopolistic cartels would no longer be able to utilize their economic dominance to distort market pricing. '*The most original feature of European competition policy is its explicit role within the European integration process ... Competition policy is an essential feature of any common market if that market is to provide a "level playing-field" for industrial activity.*'[13]

With Article 3 of the Treaty of Rome, calling for the creation of a common market free from distortion to competition, the establishment of both the Commission and the Directorate General for Competition (DG IV) created an institutional framework for

[10] Ibid, pg 10.
[11] Ibid.
[12] Ibid, pg 11.
[13] Ibid, pg 12.

the development of a European competition policy. Competition policy also played a key role in the subsequent steps that were taken towards European integration. '*The effect of the single market project on the development of competition policy was unequivocal. Although supplementary to the 1992 programme, competition policy was always going to be a necessary condition for its success.*'[14]

Historically wise, European competition policy had mainly focused on three major issues: '*the conclusion of anti-competitive agreements (trusts, cartels) and the abuse of market power, mergers that provide companies with an exclusive position in catering to certain markets, and the granting of state subsidies conferring advantage on particular companies*'.[15] Although not officially part of competition policy, transport costs became of crucial importance if companies wanted to compete in the European market, and thus the transportation sector was among the first to be subjected to liberalization. However, despite the drastic reduction in transport prices, most especially road transport, so that companies would concentrate production and expand distribution costs, in the end, transport costs did not experience the same reduction, being instead redistributed from transport consumers to a wider public. One of the worst generalized direct results was that rail transport lost market share, as cargo customers opted for cheaper road transport. Soon after, in response to the falling share of rail transport in total transport, in accordance with the neoliberal credo that only the '*injection of more market*' solves problems, such '*marketization*' troubles made the Commission propose the liberalization of the railway sector.[16]

The process of European neoliberalization did not limit itself to the privatization of transport. The liberalization of public services became the fourth major concern of European competition policy. While the European and UK public sectors included nationalized industries, as well as public services, during the 1980s, the UK led by Thatcher paved the way for the European privatization of state-owned and public companies, just as it had previously done with trade liberalization. Although during the 1980s, the UK privatized various public entities, such as British Telecom and British Gas, it was not until the 1990s that the European liberalization of public companies gained momentum. With the adoption of a series of directives demanding the liberalization of public services, the telecommunications sector was privatized in 1990, the railway sector was privatized in 1991, and the postal services and the gas sector were respectively privatized in 1992 and 1996. It was affirmed that '*there is a fundamental belief running through all these provisions that the liberalisation of these sectors will create competition and there is a further assumption that ... competition will benefit consumers*'.[17] Throughout the whole process and henceforth, with the Commission's consumer-orientated action presenting a very lucrative business

[14] Ibid.
[15] Ibid.
[16] Ibid, pgs 12–13.
[17] Ibid, pg 14.

opportunity for private capital, Brussels became plagued with private companies lobbying strongly in favour of liberalization.[18]

The European Union's Economic and Monetary Integration

The year the Single Market was achieved generated a whole new phase in the European Union's integration process, with the establishment of the Economic and Monetary Union (EMU). Although there had been a first proposal made in 1970 in order to adjust monetary policies, and that in 1979, the European Monetary System (EMS) was established, in 1980, the idea of a common monetary area was still far from becoming a reality. The 1970s evolved quite turbulently in monetary terms, as many European currencies *'struggled with the volatility of currency markets and increasing inflationary pressures. In response to these problems, member states reverted to national strategies to tackle the economic crisis'*.[19] However, in 1989, due to the little effect of national solutions, together with the tensions they created in the international monetary system, along with a weakened Deutsche Mark, the Commission made a fresh approach to the monetary union, with the Delors Report. The new initiative marked a new phase of intense negotiations, and in 1992, with the European Treaty being adopted at the Council of Maastricht, *'member states committed themselves to the establishment of monetary union and the introduction of a common European currency by 2002'*.[20]

Within the framework of the European 'neoliberalization' process, the EMU is widely considered the most blatant expression of neoliberal restructuring. While, on one hand, the SEA guarantees *'free trade'* and *'capital mobility'* within Europe, on the other hand, the EMU forces EMU member states into a *'fiscal straitjacket'*, which thus and in turn restrengthens the principles of monetary restraint and budgetary austerity.[21]

> *The EMU, can be comprehended as part of a set of policies that has shifted the European Union towards a neoliberal and financial, as opposed to social market or social democratic, model of capitalism. This viewpoint favours tight monetary and financial discipline in a rules-based economic constitution as a means to deliver low inflation rates and protect savings. The draft European constitution, rejected by French and Dutch voters in spring 2005, confirms this view. Economic policy, according to the constitution, shall entail compliance with the following principles: stable prices, sound public finances and monetary conditions and a stable balance of payments.*[22]

Accordingly, in 1995, at the Council of Madrid, further details about the structure and functioning of the EMU and the Euro were negotiated, and in 1997, at the

[18] Ibid.
[19] Ibid, pgs 14–15.
[20] Ibid, pg 15.
[21] Ibid, pg 16.
[22] Ibid.

Table 4 The Maastricht Treaty's Five Convergence Criteria

- A nation's annual budget deficit has to be below 3% of GDP.
- A nation's public debt has to be less than 60% of GDP (the public debt is the cumulative total of annual budget deficits).
- A nation should have an inflation rate within 1.5% of the three EU countries with the lowest rate.
- Long-term interest rates must be within 2% of the three lowest interest rates in the EU:
- Exchange rates must be kept within moderate fluctuation margins of Europe's exchange-rate mechanism.

Source: STEGER, M.B. and RAVI, K.R. '*Neoliberalism: A Very Short Introduction*', pg 69.

Council of Amsterdam, such details were adopted through the Growth and Stability Pact (GSP). Due to pressure stemming from German worries about the stability of a common European currency, the GSP therefore defined '*convergence criteria*', which established the conditions to be met by member states, in order to be allowed to join the new economic and monetary area. '*These criteria included the three per cent limit for government deficits per year and the 60 per cent cap on accumulated debt (both as proportion of national GDP). The European Treaty also clarified the role of the European Central Bank, following blueprints largely modelled on the German Bundesbank. According to its statute neither the ECB nor a national central bank, nor any member of their decision-making bodies shall seek or take instructions from Community Institutions or bodies, from any government of a Member State or from any other body.*'[23]

The main objective of the establishment of the ECB was fundamentally in order '*to maintain price stability*', with price stability being set as an inflation rate of less than 2 per cent. As a direct result of such measure, today, the ECB enjoys not only more independence than the New York Federal Reserve, but also probably the most independence than any other bank in the world. However and although the ECB is independent from political parties and national governments, '*it is not independent in the sense that it adheres to a particular ideology concerning the operation of economic policy*'.[24]

Regardless of the fact that it is sometimes assumed that the main profiteers of monetary integration have been industrial concerns, it was not only the corporations involved in the process, which pressured for monetary union. For example, the Association for the Monetary Union of Europe (AMUE) is in that respect viewed as the main pressure group that lobbied for EMU. Founded in 1987, by five of the largest European companies, the majority of its 300 current members now come from the financial and

[23] Ibid, pg 15.
[24] Ibid.

banking sector. Throughout the turbulent history of European monetary integration, it was the AMUE, which continuously urged the Commission and national governments to adhere to their commitment of establishing a European zone of common economic policy and currency. *'When politicians couldn't agree about whether they would set precise dates for EMU implementation in the Maastricht Treaty, the AMUE, the ERT and the other corporate lobby groups successfully pressed for the inclusion of a well-defined time-schedule.'*[25]

Although the Commission continues to advocate price stability and fiscal austerity as the most effective growth-promoting measures, the actual outcomes of such policies have unfortunately been slow growth rates, outright stagnation, quite moderate real income increases, as well as a very high unemployment rate across the Union. In accordance with many progressive economists, the ECB's diligence on price stability has been the main cause behind the European economy's non-achievement of higher growth rates. It is widely believed that the consideration of lower interest rates, as well as higher budget deficits, could have stimulated investment and aggregate demand.[26]

The European Employment Strategy

Regardless of the progress made by the EU's market and monetary integration, the aggravation caused by the EU's neoliberal restructuring has generated much criticism, facing continuous challenges posed by its on-going democratic, social and unemployment deficits. In 1992, in order to counter-punch such forces, as well as to rally more support for the common market project, the European Treaty was complemented with a '*social chapter*'.

The social chapter established the possibility for social-partner agreements at the European level, *'which would then be transferred into binding EU law by directives passed by the Council of Ministers without further discussion'*.[27] In 1993, the departing Commission President Delors elaborated the *'White Paper on Growth, Competitiveness and Employment'*, which attempted to combine two objectives at the same time: *'The ambition was to meet the convergence criteria for EMU, the implications of which were deflationary, and yet to achieve higher levels of employment'*.[28] The White Paper initiative served as a vital springboard for the consequent European Employment Strategy.[29]

Between 1990 and 1994, largely due to the failure of neoliberal macro-economic policies of supporting unemployment, unemployment in Europe rose rapidly, which

[25] Ibid, pg 17.
[26] Ibid, pg 16.
[27] Ibid, pg 18.
[28] Ibid.
[29] Ibid.

became a major issue at the 1994 Council of Essen. As a direct result, the Council identified five employment priorities to be transformed by member states into a '*multi-year employment programme*'. While, on one hand, the Council also introduced some first steps for a multilateral monitoring procedure, with member states having to report back to the Commission, on the other hand and henceforth, the Commission, the Employment and Social Affairs Council and the ECOFIN Council were put in charge of examining national employment policies, as well as of drafting a joint report for the European Council. '*The Essen Council endorsed the employment policy agenda of the Delors White Paper; what it did not do, however, was to consent to a major allocation of competence over employment policy to the Commission. Instead, it could be argued, that having "discovered" employment policy as matter of concern for the EU as a whole, the Essen Council marked the beginning of a process whereby political initiatives was shifted from the Community institutions to the member states.*'[30]

Despite the fact that during the following years unemployment in Europe decreased, it remained a major issue in some countries, like France, where the Left-winged coalition won, partly due to the Conservatives not being able to stop the rising unemployment. At the 1997 Council of Amsterdam, the unemployment issue dominated the itinerary, as even though unemployment had not originally been on the agenda, the failure of the previous integration process to tackle the unemployment issue had made the theme imperative. It had become evident that measures had to be seriously taken '*if the EMU project, or at least the planned timetable, was not to be at risk*'.[31]

With the Treaty of Amsterdam, unemployment officially became a major European policy area. Through the process called the Open Method of Coordination (OMC), a flexible alternative to the usual approach of finding a compromise among member states was established, with member states being ultimately responsible of employment issues. Every year, following recommendations by the Commission, the Council adopts a new set of employment guidelines. Subsequently, member states are then expected to account for those objectives in their national employment strategies, as well as to report to the Commission both on the implementation processes and on the effects of their respective measures. The Commission then reviews the National Action Plans (NAPs) and, together with the Council, produces a joint employment report. Based on that report, the Council with a qualified majority can then issue recommendations to specific member states, although they do not have any binding legal force.[32]

In 1997, in Luxembourg, the Extraordinary Council on Employment adopted the first set of employment policies, which mainly specified '*employability, entrepreneurship, adaptability and equal opportunity*'. While the first three objectives reflect the strong

[30] Ibid.
[31] Ibid, pg 19.
[32] Ibid.

bias towards the overall aim of employment flexibility, the last point clearly stands out as a social justice issue. Employability represents, in quantitative terms, the central pillar of the employment strategy. '*What the areas of intervention ... had in common was an emphasis on supply-side measures or "structural reforms" aimed at making the allocative function of the market work more effectively'. The emphasis on supply-side measures ensures that the employment strategy is subordinated to the general economic policy of Maastricht imprinting".*

Although the European Employment Strategy was of crucial importance for the maintenance of sufficient support for market and monetary integration, job outcomes have, nonetheless, been quite moderate. Based on the neoliberal conviction that '*problems can only be solved with more market*', the ECB, ECOFIN and the Commission have incessantly pressed for further labour market flexibilization in their official policy statements.[33] '*European employment policy was made to fit the existing integration project and thus became one of the pillars of supply-side-oriented neoliberal restructuring. Yet in contrast to the monetary and budgetary policies, in the case of labour market flexibility ... the EU level can encourage but only national politicians can deliver.*'[34]

[33] Ibid, pg 20.
[34] Ibid.

16

First-Wave Neoliberalization in the 1980s: *Reaganomics and Thatcherism*

The substitution of Keynesian economics and the Bretton Woods system of fixed exchange rates and embedded liberalism for the neoliberal free-market economy and the international financial monetary system (IFMS) of flexible exchange rates was carried out at different intervals and in differing ways. The process of neoliberalization of the capitalist world or process of '*global neoliberalization*' was fulfilled through a series of different multi-levelled phases, together with its gradual implementation in key strategic sectors and areas.

From a wide-ranging perspective, the main driving force of neoliberalism revolved around the promotion of '*free trade*' and '*unrestricted capital mobility*', combined with dramatically reduced costs in transportation and the information revolution. The process of global neoliberalization began through the flexibilization of labour markets and the repression of wage demands, the privatization of public companies and services, together with the '*workfarist*' restructuring of welfare states.[1] The entire process was carried out through two huge successive waves of neoliberalization, which together and gradually, set up and established the global neoliberal architecture.

First-wave neoliberalization, which this chapter will focus on, was carried out during the 1980s by the Reagan and Thatcher administrations. First-wave neoliberalization began setting up the neoliberal stage, through the application of the first neoliberal agendas and programmes, which were mainly based on the liberalization of markets and widespread deregulations and privatizations at the national and international levels.[2]

Over the neoliberal bedrock established by first-wave neoliberalization, as the next chapter will reflect upon, a more modernized, second-wave neoliberalization was generated in the 1990s by the Clinton and Blair administrations, which had a massive impact on the post-1990s international landscape. Second-wave neoliberalism synthesized market-orientated economic growth, within an ethical framework of

1 FORBA. FORBA Discussion Paper 3/2007. HERMANN, C. *Neoliberalism in the European Union*, pgs 1–2. http://www.forschungsnetzwerk.at/downloadpub/neoliberalism_eu_SR%2003-07.pdf
2 STEGER, M.B. and RAVI, K.R. *Neoliberalism: A Very Short Introduction*, pgs 26–75.

social justice and human rights. It spearheaded the worldwide unification of efforts and attempts, which liberalized trade relations, as well as integrated national economies into one single, global market.[3]

> *The reduction of trade barriers and enhanced capital mobility together with the application of new information-based technologies, facilitated the emergence of less constrained multinational corporations able to negotiate the very favourable terms of investment with national governments. The process of corporate internationalisation was accompanied by the adaptation of dominant Anglo-American corporate governance structures and an increasing dependence on capital markets as the predominant mode of financing corporate debt. The shift from borrowing through bank credits to selling stock options was facilitated by a sustained period of high interest rates. The result was a shift in the focus of managers from the 'stakeholder' to the 'shareholder value'.*[4]

In very broad terms, the overall process of 'global neoliberalization' can be considered to have been triggered by the crumbling of the Bretton Woods system of fixed exchange rates and the liberalization of exchange rates, which began liberalizing financial systems, thus allowing the free flow of capital. Both the late 1960s devaluation of the US dollar and the 1973 collapse of the Bretton Woods system of fixed exchange rates encouraged the flow of '*cheap*' money from the United States to Europe and less-developed countries. In general, *'the abolition of barriers to capital mobility together with the rise in interest rates led to a dramatic reversal of financial flows on a global scale'.*[5] During the 1980s and 1990s, the United States' rising interest rates and a reinvigorated dollar made money pour back into the country to finance a swelling current account deficit, with most of the bulk of the deficit being financed by Asian countries and some European countries, like France and Germany, which also net-exported capital. The attractiveness of the US economy for foreign capital gave it a decisive advantage compared to other countries, which partly explains the employment gap between the United States and Europe. Since the United States printed the dominant world currency, the US dollar, it had the sole privileged option of running such a huge current account deficit.[6]

A second key trigger of the whole process of neoliberalization of the capitalist world was the unprecedented international expansion of the US-dominated financial sector, in terms of it as proportionate of economic activity, as well as of the volume of money transactions. *'Monetarism was accompanied by a simultaneous abolition and erosion of regulations that restricted entrepreneurial freedom and therefore were purported to hamper overall market efficiency.'*[7] One of the main targets of neoliberal deregulation

[3] Ibid.
[4] FORBA. FORBA Discussion Paper 3/2007. HERMANN, C. *Neoliberalism in the European Union*, pg 2.
[5] Ibid, pg 3.
[6] Ibid.
[7] Ibid.

was labour markets. The developing neoliberal project involved an '*open assault on organized labour*', which is considered the main reason for labour-market rigidity. While in the UK '*the political and economic war on labour led to successive erosion of trade unions and a sharp decline in overall trade union membership*',[8] in the United States, its gradual decline took a longer time, and in less-developed countries, the attack on labour was even worse, very often being overlooked. The supposed rigidity of labour markets was regarded as the main cause of inflationary pressures, as well as of the latter massive increase in unemployment, although other more probable reasons can likewise be attributed to low levels of investment, as well as a rise in interest rates.[9]

The pressure to deregulate labour markets was more intense in less-developed countries, which had adverse effects. Such countries, together with peripheral EU states, traditionally utilized their currency devaluations to compete with advanced capitalist countries, although with prices becoming a top priority, such strategy was no longer feasible. Thus, their only alternative to maintain some degree of competitiveness in international markets was to reduce wages and extend working hours. However, due to the effectiveness of flexibilized labour markets critically depending on the general incentive of accepting deregulated forms of employment, part-time jobs and fixed-term contracts or self-employed work, social security systems also needed to be adapted to support such a purpose. The overall result was a shift from the general provision of benefits to '*a means-tested access to public allowances*', and henceforth, benefits were thus no longer perceived as social rights, but as '*temporary support for unemployed individuals to find employment*'.[10]

The individualization of the unemployment problem is also described as a shift '*from welfare to workfare-orientated social policies*'. While the general drive to shift the employment responsibility from the macro to the micro level involved measures like further training or lifelong-learning, at the same time, budgetary and fiscal austerity magnified the '*workfarist*' turn. All combined, labour market flexibilization and the workfarist restructuring of welfare support increased insecurity for those who lacked access to alternative sources of income. Another key distinguishing feature of neoliberalization was the established, '*budgetary austerity*', with four main outstanding arguments in favour of it, which rotated around '*deficit-spending is seen as an additional element that drives up inflation rates; deficit expenditures depend on high tax revenues and hence on elevated tax rates funded by middle and upper-class citizens; higher interest rates render deficit spending increasingly expensive; growing unemployment multiplies the cost of an encompassing and effective unemployment benefit system*'.[11]

The neoliberalization project's expansion of markets and budgetary restrictions had another key distinguishing trait related to its embracement of the '*privatisations*

8 Ibid.
9 Ibid.
10 Ibid, pg 4.
11 Ibid.

of public companies, services and pension systems'. Whereas in the United States privatization was secondary due to the modest starting point of the state sector, services and other public provisions, in the UK, it however became a main focus point of neoliberal restructuring during the second Thatcher mandate. While in 1975, 20 per cent of British GDP was produced by the public sector, by the year 2000 the state had sold off virtually all of its infrastructure and service operations. Together with budgetary restraint and chronic underfunding of services, both the incidence and price of user-fees surged, which in turn narrowed access to service provision even more. A shared feature of the neoliberal restructuring in Latin America (LA) was the privatization of state-owned companies, which had an important role in the 1950s and 1960s domestically orientated growth strategies. Nonetheless, within the context of families relying on the income of one member in the state-sector, the effects of letting go of thousands of employees were multiplied manifold. Additionally, the reduced inflow of tax revenues increased the pressure on regional and local administrations to cut expenses, which thus created an equal increase in communities hiring private companies that fulfilled an increasing range of public tasks at cheaper costs. That way and from then onwards, '*public-private partnerships*' and endeavours hence became another very innovative and popular neoliberal characteristic.[12]

As a whole, the neoliberal project was very pressed forward by the deregulation and privatization of public pension systems, with countries in LA being early adopters of such a policy change in that direction. '*The establishment and extension of private pension funds generated substantial amounts of money required for the sale of newly privatised companies and for financing corporate and public debt. The growing reliance on stock and bond markets also had the additional impact of drawing workers closer to the profit-making perspective of capital owners, and partially dissipated reaction to downward pressure on wages and lay-offs.*'[13]

Against such a backdrop of neoliberal initiatives, the capitalist world began to be gradually and progressively neoliberalized through a series of '*gyrations and chaotic experiments*', which, during the 1990s, all finally converged into a new orthodoxy, with the articulation of the Washington Consensus. Although the geographical development of neoliberalization is considered to have been carried out unevenly, the gradual '*frequently partial and lop-sided application from one state and social formation to another*'[14] witnessed how neoliberal solutions began progressively transcending in very complex ways, historical traditions, existing institutional framework arrangements, international political forces and capital structures.[15] The neoliberalization process is generally interpreted as either a '*utopian project*', in order to fulfil a theoretical design for the reorganization of international capitalism, or as a '*political project*', for the re-

[12] Ibid, pgs 4–5.
[13] Ibid, pg 5.
[14] HARVEY, D. *A Brief History of Neoliberalism*, pg 13.
[15] Ibid.

establishment of conditions for capital accumulation and the restoration of the power of ruling elites. Despite the fact that neoliberalization has not been very successful in revitalizing global capital accumulation, nevertheless and conversely, it has been very effective in restoring and in some cases creating the power of an economic elite.[16]

The theoretical utopianism of neoliberal reasoning has for many chiefly worked as '*a system of justification and legitimisation*', for whatever means were necessary in order to achieve its goal. It is suggested by evidence that when neoliberal principles clashed with the restoration or sustainment of elite power, such principles were either abandoned or became unrecognizably twisted. In no way undermining the force of the power of ideas to influence historical-geographical change, an undeniable creative tension has, nonetheless, characterized the power of neoliberal ideas and the actual neoliberal practices, which have transformed so much the way global capitalism has been working over the last four decades.[17]

While Friedrich Hayek argued presciently in favour of the neoliberal collective by pointing out that the battle of ideas was key, he, nevertheless, always pointed out that it would take at least a generation for the battle to be won, '*not only against Marxism but against socialism, state planning and Keynesian interventionism*'.[18] With the Mont Pelerin contingent beginning to gather more and more financial and political support, especially in the United States, many other powerful and wealthy individuals and corporate leaders viscerally opposed to any sort of state intervention, regulation or even internationalization, likewise began organizing a very strong opposition to what they considered as an emerging consensus for the pursuit of a mixed economy. Fearful of the political outcome that the alliance with the Soviet Union and the command economy, constructed during the Second World War within the United States, would have in a post-war setting, such progressive people were more than willing to embrace whatever different approach that would protect and enhance their power – from McCarthyism to neoliberal think tanks. Although the neoliberal movement remained subjacent to policy and academic influence until the 1970s, from then onwards it began to rapidly move much more centre stage, most especially in the United States and Britain.[19] With the cultivation of neoliberalism within an enlarged network of well-financed think tanks – offspring of the Mont Pelerin Society, like the Heritage Foundation in Washington and the Institute of Economic Affairs in London – neoliberal influence began to grow stronger in academia through the University of Chicago, where Milton Friedman dominated the Chicago School's monetarist orientation. Neoliberalism also gained much more academic respectability when Hayek was awarded the Nobel Prize in economics in 1974 and Friedman in 1976. Through its monetarist guise, neoliberalism began to gradually exert more and more practical influence in various policy fields.

16 Ibid, pg 19.
17 Ibid.
18 Ibid.
19 Ibid, pgs 21–2.

For example, during the Carter administration, the deregulation of the economy was proposed as a solution to the chronic stagflation that prevailed in the United States during the 1970s, with some first deregulating incursions carried out in the airlines and trucking sectors. However, the true and final consolidation of neoliberalism '*as a new economic orthodoxy regulating public policy at the state level in the advanced capitalist world occurred in the United States and Britain*'.[20]

The definite rise of neoliberalism to international practice status is most usually associated with US President Ronald Reagan (1981–8) and British Prime Minister Margaret Thatcher (1979–90). Their zealous battle against Keynesian-style '*big government*' was equally shared by Australian Prime Minister Malcolm Fraser (1975–83) and Canadian Prime Minister Brian Mulroney (1984–93), who all articulated the core ideological claims of neoliberalism and converted them into public programmes and policies.[21] Although both Reagan and Thatcher cut and shaped their approaches from the same neoliberal mould, their different views inspired diverging policy agendas.[22] On one hand, Reagan was a staunch supporter of neoliberal supply-side economics and believed that high taxes were the main cause of poor economic performance, so he promoted policies aimed at private-sector-led growth. On the other hand, Thatcher was much more of a monetarist economist, and as such, believed that the growth of the money supply was the main culprit of bad economic performance, so she focused much more on neoliberal policies that targeted the reduction of taxes, deregulation, privatization of public industries and the reduction of labour union power. However, and in general, neoliberalization occurred through the combination of both the adoption of monetarism and the unfolding of government policies in many areas.[23]

During the 1980s, first-wave neoliberalization is widely considered to have been a successful ideological crusade against Keynesian-style '*big government*' and state interference in the market. Although Reaganomics and Thatcherism represented very unique responses to an increasing globalized economic and political context, they were both, however, anchored in common principles focused on the release of the entrepreneurial energies of the individual. While both administrations advocated a reduced role of government, they reflected two variations of the neoliberal theme that took distinct approaches to issues, such as the relative importance placed on budget deficits and taxes. With their economic initiatives depending '*on the muscle of state-imposed neoliberal reforms on local and regional authorities*',[24] it is generally believed that the ascension of neoliberalism would not have been possible without strong governmental action. Similarly, whereas both Reaganomics and Thatcherism supported increases in military spending, the two, however, espoused cuts in public expenditures

[20] Ibid, pg 22.
[21] STEGER, M.B. and RAVI, K.R. *Neoliberalism: A Very Short Introduction*, pg 21.
[22] Ibid, pgs 23–4.
[23] HARVEY, D. *A Brief History of Neoliberalism*, pg 23.
[24] STEGER, M.B. and RAVI, K.R. *Neoliberalism: A Very Short Introduction*, pg 49.

for social programmes. Despite their ideological tensions and contradictions, by the late 1980s, the two variants of neoliberalism already enjoyed a very broad appeal. Furthermore, the power of Reaganomics and Thatcherism also much influenced the forces of the democratic Left to '*incorporate major portions of the neoliberal agenda into their political programmes*'.[25]

Reaganomics

Upon taking office in 1981, President Ronald Reagan proclaimed his Program for Economic Recovery, which was mostly based on neoliberal principles and '*supply-side economics*'. The president's '*Reaganomics*' programme quickly set out to combat the toxic mixture of stagflation inherited from the Carter administration, by mainly focusing on the reduction of marginal tax rates.

With an equal firm determination to tackle deficit spending and existing government regulations, the only area in which Reagan increased spending was military defence, due to the waging Cold War against the Soviet '*Evil Empire*' and other '*communist aggressors*' around the world.[26] However, when Reaganomics failed to end deficit spending, the president's budget director, David Stockman, a traditional fiscal conservative, challenged his economic strategy. Stockman publicly warned that deep tax cuts and increased military spending would entail large deficits with disastrous consequences and advised Reagan to channel funding towards social programmes, like Medicare and Medicaid. Notwithstanding, the president continued undeterred down his economic path.[27]

Although both Reagan and Thatcher perceived inflation as an obstruction to growth, supply-siders, like the US president, portrayed monetarism as the '*politics of austerity*'. Believing that the money supply would adjust naturally to market imperatives, Reagan diverged from Thatcher's monetarist sense of worry over budget deficits. He instead asserted that lower taxes promoted increased growth, which would in turn automatically generate enough revenues to cover existing spending public programmes' spending.[28]

'Supply-side economics' was primarily advocated by neoliberal economists, like Arthur Laffer. It bases itself on the assumption that long-term economic growth depends on '*freeing-up*' the amount of capital available for private investment. The '*Laffer Curve*' is a key theoretical component that illustrates graphically the thesis that '*increases in taxation rates will not always lead to an increase in taxation revenue*'.[29] The

[25] Ibid.
[26] Ibid, pgs 26–7.
[27] Ibid, pg 27.
[28] Ibid.
[29] Ibid, pg 24.

curve suggests that as tax rates near 100 per cent, revenue will drop, as there are no incentives for citizens to work harder. Supply-side economics reflects a single-minded commitment towards the reduction of taxes on private income. Its advocates, based on the Laffer Curve, uphold that added investment will produce new economic growth that will automatically generate large enough tax revenue surpluses, which could in turn, be utilized by governments to clear off debts and balance out their budgets. Supply-side economics is also referred to as '*trickle-down economics*'.[30]

Although from a short-term perspective, Reagan's tax cuts had little to do with a neoliberal revolution, from a broader standpoint, however, their cumulative effect reflected a full-blown assault on state-led redistribution of private wealth, which eventually led to a dramatic widening of the income gap between the middle class and the wealthy. Most particularly, the 1986 Tax Reform Act, '*reduced the tax brackets to four while reducing the average individual income tax rate by about 6%. In an attempt to address mounting fears over the growing budget deficit, the Tax Reform Act raised corporate taxes to offset cuts in personal income taxes, thus seeking to make the latter "revenue neutral"*'.[31] Reagan's early 1980s initial tax cuts led to both a decline in government revenues intended to cover existing spending commitments in social policy and dramatic increases in military expenditure, which thus forced the administration to resort to huge levels of deficit spending in order to cover the revenue shortfalls. The intense pressure from traditional conservatives eventually obliged Reagan to deal with what turned out to be the largest budget deficit in US history.[32]

Reagan's long-standing antipathy against government growth paved the way for the historic enactment denominated as the '*Gramm-Rudman-Hollings Deficit Reduction Initiative (GRH)*' or Balanced Budget and Emergency Control Act, which was largely sponsored by Republican Senators Phil Gramm and Warren Rudman.[33] It was a Congress-instrumented method of controlling the Reagan administration's excessive government spending, which mainly outlined a series of spending targets to eliminate the deficit by 1991, and generated a huge demand to cut social spending and restrict military spending so that it paralleled reduction schemes in social programmes. While not all the measures of the GRH were implemented, the neoliberal stimulus nevertheless ended lasting.[34]

Although Reagan's neoliberal agenda did not include monetary policy as a top priority, his firm commitment to monetarism soon became very evident. The US Federal Reserve Bank had for a long time been enjoying relative independence in setting monetary policy, especially as regards interest rates.[35] What became

30 Ibid.
31 Ibid.
32 Ibid, pg 28.
33 Ibid.
34 Ibid.
35 Ibid, pg 29.

denominated as the '*Volcker Shock*', marked one of the biggest steps forward towards neoliberalization. In October 1979, still under President Carter, the chairman of the US Federal Reserve Bank, Paul Volcker, produced what was denominated as a '*draconian shift in US monetary policy*'. The US liberal democratic state and its long-standing commitment to the principles of the New Deal, based on Keynesian fiscal and monetary policies with full employment as the main objective, was substituted by a policy designed to quell inflation, regardless of its effects on employment. The real interest rate, which was often negative during the double-digit inflationary surge of the 1970s, was deemed positive by fiat of the Federal Reserve, with the nominal interest rate being raised overnight, which by July 1981 and after a few ups and downs, stood nearly at 20 per cent. Although Volcker held that it was the only way out of the grubby crisis of stagflation, which prevailed during the 1970s in the United States and much of the global economy, it nonetheless triggered '*a long deep recession that would empty factories and break unions in the US and drive debtor countries to the brink of insolvency, beginning the long era of structural adjustment*'.[36] In 1983, Reagan re-appointed Volcker as chairman of the Federal Reserve, and in 1987, appointed the renowned monetarist, Alan Greenspan. Whereas by 1986 Volcker's monetarist measures had reduced inflation by nearly 50 per cent, the reduction, however, brought about very negative consequences onto many American citizens. With exorbitant interest rates on mortgages and private loans, the financing of new homes and cars became nearly impossible for middle- and low-income earners, which gained Reagan much unpopularity. In contrast, after the economy picked up again from the mid-1980s onwards, it reached historical record highs.[37]

Reagan's fiscal policy, involving the reduction of taxes and the increase in military expenditure combined with the simultaneous balancing of the budget, proved to have inconsistent objectives. Most particularly within the tax policy area, the cuts in income taxes led to increases in corporate tax revenues, which all in all ended fuelling volatile exchange rates. Despite that in 1980, the US dollar reached its highest point in 1988, during Reagan's last year in office it fell to its lowest level. The main causes for such volatility were mainly related to the initial tax cuts, which complemented the Federal Reserve's tight monetary policy and thus helped create a strong dollar. Although the early tax cuts encouraged international investment and stimulated investor demand for US portfolio assets and treasury bonds, the subsequent increases in tax rates, especially when levied on corporate income '*reduced the foreign investment and caused the dollar's depreciation toward the end of Reagan's second term*'.[38] Nevertheless and more positively, Reagan's currency volatility made the dollar weak which in turn made foreign imports more expensive, with American goods and products becoming more desirable to both domestic and foreign consumers.[39]

[36] HARVEY, D. *A Brief History of Neoliberalism*, pg 23.
[37] STEGER, M.B. and RAVI, K.R. *Neoliberalism: A Very Short Introduction*, pg 29.
[38] Ibid.
[39] Ibid, pgs 29–30.

Another key distinguishing policy of Reaganomics was a wide-arching regulatory reform, which included much strategic deregulation in key sectors. The reform formed part of Reagan's ideological commitment to the '*New Federalism*' and was rooted in the theories of the Public Choice School of Economics. The New Federalism was principally inspired by the neoliberal tenets of decentralization and individual choice, and considered politics '*as a rational enterprise devoted to winning a maximum of votes rather than a messy strategy of governing in the public interest*'.[40] Public choice economists regarded '*smaller, decentralized government*', to be better in terms of economic effectiveness and market efficiency. Furthermore, new federalists viewed small governments less likely to regulate the market, with their neoliberal slogan, '*less is more*', clearly professing that.[41]

Reagan was attracted to the public choice/new-federalist approach due to its appealing rationale for regulatory restraint. Basing himself on the value of rigorous economic statistical tools for the assessment of policy decisions, he signed '*Executive Order 12291*', which required federal agencies to utilize the cost-benefit analysis methodology for appraising government regulation proposals. Whereas numerous existing regulations were highlighted for possible elimination, the regulatory powers of governmental organizations, such as the Environmental Protection Agency (EPA), were also diminished. Such initiatives proved quite revealing, as they confirmed the ability of neoliberalism to function both as an ideology or set of policies and as a distinct mode of governance, which ran consistent with the principles of new public management and public choice theory.[42]

Within the framework of Reagan's New Federalism Initiative, federal regulatory powers were transferred to the states, although they often lacked enough provision of resources for the proper accomplishment of their functions and mandates. Further deregulation measures were also applied to key sectors like banking, communications and transportation. One of the most transcending deregulations of the telecommunications industry was the authorization by the administration to settle the never-ending lawsuit filed by the Department of Justice against American Telephone and Telegraph (AT&T), which broke up the Bell system monopoly of local telephone services into different telephone companies. Although under the new terms of the deregulation deal, rates remained regulated, the areas of services and products (including long-distance service and equipment leasing) were left subject to market forces.[43]

Reaganomics's most controversial neoliberal deregulation initiative was the deregulation of the Savings and Loans (S&L) industry, which had been providing savings accounts to depositors and passing on those funds as loans for home mortgages.

[40] Ibid, pg 30.
[41] Ibid.
[42] Ibid.
[43] Ibid, pg 31.

S&L was considered a prudent and secure industry that was heavily regulated, with its customer's savings insured by the federal government. President Reagan focused his deregulation objectives onto S&L, aiming to give the industry the possibility of competing more aggressively with other commercial banks and security markets, by providing it more freedom to seek new forms of financing for their pursuit of higher short-term profits.[44]

Such neoliberal measures also affected the finance sector, sparking off a series of mergers, acquisitions and leverage buyouts, which involved some of the country's largest corporations. Many of such takeovers were funded through innovative financing tools, like '*junk bonds*', which were sold to investors for such actions. Underperforming companies with lucrative assets, including employee pensions, became common targets by corporate raiders that initiated hostile takeovers and then sold off their assets for huge profits, which often led to significant layoffs.[45] '*Thus, speculators and stockholders thrived during the legendary Wall Street-driven Bull Market that lasted from 1984 to the autumn of 1987. Lured by the promise of quick profits and high returns, short-term investors often overlooked the substantial risks involved in such transactions. Thus, by October 1987, most stock values were seriously inflated. The disastrous correction came swiftly with the "Black Monday" crash of the New York stock market, which lost a third of its value overnight.*'[46]

Although the crisis generated a massive outcry to reinstate strict regulatory oversight, with much anti-takeover legislation was pressed forward, the Reagan administration refused to support any of them, preferring instead to stick to the new-federalist premise, which classified corporate regulation as a state prerogative. In 1991, rising interest rates put a drastic end to another speculation-driven phenomenon: the real estate bubble, which had been expanding during the 1980s and that caused the collapse of hundreds of S&L. With the federal bailout costing over $100 billion, the effects of the financial crisis were hard-felt for years. Ironically, the global financial crisis of 2007–15 was likewise caused by the exact same dynamics related to the deregulation of the financial sector and the swelling up of a gigantic real estate bubble due to bad subprime mortgages.[47]

Reaganomics also further amplified some early neoliberal policies of the previous Carter administration. For example, he expanded the Airline Deregulation Act of 1978, which eviscerated the Civil Aeronautics Board's regulatory power, with its legislation eventually promoting competitive bidding for route destinations although it had mixed results. While, on one hand, it expanded airline services and boosted competition, on the other hand, it increased air traffic radically and reduced federal

[44] Ibid.
[45] Ibid, pgs 31–2.
[46] Ibid, pg 32.
[47] Ibid, pgs 32–3.

funding for infrastructure. The dishevelled existing resources plus the extra work caused protests from the Professional Air Traffic Controllers Association, as well as large-scale strikes and many workers' demands. Reagan considered the demands too radical and he ended firing about 11,000 employees. Although his anti-labour measure scared many unions, it, however, also forced them to accept the new neoliberal era's business-orientated imperatives.[48]

Another of the Reagan administration's symbolically important neoliberal reforms included its attempt to privatize big portions of federally owned land. Although such initiatives did not actually transcend, they clearly highlighted the huge emphasis neoliberalism put on private ownership. President Reagan's argument held that 50 per cent of the '*underused*' land, west of the Rocky Mountains, which belonged to the US federal government, should be transferred to private hands, so as to enjoy a much better management and productivity. The argument also ran in close parallel to Thatcher's neoliberal claim that the transfer of public resources to private investors improved management and increased productivity. Reagan further highlighted that the revenues from the land would be useful to service public debt. In 1983, however, the privatization scheme was abandoned due to the extreme opposition from many federal legislators and officials in the executive branch, who were extremely reluctant to sell off property they controlled and managed.[49]

Reagan's neoliberal mode of governance also delved into the social policy realm, with the social policy area likewise experiencing major reform initiatives. Many programmes and policies aimed at the poor were passed on to the states, such as Medicaid, Aid to Families with Dependent Children and school lunch programmes. The utilization of a budgetary tool denominated as '*block grants*', for the provision of federal funds to states, was even further increased in order to facilitate the discreet implementation of such reforms. Although the federal government continued to manage and administer major entitlement programmes, like Social Security and Medicare, the Reagan administration also subjected such Keynesian-era social programmes to neoliberal reforms.[50] While experiments like the '*voucher experiment*', which sought '*to introduce a lean voucher system in the Medicare programme to boost competition and efficiency in the name of reducing public expenditures*',[51] did not produce the desired results, they nonetheless represented a strong neoliberal signal for the application of market principles for the deliverance of social services.[52]

Reagan's promotion of trade policy was contrariwise perceived as disappointing by hardcore free-trade neoliberals, being often perceived as more protectionist-like. His free-trade agenda was in fact regarded as quite modest, characterized

[48] Ibid, pgs 33–4.
[49] Ibid, pg 34.
[50] Ibid, pgs 34–5.
[51] Ibid, pg 35.
[52] Ibid.

by piecemeal attempts to retune or readjust existing trade agreements in areas like agricultural commodities and high-technology products, together with the adoption of protectionist stances towards Japanese automobiles. Notwithstanding, from a strong free-trade standpoint, Reaganomics undertook three crucial initiatives which put together triggered the official projection of the free-trade legacy. Those first three neoliberal actions, mainly conducted through major regional and international trade liberalization agreements, completed the partial establishment of a global single market. The whole trade liberalization crusade was spearheaded by many Northern rich industrialized countries, which sought the creation of a single global market.[53]

The first of those three actions, revolved around the Reagan administration's long-time involvement with the 1982 General Agreement on Tariffs and Trade (GATT) negotiations, which sought the liberalization of trade in the agriculture and services sectors. Although in 1982 Reagan left the discussions, GATT expanded successfully to include about 120 countries and as a direct result of the eight rounds of GATT negotiations, tens of thousands of tariff concessions fuelled international transactions worth of tens of billions of dollars.[54]

The second pro-free-trade initiative hinged on the Uruguay Round (1986–94), a comprehensive set of multilateral trade negotiations, which covered a wide range of areas from agriculture and services to intellectual property rights. The Uruguay Round negotiations represented a major force behind the ensuing 1990s free-trade trajectory. More transcendently, the negotiations established the basis for the creation in 1995 of the World Trade Organization (WTO).[55] With its headquarters in Switzerland, the WTO provides a forum for '*implementing and enforcing trade agreements, managing trade disputes, monitoring national trade policies, and providing expertise and training for its members*'.[56]

The third and final big free-trade step forward taken by the Reagan administration was the Free Trade Agreement (FTA) successfully negotiated with Canada, which later also included Mexico. In 1994, President Bill Clinton completed the process with the signature of the North American Free Trade Agreement (NAFTA).[57] NAFTA constitutes a '*comprehensive set of agreements that eliminated tariffs and duties on a variety of important products, ranging from automobiles to textiles and agricultural products. It ultimately covered protections on intellectual property and sought the removal of capital controls on financial capital*'.[58] (Big efforts were consequently made to include many other Latin American countries into what would have been the Free

[53] Ibid
[54] Ibid, pg 37.
[55] Ibid.
[56] Ibid, pgs 37–8.
[57] Ibid, pg 37.
[58] Ibid, pg 38.

Trade Area of the Americas (FTAA), although Latin American Leftist progressive countries continuously trumped such initiatives.)[59]

Thatcherism

In contrast to the Reagan administration (1979–90), Margaret Thatcher government took a very different neoliberal approach for tackling a series of issues. Prime Minister Margaret Thatcher was ideologically much influenced by both Friedrich Hayek and Milton Friedman, as she had read books of Hayek while studying at Oxford University, as well as maintained long personal conversations with him regarding his neoliberal thought and free-market ideas. Similarly, Milton Friedman also influenced her monetarist mentality considerably.

Prime Minister Thatcher deplored her perceived link between the growth of government and public spending increases, as well as vehemently opposed Keynesian increase of taxes on private wealth for the financing of '*burgeoning state bureaucracies*'. She disliked even more the negative effect of monetary growth on overall economic stability. Accordingly, basing herself on such a '*monetarist maxim*' throughout her mandate, Thatcher unleashed a comprehensive set of neoliberal reforms, targeting the reduction of taxes, liberalization of exchange rate controls, reduction of regulations, privatization of national industries and the radical diminishment of the power of labour unions.[60]

Thatcher's fight against inflation set rigorous draconian monetary growth targets. The central importance that she placed on monetary policy was even institutionalized, with the adoption of the Medium Term Financial Strategy (MTFS), which aimed at shifting the focus of economic policy reform from a '*short-term tax-and-spend*' strategy to a '*long-term monetary scheme*'.[61] The MTFS, undertook a '*comprehensive approach to economic policymaking by linking the growth of the money supply to the rising national deficit*',[62] hence establishing a direct relation between deficit spending and high interest rates. Thatcher's MTFS contrasted with Reagan's vague strategies of deficit expenditure, as it contained explicit language on how those reductions should be achieved. Ultimately, Thatcher's blatant fixation on her monetarist objectives led her to both raise the value-added tax (VAT), which gained her much unpopularity, and impose new taxes on revenues from the North Sea oil in order to reduce deficit spending.[63]

While both Thatcherism and Reaganomics disliked '*big government*', Thatcherism also showed little affection for decentralization and local government virtues, with the latter

[59] Ibid.
[60] Ibid.
[61] Ibid, pgs 38–40.
[62] Ibid, pg 40.
[63] Ibid.

being regarded as inefficient and susceptible to corruption from political patronage. Thatcher went as far as abolishing local tax rates or council taxes, by substituting them with the infamous '*poll tax*' or '*community charge*' charged per head. However, in 1993, following much public and political criticism, the poll tax was again replaced by the same previous council taxes.[64]

Very much in line with Friedman's economic theories, Thatcher did not support fixed exchange rates either. Notwithstanding, during the second half of the 1980s, Thatcher's Treasury made exchange rates follow the German mark until the pound began to lose value. Although in 1990 Thatcher joined the European Community's Exchange Rate Mechanism (ERM), which officially pegged the pound to the mark, in 1992 when faced with the possibility of a serious economic downturn due to German reunification causing inflation and of driving interest rates up, John Major ultimately withdrew from it.[65]

Another key distinguishing trait of Thatcherism was its intense neoliberal privatization drive, which sold substantial state assets to the private sector. The privatization campaign began in 1980 with the sale of the National Freight Corporation, British Aerospace, several cable and wireless services, British Rail and Associated British Ports. The campaign continued with the sale of Rolls Royce Aircraft Engines, British Airports, British Petroleum and British Steel, as well as various water and power companies. Many of such state-owned industries were sold to corporations and private investors at low prices, with the objective of upgrading facilities to compete globally.[66]

One of Thatcherism's star social programmes was the sale of huge amounts of housing units or '*council flats*', although it generated many considerable social costs. Despite the fact that councils oversaw the construction, administration and management of millions of properties, Thatcher, however, found them inefficient and unresponsive to tenants' needs. Although the 1980 Housing Act provided tenants the right to buy option, many, however, could not afford them in appealing neighbourhoods, being thus relegated to more peripheral and unattractive areas. In general, the whole issue exacerbated even more the already-existing disparities between social classes and groups.[67]

The wide-ranging de-industrialization process soon caused massive structural unemployment, which made Thatcher call upon the free-market in order to determine which jobs should be saved or sacrificed. However, she undermined the fact that job cuts in the manufacturing sector would lead to a further decline of union power. Thatcher believed that Britain's competitive advantage resided in the financial sector services, which were most specially centred in the '*City*' of London. Thus, and in order

64 Ibid.
65 Ibid, pgs 40–1.
66 Ibid, pg 41.
67 Ibid.

to expedite the structural shift that led to the rebirth of the City, she closed many manufacturing plants, coal pits and mines, which did not meet the private-sector performance standards.[68]

Thatcherism's economic financialization approach subjected London's financial system to a massive neoliberal transformation. Since prior to late 1986, the City's trading system had been technologically outmoded and placed under strict government rules and regulations, with high commissions imposed on investors, it had been difficult for it to compete with New York, where commissions were much lower. Most particularly, foreign firms ready to deal at better rates were not allowed to participate in the London stock and securities trading system. On 27 October 1986, the whole financial sector was radically deregulated, with the event becoming denominated as the '*Big bang*', since it erased all such rules and exclusions. With the neoliberal prime minister reflecting her firm belief in a '*no-holds-barred competition*', London quickly metamorphosed into a much-revitalized global financial epicentre. Just like the New York Stock Exchange (NYSE), the London Stock Exchange became one of the world's best and most important financial epicentres, being upgraded to electronic screen-based trading, as well as providing an excellent environment for the free and aggressive interaction of a wide array of international investors. However, one of its worst downsides was that the City's financial deregulation coincided with the massive overvaluation of stocks, which altogether contributed to the Black Monday worldwide crash.[69]

Thatcher firmly believed that England's competitive advantage in the ever-growing globalized '*new economy*', depended on a '*flexible and skilled workforce*', which thus drove her to '*shift the responsibility of employment from the state to the individual, arguing that well-trained and highly skilled workers would be easily employable while those with limited or outmoded skills would find themselves left behind*'. In accordance with that belief, Thatcher laid the foundation of her well-known '*workfare*' or '*welfare to work*' programme by diminishing the role of unions in favour of a network of service-sector employers, named the Training and Enterprise Councils.[70]

Thatcherism also considered economic inefficiency to be closely related to state welfare policy, and hence also tried to cut state expenditures through several policies and programmes, such as amongst others, child benefit provisions. Notwithstanding, the agenda was abandoned due to the realization that Keynesian social security and child benefit programmes were so imbued in the socio-political fabric of British society that they were deemed politically untouchable.[71]

Thatcherism's public pension reforms were also seen through the same neoliberal prism as labour market training, and were thus aimed at making them more flexible

[68] Ibid, pg 42.
[69] Ibid.
[70] Ibid, pg 43.
[71] Ibid.

Table 5 Reaganomics and Thatcherism: Supply-Side and Monetarist Neoliberalism

REAGAN Supply-Side Economist	**Core Neoliberal Beliefs** Government is inefficient. Government predation leads to poor economic performance.	**Secondary Beliefs** Monetary and fiscal stability is necessary for economic growth.	**Core Neoliberal Policy Issue** Restrict the extent of government predation through minimal taxation.	**Secondary Policy Issue** Create economic stability through deficit reduction and spending restraint.
THATCHER Monetarist Economist	Government is inefficient. Monetary and fiscal stability is necessary for economic growth.	Government predation leads to poor economic performance.	Create economic stability through deficit reduction and spending restraint.	Restrict the extent of predation through minimal taxation.

Source: STEGER, M.B. and RAVI, K.R. '*Neoliberalism: A Very Short Introduction*', pg 25.

and '*responsive to shifting market conditions*'. However, and once again, the same intractable electorate, which was still very attached to the Keynesian legacy, countered Thatcher, making her thus settle for more modest social reforms.[72] '*Thus, she limited the bulk of her reform strategy to streamlining rules and procedures and instituting greater consistency among departments in the managing of means-testing eligibility requirements for those drawing on social benefits. At the same time, these administrative reforms were part of an attempt to change the motivational logic at the root of what she saw as bureaucratic inertia*".[73]

Prime Minister Thatcher also subdued the British National Health Service (NHS) to market-based practices by exposing hospitals to many competitive bids from the private sector for many services. '*The end of the decade of Thatcherism saw the passage of neoliberal reform legislation that gave local health authorities increased discretion and administrative powers over healthcare services – including the power to manage costs by contracting with doctors and hospitals to provide services*'.[74]

Quite markedly, both Thatcherism and Reaganomics sought the application of the public sector neoliberal management techniques to the private sector, through the principles of the '*new public management*', largely based on the clear definition of objectives and the strict measurement and assessment of results in relation to costs.

[72] Ibid, pgs 43–4.
[73] Ibid, pg 44.
[74] Ibid, pgs 44–5.

However, the introduction of such a new neoliberal mode of governance proved quite fatal on many social programmes, whose true benefits were only appreciated in the long run, and even then not too easily quantifiable.[75]

In relation to foreign affairs, both Thatcherism and Reaganomics were likewise very flagrantly attached to an imaginary, which very much adhered to '*torch-bearers*' of '*an Anglo-American civilization anchored in the ideals of political liberty, free-market commerce, and love of country*'. Such tension between the national and the global imaginaries was very clearly reflected by Thatcher's 1982 bigoted Falklands War and Reagan's 1983 invasion of the Caribbean's small Grenada Island.[76]

During the 1980s, first-wave neoliberalism was very interlaced with world events and most especially with the geopolitical imperative to impede the spread of communism and socialist developmentalism in the Third World. The decades-long '*Cold War hostility and mistrust between the capitalist West and the communist East only intensified Reagan's and Thatcher's desire to stand up to the "Evil Empire"*'.[77] Paradoxically, the 1985 election to the Soviet Politburo of Mikhail Gorvachev paved the way for some modest market-orientated reforms carried out in Russia, from '*within*', which also reflected neoliberal tendencies in the communist East. Reagan and Thatcher publicly endorsed Gorvachev's comprehensive economic and political restructuring programme, or '*perestroika*', as well as his cultural revolution or '*glasnost*' (openness about public affairs). Thanks to the Soviet leader's willingness to undertake market-orientated reforms, his Western counterparts were able to work closely with him in order to build a whole new relationship, largely based on neoliberal ideas. With the new ideological framework and rapprochement becoming evident with the consequent breakthroughs in arms-control disarmaments that were carried out, Gorvachev's reforms finally led to the unravelling of the Soviet Union and the political independence of its Eastern European client States.[78]

Such a historic opportunity offered by Gorvachev's new ideological outlook was indeed quickly perceived and recognized by the neoliberal pioneers, Reagan and Thatcher, who, with the rapid decline and collapse of the Soviet '*Evil Empire*', were able to further confirm their strong belief in the superiority of free-markets and their liberal-democratic political systems.[79]

[75] Ibid, pg 44.
[76] Ibid, pg 45.
[77] Ibid.
[78] Ibid, pgs 46–7.
[79] Ibid, pg 47.

17

Second-Wave Neoliberalization in the 1990s: *Clinton's Market Globalism and Blair's Third Way*

During the 1990s, President Bill Clinton and Prime Minister Tony Blair adopted ideological positions, which reflected a halfway approach that embraced major portions of neoliberalism, while at the same time, pursued the incorporation of parts of a socially progressive agenda, usually associated with democratic left-wing political parties.[1] The two leaders became very closely intertwined by their common will of refining neoliberalism, by stripping-off some of its first-wave neo-conservative accretions, such as hyperpatriotism and militarism, its '*antiquated family values*', its dislike of multiculturalism, as well as its neglect of ecological issues. They hoped that their '*purified product – a socially conscious market globalism*', would drive the world into a '*new age of technological progress and prosperity*'.[2]

The 1990s, more '*modernized*', second-wave neoliberalism had a huge impact on the decade's post-communist political landscape. After more than ten years of Reaganomics and Thatcherism, neoliberalism conveyed an attractive model for progressive political forces eager to return to power. By the year 2000, and from then onwards, many leaders of European traditional social-democratic parties, like German Chancellor Gerhard Schröder, Dutch Prime Minister Wim Kok, French Prime Ministers Pierre Beregovoy and Lionel Jospin, and Italian Prime Ministers Romano Prodi and Massimo D'Alema, had adopted the new left-centre agenda. Together, President Clinton and Prime Minister Blair spearheaded the generalized unification of efforts and attempts, which liberalized trade relations and integrated national economies into one global single market. Those two political leaders are also largely accredited for producing the economic boom of the '*Roaring Nineties*'.[3]

The 1990s second-wave neoliberalization was very tightly latched to the imperative of making the economy grow, without falling prey to the divisiveness of '*old-style partisan politics*', by way of putting forward an innovative mélange of market-orientated thought and moderate social policies. Both Bill Clinton's market globalism and Tony

[1] Ibid, pg 50.
[2] Ibid, pg 51.
[3] Ibid.

Blair's Third Way synthesized market-orientated economic growth within an ethical framework of social justice and human rights. Their programmes clearly reflected a big change of mind, regarding the passing away of the age of relatively sheltered national economies, with countries and their economies being drawn into the dynamics of corporate-led globalization.[4]

Second-wave neoliberalism, has, nonetheless, also been very widely criticized by the political Left for its usage of a '*largely symbolic rhetoric of community*', while at the same time, continuing with the '*turbo-capitalist*' projects of Reaganomics and Thatcherism. Although the economic vibrancy of the Roaring Nineties is widely acknowledged, the Global North's and South's extreme levels of inequality reflect the skewed prosperity that second-wave neoliberal policies produced.[5] In contrast, supporters of market globalism have, however, praised the second-wave's ability to generate robust economic growth, as well as to supply consumers in developing regions with cheap consumer goods from the developed world, which have considerably raised living standards in such disadvantaged regions.[6]

At one stage or another of their mandates both President Clinton and Prime Minister Blair publicly acknowledged the neoliberal nature of their agendas. In 1996, President Clinton announced at his State of the Union Address that the era of big government was over, as well as indirectly transmitted his strong belief that in the '*global age*', '*trimmed-down, activist governments operating more efficiently by embracing a neoliberal mode of governance*' would have a very dynamic role.[7] Clinton firmly believed that what some neoliberals dubbed as '*super-capitalism*' or '*turbo-capitalism*' could nonetheless work well, combined with greater corporate responsibility and moderate social welfare provisions.[8]

Similarly, Prime Minister Blair's reformed '*New Labour*' Party sought to broaden its appeal to all social classes by arguing that the New Labour stood for '*social advancement through individual achievement*'.[9] In 1998, Blair declared his intention to '*create a global network of "centre-left" parties that would develop a joint policy framework capable of responding to the challenges of the post-Cold War world. The key to forging such a "Third Way" beyond the time-worn agendas of the old Keynesian Left and the new Thatcherist Right ... was a commitment to the centre-left principle of strengthening social solidarity without dropping the neoliberal ideal of market-orientated entrepreneurship.*'[10]

4 Ibid, pgs 74–5.
5 Ibid, pg 75.
6 Ibid.
7 Ibid, pg 51.
8 Ibid.
9 Ibid, pg 50.
10 Ibid.

Clinton's Market Globalism

From the very beginning of his presidential mandate President Bill Clinton confirmed his strong belief that the American economy was inextricably linked to a series of processes, which would make the world much more interconnected and interdependent. A '*new economy*' of global reach was very quickly evolving, being muscularly driven by irresistible market forces. During the 1990s, the new buzzword – '*globalization*' – emerged, becoming henceforth established as the main reference to the way economic relations across the planet had expanded and intensified.[11]

The late twentieth century's process of compression of time and space was carried out very tightly hinged on the close interrelation between the globalization phenomenon and economics, which all in all '*would have been impossible without the worldwide expansion of markets, the rise of transnational corporations (TNCs), and the intensification of economic flows across the globe. Moreover, these economic developments were facilitated by the rapid transformation of information, communication, and transportation technology – a digital revolution epitomized by the proliferation of personal computers, the Internet, satellite TV, standardized containers, fibre-optic cables, electronic barcodes, and global supply chains.*'[12]

Beyond the realms of commerce and technology, the unfolding of globalization was also a direct consequence of the worldwide dominance of the neoliberal ideology following the 1989–91 collapse of Soviet communism. Globalization as an economic phenomenon, driven by the irreversible dynamics of the free market and cutting-edge technology, was highly fuelled at the same time by political leaders like Bill Clinton and Tony Blair, high-level executives of large transnational corporations, corporate lobbyists, prominent journalists and public-relations specialists, cultural elites and entertainment celebrities, who within the globalist framework, articulated vigorously their neoliberal agenda.[13]

The gradual imbuement of globalization was to a large extent carried out by such global power elites with neoliberal ideas and meanings, who made their influential ideological narrative of market globalism deeply transcend national and cultural boundaries. Neoliberal '*transnationalization*' was spurred by various claims. One claim projected the creation of globally integrating markets, based on a rational process that increased individual freedom and material progress in the world. The claim's underlying assumption held that markets and consumerist principles are universally applicable, as they appeal to every single (self-interested) human being, disregarding

[11] Ibid, pgs 51–2.
[12] Ibid, pg 52.
[13] Ibid, pg 53.

their social context. Stark cultural differences should likewise neither obstruct nor impede, the establishment of a single global free-market of goods, services and capital. Another accompanying interrelated claim assured that the liberalization of trade and the global integration of markets would benefit everyone materially. Such assertion much boosted the global appeal of neoliberalism, by assuring people that the creation of a single global market would '*lift regions out of poverty*'. The latter allegation was very strongly supported and promoted by international economic organizations, like the International Monetary Fund (IMF) and the World Bank (WB), through their imposition on less developed countries of structural adjustment programmes, circumscribed as '*poverty alleviation*'.[14]

Another of the neoliberal prerogatives projected the liberalization and global integration of markets as inevitably irreversible, or something like a '*natural force such as the weather or gravity*'. It made the neoliberal discourse more convincing to people, whom for the sake of survival or prosperity, needed to adapt to the inherent rules of the free-market. One last neoliberal contention linked the notion of globally expanding self-regulating markets to democracy and individual choice, thereby implying that economic and political forms of freedom are interconnected. Contradictorily, the main neoliberal belief sustains that free-market economics will establish democracy and not the other way around.[15]

President Clinton was a staunch market globalist and he therefore believed that the economic vitality of the global economy was the key for a sustained expansion of the US economy. Clinton's main economic strategy was primarily based on trade, since he perceived the huge possibilities for mutual growth that would entail furthering trade ties with the '*emerging economies of the Global South*'. Although he still supported America's world leadership, he nonetheless envisioned a world interweaved by trade relationships, through the exertion of '*soft power*' rather than '*hard power*',[16] which would not only benefit America's interests, but also complement old military-based alliances, like the North Atlantic Treaty Organization (NATO).[17]

President Clinton's market globalism framework was largely based on the neoliberal thesis that free trade would produce unprecedented prosperity to both the developed and the developing worlds. While Clinton always held that government programmes and policies were ad-hoc when free-markets destabilized existing social networks,

[14] Ibid.

[15] Ibid, pgs 53–4.

[16] Joseph Nye Jr., an international relations expert and Clinton administration official, coined such terminology. '*Hard power*', refers to military and economic prowess, which through inducements or threats – '*carrots and sticks*' – changes other nations' or political actors' positions. '*Soft power*', involves the use of cultural and ideological appeals, to obtain desired results without commanding allegiance or the use of force. Ibid, pg 55.

[17] Ibid, pg 54.

his administration, however, was extremely supportive of international institutions, like the IMF and WB, imposing radical market-orientated structural adjustment programmes on developing countries.[18] Although the United States claimed that such trade policies were for the benefit of the whole global community of nations, it is nonetheless argued that Clinton's market globalism was only sought after in order to perpetuate US hegemony, rather than for truly providing '*genuine multilateral agreements or providing a forum for an open dialogue of alternative views*'.[19]

The same perception surrounds Clinton's grand stratagem of promoting the North America Free Trade Agreement (NAFTA), the General Agreement on Tariffs and Trade (GATT) and the Uruguay Trade Round negotiations, begun by his predecessors and ultimately signed by him in 1994, in Morocco, Marrakech. '*The Treaty allowed for a tightening of neoliberal rules governing the international economic system and established the powerful WTO in the place of the old GATT. It further reduced trade barriers on goods, expanded trade liberalization of services, provided clarification of what counted as "unfair trade" practices, and promoted an international agreement on intellectual property rights (TRIPs). Clinton made sure that the new provisions – especially the liberalisation of the service industry and intellectual property rights (where the US enjoyed a major comparative advantage) – became the cornerstone of the Marrakech Agreement.*'[20] Contrariwise, with the objective of balancing neoliberal policies, which promoted competitive markets through free trade vis-à-vis social and environmental justice concerns, Clinton's executive power also negotiated amendments on issues that covered international labour and environmental standards.[21]

The worldwide promotion of the neoliberal Washington Consensus by President Clinton was most specially reflected through his economic strategy towards the former Soviet Union's successor states. The strong relationship between Clinton and the increasingly problematic Russian president, Boris Yeltsin, allowed Clinton to channel into the country many American advisors to direct its transition from communism to capitalism.[22] Furthermore, the US president supported the G-7 and the IMF in their recommendations for the shock therapy imposed on Russia, which persisted with the '*big bang*' approach to the economic transition demanding the '*lifting of price controls, the privatisation of nearly 250,000 state-owned companies, and the liberalisation of trade. The reward for staying on the course was to be the continuation of massive loans from the IMF and other international economic institutions*'.[23]

By the late 1990s, the negative consequences of Russia's shock therapy were clearly exposed by the dramatic widening of economic inequality, with only a tiny power

[18] Ibid.
[19] Ibid, pg 56.
[20] Ibid.
[21] Ibid.
[22] Ibid, pgs 56–7.
[23] Ibid, pg 57.

elite of '*oligarchs*' reaping most of the benefits. Although to the outside observer, the neoliberal reforms deserved merit and praise, President Yeltsin, however, increased his internal authoritarian actions through the dissolution of Parliament, suspension of the Constitutional Court, pervasive censorship and the escalation of the Chechnyan conflict into a full-blown war. As a result of the 1997–8 Asian Financial Crisis, Russia's earnings from oil and other resources declined sharply and foreign investors quickly withdrew capital from Russian markets, which in general caused serious inflation and the breakdown of Russia's banking system. While the Yeltsin government was forced to devaluate the Russian ruble and stop the payment on US$40 billion in ruble bonds, despite the economy's recovery, the country suffered severe blows to its young democracy, which are still very visible through the continued oligarch rule of the country.[24]

The domestic policy of President Clinton was also a clear reflection of his market globalism approach, with a very strong focus being placed on retrieving the US economy's former glory. The 1991 severe fiscal crisis, induced by the S&L crisis, had made the annual fiscal deficit during the end of the Reagan administration nearly approach US$150 billion, which by the early 1990s had ascended to about US$300 billion. Thus, President Clinton was urged by his advisors to place the reduction of the budget deficit at the top of his economic agenda. Whilst they believed that excessive levels of public borrowing would deter private investment, the negative effect of long-term interest rates was also emphasized upon, which pointed to the control of the growth of federal deficit for their lowering.[25]

As soon as President Clinton assumed office in January 1993, he committed his administration to the neoliberal economic drive towards fiscal stability.

Clinton's large economic team was formed by '*deficit hawks*'', with strong ties to Wall Street, like Alice Rivlin, Lloyd Bentsen, Robert Rubin, Lawrence Summers and Leon Panetta. Clinton also sought the advice of Federal Reserve chairman, Alan Greenspan, who further convinced him to put into practice an economically feasible, five-year massive federal deficit reduction plan of US$500 billion. Thus and accordingly, Clinton established draconian spending limits, as well as set an ambitious inflation target of 3 to 3.5 per cent. Furthermore, he also offered Greenspan unqualified discretion and the Federal Reserve independent authority regarding monetary policy and the setting of interest rates, which reflected his willingness not to influence Federal Reserve policy for political purposes.[26] By the mid-1990s, the neoliberal combination of fiscal and monetary policies began having very positive effects without overheating the economy or weakening the dollar, with the budget deficit declining and long-interest rates falling. *'As a result, the US attracted new international investment from East Asia, the stocks from American high-tech companies skyrocketed and Silicon Valley experienced*

[24] Ibid.
[25] Ibid, pgs 57–8.
[26] Ibid, pg 58.

an unprecedented boom. During that period, a number of Asian and Latin American countries adopted fixed exchange rates that were pegged to the stable US dollar, making it more attractive for those nations to buy US bonds and other assets. Flush with cash, Americans consumed like never before, targeting, in particular, big-ticket items like computers, appliances, automobiles, and real estate. At the same time, however, this new-found prosperity resulted in political pressure to reduce taxes as voices echoing the principles of Reaganomics grew louder.'[27]

President Clinton's tax cuts were aimed at '*capital gains investments by homeowners in real property, and securities and stocks, as well as businesses investing in new research and development in high-technology sectors*'.[28]

The administration, consistent with the second-wave neoliberal objectives of mixing market initiatives with social concerns, held that tax breaks for American venture capitalists and start-up companies would encourage breakthroughs and advancements in technology and medical research that would ultimately benefit the whole global community. In accordance with such approach, in 1997, the Federal Budget included more than US$10 billion of business and capital gains tax relief over a five-year span. In 1998, President Clinton signed a massive tax cut package totalling nearly US$100 billion, which provided more relief for capital gains and estate taxes, and at the same time provided limited tax relief for working families that earned less than US$100,000 a year. On the other hand, such tax cuts also benefitted powerful US corporations, like Hewlett-Packard, Johnson and Johnson and Microsoft. Whereas during the 1990s compensation packages of American CEOs reached new heights, with wages stagnating and only growing marginally, by the turn of the millennium economic disparities in the country had dramatically widened.[29]

The most radical neoliberal measures of the Clinton administration, however, are considered to have been the ones connected to the further deregulation of the economy. Clinton carried out some of the most comprehensive deregulatory reforms of the twentieth century, as '*antiquated regulatory policies*' were perceived to be curtailing entrepreneurial initiatives, assisted by both technological breakthroughs in telecommunications and the development of new international financial instruments. Although the inherent flaws of such deep deregulations in the finance sector only became evident with the global financial crisis of 2007–15, with the 1999 Financial Services Modernization Act, the legal divisions between commercial and investment banking were removed, as well as the ones between insurance companies and brokerage houses. Other deregulatory measures likewise ended in a flood of mergers in the telecommunications industry. Clinton's 1996 Telecommunications Act led to spectacular mega-mergers, like the ones involving SBC-Pacific Bell-Ameritech, Bell

[27] Ibid, pg 59.
[28] Ibid.
[29] Ibid, pgs 59–60.

Atlantic-Nynex-GTE, Quest US West, AOL-Time Warner, AT&T-TCI, plus the now-defunct World-MCI, which allowed Bell companies to compete in long-distance services and cable TV delivery.[30] While the Clinton administration was dead set on undercutting monopolies by encouraging rigorous competition, the president supported vigorous anti-trust campaigns, involving high-profile government lawsuits against Microsoft, Intel Corp and American Airlines, which clearly indicated that President Clinton's neoliberal approach was very strongly committed to the defence of free-markets and to the encouragement of competition.[31]

A last crucial aspect of President Clinton's market globalism framework of neoliberal policies in the areas of trade and fiscal policy was that they clearly demonstrated that his pro-business policies were intricately interwoven with progressive social programmes. A lot of Clinton's neoliberal ideas on social policy, stemmed from his affiliation with a rising party faction named the '*New Democrats*', which strongly embraced the neoliberal principles of '*individual responsibility*' and '*accountability*', instead of the old Left's credo of '*collective welfare*'.[32] In 1996, Clinton signed the Welfare Reform Act, which presented a new version of '*welfare*', requiring work in exchange for assistance. '*A maximum of two years of benefits were delivered before parents were compelled to work or engage in job (re)training. No recipient was permitted more than five years of cumulative assistance. However, there were a number of special considerations, which included provisions for childcare and medical insurance for short-term unemployed mothers*'.[33] The Act, however, reduced allocations, as well as limited the duration of the welfare payments, which thus often forced welfare recipients to accept short-term, low-pay work in the service sector.[34]

Quite evidently, President Clinton maintained Reagan's approach of '*re-inventing government*' very consistent by way of implementing a neoliberal mode of governance, through which success was measured mainly in terms of efficiency and profitability. Clinton, therefore also supported initiatives for contracting many public services to private sector companies, ministered by county and municipal authorities. Despite facing criticism due to the sometimes difficult proper oversight of worker compliance and the complex coordination between governmental agencies and the private sector, the Clinton administration supported some important centre-left programmes, such as increases in the minimum federal wage, as well as an Earned Income Tax Credit, which provided economic assistance to America's working poor. Additionally, both Bill and Hillary Clinton also put huge efforts into a universal healthcare initiative, which although did not materialize would have covered over 40 million uninsured working Americans.[35]

[30] Ibid, pg 60.
[31] Ibid, pgs 62–3.
[32] Ibid, pgs 64–5.
[33] Ibid, pg 65.
[34] Ibid.
[35] Ibid, pgs 65–6.

Blair's Third Way

In 1997, one of Prime Minister Tony Blair's most trusted advisors, the then director of the London School of Economics, Anthony Giddens, recommended the new government to forge a '*Third Way*', sensitive to the challenges posed by the dawning of the global age and its '*New Economy*'.[36] Such an innovative approach was intended to transcend '*the vexing political dualisms of the past but also bridge the stark divide between free-market dynamics and concerns for public good*'.[37]

> *The Third Way involves a balance between regulation and deregulation, on transnational as well as national and local levels; and a balance between the economic and non-economic life of the society. The second of these is at least as important as the first, but attained in some part through it.*[38]

Prime Minister Tony Blair promised the British that through his '*Third Way*' he would put an end to the old politics of '*class warfare*' by reconciling middle-class concerns with business interests. Blair used his political skills to forge new coalitions and bipartisan networks, which brought together groups and individuals from a broad ideological spectrum. His drive towards the political centre awakened a new generation of Labour leaders, like himself and Gordon Brown, who embraced neoliberal ideas in order to fundamentally change the relationship between government and the marketplace. Under the '*New Labour*' logo, Blair and Brown abandoned their party's socialist heritage so as to broaden its political base, seeking to attain prosperity and promote employment through the control of government expenditures instead of through the redistribution of wealth.[39]

In a big way, Prime Minister Blair's shift towards neoliberalism was profoundly inspired by the electoral success of Bill Clinton and the New Democrats. Both the Clinton and Blair administrations seemed to have perceived quite well the new emerging global economic interdependent paradigm. In the autumn of 1997, the Blair government met up with a contingency of top representatives of the Clinton administration, which included Deputy Treasury Secretary Larry Summers and First Lady Hillary Clinton, in order to discuss economic policy. Soon after, it became obvious that the Blair '*Third-Way modernizers*' had readily embraced the basic principles of Clinton's market globalism, with the New Labour government emphasizing strongly on the values of individual ownership and entrepreneurship.[40] Basing himself on strong neoliberal values, '*the Prime Minister argued that remaining social inequalities could best be tackled*

[36] Ibid, pg 66.
[37] Ibid, pg 67.
[38] Ibid.
[39] Ibid.
[40] Ibid.

by fundamentally changing the "paternalistic" relationship between state and society to one based on a "social partnership" among individuals'.[41]

Running in parallel to President Clinton's market globalism, Prime Minister Blair's Third Way highlighted the importance of global cooperation and consensus building through international institutions, with Blair showing new sympathetic sentiments towards the ongoing process of European integration, which contrasted with his Conservative predecessors. Initially, Blair had high hopes for British participation in the single-currency European Monetary Union, as delineated in the 1992 Maastricht Treaty, and thus directed the Treasury to set up various '*Euro forums*', spearheaded by renowned business leaders already working for regional convergence. Furthermore, the government enacted customs reforms, enabling British firms to pay taxes, issue shares and receive certain grants in Euros. Blair was convinced that Euro membership within the Eurozone would fuel huge opportunities for British business and financial markets court new investments.[42]

Notwithstanding, Prime Minister Blair's attitude changed radically when the Eurozone's economic performance did not meet its high expectations. While his New Labour government had limited public spending drastically, other countries, like Germany and France, had by far exceeded deficit spending limits outlined in the Maastricht Treaty, thus making the Treaty's stability and growth strategy lose much credibility. Ultimately, believing and trusting the stable British pound much more than an apparently tenuous and fluctuating Euro, Blair decided to remain outside the Eurozone. In the short-term, his decision was vindicated by the massive uprise of foreign direct investment in Britain from US$20 billion per annum in the 1990s to US$80 billion per annum in 2001.[43]

Very clearly mirroring President Clinton's market globalism, Prime Minister Blair specified that the only way for Britain to enhance its global competitiveness was through the adoption of a coherent macroeconomic framework for taxation and spending practices. Blair confirmed his neoliberal mode of governance with the implementation of a Code for Fiscal Stability, '*which institutionalised the five principles of prudent fiscal management: transparency, stability, responsibility, fairness and efficiency*'.[44] While it reassured investors of his commitment to managing the State coffers in a neoliberal fashion, it also required the prime minister and his government to '*adhere to clearly stated objectives and rules that had to be reported to and discussed with the business community*'.[45] The new fiscal policy rules-based approach eventually also led to the instauration of periodical Comprehensive Spending Reviews, which outlined departmental spending planification and objectives, based on strict cost-benefit calculations. Blair's neoliberal policy framework was even more fine-tuned

[41] Ibid, pg 68.
[42] Ibid.
[43] Ibid, pgs 68–9.
[44] Ibid, pg 69.
[45] Ibid.

with the Third Way philosophy's strong emphasis on the importance of inclusiveness and consensus-building, directing the '*Treasury to consult with spending departments, cabinet committees, and business groups … Formalizing these relationships required the establishment of over 300 task forces dedicated to facilitating greater coordination both within and among central government departments*'.[46]

Clearly emulating President Bill Clinton (who had won himself the support of the business community and the middle class, by blaming the 1991–2 economic recession on the Reagan/Bush era's failed policies) once again, Prime Minister Blair linked the volatile '*boom-bust*' cycles of the Thatcher/Major years, to their '*ineffective fiscal and monetary strategies*'. Just after being elected prime minister, one of Blair's first major economic initiatives in order to encourage investment and growth granted the Monetary Policy Committee '*full operational independence in setting short-term interest rates while retaining the government's prerogative to set an ambitious inflation target of 2.5%*'.[47] Following the setting of such a course of action, Chancellor of the Exchequer Gordon Brown, after consulting with the US Federal Reserve Chairman Alan Greenspan, eventually granted the Bank of England policy independence. Additionally, both the Confederation of British Industry and the British Chambers of Commerce were delighted to learn that denouncements were made due to '*aggressive union wage bargaining practices allegedly threatening economic growth*'.[48]

The fiscal strategies of the New Labour's Third Way were consciously designed to reduce government borrowing, and at the same time, bolster opportunities for business and the middle class. Prime Minister Blair's entrepreneurial sympathies lay most especially with companies and individuals able to generate new venture capital, to invest in new technologies, and to fuel research and development. While the government's neoliberal reforms were successful in broadening the tax base, they equally cut top income and business tax rates in order to provide investors with incentives. Additionally, Blair also formulated the '*Golden Rule*', which was a measure that directed the Treasury not to exceed public debt over 40 per cent of GDP. What is more, Blair also declared that no additional spending would be sought for health, education or social security, as the welfare reform was to be implemented with no increase in public expenditure or raise of taxes. Making one exception to such assertion and modelled on Clinton's workfare programme, Blair endorsed a new '*welfare-to-work*' programme, issuing a one-time '*windfall tax*' on privatized utilities. Considering Blair's commitment to '*social justice*', although both Blair and Brown had clearly emphasized that the government's welfare provisions would require '*accountability*' and '*responsibility*' from its participants, Blair's commitment to '*social justice*', as implemented through his neoliberal social policy agenda, shocked many working-class supporters.[49]

[46] Ibid, pg 70.
[47] Ibid.
[48] Ibid.
[49] Ibid, pgs 70–1.

The New Labour social policy mainly focused on the reconfiguration of three basic services: reform of the National Health Service, assistance to the unemployed and assistance to the poor. Prime Minister Blair sought the transformation of the '*paternalistic*' British welfare system into an American-style neoliberal programme, named '*New Deal*'. Notwithstanding and in stark contrast to the FDR's Keynesian-based programme, Blair's New Deal liberalized work-training schemes even more, replacing Thatcher's Training and Enterprise Council, with a much more neoliberal '*partnership*' model. The Blair government, also promoted progressive initiatives, like the Working Families Tax Credit, in aid of the working poor, as well as adopted a national minimum wage, in order to assist low-income workers. However, such divergent social policy strategies likewise reflected the difficulties of building a viable Third Way, which went beyond the Left and Right.[50]

As regards second-wave neoliberal foreign policy, the preferences of the two leaders very clearly harboured many sympathies for '*neoliberal institutionalism*', which emphasized on ethics and humanitarian dynamics, as tools for advancing national power, in opposition to realist models, that took military and diplomatic policy as their preferred instruments. Market globalists, like Clinton and Blair, strongly believed in the link between the global expansion of commerce and a more peaceful world, and thus during the time moral values like reciprocity and human rights played a chief role in international relations. Both presidents worked closely together in the redefinition of the role of international institutions, like NATO, from a Western military alliance created to keep the Soviet bloc at bay, to a global multi-purpose organization devoted to enhance international security, through the protection of human rights and its peacekeeping missions. The European Union (EU) was also much relied upon for such undertakings.[51]

A clear example of the influence of such neoliberal institutionalism was the 1991–9 Balkan Wars. Despite the fact that during its early stages the EU was called upon to use its entire diplomatic and non-interventionist means at its disposal in order to bring the conflict to an end, the conflict eventually ended with the NATO intervention in Kosovo. Despite the failure of the EU's diplomatic measures to end the conflict, the new rationale for the NATO intervention in Kosovo was very markedly '*couched in the liberal language of "moral imperative" rather than the realist idiom of "national interest" … The campaign was justified explicitly on humanitarian grounds: to prevent ethnic cleansing and protect the Kosovar Albanian majority in the Serb-ruled province*'.[52] Foreign policy, especially in relation to military interventions, had clearly adopted a new approach, which was proposed by Prime Minister Blair as '*a "doctrine of international community" based on traditional Christian just-war teachings that permitted collective acts of violence against implacable aggressors to prevent humanitarian disasters*'.[53]

[50] Ibid, pgs 71–2.
[51] Ibid, pg 72.
[52] Ibid, pg 74.
[53] Ibid.

18

The 2007–15 Global Financial Crisis: *The Neoliberal Crisis*

Since the beginning of the process of 'global neoliberalization', although there was quite evidently a clearly established international neoliberal project, there was, however, no clearly defined neoliberal strategy as such or in itself. Despite the fact that neoliberal policies have been applied in multiple levels, as well as transcended a wide array of areas, neoliberalism has, nonetheless, proven to be based on a poorly developed and incoherent strategy. Many of the neoliberal project's policies are considered to have been '*contradictory and pragmatic responses to the antinomies of neoliberal assumptions as formulated in the Washington Consensus*'.[1] Irrespective of neoliberalism's international agenda, the actual implementation of neoliberal policies was highly dependent on local struggles and compromises. '*There is an obvious conflict between the logic of capital accumulation, which drives politics in all states with free elections*'.[2] The requirements of international capital and the demands of local electorates or local struggles created an ongoing tension, which opened the way for '*state-to-state*' variation. '*Neoliberal policies have been resisted and contested at every step and at every level, from collective agreements to welfare policies to trade agreements, thus existing social forces and institutions have mediated their implementation in many unexpected ways*'.[3]

Across the international landscape, most particularly within Europe, the importance of the different national peculiarities, together with the differing '*varieties of neoliberalism*' approach, has often been underestimated by neo-Gramscian accounts and their highlights on transnational class struggles. However, advocates of the '*varieties of capitalist societies*' approach have recognized the rather unique ways in which capitalist societies have responded to neoliberal challenges, although they have falsely assumed that the forces of change have been external to national models. Undeniably however, the struggle for neoliberalism occurred simultaneously both within national societies and outside them.[4]

1 FORBA. FORBA Discussion Paper 3/2007. HERMANN, C. *Neoliberalism in the European Union*, pg 6. http://www.forschungsnetzwerk.at/downloadpub/neoliberalism_eu_SR%2003-07.pdf
2 Ibid.
3 Ibid.
4 Ibid.

Despite the existence of many internal contradictions and countless variations of neoliberal policies, the actual outcomes have always been the result of deliberate political choices, rather than the workings of abstract forces, such as globalization and market competition. One clear example of such neoliberal policies was provided by the US hike in interest rates, which was not the only existing viable solution for controlling runaway inflation, as price-controls could have been another possible alternative measure to achieve the same end.[5] *'The Federal Reserve's decision to increase interest rates was not a technical but political choice and based on ideological conviction that the crisis could only be resolved by more, rather than less, market activity and competition. Neoliberal preferences for "free trade" and "free" capital mobility, monetary restraint and budgetary austerity, flexibilization of labour markets, downward pressure on wages, privatisation of public companies and services and the "workfarist" restructuring of welfare states were not random policy prescriptions.'*[6] Together, however, they produced the same outcome with countries subjected to neoliberal restructuring experiencing both a redistribution of wealth, which has gone from work-dependent wage earners to owners of financial assets, and a substantial increase in inequality among salaried employees.[7]

The 2007–15 Global Financial Crisis, '*Great Recession*' or '*Neoliberal Crisis*', was the direct result of the huge bundle of neoliberal political choices, which in turn created so many technical flaws. The unregulated economic and financial system created so much opacity within it that anarchic financial free-will, malpraxis, speculative irrational behaviour, financial crimes and fiscal and tax offences became widespread, eventually leading to the breakdown of stock exchanges, banks and markets. Compared in its viciousness to the Great Depression, the '*Great Recession*' caused the quasi-total collapse of the system, the bankruptcy of countries, like Iceland, the economic rescuing of countries, like Ireland, Greece and Portugal, the financial assistance of Spain, as well as the downfall of many heads of state and government, presidents of economic and financial institutions and other world leaders. Likewise, a never-ending list of multinationals, financial entities and historically established companies and firms also ceased to exist.

> *The Global financial crisis is a crisis which is simultaneously individual, national and global. It is a crisis of both the developed and the developing world. It is a crisis which is at once institutional, intellectual and ideological. It has called into question the prevailing neoliberal economic orthodoxy of the past 30 years – the orthodoxy that has underpinned the national and global regulatory frameworks that have so spectacularly failed to prevent the economic mayhem which has visited upon us.*[8]

[5] Ibid, pgs 6–7.
[6] Ibid, pg 7.
[7] Ibid.
[8] STEGER, M.B. and RAVI, K.R. *Neoliberalism: A Very Short Introduction*, pg 133.

To a great extent, the wide-ranging neoliberal deregulation measures, which both first-wave and second-wave neoliberalism generated, set the stage for such a financial catastrophe. During the 1980s and 1990s, three consecutive neoliberal governments raised borrowing limits and reduced asset requirements for loans, which much stimulated US mortgage markets. Begun by the Reagan administration, the three governments deregulated significantly the US financial services industry. In 1999, Congress repealed the 1933 Glass-Steagall Act, which had since the 1929 Crash and the ensuing Great Depression prohibited commercial banks from engaging in investment activities in Wall Street.[9] The Federal Reserve had been for some time reasoning that since the dark days of the Great Depression there were three established effective checks on corporate speculation, which already provided more security to the financial-banking sector: '*(1) An "effective" Securities Exchange Commission (SEC); (2) the higher sophistication level of most investors; (3) independent rating credit agencies like Moody's Investors Services that delivered accurate and reliable information to investors.*'[10] Thus, in 1999, President Clinton signed the new legislation, and henceforth all restrictions on commercial bank ownership of investment banks were removed.[11]

Such a series of neoliberal deregulations in the financial-banking sector consequently generated a frenzy of mergers, which in turn created huge financial-services conglomerates, very eager to plunge into securities ventures in areas outside their underlying business. '*Derivatives, financial futures, credit default swaps, and related instruments became extremely popular when new computer-based mathematical models suggested more secure ways of managing the risk involved in buying an asset in the future at a price agreed to in the present. Relying far less on savings deposits, financial institutions borrowed from each other and sold these loans as securities, thus passing the risk on to investors into these securities. Other "innovative" financial instruments such as "hedge funds" leveraged with borrowed funds fuelled a variety of speculative activities, including full-scale attacks on national currencies. Billions of investment dollars flowed into complex 'residential mortgage-backed securities' that promised investors up to 25% return on equity.*'[12]

The assurance by Chairman Alan Greenspan's monetarist policies of maintaining interest rates low and credit flowing eventually made investment banks expand their search for capital by buying '*subprime*' loans from mortgage brokers, who seduced by the big commissions they would receive began accepting applications for housing mortgages, with hardly any or no down payment at all and without credit checks. Such loans became extremely popular in the United States, with most of them being adjustable-rate mortgages tied to fluctuations of short-term interest rates. Investment banks, quickly grabbed the high-risk loans, being perfectly aware that they could resell

9 Ibid, pgs 123–4.
10 Ibid, pg 124.
11 Ibid.
12 Ibid, pgs 124–5.

the assets including the involved risk, by bundling them into composite securities without government regulation. One of the most complex innovative instruments of securitization were the so-called'*collateralized debt obligations*', which often hid the problematic loans by way of grouping them together with lower-risk assets, and subsequently reselling them to unsuspecting investors.[13]

There are three main reasons which stand out the most for the continuous purchase of those mortgage-backed securities by institutional and individual investors. In the first place, such esoteric forms of securities often veiled the degree of risk involved and investors did not fully grasp the actual complexity of the new investment funds. Secondly, investors relied heavily on the impeccable reputation of such financial giants like the Bank of America and Citicorp. Thirdly, investors trusted the positive credit ratings reports of Standard and Poor's and Moody's, not realizing the extent to which such credit ratings giants were also implicated in the expanding speculative bubble. Such firms likewise sought to maximize their profits with their vested interests in the growth of securities markets by making them provide '*rosy*' assessments of inherent risks.[14]

With more and more investors from all over the world being attracted by the high yields flowing from the new securities funds, very soon over a US$ trillion worth of '*toxic assets*' were globalized, thereby highly contaminating the system. By mid-2007, the financial steamroller completely ran out of fuel when the seriously overvalued American real estate began to plummet and foreclosures dramatically upsurge. Investors soon realized the serious risks associated with the securities market and lost all confidence in it, with the consequential drop in the value of securitized mortgage funds, ultimately making banks to desperately try to somehow eliminate their debts in vain by showing their balance sheets.[15]

The atmosphere of chaos and disorder that soon established itself within the US national system and the international financial system tragically witnessed how some of the oldest and most classical financial institutions, insurance companies and government-sponsored underwriters of mortgages, either declared themselves bankrupt or had to be rescued through '*nationalizations*'. The entire event and its consequences, turned out to represent the United States' most spectacular nationalization drive since the Great Depression. It included amongst many others: Lehman Brothers, Bear Stearns, Merrill Lynch, Goldman Sachs, AIG, Citicorp, J.P. Morgan Chase, IndyMac Bank, Morgan Stanley, Fannie Mae and Freddie Mac. Ironically, the conservative Bush administration offered to purchase up to US$700 billion in distressed mortgage securities in return for a government share in the business outcome. Soon, most advanced industrialized countries, such as Great Britain, '*followed suit with their own multi-billion bailout*

[13] Ibid, pg 125
[14] Ibid, pgs 125–6.
[15] Ibid, pg 127.

packages, hoping that such massive injections of capital into ailing financial markets would help to prop up financial institutions deemed "too large to be allowed to fail". But these generous rescue packages allowed large financial conglomerates to lose even more money without having to declare bankruptcy. The cost passed on to the world's taxpayers is truly staggering: future generations will have to repay trillions of dollars used for financing these bailout packages.'

Probably one of the worst consequences caused by the defaulting financial system was that banks that tried to rebuild their capital base could no longer afford carrying on lending large amounts of money. Thus and very quickly, the flow of credit quickly froze to a mere trickle and businesses and individuals relying on credit found it much harder to obtain. In turn, the overall credit shortage impacted heavily on businesses, forcing upon them into a huge reduction of production and enormous lay-off workers. Consequently, the dramatic drop of stock markets caused an upsurge of unemployment, the spiraling down of national indexes, together with a rapid decline of national industrial outputs, which all in all made the economies of countries around the world very quickly slide into recession. That way and soon after the global '*financial*' crisis quickly turned into a global '*economic*' crisis.[16]

By way of domino effect, from October 2007 to early 2009, the Dow Jones Industrial Average dropped from 14,000 to below 7,000; from June 2007 to early 2009, the Paris CAC 40 fell from 6,000 to around 3,000; and from July 2007 to early 2008, Japan's Nikkei index fell from 18,000 to 8,000. By early 2009, the crisis had wiped out 33 per cent or $14.3 trillion of the value of the world's companies.[17]

Likewise, in 2008 industrial output declined sharply in Brazil by 14 per cent, in Germany by 12 per cent, in Italy by 14 per cent, in Russia by 16 per cent, in Korea by 26 per cent and in Japan by 31 per cent. In 2009, the World Bank forecasted correctly that for the first time since the Second World War, both the global economy and the volume of foreign trade would shrink substantially, with the developing world especially being hit hard facing a financial shortfall by the end of 2010 of US$700 billion. Furthermore, the International Labour Organization predicted that by the end of 2009 the crisis would wipe out 20 million jobs, thus elevating the global unemployment figure to the unprecedented figure of over 200 million. Lastly, the Zagat's Hotels, Resorts and Spas Survey also predicted a huge decline in 2009 in business travel of about 30 per cent.[18]

16 Ibid, pgs 129–31.
17 Ibid, pg 130.
18 Ibid, pg 131.

19

The European Sovereign Debt Crisis: *The Eurozone Crisis*

The intense shockwaves that the 2007–15 global financial crisis sent ripping through the international economic-financial system very nearly caused its total collapse. From 2009 onwards, one of the most hard-hit and afflicted areas was the EU's '*Eurozone*', where the financial and banking crisis quickly turned into a '*sovereign debt crisis*'.

The '*Eurozone Crisis*' mostly stemmed from the structural problem of the Eurozone plus a combination of other complex factors like most significantly: a weak structure of the Eurozone as a single currency union, which completely lacked fiscal union (like different tax and pension rules among its member states); fiscal policy choices related to government revenues and expenses; European banks owning a significant amount of sovereign debt, as well as the approaches used by member states to bail out troubled banking industries and private bondholders, which assumed private debt burdens or socialized losses.[1]

During the 2000s, some EU member states failed to stay within the confines of the Maastricht Treaty's criteria for limiting member states deficit spending and debt levels, thus sidestepping best practice and ignoring international standards by turning to securitizing future government revenues in order to reduce their debts and/or deficits. The highly unregulated Eurozone, permitted sovereigns to mask their deficit and debt levels through a combination of established techniques, which included inconsistent accounting, off-balance-sheet transactions and the utilization of complex currency and credit derivatives structures. Eurozone countries had provided easy credit conditions encouraging high-risk lending and borrowing practices, but when in several countries property bubbles made private debts arise such debts were then transferred to sovereign debt. The Eurozone sovereign debt crisis was triggered in 2008 with Iceland's declaration of bankruptcy, due to the collapse of its entire banking system, and subsequently it quickly began spreading out to other Eurozone member states, such as Portugal, Italy, Greece and Ireland, and in 2009 to Spain. When those Eurozone countries soon defaulted unable to repay or refinance their government

1 LANE, P. *The European Sovereign Debt Crisis*, pgs 1–13. https://pubs.aeaweb.org/doi/pdfplus/10.1257/jep.26.3.49

debt or bail out over-indebted banks under their national supervision, the fear of the collapse of the Euro and of financial contagion, prompted their rescue or assistance by either other Eurozone countries, the EU, the European Central Bank (ECB) or the International Monetary Fund (IMF).[2]

Compared to the rest of the world, between 1999 and 2007, the Eurozone maintained a roughly balanced current account, although there were large and sustained imbalances within the area. Whereas some countries, such as Greece, Portugal, Spain and to a lesser extent Ireland, incurred substantial current account deficits, other countries like Germany, Luxembourg and the Netherlands ran current account surpluses. Between 1999 and 2007, per capita GDP in the Euro Area grew 1.7 per cent a year.[3]

There were very marked differences in the sources of economic growth across countries, with Germany and Ireland having their economic growth led by exports, Greece and Portugal having their growth led by a boom in private consumption, and Spain having its growth led by both private consumption and investment.[4]

Greece, Ireland, Portugal and Spain financed their current account deficits through cross-border financial and capital movements, which were facilitated by the adoption of the common currency in 1999 (thus eliminating currency risk de facto), as well as the expansion of financial activities, most notably by French and German banks.[5]

Variations were also present in the sources of the large and widening current account deficits across countries. In Greece and Portugal, the external gap stemmed mainly from a low savings rate, which in turn reflected high public and private consumption rates between 1999 and 2007. Greece's current account deficit increased from 7.0 per cent to 14.7 per cent of GDP. The deficit widening was caused by a decline in the saving rate from 15.0 per cent to 7.6 per cent, of GDP, with the decline comprising a 4.2 per cent drop in the public savings rate and a 3.3 per cent drop in the private savings rate. Although from 1999 to 2007 the investment rate remained fairly stable between 2007 and 2009 it fell by 4 per cent of GDP.[6]

[2] Investopedia. *European Sovereign Debt Crisis.* https://www.investopedia.com/terms/e/european-sovereign-debt-crisis.asp; The Balance. *The Eurozone Crisis: Causes and Potential Solutions.* https://www.thebalance.com/the-eurozone-crisis-causes-and-potential-solutions-1978970; The Balance. *What Is the European Debt Crisis?.* https://www.thebalance.com/what-is-the-european-debt-crisis-416918

[3] The World Bank. PRIMO BRAGA, C.A. and VINCELETTE, G.A. (Eds). *Sovereign Debt and the Financial Crisis. Will This Time Be Different?* FAVARO, E., LI, Y., PRADELLI, J. and VAN DOORN, R. *Europe's Crisis: Origins and Policy Challenges*, pg 222. http://documents.worldbank.org/curated/en/217391468151502378/pdf/Sovereign-debt-and-the-financial-crisis-will-this-time-be-different.pdf

[4] Ibid.

[5] Ibid, pgs 222–3.

[6] Ibid, pgs 223–4.

In Portugal, while the 1999 current account deficit was 8.9 per cent of GDP, in 2007 it increased to 9.8 per cent. During the same period, the country's savings declined from 18.9 per cent to 12.4 per cent of GDP, due to a decrease in investments from 27.8 per cent of GDP to 22.2 per cent, with the public sector accounting for 1.4 per cent of the 6.5 per cent decline in the savings rate. In Ireland and Spain, the current account deficits were caused by an investment boom, and in 1999, Ireland's current account balance fell from a surplus of 0.3 per cent to a deficit of 4.3 per cent of GDP in 2007. Such deterioration was caused by increases in investment rates and decreases in savings rates. Likewise, while in 1999 investment in construction rose from 14.7 per cent to 20.2 per cent of GDP in 2007, during the crisis, the investment rate contracted 12 per cent and the savings rate fell 10.2 per cent, mainly due to a 12.1 per cent decline in public savings.[7]

Similarly, whereas in 1999 Spain's current account deficit was 2.7 per cent of GDP, in 2007 it increased to 10.0 per cent. Such widening of the deficit was due to an increase in the investment rate from 25.1 per cent to 31.0 per cent of GDP, resulting from a 5.3 per cent increase in construction. While from 1999 to 2007, the savings rate remained constant, the composition of savings changed dramatically, with an increase in the public savings rate offsetting a decrease in the private savings rate.[8]

External imbalances in the Eurozone also projected different exports patterns. While in 1999 Germany's export share in GDP was 29.1 per cent, in 2007 it had increased to 47.5 per cent. Throughout the same period, whereas in Greece and Spain the share of exports in GDP remained roughly constant, in Portugal it increased slightly and in Ireland it fell. In Germany, exports expanded because of gains in China, India and Eastern Europe, and not because of market share gains within the Eurozone. German exports also increased even after the observed since 2002 gradual appreciation of the euro, which had caused a reduction of the external competitiveness of all Eurozone countries.[9]

The huge disparities in the economic growth strategies and wage and labour policies pursued by European countries account for their differences in export performance. Whereas Germany's growth strategy was export led, the strategies of Greece, Portugal and Spain were mostly based on domestic demand expansion. '*Wage and labour policies supported growth strategies and eventually gave rise to wide differences in competitiveness. The dynamics of productivity growth and nominal wage inflation in Greece, Ireland, Portugal, and Spain with respect to Germany resulted in a steady increase in productivity-adjusted labour costs in those countries and flat labour costs in Germany.*'[10]

[7] Ibid, pgs 224–5.
[8] Ibid, pg 225.
[9] Ibid, pg 226.
[10] Ibid.

In Greece, Ireland, Portugal and Spain, the counterpart of protracted current account deficits represented the accumulation of financial and equity claims by foreign investors (mainly residents in exporting/lending countries) on income generated domestically in the importing/borrowing countries. Such an inflow of capital caused a fall in the net foreign asset position of Greece, Ireland, Portugal and Spain, as well as a sustained increase in the net factor income paid to foreigners. Although in the late 1990s Greece and Portugal were net recipients of factor income, the build-up of external liabilities reversed income flows. By 2007, net payments abroad amounted to 3.6 per cent of GDP in Greece and 2.3 per cent in Portugal, which represented one-quarter of the current account deficits in both countries. In Spain, net payments abroad rose from 1.0 per cent of GDP in 1999 to 3.2 per cent in 2007, representing one-quarter of the external deficit. Due to foreign direct investment and foreign firms operating in Ireland, net payments abroad have always been sizable, averaging from 1999 to 2007 15 per cent of GDP, which absorbed most of the trade surplus.[11]

> *The global economic crisis put severe strain on government budgets and public debt, raising concerns about fiscal sustainability as well as external imbalances. The increase in fiscal deficits and the virtual explosion of public debt were immediate consequences of the crisis and the strong policy responses to cope with it. European governments resorted to automatic stabilizers and stimulus packages to partly offset the sudden contraction in private sector demand. The large increase in debt in Ireland was caused largely by the nationalization of its major banks. Expansionary fiscal policies eventually limited the decline in output and employment but left government with debt burdens of an unprecedented magnitude.*[12]

The European sovereign debt crisis officially erupted around late 2009, in the wake of the Great Recession and within the European context of overly high government structural deficits and accelerating debt levels. One of the worst repercussions of the Great Recession fell on the banking sector, with the relatively fragile banking sector suffering large capital losses due to the strong linkage between its survival and the financial stability of the economy, which made most states in Europe bail out several of their most affected banks, with some supporting recapitalization loans. As of January 2009, a group of ten Central and Eastern European banks had already asked for a bailout. At the time, the European Commission's (EC) declining forecast for the 2009 EU economic output provided an even worse outlook for banks. The many public-funded bank recapitalizations were one of the reasons behind the sharply deteriorated debt-to-GDP ratios experienced by several European countries in the wake of the Great Recession. The main causes for the four sovereign debt crises that were detonated in Europe are considered to be rooted at the same time in a mixture of weak actual and potential growth, competitive weakness, liquidation of banks and sovereigns' large

[11] Ibid, pg 227.
[12] Ibid, pgs 227–8.

pre-existing debt-to-GDP ratios, together with considerable government and private and non-private sector liability stocks.[13]

During the first weeks of 2010, the regional renewed anxiety about excessive national debt made lenders demand ever-higher interest rates from several countries with higher debt levels, deficits and current account deficits. In turn, that made it difficult for the governments of Greece, Portugal, Ireland and Spain to finance further budget deficits and repay or refinance existing government debt, particularly when economic growth rates were low and a high percentage of debt was in the hands of foreign creditors, as was the case of Greece and Portugal. The states that were adversely affected by the crisis faced a strong rise in interest rate spreads for government bonds as a result of investor concerns about their future debt sustainability. Greece, Portugal and Ireland had to be rescued by sovereign bailout programmes, which were provided jointly by the IMF and the EC, with additional support at the technical level from the ECB. Those three international organizations that represented the bailout creditors became dubbed as the '*Troika*'. Spain was likewise also earmarked for a bank recapitalization fund, which did not, however, include financial support for the government itself.[14]

From 2010 and thereafter, the main series of financial support measures implemented by European countries included the European Financial Stability Facility (EFSF) and the European Financial Stabilization Mechanism (EFSM), together with the successor of those two – the European Stability Mechanism (ESM). The ECB also lowered interest rates and provided cheap loans totalling more than a trillion euro in order to maintain money flows between European banks. Additionally, in September 2012, the ECB calmed financial markets with the announcement of free unlimited support for all Eurozone countries involved in a sovereign State bailout/precautionary programme from the EFSF/ESM, through yield lowering Outright Monetary Transactions (OMT). Other measures also included the initiation in March 2011 of the Stability and Growth Pact or '*European Fiscal Compact*', which adopted an automatic procedure for imposing penalties in case of breaches of either the 3 per cent deficit or the 60 per cent debt rules, as well as the planning of the reorganization of the European banking system.[15]

On 9 May 2010 the twenty-seven EU member states agreed on the creation of the EFSF, which was a legal instrument for the preservation of financial stability in Europe through the provision of financial assistance to Eurozone states in difficulty. The EFSF issued bonds and other debt instruments in the market, with the support of the German Debt Management Office, in order to raise needed funds to provide loans to Eurozone countries in financial troubles, recapitalize banks or buy sovereign debt. The

[13] Scielo. WEBER, C. *La Euro Crisis: Causas y Síntomas.* http://www.scielo.org.mx/scielo.php?script=sci_arttext&pid=S0187-69612015000200009

[14] Ibid.

[15] BORRELL FONTELLES, J. *Euro Crisis Timeline.* https://www.ucm.es/data/cont/docs/518-2015-04-15-TIMELINE%20OCT%202009%20MAYO%202013_ampliado.pdf

emissions of such bonds were backed by guarantees given by the Eurozone member states in proportion to their share in the paid-up capital of the ECB. The €440 billion lending capacity of the facility was jointly and severally guaranteed by the Eurozone countries' governments, and could be combined with loans up to €60 billion from the EFSM (reliant on funds raised by the EC using the EU budget as collateral), and up to €250 billion from the IMF in order to obtain a '*financial safety net*' of up to €750 billion.[16]

On 5 January 2011 the European Union created the EFSM, an emergency-funding programme reliant upon funds raised on financial markets and guaranteed by the EC, using the budget of the EU as collateral. The EC supervised the EFSM, aiming to preserve financial stability in Europe by providing financial assistance to EU member states in economic difficulty. The EC fund had the authority to raise up to €60 billion and was rated AAA by Fitch, Moody's and Standard & Poor's. Under the EFSM, the EU successfully placed in the capital markets a €5 billion issue of bonds as part of the financial support package agreed for Ireland at a borrowing cost for the EFSM of 2.59 per cent.[17]

In September 2012, just like the EFSF, a permanent rescue-funding programme, the European Stability Mechanism (ESM), replaced the EFSM. The ESM now serves as a '*financial firewall*', in order to avoid that the default of any country rips through the entire financial system. It mainly ensures that downstream nations and banking systems are protected by guaranteeing some or all of their obligations, with the possibility of one single default being managed while limiting financial contagion. Whereas on 16 December 2010 the European Council agreed on a two-line amendment to the EU Treaty of Lisbon, in order to allow for a permanent bailout mechanism to be established including stronger sanctions, in March 2011 the European Parliament approved the treaty amendment after receiving assurances that the EC, rather than EU states, would play '*a central role*' in running the ESM. The ESM is an intergovernmental organization under public international law, with its headquarters located in Luxembourg.[18]

In order to fight the crisis, some governments primarily focused on raising taxes and lowering expenditures, which all in all contributed to much social unrest and significant debate among economists, many of who advocated greater deficits with struggling economies. Especially in countries where budget deficits and sovereign debts increased sharply, a crisis of confidence also emerged, with the widening of bond yield spreads and risk insurance on Credit Default Swaps (CDS), between those countries and other EU member states, most importantly Germany.[19]

16 European Voice. *Spain Seeks to Reassure EU Leaders.* https://www.politico.eu/article/spain-seeks-to-reassure-eu-leaders/

17 BORRELL FONTELLES, J. *Euro Crisis Timeline.* https://www.ucm.es/data/cont/docs/518-2015-04-15-TIMELINE%20OCT%202009%20MAYO%202013_ampliado.pdf

18 European Stability Mechanism. https://www.esm.europa.eu/

19 AKALA, I. *The Euro-zone Financial Crisis: Causes, Consequences and Policy Responses.* http://www.naturalspublishing.com/files/published/3zl7oij137v39s.pdf

Despite sovereign debt having risen substantially in only a few eurozone countries, with the three most affected countries, Greece, Ireland and Portugal, collectively only accounting to 6 per cent of the Eurozone's GDP, the issue became a big problem for the whole area. Soon, Europe found itself permeated by much speculation of more contagion from other European countries, as well as facing a possible break-up of the Eurozone. By the end of 2012, the debt crisis had forced 5 out of 17 Eurozone countries to seek help from other nations.[20]

However, by early January 2013 successful sovereign debt auctions across the Eurozone, most importantly in Ireland, Spain and Portugal, reflected that investors believed that the '*ECB-backstop*' had worked. While financial stability in the Eurozone improved significantly, interest rates likewise fell steadily. In November 2013, the ECB lowered its bank rate to only 0.25 per cent, in order to assist recovery in the Eurozone. As of May 2014, only Greece and Cyprus continued needing help from third parties.[21]

Notwithstanding, there were other underlying factors, which soon exacerbated the situation. The large amount of money assigned to rescue packages, together with the strong overall decline in tax revenue income, forced some governments to implement safeguarding economic austerity programmes. In most countries, such programmes involved many social cuts, which provoked both social unrest and an increase in the generalized state of poverty. With most countries being flung into recession, in some countries, like Spain, the bursting of a big construction and housing bubble aggravated the crisis even more. In general, the crisis had many adverse economic and labour market effects, which together caused the extreme economic growth slowdown of the Eurozone. Whilst unemployment rates in Greece and Spain reached 27 per cent, the crisis-induced European economic and social deterioration had a terrible political impact on the ruling governments of 10 out of 19 Eurozone countries, which contributed to significant power shifts in Greece, Ireland, France, Italy, Portugal, Spain, Slovenia, Belgium and the Netherlands, as well as outside the Eurozone, like in the UK.[22]

Spain's Savings Banks Fiasco

Out of all the crisis-affected European countries, Spain represents a particularly interesting study case of one of the Eurozone countries that was affected by the crisis at different intervals, as well as in different ways. Although when the 2007–15 global financial crisis broke out, Spain's strong and robust banking sector absorbed the shocks relatively well, a few years into the crisis the base of the banking system's structure, formed by highly politicized, unregulated and uncontrolled savings banks and other financial entities, collapsed, which in turn took down with it the entire banking

[20] Ibid.
[21] Ibid.
[22] Ibid.

structure. The bursting of a big construction and housing bubble, which consequently spurred an acute socioeconomic crisis, aggravated the financial-banking crisis even more. With Spain's banking system having to be recapitalized by a fund provided by the ESM, the country's political theatre soon also witnessed the apparition of many Left-wing parties, which dramatically changed the political scenario forever.

Up until the first years of the Great Recession and the Eurozone Crisis, Spain's central bank or Banco de España (BE) had maintained a strict regulation of the banking system. It had most especially closely monitored the top and the middle of the banking structure, formed by big and medium-sized banks, such as most notably the Banco Santander, Banco Bilbao Vizcaya, Banco Popular, Banco Sabadell and Bankinter. When the global financial crisis's shockwaves shook the Eurozone's financial and banking system, Spain was in fact congratulated by the IMF in view of the strength and robustness of its banking structure, which absorbed the thrusts really well. However, only a few years later, the base of the structure of Spain's banking system, formed by the politicized and unregulated savings banks and other financial entities, revealed

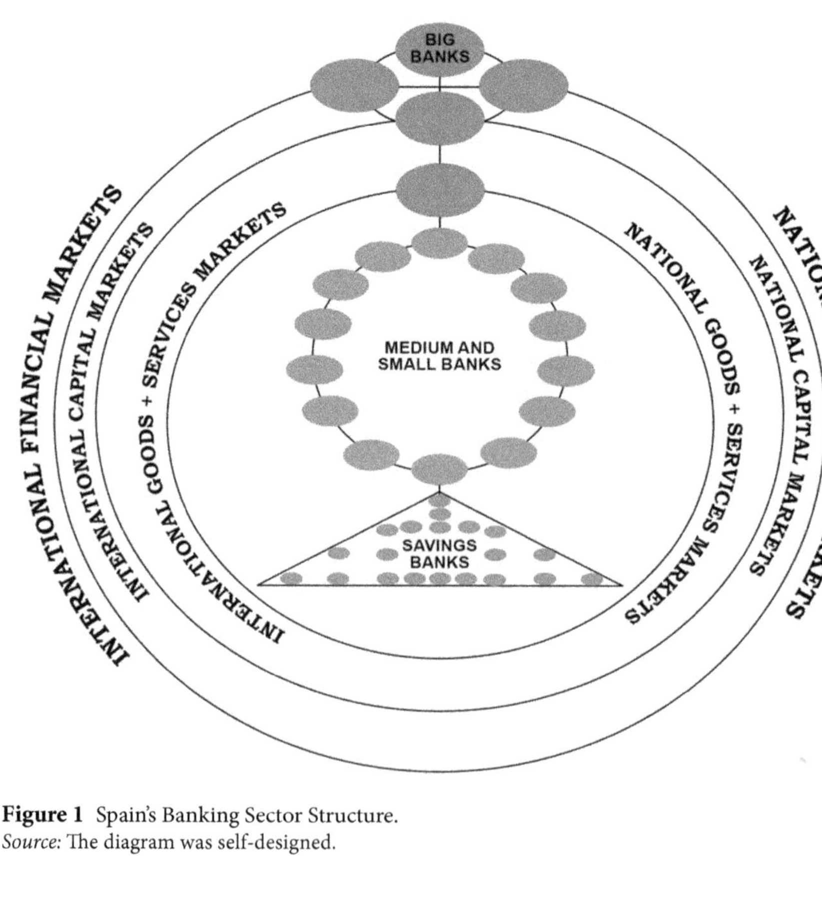

Figure 1 Spain's Banking Sector Structure.
Source: The diagram was self-designed.

extremely high levels of indebtedness due to an entangled web of corruption, which made it breakdown and bring down with it a big part of the banking system. Some of the savings banks involved were Caja de Castilla-La Mancha, Caixanova, Caixa Galicia, Caja Sur, Caja de Ahorros del Mediterráneo (CAM) and Catalunya Caixa.[23]

In Spain, institutions and entities, such as savings banks, were created during the reign of Queen Isabel II, with the main objective of offering reduced interest rates while assuring a high level of security to the deposits of its clients. To that effect, they successfully mixed their local character with social work. After 1977 and the return of Spain to democracy, however, savings banks began to carry out their activities outside of their realms of influence, until their absolute liberalization when Spain entered the European Common Market. Soon after, they quickly multiplied in number, with their presence across the Spanish territory expanding tremendously, eventually taking up about 50 per cent of Spain's banking business.[24]

However, the dependency of the savings banks on local powers, together with the lack of banking regulation and the 2005-onwards runaway credit expansion, made such institutions extremely vulnerable. What is more, rising above private banking, savings banks acquired most of the credit from real estate, experiencing a huge increase in 2002 of 21 per cent, as well as another increase in 2007 of 41.8 per cent. Following the same trend as the case of the US subprime loans, between 2007 and 2008, delinquent and non-performing loans provided by savings banks grew disproportionally, with a big 326 per cent upsurge in savings banks compared to a 265 per cent growth of banks and a 184 per cent increase in other credit entities and institutions. The fact that many savings banks were later transformed into banks, or that many of them found themselves obliged to fuse or merge, did not improve the situation. Soon, while the entire system broke down, mainly due to the politicization and incompetence of such entities, they have today completely lost their primary function as social instruments.[25]

Within such a chaotic and disordered banking context, one of the most paradoxical cases was the rise and fall of Bankia Bank. Bankia Bank was formed through the integration of Caja Madrid and Bancaja, as well as five other small institutions namely Caixa Laietana, Caja Canarias, Caja Rioja, Caja Ávila and Caja Segovia. The new Bankia Bank was practically completely nationalized since its genesis by way of receiving €4.500 million from the newly created '*Fondo de Reestructuración Ordenada Bancaria (FROB)*' or Ordered Banking Restructuration Fund. By mid-2012, Bankia Bank had become Spain's fourth biggest bank by market share, with 10 million clients and €340,000 million in assets.

23 OLIER, E. *Codicia Financiera*, pgs 73–4.
24 Ibid, pg 73.
25 Ibid.

Whereas the downfall of Bankia Bank could have easily brought down with it Spain's entire financial system and banking structure, it ended dragging down with it the following entities: Caja Castilla-La Mancha (CCM), which was integrated into Liberbank, requiring more than €7.000 million from the state; Novacaixagalicia (the fusion of Caixanova and Caixa Galicia); Caja Sur, which is today in BBK Bank; Caja de Ahorros del Mediterráneo (CAM), which was intervened by the State in July 2011; as well as Catalunya Caixa, which received an FROB injection of €1.718 million.[26]

The main reasons for the collapse of Spain's savings banks are considered to be a mixture of economic issues linked to the politicization of such entities, together with a generalized lack of regulation and control. Ever since Spain had adopted the euro, savings banks had changed from being lenders of credit in the inter-banking system, to being actual savings banks in the European market. Due to the fact that such entities were not anonymous societies, they could not, therefore, technically acquire capital. Consequently, the inability of savings banks to recapitalize, together with the fluctuations of financial markets and the crisis, triggered the whole fiasco.[27]

Since years before the crisis, the savings-banking sector had become extremely politicized and unregulated, infested with politically appointed presidents, directors and managers, who totally lacked professional know-how and capabilities. In most cases, such appointees merely represented the individual pawns of national or local political powers, with no real control over management, as well as very dependent of a corporatist government full of influences, which undoubtedly made them grow disproportionally. Such growth was equally accompanied by the promotion of politically driven, imprudent business and entrepreneurial ventures with no real future, together with the uncontrolled haywire lending of delinquent and non-performing loans.[28] The badly managed financial entities also hid accounting sheets, losses and earnings volatility, as well as misled analysts and investors. Moreover, the frequently established corruption networks in the sector saw outgoing managers being adjudicated with multimillion compensations, although many of them were in the end prosecuted.[29] The patterns of behaviour found within the savings banks sector, which to a great extent caused its collapse and the shaking down of the whole banking sector's structure, were a clear reflection of John Stuart Mill's self-interested and greedy '*Homo Economicus*'. As Mill wrote in his 1848 '*Essays on some Unsettled Questions of Political Economy*' and full-fledged during the same year in his '*Principles of Political Economy*':

> *[Political economy] does not treat the whole of man's nature as modified by the social state, nor of the whole conduct of man in society. It is concerned with him solely as a being who desires to possess wealth, and who is capable of judging of the comparative*

[26] Ibid, pgs 73–4.
[27] Ibid, pg 74.
[28] Ibid.
[29] Ibid.

> *efficacy of means for obtaining that end. It predicts only such of the phenomena of the social state as take place in consequence of the pursuit of wealth. It makes entire abstraction of every other human passion or motive; except those which may be regarded as perpetually antagonizing principles to the desire of wealth, namely, aversion to labour, and desire of the present enjoyment of costly indulgences.*[30]

The overall disastrous results that swept through Spain were manifold. Not only did savings banks lose their traditional raison d'être and functions, but they also dilated the capillarity of the financial sector of territorial cohesion and of the fight against economic exclusion.[31] During the decade before the crisis Spain's economy thrived at a faster pace than Europe, enjoying very high employment rates. Between 1997 and 2008, there was a huge construction boom with housing prices nearly tripling. Notwithstanding, the bubble was inflated by easy loans from banks, most particularly savings banks. When the '*credit crunch hit*', real estate prices plummeted, with banks, most especially savings banks, being left with huge losses and debts from unsecured loans as clients struggled to repay mortgages, while at the same time also losing their ability to borrow money or raise capital. Whereas in 2009 the Spanish budget deficit rose to 11 per cent of GDP, thus making Spain enter a first recession, in 2011 the country entered a second recession, which affected the livelihoods of much of its citizens. The Spanish government was left with both a stretched budget and very little room to manoeuvre. Although the country never lost access to market financing, its capability to raise money became increasingly expensive. Thus and in a bid to calm uncertainty, while in 2010 the government subjected its banking sector to a deep restructuring process, in 2012 it requested assistance from the ESM, in order to recapitalize the sector.[32]

Starting in 2010, Spain's whole banking sector, especially savings banks, was subjected to a series of restructuring operations, which included interventions from the BE, fusions, acquisitions and transformations of savings banks into banks. Most savings banks were converted into banks, with the amount of financial entities being reduced significantly. Furthermore, whilst the individual financial value of financial entities was increased, structural costs and the number of branches and employees were decreased. After a further two major fusions of big banks, Spain's banking sector was totally reconfigured. In 2010, the '*Banco Sabadell*' fused with '*Banco Guipuzcoano*' and in 2011 '*Banco Popular*' fused with '*Banco Pastor.*'[33]

In 2012, Spain asked the ESM for assistance in recapitalizing its banking sector. The ESM made available to Spain up to €100 billion in assistance although in the end it only

30 RODRIGUEZ-SICKERT, C. *Homo Economicus*, pg 1. https://complejidadsocial.udd.cl/wp-content/uploads/2012/05/Homo-economicus-Handbook-E.Elgar_.pdf
31 OLIER, E. *Codicia Financiera*, pg 74.
32 European Stability Mechanism. Financial Assistance. *Spain*. https://www.esm.europa.eu/assistance/spain#spain:_a_fast_and_effective_programme
33 Tatum. *Reestructuración del Mapa Financiero Español*. http://www.gref.org/nuevo/articulos/art_131211.pdf

Table 6 Spain's Post-Crisis Restructured Banking Sector

Main National Big and Medium Banks	
SANTANDER	
BBVA	
SABADELL	
BANCO POPULAR-BANCO PASTOR	
BANESTO	
BANKINTER	
BANCO DE VALENCIA	
BANCA MARCH	
Group of Savings Banks and Small Financial Entities	**New Financial Entity**
La Caixa / Caixa Girona	CAIXA BANK
Caja Madrid / Caja Ávila / Caja Segovia / Caixa Laietana / La Caja de Canarias / Caja Rioja / Bancaja	BANKIA
Cajastur / Caja Cantabria / Caja Extremadura / CCM	Liberbank
Caixa Catalunya / Caixa Tarragona / Caixa Manresa	CXCatalunyaCaixa
Caixanova / Caixa Galicia	ABANCA
Caixa Penedés / Cajamurcia / Sa Nostra / Caja Granada	BMN
Caja España / Caja Duero / Unicaja	Caja España-Caja Duero-Unicaja
CAN / CajaBurgos / Caja Canarias / Cajasol (Guadalajara)	BANCA CIVICA
BBK /Kutxa /Caja Vital	BBKBank
Caixa Sabadell / Caixa Terrasa / Caixa Manlleu	Unnim
CAI / Caja Círculo / Caja Badajoz	Caja 3

Source: Data from Tatum. '*Reestructuración del Mapa Financiero Español*'. http://www.gref.org/nuevo/articulos/art_131211.pdf

needed €41.3 billion. The funds were lent to the Spanish government, which meant that no ESM cash was disbursed directly to the banks. Two disbursements were made: one in December 2012 of €39.468 billion and another in February 2013 of €1.865 billion. '*In return for the financial assistance, Spain modernised the sector, a process that had already started before the programme. Ownership structures were reformed, and risk management practices were improved. Spain successfully exited its programme in December 2013 and gave a strong signal of returning to normal by voluntarily starting to repay the ESM loans earlier than required.*'[34]

[34] European Stability Mechanism. Financial Assistance. *Spain*. https://www.esm.europa.eu/assistance/spain#spain:_a_fast_and_effective_programme

The overall effects of the banking crisis were devastating for Spain, which additionally also suffered a generalized economic crisis to the detrimental expense of its citizens due to the bankruptcy of big and small companies and firms, the dropping of its GDP to around 8 per cent, a drastic increase in unemployment which reached an unprecedented 27 per cent, together with the raising of taxes and many social cuts.[35]

The overall socio-economic effects also had extremely serious political repercussions. The political scenario, formed by traditional political parties, witnessed the bursting into the scene of new political groups and factions, some of which are very Left-wing, progressive and populist, such as '*Unidas Podemos*', '*Ciudadanos*', '*Vox*' and '*ERC-Soviranistes*'. Between 2018 and 2019, Spain underwent two general elections and from January 2020 up until the end of 2023, the centre-left Socialist (PSOE) and hard-left Unidas Podemos (UP) parties made up Spain's first coalition government since the pre-Franco era. Following the November 2023 general elections, President Pedro Sanchez was again re-elected. The unknown coalition for the formation of a government of very differing ideologies has one head of government or president, four vice-presidents and a total of twenty-three female and male ministers, thus making however simple the decision-making extremely complicated.[36]

The new government in Spain took office within a much more complicated context of wider circumstances than ever before. Although Spanish politics used to enjoy almost German levels of stability, a series of four interlocking crises – the banking and socioeconomic crises, corruption scandals and the rise of Catalan separatism – have all in all left the old political landscape severely fractured.[37]

In 2020, there were further banking fusions between Caixabank and Bankia and between Unicaja and Liberbank. The latter fusión has created the new '*Unicaja Banco*'.[38]

[35] OLIER, E. *Codicia Financiera,* pg 74.

[36] Nueva Tribuna.es BARRA GALAN, C. *Gobierno de Progreso en Tiempos Inciertos.* https://www.nuevatribuna.es/articulo/actualidad/gobierno-progreso-tiempos-inciertos-psoe-pedro-sanchez/20231120105238219729.html

[37] Ibid.

[38] Statista. Statista Research Department. *Principales Bancos en España tras las Fusiones Bancarias planeadas en 2020.* https://es.statista.com/estadisticas/1188317/ranking-principales-entidades-bancarias-tras-fusiones-bancarias-espana-segun-volumen-activos/

Dimension Three

Neoliberalism in Latin America: *Neoliberalism as the Basis of Development and Integration Processes*

20

Neoliberalism in Latin America

Since its discovery in 1492, the subcontinent of Latin America (LA) has always represented a key region of the international community. Today, most especially, LA is considered an extremely relevant, influential and equilibrating pole of the international system. Its geographical position makes it crucial for world equilibrium, not just in terms of security, but much more so as regards political, economic, social, cultural, scientific and technological, religious, demographic and environmental issues. The integration of LA into the international system is a very transcendental question, which has for a long time been gradually but progressively taking place. Since the 1970s–80s, the neoliberal economic model, based on the Washington Consensus, has been leading the different regional, sub-regional and intra-regional, development and integration processes into the international system.

However, in recent decades, LA has experienced a big anti-neoliberal swing, mainly due to the negative results neoliberalism has been producing throughout the region. The neoliberal economic model has produced a highly disproportioned and unequal economic growth, as well as an extremely uneven and disproportioned development. Moreover, the region's underlying sub-development, which is much more widespread than the generalized development, has been left totally unattended and ignored. All those factors put together have had very grave consequences for the whole region. While many countries have gone as far as completely abandoning the neoliberal economic model, they have generated and put into practice other heterodox economic currents, some of which have had excellent results and continue doing so.

> *What is often referred to as the 'globalization,' or the increasing integration, of the Latin American and Caribbean region (as well as other regions) into the contemporary global capitalist system has not propelled the people living in this important part of the world into a new era of postmodernity. Many of the 'old' problems and issues confronted by the societies in this region during the twentieth century persist. In fact, the effects of contemporary globalization – perhaps best defined as the global expansion of late-twentieth-century capitalism or what has been called 'turbo-capitalism', have aggravated most of the chronic problems of the Latin American and Caribbean societies while adding new ones. Most of these problems are still best characterized in terms of such 'classical' or 'modernist' concepts as corporate*

> *capitalism, imperialism, neocolonialism, economic exploitation, political repression, social inequality, and social injustice.*[1]

The emergence of neoliberalism in LA dates back to the 1950s and 1960s, when Latin American economic practices became the constant target of non-stop academic attacks. During those decades, development in LA was primarily driven by '*developmentalism*'. 'Devopmentalism' was largely derived from principles of economic nationalism and based on the same successful developmental path followed by most West European and North American countries during the late nineteenth and early twentieth centuries. Developmentalist economists, like most particularly the Argentinian economist, Raul Prebisch, recommended that economic progress in the region should be dependent on internal industrialization and protected by high tariffs and limited trade instead of on the exportation of natural resources to a global market where large European and North American corporations controlled its prices. With the conversion of those theories by developmentalist politicians into economic policy through the nationalization of key industries, like mining and transportation, states also began offering incentives to private enterprises for their support of such state-directed development projects, such as public subsidies for the construction of factories or the hiring of workers. Additionally, they likewise also placed stringent price controls on food and other basic products. Thus and in accordance, highly centralized and interventionist governments were therefore established for the successful execution of such economic objectives, which were very committed to national autonomy and basic welfare provisions, like social services and public education.[2]

In the 1973, after years of much criticism and opposition to the developmentalist model, neoliberalism, based on the Washington Consensus, was applied in Chile for the first time. The Chilean experience generated a powerful neoliberal wave, which eventually splashed onto the whole region, establishing neoliberalism as the main economic model in order to run the region's economic development and integration processes.

Notwithstanding, towards the end of the 1990s and beginning of the twenty-first century, Latin American development and integration, together with its neoliberal economic hermeneutics, were trumped and slowed down by the resurgence of a radical and extremist, political progressive and populist Left. Since then, a dichotomy has been created and established by countries of the so-called, 'positive Left', such as Mexico, Brazil and Chile, and by countries of the progressive and populist, 'negative Left', like Argentina, Bolivia, Ecuador and Venezuela.

In countries of the 'negative Left', the political economy against '*American imperialism*' and foreign influence induced both the abandonment of the neoliberal economic model

[1] HARRIS, R.L. *Resistance and Alternatives to Globalization in Latin America and the Caribbean*, pg 1.
[2] STEGER, M.B. and RAVI, K.R. *Neoliberalism: A Very Short Introduction*, pg 99.

and the emergence of heterodox economic currents, such as most predominantly 'Neo-Structuralism', 'Neo-Extractivism' and the 'Social Communitarian Productive Economic Model'.

Such an agitated atmosphere of substitution of economic models and experimentation with heterodox currents has had very negative effects in LA for its different development and integration processes, as well as had adverse effects in its reception of commercial initiatives and Foreign Direct Investment (FDI). The anti-neoliberal turn saw how many big foreign firms, like the Spanish Repsol, YPF, Endesa and Red Eléctrica, were either expropriated or bought-out in several of those countries.

In some countries the substitution of neoliberalism for other alternative models has affected their membership and role in the various neoliberal development and integration processes, such as, most significantly, the 'Mercado Común del Cono Sur (MERCOSUR)', the 'Comunidad Andina de Naciones (CAN)', the 'Comunidad del Caribe (CARICOM)', the 'Mercado Común Centroamericano (MCCEAM)' and the 'Tratado de Libre Comercio de las Américas (TLCAN)' or 'Free Trade Agreement of the Americas (FTAA)'. Conversely, the switch of economic models, has, nonetheless, been extremely successful in some countries of the 'negative Left', such as, most significantly, Bolivia. Since Bolivia's adoption of the 'Social Communitarian Productive Economic Model', a home-grown model to fit its national multi-ethnic characteristics, Bolivia has produced the so-called *'Bolivian Economic Miracle'*.

Despite such a hard-felt anti-neoliberal swing, LA is enjoying another period of FDI upsurge and commercial bonanza. While, on one hand, the 'Alianza del Pacífico' or 'Pacific Alliance' is providing LA with many trade opening opportunities both inwards and outwards, on the other hand, the EU and Spain continue leading foreign cooperation and investment. Likewise, countries like China and Russia have equally incremented their interest in the region due to its economic performance, its immense commercial attraction and its ever-bulging '*Oil and Gas*' sector.

The Chile Experiment

By the 1970s, the Latin American state-led 'developmentalist' model, which had been dominated by policies of import substitution that fostered national industries through subsidies or tariff protections, had begun to become quite unpopular, most especially in Chile, where such policies had never worked well.

Ever since the 1950s, Chicago School economists had been extending their public criticism of Keynesian macroeconomic policies to countries in LA. Milton Friedman and his colleague Arnold Harberger strongly opposed the state-led 'developmentalist' model and with the help of the University of Chicago, the US State Department, several large corporations and the Ford Foundation, they launched various neoliberal academic programmes in the region.

One of those programmes was named the '*Chile Project*', and it trained hundreds of Chilean economic students through the University of Chicago and Santiago's Catholic University in accordance with free-market principles. During the 1960s, such programmes were applied across LA, with many of the students rising to prominent academic and professional positions in different countries, like Argentina, Uruguay and Brazil.

At the beginning of the 1970s, in the wake of the Oil Crisis and with the whole world dipping into recession, a new economic approach was called for LA.[3] With the United States supporting the 1973 coup d'etat in Chile, led by General Augusto Pinochet, it was able to subsequently apply the neoliberal economic model in the country. That way, Chile became the first country in the world to put neoliberalism into practice at a national scale. It became the first national '*neoliberal testing ground*' in history.

On 11 September 1973 General Augusto Pinochet carried out a coup d'état against the democratically elected government of Salvador Allende, a strong supporter of the developmentalist school. The coup was promoted by domestic business elites that felt threatened by Allende's developmentalist beliefs and drive towards socialism. However and most importantly, the coup was backed and supported by the CIA, US corporations and the US Secretary of State Henry Kissinger. Whereas political organizations of the Left and social movements were violently repressed, all forms of popular organization, like community health centres in poor neighbourhoods, were also dismantled.[4]

Immediately after the coup, Pinochet's team of Chicago Boys, elaborated '*The Brick*', a 500-page economic programme for the country's economy, which '*called for extensive and immediate deregulation and privatization measures as well as deep cuts to social spending, the reduction of tariffs, and the lifting of price-controls – ostensibly for the purpose of fighting Chile's runaway inflation*'.[5] Pinochet and his team of Chicago Boys spearheaded a sweeping national neoliberal reform.

While General Pinochet clamped down very hard on his political opponents, he accepted the majority of the neoliberal programme and imposed its policies very quickly. Although Friedrich Hayek and Milton Friedman's libertarian ideals clashed markedly with the General's brutal methods of political repression, they nevertheless argued that such neoliberal '*shock treatments*' should be given a '*fair chance*', strongly believing that their swift application '*would return Chile to democracy, freedom, and unprecedented levels of prosperity*'.[6]

[3] HARVEY, D. *A Brief History of Neoliberalism*, pg 8.

[4] Ibid, pgs 7–8.

[5] STEGER, M.B. and RAVI, K.R. *Neoliberalism: A Very Short Introduction*, pg 100.

[6] Ibid.

During the next two decades, General Pinochet ruled with extensive and repressive dictatorial powers with many frequent disappearances of political dissidents, tortures and many other systematic human rights violations. Notwithstanding, Chile's economy stabilized in terms of inflation and GDP growth rate, although the dramatic increase in economic inequality also made the middle and lower classes lose much ground. During those decades, the gap between the rich and the poor became much more pronounced, with the country's richest 10 per cent benefitting the most from the neoliberal reforms, which almost doubled their incomes.[7] Today, Chile has the widest breach between rich and poor people in the whole of LA.

Despite the dictatorial regime's authoritarian and repressive rule, the neoliberal economic model's main objectives of economic liberalization, privatization of state-owned companies and stabilization of inflation were nonetheless carried out very successfully.[8] The Chilean experience generated a very powerful neoliberal wave, which eventually splashed onto the whole region. Through the Washington Consensus, neoliberalism was henceforth established as the main economic model to run the region's economic development and integration processes into the international system.

The Washington Consensus

Following the first 1970s successful Chilean neoliberal experience, Argentina and Mexico soon followed suit, adopting the neoliberal model. That way and thereafter, neoliberal thought began to flow much more vigorously through LA, eventually establishing neoliberalism as the main regional economic development and integration model. Through the US-devised '*Washington Consensus*' together with its neoliberal framework, neoliberalism became and still is the chief economic model leading the region's economic integration process into the international system, as well as most other sub-regional and intra-regional development processes.

The 1970s oil debt crisis impacted very heavily on LA. When in 1982 Mexico was finally unable to comply with its debt payments it provoked the overall '*drying up*' of lending to the region. The prevailing regional '*developmentalism*' and its Import-Substitution Industrialization (ISI) economic model had created huge macroeconomic imbalances with disastrous effects.[9] All combined, the deeply indebted countries were obliged to renegotiate their debts with the International Monetary Fund (IMF) and the World Bank (WB) or ask for either extended or new loans. However, the IMF and the WB established a new set of dictums for those indebted countries and the renegotiations of

7 Ibid, pgs 100–1.
8 Ibid, pgs 99–101.
9 KINGSTONE, P. *The Political Economy of Latin America: Reflections on Neoliberalism and Development*, pg 45.

their debts and new loan applications. Both institutions mandated that loan-receiving governments restructure their economies according to a neoliberal framework of policies, linking all loan guarantees to '*structural adjustment programs (SAPs)*'. The setup of such a neoliberal framework in countries was based on structural changes to their production patterns, which ceased to be ISI models and began functioning as open economy models.[10] Thus, the adoption of neoliberalism by countries in LA became an obligatory pre-requisite or condition imposed by the IMF and WB onto those countries that hoped to be able to re-negotiate their debts or attain any loans.

The neoliberal principles embraced included '*putting more emphasis on production for export rather than on meeting the needs of national and local markets; severe spending cuts – especially for social programmes; sweeping privatisation measures; reduced regulation on the activities of transnational corporations; and, in a number of cases, significant currency devaluations*'.[11] Furthermore, both institutions likewise assured themselves that a large portion of those loans were specifically assigned for paying off the external debts such countries had accumulated due to a number of factors, some of which had become very negatively imbued in their national systems and general developmental practice. Most particularly, '*deep-seated patterns of social domination left behind by colonialism; misguided development strategies often devised by First World aid agencies; the dramatic oil price hikes of the 1970s; the rise of global interest rates in the early 1980s, waning global demand for Third World products; decreasing importance of domestic markets; ill-considered and wasteful mega-construction projects; and widespread corruption among domestic governing elites*'.[12]

Accordingly, in 1989 a summit took place in the Washington DC, promoted by the IMF and the WB. The summit counted with the presence of officials from the US Department of State, finance ministers of industrialized countries, presidents of important international banks and many other renowned economists.

At the summit, the British economist, John Williamson, presented his self-elaborated '*Washington Consensus*' and its '*10 Points*', which put together a series of neoliberal '*recommendations*' for those indebted Latin American countries that requested re-negotiations of their debts or new loans from the IMF and the WB. Since then, the Washington Consensus and its 10 recommendations have provided LA with its neoliberal framework and dynamics, which still prevail throughout the region. The ten recommendations are the following:

10 Biblioteca Virtual de Derecho, Economía y Ciencias Sociales. *Consenso de Washington*. http://www.eumed.net/libros-gratis/2007a/252/9.htm

11 STEGER, M.B. and RAVI, K.R. *Neoliberalism: A Very Short Introduction*, pg 98.

12 Ibid.

Table 7 The Washington Consensus: John Williamson's 10-Point Recommendations

'Fiscal Discipline: *Large and sustained fiscal deficits contribute to inflation and capital flight. Therefore, governments should keep them to a minimum.*
Public Expenditure Priorities: *Subsidies need to be reduced or eliminated. Government spending should be redirected toward education, health, and infrastructure development.*
Tax Reform: *The tax base "should be broad" and marginal tax rates "should be moderate."*
Interest Rates: *Domestic financial markets should determine a country's interest rates. Positive real interest rates discourage capital flight and increase savings.*
Exchange Rates: *Developing countries must adopt a "competitive" exchange rate that will bolster exports by making them cheaper abroad.*
Trade Liberalization: *Tariffs should be minimized and should never be applied toward intermediate goods needed to produce exports.*
Foreign Direct Investment: *Foreign investment can bring needed capital and skills and, therefore, should be encouraged.*
Privatization: *Private industry operates more efficiently because managers either have a "direct personal stake in the profits of an enterprise or are accountable to those who do." State-owned enterprises ought to be privatized.*
Deregulation: *Excessive government regulation can promote corruption and discriminate against smaller enterprises that have minimal access to the higher reaches of the bureaucracy. Governments have to deregulate the economy.*
Property Rights: *Property rights must be enforced. Weak laws and poor judicial systems reduce incentives to save and accumulate wealth'.*

Source: New Voices in Public Policy. SYMONIAC, J.D. '*The Washington Consensus*'. http://journals.gmu.edu/newvoices/article/viewFile/14/14

21

The Re-Emergence of the Left in Latin America

Despite the prevalence of the Washington Consensus throughout LA, most especially since the end of the twentieth and the beginning of the twenty-first centuries, the region has experienced a re-emergence of the Left, most particularly a radical and extreme, progressive and populist political Left. A schism has been created by the established dichotomy between the so-called '*positive Left*' and the '*negative Left*'. Countries like Mexico, Brazil and Chile are considered part of the '*positive Left*', while countries like Argentina, Bolivia, Ecuador and Venezuela are regarded as the group of the '*negative Left*', due to their types of government and political ideologies being based on extreme and radical progressivism and populism. Much more transcendentally, the negative Left completely abandoned the neoliberal economic model and put into practice other types of heterodox economic currents.

The main reasons for the anti-neoliberal turn are mostly rooted in the fact that the Left, most particularly the negative Left, detected serious faultlines in the obtainment of positive neoliberal results related to economic development and its expected economic and social benefits. For the negative Left, neoliberalism and its dictums have produced extremely bad results, mostly associated to an extremely disproportioned economic growth, as well as to a very uneven economic and socially exclusive development. For them, neoliberalism has only widened and deepened the breach between the rich and the poor, obtaining very good results with reaping benefits for the rich, making them richer, but likewise producing very bad results with hardly any benefits for the poor, making them poorer. In general, economic growth has not alleviated poverty and social equality issues, with the widespread privatizations of public firms, having the worst and most disastrous results for the poor. Going further, economic growth and national development have totally disregarded the much more widespread and established '*sub-development*' which predominates in most countries, yet not being attended satisfactorily.[1]

LA has witnessed the resurgence of a new breed of '*pragmatic Leftists*' very strongly devoted to the combination of '*good-hearted*' social objectives and a complete new appreciation for economic calculation. The region's '*new development*' has been

[1] LEIVA, F.I. *Latin American Neostructuralism: The Contradictions of Post-Neoliberal Development*, pgs XVII–1.

elevated to a much higher dimension, with an increase in Leftist governments and the continued presence of powerful social movements, which clearly point to a historical process of political and intellectual re-grouping. Ever since 1990, when the Comisión Económica para América Latina (CEPAL) or Economic Comission for Latin America and the Caribbean (ECLAC) published its '*Transformación Productiva con Equidad. La Tarea Prioritaria de América Latina y el Caribe en los Años Noventa*', the new Latin American Left has sought both the replacement of '*market fundamentalism*' and the '*humanisation of wild capitalism*', which has been imposed incessantly since many decades ago in the region by the dogmatism of neoliberal laissez-faire. The search continues restlessly in order to find a suitable formula that combines political democracy, economic growth and social equality in such a way that LA can at the same time take full advantage of, as well as profit from, the economic opportunities rendered by globalization.[2]

Neoliberals still strongly insist that the market and the price-signalling mechanism continue representing the best fundamental tools in order to reform economies in LA and achieve international competitiveness. The new Left, however, counter-argues that although market forces are still priorities, governmental intervention and policies are imperatives for the construction of a '*systemic competitiveness*' (including the whole of society) necessary to compete successfully in international markets. For them, institutional and political interventionism is essential for the generation of the synergy formed by the levels of coordination and social harmony, indispensable for a fluid and quick integration into the process of globalization. The Left has high hopes of transforming LA, through the substitution of neoliberalism and its market dogmatism, for a more holistic approximation that re-establishes itself in the regional economic development, institutional, political, social and cultural dimensions. Most especially, the Left aims to juxtapose economic growth with social equity.[3]

Within such an ever-changing context, the '*post-neoliberal*' swing has likewise and in turn generated both a 'new development' and the flow of other heterodox and alternative economic currents, such as '*Neo-Structuralism*', '*Neo-Extractivism*' and until recently, the very successful '*Social Communitarian Productive Economic Model*'. Although the 'new development' has integrated previously left out important sub-development aspects, in general terms, it has, however, had mixed results.

Whereas Argentina has experienced very negative results with its new economic framework, Venezuela has experienced even more disastrous results. In contrast, in Brazil, and most especially in Chile, Neo-Structuralism has been very successful in achieving the transformation of its economies and of its individual exporting firms by allowing them to enjoy the national generalization of economic, social and technological benefits derived from globalization. Whilst in Ecuador Neo-Extractivism has attended

[2] Ibid.
[3] Ibid.

satisfactorily social and environmental demands, in Bolivia the Social Communitarian Productive Economic Model managed to integrate and involve previously ignored ethnic-indigenous groups in its national process of economic development and growth. The economic results of Bolivia have, until recently, likewise proved to be extremely impressive and historically unprecedented. At the same time, key elements of each of the new currents can also be discerned and identified in most of those countries, although they might not officially adhere to them.

Neo-Structuralism

Since the beginning of the twenty-first century, one of the main new heterodox economic currents that flow through LA is '*Neo-Structuralism*'. Both the CEPAL's report '*Transformación Productiva con Equidad. La Tarea Prioritaria de América Latina y el Caribe en los Años Noventa*' and the book '*Neoestructuralismo y Corrientes Heterodoxas en América Latina y el Caribe a Inicios del Siglo XXI*' include in their recommendations for LA a totally different diagnostic to the one offered by the neoliberal economic model.

In basic terms, neo-structural thought and its general concepts, mainly base themselves on criteria related to a '*group of productive and managerial structures that facilitate economic dynamism and more equality, together with strategies and policies that make possible a bigger national autonomy; a basic continuation of structuralism, with some adjustments deriving from new national and international realities; the transformation of production with equity, that is, the achievement of growth with equity, through changes in the productive structure, guarding financial equilibriums and articulating democratic social support to those transformations*'.[4]

Neo-Structuralism has produced a very deep change in tackling development and sub-development problems based on an equitable transformation of production. It has articulated a traditional macroeconomic focus, but with a microeconomic vision of investment, as well as generated productive employment. It has aimed to create new sources of dynamism which allow the reaching of the objectives of the new developmentalist concept, the consolidation through democratization processes, the acquisition of a wider autonomy, equitable economic growth, an improvement in income distribution, the creation of conditions that stop environmental degradation, and the overall uplifting of the population's quality of life.[5]

[4] ODIO-AYALA, M.M. *Enfoques Principales del Neoestructuralismo como Corriente del Pensamiento Económico Latinoamericano*, pgs 3–4.ojs.uo.edu.cu/index.php/aeco/article/download/674/648. See also, BÁRCENA, A. and PRADO, A. (Eds). *Neoestructuralismo y Corrientes Heterodoxas en América Latina y el Caribe a inicios del siglo XXI.*

[5] ODIO-AYALA, M.M. *Enfoques Principales del Neoestructuralismo como Corriente del Pensamiento Económico Latinoamericano*, pg 8.

> *The neostructuralist State intends to abandon many functions, mainly in the productive sphere, and to assume more rigorously macroeconomic management, social and distributive investment, support for international integration and the incorporation of progress to the production process, and the defence of the environment. A structuralist macroeconomics is emerging that aims to strengthen the State based on raising its collection capacity and making its spending capacity more efficient. The fiscal policy of the neostructuralist state increases national savings and, therefore, growth and productive employment, so it is important to be able to consolidate the fiscal balance on solid and more permanent bases. A good part of the potential effort of social policies should be directed at investment in human capital (education, training, health and nutrition) as well as social security; but this will depend on the good collection of sufficient resources to allocate for these purposes. Hence, it is proposed to achieve a fiscal balance based on a reasonable level of collection, and not just a reduction in spending.*[6]

Neo-Structuralism is today present in Brazil, and most markedly in Chile. It has had very successful results transforming their economies and individual exporting firms, by way of allowing them to enjoy the economic, social and technological benefits that have derived from globalization.

The main focus of Neo-Structuralism is placed upon the following aspects:

"1. <u>Industry Transformation and Productive Modernization Strategy:</u> *The need for the creation of an institutional framework that stimulates the creativity and dynamism of productive actors and the capacity for concentration and coordination between them is considered. It entails policies to overcome inequity, ensure the macroeconomic stability indispensable in productive management, as well as technological innovations that advocate for high productive returns in both industry and agriculture. This also means guaranteeing subsidies for exports of companies introducing products to the external market; lowering tariffs to facilitate export and competitiveness; take advantage of the international trading network, market signals and international competition.*
2. <u>Technology and Innovation Strategy:</u> *The systematic and organized work of companies in research and development should be carried out and public policies should be established to socialize the results achieved in the processes. Create a scientific and technological infrastructure developed and articulated with the productive sectors within the framework of long-term specialization decisions. It is also necessary to have a close relationship between the public and private sectors and between organisations, workers and employers and between companies in the same sector.*
3. <u>Capital Formation Strategy:</u> *It is necessary to regulate capital movements, the exchange rate, trade policy and interest rate in order to generate a*

[6] Ibid, pg 6.

macroeconomic framework conducive to the transformation of capital and the acquisition of comparative advantages to take advantage of them and generate greater opportunities for investment and innovation. In addition, a functional macroeconomic balance for productive development should be established; reduce net transfer abroad; increase the availability of technology and savings; put the financial system at the service of productive development by reducing speculation and risk and promoting the generation of new dynamic comparative advantages in the production of exportable goods.

4. Role of the State Renewal Strategy: *The State needs to be perceived as concerted, with the aim of establishing policies aimed at achieving democratic openness of adjustments to the development strategy, maintaining macroeconomic balances and equity. The State must ensure minimum transport, communication, health, housing and education infrastructure, as well as a scientific and technological infrastructure, and must also eliminate market failures and support the structural competitiveness of the economy".*[7]

Neo-Extractivism

Another new alternative economic current adopted in the early twenty-first century in LA has been '*Neo-Extractivism*'. 'Neo-Extractivism' is most especially present in Ecuador, where it has attended satisfactorily many social and environmental demands.

Neo-Extractivism, just like its predecessor pure conventional 'Extractivism', also orientates the economy towards activities related to the exploitation of nature and the extraction of unprocessed resources, such as oil and gas, with the primary objective of exporting them. However, in stark contrast to conventional Extractivism, Neo-Extractivism differs from it mainly in relation to the leading role that the state acquires in the production process. The participation of the state has several primary protagonist areas and facets. State participation can either be direct through state-owned enterprises or indirect through taxation and other regulatory mechanisms. Similarly, such form of interventionism allows for a greater percentage of income for the state coffers. However, a much more crucial and transcendental fact is that a portion of those benefits and resources is reserved and earmarked for the implementation of social programmes and projects, as well as other initiatives, which provide those governments with a certain degree of legitimacy.[8]

So far, the effects of Neo-Extractivism have been positive. On one hand, Neo-Extractivism has produced an increased public control of the most profitable productive activities in the countries of the south, which has thus allowed the financing of multiple

[7] Ibid, pgs 7–8.
[8] Observatorio de Multinacionales en América Latina. *Neoextractivismo.* http://omal.info/spip.php?article4847

social welfare initiatives and programmes. On the other hand, it has equally produced a substantial improvement in the quality of life of both layers of the population. Its economic policy must be understood as part of a process of overall empowerment of those societies, which have erected and sustained those democratic governments capable of placing market forces at the service of development processes equitable and beneficial for all social strata. The overarching framework of such political processes embodies the true understanding of Neo-Extractivism's analysis as a contributing factor to the break-up with models of the past.[9]

Bolivia and the Social Communitarian Productive Economic Model

Profoundly enmeshed by the schism provoked by the Left's dichotomy, in 2005 in Bolivia the former leader of the Movimiento al Socialismo (MAS), and previous president of Bolivia, Evo Morales, generated a '*Proceso de Cambio*' or process of change, which, until recently, managed to radically transform the country politically, economically and socially in an extremely positive way. While Bolivia was provided with a new political constitution, which recognizes and identifies all the different ethnic groups and ethno-linguistic families in the country, economically, it likewise substituted the neoliberal economic model for the '*Social Communitarian Productive Economic Model*'. In social terms, it also managed to integrate and involve in the process of change most previously excluded groups and collectives.

The new Constitution of the Plurinational State of Bolivia now integrates and involves all 36 ethnic groups and 10 ethno-linguistic families in the overall process of change. President Morales also produced in Bolivia one of the most important changes to its economic system and model in its recent history.[10] From 2006 to 2019, the Morales administration spurred historically unprecedented political, and most especially, socio-economic changes throughout the country. Bolivia's impressive economic progresses and achievements were even termed as '*Bolivia's Economic Miracle*', with its economic success attracting much worldwide admiration.[11]

In 2020–5, President Luis Arce continued with the same economic model spawned by his predecessor President Morales. During the Morales administration, Arce had acted as finance minister and had in fact designed and fashioned the new economic model in accordance with Bolivia's needs.

[9] Ibid.

[10] ZURITA, A. *La Sociedad Multiétnica Boliviana: Riesgos de Fragmentación Social y Amenazas a la Formación de la Identidad Nacional.*

[11] Notimérica.com. *Bolivia, a la cabeza del crecimiento económico en Iberoamérica este 2019.* https://www.notimerica.com/economia/noticia-bolivia-cabeza-crecimiento-economico-iberoamerica-2019-20190410143507.html

In the August 2025 general elections held in Bolivia and after two decades and two different *'Masinian'* administrations, the winds of change have begun blowing strong across the country. The elections were clearly marked by an acute nationwide economic crisis, mainly caused by the huge dramatic drop in oil prices, which affected very negatively Bolivia's hydrocarbons sector, together with a much lower hydrocarbons sector production level, the deep fractures and rifts within the Left and the MAS party (now splintered into three distinct factions), plus a very divided opposition. It is expected that by the second round of elections in October 2025, the MAS political party and the Bolivian Left will lose their power and control of the country after twenty years of governance, either to the Centre or to the Conservative Right.[12]

While both new presidential candidates, Senator Rodrigo Paz Pereira and ex-President Jorge Quiroga, compete to overcome the acute economic crisis, as well as to close the political cycle of the MAS party, they are carrying it out, however, with different styles. Whereas Paz incarnates a more renovating and moderate stance, Quiroga offers a much more ideological and conservative political discourse.

Notwithstanding, the changes Bolivia has experienced from 2006 to 2025, due to the anti-neoliberal swing and mastered and commanded by the *'Social Communitarian Productive Economic Model'*, together with the 'Bolivian economic miracle' it produced, represent an excellent example of a very innovative, home-grown, anti-neoliberal economic counter-current, which has had tremendous success.

Back in 2006, President Morales put into motion the process of change by replacing the neoliberal economic system that prevailed in the country, with a *'Plural Economic System'*. Whereas the new economic model was founded on a plural economy and based on a very interrelated economic, community, state, private and cooperative social organization, it was likewise very deeply rooted in the *'Social Communitarian Productive Economic Model'*. Within the new model of mixed economy, the state exercised the integral direction of economic development and its planning processes, while being at the same time, governed by different production models, such as the pre-capitalist, the capitalist and the social models. The state also combined economic balance with structural and social change, thus having a very broad and deep presence in the economy through public and private enterprises, which therefore ensured a strong economy for the supply of mass-consumption food. State interventionism in strategic sectors was linked to the National Development Plan, which also generated more space for the good development of private-peasant, community and business activities, together with the reduction of fiscal and monetary pressures, which in turn increased domestic supply and exports.[13]

[12] BBC.com. News Mundo. 18 August 2025. AMERISE, A. and OLIVA, A. *El Senador Rodrigo Paz y el expresidente Quiroga se Disputarán la Presidencia de Bolivia en segunda vuelta, poniendo fin a 20 Años de Gobierno del MAS.* https://www.bbc.com

[13] Universidad Nacional Siglo XX. Centro de Altos Estudios Nacionales Federico Ahlfeld. *Bolivia Frente al Modelo Neoliberal.* http://cadimavictor.blogspot.com.es/

The Social Communitarian Productive Economic Model very successfully both generated the surplus and redistributed it into previously excluded sectors. The state assumed the role of redistributor and head-of-charge in such a positive way that the generation of wealth, together with the distribution of income and profits, reached previously marginalized and excluded economic agents from society. Likewise, the state was also able to transfer resources from surplus sectors to employment-generating sectors.[14]

Table 8 Main Differences between the Neoliberal Economic Model and the Social Communitarian Productive Economic Model

Neoliberal Economic Model	**Social Communitarian Productive Economic Model**
1) Free Market. The market is the resource allocator and imbalance correction mechanism. Efficient market hypothesis. **2)** State has Gendarme status. Observer State. The market is the self-regulatory mechanism of the economic process.	**1)** The State intervenes to correct market failures (the absence of wealth redistribution and transnational monopoly of strategic enterprises). **2)** Active participation of the State in the economy. The State must intervene in the economy through its seven facets: Planner, Entrepreneur, Investor, Regulator, Benefactor, Promoter and Banker.
3) Privatizing state, which transfers surpluses abroad and does not pre-precaution natural resources.	**3)** Nationalization and control of strategic natural resources.
4) Primary Development Exporting Pattern.	**4)** Industrializing Pattern and Productive Development.
5) Concentration of income, sectors excluded from society.	**5)** State re-distributes income.
6) Centralized economy in private initiative.	**6)** State promotes de Plural Economy.
7) Growth is based on external demand alone.	**7)** Growth based on external demand and domestic demand.
8) Dependence on external savings for investment, increased indebtedness and fiscal deficit.	**8)** Generation of domestic resources for investment, lower indebtedness and fiscal surplus.
9) Stagnation, poverty, wealth and opportunity inequality.	**9)** Increased development, redistribution and job creation.
10) Macroeconomic stability as an end in itself.	**10)** Preserve macroeconomic stability as a social heritage and boost economic development.

Source: Estado Plurinacional de Bolivia. Ministerio de Economía y Finanzas Publicas. '*El Nuevo Modelo Económico en Bolivia*'. https://medios.economiayfinanzas.gob.bo/MH/documentos/Materiales_UCS/Revistas/Revista_01.pdf

[14] SENAPE. *Rendición de Cuentas Parcial. 5 de octubre 2011*, pg 2. http://www.senape.gob.bo/docs/rendicion-cuentas-pre.pdf

Within the new economic setup, the state acted as promoter of the economy, thereby representing the most important actor. Since its genesis, the new Social Communitarian Productive Economic Model more than proved that it had the necessary elements for the generation of wealth in each and every economic ramification of Bolivian society – the state branch, the private branch and the cooperative and communitarian branch. Bolivia's new supercharged engine, indeed turbo-boosted its economy into a historically unprecedented, prolific path of economic growth and equitable socio-economic development and prosperity.[15]

Thanks to the Social Communitarian Productive Economic Model and the new adopted role of the state in the economy, the priority of the state apparatus managed to fully assure that its institutional heritage was properly managed. In order to fully enjoy its perfected proprietary right over real estate and vehicles, the state apparatus likewise began a parallel continuous and progressive sanitation process. Similarly, another priority was also focused upon insuring that public entities did not have unproductive remnants that generated superfluous administrative costs.[16]

During the two decades that the neoliberal economic model was substituted by the Social Communitarian Productive Economic Model, Bolivia's economy performed spectacularly. Both a favourable external environment and prudent macroeconomic policies managed to generate both fiscal and current account surpluses, a relatively strong and robust financial system, as well as an increase in international reserves. The combination of all such factors allowed Bolivia in 2008–9 to deal with the global financial crisis with very good macroeconomic fundamentals, which together with the country's relative isolation from international financial markets, made it overcome the crisis in good condition. After fourteen and a half years of leading the government, President Morales made Bolivia enjoy a historically unprecedented economic cycle with record macroeconomic indicators.[17] For the first time in the history of LA and of Bolivia, in 2009, 2014, 2015, and during the first semester of 2016, Bolivia projected the best regional economic performance in terms of real GDP growth, with a 3.4 per cent, 5.5 per cent, 4.8 per cent and 4.2 per cent, respectively. Likewise, during 2016, Bolivia maintained the same impressive economic performance. According to the IMF, in October 2016, Bolivia had the best performance in LA with a real GDP growth rate of 3.7 per cent.[18] The following years, Bolivia carried on with its continued growth. Concurring with the IMF and its *'Perspectives on the World Economy'* report, in 2019

[15] Ibid, pg 3.

[16] Ibid.

[17] Banco Mundial. *Banco Mundial- Socios de Bolivia- Alianza Estratégica con el País 2012–2015*, pg 8. http://www-wds.worldbank.org/external/default/WDSContentServer/WDSP/IB/2012/03/09/000386194_20120309024133/Rendered/PDF/651080SPANISH00ianza0print0digital0.pdf

[18] Gobierno de Bolivia. Ministerio de Economía y Finanzas Públicas. *Balance de la Economía Boliviana 2016*, pgs 8–9. http://www.economiayfinanzas.gob.bo/index.php?opcion=com_contenido&ver=contenido&id=3809&id_item=774&seccion=269&categoria=1576

Bolivia had the highest economic growth rate in Iberoamerica, followed by Peru.[19] Bolivia's impressive performance was even denominated as the *'Bolivian Economic Miracle'* and President Arce assured the continuation of such a positive evolution. *'GDP Annual Growth Rate in Bolivia averaged 3.79 per cent from 1991 until 2022, reaching an all time high of 23.09 per cent in the second quarter of 2021 and a record low of -24.74 per cent in the second quarter of 2020'*.[20]

However and probably one of the worst downsides of the anti-neoliberal shift in LA and its experimentation with heterodox economic currents was that it likewise and in turn generated a massive wave of expropriations and evictions of foreign companies and firms, which affected the business and commercial environment very negatively, with equally profound repercussions on the ongoing development and integration processes. Among many of the multinationals and companies expropriated in those countries, it is worth highlighting the seven major *'nationalizations'* of large Spanish companies: Gas Natural by the Colombian government; the withdrawal of the water business in Argentina to Aguas de Barcelona, together with the expropriation of Repsol-YPF and the expropriation of the airlines of the Marsans Group, Aerolíneas Argentinas and Austral; the purchase of Banco de Santander by the Venezuelan government; the appropriation by the Government of Bolivia of the subsidiary of Red Eléctrica. Lastly and also in Bolivia, the nationalization of the hydrocarbons sector affected Repsol and YPF very negatively.

In addition and descending in chronological order, in 2016 in Colombia, the Spanish subsidiary of Gas Natural was intervened by the government. In 2012 in Argentina, the government of Cristina Fernández de Kirchner declared as public utility and therefore subject to expropriation 51 per cent of Repsol-YPF's shares. Whereas more than half of that percentage became property of the Argentine government, the remaining percentage was divided between the ten Argentine provinces where hydrocarbons are produced. Likewise, in 2012 Bolivia's President Evo Morales ordered by decree the nationalization of Transportadora de Electricidad (TDE), a subsidiary of Red Eléctrica Española, which had control of three quarters of the country's electricity transmission lines. While the initial compensation was of 29.2 million euros, in 2014 Red Eléctrica valued favourably the impact of the operation to their profit of 52 million euros. In 2009 in Venezuela and after a year of negotiations the government of Hugo Chávez bought the Santander entity in the country for $1.05 billion. While such amount was 100 million short from what the Banco Santander had requested, the Spanish bank however earned capital gains of more than 300 million euros from the alleged *'divestment'*. At the end of 2009, in Argentina and after months of strikes and cancellation of flights, the Senate allowed the expropriation without any refund

[19] Notimérica.com. *Bolivia, a la cabeza del crecimiento económico en Iberoamérica este 2019.* https://www.notimerica.com/economia/noticia-bolivia-cabeza-crecimiento-economico-iberoamerica-2019-20190410143507.html

[20] Trading Economics. *Bolivia GDP Annual Growth Rate.* https://tradingeconomics.com/bolivia/gdp-growth-annual

of the companies of the Marsans group, Aerolíneas Argentinas and Austral. Shortly after, in 2010 the Marsans Group suspended payments in Spain. In 2006, in Argentina the government led by Néstor Kirchner decided to terminate its contract with Aguas Argentinas in Buenos Aires, which had among its shareholders Aguas de Barcelona (AGBAR), a company controlled in turn by Caixa with 25 per cent. However, five years later, Suez Environment, owner of AGBAR, was compensated with 375 million euros. Lastly, when in 2006 Bolivia decreed the nationalization of the hydrocarbons sector and the state assumed full control of hydrocarbons in the country, all foreign companies were obliged to hand over all their production to Yacimientos Petrolíferos Estatales, cutting their profits from 82 per cent to 18 per cent. Such actions greatly affected Repsol YPF, although it soon signed an agreement with the state guaranteeing the security of its investments.[21]

Implications of the Anti-Neoliberal Turn for Latin American Foreign Direct Investment Flows

Despite the anti-neoliberal turn in LA and the strong flow of alternative economic models, the region continues to represent an immense vessel full of natural, human and mineral resources. LA has also become a very active laboratory for myriad economic–commercial–financial experiments, together with many other political, social and cultural trials. The region has become a large recipient and issuer of FDI to and fro most regions and countries of the world. Its very good economic performance, huge commercial attraction and its rich and prosperous '*Oil and Gas*' sector have produced a very positive increase in FDI round-trip flows. In much the same way, while the '*Alianza del Pacífico*' or Pacific Alliance has for some years now been providing LA with greater openness of trade in and out of the region, at the same time, the EU represents the first development cooperation donor and the first Latin America and the Caribbean (LAC) trading partner. Likewise, the historical and linguistic ties between Spain and LA have also united them greatly, making Spain the third donor country in the region. Similarly, China's presence in LA has also expanded greatly and even levelled up to the EU as the region's first trading partner. Similarly, Russia has also increased its interest in LA, inexorably linked to the Oil and Gas sector.

The Pacific Alliance (PA) has been the most recent integration mechanism added to the list of integration processes in force in LA. The PA is formed by Chile, Colombia, Mexico and Peru. The nominations for membership have the worldwide participation of forty-nine nations as observer countries. The PA was established in April 2011, being formally and legally constituted on 6 June 2012, with the conclusion of a Framework Agreement.[22]

[21] El Español.com. *Las seis grandes 'nacionalizaciones' de empresas españolas en América Latina*, pgs 1–7. http://www.elespanol.com/economia/empresas/20161115/170983362_0.html

[22] Alianza del Pacífico. *Abecé. Alianza del Pacífico*, pgs 1–3. https://alianzapacifico.net/?wpdmdl=4441

The main objectives of the PA are the following:

- *"To build, in a participatory and consensual way, a deep area of integration to progressively move towards the free movement of goods, services, capital and people;*
- *To promote greater growth, development and competitiveness of the economies of the Parties, with a view to achieving greater well-being, overcoming socio-economic inequality and the social inclusion of its inhabitants;*
- *Become a platform of political articulation; economic and trade integration; and projection to the world, with special emphasis on the Asia Pacific".*[23]

While the PA represents a regional integration initiative with the primary objective of benefitting the population through the free movement of people, capital, goods and services, its Trade Agreement facilitates *'trade between the four countries through tariff reduction, the reduction of barriers to trade, the settlement of disputes, the streamlining of import and export operations, and the facilitation of trade in services, among others. In addition, it provides scholarships to students from all four countries to fortify human capital, and has achieved a free flow of people for tourism and business through the elimination of visas'.*[24]

Three of the PA's member countries are at the top of the World Bank's ease-to-do business ranking – (1) Chile, (2) Peru and (3) Colombia, and the GDP of all member countries represents about 39 per cent of LA's total GDP. All-combined, they account for about 50 per cent of LA's foreign trade, as well as account for around 41 per cent of LA's total inward FDI flows.[25]

The PA in accordance with its 'Pacific Alliance 2030 Vision' report projects to become a commercial bloc for the year 2030, which grows sustainably and that will depend less on primary resources, counting with a much more competitive, efficient, productive and fully integrated market. It will also have a fiscal, tax and financial regulatory framework, which favours an integrated market that allows financing infrastructure projects and dealing with natural disasters; the development of an electronic market and the promotion of the participation of institutional investors from the PA countries in the capital markets of the four countries.[26]

The bi-regional relationship between the EU and LA is excellent. The EU represents the first development cooperation donor in LAC, with its presence in the region being broad and deep. The relationship between the two blocs includes different dimensions and different levels. The EU interacts with the region through the bi-regional European Union-Latin America and the Caribbean Summits of Heads of State and Government.

[23] Ibid, pg 4.
[24] Ibid.
[25] Ibid.
[26] Alianza del Pacifico. *Alianza del Pacífico Visión 2030.* https://alianzapacifico.net/download-category/alianza-del-pacifico-proyeccion-2030/

It also interacts with Central America, the Andean Community and MERCOSUR. With other countries, the EU also has extensive association, cooperation and commercial agreements. Equally, the EU has Mixed Parliamentary Commissions, established for a better follow-up of its relations with all the different countries and commercial blocs.

Since a long time ago, the EU and Latin America and the Caribbean (LAC) find themselves at a true economic-commercial and social juncture. While their relations have always been good, they also continue to increase annually in various economic-commercial areas, as well as in development cooperation.

Although commerce between the EU and LA suffered a contraction during three years due to the international trade drawbacks created by the United States and Britain, in 2017 however, it began improving once again. LA continues to be an increasing net receptor of global concentrated FDI currents, with an 11 per cent of inflows and a 2 per cent of outflows.[27]

Due to their many historical, human, commercial, political, economic, social, and most especially, cultural-linguistic bonds and ties, Spain and LA have always enjoyed very good relations. Their interactions have continuously increased in the economic and commercial areas, as well as in many other fields, like most particularly, development and cooperation. Relations between Spain and LA are largely framed in the bi-annually held 'Iberoamerican Summits' of Heads of State and Government, together with many other economic-trade and development cooperation agreements. The *'Secretaria General Iberoamericana (SEGIB)* or the Iberoamerican General Secretariat, headquartered in Spain, Madrid, represents their main mediating body, as well as a fundamental and strengthening pillar of cooperation. The Spanish Agency for International Cooperation (AECID), which ranks as the world's number one in development cooperation in LA, also much cooperates, collaborates and interacts with the region. Spain is the number one cooperating country in LA and continues to project strong wills to achieve balanced and firm relations, based on equality. Moreover, Spain is a key player in relations between Europe and the countries of the region.

King Juan Carlos I of Spain proposed and induced Iberoamerican countries to organize amongst and for their own benefit, a discussion forum to deliberate on, as well as to further improve on political, economic, social and cultural issues. Such forum of interaction has generated, in accordance with the needs of the times, many Iberoamerican initiatives in all those areas, as well as a much-increased cooperation. In 1991, the first Iberoamerican Summit of Heads of State and Government was held in Colombia, Cartagena de Indias. Since then, they continue to be held biannually, with

[27] CEPAL. *La Unión Europea y América Latina y el Caribe: Estrategias Convergentes y Sostenibles ante la Coyuntura Global,* pg 96. https://repositorio.cepal.org/bitstream/handle/11362/43740/6/S1800903_es.pdf

the SEGIB representing the main international mediating body for the Iberoamerican Summits, as well as the General Secretariat for those and other interrelated issues.

Spain also maintains economic-commercial and cooperation relations with other regional organisms, such as '*MERCOSUR*', the '*Andean Community of Nations*', the '*Caribbean Community*', the '*South American Union of Nations*', the '*Central American Integration System*' and the '*Alianza Bolivariana para América*'.

From 1990 onwards, Spanish companies focused their international expansion much more towards LA, and in a short period of time, Spain soon also became the world's number 2 country in direct investments in the region, ranking only second to the United States.

> *The features of FDI in Latin America over the past 20 years make it possible to point out that a leading group of Spanish companies have built a relevant network of interdependence in direct investments, with a wide number of countries in the region. Hence, despite the strong negative impact of the international financial crisis, Spain will continue to be positioned as the second investor after the US.*[28]

> *Latin America has been configured in recent years as one of the main destinations for Spanish investment, especially in sectors such as infrastructure, which has redirected its efforts outside Spain in the face of the halting of civil works during the recession and subsequently. Beyond that sector, Spanish investment in Latin America has also been directed to telecommunications, manufacturing, financial activities and energy generation and supply. In addition, it should be noted that other activities, such as trade or catering, have also been maintained despite economic swings. Looking to the future … Spanish companies have improved their economic expectations for this region, to the point that three out of four companies … plans to increase its investments in Latin America and the Caribbean.*[29]

Since more than a decade ago, China has also been expanding its presence throughout LA, and Russia likewise greatly increasing its interest in the region.

While on one hand, some argue that the relationship between China and LA is exclusively tied to economic and energy issues, on the other hand, however, others contend that China's foreign policy is primarily driven by geopolitical concerns.[30]

[28] Política Exterior. *Las Inversiones españolas en América Latina en el periodo 2009–2016.* http://www.politicaexterior.com/articulos/economia-exterior/las-inversiones-directas-espanolas-en-america-latina-en-el-periodo-2009-16/

[29] Dirigentesdigital.com. *Aumenta la Inversión Española en América Latina.* https://dirigentesdigital.com/hemeroteca/aumenta_la_inversion_espanola_en_america_latina-DPDD72948

[30] ROETT, R. and PAZ, G. (Eds). *China's Expansion into the Western Hemisphere – Implications for Latin America and the United States.*

Nonetheless, the overall opinion emphasizes that China's growing presence in the region and its ever-deepening interactions have been established with the '*positive Left*' rather than the '*negative Left*'. China has been commercially very cautious in establishing its relations primarily with countries of the '*positive Left*', such as Chile and Brazil, which offer the richest variety of commodities and raw materials. At the same time, China has also been very discreet in its correct and courteous relations with countries of the '*negative Left*', such as Bolivia, Cuba and Venezuela, although lately there is much more rapprochement with Bolivia due to its prosperous Oil and Gas sector. However and in that sense, critics point to the fact that considering that the US factor is crucial for China-LA relations, China cannot circumvent the geostrategic implications of its ties with LA.[31] Notwithstanding and despite the variety of perceptions surrounding China's intentions in LA, it is however stressed that the United States should take stock of the high-level bilateral policy relationship positively and not be misguided by negative ideas about China's goals and objectives in AL.[32] '*China's expanding role in LA should be seen as a unique opportunity to strengthen the three China-US-LA triangle relations*'.[33]

As regards relations between Russia and LA, it should be highlighted that given Russia's growing importance and interest in the Oil and Gas market, relations between Russia and hydrocarbon-producing countries, like most especially Bolivia, have greatly increased.[34] The relationship between Russia and Bolivia has grown stronger since the 2016 signature of a cooperation agreement between the two countries. Whereas their bilateral cooperation has increased in the commercial, economic and investment fields, both countries have also made much progress in agricultural security and cooperation development.[35]

Most particularly through the 2016 Bolivia-Russia Cooperation Agreement, both countries agreed on the development of nuclear projects with pacific ends. Their main ongoing nuclear project in Bolivia has built a research centre at 4,000 metres above sea level, destined for the development of technology, based on atomic energy, with medicinal, agro-industrial and research objectives. It is currently envisaging the exploitation of the huge Bolivian concentration of lithium reserves there.[36] Since August 2021, '*the Cyclotron Radiopharmacy Preclinical Complex (CRPC) and the Multipurpose Irradiation Centre (MIC) at the Centre for Research and Development in Nuclear Technology in Bolivia, have been put into trial operation*'.[37]

[31] Ibid, pgs 19–20.

[32] Ibid.

[33] Ibid.

[34] Ibid.

[35] Notimérica. *¿Cuáles son los nuevos acuerdos firmados entre Bolivia y Rusia?*. https://www.notimerica.com/politica/noticia-cuales-son-nuevos-acuerdos-firmados-bolivia-rusia-20190712171021.html

[36] Ibid.

[37] World Nuclear News. *Nuclear Research and Technology Centre in Bolivia into Pilot Operation.* https://www.world-nuclear-news.org/Articles/Nuclear-research-and-technology-centre-in-Bolivia

The Latin American paradigm reflects a region, which, despite the many drawbacks and setbacks, is still full of fervent tendencies, sub-regional integration processes and commercial initiatives. It also continues to represent a very strong receptor and generator of FDI flows inwards towards its domestic market, as well as outwards towards other continents and parts of the world. Despite the Left's anti-neoliberal swing and its experimentation with heterodox currents, some of which are still flowing vigorously through several countries, neoliberalism continues to prevail in LA as the chief economic model, with most of the regional neoliberal integration processes continuing to expand their borders and benefits for the involved sub-regions. The growing flows of FDI from and to LA also clearly reassure the excellent source of economic-commercial possibilities that the region represents both for itself and for the entire world.

Notwithstanding, at the same time, the signs of change in LA are also very perceptible. The negative Left's anti-neoliberal swing has already witnessed the generation of a 'new development', which has spawned a series of new heterodox currents, such as 'Neo-Structuralism' and 'Neo-Extractivism', as well as until recent, the very successful 'Social Communitarian Productive Economic Model', which continue to flow vigorously through Venezuela, Brazil, Ecuador and Chile. Nonetheless, with Argentina having recently once again re-adopted neoliberalism led by President Milei, the amount of neoliberal countries continues topping non-neoliberal countries.

The achievements and benefits of LA are favourable to all those involved: the international community, LA and the different actors at play in the international, regional, national and local public and private sectors. With time, all of such efforts are likely to grow in both number and intensity, as well as in width and depth. Although the economic growth prospects for LA for the coming years are good, economic caution must however prevail, most especially in view of the political-social changes and alterations, which are and will probably continue taking place in the region. The international economic landscape is also currently dealing with the apparition of many new types of '*economic phenomena*', which will undoubtedly generate even more transformations.

Dimension Four

The European Union's Financial Reform: *The Ordo-Neoliberalization of the European Union*

22

The European Union's Financial Reform: *The EU Financial Regulatory Framework*

Following the 2007–15 global financial crisis, the prevailing neoliberal orthodoxy was put under a lot of scrutiny and into very serious questioning. By early 2009, the predominating worldwide opinion amongst experts had concluded that the global financial crisis was fundamentally deep-rooted in neoliberalism. Compared to the Great Depression, it was labelled as the '*Great Recession*', although it was more appropriately also tagged as the '*Neoliberal Crisis*'.

While many Wall Street bankers were blamed for triggering the crisis, most of the culpability fell on global financial elites for adhering so strongly to such a deeply ingrained neoliberal orthodoxy and dogmatism. Since then, most political and economic leaders began to critically question the foundations of neoliberalism, as well as to demand more regulation from national and international institutions. Whereas new regulations and rules were soon applied by G-20 agreements to the international financial system, the European Union and its severely battered Eurozone were most especially transformed through a wide-arching financial reform. The EU Financial Reform, together with the establishment of the EU Financial Regulatory Framework, has successfully provided the region with many new economic, financial and banking supervising entities, together with a new set of interventionist procedures and strict regulations and rules.

Bearing in mind that the EU was constructed over a very solid neoliberal bedrock, the ordoliberal restructuring, which the financial banking sector has been subjected to, has even gained it the moniker the '*ordo-neo-liberalization*' of the EU. In view of the new and much stricter EU regulating rules-based order, the new financial-banking structure has likewise been dubbed by critics and observers as '*Europe's ordoliberal iron cage*'.[1]

During the first months of 2009, at the international level former Federal Reserve Chairman, Alan Greenspan, officially declared, that '*his neoliberal ideology was no*

[1] RYNER, M. *Europe's Ordoliberal Iron Cage: Critical Political Economy, the Euro Area Crisis and Its Management.* https://www.semanticscholar.org/paper/Europe%27s-ordoliberal-iron-cage%3A-critical-political-Ryner/db0d9f47d024e4ab13910fd512b10f333615c2cc

longer working'.[2] Many other critics likewise conceded '*that free markets were not self-regulating and perfectly efficient and people were not always good guardians of their own self-interest*'.[3] Additionally, in March 2009, the United Nations Conference on Trade and Development (UNCTAD), provided the most '*comprehensive and sophisticated criticism of the neoliberal model*',[4] through a sixty-five-page report titled '*The Global Economic Crisis: Systematic Failures and Multilateral Remedies*'. The UNCTAD Report contained four key messages or insights, which summed up the main neoliberal defects. The first message, emphasized that the '*market fundamentalist laissez-faire*' of previous decades had failed miserably in its first real-world application and that '*financial deregulation had created the build-up of huge financial risks whose unwinding had pushed the global economy into debt deflation that, ultimately, could only be countered by government debt inflation*'.[5] The second message reflected that '*blind faith in the efficiency of deregulated financial markets and the absence of a cooperative financial and monetary system had created an illusion of risk-free profits and licensed profligacy through speculative finance*'.[6] The third insight highlighted that '*the growing role of financial conglomerates on commodities and derivatives had led to extreme volatility and the emergence of speculative commodity "bubbles" such as the US housing bubble*'.[7] The fourth and last insight mirrored that '*similar to the 1997–8 Asian Crisis, the absence of a cooperative international system to manage exchange rates fluctuations had facilitated rampant currency speculations and increased global imbalances, thus bringing a number of countries to the verge of default*'.[8]

The UNCTAD Report, which paradoxically much resembled an '*obituary of neoliberalism*', also proposed three additional remedies to improve the generalized state of affairs:

1) *"Comprehensive re-regulation of the global financial system with the world's governments working in unison to achieve this goal;*
2) *government-private sector cooperation to stimulate economic growth;*
3) *developing countries should no longer be subjected to the kind of neoliberal logic that caused the current crisis in the first place"*.[9]

Only one month after the publication of the UNCTAD Report, the international community organized a G-20 Heads of State meeting at a Summit in London in order to discuss and develop a common strategy on how to tackle the neoliberal hulabaloo. British Prime Minister Gordon Brown observed that the meeting was

[2] STEGER, M.B. and RAVI, K.R. *Neoliberalism: A Very Short Introduction*, pg 131.
[3] Ibid.
[4] Ibid.
[5] Ibid, pg 133.
[6] Ibid.
[7] Ibid.
[8] Ibid, pgs 133–4.
[9] Ibid, pg 134.

'a historic opportunity to establish a new world order'.[10] However, throughout the Summit, two factions were formed, which split the meeting amid different opinions regarding the actions to be taken. One faction, represented by President Nicolas Sarkozy and Chancellor Angela Merkel, favoured applying stronger global regulatory controls. Another faction, led by President Barack Obama, Prime Minister Brown and Japanese Prime Minister Taro Aso, supported providing further stimulus packages. Consequently, on 2 April 2009 the G-20 published a joint communiqué with a new set of general principles regarding stricter and tighter rules, regulations and security mechanisms for the global banking system.[11]

Although the G-20 Agreement was considered fundamental for the repair of the world's financial infrastructure, such reforms, however, were regarded as quite moderate, since, in general, they lacked specificity as they were absent of any concrete measures to combat the global climate change. What is more, the communiqué left the required reforms of the banking system the sole responsibility of national governments to act on a *'case-by-case'* basis, a measure which was met by much resistance, as banking executives believed that the regulation pendulum would tilt too heavily against the financial sector. Moreover, the new established Financial Stability Board was not adjudicated with any enforcement powers either, with its functions being merely limited to *'advising members, monitoring regulations, and collaborating with the IMF to create early-warning mechanisms aimed at preventing the next financial crisis'*.[12]

Table 9 The Six Key Points of the G-20 Agreements

1. Reform of the global banking system, with controls on hedge funds, better accounting standards, tighter rules for credit-rating agencies, curbs on excessive executive remuneration, and the naming-and-shaming of tax havens that fail to share information.
2. A new Financial Stability Board will be set up to work with the IMF to ensure cooperation across boarders and provide an early warning mechanism for the financial system. Its members will include finance ministries, regulators, and central banks from G-20 countries.
3. A $1.1 trillion package to supplement the $5 trillion stimulus to the global economy by individual countries. $750 billion – the lion's share of the 1.1 trillion – will go to the IMF, the rest to the World Bank and other institutions to restore credit, jobs, and increase lending to vulnerable.
4. More power for leading developing countries such as China and India to determine IMF and World Bank policies.
5. $200 billion of trade finance over 2009–10 to help reverse the decline in world trade.
6. A pledge that part of the fiscal stimulus, including the sale of gold by the World Bank to raise $6 billion, will be used to help the poorest nations as well as to create 'green' jobs.

Source: STEGER, M.B. and RAVI, K.R. *'Neoliberalism: A Very Short Introduction'*, pg 135.

[10] Ibid.
[11] Ibid.
[12] Ibid, pg 135.

However and despite the IMF being given a pivotal role in the whole reform process, the neoliberal rationale and logic are so deeply ingrained in the institution's mindframe, that such reforms have not managed to neither change nor alter much the international financial system or let alone its free-market dynamics.[13]

The EU Financial Regulatory Framework

In stark contrast, the post-crisis reforms carried out in Europe have been much more thorough, as well as far more far reaching. Once the crisis spread and hit Europe hard, the Eurozone crisis that ensued saw Member States showing immense solidarity to prevent the collapse of the monetary union. From then onwards, the Council of the EU (the Council), comprising the heads of government of the '*Euro Club*' began representing the political executive committee for managing the common affairs of the Eurozone. Since 2010, it has closely overseen the hardening of the whole system of fiscal governance through new fiscal rules, much stricter supervision, stiff regulation and periodic stress-tests. In a relatively short period of time, the EU has set up and established in the Eurozone a very rigid and rule-binding framework of economic, fiscal and financial supervision and regulation.[14]

In view of the many failures of financial supervision exposed by the financial crisis, the European Commission (EC or the Commission) mandated the '*de Larosière*' expert group to provide advice on how to strengthen European supervisory arrangements. Based on the proposals of the '*Commission Communication on Financial Supervision*', together with the recommendations of the expert group, the EU set up a specific supervisory architecture – the European System of Financial Supervision (ESFS). The ESFS consists of one European Systemic Risk Board (ESRB) in order to monitor systemic risks and three European Supervising Authorities (ESAs). Following the adoption of a package of legislative acts, the ESRB and the three ESAs began operating in January 2011.[15]

The new European System of Financial Supervision (ESFS) is formed by the following:

- *"European Systemic Risk Board (ESRB)*
- *European Banking Authority (EBA)*
- *European Securities and Markets Authority (ESMA)*
- *European Insurance and Occupational Pensions Authority (EIOPA)"*[16]

[13] Ibid.

[14] RYNER, M. *Europe's Ordoliberal Iron Cage: Critical Political Economy, the Euro Area Crisis and Its Management.* https://www.semanticscholar.org/paper/Europe%27s-ordoliberal-iron-cage%3A-critical-political-Ryner/db0d9f47d024e4ab13910fd512b10f333615c2cc

[15] European Commission. *European System of Financial Supervision,* pgs 1–2. https://ec.europa.eu/info/business-economy-euro/banking-and-finance/financial-supervision-and-risk-management/european-system-financial-supervision_en

[16] Ibid, pg 1.

In September 2017, the EC adopted a new package of proposals to further strengthen the ESFS, which much improved the mandates, governance and funding of the three ESAs, as well as the functioning of the ESRB. Altogether, they are successfully ensuring a stronger and more integrated financial supervision across the EU.[17]

Additionally, in September 2018 the EC took yet another very important step to assure a fully functioning '*Capital Markets Union*', in order to reinforce '*the role and powers of the European Supervisory Agencies, including that of the European Banking Authority, by strengthening its role in the area of anti-money laundering*'. Following President Juncker's State of the Union address, the EC published a '*Communication on Strengthening the Union Framework for Prudential and Anti-money Laundering Supervision*', which introduced '*a proposal for a regulation amending a series of regulations and directives aiming to concentrate anti-money laundering powers related to the financial sector into the European Banking Authority (EBA). The proposal furthermore aims at strengthening the EBA's mandate to ensure that all relevant authorities effectively and consistently supervise the risks of money-laundering and that they cooperate and share information*'.[18]

In April 2019, the European Parliament reflected the advances of the process, with the endorsement of legislation that laid down the building blocks for the Capital Markets Union, as well as an assessing review of the ESFS.[19]

Likewise, the EU has also strengthened its economic governance framework by refining its '*Stability and Growth Pact*' *(SGP)* through a set of legislative measures, which have enhanced fiscal and macroeconomic surveillance. The so-called '*Sixpack*' both reformed the established SGP and established greater macroeconomic surveillance. The newly established 'six regulations' have strengthened the procedures to reduce public deficits and address macroeconomic imbalances. Similarly, fiscal discipline has also been reinforced with an extra two regulations to increase fiscal discipline, which are termed as '*Two-pack*'. Furthermore, the '*Treaty on the Functioning of the European Union*' amended its Article 136, as well as established a stability mechanism for Member States whose currency is the euro. The '*Treaty on Stability, Coordination and Governance in the Economic and Monetary Union*' *(TSCG)* or also called '*Fiscal Compact*' has further strengthened the budgetary targets set by the SGP's Preventive Arm (the Medium-Term budgetary Objectives).[20]

The '*Sixpack*' entered into force in November 2011. In accordance with its guidelines, all Member States are committed to implement fiscal policies, which stay within the

[17] Ibid, pg 2.
[18] Ibid.
[19] Ibid.
[20] European Commission. *The EU's Economic Governance Explained.* https://ec.europa.eu/info/business-economy-euro/economic-and-fiscal-policy-coordination/eu-economic-governance-monitoring-prevention-correction/european-semester/framework/eus-economic-governance-explained_en

limits of government deficit, set at 3 per cent of GDP, and debt, set at 60 per cent of GDP. In the case of debt levels rise above 60 per cent, they are in turn expected to have a declining trend each following year. Member states are also obliged to submit yearly SGP compliance reports or so-called '*stability programmes*' for Eurozone Member States and '*convergence programmes*' for non-Eurozone Member States, in order to present the country's expected fiscal development for the current and subsequent three years. The EC and the Council are in charge of evaluating the contents. The '*stability programmes*' have also included '*Medium-Term budgetary Objectives*' *(MTOs)*, which are individually calculated for each Member State as the medium-term sustainable average-limit for the country's structural deficit. It also obliges Member States to outline the measures they intend to implement to attain their MTOs. In the case that a non-compliance were to occur with either the deficit limit or the debt limit from any of the EU Member States, the '*Excessive Deficit Procedure*' *(EDP)* is then initiated with a deadline to comply, which outlines an '*adjustment path towards reaching the MTO*'.[21]

In November 2013, in addition to the EU '*Sixpack*', the EU '*Two-pack*' introduced urther integration of fiscal policies and tighter budgetary surveillance matters, as well as closer collaboration on fiscal matters between Member States sharing the same currency. Whereas the '*Two-pack*' regulations apply to all Eurozone Member States, together, the two packs form much stronger budgetary governance, with a tighter system of monitoring and surveillance by the EC.[22]

Table 10 Main Objectives of the EU '*Sixpack*'

- '...*Bring the surveillance of fiscal and economic policies under the European Semester, to ensure that the policy advice given to Member States is consistent;*
- *introduce an expenditure benchmark, linked to a country's medium-term budgetary objective (MTO), that places a cap on the annual growth of a country's expenditure;*
- *enhance country surveillance, through examining not only countries with current account deficits, but also those with current account surpluses;*
- *permit the excessive deficit procedure to be opened on the sole basis of the debt criterion (60% of GDP);*
- *introduce a macroeconomic imbalance procedure relying on an early-warning system and enforcement regime, and allows the Commission and the Council to insert preventive recommendations in the country-specific recommendations, before the imbalances of a Member State become too large, or if this fails, to open an excessive imbalance procedure and oblige it to follow a corrective action plan;*
- *impose graduated financial sanctions, which may eventually reach 0.5% of GDP*'.

Source: European Parliament. '*Review of the "six-pack" and "two-pack"*'. http://www.europarl.europa.eu/EPRS/EPRS-AaG-542182-Review-six-pack-two-pack-FINAL.pdf

[21] European Parliament. *Review of the 'Six-pack' and 'Two-pack'*. http://www.europarl.europa.eu/EPRS/EPRS-AaG-542182-Review-six-pack-two-pack-FINAL.pdf

[22] Ibid.

On the other hand and with the amendment of Article 136 of the *'Treaty on the Functioning of the European Union'*, the EU has equally improved and strengthened its provisions specific to its Member States whose currency is the euro, with the establishment of a euro-solidary permanent crisis resolution mechanism. The amendment adds an extra third paragraph to Article 136, which reads as follows:

> *The Member States whose currency is the euro may establish a stability mechanism to be activated if indispensable to safeguard the stability of the euro area as a whole. The granting of any required financial assistance under the mechanism will be made subject to strict conditionality.*[23]

Going even further, the *'Treaty on Stability, Coordination and Governance in the Economic and Monetary Union'* *(TSCG)* or *'Fiscal Compact'* has much legally reinforced

Table 11 Common Principles and Rules of the *'European Fiscal Compact'*

- *'Member states bound by the Fiscal Compact have to transpose into national legal order the provisions of the Fiscal Compact. In particular, national budget has to be in balance or surplus under the treaty's definition. An automatic correction mechanism has to be established to correct potential significant deviations. A national independent monitoring institution should be mandated to provide fiscal surveillance. The treaty defines a balanced budget as a general budget deficit not exceeding 3.0% of the gross domestic product (GDP), and a structural deficit not exceeding a country-specific Medium-Term budgetary Objective (MTO) which at most can be set to 0.5% of GDP for states with a debt-to-GDP ratio exceeding 60% – or at most 1.0% of GDP for states with debt levels within the 60%-limit. The country-specific MTOs are recalculated every third year and might be set at stricter levels compared to what the treaty allows at most. The treaty also contains a direct copy of the "debt brake" criteria outlined in the Stability and Growth Pact, which defines the rate at which debt levels above the limit of 60% of GDP shall decrease.*
- *If the budget or estimated fiscal account for any ratifying state is found to be noncompliant with the deficit or debt criteria, the state is obliged to rectify the issue. If a state is in breach at the time of the treaty's entry into force, the correction will be deemed to be sufficient if it delivers sufficiently large annual improvements to remain on a country specific predefined 'adjustment path' towards the limits at a midterm horizon. Should a state suffer a significant recession, it will be exempted from the requirement to deliver a fiscal correction for as long as it lasts.*
- *Despite being an International treaty outside the EU legal framework, all treaty provisions function as an extension to existing EU regulations, utilising the same reporting instruments and organisational structures already created within EU in the three areas: Budget discipline enforced by Stability and Growth Pact (extended by Title III), Coordination of economic policies (extended by Title IV), and Governance within the EMU (extended by Title V)'.*

Source: Citizens Information. *'Summary of the Fiscal Stability Treaty'.* https://web.archive.org/web/20120603055020/http://www.citizensinformation.ie/en/government_in_ireland/european_government/fiscal_stability_treaty/fiscal_treatysummary.html

[23] EUR-Lex. *European Council Decision of 25 March 2011 Amending Article 136 of the Treaty on the Functioning of the European Union with Regard to a Stability Mechanism for Member States Whose Currency Is the Euro.* https://eur-lex.europa.eu/legal-content/en/ALL/?uri=CELEX%3A32011D0199

the SGP. The *'Fiscal Compact'* came into force in January 2016, with its all-binding set of common principles and rules articulating in the Eurozone an economic and budgetary supervision mechanism, in order to ensure more financial security and stability to Member States.[24]

Notwithstanding and in accordance with many experts, the COVID-19 crisis further exposed and put into highlight several defects inherent to the new fiscal framework, with many calls being made since then to reform it. The reform of the EU fiscal framework is most especially recommended, considering that the current fiscal rules are asymmetric and pro-cyclically biased and that they lack transparency and political ownership in Member States. Further adding to the already-existing deficiencies of the Stability and Growth Pact, the current macroeconomic scenario has debt levels that exceed 100 per cent of GDP, which points to the irrefutable fact that substantial changes will have to be brought about soon to the fiscal framework.[25] Some of the options pressed forward in order to improve the current framework include the reform of *'the mechanisms and institutions created over the past decade, which would prevent fiscal profligacy, stimulate economic growth through reforms and ensure ownership of the process at the national level, while increasing risk sharing and control'*.[26]

> *The overarching element of the reform would be a permanent central fiscal capacity, consolidating and institutionalising the Next Generation EU instrument, transformed into a new pan-European investment mechanism. It would finance EU public goods (especially green and digital investments, with considerable external effects) and would also ease the path of adjustment of member states towards a solid and sustainable fiscal position, no longer defined by arbitrary reference values (such as the 60% debt rule), but as the result of a process of analysis and permanent interaction with EU institutions.*[27]

The main objective of the proposed reform is to be able to return to balanced fiscal positions. It is strongly held that once such objective is achieved, *'the preventive arm would be based on a simple and observable primary expenditure rule (complemented with a safeguard for highly indebted countries) which would replace other indicators such as the structural balance or the expenditure benchmark. The reform of the preventive arm would be complemented with a strengthening of the accountability of national Stability and Convergence Programmes and Draft Budgetary Plans, as well as with*

[24] Citizens Information. *Summary of the Fiscal Stability Treaty.* https://web.archive.org/web/20120603055020/http://www.citizensinformation.ie/en/government_in_ireland/european_government/fiscal_stability_treaty/fiscal_treaty_summary.html

[25] Real Instituto Elcano. Elcano Policy Paper. FEÁS, E., MARTÍNEZ MONGAY, C., OTERO-IGLESIAS, M., STEINBERG, F. and TAMAMES, J. *A Proposal to Reform the EU's Fiscal Rules,* pg 5. https://www.realinstitutoelcano.org/en/policy-paper/a-proposal-to-reform-the-eus-fiscal-rules/

[26] Ibid.

[27] Ibid.

an enhancement of member states' fiscal policy assessments through a newly created European System of Independent Fiscal Institutions'.[28]

> *On the corrective arm, we propose suppressing the 1/20th debt reduction rule and reforming the Excessive Deficit Procedure so that it can only be triggered by a simultaneous consideration of both debt and deficit indicators. Recommendations should concentrate on fiscal structural factors behind excessive deficits, and would not be required if the excessive deficit derives from asymmetric downturns.*[29]

There are also more calls being increasingly made in order to tackle other aspects of the Eurozone governance. Some of those include '*additional EU own resources and debt issuance. Democratic accountability must be reinforced by strengthening the European Parliament's oversight over fiscal policy and taxation, reverting the intergovernmental tide. The European Stability Mechanism and other intergovernmental bodies must be fully included into the EU treaties, institutionalising and merging the figure of a Euro Finance Minister/Vice-president of the Commission, permanent President of the Eurogroup/Ecofin, and single representative of the Euro in international forums*'.[30]

The Banking Union

Within the framework of the EU Economic and Monetary Union (EMU) and as a complement to the internal market for capital and the single currency, EU policymakers have long sought the integration of bank regulation. In 2012, the response to the Eurozone crisis greatly stimulated the motivation for an EU Banking Union, which transferred the responsibility for banking policy from the national to the EU level amongst EU Member States. A big part of such motivation came from the fragility of numerous banks in the Eurozone, together with the identification of a vicious circle between credit conditions for those banks and the sovereign credit of their respective home countries. During the Eurozone crisis, the deterioration of credit conditions and the contagion of financial instability to larger Member States of the Euro Area further encouraged the interdependence between banking policy, financial integration and financial stability.[31]

Since October 2014, and founded on the EU's '*Single Rulebook*' or common financial regulatory framework, the Banking Union rests upon two main pillars: the '*Single Supervisory Mechanism (SSM)*' and the '*Single Resolution Mechanism (SRM)*'. A

[28] Ibid.
[29] Ibid.
[30] Ibid.
[31] European Central Bank. Banking Supervision. *Banking Union.* https://www.bankingsupervision.europa.eu/about/bankingunion/html/index.en.html

third pillar, the *'European Deposit Insurance Scheme (EDIS)'*, is also currently being developed. Once the EDIS is finalized and established, the three pillars of the Banking Union will provide more supervision, resolution and deposit protection throughout the whole Eurozone banking system. Whereas the SSM began exercising its authority on 4 November 2014, the SRM entered into full force on 1 January 2016, with Eurozone Member States participation being automatic.[32] On one hand and directly at the European level, the SSM supervises the largest and most important banks in the Euro Area. On the other hand, the primary purpose of the SRM is to resolve failing banks in an orderly manner with minimal costs for taxpayers and for the real economy.

The main purpose and objectives of the European Banking Union are to make European banking '*more transparent, by consistently applying common rules and administrative standards for supervision, recovery and resolution of banks; unified, by treating national and cross-border banking activities equally and by delinking the financial health of banks from the countries in which they are located; safer, by intervening early if banks face problems in order to help prevent them from failing, and – if necessary – by resolving banks efficiently.*'[33]

The EU's *'Single Rulebook'* represents the financial regulatory framework, which comprises the EU laws that govern collectively the financial sector across the whole of the EU. '*This set of rules provides legal and administrative standards to regulate, supervise and govern the financial sector in all EU countries more efficiently. It includes rules on capital requirements, recovery and resolution processes and a system of harmonised national Deposit Guarantee Schemes.*'[34]

The *'Single Supervisory Mechanism (SSM)'* is the new system of banking supervision which has been established in Europe. It comprises the European Central Bank (ECB) and the national supervisory authorities of the participating countries. Its main objectives are to '*ensure the safety and soundness of the European banking system; increase financial integration and stability; and ensure consistent supervision*'. While the ECB has the authority to take over direct supervision of any Eurozone bank, its monitoring regime includes conducting periodic stress tests on financial institutions.[35]

The *'Single Resolution Mechanism (SRM)'* has the main purpose of ensuring '*the efficient resolution of failing banks with minimal costs for taxpayers and to the real economy. A Single Resolution Board ensures swift decision-making procedures, allowing any bank to be resolved over a weekend. As a supervisor, the ECB has an important role in*

[32] European Parliament. Fact Sheets of the European Union. *Banking Union.* http://www.europarl.europa.eu/factsheets/en/sheet/88/banking-union

[33] European Central Bank. Banking Supervision. *Banking Union.* https://www.bankingsupervision.europa.eu/about/bankingunion/html/index.en.html

[34] Ibid.

[35] European Central Bank. Banking Supervision. *Single Supervisory Mechanism.* https://www.bankingsupervision.europa.eu/about/thessm/html/index.en.html

deciding whether a bank is failing or likely to fail. A Single Resolution Fund, financed by contributions from banks, is available to pay for resolution measures'.[36] The SRM provides strong, centralized and independent decision-making, which ensures that '*resolution decisions across participating member states of the Banking Union are taken effectively and quickly, avoiding uncoordinated action, minimising negative impact on financial stability, limiting the need for public financial support and ensuring a level playing field*'.[37]

In June 2019, the EU '*Banking Package*', '*Banking Reform Package*' or '*Risk Reduction Package*' came into force marking a big milestone towards the completion of the EU post-crisis regulatory reforms by drawing on a series of international standards agreed on by the Basel Committee, the Financial Stability Board and the G-20. The Banking Package focuses on small and medium-sized firms, sustainable financing and infrastructure financing, as well as on the treatment of software in recognition of the rise of digitalization. The package updates the post-crisis established framework of harmonised rules. It also introduces changes to the Capital Requirements Regulation (CRR), the Fourth Capital Requirements Directive (CRD), the Bank Recovery and Resolution Directive (BRRD) and the Single Resolution Mechanism Regulation.[38]

The EU is also making much progress with the current development of the third and last pillar of the Banking Union, the 'European Deposit Insurance Scheme (EDIS)'. The EDIS proposal builds on existing national deposit guarantee schemes. It was conceived as a cost-neutral overall for the banking sector, suggesting complementary safeguards and measures to reduce banking risks.

> *At the 25 June 2021 Euro Summit, leaders reiterated their full commitment to the completion of the BU and invited the Eurogroup in inclusive format to 'agree without delay on a stepwise and time-bound work plan'*.[39]

The EDIS '*will be introduced in three stages over a number of years. First will be a re-insurance of national deposit guarantee schemes. After three years, bank deposits will be co-insured by national deposit guarantee schemes and EDIS, with the contribution of EDIS increasing progressively over time. In the final stage, planned for 2024, all bank deposits in the euro area will be insured by EDIS*'.[40]

36 European Central Bank. Banking Supervision. *Single Resolution Mechanism*. https://www.bankingsupervision.europa.eu/about/bankingunion/html/index.en.html

37 Ibid.

38 White and Case. Financial Regulatory Observer – June 2019. *EU Banking Reforms Imminent*. https://www.whitecase.com/publications/insight/eu-banking-reforms-imminent

39 European Parliament. Legislative Train. 04.2022. *European Deposit Insurance Scheme (EDIS)*. https://www.europarl.europa.eu/legislative-train/carriage/jd-european-deposit-insurance-scheme-(edis)/report?sid=5801

40 European Commission. Newsroom. *Policy in Focus: European Deposit Insurance Scheme (EDIS)*. https://ec.europa.eu/newsroom/fisma/items/27568/en

23

Ordoliberal Ideational Influence in the European Union

Since the beginning of the making of the European Union, neoliberalism always provided the solid bedrock over which the European integration project was built upon. Moreover, since the 1980s Anglo-American financial-monetarism has most especially been a main key driver of the process.

Notwithstanding, ordoliberalism has always equally been very present as regards the integration process, as well as exerted much considerable ideational influence in the EU. Such ordoliberal ideational influence is most particularly expressed in the fields of EU competition policy and EU economic and monetary policy. During recent years, the interrelationship between neoliberalism and ordoliberalism has in fact been further re-strengthened. The responses to the Eurozone crisis highlight much more the EU ordoliberal commitment to the rule of law through the generation of the various discretionary emergency measures, which have been implemented throughout the region.[1]

The influence of ordoliberalism in the EU is primarily discernible since the beginning of the integration process in amongst other areas competition policy and economic and monetary policy. Most of the recent features of the new financial supervising, regulating and rules-based order have chiselled into the region many more ordoliberal features and traits.[2] Moreover, the new European financial order is being further deepened through a proposal, which is making lots of progress for the creation of a '*European Monetary Fund (EMF)*', which would act like the International Monetary Fund (IMF), but at the EU level. The EMF would likewise and eventually, also enjoy many more supervising and interventionist rights over its member countries.

Although after the German economic miracle most of the Germanic literature on ordoliberalism became lost in the annals of German history, the responses to the

1 EUI Working Papers. Department of Law. HIEN, J. and JOERGES, C. *Dead Man Walking: Current Interest in the Ordoliberal Tradition,* pg 1. https://cadmus.eui.eu/bitstream/handle/1814/51226/LAW_2018_03.pdf?sequence=1

2 NEDERGAARD, P. *The Influence of Ordoliberalism in European Integration Processes – A Framework for Ideational Influence with Competition Policy and the Economic and Monetary Policy as Examples,* pgs 1–32. https://mpra.ub.uni-muenchen.de/52331/1/MPRA_paper_52331.pdf

Eurozone crisis, however, induced a very powerful and transcendental ordoliberal revival. The crisis-response, management and resolution policies of Germany, together with the ordoliberal-like measures introduced in the EU, were equally accompanied by an abundant production of literature on ordoliberalism, which have provided the region with much more of an ordoliberal character and personality. The recent resuscitation of ordoliberalism at the EU level has been so far reaching that it is even referred to by many observers as the '*ordo-neo-liberalization*' or the '*ordoliberalization*' of Europe.[3]

Since many years ago, ordoliberalism has been very clearly present in the EU, as well as gradually been imbedding itself within it in a very deep way. The abundant literature that has been recently flourishing on the subject likewise reflects an unmistakable governing of the ordoliberal approach in the policy-making of Germany during the Eurozone crisis. Notwithstanding, from a broader perspective, the influence of ordoliberalism has always helped shape the institutions of economic governance in the Eurozone at different key points of the integration process.[4]

Although after the German Economic Miracle, ordoliberalism and '*Ordnungstheorie*' remained unheard of outside Germany, ordoliberalism was, nonetheless, very markedly present and influential in the overall process of construction of the EU since its initiation. Harking back to the '*early formative phase*' of the '*constitutionalization*' of the European Economic Community (EEC) Treaty, the interdependent relationship between the legal and the economic realms became very clearly stressed upon and established by the mere fact that it was legal scholars and law courts who began setting the tone in shaping the integration project in the first place. Moreover, the EEC Treaty was also significantly permeated with ordoliberalism. For example, many of the early and ground-setting features and characteristics of the integration project, such as the freedoms the EEC Treaty guaranteed, the opening up of national economies, the bans on discrimination and the commitment to a system of undistorted competition, can be unmistakenly interpreted as being very much in favour of an ordoliberal '*Economic Constitution*', conforming the underlying conditions of a market-based order.[5]

During the early days of the EEC, the first president of the European Commission (EC, or the Commission), Walter Hallstein, acknowledged that '*what Europe is integrating is the role of the state in establishing the framework within which economic activity goes*

[3] White Rose Research Online. Critical Sociology. BONEFELD, W. *Ordoliberalism, European Monetary Union and State Power*, pg 2. http://eprints.whiterose.ac.uk/141922/2/_system_appendPDF_proof_hi.pdf

[4] Ibid, pg 6.

[5] EUI Working Papers. Department of Law. HIEN, J. and JOERGES, C. *Dead Man Walking: Current Interest in the Ordoliberal Tradition*, pgs 9–10. https://cadmus.eui.eu/bitstream/handle/1814/51226/LAW_2018_03.pdf?sequence=1

on'[6] – which fits perfectly into the framework of the ordoliberal concept of an *'Economic Constitution'*. From the very beginning, the European Union has always represented a project based on a monetary union, a market union and a legal union. It thereby and thus established the *'regulative media of the free labour economy at a supranational level beyond the direct control of its member states, who are however bound in their politics by supranational policy commitments and requirements, rules and regulations'*.[7] European institutions have also been always tasked with producing monetary policy, with establishing the framework conditions for the austere conduct of fiscal policy in member states, as well as with the imposition of the condition of enhanced market competition upon Member States, which have implemented Union requirements.[8]

With the EU's Economic and Monetary Union (EMU) being largely regarded as the pinnacle of the project of the internal market, the Monetary Union was a construct, which in itself was drenched with ordoliberalism. While some of the most distinguishing ordoliberal features of the EMU are reflected by the existence of an independent central bank, the commitment to price stability, as well as by the support for the currency through the Stability Pact, the first two of those traits most particularly corroborate both the institutional and the factual influence of ordoliberalism. On one hand, the establishment of the European Central Bank (ECB) and its endowment provides the institutional indicator, with a greater degree of independence than, for example, the German Bundesbank. On the other hand, the factual pointer rests upon the strict commitment of monetary policy towards price stability, as well as on the '*stability*' of the *'community of stability'*, being a sine-qua-none of its binding nature with member countries. All-combined, those key elements were originally equally established so as to ensure a corresponding '*order*' in the monetary field.[9]

The recent EU financial reform and the establishment of a EU Financial Regulatory Framework clearly reflect that the new forms of economic governance have been further transformed into an '*Ordnungspolitik*' or '*Politics of Ordering*', with its most specific feature being the legal force as the basis of the interdependency, of both the legal order and the economic order. In 1979, Michel Foucault discussed ordoliberalism at the College de France, in 5 of his 12 lectures on *'The Birth of Biopolitics'*, which provided some excellent early insights stressing on the crucial importance of such an interdependent relationship. '*What does applying the principle of the rule of law in the economic order mean? Roughly, I think it means that the state can make legal interventions in the economic order only if these legal interventions take the form solely of the introduction of formal principles. There can only be formal economic legislation. This is the principle of the rule of law in the economic order.*'[10]

[6] White Rose Research Online. Critical Sociology. BONEFELD, W. *Ordoliberalism, European Monetary Union and State Power*, pg 3. http://eprints.whiterose.ac.uk/141922/2/_system_appendPDF_proof_hi.pdf

[7] Ibid.

[8] Ibid, pg 5.

[9] EUI Working Papers. Department of Law. HIEN, J. and JOERGES, C. *Dead Man Walking: Current Interest in the Ordoliberal Tradition*, pgs 14–15. https://cadmus.eui.eu/bitstream/handle/1814/51226/LAW_2018_03.pdf?sequence=1

[10] Ibid, pg 16.

At present, such insights have become increasingly visible throughout the EU. The EU Financial Regulatory Framework represents a blatantly obvious indication that today economic policies being bound to justice-based criteria are perceived as strictly indispensable. As Foucault further echoed in his lectures, *'the juridical gives form to the economic, and the economic would not be what it is without the juridical'.*[11] With more and more ordoliberal ideals being implemented in the EU reinforcing the interrelated legal, economic and financial-banking realms, a much higher level of ordoliberal consciousness has very positively transcended Europe.

Ordoliberal Influence in the European Union's Competition Policy

In view of its mere nature, competition policy is fundamentally viewed as a government policy designed for the prevention of market distortions within a competitive environment – *'it is a policy policing the market'.* Although during the 1950s, EU competition law was inspired by US antitrust regulations (as applied through the principle of free competition that was incorporated by Allied Forces through the anti-cartel law in West Germany), over time, the ideational influence of ordoliberalism in EU competition law became both more prominent and more varied. Such ideational influence is most especially perceptible from 1985 onwards, being primarily related to some key elements of competition policy, such as the *'role of the state, economic freedom, market forces, role of consumers and mergers'.*[12]

In relation to the *'role of the state'*, EU competition policy has always rotated around the general concept that if the market is left to itself, risks will undoubtedly arise related to various elements that undermine competition. While such line of reasoning runs in close parallel to both ordoliberalism and US antitrust regulations, at present EU competition policy has expanded much more, covering antitrust measures, as well as through its fight against cartels, state aid, and since 1989, mergers. Within such a framework and in direct accordance with the ordoliberal concept of a *'strong state'*, the General Directorate for Competition of the EC can analogically be considered as playing a strong and central role overseeing the proper implementation of EU competition policy. The different EU treaties stipulate that the Commission is also free to investigate rules, force firms to present documentation, carry out raids on companies without prior warning, as well as when deemed necessary and at their own discretion, order the enforcement or the imposition of fines.[13]

The EC has always represented a potentially strong state in the field of competition policy. It was initially *'elected not to enforce vigorously the provision of state aid, government monopolies and government facilitation of private anti-competitive conduct*

[11] Ibid, pg 2.

[12] NEDERGAARD, P. *The Influence of Ordoliberalism in European Integration Processes – A Framework for Ideational Influence with Competition Policy and the Economic and Monetary Policy as Examples*, pgs 11–17. https://mpra.ub.uni-muenchen.de/52331/1/MPRA_paper_52331.pdf

[13] Ibid, pgs 11–12.

in the foundational period ... it was only with the launch of the internal market programme that the Commission directed attention to government interference in competition'.[14] However, from 2004 onwards, as a prolongation of the Single Market programme, EU competition policy was reformed, thereby establishing a more effective division of tasks. Thereafter and signalling an even stronger state in EU competition policy, the EC, national competition authorities and national courts have shared responsibility in enforcing EU antitrust rules, with the EC focusing primarily on infringements, which present the biggest risk of distortion at the EU level. The fact that it has only been during recent years that the EC has imposed the biggest fines in cartel cases, and that only since 2007 it has executed nine of the largest ever imposed fines distinctively reflects an intensification of ordoliberal thought in EU competition policy. In contrast, however, since the Eurozone crisis, the attitude towards state aid has relaxed significantly.[15]

A very strong state attitude in EU competition policy evidently prevails in the form of the EC, which, depending on the situation or circumstances, even acts as a strong state. What began in the 1950s, with the ideational influence of US antitrust regulations was in fact re-strengthened years later. From 1985 onwards, there has been more of an ordoliberal ideational influence regarding a strong state, although it has both functioned adversely towards selective interventions in the economy and varied over time and between the three main elements of EU competition policy.[16]

The ordoliberal concept of '*economic freedom*' being strictly based on '*orderly*' economic freedom has also since the beginning always ideationally influenced EU competition policy. Notwithstanding, it was only since the adoption of the Single Market programme, and most especially from the 1990s onwards, when globalization processes began gaining much more impetus, that the concept became more strongly embedded in the rhetoric of EU policymakers. '*Large firms have to behave "as if" they were subject to market competition*'.[17]

Since the Eurozone crisis, EU leaders and decision-makers are stressing much more emphatically on the importance of 'ordered' economic freedom. '*We need a clear level playing field for European consumers and businesses, not a jungle. But a jungle is what we would get if we suspended or abandoned competition policy ... Without a solid competition policy, the European economy would descend into chaos.*'[18]

Although when breaking up the above quote the terms '*jungle*' and '*chaos*' can at the same time refer to two completely different things – to both a '*market without regulations*' and to a '*market being victim of interventionist or competition distorting national measures*' – together, however, they strongly infer the necessity of '*order*' in economic freedom. Since the Eurozone crisis and most especially at the rhetorical

14 Ibid, pg 12.
15 Ibid.
16 Ibid, pgs 12–13.
17 Ibid, pg 13.
18 Ibid.

level, ordoliberal ideational influence in EU competition policy regarding economic freedom prevails much more.[19]

Ordoliberalism also holds that a strong state should unfold *'market forces'* in an orderly manner. Since the mid-1980s, the EU's competition policy has always been instrumental in the neoliberal opening up of markets and deregulation measures, as it demonstrated with the postal services and the transportation and telecommunication sectors. Such actions, were, however, soon followed by an ordoliberal process of *'re-regulation', 'in the form of consumer protection and minimum health and safety standards'*.[20]

Even though from the 1980s onwards the Single Market programme was carried out in accordance with neoliberal principles, at the same time, however, its implementation was very carefully *'gardened'* by the EU in much more of an ordoliberal, *'orderly'* manner. Although the Single Market was based on *'negative integration'* (deregulation), it was also accompanied by many *'positive integration'* (re-regulation) measures. Considering that ordoliberalism operates hinged on such a delicate balance, the special EU balance that was placed between the different positive and negative integration elements reflects by correlation, a medium to strong influence of ordoliberal ideals.[21]

In association with the *'role of consumers'*, although from the start and at the rhetorical level, EU competition policy has always looked after consumer's interests, it was only after the Single Market programme that such rhetoric actually materialized. In contrast to neoliberalism, it was the ordoliberal promotion of consumer sovereignty directly and without further purposes, which in fact influenced EU decision-makers in coining the idea in the first place.[22]

In relation to *'mergers'*, it was only when the Single Market programme was generated that the regulation of mergers to protect competition policy for the benefit of consumers came into proper existence. However and in divergence with other theoretical proposals that recommended no merger legislation, with a medium-strong regulation being implemented throughout the EU, ordoliberal thought has manifestly increasingly taken root among EU decision-makers.[23]

Ordoliberal Influence in the European Union's Economic and Monetary Policy

Considering that up until 1970 more or less, most Western countries were integrated into the Bretton Woods System of fixed exchange rates vis-à-vis the dollar, within the

[19] Ibid, pgs 13–14.
[20] Ibid, pg 14.
[21] Ibid, pg 25.
[22] Ibid.
[23] Ibid, pg 26.

EC, monetary policies thus did not exist. It was only when the Bretton Woods system broke down, that EU policymakers began to really speculate on future EU monetary policy.

Before 1992, however, there had been several attempts to achieve full economic and monetary union by 1980, which were soaked with ordoliberalism. One of the first of those main attempts was an arrangement of the EU named '*the snake in the tunnel*' or the '*snake*'. In 1979, the '*snake*' was in turn transformed into a more institutionalized form of European Monetary System (EMS), which was of a mixed exchange rate nature, since it blended both fixed and adjustable exchange rates. The EMS was '*also based on fixed but adjustable exchange rates as well as a system of monetary cooperation with short and medium term credits to defend the semi fixed exchange rates*'. It was only with the failure of the EMS, however, that the idea of a EU monetary union was in fact revitalized. Eventually, that same idea gave way to the adoption in 1992 of the Maastricht Treaty and the establishment of the European Monetary Union (EMU).[24]

All-combined, the snake, the EMS and the EMU, represent a blatant indication of a very strong ideational ordoliberal influence. The main objective of their establishment was to create more '*order*' in the EU financial monetary system. Even the declaration about the main objective of the EMU was written with loud and clear ordoliberal vocabulary, since its 'reason of being' and establishment were precisely in order to '*make of Europe a zone of stability*'.[25] In the end, however, although the EMU's Stability and Growth Pact '*was made to ensure that these countries exerted a responsible economic policy as the concept is understood according to ordoliberalism*',[26] both a weak regulatory framework necessary to ensure the '*harmonisation of economic policies*' and the cancellation of sanctions of the Stability and Growth Pact for countries with excessive deficit procedures unfortunately represented some of the main key triggers of the Eurozone crisis.[27]

At present, the recent EU financial reform, together with the establishment of a EU financial regulatory framework, represents the most obvious indications that a fundamental re-configuration of ordoliberal thought has transcended the EU, most especially, as regards the notion of an '*economic constitution*', as well as within the areas of '*public deficits, inflation, central bank independence, short-term or long-term views*'.[28]

The influence of the notion of an '*economic constitution*' has always been extremely evident in the EMU. Both the Maastricht Treaty and the EMU have always been very much in line with the idea of an ordoliberal economic constitution, for the establishment of order and stability. On one hand, the non-adherence to the Stability

[24] Ibid, pg 17.
[25] Ibid.
[26] Ibid.
[27] Ibid, pg 19.
[28] Ibid, pgs 18–23.

and Growth Pact's weak regulation and rules partly brought about the Eurozone crisis. On the other hand, the Fiscal Compact, the European Stability Mechanism (ESM), as well as the nearly completed Banking Union reflect the immense reliance on ordoliberal thought, which has produced a much stricter rules-based economic constitution for the establishment of economic and monetary order and stability in the Eurozone.[29] Although the Fiscal Compact is simply an intergovernmental agreement that is not actually part of the EU treaties and therefore not in complete direct alignment with ordoliberal recommendations, the Banking Union constitutes another initiative, which will much further strengthen the EMU and its institutions. As a whole, the new EU financial regulatory framework is a very clear expression of a much more reinforced, ordoliberal economic constitution in the Eurozone.[30]

Ever since the 1970s, EU decision-makers of monetary policy have always been very influenced by ordoliberalism, most particularly in connection to the area of '*public deficits*'. The new policy on public deficits, together with the strengthening of rules and their sanctioning, clearly reveals that ordoliberal thought has once again strongly influenced EU decision-makers. Within the recently established rules-based order, countries are today much more easily fined and the new procedures make it harder for countries to diverge from it.[31] The mere establishment of the snake, the EMS and the EMU, with the aim of creating more order in the area, is a very clear indication that from the beginning ordoliberal principles were at the very top of the agenda. Although countries, such as even Germany and France, did not always follow the ordoliberal prescripts, and that throughout the 1990s violations of the weak rules on public deficits became more widespread, things have now radically changed. The EU financial reform and the strict financial regulatory framework based on ordoliberal ideals have much transformed the Eurozone's context. During the last decade, the ordoliberal austerity line concerning public deficits has totally changed the rules of the game. On one hand, cooperation on economic policy has been strengthened in the EU and the EMU with the comprehensive EU legal acts – Six-Pack and Two-Pack – which automatically sanction any violations of the EMU rules. On the other hand, national budgets now also have to be discussed at the European level. Furthermore, the intergovernmental agreement – the Fiscal Compact – has equally reinforced the rules on public debt.[32]

In relation with the area of '*inflation*', the EMU was from its offset established with the aim of achieving low inflation, which is an important accession criterion that forms part of the statutes and policy of the ECB. That area has also been heavily influenced by ordoliberalism. The fact that '*the goal of the ECB is first and foremost to independently ensure price stability*' is an obvious expression of the ordoliberal recommendation on monetary policy, which also coincides with monetarism. Although monetarism only became an international trendsetting economic theory many decades after

[29] Ibid, pgs 22–3.
[30] Ibid.
[31] Ibid.
[32] Ibid, pg 26.

ordoliberalism led Germany's social market economy, *'monetarism further strengthened the ordoliberal agenda in the making of the EMU and its guidelines'*.[33]

The idea of *'central bank independence'* is also extremely ordoliberal. From the beginning of the integration project, the Maastricht Treaty postulated that the ECB would be independent, with its main task being directed towards conducting long-term stability-orientated monetary policy. While the independence of the ECB forms part and parcel of an ordoliberal *'Ordnungspolitik'*, from an ordoliberal perspective its *'independent status'* also provides the ECB with both *'credibility'* and *'stability'*. Furthermore, the fact that the ECB has been cautious not to assume the role of *'lender of last resort'* as most central banks do, equally provides a strong ordoliberal guarantee within the EMU, *'against non-ordoliberal disorder'*.[34] Although especially during the Eurozone crisis some political pressure was put on the ECB, its independence is one of the most blatant expressions of medium-strong to strong ordoliberal influence.[35]

The areas of *'short-term'* and *'long-term views'* equally run in tight parallel to ordoliberal thought. Although the EMU orientation is based much more on a long-term view, in practice however both the ECB and EU decision-makers have also made many short-term-orientated decisions.[36]

The Financial Reform and Its Enhancement of Financial Stability

Since the first post-crisis reforms were begun in the EU, the policy actions taken to stabilize the economy and the financial system have proved effective with the return of stability to the region. Whereas the EU financial regulatory framework places more emphasis on identifying and addressing system-wide risks, the establishment of the European System of Financial Stability (ESFS) and the creation of macroprudential instruments assigned to public authorities have been effective making the financial system more stable.[37] On one hand, the rules-based order has improved market discipline without generating significant costs to the overall economy. On the other hand, the new mandates and tools that authorities have been provided with in order to tackle risks in the banking sector have made it more resilient and have created a financial system that poses less risks to the real economy. The full integration of the financial system will be completely achieved with the completion of the Banking Union and the further development of a Capital Markets Union, which is underway.[38]

[33] Ibid, pgs 20–1.
[34] Ibid, pg 21.
[35] Ibid.
[36] Ibid, pg 27.
[37] European Central Bank. *Building on the Achievements of Post-Crisis Reforms*, pgs 1–4. https://www.ecb.europa.eu/press/key/date/2017/html/ecb.sp170921.en.html
[38] Federal Ministry of Finance. *Ten Years after the Financial Crisis: Have Regulatory Reforms Made the Financial Sector More Resilient to Crisis?*, pgs 1–7. https://www.bundesfinanzministerium.de/Content/EN/Standardartikel/Topics/Financial_markets/Articles/2019-04-15-ten-years-financial-crisis.html

The EU financial reforms have successfully reinforced financial stability with no measurable adverse impact on the real economy. The build-up of additional capital has not led to either a reduction in lending or to a substantial increase of lending costs. Furthermore, and as a direct result of the implemented reforms, different hypothetical crisis scenarios to simulate losses that might affect the banking system have proven that depending on the respective scenario, projected losses have declined significantly in recent years or even dropped to zero.[39]

From one angle, the recent EU's revised *'Markets in Financial Instruments Directive (MiFID II)'* has made much progress in advancing European financial market integration and improving supervisory transparency and control.[40] From another angle, the European resolution regime has also led to a marked improvement in the functioning of market mechanisms. *'There is now a high level of confidence that banks with low capital adequacy can be wound down successfully'*,[41] although warnings have been emitted against an excessive concentration of risk in the private sector and the banking sector from liabilities eligible for '*bail-in*'. Such enhanced liquidity requirements will have a positive effect across the whole of Europe and will in turn reduce the level of risk exposure in the European banking sector.[42]

More recently, much progress has been made as regards the Banking Union, with the adoption in 2019 of the '*Banking Package*' to further reduce risks and strengthen the resilience of European banks. The law package has changed the rules of '*Capital Requirements and Recovery and Resolution*',[43] with some of the most important changes including:

- *More risk-sensitive capital requirements for banks (risky businesses require more own capital – less risks less capital);*
- *binding rules for the ratio between debt and equity;*
- *new liquidity requirements;*
- *additional requirement for systemically important banks to hold minimum levels of capital;*
- *harmonised rules on the position of bondholders in the bank creditors' hierarchy in insolvency (who gets money first, when a bank fails etc.);*
- *more proportionate and flexible reporting and remuneration requirements for smaller and less complex banks (to reduce bureaucracy and make it easier for small banks to lend to SMEs).*[44]

[39] Ibid, pgs 5–7.
[40] Ibid, pg 5.
[41] Ibid, pg 4.
[42] Ibid.
[43] EPP Group in the European Parliament. *Banking Reform*, pg 1. https://www.eppgroup.eu/what-we-stand-for/campaigns/eu-elections-2019/achievements/achievement/banking-reform
[44] Ibid, pg 2.

Within the framework of the 2017 '*Action Plan to Tackle Non-Performing Loans in Europe*', a new law was adopted in 2019, '*requiring European banks to reduce the number of non-performing loans and avoid the future accumulation of such loans in their balance sheets*'.[45]

At present, the first two pillars of the Banking Union – the Single Supervisory Mechanism (SSM) and the Single Resolution Mechanism (SRM) – have been erected and are fully operational. The eventual full implementation of the third and last pillar – the European Deposit Insurance Scheme (EDIS) – will both provide the Banking Union with a common system for bank deposit protection, as well as complete its structure.[46]

With the completion of the Banking Union, together with the subsequent Capital Markets Union, the EU financial system will be totally integrated. In turn, a fully integrated EU financial system will further strengthen and support the EMU, as well as the international role of the Euro.[47]

Creation of a European Monetary Fund (EMF)

One of the last and most innovative proposals being pressed forward for strengthening the EMU even more revolves around the creation and establishment of an equivalent to the International Monetary Fund (IMF), but at the European level.

The EC proposal aims to transform the intergovernmental European Stability Mechanism (ESM) into a '*European Monetary Fund (EMF)*' under EU law. In turn and likewise, the EMF would be provided with both wide-ranging supervising tasks and interventionist rights over its member countries. Since the proposal involves the extension of the prerogatives of the ESM, it would thus transform the ESM into an EMF, with new and more extensive powers.[48]

The main elements of the proposal primarily aim to integrate the ESM into EU law, with only a few, but substantial elements. While the name European Stability Mechanism (ESM) would be changed to European Monetary Fund (EMF), it would also become a Union body with legal character, substituting the ESM and its legal position, as well as assuming all its rights and obligations. The integration of the EMF into EU law would also change the structure of democratic accountability. Some of the de facto veto rights of the national parliaments in the decision-making framework of the ESM

45 Ibid.
46 Ibid.
47 Ibid.
48 European Parliament. *Establishment of a European Monetary Fund (EMF)*, pgs 1–2. http://www.europarl.europa.eu/RegData/etudes/BRIE/2019/635556/EPRS_BRI(2019)635556_EN.pdf

Table 12 Provisions of the European Monetary Fund

- *'The EMF would become a backstop to the Single Resolution Fund, with a maximum amount set at €60 billion, although that ceiling may be increased. The fund would also be given a role in negotiating and signing MoUs.*
- *Concerning decision-making, although the ESM's categories of voting rules would remain the same, substantial changes would be made concerning decisions related to granting financial support or disbursements, where a reinforced qualified majority (85%) would be applied, replacing unanimity.*
- *However, decisions taken by the Board of Governors regarding, for instance, financial assistance facility agreements could enter into force only if they were approved by Council, acting by qualified majority.*
- *In urgent cases, decisions on stability support could be taken under an emergency procedure that would restrict Council's powers'.*

Source: European Parliament. *Establishment of a European Monetary Fund (EMF)*, pg 6. http://www.europarl.europa.eu/RegData/etudes/BRIE/2019/635556/EPRS_BRI(2019)635556_EN.pdf

would equally be curtailed to information rights. The EMF would be accountable to both the European Parliament (which does not have a veto right) and to the Council. It would likewise, but to a lesser degree, be accountable to the EC, for which it would produce an annual report. The European Parliament would also have a consultative role in the nomination of the managing director.[49]

The main tasks of the EMF would remain the same as the present ones, especially as regards its role as '*lender to governments which have lost – or about to lose – access to the financial markets*'.[50] The EMF, would have independency status from the EU and not be linked to it. While the EMF would still be able to directly recapitalize banks, its lending, however, would still be subject to strict conditionality, like, through the signing and implementing of a memorandum. The EMF would have its capital subscribed by Eurozone Member States, with the capital already paid into the ESM being transferred to the EMF.[51]

Although since the very beginning of the European integration project neoliberalism formed the solid bedrock over which the different processes were built upon, the influence of ordoliberalism has, nonetheless, also been in many ways very deep and profound. Such fact has today been much further reinforced. Undoubtedly and compared to neoliberalism, the influence of ordoliberalism has varied in intensity, most especially as regards the areas of EU competition policy and EU economic and monetary policy. However, the recent EU readjustments at the EU level clearly point to the establishment of a very powerful and positive synergy created by the mixing and blending of both neoliberal and ordoliberal features and traits.

[49] Ibid, pg 6.
[50] Ibid.
[51] Ibid.

The fact that the financial and banking readjustments of the Eurozone have focused on the establishment of legally binding rules-based ideals points to a much stronger and increasing ordoliberal presence and influence, which has made the financial-banking sector more stable and resilient. The new EU Financial Regulatory Framework or ordoliberal '*Economic Constitution*' has much improved the area's stable performance. The reconstruction of ordoliberal reasoning, which has taken place in the EU, has more than assured the firm establishment of ordoliberalism throughout the Eurozone's financial and banking rules-based order. Over the pre-established neoliberal bedrock, the new rules based order indeed promises continuity.

The eventual completion of the Banking Union as well as of the Capital Markets Union, together with a potential EMF, will not only further re-strengthen such a positive triad by providing more supervision and regulation to the EMU, but equally and in turn much enhance its stability and resilience.

Dimension Five

The State of the Neoliberal World Order

24

The Prevalence of the Neoliberal World Order

In recapitulation, as far and as much neoliberalism and ordoliberalism were very joined at the hip during the early years of the process of construction of neoliberal thought, things radically changed between the first and the second phase of the Mont Pelerin Society. Neoliberalism ended up eclipsing ordoliberalism, probably as much as thereafter, Anglo-American neoliberalism ended up controlling the neoliberal collective's pendulum of influence within and outside the new liberal institution's academic and professional networks. Since then and throughout its two successive waves, neoliberalism has swept the world across diverse landscapes to such an extent that today it not only functions as an ideology but also as a mode of governance and policy package rotating around the pivotal role of free markets and private enterprise.

Beginning in the 1980s in the United States and the UK, first-wave neoliberalism saw how Reaganomics and Thatcherism boldly put Hayek's and Friedman's economic ideas into practice. During the process, they also managed to successfully shatter the Keynesian paradigm and dismantle embedded liberalism, which had dominated economic theory and practice since the dark years of the Great Depression. Although those two first-wave neoliberal variants had their own individual set of supply-side and monetarist policy preferences, they, nonetheless, shared the same common desire to reshape their respective societies in accordance with the neoliberal formula of liberalization, deregulation and privatization.[1]

During the following 1990s, or the *'Roaring Nineties'*, second-wave neoliberalism, espoused by Bill Clinton's and Tony Blair's centre-left political agendas, balanced free-market thought with some sense of social responsibility and community. At the same time, while the soft power of the International Monetary Fund (IMF) and the World Bank (WB) was equally utilized to spread the Washington Consensus throughout the world, the firm commitment to a global economy led by transnational trade, likewise resulted in many free-trade agreements. What is more, the creation of the World Trade Organization (WTO) established its role as the powerful watchdog and enforcer of market globalism's liberalization project.[2]

[1] STEGER, M.B. and RAVI, K.R. *Neoliberalism: A Very Short Introduction*, pg 136.
[2] Ibid.

Since then, the neoliberal tsunami has taken the world by storm. If the Bretton Woods system of Keynesian economics and embedded liberalism dictated the first-ever international financial-monetary order from 1945 up until the 1980s, from the 1980s onwards, the all-embracing might of the '*Neoliberal World Order*' (NLWO) has been far more transcendental. Although Keynes's economic influence throughout the twentieth century is unquestionable, the legacies of Hayek and Friedman have, however, proved much more dominant in not only the economic realm but also probed far deeper, surpassing into many other interrelated political, social and cultural domains.

Notwithstanding, for the first time in forty years, at the beginning of the twenty-first century, the '*unrivalled reign*' of neoliberalism has been severely destabilized by, amongst other challenges, the 2007–15 global financial crisis, which was fundamentally triggered by neoliberalism's intrinsic flaws, as well as by the COVID-19 crisis, since it further highlighted neoliberalism's defects and imperfections. In other world regions, like Latin America (LA), neoliberalism has similarly also suffered many drawbacks, with the anti-neoliberal turn witnessing the complete abandonment of neoliberalism in various countries and its substitution by other heterodox currents. Altering the Latin American neoliberal consensus even more, although today the number of neoliberal countries continues to top non-neoliberal ones, the recent new wave of social uprisings is seeing how more anti-neoliberal governments are taking power once again.

Despite the many setbacks, however, the NLWO is still standing strong and continues to prevail. The majority of the responses to the global financial crisis evidently point to the predominance of the neoliberal paradigm and orthodoxy, with its free market and financial monetary dynamics. On the one hand, the G-20 agreements have readjusted the international financial system, with new rules and regulations being established. On the other hand, the European Union's (EU) ordoliberal revival has curiously seen the implementation of a lot of the regulating features and rules-based order ideals, which formed part of the original new liberal joint project between ordoliberalism and neoliberalism during their first years of existence. The fact that neoliberal Europe has resorted to ordoliberal traits to stabilize and improve its financial-banking sector is interesting, as it reveals how both currents are interacting once again – just like they did during the first phases of the process of construction of neoliberal thought. So far, '*Europe's ordoliberal iron cage*' and the '*ordoliberalization*' of Europe have proven very effective in making the Eurozone's financial system more stable and the banking sector more resilient. Moreover, the completion of the Banking Union and the Capital Markets Union, together with the prospect of a European Monetary Fund, promises to reinforce the economic and monetary union (EMU) much more.

Running in parallel to such a line of reasoning, although after the global financial crisis many prolific neoliberal intellectuals, scholars and critics proclaimed the imminent death of neoliberalism, with mantras like *'neoliberalism is dead'*,[3] *'neoliberalism must be pronounced dead and buried'*[4] or *'neoliberal capitalism at a dead end'*,[5] others, however, cannot negate the inescapable truth, that across-the-board neoliberalism is very alive and kicking. In his acclaimed book *'The Strange Non-Death of Neoliberalism'*, Colin Crouch avows that although the crisis has posed a fundamental challenge to the neoliberal body of ideas, which for the last forty years have constituted the political orthodoxy of most advanced economies, neoliberalism has, nevertheless, become very deep-rooted in governance, public management, international organizations, corporations and corporatism. New, inter-associated terminology, such as *'neo-corporatism'*, further corroborates the fact that neoliberalism is so profoundly ingrained within the system that it will not be easily uprooted, untangled or let alone removed.[6] David Harvey, author of *'A Brief History of Neoliberalism'*, concurs with Crouch and others, avowing the *'persistence of neoliberalism despite its loss of legitimacy'*.[7] For Harvey, even though neoliberalism has lost legitimacy as an ideology, having even penetrated progressive thinking, it nonetheless continues to be extremely embedded in transnational and national institutions.[8]

Although the global financial crisis has retired free-market fundamentalism, free trade is still standing strong, having been *'reaffirmed as indispensable by political and economic elites around the world'*,[9] with many diverse varieties of neoliberalism having imbedded themselves further in countless other different social contexts in Africa, Asia and Australia. Above all and most importantly, neoliberalism has become very deeply imbued within the institutional frameworks that uphold and supervise the neoliberal order, as well as within the multilateral economic structures that they represent and assist. Irrespective of the fact that new progressive thought and practice have shifted neoliberalism considerably, they simply cannot compete against the NLWO's rigid architecture or its wide-ranging infrastructure formed by academia, non-profit organizations, non-governmental organizations (NGOs), think-tanks, banks, wealthy backers, Wall Street and the public press. The complete dismantlement of the neoliberal order's wide-arching scaffolding and deep-reaching webwork would undoubtedly prove to be a very complex and arduous task, as well as an extremely difficult one to accomplish in just a few years.

3 Alternet.org. ATCHESON, J. *Neoliberalism Is Dead – but the Neoliberal Elite Still Haven't Gotten the Memo.* https://www.alternet.org/2019/06/neoliberalism-is-dead-but-the-neoliberal-elite-still-havent-gotten-the-memo/

4 The Guardian.com. STIGLITZ, J. *Neoliberalism Must Be Pronounced Dead and Buried. Where Next?* https://www.theguardian.com/business/2019/may/30/neoliberalism-must-be-pronouced-dead-and-buried-where-next

5 Monthly Review.org. PATNAIK, U. and PATNAIK, P. *Neoliberal Capitalism at a Dead End.* https://monthlyreview.org/2019/07/01/neoliberal-capitalism-at-a-dead-end/

6 CROUCH, C. *The Strange Non-Death of Neoliberalism.*

7 David Harvey.org. HARVEY, D. *The Persistence of Neoliberalism Despite Its Loss of Legitimacy.* http://davidharvey.org/2019/07/video-david-harvey-the-persistence-of-neoliberalism-despite-its-loss-of-legitimacy-real-news-network/

8 Ibid.

9 Ibid.

However, regardless of the still strong prevalence of the NLWO, both the neoliberal paradigm and orthodoxy have, nonetheless, been irredeemably shifted and displaced by new progressive thought and practice. The structure of the NLWO is being increasingly destabilized and weakened by both the clash between the old and new economic and financial models and by flaws inherent to the financial monetary system. As the following chapters will reveal, the two neoliberal scenarios clearly reflect that while the intellectual collapse of neoliberalism has produced an irreversible shift and displacement of neoliberal thought and practice, the current financial monetary system is similarly on the verge of being monetarily overridden, which is steadfastly increasing the risks of a 'Global Liquidity Trap'.

The first neoliberal scenario shrouds the ongoing intense and virulent clash between the old and still-standing neoliberal economic and financial models and the new progressive models threatening to debunk them. On the one hand, the NLWO has been seriously damaged and debilitated by the revival and growing expansion of mercantilist, protectionist-isolationist models, such as, most predominantly, 'Neo-Nationalism' or 'New Nationalism'. On the other hand, although to a lesser extent, the financial monetary model mechanizing the international financial system has also experienced a displacement by new progressive financial models, such as the very salient 'Modern Monetary Theory (MMT)'. In much the same way, at the underlying academic sector, the scorching criticism surrounding stakeholder capitalism has equally spurred a strong outburst of counter-reactive capitalist reformulations challenging and contesting it, such as Joseph Stiglitz's 'Progressive Capitalism', which are gaining more and more ground in international fora. More recently, President Trump has also put into practice his self-designed 'Techno-Feudal and Oligopolistic Capitalism', which is tearing through the international landscape with much vigour.

The second neoliberal scenario, unfortunately, also conceals more negative forecasts for the international financial monetary system (IFMS) due to its development of several deep flaws at its core. Owing to the IFMS having produced such vast amounts of money, there is way too much liquidity flowing through the system that could end up clogging it at any given moment. While the orthodoxy of monetary policy is being endangered by such schisms within the system itself, the global economy could be drifting towards yet another huge crisis. With the financial monetary system finding itself on the verge of being monetarily overridden, the growth of such a destabilizing asymmetry at the heart of the system is steadfastly increasing the risks of a 'Global Liquidity Trap', which could easily spark off yet another massive global crisis, or as already labelled, 'Great Stagnation'.

Neoliberalism's Deep Imbuement in Institutional Frameworks and Economic Multilateral Structures

Most probably, what constitutes the main reason for the indisputable hegemony of neoliberalism is tied to the fact, that since the 1980s, neoliberalism has become much more deeply imbued within the globalized free-market economic order and the IFMS, as well as other interrelated areas, than Keynesian economics ever did. The best explanation for that is found in the way neoliberal thought and practice have been progressively adopted and promoted by the institutional frameworks that uphold and supervise the system, as well as in the way it has become increasingly imbedded in the different economic multilateral structures that the system represents and assists.

When the Bretton Woods system was established in 1945, international financial institutions (IFIs), such as the IMF and the WB, were created at the same time, with the key and specific role of acting as '*guardians*' of the system. From then onwards and within the frameworks of both past and current systems, IFIs have therefore always had a very prominent role in assuring balance and order within the context of the prevailing economic orthodoxy. Within the framework of the Bretton Woods financial monetary system of fixed exchange rates, IFIs had a key role assuring the balance and order of the Keynesian consensus. However, once the system changed to a neoliberal free-market economy of flexible exchange rates, IFIs changed too, henceforth assuming the new system's neoliberal nature. Since then, the current framework of the NLWO has been, and still is kept and maintained in equilibrium due to the role IFIs have as supervisors or overseers of the international economic-financial system. That way, neoliberal thought and practice gradually became, and still remain very deeply imbued within institutional frameworks and economic multilateral structures.

Within the framework of the globalized free-market economy, IFIs have established themselves as key influencing figures in times of change, reform, progress and crisis management. Some of the most prominent IFIs include the IMF, WB, WTO, the Inter-American Development Bank (IDB), the Central American Bank for Economic Integration (CABEI), the European Investment Bank (EIB), African and Asian Development Banks, and other subregional banks. Through time, IFIs have come to be defined as '*the world's most powerful agents of economic reforms*',[10] providing advice, financing and support to national governments all around the world. The three most prominent ones – the IMF, the WB and the WTO – have come to be regarded both as '*agents of neoliberalism*', and '*prefects*' of the globalized free-market economy. Especially since the 1980s, together with the latter 1995 creation of the WTO, the three IFIs began enjoying unprecedented neoliberal influence over the economies of world regions and countries that asked for their assistance and support. Henceforth, they began making access to their resources '*conditional*', on the adaptation to neoliberal prescriptions, based on a range of market-oriented institutional reforms and extensive domestic policy reforms. Most particularly, the opening up to trade and international finance, the deregulation of economic activities, the privatization of natural resources and state-owned enterprises and the reformation of the provision of social services.[11]

[10] CAHILL, D., COOPER, M., KONINGS, M. and PRIMROSE, D. *The SAGE Handbook of Neoliberalism*. BABB, S. and KENTIKELENIS, A. *International Financial Institutions as Agents of Neoliberalism*, pg 16.

[11] Ibid.

Regardless of the fact that in recent years the term neoliberalism has lost a lot of precision due to overuse, with its conceptual definition pivoting around much ambiguous abstraction, the relationship between the two most powerful IFIs, the IMF and the WB and neoliberalism continues to be very up-close and personal. Both IFIs continue to actively implement neoliberal policies, based on measures *'intended to reduce the role of states and enhance the role of markets in at least one national economy'*.[12] Although with the passing of time, the original raisons d'être and mandates of the IMF and the WB have been modified, they have, nonetheless, both been extremely critical in the emergence of neoliberalism and in the promotion of neoliberal policy reforms throughout the world. At present, despite the field of international policymaking having experienced some transformations, both IFIs continue operating as very active *'agents of neoliberalism'*, *'prefects'* of the globalized free-market economy, as well as *'guardians and supervisors'* of the IFMS.[13]

When the Bretton Woods conference founded the first-ever system of global financial and monetary governance based on Keynesian economics, world leaders envisioned *'a system of "free and stable exchanges": freedom was guaranteed by the removal of exchange controls and other restrictions; stability was underpinned by adjustable pegs to the US dollar, and ultimately backed by gold. At the same time, countries were guaranteed adequate policy space to adjust their exchange rates and to keep their economies at full employment'*.[14] As previously explained, during the same conference, it was also acknowledged that the system needed assistance for international public financing for economic reconstruction and post-war reconstruction. Thus, the IMF and the International Bank for Reconstruction and Development (IBRD), which soon became simply known as the World Bank, were therefore created and established in order to supervise and uphold the new system. From then onwards, both IFIs were labelled as *'The Bretton Woods Twins'*.[15]

On the one hand, the main task of the IMF was to supervise and support the Bretton Woods system of pegged exchange rates by carrying out two main functions: *'overseeing the exchange rates of member governments; and making its financial resources temporarily available to [members] under adequate safeguards, thus providing them with opportunity to correct maladjustments in their balance of payments without resorting to measures destructive of national or international prosperity'*.[16] However, when by 1973, the system changed and countries moved towards floating exchange rates, the first component of the IMF's operations was dropped, and today, only the second aspect of its original mandate survives.[17]

[12] Ibid.
[13] Ibid.
[14] Ibid, pg 17.
[15] Ibid.
[16] Ibid.
[17] Ibid.

On the other hand, the original role of the WB was to provide investment capital for post-war reconstruction and economic development, with its main specialization focusing on lending for tangible, profitable infrastructure projects such as ports, railroads and hydroelectric dams. Although development was a prime aspect of the WB's mandate, since it was at first focused on post-war reconstruction and poorer countries could not afford the IBRD's interest rates, its impact on developing countries was initially quite limited. In 1960, and in response to demands from developing countries, world leaders established within the WB the International Development Association (IDA), with the mandate of improving living standards in least developed countries, as well as providing loans at subsidized interest rates. The IDA made the WB much more of a development-focused organization. From 1968 to 1990, under the leadership of the WB president Robert McNamara, the WB's mandate was further expanded to encompass both infrastructural project lending and the eradication of global poverty.[18]

Since 1944 and for more than three decades, the IMF and the WB kept balance and order within the Bretton Woods system by concentrating solely on Keynesian policies, with neither one of them promoting neoliberal policies. Within the Bretton Woods system, while the IMF practiced conditionality with its infamous stabilization programmes designed to steady the value of national currencies, the WB specialized in financing development projects rather than providing policy-conditional loans.

However, from the 1980s onwards, with the shift from the Keynesian paradigm to the Hayekian and Friedmanian neoliberal paradigm, things totally changed. In accordance with the new system's neoliberal nature and the adoption by both IFIs of the neoliberal dictums, they became famous for the utilization of 'conditionality' for the promotion of market-liberalizing reforms. The switch was much assisted by the Third World debt crisis, which in turn coincided with the changing political context of rising neoliberal conservative governments in the United States and the UK. Henceforth, the Reagan and Thatcher administrations steered away from Keynesian economics, adopting much greater confidence and faith in the '*magic of the marketplace*' and the private sector, which since then began gradually taking over and ultimately ended up prevailing worldwide.[19]

With the outbreak of the Third World debt crisis, '*governments, such as those of Mexico and Brazil – which had borrowed from private banks when interest rates were low in the 1970s – suddenly found their debts to be unpayable with the higher interest rates of the 1980s. To manage the multiple crises that ensued, governments turned to the IMF, which coordinated creditors' claims, lent to allow governments to keep*

[18] Ibid.
[19] Ibid, pg 19.

servicing their debts, and required its familiar belt-tightening stabilization, leading to a "lost decade" for growth in Latin America'.[20]

As a direct response, in 1985, US Treasury Secretary James Baker proposed his '*Program for Sustained Growth*'. The Baker Plan suggested that '*private banks would increase their lending to developing countries, and the IMF, World Bank, and regional development banks would engage in coordinated "structural adjustment" lending aimed at market liberalizing policy reforms. The premise was that by accessing more liquidity and liberalizing their economies under the supervision of IFIs, these countries would be able to restore growth – and this growth, in turn, would make their debts sustainable once again*'.[21] However, the Baker Plan's failure to get private banks to increase their lending to developing countries, together with the ultimate failure to either solve the debt crisis or restore growth in indebted countries, led to the demise of the '*Washington Consensus*'. The Baker Plan did, nevertheless, manage to legitimize a new role for the IFIs, the basic contours of which were immortalized in John Williamson's Washington Consensus. Williamson had worked for the IMF and the WB. In 1989, the Washington Consensus and its ten-point list of market-liberalizing policy reforms grouped together the recommendations for developing-country governments from Washington policymakers at the US Treasury, the IMF and the WB. In accordance with Williamson, '*no statement about how to deal with the debt crisis in Latin America would be complete without a call for the debtors to fulfil their part of the proposed bargain by "setting their houses in order," "undertaking policy reforms," or "submitting to strong conditionality"*'.[22] Since then, Washington's recommendations have assumed more importance, as they became tied to the practice of policy leverage and were promoted worldwide. '*The economic policies that Washington urges on the rest of the world may be summarized as prudent macroeconomic policies, outward orientation, and free-market capitalism.*'[23]

In the meantime, the WB's research publications became one of the most important platforms for the promotion of Washington Consensus's ideas and norms. From the 1980s onwards, the WB's research became much more critical of '*distortionary state economic interventions … less tolerant of dissent … and devoted quite disproportionate effort to the documentation of the errors of governments and the advantages of reliance upon markets*'.[24] Although during the next decades, the scope of the WB research broadened once again, the WB has always '*nevertheless maintained a reputation for its skilled paradigm maintenance*'.[25]

During the same decade, the WB also began devoting a much larger portion of its resources to programme lending, or lending for policy reforms, rather than for

20 Ibid.
21 Ibid.
22 Ibid.
23 Ibid.
24 Ibid, pgs 19–20.
25 Ibid, pg 20.

development projects. '*For its part, the IMF became, for all intents and purposes, a development institution that collaborated with the World Bank to require its borrowers to engage in 'structural' reforms, such as privatizing state-owned industries and lifting trade barriers. Compliance with these reforms was encouraged not only by a closer relationship between the IMF and World Bank, but also between the World Bank and regional development banks, which harmonized and upheld one another's conditions, and between the IMF and private creditors. The presence of IFI agreements also served as a 'stamp of approval' that translated to additional aid flows, such as bilateral assistance from donor governments. Among the World Bank and regional development banks, policy leverage was also implemented through greater 'selectivity' – the awarding of project loans to countries that were demonstrably compliant with Washington Consensus policies.*'[26]

One of the most important features of the Washington Consensus, besides the original list of policies prescribed to governments, was the innovative premise, which allowed IFIs to utilize their resources to transform the policy architecture of developing economies around the world. It was such policies that were classified as pertaining to '*market fundamentalism*' that were so widely criticized. The new role of IFIs was very permissive of 'market fundamentalism', as conditionality was utilized to promote trade liberalization, as well as more radical policies, '*such as public pension privatization, replacing progressive tax systems with more regressive value-added tax systems, or health policy reforms*'.[27]

Market fundamentalism was rooted in the fact that the Washington Consensus had tasked the WB and the IMF with persuading governments to carry out very politically difficult and painstaking structural reforms, which would eventually be justified by sustained growth. In many ways, the natural experiment on the effectiveness of neoliberal policies in developing countries failed miserably.

During the 1990s, a series of devastating financial crises in Mexico, Argentina, Russia and Asia indicated that the Consensus was flawed, most especially in LA, where economic growth had proven to be very unequal and development even more uneven. Thus, the Washington Consensus was broadened and deepened, with more emphasis being placed on '*governance ... institutional frameworks that allow markets to function, such as laws and judicial systems*',[28] as well as on '*establishing and strengthening social safety nets and reducing poverty*'.[29] In fundamental terms, it evolved into an '*augmented Washington Consensus*' or '*second-generation reforms*'.[30]

Although the augmented Consensus reflected a '*kinder*' and '*gentler*' version, which assumed that markets did not work perfectly and that could appropriately address

[26] Ibid.
[27] Ibid.
[28] Ibid.
[29] Ibid.
[30] Ibid.

issues of the poor, it, however, made the conditional list of IFIs become progressively longer and more constraining. For example, during the Asian financial crisis, the IMF '*ordered the South Korean government to make its central bank independent, and specified the level of debts that Korean companies were allowed to accrue. One IMF Letter of Intent in 1997 committed the Indonesian government to more than 100 policy conditions – including, for example, privatization, the removal of price controls and trade barriers, the revision of national bankruptcy legislation, and changing laws governing corporate mergers and acquisitions (Indonesia Letter of Intent reproduced in US Congress)*'.[31] Likewise, the WB's '*Country Policy and Institutional Assessment (CPIA)*' index, on which it bases eligibility for obtaining loans, '*rates potential borrowers according to a detailed list of measures of market friendliness, institutional quality, and social inclusion/equity*'.[32] With the end of the Cold War, IFIs became much more explicit in utilizing all their possible resources for leveraging sensitive and political policy reforms.[33]

IFIs have a vast array of resources and means for the promotion of neoliberalism throughout the world, although they have both developed different organizational cultures. The IMF emphasizes '*primarily on addressing short- and medium-term issues, like pressing financial crises*'.[34] The WB focuses more on long-term strategies in its '*development and poverty eradication objectives*'.[35] Nonetheless, they share very similar organizational similarities, which is precisely what enables their joint worldwide neoliberal influence, outreach and diffusion. First of all, bureaucrats educated in elite universities, most usually in the United States and the UK, staff both. With the IMF's managing director being European and the WB's president being from the United States, they both have considerable authority in world economic affairs. The day-to-day activities of both organizations are governed by their executive boards, which are composed of government representatives, who ultimately '*decide on a wide range of key issues, including the approval of loans and the establishment of new organizational policies*'.[36]

Probably one of the most influential aspects of the two IFIs is that they are both located in Washington, DC, and thus, '*dominated by the US, as well as other wealthy countries that contribute most to their capital base. Since the founding of these organizations, the United States has held the largest block of weighted voting shares in both (as of 2015, 16.7% at the IMF and 16.1% at the World Bank), followed by other developed countries, such as Japan, Germany, France and the United Kingdom, who together control more than 60% of voting shares*'.[37] In addition, the US Treasury, which is the federal reserve agency in charge of American foreign policy towards IFIs, equally exercises much

31 Ibid.
32 Ibid.
33 Ibid, pgs 21–2.
34 Ibid, pg 17.
35 Ibid.
36 Ibid, pgs 17–18.
37 Ibid, pg 18.

influence, due to, of course, its voting share, but also due to its *'geographical proximity and the incredible threat of withholding approval for IFI contributions'*.[38]

One of the most influential means that IFIs have for persuading governments to adopt reforms is through indirect forms of influence, the most established of which is *'conditionality: the practice of requiring policy reforms in exchange for access to resources.*[39] Conditionality became much more widespread and influential during the 1980s when it was utilized by the IMF, the WB and other multilateral and bilateral '*lenders*', as an excellent means to promote neoliberal policies. It is the most established and best-known mechanism through which IFIs affect domestic policies. *'In conditional lending arrangements with IFIs, policy reforms are outlined in documents specifying timetables for their introduction and are assessed on a regular basis. Non-implementation can result in delays in loan disbursements and – ultimately – the suspension of lending altogether.'*[40]

Besides conditionality, other ways through which IFIs reach out and affect courses of action and policies are through their well-trained and established expert professionals. *'Argentinian officials in the 1960s and 1970s agreed to IMF recommendations in their routine encounters with IMF officials, who had far greater knowledge and experience.'*[41] Likewise, many governments often invite IFIs to carry out technical assistance missions for the transfer of knowledge, know-how and skills. *'In the 1990s many member governments transitioning from state socialism asked for IMF missions to help them reform their central banks and financial institutions.'*[42] IFIs and their expert reputation also very often engage in the '*transnational socialisation of government officials*'. The WB's Economic Development Institute (now the World Bank Institute) has, since its establishment in 1956, always been an important source of training for senior government functionaries. Likewise, the IMF's Institute for Capacity Development has similar programmes, mainly for Ministry of Finance and Central Bank officials. Such socialization programs inculcate norms and routine practices, which inform policymakers' work.[43] At the same time, such training programmes accumulate for IFIs widespread social capital *'in the form of a network of like-minded officials throughout the governments of medium and low-income developing countries. Once back home, these officials may serve as "sympathetic interlocutors," in their governments' negotiations with IFIs, a factor observed to make compliance with IFI-prescribed policies more likely'*.[44]

Other subtler means of persuasion and resources of diffusion, which IFIs have are their renowned expert authority and their very well-informed technical research departments. The Bretton Woods Twins are very permeated with much academic

[38] Ibid.
[39] Ibid.
[40] Ibid.
[41] Ibid.
[42] Ibid.
[43] Ibid.
[44] Ibid, pg 19.

and professional expertise. Whereas the IMF employs over 2,400 individuals who are mostly economists, the WB's diverse staff includes over 10,000 economists, social scientists and engineers. Both organizations have research departments, usually headed by prominent academic economists, which produce tons of influential research papers and reports on world, regional and individual country issues. The publications of both IFIs are widely read by scholars and policymakers around the world. On the one hand, the IMF's flagship publication, the '*World Economic Outlook*', provides short- and medium-term economic growth and inflation forecasts, which are highly influential among policy elites. On the other hand, the WB's annually elaborated '*World Development Report*' is probably the most widely read publication in the development arena. In general, the WB's research pretty much sets the terms of international development debates.[45]

During the late 1990s, the IMF's role in the Asian financial crisis, put IFIs under great scrutiny, being widely criticized by academics and policymakers for its handling of the crisis and the promotion of policy reforms that swayed far from its core areas of expertise. Such criticism stemmed from all sides of the political spectrum and marked the beginning of a period of organizational crisis. For example, by the mid-2000s, middle-income and rapidly growing countries, like China, had stopped relying on the IMF's management of their balance of payments, preferring instead to '*self-insure*', through the accumulation of large stocks of hard currency. Criticism of the WB was more long-winded, '*but over time it became clear that emerging-market governments with access to private capital markets were similarly avoiding the Bank's conditionality: they had become "increasingly selective about the [policy-conditional lending] areas in which they invite Bank engagement"*'.[46]

In response to those and other challenges, the Bretton Woods Twins carried out a series of organizational transformations and changes '*intended to challenge the perception that they were single-minded advocates of one-size-fits-all neoliberal economic reforms*'.[47] They both adopted new language, like '*country ownership, on the theory that reforms could only succeed where they had strong support from domestic governments and other stakeholders*'.[48] They also began renaming the making of reforms as '*pro-poor*'. The IMF likewise acknowledged that the practice of conditionality had become '*unwieldly*' and unfocused and thus began '*streamlining*' it in order to provide valuable space to countries with lending programmes. In addition, there was also a shift in the research publications of both organizations, with the WB acknowledging that '*there is no unique universal set of rules*',[49] as well as calling for '*humility and respect for diversity in the prescription of development policies*'.[50] The IMF '*partially disavowed its previously*

[45] Ibid, pg 18.
[46] Ibid, pg 21.
[47] Ibid.
[48] Ibid.
[49] Ibid.
[50] Ibid.

militant stance toward eliminating inflation, and called for fiscal stimuli to forestall global economic recession'.[51] As part of the transformation process, both IFIs similarly rebranded their '*structural adjustment*' facilities, opting instead for new nondescript terminology, such as '*extended credit*' and '*development policy*' loans. Moreover, whereas the WB also began targeting more of its lending programmes towards the direct benefit of the poor, the IMF equally began obliging social spending targets in its loan conditionality.[52]

Notwithstanding and regardless of the fact that IFIs have carried out some organizational transformations and changes in their practices, evidence suggests, however, that beneath the IFI's post-neoliberal rhetoric and reforms, much neoliberal substance still prevails. Research studies on conditionality, clearly reflect that the IFIs' organizational changes simply represent mere '*window-dressing*', with not much departure from their standard neoliberal policy advice.[53] While the IMF's own Independent Evaluation Office has concluded that '*conditionality remained very detailed, not obviously critical, and often felt to be intrusive*',[54] labour market reforms, a keystone of neoliberal restructuring across the world, '*are still part of IMF lending programs and include public sector layoffs, pension reductions, and the dismantling of collective wage agreements*'.[55] Likewise, the WB's '*development policy loans*' – its new term for policy-conditional lending – still account for more than a third of its portfolio, with many of the WB's conditions still rotating around privatization and commercialization. Furthermore, '*the Bank also continues to allocate access to loans on the basis of the Country Policy and Institutional Assessment (CPIA) rating system, which places considerable weight on the degree of market liberalization (in order to get access to World Bank program loans governments usually need to receive an average or better CPIA rating)*'.[56] Lastly, '*the Bank's "Doing Business" report, which similarly ranks countries' business environments based on such factors as corporate taxation and labor market policies, has drawn criticism from civil society groups for its emphasis on market deregulation*'.[57]

Moreover, the 2007–15 global financial crisis re-strengthened and re-established the IMF as the '*central crisis-management institution*' of the multilateral economic structures that it represents, assists and supports, like the EU. Throughout the crisis, the IMF disbursed in collaboration with EU institutions, some of the largest loans ever expended by it to countries, like Greece, Portugal, Ireland and Cyprus.[58]

However, over the past decade and a half, the world's balance of economic power has begun to tilt significantly from West to East, towards Asia, with more economic

51 Ibid.
52 Ibid.
53 Ibid.
54 Ibid, pg 22.
55 Ibid.
56 Ibid.
57 Ibid.
58 Ibid.

influence increasingly concentrated there. In a way, the growth of such a trend could start eroding the role of the Bretton Woods Twins as worldwide promoters of neoliberalism.[59]

The reasons for such a shift in the balance of power from West to East are varied. On the one hand, the IMF and the WB have been put under much pressure by other powerful economies and emerging-market governments. BRICS countries, like Brazil, Russia, India, South Africa and China, have now become extremely internationally empowered, even topping G7 countries in terms of world GDP. '*The BRICS countries overtook the G7 countries share of the world's total gross domestic product (GDP) in terms of purchasing power parity (PPP) in 2020. By 2023, the difference had increased even further, the BRICS now holding a total 32 per cent of the world's GDP compared to 30 per cent held by the G7 countries.*'[60] BRICS nations have also become aid donors themselves, partly through '*their ability to avoid IFI conditionality – whether through accumulating central reserves (rather than relying on the IMF), or by borrowing from private capital markets (rather than from the World Bank)*'.[61] They now '*provide development assistance to low-income countries, thereby weakening the influence of IFIs in the world's poorest regions*'. With the new '*south-south*' development assistance being completely focused on development financial assistance, it eschews making policy recommendations to recipient countries.[62]

On the other hand, BRICS nations have likewise evolved much and also created their own new IFIs. Due to the failure of BRICS governments to influence the reform of the governance structures of the Bretton Woods Twins, as well as other letdowns to grant greater representation and voice to developing countries, together with the greatly unsatisfied need for development financing, they were obliged to create their own parallel IFIs in order to provide help with balance-of-payments and development assistance. Two of those new IFIs are the New Development Bank (NDB) and the Asian Infrastructure Investment Bank (AIIB). Paradoxically, and reflecting the shift in the balance of economic power from West to East, and in contrast to the US-based Bretton Woods Twins, the two new organizations are headquartered in China.[63] Whereas the NDB, or better known as the '*BRICS Bank*', has, akin to the IMF's operations, a balance-of-payments support mechanism, it also has, like the WB, a development finance arm. Influential observers have already pointed out that the NDB represents '*a catalyst for further reforms in the international financial and development architecture that favour*

[59] Ibid.

[60] Statista. *BRICS and G7 Countries' Share of the World's GDP in PPP 2000–2023*. https://www.statista.com/statistics/1412425/gdp-ppp-share-world-gdp-g7-brics/#:~:text=By%202023%2C%20the%20difference%20had,held%20by%20the%20G7%20countries

[61] CAHILL, D., COOPER, M., KONINGS, M. and PRIMROSE, D. *The SAGE Handbook of Neoliberalism*. BABB, S. and KENTIKELENIS, A. *International Financial Institutions as Agents of Neoliberalism*, pg 22.

[62] Ibid.

[63] The Association of Southeast Asian Nations (ASEAN) is another very influential international organization with its secretariat based in Jakarta, Indonesia.

developing and emerging countries'.[64] The China-led AIIB has already managed to raise well over '*$100 billion of seed capital for infrastructure projects in Asia*'.[65]

Whether or not the new emerging Asian IFIs end up completely eclipsing the Western IFIs neoliberal influence, so far, the two new Asian organizations are directing their focuses more towards lending for infrastructure projects rather than towards policy reforms, offering alternative forms of financing untrammelled by the conditionality of the Western IFIs. However, at the same time, more competition in the international finance arena equally implies that it will be more difficult for the Western IFIs to promote market-liberalizing reforms.[66]

Although it is still far too soon to be able to truly predict the future demise of the Breton Woods Twins, as far and as much as the Western hemisphere is concerned, the IMF and the WB, together with other regional organizations under their financial assistance, development and cooperation umbrella, continue prevailing as the main pillars of the institutional framework of the globalized neoliberal free-market economy. Likewise and correspondingly, their neoliberal free market and financial monetary orthodoxy remain very deeply instilled within the different economic multilateral structures, which they represent, assist and support.

[64] Ibid.
[65] Ibid.
[66] Ibid, pgs 22–3.

25

The Clash of Economic Models: *Neoliberalism vs Neo-Nationalism; Financial Monetarism vs Modern Monetary Theory; Stakeholder Capitalism vs Progressive Capitalism*

Regardless of the still-strong hegemony of the Neoliberal World Order (NLWO), the skewed development and disparate benefits that neoliberalism has produced have turned a huge legion of unsatisfied losers against it, who are much more in favour of other newer, heterodox models. We find ourselves at a very delicate economic threshold, wherein the shift and displacement of the free market model and the financial monetary model by new progressive thought and practice have critically destabilized both the NLWO and the established neoliberal paradigm and orthodoxy.

The first neoliberal scenario shrouds the ongoing intense and virulent clash between the old and still-standing economic and financial monetary models and the new countering models threatening to debunk them. The free market economic model, which has since the 1980s been churning the machinery of the globalized free market economy, has been seriously shifted and displaced by the revival of and growing preference for mercantilist, protectionist-isolationist economic models, such as most particularly 'Neo-nationalism'. In the United States, where neo-nationalism is expressed in its freest and most savage form, President Trump's protectionist-isolationist stance had some very impressive internal results during his first Presidential Mandate from 2017 to 2021, with surprisingly high economic indicators in some areas. However, his 'Fair Trade vs. Free Trade' strategy also had negative repercussions on many other political, economic and military issues. For example, the withdrawal of the United States from the global trading system and many other major trade pacts, plus the US-China trade war, left the structure of the globalized free market economy severely destabilized. Since the beginning of his second Presidential Mandate in January 2025, President Trump has resurfaced but with a much more reinvigorated, bitter and much more aggressive global neo-nationalist agenda, which has already begun re-stirring the international waters much more. Trump's 'Make America Great Again (MAGA)' project has gone much more global both at home and abroad, entailing a much wider and deeper neo-national geostrategy. Apart from many other new-fangled political motives and interests, 'global MAGA' has triggered much more aggressive and harsher trade wars with the EU and China, as well as many other countries.

At the same time, with the structure of the NLWO having lost one of its main founding pillars and been left severely dislocated, the ongoing clash between the neoliberal and neo-national economic models has inevitably produced a huge geo-economic reconfiguration, which has in turn instigated a big geopolitical realignment. Such an enormous re-shuffling, combined with other exacerbating factors, such as the Russia-Ukraine war, plus the rising tensions in the Middle East and the escalation of the China-Taiwan conflict, is altering the aspect of the international landscape incredibly quickly.

In much the same vein, although to a lesser extent, the financial monetary model has also been shifted by the up and rising 'Modern Monetary Theory (MMT)' in some countries, like the United States and Japan. MMT is progressively gaining traction, especially in the United States, where it has become a big part of the Trump administration's economic programme, with Trump being dubbed as the *'most MMT-like-President ever elected'*.[1] Since many years ago, Japan has also been very successfully applying MMT, with its latest 'Abenomics', 'Suganomics' and 'Kishidanomics' economic revitalization strategies, based on expansionary monetary policies, making its economy recover very quickly, rendering very high standards of living. The new prime minister, Shigeru Ishiba, is through his 'Ishibanomics' economic strategy equally continuing along the same economic policy direction.[2] Similarly, Europe is also becoming increasingly more supportive of MMT, with many calls being made about the need to experiment with *'helicopter money/MMT-type policies'*.[3]

Correspondingly, at the underlying academic sector, stakeholder capitalism is also being increasingly challenged and contested by new revised forms of capitalism, which are very rapidly gaining more credit and recognition in both academia and international fora. Joseph Stiglitz's Progressive Capitalism represents one of the most challenging capitalist reformulations currently rivalling stakeholder capitalism. Moreover, the latest editions of the World Economic Forum (WEF) are likewise continuing pressing forward more humane forms of capitalism, such as 'Equitable Capitalism' and 'Egalitarian Capitalism'. Most recently, President Trump has also generated his own home-grown 'Techno-Feudal and Oligopolistic Capitalism', which has already begun ripping aggressively across the international landscape.

[1] MEDIUM. *TRUMP: The First MMT President.* https://medium.com/@kevin_640/trump-the-first-mmt-president-9df44bd0784d

[2] Bloomberg News. Politics. Economics. *Japan's Kishida Set to Stay on Kuroda Path, Party Official Says.* https://www.bloomberg.com/news/articles/2022-06-05/japan-s-kishida-set-to-stay-on-kuroda-path-party-official-says

[3] Investopedia. Economy. Government and Policy. *Modern Monetary Theory (MMT).* https://www.investopedia.com/modern-monetary-theory-mmt-4588060

The Renaissance of Mercantilist, Protectionist-Isolationist Economic Models: Neo-Nationalism

At present, the renaissance of mercantilist protectionist-isolationist economic models riding on strong anti-globalization and anti-free-market feelings currently represents the most powerful counterforce threatening the stability of the NLWO. The new phenomenon's front-running prototype '*Neo-nationalism*', '*New Nationalism*', '*Illiberal Democracy*' or '*Right-Wing Nationalism*' has become huge in the United States and is becoming increasingly embraced throughout Europe. Since the 2007–15 global economic meltdown, the new '*neo-tribal*' nationalism has been progressively boiling up in United States and European politics closing borders and restoring societies to a past homogeneity. Together with the UK's Brexit and China's hegemonic rise in Asia, the geo-economic reconfiguration and geopolitical realignment that neo-nationalism has provoked have badly shaken the foundations of the world's neoliberal architecture.

For more than two decades now, the world has been witnessing a sharp spike in nationalist tensions, paralleled by flare-ups in xenophobia and nativism. The neo-national '*broad nativist revolt*' runs totally against *'post-Cold War politics long characterised by an orthodoxy of free trade, nurturing the service economy, neoliberal trading arrangements, and liberalised immigration policies'*.[4] While academics have perceived that *'economic stagnation among lower- and middle-class whites has been a main driver for nationalism's rise around the globe'*,[5] neo-nationalism has, at the same time, strongly set *'the nation-state against supranational, liberal regimes like the EU or NAFTA, and local customs and traditions, including religious traditions, against alien, outside trends'*.[6] Although the main conservative argument against new nationalism considers it an elevation of nationalism, with a focus on its own nation and people at the expense of the more global agenda, others perceive it as a '*return*'.[7]

It was not until the presidency of Donald Trump together with the UK's Brexit that intellectuals, academics and journalists really began to come to grips with and grasp the magnitude of the global rise of neo-nationalism. It is all quite understandable, considering that such profound political-economic changes have only occurred recently within the world's leading superpower, as well as within leading countries of the EU. Since then, the neo-national family tree has continued to ramify evermore

4 The Week. DOUGHERTY, M.B. *A New Nationalism Is Rising. Don't Let Donald Trump Destroy It.* https://theweek.com/articles/638440/new-nationalism-rising-dont-let-donald-trump-destroy

5 NPR. DETROW, S. *From Brexit to Trump, Nationalist Movements Gain Momentum around World.* https://www.npr.org/2016/06/25/483400958/from-brexit-to-trump-nationalist-movements-gain-momentum-around-world

6 Law and Liberty. MOVSESIAN, M. *The New Nationalism.* https://www.lawliberty.org/2016/12/08/the-new-nationalism/

7 National Review. BROG, D. and HAZONY, Y. *The Nationalist Spirit of 2016.: A Conservative Spring.* https://www.nationalreview.com/2016/12/conservatives-nationalists-2106-brexit-donald-trump-internationalism/

extensively, with some of the most outstanding neo-nationalist figures including Donald Trump, Nigel Farage, Georgia Meloni, Marine Le Pen and Geert Wilders. Other notable inclusions likewise range from Hungary's Viktor Orbán to Poland's Andrzej Duda, India's Narendra Modi and lastly to the Philippines's Rodrigo Duterte.[8]

The rise of '*illiberal democracy*' was announced as far back as twenty years ago. Many democratic elections that took place in South America, North Africa, the Middle East, the Balkans and South and South-East Asia (sometimes internationally unperceived) gave rise to authoritarian ultra-nationalist regimes, which quickly eviscerated their opponents' civil liberties and rights from their nationalist programmes. Apart from the Balkans case, whereas the phenomenon did not really appear to affect Western countries, the fall of the Berlin Wall gave rise to a new powerful geopolitical narrative. The discourse praised how the destruction of walls and barriers across the globe and the '*irresistible melding of societies*' benefitted the new transnational powers. In addition and favoured by international companies, as well as supported by NGOs, economic liberalization went hand in hand with political liberalization.[9]

Seen through that prism, although illiberal democracy was then considered a side concern, as it has turned out, while it was formerly a peripheral and secondary issue, it has now become a much more substantial one that has broken through the mental barriers meant to contain it. Signs of the coming '*globalised nationalism*' have projected new improbable yet highly effective transnational ties between nativists, with very strong signals having been emitted by Japan's latest Prime Ministers Shinzo Abe, Yoshihide Suga, Fumio Kishida and Shigeru Ishiba, as well as by Russia's President Vladimir Putin. In Russia, '*Pan-Russian hyper-nationalism*' now much permeates both the Kremlin and Putin's official discourse.[10]

Even the alliance created by Brazil, Russia, India and South Africa, or the BRICS forum, was in some respects viewed as a combining force of militant nationalism '*ill at ease with global governing bodies that were perceived as too intrusive*'.[11] Such assertion is today further reinforced by the recent nationalist escalation in Brazil, Russia, India and China. Furthermore, President Putin's support of President Trump reflects how the alliance between neo-nationalist leaders is ripping through the Western and non-Western divide. An extremely powerful worldwide narrative has quite evidently developed in strong opposition of the post–Cold War optimistic globalization period.[12]

Ironically, globalization's ultimate tools – the Internet and social media – are in fact assisting with the projection of a '*world crisscrossed with walls*', by means of its '*hi-*

8 The Conversation. POSTEL-VINAY, K. *How Neo-Nationalism Went Global*. https://theconversation.com/how-neo-nationalism-went-global-74095
9 Ibid.
10 Ibid.
11 Ibid.
12 Ibid.

tech populism'. Although a decade ago neo-nationalist convictions hung loosely on the fringe, nowadays the internet and access to mainstream media outlets have increased the possibilities of communication, with non-stop rallying and sharing of all sorts. The main figures of the new nationalist populism have become '*masters of hi-tech populism*', as clearly reflected by the new modus operandi of India's Narendra Modi and the United States' President Trump. With political tweets being widely read and interactively followed more rapidly than traditional headlines, new nationalists are today much better interconnected than traditional politicians.[13]

There are various predominant explanations for the rise of the neo-nationalist phenomenon and its destabilization of the NLWO, which are primarily rooted in the history of nationalism and its gradual transition to neo-nationalism, in the '*bankruptcy of the Left*', as well as in national sovereignty and immigration issues.[14]

Back in the seventeenth and eighteenth centuries, when the modern nation-state emerged, it '*played an important role in the development of the system of the market economy and vice versa. However, whereas the "nationalization" of the market was necessary for the development of the "market system" out of the markets of the past, once capital was internationalized and therefore the market system itself was internationalized, the nation state became an impediment to further "progress" of the market system*'.[15]

That is how the NLWO arose, and it involved at the same time '*a radical restructuring not only of the economy, with the rise of Transnational Corporations, but also of polity, with the present phasing out of nation-states and national sovereignty*'.[16]

The phasing out of the nation-state and national sovereignty inevitably induced the development of a new movement for self-determination, which thus and in turn, saw the consequential blooming of neo-nationalism. With the disappearance of a world dominated by nation-states, within which communities sharing a common culture, language and customs could express themselves, the nation-state has once again become the means for self-determination although it has, however, done so with a completely different concept of culture. While the neoliberal culture or '*globalist culture*' is imposed from above by transnational elites and is based on multiculturalism and the protection of human rights, the neo-national culture is however, ingrained much deeper within the national psyche and constructed around issues related to economic, political and cultural sovereignty. Neo-nationalism strictly opposes the globalist culture and the globalization ideology of multiculturalism and protection of human rights, through which during the last thirty years so many wars have been waged in

[13] Ibid.

[14] Global Research. FOTOPOULOS, T. *Globalisation, Rise of Neo-Nationalism and the Bankruptcy of the Left*. https://www.globalresearch.ca/globalization-the-massive-rise-of-neo-nationalism-and-the-bankruptcy-of-the-left/5527157

[15] Ibid, pg 1.

[16] Ibid.

order '*to protect human rights*' (like in Yugoslavia, Iraq, Afghanistan and Libya) that have led to millions of deaths and dislocations of populations. That is the exact reason why globalist ideologists have classified the emergence of neo-nationalism as the rise of '*illiberalism*' or '*illiberal democracy*'.[17]

Neo-nationalism differs very much from classical nationalism, with both ideologies being separated by several main distinctions. Although due to their similar origins, many neo-national parties and their supporters have incorporated some elements of classical nationalism, such as Islamophobic or anti-immigration trends, they are nonetheless mostly motivated by economic, political and cultural sovereignty issues, which have been phased out by the globalization process.[18] '*Neo-nationalism is basically a movement that arose from the effects of globalisation*'[19] as the global liberalization of markets intended to make labour more competitive produced a '*continuous squeezing of employees' real incomes*'.[20] In Great Britain, for example, '*unemployment is low, largely because British workers have been willing to stomach the biggest real-terms pay cut since the Victorian era*'.[21] In the words of Marine Le Pen, '*globalization is a barbarity, it is the country which should limit its abuses and regulate it (globalization) ... Today the world is in the hands of multinational corporations and large international finance ... Immigration "weighs down on wages," while the minimum wage is now becoming the maximum wage*'.[22]

Table 13 Classical Nationalism vs. Neo-Nationalism

• *'Nationalism developed in the era of nation-states as a movement for uniting communities with a common history, culture and usually language under the common roof of nation-states that were emerging at the time but also even in the 20th century when national liberation movements against colonialist empires were fighting for their own nation states.* • *Nationalism's emphasis was on the nation-state, or the aspiration for one.*	• *Neo-nationalism developed in the era of globalization with the aim of protecting the national sovereignty of nations, which was under extinction because of the integration of their states into the NWO.* • *Neo-nationalism's emphasis is not so much on the nation but rather on sovereignty at the economic but also at the political and cultural levels, which has been phased out in the globalization process.*
Unlike old nationalism, neo-nationalism raises also demands that in the past were an essential part of the Left agenda, such as the demand for greater equality (within the nation-state and between nation-states), the demand to minimize the power of the elites, even anti-war demands'.	

Source: Global Research. FOTOPOULOS, T. *Globalisation, Rise of Neo-Nationalism and the Bankruptcy of the Left*. https://www.globalresearch.ca/globalization-the-massive-rise-of-neo-nationalism-and-the-bankruptcy-of-the-left/5527157

17 Ibid.
18 Ibid.
19 Ibid, pg 2.
20 Ibid.
21 Ibid.
22 Ibid.

Although the NLWO's transnational elite has concentrated much political and economic power against neo-nationalist movements, the latter are slowly but gradually taking over accompanied by much social dissent, which is battling the phasing out of national sovereignty. Neo-nationalism has laid down very strong roots that stretch out from the United States to the UK, Italy, France, Hungary, Poland and Austria, and even as far out as Russia and Australia.[23]

The neo-nationalist process is not only spreading out thick across Europe, but equally deepening, leading particularly working-class people to turn to the rising neo-nationalist Right. People have not suddenly become '*nationalists*' or let alone '*fascists*', as the globalist Left accuses them of in order to ostracize them. It is just that the globalist Left is so fully integrated into the NLWO that it does not question any of its institutions, like the EU. Although the current globalist Left does not wish to lead the struggle against globalization, '*globalisation and membership in the NLWO's institutions are incompatible with national sovereignty*'.[24] With so many unsatisfied voices not being satisfactorily heard in the NLWO's institutions, '*the popular strata have realised that national and economic sovereignty is incompatible with globalisation*'.[25]

As the French National Front's vice-president, Florian Philippot, described the Left-to-Right shift, '*the people who always voted for the left, who believed in the left and who thought that it represented an improvement in salaries and pensions, social and economic progress, industrial policies ... have realized that they were misled*'.[26]

What began with the UK's Brexit has now spread throughout the European landscape, inundating it with many other neo-national economic policy proposals. While many of the new proposals '*include exiting the euro and throwing up trade barriers to protect industry*',[27] others champion public services instead, as well as hail the protection '*of workers and farmers in the face of wild and anarchic globalisation ... which has brought more pain than happiness*'.[28]

'*Eurocrats*' were very taken aback when the Prawo i Sprawiedliwosk (PiS) or the Law and Justice Party won the 2015 elections in Poland. However, it was not really that surprising considering that since Poland joined the EU in 2004 more than two million Poles have emigrated mostly to the UK. Traditional Polish voters were obviously tired '*of the bulldozing of their values by the ideology of globalisation*'.[29]

> *The nationalist, pro-religion, protectionist, xenophobic PiS has attracted these disappointed people with an ambitious welfare programme: a family allowance of*

[23] Ibid.
[24] Ibid.
[25] Ibid.
[26] Ibid.
[27] Ibid.
[28] Ibid, pgs 2–3.
[29] Ibid, pg 3.

> *500 zloty ($130) a month per child, funded through a tax on banks and big business; a minimum wage; and a return to a retirement age of 60 for women and 65 for men (PO had planned to raise it to 67 for both). In fact, PiS used to be a conservative pro-EU party when they were in power between 2005 and 2007, following faithfully the neoliberal program, and since then they have become increasingly populist and Eurosceptic. As a result, in the last elections they won the parliamentary elections in both the lower house (Sejm) and the Senate, with 37.6% of the vote, against 24.1% for the neoliberals and 8.8% for the populist Kukiz while the 'progressive' camp failed to clear the threshold (5% for parties, 8% for coalitions) and have no parliamentary representation at all!.*[30]

In broad terms, the devastating economic and social consequences of the globalization process on much of the world population have inevitably led to the '*bankruptcy of the Left*'. At the same time, the crusade carried out by the NLWO's transnational elite has likewise provoked many parallel political and cultural transformations, in order '*to integrate any country resisting integration ... defined by neoliberal globalization (Yugoslavia, Iraq, Afghanistan, Libya and Syria)*'.[31]

In Europe, the ultimate causes of the rise of a neo-nationalist movement are mostly found in '*the intellectual failure of the Left to grasp the real significance of a new systemic phenomenon, (i.e. the rise of the Transnational Corporation that has led to the emergence of the globalization era) and its consequent political bankruptcy*'.[32]

With the Left having espoused and become an integral part of the economic, political and cultural globalization of the NLWO, the main embracers of the neo-national movement are the victims of globalization, most especially the working class that used to support the Left. Although the activities of the Left have managed to emasculate other anti-globalization anti-systemic movements, the fight against globalization, particularly against the EU, has now been taken over by the neo-nationalist movement.[33]

Due to the NLWO's transnational elite's military campaigns against Muslim countries (like Iraq, Afghanistan, Libya and Syria), some neo-nationalist movements have developed worrying Islamophobic trends, some of which have turned their old anti-Semitism to Islamophobia, even being supported by some Zionists. Despite Marine Le Pen's misperception that '*there is no Islamophobia in France ... but there is a rise in anti-Semitism*',[34] Islamophobia has been growing there since before the Charlie Hebdo case, with frequent attacks against Islamic immigrants living in squalid conditions in

30 Ibid.
31 Ibid.
32 Ibid.
33 Ibid.
34 Ibid.

virtual ghettos. In the United States and the UK, such trends also affect the Jewish community as they are economically considerably well off, and in disproportion to their size share a big part of the countries' political and economic power.[35]

The 2022 General Elections in France very manifestly reflected how divided the country has become and how polarized society is, with Marine Le Pen and her extreme Right party, the National Rally, achieving 41.45 per cent of national votes.[36] Italy has gone even further and completely converted to neo-nationalism, with the 2022 General Elections being won by the far Right leader of the Brothers of Italy party, Georgia Meloni.[37]

The British Brexit issue is not just a case about free trade versus protectionism. It is a case against globalization '*which has led to the present mass economic violence against the vast majority of the world population*'[38] and accompanied it with military violence. The Leftist trends hide that globalization is basically a '*class issue*'. However, that is precisely '*the essence of the bankruptcy of the "Left", which is reflected in the fact that, today, it is the neo-nationalist Right which has replaced the Left in its role of representing the victims of the system in its globalized form, while the Left mainly represents those in the middle class or the petty bourgeoisie who benefit from globalization … The millions of European voters who turn their back towards this degraded "Left" are far from racists or fascists but simply want to control their way of life rather than letting it to be determined by the free movement of capital, labor and commodities, as the various Soroses of this world demand!*.'[39]

The '*intellectual and political bankruptcy of the Left*' is reflected by the fact that the neo-nationalist movement has been increasingly adopted all over Europe by most of the victims of globalization, especially the working class who used to support the Left – a kind of Left that has totally embraced the NLWO's full integration of not just economic globalization, but also of political, ideological and cultural globalization. '*It is therefore clear that the neo-nationalist parties which are, in fact, all under attack by the transnational elites, constitute cases of movements that have simply filled the huge gap created by the globalist "Left". Thus, this "Left", instead of placing itself in the front line among all those peoples fighting globalization and the phasing out of their economic and national sovereignty, it has indirectly promoted globalization, using arguments based on an anachronistic internationalism, supposedly founded on Marxism.*'[40]

35 Ibid.

36 *The Guardian. French Election 2022: Full Second Round Results.* https://www.theguardian.com/world/ng-interactive/2022/apr/24/french-election-2022-live-results-projection-second-round-emmanuel-macron-marine-le-pen

37 BBC News. *Georgia Meloni: Italy's Far Right Wins Election and Vows to Govern All.* https://www.bbc.com/news/world-europe-63029909

38 Ibid.

39 Ibid, pgs 3–4.

40 Ibid, pg 4.

The main and foremost unifying element of neo-nationalism is the struggle for national sovereignty, which is perceived to be disappearing in the era of globalization. Although neo-nationalists battle against immigration, their true-gritted war, however, is against globalization. They blame globalization for the *'opening of all markets, including the labor markets, particularly within economic unions like the EU, which is the direct cause of their own unemployment or low-wage employment, as well as of the deterioration of the welfare state, given that the elites are not prepared to expand social expenditure to accommodate the influx of immigrants'*.[41] Neo-nationalism is not, however, perceived as a racist movement, but purely as an economic movement.

In their book, *'Neo-Nationalism in Europe and beyond. Perspectives from Social Anthropology'*, Andre Gingrich and Marcus Banks strongly highlight how neo-nationalism has in many instances become quite radical, having even mutated to '*Ethno-Nationalism*' in some countries, such as Norway. In Norway, immigrant discrimination has made *'descent'* come to play a huge role in the re-articulation of Norwegian ethno-nationalism.[42] *'Many "non-Western immigrants" work in unskilled and semi-skilled service occupations, doing many of the jobs that "Norwegians no longer want". They earn considerably less than native Norwegians at the same age and with the same educational level. During the first years after arrival this difference in income is 40 per cent, after twenty-five years it is 20 per cent. Educated "immigrants" often experience difficulties when attempting to obtain appropriate jobs. For white Norwegian employers, a "strange name" or "non-Norwegian looks" often signal not sharing basic values and assumptions. Unemployment is three times as high as among majority Norwegians. Both personal narratives document the considerable discrimination that is taking place in the housing market, the labour market and in everyday life. These studies suggest that the main problem is not violent extremist and racist groups, but "more subtle forms of everyday discrimination". It is argued that this is due to a discrepancy between "official and unofficial attitudes". In other words, that people say one thing officially and do something else unofficially.'*[43]

Ethno-nationalism is also present in other parts of the world, such as in Bolivia where it has become very pronounced and radical. With the country being deeply immersed in a very dense process of construction of its multi-ethnic national identity, ethno-nationalism has only widened the breaches of Bolivia's fragmented social sphere even more. Likewise, it has equally fuelled the confrontational spirit between two of the country's most prominent political movements – the Movimiento al Socialismo (MAS) and the Movimiento Indígena Pachakuti (MIP).[44]

41 Ibid.

42 GINGRICH, A. and BANKS, M. (Eds). *Neo-Nationalism in Europe and Beyond: Perspectives from Social Anthropology*. GULLESTAD, M. *Imagined Kinship: The Role of Descent in the Rearticulation of Norwegian Ethno-nationalism*, pgs 69–91.

43 Ibid, pgs 71–2.

44 ZURITA, A. *La Sociedad Multiétnica Boliviana: Riesgos de Fragmentación Social y Amenazas a la Formación de la Identidad Nacional*, pgs 151–72.

The NLWO and the transnational elite find themselves at a historical juncture, wherein neo-nationalism and the victims of globalization are increasingly disrupting the process of neoliberal globalization. Neo-nationalism, together with its social struggle, has become much more widespread and established throughout Europe and other world regions, aiming to break away from the NLWO in order to build a new global democratic community, based on the restoration of economic, political and cultural national sovereignty.[45]

Neoliberalism vs Neo-Nationalism

Following the 2007–15 global financial crisis, the hardest and most destabilizing blow to the NLWO came through the 2016 US shift from a free-market economy to a neo-nationalist isolationist-protectionist economy. The US abandonment of the neoliberal model and its substitution by the neo-national model, through President Trump's *'Fair Trade versus Free Trade'* strategy, severely weakened and dislocated the structure of the globalized free-market economy. It was an awfully unexpected and ironic swing, considering that throughout the 1980s and 1990s, the United States, together with the UK, spearheaded the two waves of neoliberalization, which lay down the foundations of the NLWO, thereby establishing the neoliberal paradigm and orthodoxy.

Although since the 1980s the United States has always been the world's chief embracer of free trade and front-running promoter of free-market economics, at present the United States is where neo-nationalism is expressed in its freest and wildest form, having seriously divided the country and completely polarized society. While during his first term in office from 2017 to 2021, President Trump generated an initial, hard-core neo-national crusade, since the beginning of his second term in office in 2025, President Trump has re-merged but with a much more bitter and aggressive, global MAGA campaign, which goes far beyond the economic and financial waters.

Since the very beginning of his first presidential campaign, President Trump always made it clear that he intended to '*Make America Great Again (MAGA)*'. His approach, however, has to be understood from the perspective of his own personal, educational and professional background. Donald Trump always represented the complete opposite of the classical Capitol Hill mould of '*politically correct*' prototype of US presidents, having been mostly bred as an '*economic animal*', rather than as a '*political animal*'. He thus embarked on his own personal crusade to achieve his goals. Finding himself with an economically deteriorated United States and a very unsatisfied citizenship, together with his perception of China and some of the United States' trading partners

45 Global Research. FOTOPOULOS, T. *Globalisation, Rise of Neo-Nationalism and the Bankruptcy of the Left*, pg 5. https://www.globalresearch.ca/globalization-the-massive-rise-of-neo-nationalism-and-the-bankruptcy-of-the-left/5527157

of taking unfair advantage of the country's open market for decades, intentionally dumping goods into US markets that were priced unfairly due to lower labour costs and government assistance to business in those nations, he changed the situation completely.[46]

Starting off with his first presidential inaugural address, Trump openly stressed that *'we must protect our borders from the ravages of other countries making our products, stealing our companies, and destroying our jobs. Protection will lead to great prosperity and strength'*.[47]

President Donald Trump's 'fair-trade versus free-trade' strategy immediately closed the borders of the '*land of freedom and opportunities*' and the haven of parallel markets. He walked out of big trade pacts, renegotiated others and imposed stiff tariffs on tonnes of foreign goods entering the country. Altogether, the Trump-led nation of the '*fair, the strong and the wise*' indeed soon made '*America Great Again*'. Trump dropped the established US consensus of open international trade policies, which prevailed in US politics since the debacle of the Smoot-Hawley tariff of the 1930s and the Great Depression that ensued.

With a very wide base of American followers which has grown strong to support Trump's isolationist-protectionist stance, neo-nationalism has now become extremely profoundly imbued within the American socioeconomic fabric. In strict accordance with the neo-nationalist ideals of economic, political and cultural sovereignty, the United States, turn to protectionism was driven by economic distress, as well as by an extremely anxious American white population, over its loss of cultural status and political control *'both as the dominant group at home and in America's standing abroad'*.[48]

Although President Trump's attitudes towards international trade and domestic minorities diverged extremely from traditional American principles and values of equality and respect for multicultural and racial diversity, they nevertheless proved to be a very powerful self-reinforcing synergy. The first so-called '*White President's*' articulation of protectionism, together with a racially charged, anti-immigrant and Islamophobic approach, provided America many historically unprecedented economic results. Trump definitely delivered on his campaign promises by quickly making America great again, with his new internal and external attitude rendering very impressive socio-economic results. Notwithstanding, the US swing of both economic

[46] Chron. TEEBOOM, L. *Free Trade vs Protectionism*, pg 1. https://smallbusiness.chron.com/trade-vs-protectionism-3830.html

[47] Peterson Institute for International Economics. NOLAND, M. *Protectionism under Trump: The China Shock, Intolerance, and the 'First White President'*, pg 2. https://www.piie.com/system/files/documents/wp19-10.pdf

[48] Peterson Institute for International Economics. NOLAND, M. *Protectionism under Trump: Policy, Identity, and Anxiety.* https://www.piie.com/experts/senior-research-staff/marcus-noland

nature and direction has severely damaged and weakened the structure of the NLWO, as well as provoked a huge geo-economic reconfiguration, which has in turn instigated a big geopolitical realignment.

Soon after his November 2016 election, President Trump began to quickly break the United States away from the framework of the globalized free-market economy, hence giving way to his splendid *'isolation'*. During his first week in office, Trump pulled the United States out of the Trans-Pacific Partnership initiative, as well as subsequently moved the American Free Trade Agreement and the Korea-US Free Trade Agreement out of free trade, through renegotiations that tightened the rules of origin and the lengthening of liberalization timelines.[49] While in January 2020, President Trump also abandoned the North American Free Trade Agreement (NAFTA), signing into law a brand-new US-Mexico-Canada Agreement (USMCA),[50] he equally ignited very aggressive trade wars with China, as well as other commercial partners like the EU and France.[51]

Although the US trade wars made applied protection upsurge, at the same time US exports also suffered the equal imposition of retaliatory tariffs, which cost the United States billions of dollars. The Trump administration foisted several rounds of tariffs, with around 40 per cent of US imports being put under special protection. Some of those included the following: in March 2018, through Section 232 of the 1962 Trade Expansion Act, President Trump announced that he would impose a 25 per cent tariff on imported steel and a 10 per cent tariff on imported aluminium, although in May 2019 he lifted the imposition of those tariffs on Canada and Mexico. Through Section 301, the United States imposed a 25 per cent tariff on approximately $250 billion of imports from China and a 15 per cent tariff on approximately $112 billion worth of imports from China, although in December 2019 it was agreed to reduce the 15 per cent tariff to 7.5 per cent at a near-future date. In October 2019, the United States won a nearly fifteen-year-long dispute in the World Trade Organization (WTO) against the EU. The WTO ruling authorized the United States to impose tariffs of up to 100 per cent on $7.5 billion worth of EU goods. Beginning on 18 October, tariffs of 10 per cent were to be applied to aircrafts and of 25 per cent to agricultural and other products. In October 2018, the United States had likewise announced that it would equally be imposing tariffs on solar cells and modules and washing machines imports. There were also other pending tariffs on automobile and parts, as well as on a list of products

[49] Peterson Institute for International Economics. NOLAND, M. *Protectionism under Trump: The China Shock, Intolerance, and the First 'White President'*, pg 2. https://www.piie.com/system/files/documents/wp19-10.pdf

[50] The White House. Economy and Jobs. *Remarks by President Trump at a Signing Ceremony for the United States-Mexico-Canada Trade Agreement.* https://www.whitehouse.gov/briefings-statements/remarks-president-trump-signing-ceremony-united-states-mexico-canada-trade-agreement/

[51] Peterson Institute for International Economics. NOLAND, M. *Protectionism under Trump: The China Shock, Intolerance, and the First 'White President'*, pg 2. https://www.piie.com/system/files/documents/wp19-10.pdf

from France. Likewise, there were equally a wide range of threatened tariffs on many more products from China and the EU. In contrast and stemming from the actions of Section 232 and Section 301, retaliatory tariffs amounted to an approximate total of $18.6 billion, a figure that is still rising. However, the latter tariffs are not supposed to be paid to the US government, but to the governments imposing those tariffs.[52]

There are two predominant explanations for the rise of neo-nationalism in the United States. The first one is based on the country's gradual economic deterioration during the past decades. The second one is rooted in the distress felt by a huge amount of American '*whites*' over their loss of cultural and political status, both as the dominant majority at home and in relation to America's standing abroad.[53]

One of the first main reasons for the US turn to protectionism is strongly attributed to much of the citizenship's economic distress caused by an enhanced import competition. Many US citizens, most particularly '*white male voters*' in areas with high levels of manufacturing employment, have shifted towards protectionism due to a heightened import competition associated specifically to competition from China. For over two generations, the huge increase in globalization experienced by the US economy had seen a steady rise of the share of international trade in national income. From 1960 to 2017, it roughly tripled from 9 per cent to 27 per cent. In the United States, the expansion of trade has always tended *'to depress the wages of low-skilled workers, increase the wages of some skill classes, and may well increase the returns to capital, land, and other natural resources'*.[54] It is widely believed that the so-called 1990s '*China shock*', together with the granting of permanent normal trade relations status to China after its 2001 accession to the WTO, as well as a period of Chinese currency devaluation, greatly contributed to an upsurge in manufactured goods, which much harmed employment in the US manufacturing sector. Considering that during the period 2000–2010, 88 per cent of the US job losses in the manufacturing sector were accounted for by the productivity change, international trade policy thus became the scapegoat for unsatisfied citizens with the prevailing economic trends. That way, citizens' perceptions of American global dominance and the domestic group position of '*whites*' became extremely influencing factors for the generalized swing to protectionism.[55]

On the other hand, a pre-election survey also found that *'"fears about immigrants and cultural displacement" were more important than economic concerns in predicting support for Trump'*.[56] The survey results clearly reflected that about two-thirds of '*white*

[52] The Tax Foundation. YORK, E. *Tracking the Economic Impact of U.S. Tariffs and Retaliatory Actions.* https://taxfoundation.org/tariffs-trump-trade-war/

[53] Peterson Institute for International Economics. NOLAND, M. *Protectionism under Trump: The China Shock, Intolerance, and the First 'White President'*, pgs 2–3. https://www.piie.com/system/files/documents/wp19-10.pdf

[54] Ibid, pg 3.

[55] Ibid.

[56] Ibid, pg 4.

working-class' voters strongly believed that American culture and way of life had since the 1950s deteriorated, with almost half of them stressing that they '*often feel like a stranger in my own country*'.[57] More than two-thirds of those surveyed, believed that America needed to be protected from foreign influence, which is substantially more than the 44 per cent of college-educated Americans holding the same views. While such white working-class voters believed '*that immigrants threaten America at more than twice the rate that they believe immigrants strengthen it ... more than half believe that discrimination against whites is now as big a problem as discrimination against blacks and other minorities, while 70 per cent of college-educated whites disagree with this proposition*'.[58] Lastly and in general, 60 per cent of white working-class voters, which nearly doubled the rate of college students, also believed that the country was so off track that it needed a new strong leader willing to break the rules. All-combined, and quite evidently, anti-immigrant and racist sentiments represented very important motives for the US shift to protectionism.[59]

There is considerable evidence indicating that attitudes towards international trade and towards domestic minorities go hand in hand. Whilst some conclusions find that '*prejudicial attitudes toward domestic minorities is a better predictor of trade policy attitudes than occupational or employment status*', others reflect that '*individuals in regions exposed to the "China shock" have harsher attitudes towards immigrants and racial minorities and tend to gravitate toward more extreme forms of their own religion*'.[60] It has been demonstrated that such individuals tend to harvest favourable attitudes towards the '*in-group*' religion, like Christian fundamentalism, and negative attitudes towards the '*out-group*' foreign Muslim religion. Since the Muslim population only makes up about 1 per cent of the US population, arguments in favour of such sociotropic views being the product of competition over scarce resources or labour market outcomes simply do not curdle. Evidence suggests that the salience of such issues was increased by Trump's emphasis on immigration and trade, which together with '*his superior alignment with shifting voter preferences*', won him many votes, as well as much influenced the US protectionist turn.[61] President Trump's '*campaign's articulation of protectionist positions and the use of racially charged, anti-immigrant, and Islamophobic political language ... amounted to a self-reinforcing package*'.[62]

It has also been revealed that economic and cultural explanations are mutually inclusive and thus very interrelated. '*Political polarization is intimately tied not just to economic displacement due to trade shocks but also specifically to industries employing large numbers of white males. White male voters likely experience such distress most*

[57] Ibid.
[58] Ibid.
[59] Ibid.
[60] Ibid, pgs 4–5.
[61] Ibid, pg 5.
[62] Ibid.

acutely, insofar as they perceived threats to dominance both domestically and globally.'[63] Similarly, the impact of trade as an influencing voting factor was conditional on the racial composition of the county in question. Although trade shocks may provide attractive economic reasons for the protectionist swing, the perception of US citizens of trade effects was certainly equally intimately tied to a nexus of issues related to race, education and status.[64]

Much survey literature has similarly highlighted the unease felt by the US working-class white population with ethnic and religious minorities as a protectionist influencing issue. In the development arena, '*ethno-linguistic fractionalisation (ELF)*', which is a '*measure of the probability that two random individuals in an area do not share the same cultural identity*',[65] can be related to intense political competition over rents that the political system has generated and allocated. It assumes that citizens in a certain fractioned polity will mainly support the provision of goods that are going to directly benefit them and not goods destined to benefit '*out-groups*'. Thus, in connection with Trump's election, it can therefore be presumed that a rising ELF played a very significant role in white citizens' discomfort and their move to protectionism.[66]

The 2016 US turn to neo-national isolationist-protectionism represented a huge paradoxical break from its historically established neoliberal norm. As previously detailed, the predominant explanations for such a drastic twist mainly pivoted on the economic effects of globalization on the US economy and the China shock, together with the anxiety of white citizens over their loss of political and cultural status within the United States, as well as with the country's loss of standing abroad. While the two hypotheses are closely intertwined and hard to disentangle, US citizens have clearly mixed together features associated with trade, racial and religious minorities and immigrants and foreigners in their roll to protectionism. Although trade exposure has evidently played a key role in the shifting patterns, it has, however, done so through the prisms of race, diversity, education and age.[67]

The US-China trade war begun by Trump agitated the international commercial waters very much, although at the beginning of 2020 it was, however, somewhat appeased. An initial trade deal between the United States and China capped more than two years of tense negotiations and escalating threats that many a time seemed to plunge the two countries into a long-winded economic war, despite that possibility still remaining open on many commercial fronts. The signing on 14 January 2020 by President Trump and Vice Premier Liu He of the first phase of a multi-phased trade deal between the

63 Ibid.
64 Ibid.
65 Ibid, pg 8.
66 Ibid.
67 Ibid, pg 12.

two powers brought the first chapter of a protracted and economically damaging fight with the world's second largest economy to a close.[68]

The US-China trade agreement marked both a key significant turning point in American foreign policy and a total break from the previous neoliberal free-trade agreements the United States had typically supported. Instead of being based on the old-style neoliberal lowering of tariffs for the free flow of goods and services to meet market demand, the heterodox neo-national deal left a record level of tariffs in place and obliged China to purchase $200 billion worth of specific products within two years. Whilst many critics have highlighted that the deal represents the sort of trade approach that the United States had criticized for a long time, especially in relation to China and its control over its economy, President Trump and many of his supporters viewed it as a correction of past trade deals, which had enabled corporate outsourcing and led to the loss of countless jobs and industries.[69] While it is expected that the purchase commitments will '*strengthen the role of the state in the economy*',[70] China's President Xi Jinping conveyed that the deal was '*beneficial to both China, the US – and the world*'.[71]

The trade pact was '*intended to open Chinese markets to more American companies, increase farm and energy exports and provide greater protection for American technology and trade secrets*'.[72] Nonetheless, it '*preserves the bulk of the tariffs that Mr. Trump has placed on $360 billion worth of Chinese goods, and it maintains the threat of additional punishment if Beijing does not live up to the terms of the deal*'.[73]

Leaving aside explanations for both the US turn to neo-nationalism and the US-China trade war, President Trump's period of '*getting his house in order*' indeed quickly made America great again. His first term in office rendered the country historically unprecedented skyrocketing socio-economic results. Although the US economy did not grow as much as President Trump had promised it would, it did however grow faster since his election. Whereas real (inflation-adjusted) GDP during the third quarter of 2019 was growing at an annual rate of 2.1 per cent, in 2020 the growth rate slowed down somewhat due to the COVID-19 Crisis.[74] While under President Trump the growth of federal regulation stopped, Trump likewise eliminated some very significant rules related to the coal mining and automobile sectors.[75] After-tax corporate profits remained at near record levels, with profits running at a yearly rate

68 *The New York Times. Trump Signs China Trade Deal, Putting Economic Conflict on Pause*, pg 1. https://www.nytimes.com/2020/01/15/business/economy/china-trade-deal.html
69 Ibid, pg 2.
70 Ibid.
71 Ibid.
72 Ibid, pg 1.
73 Ibid.
74 FactCheck. *Trump's Numbers. January 2020 Update*, pgs 5–7. https://www.factcheck.org/2020/01/trumps-numbers-january-2020-update/
75 Ibid, pgs 8–9.

during the third quarter of 2019 of nearly $1.84 trillion.[76] Stock prices continued their decade-long surge since Trump began his mandate, breaking records the last two years. On 17 January 2020, Standard & Poor's 500-stock average was 47 per cent higher than at its last trading day before Trump's inauguration.[77] Although under Trump the growth of jobs somewhat slowed, the unemployment level fell to its lowest in nearly half a century. With a historical norm since 1948 of 5.6 per cent unemployment, in December 2019 it was 3.5 per cent.[78] With Trump, the median household income rose briskly by 2.3 per cent, being the highest official figure ever recorded. In turn and with the rise of income, the rate of poverty declined for its fourth consecutive year having dropped to 3.5 per cent in January 2020.[79] With job openings rising a 20.9 per cent under Trump, labour force participation rose and jobs in the manufacturing sector increased to 487,000. Likewise, jobs in the coal mining industry rose to 1,200.[80] While inflation remained in check, real wages continued on their upsurging trend with paychecks growing faster than prices.[81] Likewise, the price of homes equally soared to record levels, the consumer price index similarly rose by 6 per cent, and lastly, the percentage of home-owning Americans equally grew by 1.1 per cent.[82]

Taking into account such a record-breaking set of US in-house results, many other countries have likewise carried out further neo-national conversions. With the neoliberal paradigm and orthodoxy having been irredeemably shifted and displaced by neo-nationalism, the stable progressive evolution of the globalized free-market economy has been clearly thwarted and stalled.

Although President Joe Biden won the 2020 US Presidential Elections, thus putting a brief end to Trump's initial neo-nationalist crusade, both the electoral debacle and the election results revealed a country that was extremely geographically, ideologically and economically divided, as well as a society that was awfully polarized. It has now become crystal clear that more than half of the United States still prefers neo-nationalism to neoliberalism, having rendered incredible record-breaking economic results, as well as having become deeply ingrained in the US socioeconomic fabric. In many areas, free markets are now considered as definitely part of the past, having been substituted by the Trump-generated protectionism.

While it is widely asserted that in the United States *'free trade is over'*,[83] during President Biden's Presidential Mandate from 2021 to 2025, its administration in fact fashioned a

76 Ibid, pg 15.
77 Ibid.
78 Ibid, pgs 3–4.
79 Ibid, pgs 7–8.
80 Ibid, pgs 4–5.
81 Ibid, pg 16.
82 Ibid, pgs 17–18
83 Foreign Policy. CAMPANELLA, E. *Free Trade Is Over.* https://foreignpolicy.com/2020/11/05/protectionism-trump-biden-buy-american-tariffs/

very interesting and combined, mix and blend between the outgoing neo-nationalist model and the reinstated neoliberal model. Although President Biden regenerated US foreign policy in accordance with neoliberal principles, he however maintained many of the established protectionist measures towards China, as well as intensified the fight against illegal trade practices.

President Trump's Newly Reinvigorated, Global Neonationalist Agenda

After a devastating and crushing win over his rival presidential candidate, Kamala Harris, on 25 January 2025 Donald Trump swore in as the 47th President of the United States.[84] With the US ideological division and polarization of society having now become extremely widened as well as deepened, the pro-neo-national and anti-liberal atmosphere prevails throughout its landscape more than ever.

Donald Trump became America's 47th president after staging the most momentous comeback in political history that handed him massive, disruptive power at home and sent shockwaves around the world. Four years after leaving Washington DC as a pariah, Trump's victory defied two assassination attempts, two presidential impeachments and his criminal conviction, as well as many other criminal charges. President Trump has re-emerged with a much more resented, bitter and aggressive neo-nationalist mentality and outlook.

President Trump's newly reinvigorated neo-nationalist agenda has resurfaced but much more wide spanning and deep reaching. The new, *'global MAGA'* project, with its *'Think Big, Act Big'* slogan, encapsulates both at home and abroad, a much more aggressive and radicalized (fundamentalist) ultra-neo-nationalism, which goes far beyond the economic, financial and commercial waters, equally deep plunging into the oceans of international relations and geopolitics.

Since the beginning of President Trump's second mandate, he has clearly demonstrated that his presidency is being and will continue being extremely transformative both at home and abroad. Based on his long-held belief that liberals, democrats and foreigners are ripping off America and empowered by his MAGA-fuelled Republican majority, Trump has launched an all-out assault both internally and externally on the bastions where the power of liberals, democrats and foreigners resides. Only that way, Trump has claimed, will the United States be put back on the right track. The brute force of Trump's *'One-Size-Fits-All'* policy is already affecting Europeans, as well as many other countries.[85] While Trump's highly politicized neo-national agenda is being implemented and carried out by myriad MAGA ideologues, supporters and loyalists

[84] The White House. https://www.whitehouse.gov/administration/donald-j-trump/

[85] European Council on Foreign Relations (ECFR). *MAGA Goes Global: Trump's Plan for Europe,* pgs 2–3. https://ecfr.eu/publication/maga-goes-global-trumps-plan-for-europe/

around him, they are utilizing the same three methods: '*elimination, transformation and subjugation*'.[86]

> *At home, they seek to eliminate the 'deep state,' transform liberal America into nationalist America and subjugate opponents into submission or capitulation. Abroad, they seek to eliminate alliances and international commitments, transform Western liberal democratic allies into nationalist vassals and subjugate opponents into exploitative transactions.*[87]

President Trump's '*Big Plan at Home and Abroad*' includes strategies to enact policies in both arenas that are nearly identical. Trump's rationale lies in the fact that in order to '*Make America Great Again*' the president must be capable of taking back power, of exercising full force on his opponents and partners alike, as well as of extracting concessions from everyone.[88] '*The same way Trump is attacking the deep state that opposes his agenda in the US, he is also attacking the alliances and international institutions that obstruct his goals on the global stage. He eliminates the national and international constraints that limit his action. He transforms culture and ideas that are anathema to his political views and works to replace them. He subjugates opponents, offering those who are cornered the opportunity to bend the knee and compromise – or be gone … Trump blames the deep state for limiting his power in his first administration. He also blames alliances and international institutions for limiting his capacity to act on the world stage. The domestic mission for his second term is therefore to destroy the deep state and to contract out the federal government. The foreign one is to eliminate international commitments and free America from its allies. In pursuit of these goals, he is wresting power from Congress, the judiciary and the states; but also from international organisations, alliances and all rival centres of power. If he succeeds, he will become the sole decider of US policy – including foreign policy.*'[89]

After six months in office, President Trump has begun radically '*draining the swamp*' morphed into lambasting the '*deep state*', which obstructs his goals, including his political enemies, such as Democrats, the liberal left that continues exercising intellectual dominance, the federal bureaucracy, state and local governments of liberal states and cities, universities, science and research institutions, non-profits, and even Hollywood and the media. In 2024 Trump proclaimed, '*either the deep state destroys America, or we destroy the deep state*',[90] and for Trump and his acolytes, only a full-on assault on it can truly defeat the liberal ideology embedded in America's government, civil society and culture. For them, America needs a total and complete

86 Ibid, pg 3.
87 Ibid.
88 Ibid, pgs 11–12.
89 Ibid.
90 Ibid, pgs 7–8.

break from its past and will thus and therefore abandon its role of *'naïve trade buddy'* or *'obedient military protector'*.[91]

In a similar vein, Trump and the MAGA camp strongly believe that it has been the dominant liberal establishment that has skewed US culture towards a weak progressive ideology that provides nothing but a disservice to America. The new Trump administration is convinced that such ideology is being nurtured and fed by a *'globalist elite'*, with Europe as chief, and will thus persecute and target all liberal havens and holdouts both at home and abroad.[92]

At the internal level, some of the most outstanding governmental/administrative, political and socio-cultural transformative actions taken so far by the Trump administration include the dismantlement of the previous Biden administrative scaffolding, substituting and reforming the administrative structures in order to make them more centralized and controllable and the concentrating of executive power in the president's hands, thus making the US president much more central as well as powerful; the establishment of the *'Make America Beautiful Again (MABA)'* Commission, in order to conserve American lands and waters; the re-generation of a harsher and more aggressive war against 'illegal immigration', as well as the generation of 'culture wars' against the liberal establishment and progressive ideology, which has so much skewed US culture by providing a disservice to the country. On the other hand, some of the most outstanding economic actions taken so far by the Trump administration include the approval of the *'One Big Beautiful Bill'*, which makes many of the individual tax cuts and reforms of the 2017 Tax Cuts and Job's Act (TCJA) permanent, as well as improves others, most especially for the corporate sector, together with a very strong Trump administration investment in the digital sector and cryptocurrencies.

Soon after taking office, one of President Trump's most notorious efforts to combat the 'deep state' in order to modernize government and make it more efficient was the creation of the *'Department of Government Efficiency (DOGE)'*, helmed by billionaire Elon Musk. The main political goal of DOGE is to *'cut through the meat'* of the federal state as quickly and deeply as possible, in order to weaken the capacity of the bureaucracy to oppose Trump's agenda. The elimination of large bureaucratic structures is meant to free the Trump administration from past choices. Such elimination strategy has made the 47th US president more central and powerful than any before, as well as established a much smaller federal state, a politicized bureaucracy and the demise of independent agencies.[93]

While DOGE's initial aim was to cut federal spending in half (about one trillion dollars) in 130 days (although the ambition has since been revised significantly

[91] Ibid, pgs 18–19.
[92] Ibid.
[93] Ibid, pgs 14–15.

downward), DOGE has accessed federal payroll systems to identify *'waste'* and focus on cutting programmes and agencies, such as the Consumer Financial Protection Bureau, as well as on laying off huge chunks of the federal workforce and putting federal buildings up for sale. An additional feature is the president's new practice claim of *'Impoundment'*, which grants him the power to refuse to spend any money appropriated by Congress if he does not see fit what it is utilized for. That way, the president can also slash and cut the budgets of agencies that he does not deem fit to fund.[94] *'Impoundment allows him to "obliterate the deep state, drain the swamp, and starve the warmongers – and the globalists – out of our government." Withholding earmarked money reduces path dependency in future budget and policy decisions: Trump will not be a prisoner of the past.'*[95]

Running in parallel to such actions, the Trump camp has also wrestled hard in order to concentrate most of the executive power in the sole hands of the president. Through the articulation of the so-called *'Unitary Executive Theory'*, according to which the US Constitution (Article II–Section 1) attributes all executive powers to the president, Trump signed an 'executive order', which has clustered and put all independent federal regulatory agencies under direct presidential authority. Through that 'executive order', the president has been given the absolute power to both sack and dismiss any of those agencies' heads, as well as control all regulations that they apply. A more long-run objective of the Trump camp includes making the Supreme Court declare presidential authority over the entire federal government, which will seriously jeopardize the independence of autonomous bodies, such as the Federal Reserve.[96]

The Trump administration has also established the *'Make America Beautiful Again (MABA)'* Commission, in order to conserve the lands and waters of America, to *'cut red tape'*, as well as to drive conservation and economic growth. It is chaired by Secretary of the Interior Doug Burgum and comprised members of President Trump's administration.[97] *'The MABA Commission will work to expand access to recreation for outdoorsmen, hunters, anglers, hikers, bikers, climbers, skiers, runners, and all Americans seeking to spend time in nature ... The MABA Commission is tasked with expanding access to public lands and waters for recreation and incentivizing voluntary conservation efforts ... Using gold-standard science, the MABA Commission will promote active forest management and responsible stewardship of our public lands, while reducing bureaucratic delays that hinder effective environmental management and put our forests and rural communities at risk.'*[98]

94 Ibid.
95 Ibid, pg 15.
96 Ibid.
97 The White House. Fact Sheet. 3 July 2025. *President Trump Establishes Make America Beautiful Again Commission.* https://www.whitehouse.gov/fact-sheets/2025/07/fact-sheet-president-donald-j-trump-establishes-make-america-beautiful-again-commission/
98 Ibid.

The main objectives of the MABA Commission are to expand the access to public lands, since the Trump administration wants to preserve America's natural beauty and expand outdoor recreation for future generations, as well as to conserve American treasures by building on the legacy of conservative conservationists, such as President Teddy Roosevelt, in order to protect the nation's natural treasures.[99]

The Trump administration has equally intensified its fight against '*illegal immigration*'. US immigration continues to be one of the most hotly contested issues in Capitol Hill and in statehouses across the country, as it impacts and affects a wide swath of communities in every corner of America. Trump has framed migrants as a true existential threat to America and has thus come down hard, empowering his camp to resort to extremes.[100]

In 2018, Trump stated: '*Illegal immigration hurts American workers; burdens American taxpayers; and undermines public safety; and places enormous strain on local schools, hospitals, and communities in general, taking precious resources away from the poorest Americans who need them most. Illegal immigration costs our country billions and billions of dollars each year … And I will therefore take every lawful action at my disposal to address this crisis. And that's what we're doing.*'[101]

During his first term, President Trump enacted a series of actions that shifted immigration policy considerably. Since January 2025 and after campaigning to initiate '*the largest domestic deportation operation in American history*', the president has rolled back established protections, expedited deportations and expanded detention facilities, such as the Guantanamo Migrant Operations Center. Through the invocation of the '*1798 Alien Enemies Act*', Trump can now '*mass deport*' suspected members of Venezuelan gangs or send Salvadorians to President Nayib Bukele's mega prisons.[102]

President Donald Trump's position on immigration is extremely hard-core and his calls for '*mass deportation*', restrictions on asylum access and border reform reflect his inflexible new stance. Since January 2025, the Trump administration has rolled out several new executive orders on immigration policy, related to:

- *Border policy (detailing that the administration will "marshal all available resources and authorities" to stop illegal immigration, including establishing a physical wall and deploying "sufficient personnel along the southern border of the United States to ensure complete operational control");*
- *"Enhanced vetting and screening," including for visa applicants and foreign nationals seeking admission to the U.S.;*

[99] Ibid.
[100] Bloomberg Government. Insights. *A Guide to Immigration Policy Changes in 2025.* https://about.bgov.com/insights/federal-policy/a-guide-to-immigration-policy-changes-in-2025/
[101] Ibid.
[102] Ibid.

- *Birthright citizenship (stating that this right does not automatically extend to certain persons born in the United States);*
- *The U.S.-Mexico-Canada Agreement (as the order established an "America First Trade Policy");*
- *Enforcement policies related to illegal entry (including for those seeking asylum, as this order revoked Biden-era executive orders);*
- *"Realigning" the U.S. Refugee Admissions Program, thereby suspending immigration under this program pending formal reporting, and revoking the 2021 executive order on "Rebuilding and Enhancing Programs To Resettle Refugees and Planning for the Impact of Climate Change on Migration".*[103]

Since his return to the White House President Trump has also triggered a series of '*Culture Wars*', aiming to radically transform the cultural direction of US society. Trump is utilizing as many levers of the federal government as possible in order to steer American political culture away from liberalism and progressivism. Although the post-Obama era had seen profound societal transformations in favour of women's and LGTB+ rights, as well as in the fight against systemic racism, Trump and the MAGA camp believe that liberalism, as encapsulated in the '*Woke Agenda*', is making America weak and preventing it from being great. With the Trump camp convinced that the dominant position of liberal values in American culture is a political construct, which needs to be seriously crushed if conservatives want to restore the '*natural order*', it has clamped down hard on its fight against '*race-and-sex favouritism*', in order to re-establish '*meritocracy and a colorblind society*'.[104]

Starting from day one, President Trump has issued executive orders targeting '*the tyranny*' of diversity, equity and inclusion (DEI) initiatives, which he accuses of fostering '*anti-white racism*'. '*Trump thus ended DEI initiatives within the federal government and imposed limits on federal contractors and the private sector, which now risk being charged with violating civil rights laws if they practise positive discrimination to level the playing field in favour of minorities*'.[105]

President Trump has also targeted '*gender equality*' issues, as exemplified in his 2015 campaign book, '*Crippled America*', where he extols supposedly male-centric values of leadership like authority, force, strength and even violence. Since January 2025, President Trump '*has directed the federal government to interpret "sex" as a binary biological classification, banning accommodations for transgender people and federal support for gender affirming care. He rescinded federal funding to any educational institution or athletic association that allows transgender women to participate in women's sports*'.[106]

[103] Ibid.
[104] European Council on Foreign Relations (ECFR). *MAGA Goes Global: Trump's Plan for Europe*, pgs 19–22. https://ecfr.eu/publication/maga-goes-global-trumps-plan-for-europe/
[105] Ibid, pg 20.
[106] Ibid.

The Trump camp's *'cult of the strongman and the obsession with the weakness of the "woke culture"'* has also been extended to the Pentagon. *'Upon taking office, Trump fired the chair of the joints chiefs, General CQ Brown (a black man) and the chief of naval operations, Admiral Lisa Franchetti (a white woman). Moreover, the president signed an executive order in January 2025 that bars people from serving in the armed forces if they express a gender identity different from the one they were assigned at birth.'*[107]

Running in parallel to the Trump camp's 'elimination' strategy, 'transformation' likewise requires the new administration to both rewrite the past and reorientate the future. In relation to the first issue, Trump has promised to restore *'truth and sanity'* to American history, with a 27 March 2025 executive order stipulating that federal monuments and museums should not *'inappropriately disparage Americans past or living (including persons living in colonial times), and instead focus on the greatness of the achievements and progress of the American people or [...] the beauty, abundance, and grandeur of the American landscape'*.[108] As regards the second question, Trump has *'ordered the rescinding of federal funding of gender and race theory teachings in primary schools, claiming that schools are "imprinting anti-American, subversive, harmful, and false ideologies on our Nation's children"'*.[109]

The Trump administration has also targeted US universities and forced them into submission, as they are considered a stronghold against Trump's conservative agenda. In March 2025, President Trump accused universities of *'poor securities practices and anti-semitism'*, directing the Department of Justice to form a *'Federal Task Force to Combat Anti-Semitism'*. Focusing on the main universities, which after the October 7 attacks and Israel's subsequent war in Gaza, saw large protests, the administration has levelled the charge of reckless security practices and rampant anti-semitism against top universities, such as Harvard, Princeton and the University of Pennsylvania, likewise putting a stop to billions of dollars of federal contracts and grants. While the University of Columbia – an epicentre for pro-Palestinian mobilization – has been stripped of $400 million in federal grant money, the administration has equally targeted individual students, using their visa status as leverage, with over 1,800 students from more than 200 institutions having their visas and green cards revoked.[110]

In the economic arena, probably one of the most altering actions taken so far at home by the Trump administration has been the passing on 4 July 2025 of President Trump's *'One Big Beautiful Bill (OBBB)'*, which he claimed was one of the most successful pieces of legislation in American history that will turn the United States *'into a rocket ship'*. The OBBB delivers on two of Trump's major campaign promises – making his 2017 tax

[107] Ibid.
[108] Ibid, pg 21.
[109] Ibid.
[110] Ibid, pg 28.

cuts permanent, and lifting taxes on tips, overtime and Social Security recipients, with a total cost of $4.5 trillion over ten years.[111]

The OBBB makes many of the individual tax cuts and reforms of the 2017 Tax Cuts and Job's Act (TCJA) permanent, although it improves the TCJA by making expensing for R&D and equipment permanent. While the TCJA is not considered as a true tax reform, it however contains many laudable components and it is expected that it will boost economic growth. Whereas in basic terms the OBBB will cut taxes, it will rein in federal spending, secure permanently the US-Mexico border and reform welfare.[112]

> *The legislation makes savings through making cuts to food benefits and health care and rolling back tax breaks for clean energy projects ... About $150bn will be spent on border security, detention centres and immigration enforcement officers. Another $150bn is allocated for military expenditures, including the president's "gold dome" missile defence programme.*[113]

Although the OBBB is considered to hugely favour and boost some sectors, industries and workers, such as corporate America, manufacturers, small businesses and partnerships, high-income Americans and workers who receive tips and overtime, it however greatly disfavours others, like low-income Americans, hospitals, clean energy and EVs, together with deficit hawks.[114]

On one hand and on the winning side, corporate America is one of the sectors that will hugely benefit from the OBBB. Big business groups, including the US Chamber of Commerce and Business Roundtable, together with corporations, will benefit immensely as the legislation has made permanent the massive tax breaks in the 2017 TCJA. Likewise, the package has also restored *'a tax break from the 2017 tax package that allowed businesses to fully write off the cost of equipment in the first year it was purchased'*,[115] which had been phasing out since 2023. Additionally, *'the legislation would once again allow businesses to write off the cost of research and development in the year it was incurred'*,[116] expenses which the TCJA required to be paid off by companies over five years, starting in 2022.

The manufacturing sector is another area which will also benefit hugely from the OBBB, as it will bring about significant changes to how the US tax code treats the

[111] BBC News. 3 July 2025. *Congress Passes Trump's 'Big, Beautiful Bill' Cutting Taxes and Spending.* https://www.bbc.com/news/articles/cddz3n6vz0go
[112] Ibid.
[113] Ibid.
[114] CNN Business. 4 July 2025. *Here's Who Stands to Gain from the 'Big, Beautiful Bill'. And Who May Struggle.* https://edition.cnn.com/2025/07/03/business/trump-big-beautiful-bill-business-economy
[115] Ibid.
[116] Ibid.

construction of new manufacturing facilities. '*Businesses will be allowed to fully and immediately deduct the cost of building new manufacturing facilities. This temporary provision is retroactive to January 19, 2025 and continues for construction that begins before January 1, 2029 ... And in a bid to incentivize more chipmaking in America, the legislation would enhance tax credits for semiconductor firms building manufacturing facilities in the United States*'.[117]

The National Federation of Independent Business, the leading small business-lobbying group, as well as other business partnerships, has much praised the legislation as it has made a special deduction for the owners of certain pass-through entities who pay businesses taxes on their individual tax returns permanent. '*That deduction, which applies to small businesses and partnerships formed by lawyers, doctors and investors, would get increased in the House version of the bill from 20% to 23%. The Senate bill kept it at 20%.*'[118]

High-income Americans are equally extremely joyful with the OBBB, as the net income for the top 20 per cent of earners would increase by nearly $13,000 per year after taxes and transfers, which amounts to a 3 per cent average income increase for those households. Likewise, for the top 0.1 per cent of earners, the average annual income gain would amount to more than $290,000. '*Americans living in high-tax states should also benefit because the bill temporarily increases limits on deductions for state and local taxes for householders making up to $500,000 annually to $40,000 per year for five years ... However, millionaires who lose their jobs will not be able to collect unemployment benefits.*'[119]

Workers who receive tips and overtime are also on the winning side as certain workers will receive an extra tax break through 2028. '*Employees who work in jobs that traditionally receive tips could deduct up to $25,000 in tip income from their federal income taxes, while workers who receive overtime could deduct up to $12,500 of that extra pay. Income limits apply, however.*'[120]

On the other hand and as regards the sectors, industries and workers that the OBBB disfavours or impairs the most, low-income America, as well as many other people at the bottom of the income ladder, are some of the worse affected as the package enacts historic cuts to the country's safety net programme, most particularly Medicaid and food stamps.[121] As a whole, it is forecasted that the OBBB could result in more than 10 million people being uninsured by 2034. What is more, with the Senate tightening

[117] Ibid.
[118] Ibid.
[119] Ibid.
[120] Ibid.
[121] Ibid.

verification requirements for the Affordable Care Act's federal premium subsidies, some middle-income Americans might also be left uninsured.[122]

Some of the biggest downsides and changes to such programmes include the addition of federally mandated work requirements to Medicaid for the first time in its sixty-year history, as well as the expansion of the work mandate in the Supplemental Nutrition Assistance Program (SNAP), which is the formal name for food stamps. The implications directly affect parents of children ages fourteen and up, who would be obliged to either work, volunteer, take classes or participate in job training programmes in order to keep their benefits.[123]

The OBBB's work requirements, plus the other measures that affect Medicaid and food stamps, will make millions of low-income Americans lose their benefits. Most notably, few of those who dropped from Medicaid coverage would be able to have access to job-based health insurance.[124]

> *Those in the lowest-income group, earning less than $18,000 a year, would see a $165 reduction in their after-tax, after-transfer income, once the safety net cuts are taken into account, according to Penn Wharton. That's a 1.1% decrease. The next level, who earn between $18,000 and $53,000, would get a $30 bump in income, or 0.1%. Middle-income households would see their income rise by $1.430, or 1.8%. They earn between $53,000 and $96,000.*[125]

Hospitals are equally displeased with the OBBB's health care provisions, which will reduce the support they receive from states to care for Medicaid enrolees, thus leaving them with more uncompensated care costs for treating uninsured patients. Although the OBBB contains a $50 billion fund to help rural hospitals contend with the Medicaid cuts, the American Hospital Association is *'deeply disappointed'* with it, having stated that *'the real-life consequences of these nearly $1 trillion in Medicaid cuts – the largest ever proposed by Congress – will result in irreparable harm to our health care system, reducing access to care for all Americans and severely undermining the ability of hospitals and health systems to care for our most vulnerable patients'*.[126]

The clean energy and EV sectors are also extremely unhappy with the OBBB, as it strips tax incentives for wind, solar and other renewable energy projects by 2027, as well as applies stringent requirements to developers to claim them. The American Clean Power Association has chided the legislation as it implies a *'big step backward for American energy policy'*, which will eliminate jobs and raise electric bills.[127]

122 Ibid.
123 Ibid.
124 Ibid.
125 Ibid.
126 Ibid.
127 Ibid.

'Electric vehicle makers could also be left worse off because the GOP bill ends EV tax credits of up to $7,500 at the end of September. Previously those tax credits were scheduled to last through 2032, providing a powerful incentive for car buyers.'[128]

Deficit hawks are likewise very displeased with the OBBB, as the Senate version of the package will increase the deficit by about $3.4 trillion over the next ten years, adding trillions to the debt risks lifting already elevated interest rates. In turn, Americans will therefore find it more expensive to finance the purchase of a vehicle or a home, as well as find it harder to borrow money for their businesses to grow. What is worse, higher rates will also force the federal government to devote even greater resources in order to finance its own mountain of debt.[129]

While US federal government interest costs are expected to surpass $1 trillion per year, *'US spending on interest has already more than tripled since 2017, surpassing the federal government's entire defense budget'*.[130]

Another big transformative action taken by the Trump administration in the economic arena has been its huge bet on the digital sector and cryptocurrencies.[131] During his presidential campaign, President Trump made it crystal clear that he intended to position America as the *'global leader in cryptocurrency'*. *'Digital Assets are the future, and our Nation is going to own it. We are talking about Massive Investment, and Big Innovation'*.[132] Since then and through the signing of several Executive Orders, as well as the passing of the recent July 2025 GENIUS Act, President Trump has been delivering on his promise diligently, in order to *'make America the Crypto capital of the world'*.[133]

Since the beginning of his second presidential mandate, President Trump has been very strongly stressing the need to *'embrace digital assets to drive economic growth and technological leadership'*. While in his first week in office, President Trump signed an Executive Order to promote the leadership of the United States in digital assets, in March 2025 President Trump signed another Executive Order in order to establish both a Strategic Bitcoin Reserve and a US Digital Asset Stockpile. Through those two actions, the United States has positioned itself as one of the leading nations in government digital asset strategy.[134]

[128] Ibid.
[129] Ibid.
[130] Ibid.
[131] The White House. Fact Sheets. 18 July 2025. *President Donald J. Trump Signs GENIUS Act into Law.* https://www.whitehouse.gov/fact-sheets/2025/07/fact-sheet-president-donald-j-trump-signs-genius-act-into-law/
[132] Ibid.
[133] Ibid.
[134] Ibid.

In July 2025, with the singing of the GENIUS Act into law, President Trump has gone even further and beyond, with such a historic piece of legislation having begun paving the way for the United States to lead the global digital currency revolution. It is expected that the GENIUS Act will attract massive investment and innovation to the United States, as well as position the country as the undisputed leader in digital assets. While the GENIUS Act will prioritize consumer protection, it will likewise strengthen the US dollar's reserve currency status, as well as bolster national security.[135]

One of the most reinforcing attributes of the GENIUS Act is that it aligns State and federal stablecoin frameworks, thus ensuring fair and consistent regulation throughout the country. It provides consumers in the digital market with protection against nefarious actors in the financial markets.[136]

> *This long-overdue legislation creates the first-ever Federal regulatory system for stablecoins, ensuring their stability and trust through strong reserve requirements. The GENIUS Act requires 100% reserve backing with liquid assets like U.S. dollars or short-term Treasuries and requires issuers to make monthly, public disclosures of the composition of reserves. Stablecoin issuers must comply with strict marketing rules to protect consumers from deceptive practices. Crucially, they are forbidden from making misleading claims that their stablecoins are backed by the U.S. government, federally insured, or legal tender … In the event of insolvency of a stablecoin issuer, the GENIUS Act prioritizes stablecoin holders' claims over all other creditors, ensuring a final backstop of consumer protection.*[137]

The GENIUS Act will also ensure the strengthening of the status of the US dollar reserve currency. It is projected that by driving demand for US Treasuries, stablecoins will have a crucial role ensuring the prolongation of the global dominance of the US dollar as the world's number one reserve currency.[138]

Lastly, the GENIUS Act equally stands as a strengthening instrument for combating illicit activity in digital assets, as well as for reinforcing national security through regulation and registration of stablecoin issuers, with the coordinating assistance of the Treasury Department on sanctions enforcement.[139]

> *The GENIUS Act explicitly subjects stablecoin issuers to the Bank Secrecy Act, thereby clearly obligating them to establish effective anti-money laundering and sanctions compliance programs with risk assessments, sanctions list verification, and customer identification … This legislation improves the Treasury Department's*

[135] Ibid.
[136] Ibid.
[137] Ibid.
[138] Ibid.
[139] Ibid.

> *ability to combat illicit stablecoin activities by enhancing its sanctions evasion and money laundering enforcement capabilities ... All stablecoin issuers must possess the technical capability to seize, freeze, or burn payment stablecoins when legally required and must comply with lawful orders to do so.*[140]

The foreign policy of the new Trump administration can be considered as an extension of its domestic policy. President Trump has a brand new fangled *'Big Plan'* for America and for the world order that has been under construction for the last forty years. While the president is overhauling the way the United States works at home and functions abroad, his transforming project implies at the same time eliminating the quasi-brotherly ties that have bound the United States to Europe for such a long time, trying to transform Europe to his own image, as well as attempting to intimidate any transatlantic resistance into submission – *'Trump at home, is Trump abroad'*. His 'one-size-fits-all' politics means that domestic and foreign policy are one and the same. While Trump blames the outside world for what is happening inside the country, he views former leaders as complicit for their weakness in letting that happen. Thus, whereas Trump's domestic mission for his second mandate is to destroy the 'deep state' and to contract out the federal government, his foreign mission is to eliminate international commitments, as well as to free America from its binding ties to its allies.[141]

While Trump has long instinctively resorted to the *'populist politicization of foreign policy'*, by which foreign policy is formulated based on domestic political interests, he has equally adopted the *'anchoring technique'*, which involves making the first offer in negotiations that is outside the norm or extremely harsh, thereby ensuring that the counter-offer is already in his favour. In diplomacy, President Trump's reading of the 'anchoring technique' has translated into a sometimes-aggressive/forceful behaviour, even bordering *'imperial expansion'*, or as it has already been dubbed *'Authoritarian Neo-Imperialism'*, which has begun ripping hard through the international landscape, together with his blitzing trade war against a very big and growing number of countries. Trump's decisions on the world stage are thus best understood as an extension of US politics or as another front line in America's culture wars.[142] Ultimately, Trump aims to renegotiate deals in his sole favour – whether they are related to law firms, international trade or culture. *'Whether they like it or not, Trump's idiosyncratic worldview means Europe plays a part in the American political drama. Liberals and Democrats are the enemy within; Europeans are their extension outside. Europe is a reference, an influential player in American culture. Trump intends to contain that influence. Europe is thus a symbol of the political ideals Trump seeks to eliminate, transform and subjugate.'*[143]

[140] Ibid.

[141] European Council on Foreign Relations (ECFR). *MAGA Goes Global: Trump's Plan for Europe,* pgs 1–4. https://ecfr.eu/publication/maga-goes-global-trumps-plan-for-europe/

[142] Ibid, pgs 4–27.

[143] Ibid, pg 4.

Only six months into President Trump's second mandate, he has thus far geopolitically agitated the international waters in a very transformative way. The new wide-spanning, reinvigorated and radicalized (fundamentalist) ultra-nationalist, *'Global MAGA'* agenda is being carried out by means of an *'Authoritarian Neo-Imperialism',* most especially as regards the United States claiming of Greenland, Canada and the Panama Canal, as well as the intensification of the Mexican border issues. President Trump has equally put an end to the almost fraternal, historical US relationship with the EU; he is changing the US relationship with NATO and its allies, as well as helped increase the support for neo-nationalism within and around Europe, which is increasingly becoming a new neo-national stronghold. On another hand, probably the most transcendental economic action taken abroad so far by the Trump administration has been the gradual and swift set of a strict global protectionist framework, which is gradually imposing a new *'Trumpinian'* economic order. President Trump has generated of a very aggressive all-out trade war, with the spraying of a blitzing shower of retaliatory tariffs onto a very long and growing number of countries, such as most particularly the EU and China.

One of the first foreign policy actions President Trump took abroad soon after signing in for his second mandate (and just like he did during his first time round) was to withdraw the US membership and funding from many international agreements and organizations. After six months in office, Trump has so far withdrawn from the Paris Climate Agreement; opted out of the World Health Organization and the UN Human Rights Council; left UNESCO; discontinued the funding of the UN Agency for Palestinian Refugees (UNRWA); as well as reviewed US membership to all intergovernmental organizations, which could well end the country's participation in the WB and the IMF. Going even further, President Trump has also threatened with eliminating US contributions to the common funding of the UN and the North Atlantic Treaty Organization (NATO), as well as with shuttering dozens of American Embassies and Consulates all over the world.[144] For Trump, American foreign and development aid has also become a new battlefront. Although American foreign and development aid has always integrated human rights objectives, such as women's rights, girls' education and the defence of LGBTQ+ rights, even promoting liberal democracy in recipients' countries, Trump has so far dismantled the US main aid provider USAID, as well as mocked the concept of cooperation and ridiculed the promotion of human rights and values.[145]

If that were not enough, the new Trump administration carried on applying with astonishing speed and brutality other aspects of its 'Global MAGA' agenda, with the *'neo-imperial coveting'* of lands such as Greenland and Alaska, calling upon Canada to become the United States' 51st State, claiming he would take back the Panama Canal from the Chinese, as well as increasing very tightly the border issues with

[144] Ibid, pgs 15–16.
[145] Ibid, pg 22.

Mexico. The new Trump administration's *'Authoritarian Neo-Imperialism'* has begun ripping hard across the international landscape, although with apparent disregard for territorial integrity.[146]

For President Trump, the transatlantic relationship is not exempt either. The first quarter of 2025 witnessed an onslaught on European interests, such as a shower of indiscriminate tariffs, an increased pressure on Ukraine to accept land losses and a growing support for the increasing neo-nationalist voices in Europe.

> *In a mere three months, European citizens have come to barely recognise their biggest ally. America suddenly seems ready to bend over backwards for its strategic rival Russia; while mistreating its closest partners. The Trump administration also appears to have launched an all-out war on US society, dismantling the pillars of the country's own liberal democracy and abandoning its historic role as leader of the free world. It is as if America and Europe are not even on the same side anymore.*[147]

Trump views Europeans as *'very, very tough traders'* that *'rip off'* America, describing the EU as a *'foe'* to America, who is *'worse than China'* due to the fact that it runs high commercial imbalances. However, Trump's distaste for Europe is not only about trade competition. His perception is that the mere concept of the EU is an abomination, with its bureaucracy representing an enemy to his business instincts and interests. In 2017, when comparing Europe's bureaucracy to that of the Soviet Union's, Trump condemned the *'steady creep of government bureaucracy that drains the vitality and wealth of the people'*.[148]

> *Trump views Europe as an extension of his political opponents at home. Europeans are no better than Democrats. They, too, rip off America, they obstruct his goals and they are judgy. Worse, they are weak and they force America to support their security. The same liberal cultural political elite that has delegitimised and disrespected him in America populates the ranks of the European leadership.*[149]

Such grievance is likewise shared by Trump's whole base, even going deeper than mere resentment of bureaucratic hurdles – Europeans' ritualistic discourse of shared values that bind the United States and Europe together is completely *'alien to Trump and his MAGA supporters'*. They view the United States as having little in common with *'socialist, secular, pacifist Europeans, who preach values to the US but are unable to defend themselves'*. Trumpists are aggrieved by European criticism of their social model, their private healthcare, the death penalty or the right to bear arms. To Trump and his followers, it is all merely foreign interference in matters that do not concern Europe. It

[146] Ibid, pgs 30–3.
[147] Ibid, pg 2.
[148] Ibid, pgs 8–10.
[149] Ibid, pg 8.

does not help either that Europe, with Scandinavia in particular, often equally serves as a reference for American liberals of an ideal social democratic welfare system.[150]

As well as being judgmental, Europe, in Trump's mind, is *'weak and profiteering'*. The administration's consensus is that Europe is *'parasitic'* and will have to start paying for the services rendered. While Vice-President Vance hates the idea of *'bailing Europeans out again'*, Trump and others described Europe as *'pathetic'* when announcing his tariffs.[151] The Trumpist challenge to European democracies has become more radicalized, even accusing Europeans of anti-democratic practices. At the 2025 Munich Security Conference, Vice-President Vance denounced what he perceives as a European *'threat from within'*, as well as European restrictions of free expression.[152]

For the new Trump administration, military alliances are the worst kind of foreign commitment. For Trump, the irony is that while the United States is bound to protect countries that are too weak to defend themselves, such *'weakling states'*, meanwhile, continue to thrive and compete economically with their saviour and protector. Trump wants out of his role as *'obedient military protector'*. For Trump, while *'dependency corrupts and absolute dependency corrupts absolutely'*, the United States *'will no longer tolerate an imbalanced relationship which encourages dependency'*.[153] Whereas Ukraine occupied a special place in the Trump administration's adversarial approach to Europe, Trump dealt with the issue swift but firmly, even obliging Ukraine to give up considerable land to Russia.[154] NATO is another very thorny issue for Trump, who's *'scepticism over NATO is echoed in a new generation of American policymakers, such as Dan Caldwell who joined the administration as an advisor to Hegseth. Many such political appointees to Pentagon positions have expressed a desire to restrain American foreign policy. They are determined to shift US military resources away from Europe and back to the US or to Asia. Central to this is an aim to change the United States' relationship with its allies'*.[155]

Lastly, Trump's MAGA acolytes carry a lot of the weight in disseminating the president's anti-diversity message abroad – a message, which has begun to take hold in many more parts of Europe, emboldening leaders there to begin cultural purges of their own. MAGA's solidarity with conservative, nationalist and populist movements in Europe has one single objective, which is to find *'partners for Trump's effort to transform global culture'*. While Bannon steered the ship in Trump's first term, Musk took control of the new helm for a short period.[156]

[150] Ibid, pgs 8–10.
[151] Ibid.
[152] Ibid, pg 23.
[153] Ibid, pgs 16–17.
[154] Ibid, pgs 10–11.
[155] Ibid, pg 16.
[156] Ibid, pgs 23–6.

> *In the months leading up to Trump taking office, Musk lent his global reach via X to far-right leaders in Britain, France and Germany. This angered liberals, prompting the French president Emmanuel Macron to denounce the 'reactionary internationale' that seemed to be forming. Musk also propped up the leader of the AfD ahead of Germany's 2025 federal election, well before his outrage at the party being branded extremist. He expressed support for the Spanish far-right party Vox too, and made a video appearance at a conference of Italy's League.*[157]

Such European movements are considered *'natural partners'* for Trumpists, as they not only share the same sense of victimization, but equally share the same *'grievances against the system'*. They have even emerged with co-opt MAGA rhetoric, such as *'Make Europe Great Again'*, which was the slogan for the 'Patriots for Europe' summit held in February 2025. *'Ultranationalist Romanian presidential candidate George Simion proudly claimed to be 'perfectly aligned ideologically with the MAGA movement' ahead of his 40% win in the first round of the rescheduled election in May. In turn, US conservatives flock to Europe to support these movements. The American Conservative Union has announced that it will hold the 2025 spinoff of its major conference, 'CPAC', in Poland. Only Hungary has previously hosted the conference in Europe. Polish conservatives likely hope that CPAC will serve as a forum of cooperation for right-wing politicians and ultimately strengthen transatlantic relations.'*[158]

Notwithstanding, Trump's transformation agenda will only be truly fulfilled once the EU itself changes. While the EU is perceived by Trumpinian hard-liners as *'a supranational entity that centralises power at the expense of national sovereignty'*, proposals are circulating in order to change *'the bloc from within, as a contribution to invigorating a new era of transatlantic relations … leading to a different kind of transatlanticism that pursues a different set of priorities. Even if some European nationalists are cautious when it comes to their relationship with the US, Trump's big cultural plan for America and Europe still unites partners across the pond'*.[159]

From another perspective, probably the most transforming economic action taken abroad so far by the Trump administration has been the generation of a very aggressive and all-out *'global trade war'*, with the spraying of a blitzing shower of retaliatory tariffs onto a very long and growing number of countries, such as most particularly the EU and China. Such transcendental, economic-commercial game-changing actions are very swiftly setting up a global protectionist framework, which is seeing the gradual and progressive imposition of a brand new *'Trumpinian'* economic order.

One of the starkest examples of President Trump's imposition of *'out-of- the-ordinary demands on allies and partners to force them into either confrontation or appeasement,*

[157] Ibid, pg 23.
[158] Ibid, pgs 24–5.
[159] Ibid, pg 26.

effectively subjugating them to his will' is his all-out 'global trade war' through a blitzing shower of massive retaliatory tariffs upon most of America's trading partners.[160]

President Trump has always viewed free trade agreements as highly burdensome and he has put an end to the United States being everyone's *'naïve trade buddy'*. He dubbed 2 April 2025, the day he announced massive hikes in tariffs across the world, as *'Liberation Day'* for America. For Trump, free trade is not *'freeing'* – for him, the *'real liberation'* instead comes through his absolute liberty to impose high tariffs on trading partners and competitors.[161]

After announcing a swath of reciprocal tariffs on 2 April, Trump declared that *'we will supercharge our domestic industrial base. We will pry open foreign markets and break down foreign trade barriers ... More production at home will mean stronger competition and lower prices'*.[162] Seven months after President Trump began his campaign to rebalance global trade in America's favour many worrying ripples have been created across the world economy.

Since then, and as of 7 August 2025, Trump has imposed huge retaliatory tariffs on about ninety countries so far, including most of America's largest trading partners, such as the EU, China, Japan, South Korea, Great Britain and Vietnam.[163]

Notwithstanding, not all countries have the same tariff imposition. While Switzerland is seeking to renegotiate down to a 10 per cent tariff, Mexico has an extension to continue negotiations and Canada is already applying a 35 per cent tariff.[164]

Among the countries with the highest tariff impositions are: Brazil, with a 50 per cent tariff rate, along with India, with a 25 per cent tariff rate, plus an additional 25 per cent due to New Delhi's purchasing of Russian petrol.[165]

The minimum tariff rate of 15 per cent has been applied to about forty countries, with which the United States has a negative trade balance, such as Costa Rica, Ecuador, Venezuela and Bolivia. Countries with a positive trade balance like Chile, Colombia and Argentina have been applied the lowest tariff rate of 10 per cent. Whereas Cambodia has been applied a 19 per cent tariff rate, Vietnam has a 20 per cent tariff rate.[166]

[160] Ibid, pgs 31–2.

[161] Ibid, pg 18.

[162] Investopedia.com. HYATT, D. *What Has the US Gained from Trump's Trade Wars? It's Still up in the Air.* https://www.investopedia.com/evaluating-trump-s-trade-wars-what-has-the-us-gained-and-what-are-the-economic-costs-11793126

[163] Ibid.

[164] AS.com. MARTIN SANJUAN, L. *Los Aranceles de Trump entran en Vigor: la Lista con los Países que más van a Pagar y los que menos desde el 7 de agosto.* https://as.com/actualidad/politica/los-aranceles-de-trump-entran-en-vigor-la-lista-con-los-paises-que-mas-van-a-pagar-y-los-que-menos-desde-el-7-de-agosto-n/

[165] Ibid.

[166] Ibid.

China has agreed to a temporal agreement, with a 30 per cent tariff imposition by the United States on Chinese goods and a 10 per cent tariff by China on US goods.[167]

In the end and after a very heated round of negotiations, President Trump and President Von der Leyen have agreed on a 15 per cent tariff imposition on EU goods being exported to the United States, with no tariffs whatsoever on US goods being imported to the EU. Although the US-EU tariff pact has been lighter on the EU than expected, some sectors like the food and automobile sectors have been the most affected.[168]

Financial Monetarism vs Modern Monetary Theory (MMT)

Although to a much lesser degree than the shifting of the free market model by the isolationist-protectionist model, the financial monetary model has also experienced a displacement by the heterodox financial model *'Modern Monetary Theory' (MMT).* MMT has been in practice for years in Japan, rendering the country very impressive economic results. Likewise, in the United States, while MMT formed part of the Biden administration's economic programme, President Trump is likewise adopting some MMT policies. Similarly, the EU equally being increasingly recommended to experiment with MMT policies.

Despite the fact that much critique surrounds MMT as regards the varying ways its claims do not hold or would not work, the alternative model is nevertheless gaining more and more recognition by many renowned economists, such as Larry Randall Wray and Stephanie Kelton, with its policies also securing ground in New York.[169] The American economist, Pavlina R. Tcherneva developed the first ever mathematical framework for MMT, largely focusing on its premise of '*Job Guarantee*'.[170]

MMT evolved from German economist Georg Friedrich Knapp's '*Chartalism*', and sometimes, it is also referred to as '*Neo-Chartalism*'. Its macroeconomic policy prescriptions are considered a variant of Russian economist Abba Lerner's '*Theory of Functional Finance*'. MMT is a heterodox macroeconomic theory, which believes that governments should utilize fiscal policy for the achievement of full employment, as well as create money by themselves in order to fund government purchases. MMT advocates base their ideas on the fact that once the economy reaches full employment, inflation then becomes the primary risk, which can be tackled by the raising of taxes and the issuance of bonds for the removal of money excesses from the system.[171]

[167] Ibid.

[168] Ibid.

[169] Bloomberg. *Stephanie Kelton, Modern Monetary Theory Evangelist.* https://www.bloomberg.com/news/articles/2019-12-04/stephanie-kelton-is-the-modern-monetary-theory-mmt-evangelist

[170] World Finance. *Modern Monetary Theory Gains Traction in the US*, pgs 2–3. https://www.worldfinance.com/markets/modern-monetary-theory-continues-to-gain-traction

[171] Ibid. pgs 1–2.

The central idea of MMT sustains that governments with a fiat money system, can and should print – or in today's modern world, easily digitally create with a few keystrokes – as much money as they need to spend, since they are the monopoly issuers of money, and therefore simply cannot go broke or become insolvent, unless a political decision to do so is actually taken. The MMT macroeconomic framework is mostly recommended for monetarily sovereign countries, like the United States, the UK, Japan or Canada. It upholds that they would not have to be operationally constrained by budgets and revenues when it comes to federal government spending. In other words, since such governments are the monopoly issuers of the currency, they would not need taxes or borrowing for spending, as they would be able to print as much money as they needed.[172]

Although by its name MMT implies some kind of new modern theorem, it is in fact not that novel. Its origins trace back to, amongst others, the early-twentieth-century work of Friedrich Georg Knapp and the mid-twentieth-century work of Abba Lerner, having today been brought back to life by modern economists in revised ways. Friedrich Georg Knapp's book, '*State Theory of Money*' (also known as Chartalism), provides a synthesis of the main ideas of MMT. At the beginning of the twentieth century, physical money, such as notes and coins, was considered to have evolved from previous barter systems, which gradually became a form or medium of exchange as it represented a durable commodity that had usage value. Knapp argued that money is '*a creature of law*' rather than a commodity, contrasting his theory of money with the Gold Standard view of '*metallism*', which considered the value of a unit of currency dependent on the quantity of precious metal it contained or for which it could be exchanged. Knapp believed that the state could create pure money and make it exchangeable by recognizing it as a legal tender, with the criterion of state money, based on what is accepted at public pay offices. The ideas of Knapp much influenced Keynes and his notion on the role of the state in the economy and are referenced in the opening pages of his 1930 '*Treatise on Money*'.[173]

Likewise, in 1947, Abba Lerner, in his article '*Money as a Creature of the State*', also pressed forward his ideas on '*Functional Finance*', arguing that it was the state's responsibility to avoid inflation and depressions, since it had the ability to create or tax money away.[174]

During the 1990s, the economist Bill Mitchell coined the term '*Modern Monetary Theory*'. Today, modern-day economists, such as Warren Mosler, Larry Randall Wray and Stephanie Kelton, have revived the ideas of chartalism as an explanation of money creation, with the renewed formulation sometimes being referred to as

[172] Cato Institute. COATS, W. *Modern Monetary Theory: A Critique*. https://www.cato.org/publications/cato-journal/modern-monetary-theory-critique
[173] World Finance. *Modern Monetary Theory Gains Traction in the US*, pgs 2–3. https://www.worldfinance.com/markets/modern-monetary-theory-continues-to-gain-traction
[174] Ibid.

'*Neo-Chartalism*'. The economist Pavlina Tchernova developed the first mathematical framework for MMT, with her area of specialization primarily concentrating on the issue of '*Job Guarantee*'.[175]

MMT challenges conventional beliefs regarding the way governments interact with the economy, the nature of money, the use of taxes and the importance of budget deficits. MMT advocates hold that such beliefs are a hangover from the Gold Standard era, and thus, are no longer accurate, precise, useful or even necessary in today's modern world. MMT maintains that ever since 1971, when governments dropped the Gold Standard and switched to fiat currencies, they have no longer had the need to finance their spending through taxation or borrowing, as they are the sole issuers of currencies, and can therefore simply create more money by just printing more notes. Given that debt-servicing costs could in turn increase, governments could lower interest rates to make repayments easier, which would also ensure that in the event that investors were scared-off, capital costs remained low.[176]

MMT is based on three primordial economic principles. The first principle focuses on its belief that fiat currencies are public monopolies, as central banks are the only authorized institutions to issue them; that those currencies are the only accepted form of payment for taxes; and that countries that control their own floating currencies are not financially constrained, as they pay due obligations with the very same currency they emit and control. The second principle highlights how governments that sell bonds in a nation's currency cannot in technical terms default on their own debt, even though they may choose to do so. The third and last principle emphasizes that it is normal for governments to run deficits, as every dollar spent by the government, which exceeds the money received from taxes, represents an extra dollar for the private sector. Thus and within an MMT framework, a public deficit represents in essence a private surplus.[177]

The theoretical framework of MMT is mainly structured around what it labels and defines as '*vertical*' and '*horizontal transactions*'. '*Vertical transactions*' relate to any transactions that are carried out between the government or public sector and the non-governmental or private sector, with the government sector including the Treasury and the Central Bank. '*Horizontal transactions*' refer to any transactions within the private sector, including the expansion of the broad money supply through the extension of credits by banks. The non-government sector includes the private banking system, private domestic and foreign firms and individuals, and buyers and sellers of the currency.[178]

[175] Ibid, pgs 2–6.

[176] Ibid, pg 3. Also see KELTON, S. *The Deficit Myth: Modern Monetary Theory and the Birth of the People's Economy.*

[177] Ibid, pg 2.

[178] SSRN. FULLWILER, S.T. *Modern Monetary Theory – A Primer on the Operational Realities of the Monetary System.* https://ssrn.com/abstract=1723198 or http://dx.doi.org/10.2139/ssrn.1723198

In sovereign financial systems banks can by way of horizontal transactions create money, although such transactions do not increase net financial assets since assets are offset by liabilities. In accordance with MMT adherents, '*the balance sheet of the government does not include any domestic monetary instrument on its asset side; it owns no money. All monetary instruments issued by the government are on its liability side and are created and destroyed with spending and taxing/bond offerings, respectively*'.[179] Within the framework of MMT, '*vertical money*' enters circulation through government spending. Taxation and its legal tender are the governmental instruments utilized to discharge debt and establish the fiat money as currency, providing it with value by creating demand for it in the form of a tax obligation that must be met. In turn, fines, fees and licences create the demand for the currency. The currency can be issued either by the domestic government or by a foreign currency. Its actual value is maintained by an ongoing tax obligation, harmonious with private confidence and acceptance of the currency. MMT upholds that since governments can issue their own currencies at will, the level of taxation relative to government spending (the government's deficit spending or budget surplus) is in fact nothing else than a policy tool that regulates inflation and unemployment and not a means of funding governments' activities by itself.[180]

In accordance with '*MMT Evangelist*', Stephanie Kelton:

- *"Under MMT, fiscal policy (i.e., government taxing and spending decisions) is the primary means of achieving full employment, establishing the budget deficit at the level necessary to reach that goal. In mainstream economics, monetary policy (i.e., central bank adjustment of interest rates and its balance sheet) is the primary mechanism, assuming there is some interest rate low enough to achieve full employment ... Cutting interest rates is ineffective in a slump, because businesses expecting weak profits and few customers will not invest at even very low interest rates.*
- *Government interest expenses are proportional to interest rates, so raising rates is a form of stimulus (it increases the budget deficit and injects money into the private sector, other things equal), while cutting rates is a form of austerity.*
- *Achieving full employment can be administered via a federally funded job guarantee, which acts as an automatic stabilizer. When private sector jobs are plentiful, the government spending on guaranteed jobs is lower, and vice versa.*
- *Under MMT, expansionary fiscal policy (i.e., money creation to fund purchases) can increase bank reserves, which can lower interest rates. In mainstream economics,*

[179] Levy Economics Institute. TYMOIGNE, E. and WRAY, R. *Modern Money Theory 101: A Reply to Critics*. http://www.levyinstitute.org/pubs/wp_778.pdf

[180] MOSLER, W. *Soft Curency Economics*. http://moslereconomics.com/wp-content/uploads/2018/04/Soft-Curency-Economics-paper.pdf; ARESTIS, P. and SAWYER, M.C. (Eds). *A Handbook of Alternative Monetary Economics*. TCHERNEVA, P. *Chartalism and the Tax-Driven Approach to Money*.

> *expansionary fiscal policy (i.e., debt issuance and spending) can result in higher interest rates, crowding out economic activity".*[181]

Comprehensibly enough the fact that MMT runs completely against orthodox or conventional monetary theory has gained it much criticism in academic circles, especially from Nobel Laureate in Economics Paul Krugman. Krugman argues that MMT goes too far in its support of government budget deficits, ignoring the inflationary implications of maintaining budget deficits during times of economic growth.[182] Economists at the Cato Institute agree with him:

> *The most provocative claim of the theory is that government deficits don't matter in themselves for countries – such as the U.S. – that borrow in their own currencies ... The core tenets of MMT, and the closest it gets to a theory, are that the economy and inflation should be managed through fiscal policy, not monetary policy, and that government should put the unemployed to work.*[183]

Despite academic opposition, MMT is nonetheless definitely on the rise, gaining more and more political traction, most especially in the United States Progressive politicians on the Left of the Democratic Party, such as Alexandria Ocasio-Cortez, are pressing forward raising government expenditure to pay for new initiatives, like a '*Green New Deal*'.[184] With MMT gradually acquiring more followers, the first MMT conference was held in 2017. During the conference, the economist and MMT advocate Larry Randall Wray projected that the application of MMT would create between 14 and 19 million potential jobs, a potential increase in GDP of $500 billion to $600 billion, with less than 1 per cent potential increase in inflation.[185]

> *MMT has gained ... popularity in recent years because it has pointed out some very obvious aspects of public finance and opened up a range of economic possibilities. For a very long time, we've been told that the government must balance its books like a household, or it can go bankrupt. And therefore, the argument went, in the name of fiscal discipline, we had to sacrifice some policy priorities. Pressing economic problems, like hunger, unemployment, infrastructure degradation, we were told, could not all be financed. None of these claims [are] true.*[186]

[181] Bloomberg. KELTON, S. *Paul Krugman Asked Me about Modern Monetary Theory. Here Are 4 Answers.* https://www.bloomberg.com/opinion/articles/2019-03-01/paul-krugman-s-four-questions-about-mmt; Bloomberg. KELTON, S. *The Clock Runs Down on Keynesianism.* https://www.bloomberg.com/opinion/articles/2019-03-04/krugman-s-macroeconomics-is-no-match-for-mmt

[182] *The New York Times.* KRUGMAN, P. *Deficits and the Printing Press (Somewhat Wonkish).* https://krugman.blogs.nytimes.com/2011/03/25/deficits-and-the-printing-press-somewhat-wonkish/

[183] Cato Institute. COATS, W. *Modern Monetary Theory: A Critique,* pg 1. https://www.cato.org/publications/cato-journal/modern-monetary-theory-critique

[184] World Finance. *Modern Monetary Theory Gains Traction in the US,* pgs 3–4. https://www.worldfinance.com/markets/modern-monetary-theory-continues-to-gain-traction

[185] Ibid, pg 2.

[186] Ibid, pg 4.

Quite rightly, Tcherneva has pointed out that MMT is no longer simply a proposal, as the US government has been in fact already enacting MMT. She has highlighted how the 2017 US corporate tax cut '*is only the latest demonstration that the government funds large-scale programmes without "running out" of financial resources. The prescriptive part of MMT simply says that since we can already see that there are no limits to government spending, is there a better way to spend? Can we get more bang for our buck, so to speak? What did we get in return for the recent tax cut – more inequality, a share buyback?*'.[187]

One of MMT's primary policy proposals, which represent Tcherneva's area of specialization, is the implementation of a federal jobs guarantee. It focuses on the fact that one of the main problems in the US economy is the lack of demand, which is partly caused by underemployment. '*A jobs guarantee would, of course, be hugely costly, but it would also provide citizens with the security and spending power to increase consumption, which would feed back into the broader economy. The guarantee could even turn out to be temporary if the increase in federal spending spurs an uptick in private sector hiring.*'[188]

The fact that MMT has now penetrated both US governmental thought and practice proves just how popular and necessary MMT has become in the United States. At the beginning of his mandate, President Joe Biden created a special economic task force, the – '*Biden-Saunders Economic Unity Task Force*' – made up of senior economists, such as Dr. Stephanie Kelton and Alexandria Ocasio-Cortez, in order to '*explore possible policy initiatives in an effort to unify the Democratic Party behind a set of common goals and views. These task forces will explore areas covering climate change, criminal justice reform, economy, education, health care, and immigration*'.[189]

While President Trump has also been applying some MMT policies, he has even been dubbed as '*the most MMT President*' the United States has ever had. As far back as 2016, Trump publicly declared that the United States never has to default on debt '*because you print the money*', while trying to clarify his strategy for managing the national debt. Through the newly readjusted 2017 Job and Tax Cuts Act, President Trump has once again reflected his indirect support for MMT, most especially as regards deficit spending. Although President Trump '*isn't actually embracing MMT as a new sect of economic religion … the idea that deficits don't matter has him on the same page as MMT'ers … When you combine this balance sheet pressure with Trump's complaining about interest rate increases, it is clear that Trump wants fiscal expansion (through tax cuts) along with low interest rates and a permanently large Federal Reserve balance sheet … Trump is the most MMT-like-President ever elected*'.[190]

[187] Ibid.

[188] Ibid.

[189] Stony Brook University. College of Arts and Sciences. *Dr. Stephanie Kelton Recruited to Work on Biden/Sanders Economy Unity Task Force.* https://www.stonybrook.edu/commcms/cas/news/faculty-news/SKeltonTaskForce.php

[190] Medium. MUIR, K. *Trump: The First MMT President.* www.medium.com

Similarly, many Wall Street chief executives, managers and business analysts '*maintain that the approach offers several important and overlooked insights, and far from finding it fanciful or deranged, they are using MMT to build economic forecasts and even trading strategies*'.[191]

On one hand, one of the chief economists at Goldman Sachs, Jan Hatzius, has stated that he does not '*look at labels in terms of what's on the left and the right … I try to look at what makes me have a better chance of getting the forecast right, and I do find some of the ideas useful*'.[192] On the other hand, a former chief economist at the asset firm Pimco, Paul A. McCulley, has also stressed how '*ideas like MMT that rub against the grain of conventional economics … have for all of my career been a very useful framework for analysis. That framework helped produce billion-dollar gains for the company after the 2008 financial crisis. Dismissing alarms about outsize government debt and white-knuckle interest rates, Pimco instead bet successfully that rates would remain low. When it came to decision-making during this period … MMT and other unorthodox approaches helped him get it right*'.[193]

In a similar fashion, Europe is likewise becoming more supportive of MMT, with the European Central Bank's (ECB) ex-president Mario Draghi, having recommended at the highest levels that the ECB should be open to experiment with MMT policies.[194] In December 2019, a Deutsche Bank report on global debt also pointed out that '*"helicopter money/MMT-type policies" and "fiscal expansion" are what is needed in Europe*'.[195]

What MMT truly seeks is that governments, instead of worrying about their balance sheets, should start exploring ways to utilize resources at their disposal in the most efficient way. In accordance with MMT, it is possible to generate full employment in order to create a more equal society and to strengthen educational systems without causing rampant inflation. '*It is not a question of being able to afford it – it is a question of political will*'.[196]

> *A nation's true wealth is the sum of the real goods and services that it can create. Provided these are being exploited in an environmentally sustainable way, the most efficient use of these resources comes from full employment. If MMT can achieve this, it is certainly better than paying to have people queue up for their social security cheque.*[197]

[191] *The New York Times. Modern Monetary Theory Finds an Embrace in an Unexpected Place: Wall Street.* https://www.nytimes.com/2019/04/05/business/economy/mmt-wall-street.html

[192] Ibid.

[193] Ibid.

[194] Bloomberg News. *Draghi Says ECB Should Examine New Ideas Like MMT.* https://www.bloomberg.com/news/articles/2019-09-23/draghi-says-ecb-should-examine-new-ideas-like-mmt

[195] Investopedia. Economy. Government and Policy. *Modern Monetary Theory (MMT).* https://www.investopedia.com/modern-monetary-theory-mmt-4588060

[196] *The New York Times. Modern Monetary Theory Finds an Embrace in an Unexpected Place: Wall Street,* pg 7. https://www.nytimes.com/2019/04/05/business/economy/mmt-wall-street.html

[197] Ibid, pg 5.

Since many years ago, Japan has been applying MMT at a national scale very successfully. The case of Japan is considered both as extremely interesting and unique, due to its expansive monetary approach. The MMT trend was begun by President Shinzo Abe and his economic revitalization strategy or '*Abenomics*' programme, which was mainly based on expansionary monetary policies. MMT made its economy successfully recover, generating and establishing very high standards of living.[198] The MMT trend has also been continued by President Abe's successors, President Yoshihide Suga with his '*Suganomics*' programme, as well as by President Fumio Kishida with his '*Kishidanomics*' and by President Shigeru Ishiba with his '*Ishibanomics*' programme.

Although the Bank of Japan (BOJ) and government officials deny any official adherence to MMT, many MMT advocates point to the country as an excellent in-practice example of the theory's efficacy. In 2013, Prime Minister Shinzo Abe put into practice his economic revitalization strategy, based on an expansionary monetary policy. Despite Japan having a massive public debt, the Abenomics programme rendered the country very successful results, making its economy recover with high standards of living. Prime Minister Abe's very successful monetary policy has been equally continued by his successors, with their respective Suganomics, Kishidanomics and Ishibanomics programmes, which have been and still are, based on similar stratagems.[199]

MMT adherents view Japan's Abenomics strategy as a very unique and special case-study that bolsters their argument since Japan broke with the orthodoxy of austerity by adopting a pro-growth policy mix, regardless of its huge public debt. While Finance Minister Taro Aso has referred to MMT as '*an extreme idea and very dangerous because it would weaken fiscal discipline*',[200] BOJ Governor Haruhiko Kuroda has also expressed '*no sympathy whatsoever*'[201] with the theory. Notwithstanding, Japan's expansionary monetary policy very clearly fits perfectly into an MMT framework, having rendered it very impressive results. The MMT debate is brewing up even more in Japan, with many lawmakers arguing that with inflation still below the government's target, the country could spend more to stimulate economic growth.[202]

[198] World Economic Forum. *Does Japan Vindicate Modern Monetary Theory?*. https://www.weforum.org/agenda/2019/07/japans-answer-to-economic-deficit/

[199] World Economic Forum. *Does Japan Vindicate Modern Monetary Theory?* https://www.weforum.org/agenda/2019/07/japans-answer-to-economic-deficit/

[200] Nikkei Asian Review. TASKER, P. *Modern Monetary Theory Threatens Revolution in Economic Thinking*, pg 2. https://asia.nikkei.com/Opinion/Modern-Monetary-Theory-threatens-revolution-in-economic-thinking

[201] Ibid.

[202] Ibid.

For more than twenty years, Japan has been running large fiscal deficits, having amassed a '*Mount Fuji-sized*' heap of outstanding government debt, which by 2024 is expected to equal up to 264 per cent of Japanese GDP, and by 2025, is projected to slightly decline to 263 per cent of Japanese GDP.[203] Despite negative predictions having forecasted a bond market rebellion and soaring interest rates, Japan's interest rates have, however, practically vanished.[204] Since 2013, when Japan began implementing the Abenomics strategy things have gotten much more interesting, with Kuroda's quantitative easing programme of bond purchases making 40 per cent of all outstanding Japanese government bonds sit on the BOJ balance sheet. An MMT framework is clearly reflected by the fact that one branch of government owes a vast amount of money to another branch of government, which indicates that no debtor-creditor relationship therefore exists.[205]

Fiscal expansion was, however, not the primary cause behind Japan's public deficits, but rather a collapse in tax revenues that occurred during the '*lost decades*'. During the first year of Abenomics, the government increased public spending, making the economy rebound and inflationary expectations soar. Since then, fiscal policy has been tightened, with one unwarranted and counterproductive tax hike followed by another during the autumn of 2019, which made inflationary expectations collapse. Although before the global financial crisis, Japan's rock-bottom interest rates represented a unique and bizarre phenomenon, that is no longer the case, as now it has over $12 trillion negative-yielding bonds – including some corporate bonds – flowing through the international system.[206]

Rather than raising taxes on consumption and damaging growth, Japan could instead be '*investing in infrastructure, clean energy and fertility incentives that would increase the expected population and revive sadly depopulated regions*'.[207]

In 2021–4, President Fumio Kishida applied his economic policy programme or '*Kishidanomics*' stratagem. President Kishida vowed to replace the previous administration's neoliberal policies, which led to growing inequality in Japanese society, in order to generate and establish a '*new Japanese capitalism*'. The new Japanese capitalism distributed the profits of the nation's companies and firms more equitably among their employees, customers and sub-contractors. Despite the administration's modifications that drifted away from neoliberal policies, critics have

[203] Trading Economics.com. *Japan General Government Gross Debt to GDP.* https://tradingeconomics.com/japan/government-debt-to-gdp#:~:text=In%20the%20long%2Dterm%2C%20the,according%20to%20our%20econometric%20models.

[204] Nikkei Asian Review. TASKER, P. *Modern Monetary Theory Threatens Revolution in Economic Thinking,* pgs 2–3. https://asia.nikkei.com/Opinion/Modern-Monetary-Theory-threatens-revolution-in-economic-thinking

[205] Ibid, pg 3.

[206] Ibid, pgs 3–4.

[207] Ibid, pg 5.

pointed out that the Kishidanomics strategy was very similar in its approach to the Abenomics programme, and Japan therefore carried on along the same monetary and fiscal path[208]

Since 2024, President Shigeru Ishiba is through his Ishibanomics programme likewise following the same economic policy direction. President Ishiba announced that his *'administration will inherit the Kishida administration's policy'*, although there will be some changes in economic policy, most especially related to raising the corporate tax rate, increasing tax rates on investment income and changes connected to the nuclear energy sector.[209]

Stakeholder Capitalism vs Progressive Capitalism

Stirring the very murky neoliberal waters even more, at the underlying academic sector, *'Stakeholder Capitalism'*, is also being increasingly challenged and contested by new revised forms of capitalism, which are being progressively pressed forward in order to replace it.

Ever since the 1980s switch to the free market economy and financial monetary system, economic liberalism or liberal capitalism acquired at the same time a new hybrid form – '*neoliberal free-market capitalism*' – which is also known as *'stakeholder'* or *'shareholder capitalism'*, *'rentier capitalism'*, *'rent-seeking capitalism'* or '*corporate rent-seeking*'. Throughout its years of existence, stakeholder capitalism has equally gained itself much unpopularity, with many countering capitalist reformulations gaining more recognition both academically and in international fora.

One of the main revised capitalist undercurrents is '*Progressive Capitalism*'.[210] Widely promoted by Nobel Laureate in Economics Joseph Stiglitz, progressive capitalism provides a completely different approach to capitalism, offering instead an improved variant to substitute the current neoliberal stakeholder capitalism. It has been increasingly popularized by the US House of Representatives, Republican Ro Khanna,

[208] Center for Strategic and Contemporary Policy. REDMAN, A. *Kishidanomics – The Economic Policies of Fumio Kishida*. https://cscr.pk/explore/themes/politics-governance/kishidanomics-the-economic-policies-of-fumio-kishida/

[209] NOMURA. Economic Research View. MATSUMOTO, A. *Mr. Shigeru Ishiba Becomes the New Prime Minister*. https://www.google.es/url?sa=t&source=web&rct=j&opi=89978449&url=https://global.nomura-am.co.jp/latest-news/pdf/ecv20240930.pdf&ved=2ahUKEwiu9ZXkt6aPAxWbVqQEHWrNMa8QFnoECBUQAQ&usg=AOvVaw1I5z8mui1ta6wPvjg1wes5

[210] Another proposal flowing against neoliberal free-market capitalism is – *Anarcho-Capitalism* –, which is ironically being pressed forward by Milton Friedman's son, David Friedman.

and since 2020 it also forms part of much of the debate at the World Economic Forum, held at Davos.[211]

Running in parallel to the critique surrounding neoliberalism, Joseph Stiglitz argues that both time and experience have clearly demonstrated that *'the neoliberal fantasy that unfettered markets will deliver prosperity to everyone'*[212] has been totally false. Pretty much as erroneous and off-track as Francis Fukuyama's predictions in his book *'The End of History and the Last Man'*, which held that after the fall of the Iron Curtain, countries would be living as liberal democracies with capitalist societies.[213]

In complete divergence from the neoliberal minimalist role of the state or the socialist command-and-control role of the state, progressive capitalism strongly holds that the state should have an enabling role in the economy. Progressive capitalism sways far from stakeholder capitalism, firmly believing instead in a tripartite partnership between the federal government, the private business sector and the academic sector's research universities. It holds that such a triple alliance would fuel growth, with strategic investments increasing both the demand and supply of well-paid jobs. It also believes that the partnership would create and generate new technology, as well as provide ad hoc launch-pads for new growing businesses.[214]

Progressive capitalism has a very critical perception of capitalism and the various forms it has acquired through time, and thus proposes instead an innovative and much more refined and balanced version of it. Throughout history, capitalism has acquired four different and distinctive forms, having today mutated into yet another new hybrid form. Originally, from the sixteenth until the eighteenth century, '*mercantilism*' and its first manifestation of '*developmentalism*' gave birth to the first form of '*capitalism*', which was perceived as *'developmental capitalism'*. During the nineteenth century, capitalism was transformed once more into '*economic liberalism*' or '*liberal capitalism*'. After the Second Industrial Revolution, although Marx believed capitalism would turn into socialism, capitalism, however, changed for a third time into '*techno-bureaucratic capitalism*'. After 1945, capitalism morphed once more into its fourth form, '*socio-developmental capitalism*', thereby establishing the Golden Age of Capitalism. Lastly, since the 1980s, capitalism has mutated into its current hybrid form, – *'neoliberal free-market capitalism'* or *'stakeholder capitalism'*.[215]

[211] *The New York Times*. STIGLITZ, J. *Progressive Capitalism Is Not an Oxymoron*. https://www.nytimes.com/2019/04/19/opinion/sunday/progressive-capitalism.html
[212] Ibid, pg 4.
[213] Ibid.
[214] STIGLITZ, J. *People, Power and Profits: Progressive Capitalism for an Age of Discontent;* and, SAINSBURY, D. *Progressive Capitalism: How to Achieve Economic Growth, Liberty and Social Justice.*
[215] BRESSER-PEREIRA, L.C. *The Two Forms of Capitalism: Developmentalism and Economic Liberalism*, pgs 1–2. http://www.rep.org.br/PDF/149-2.PDF

Although originally, contemporary economic liberalism or liberal capitalism was considered the capitalism of business entrepreneurs, it has today, nonetheless, metamorphosed into yet another new type of hybrid in the form of '*capitalism of rentiers and financiers*'.[216] The current hybrid form of capitalism is the exact type of capitalism progressive capitalism is most critical of. Progressive capitalism has been mainly constructed over the solid bedrock of its chastising critique against the present-day stakeholder capitalism.[217] It equally chided US President Trump's largess to corporations for providing continuation to it, as well as continues to do so in a much more intensified way in view of the newly reinvigorated agenda of the second Trump administration. The new kind of alternative capitalism pressed forward by progressive capitalism, involves, at the same time, a careful and delicate balance formed between government, markets and civil society.[218] As Stiglitz has pointed out, '*progressive capitalism is not an oxymoron, we can indeed channel the power of the market to serve society*'.[219]

Progressive capitalism considers both neoliberalism and neo-nationalism as the main culprits, which have respectively put into practice and continued the type of free-market capitalism that has gradually warped the US social fabric. The sort of liberal capitalism both models have promoted and still promote created the stakeholder capitalist hybrid, which in turn established the present-day '*morally corrupting and self-defeating economic dogma which threatens the future of American capitalism*'.[220]

When in 1980 President Reagan began the process of neoliberalization, an increasing global competition and a flattening stock market made CEOs put into practice the currently established hybrid type of shareholder capitalism, which prioritized investor returns. In turn, since the new practice often required the help of government to achieve the radical transformation of the workings of capitalism, it ended spawning '*a new corporate agenda rooted in spurring deregulation, reducing taxes, fighting unionization, slashing benefits, vitiating antitrust enforcement, pursuing corporate consolidation, transferring the workforce overseas or into nonunion jobs, and incentivizing CEOs for maximizing shareholder value – if necessary, by suppressing wages or firing workers*'.[221]

Consequently, while the stock market rose, corporations equally began amassing lots of economic and political power, CEOs and Wall Street stock-brokers and dealmakers became '*financial stars*' and '*celebrities*', and progressively, American capitalism began

[216] Ibid.

[217] The Bulwark. NORTH PATTERSON, R. *The Case for Progressive Capitalism*. https://thebulwark.com/the-case-for-progressive-capitalism/

[218] *The New York Times*. STIGLITZ, J. *Progressive Capitalism Is Not an Oxymoron*. https://www.nytimes.com/2019/04/19/opinion/sunday/progressive-capitalism.html

[219] Ibid.

[220] The Bulwark. NORTH PATTERSON, R. *The Case for Progressive Capitalism*, pg 3. https://thebulwark.com/the-case-for-progressive-capitalism/

[221] Ibid, pg 2.

increasingly dominating the world economy. However, such a change of waters was based on three basic principles: *'that government regulation and taxation prevented corporate America from competing; that the sole purpose of public corporations was to optimize returns to investors; and that moral or societal concerns about income inequality, worker insecurity, and the maldistribution of wealth were antithetical to economic growth'.*[222] It was such a set of principles, together with the *'comforting mythology of supply-side economics'* and its assurance that the cutting of taxes would be self-rewarding since it would spur economic growth, which is mostly blamed for poisoning the economic system.[223]

The subsequent economic evolution along neoliberal dynamics made things go from bad to worse, with disparities beginning to ever-widen. Dislocations were accelerated by ensuing macroeconomic changes, *'which gutted industrial and clerical work, rewarded automation, confined growth to technologically-skilled workers, and introduced the "gig economy." Employment grew quickest in low-wage jobs. Mass employers such as Walmart paid non–supervisory workers a fraction of what General Motors had paid 50 years earlier – because they could'.*[224]

Inevitably, both corporate size and power became an economic and political problem since the swelling of private power was accompanied by much economic concentration in some of the most relevant sectors, like, amongst others, the financial, the media, the airline, the telecommunications and the information platform sectors. Concurrently, corporations turned into and became '*people*', with their own right to spend unlimited amounts of money to influence public policy, which, in turn, through their huge political spending and aggressive lobbying, became insulated from the consequences of democracy. That way and progressively, economic power gradually turned into and became political power.[225]

All-combined, corporate and shareholder domination have fed and nurtured a general lowering of moral and ethical norms. With the instalment by corporate and financial institutions of a phalanx of politicians to carry out their bidding, many Republicans are committed to the protection of corporate interests and the pressing forward of their agendas. Many Democratic candidates *'elevate liberalism on social issues over concern with concentrated power in corporate America'.*[226]

Consequentially, smaller businesses have also become infected, very often showing little or no concern for broader societal problems, such as climate change, healthcare, education, immigration and infrastructure. The 2007–15 global financial crisis

[222] Ibid, pg 3.
[223] Ibid.
[224] Ibid.
[225] Ibid.
[226] Ibid, pg 4.

provided an excellent reflection of the overall moral and ethical deterioration that has taken place, clearly mirroring how *'greed metastasised into a real estate bubble driven by financial manipulation and predatory lending'*.[227]

> *Capitalism as currently practiced erodes the basic trust and cohesion a healthy commonweal requires. Without that, civil society becomes uncivil; our politics polarized, partisan and paranoid. This results in the dysfunctional governance exemplified first by the Tea party and later by the election of Donald Trump.*[228]

Paradoxically, with corporate interests having acquired much more power and influence, antitrust laws, which used to prevent private enterprises from becoming too big to control, have in fact diminished. *'In addition to stifling competition, limiting innovation, retarding new businesses, and concentrating corporate power over important marketplaces, large corporations began dictating the terms of existence for ordinary people – which often included further depressing wages and benefits.'*[229] Big technological companies, like Google and Facebook, are particularly noteworthy of such consolidation of power instead of its dispersal, through mainly the monopolization of the collective mind, in order to influence opinion, events and outcomes.[230]

In stark contrast, whereas small businesses have drastically shrunk in both numbers as well as market share, starting new businesses has become much harder, with the number of new firms launched annually since 1980, having decreased by about two thirds.[231]

Another reason for the unequal share of economic growth has been the political subjugation of labour.[232] In general, there has been a huge decline of private sector labour union membership; a proliferation of *'state right-to-work law, which eviscerate worker bargaining power'*,[233] together with much underpayment and exploitation; the predomination of concerns of the educated urban professional class well above those of blue-collar workers; a decline of worker morale and productivity; a very uneven share of profits, as well as an increase of the fear of workers of losing of jobs.[234]

At the same time, predatory financial institutions and '*white-collar criminals*' have become immune to the law. While the widespread deregulation led to the establishment of banking '*Wild-West-style*' malpraxis allowing banks and financial institutions to

[227] Ibid.
[228] Ibid.
[229] Ibid.
[230] Ibid.
[231] Ibid.
[232] Ibid.
[233] Ibid, pg 5.
[234] Ibid.

become '*too big to fail*', the whole bacchanalia ultimately culminated in the 'Neoliberal Crisis', which ironically, even entitled banks to a government bailout at the expense of the public.[235]

Due to its mere nature, shareholder capitalism is perceived as being psychologically pathological. The emphases placed upon stakeholder value, have driven corporate buybacks '*intended to decrease the supply of publicly available shares, driving up price. This corporate obsession with satiating shareholders breeds a myopic focus on short-term quarterly results, stinting research and development, incentivizing splashy acquisitions, and reducing employees to disposable items of expense while inviting CEOs to gorge themselves on stock options*'.[236]

Inevitably, shareholder capitalism has also exacerbated income inequality much more, making the present-day concentration of income equal that of the Roaring 1920s, the precursor to the Great Depression. During the '*last five decades the top 1 per cent of Americans have nearly doubled their share of national income … America's top 10 per cent now average more than nine times as much income as the bottom 90 per cent; the top 1 per cent average 39 times as much; the top 0.1 per cent a stunning 188 times*'.[237] As a result, the US wealth gap has likewise been widened. '*The richest 1 per cent of Americans now hold more wealth than the bottom 95 per cent; the net worth of the top 10 per cent represents 70 per cent of overall household wealth. The bottom 50 per cent have virtually no net worth – the number actually approaches zero – and their share of our percentage of total wealth diminished by three-quarters in the last 30 years.*'[238]

Aggregate GDP can no longer measure the overall economic well-being of the American population. The country has wrought a '*new Gilded Age where the benefits of economic growth are being distributed more unequally than any time since before the economic reforms of the Progressive Era and the New Deal*'.[239] The oversized political influence of corporations and the wealthy have enhanced the situation much more, with ongoing changes in the tax code, such as '*cuts in the upper income tax rate, a lower capital gains rate, and slashes in the estate tax*'.[240]

The way in which corporate structures have evolved has also provided CEOs with the ability to shape their own governance boards, and thus fix their own salaries – numbers which are not in any way driven by the market or let alone a reward for enhancing worker security or looking after common concerns.[241]

[235] Ibid.
[236] Ibid.
[237] Ibid.
[238] Ibid, pg 6.
[239] Ibid.
[240] Ibid.
[241] Ibid.

The ethos of shareholder capitalism has equally spawned a ridiculous disparity in executive compensation. While '*the average CEO of the 350 largest public companies earns $15 million a year – 271 times that of the average worker in those companies*',[242] on top of executive salaries averaging in 2017, US$422,500 per annum, '*Wall Street banks gave $31.4 billion in bonuses to their roughly 177,000 New York-based employees*'.[243]

The tectonic shift of income from labour to capital guzzles its supposed benefits, thereby creating much the same disincentives as classical Marxism. The reformation of the capitalist system is even being promoted by hard-core capitalists, like Michael Bloomberg, who perceives: '*Today, Americans are questioning whether those in the private sector – and in Washington – can provide the moral leadership our country needs, both economically and politically. They see the rewards of the economy increasingly concentrated at the top. They see wealthy parents scamming the college admissions process. They see families unable to afford healthcare and housing in the world's richest country. They see decades of discrimination based on race and ethnicity trapping another generation into poverty. And they wonder: Is our economic system breaking down?*'.[244]

Bloomberg also curses shareholder capitalism, by reflecting on his own company's more humane '*modus operandi*': '*If and when you wind up in an executive position, don't make one of the fundamental mistakes I see businesses and boards make all the time: under-valuing your labor force – and overcompensating CEOs. Management often treats workers like widgets – which they are not. And boards treat CEOs like irreplaceable geniuses, which they rarely are. At Bloomberg, we pay employees very well, we invest in their training and education, and we offer industry-leading benefits. In return: Our employees pay us back ten-fold with their dedication and loyalty. And there is no better way to strengthen capitalism than to give people a greater stake in its success.*'[245]

Even though President Trump's substitution of neoliberalism for neo-nationalism did produce some record-breaking socioeconomic results, his economic approach however continued fuelling shareholder capitalism, mainly through the largess it provided corporations with. Despite Trump's neo-nationalism being orientated towards the improvement of the lifestyles of '*farmers, ranchers, energy workers, factory workers, and American workers in all 50 states*',[246] the 2017 TCJA introduced by Trump turbocharged economic inequities a lot more.[247] While his so-called act of '*fiscal profligacy*', pumped up the US deficit for the sole benefit of corporations and the wealthy, it was however justified by the resuscitation of '*the discredited notion*

[242] Ibid.
[243] Ibid.
[244] Ibid, pg 2.
[245] Ibid, pg 7.
[246] The White House. Economy. *Remarks by President Trump at a Signing Ceremony for the United States-Mexico-Canada Trade Agreement.* https://www.whitehouse.gov/briefings-statements/remarks-president-trump-signing-ceremony-united-states-mexico-canada-trade-agreement/
[247] The Bulwark. NORTH PATTERSON, R. *The Case for Progressive Capitalism*, pg 7. https://thebulwark.com/the-case-for-progressive-capitalism/

that under-taxing "wealth creators" stimulated the economy while paying for itself'.[248] Through the new Trump administration's readjustment of the 2017 tax cuts for big corporations and the ultra-rich, shareholder capitalism has once again been re-fuelled and extremely turbo-charged by Trump.

> *The bill distributed more than 80 per cent of its individual benefits to the top 1 per cent of households; the bulk of the $150 billion rebated to corporations in 2018 funded shareholder dividends and stock buy-backs – which amounted to little more than a gift to the 10 per cent of Americans who own 84 per cent of all stocks.*[249]

Throughout the last forty years, an increasingly impermeable class system has been created and firmly established, which today still over-privileges the top 10 per cent, having allowed it to become a species of its own. On one hand, the '*financial aristocracy*' enjoys '*privileged zip codes that imply shorter commutes, higher life expectancy, stronger networks, lower crime rates, and better public schools*'.[250] On the other hand, political influence enables residents the thwarting of housing projects that would allow the upgrading of others.[251]

The elite's '*happy bubble*' even provides it with secure insulation for intermarriage and longer lasting families, as well as with many more privileges for its children like '*legacy admissions*', private schools, camps, personal tutors, lessons and school stationary. All-combined, elite education likewise and consequently produces incredibly higher lifetime earnings.[252]

Despite the Trump-induced economic change of guard, Americans still intensely feel that the current practice of democracy and capitalism is inimical to collective interests. '*The middle class struggles and the poor suffer. Less-educated whites increasingly suffer death by class. Poor people die from suicide, substance abuse, or neglected health. Satisfaction with life is rising among the affluent, declining among those below.*'[253]

The '*cosmic failure*' of shareholder capitalism is that it has erased the belief in the workings of the market economy as beneficial for rising generations. The American future has been blighted by progressive polarization, the loss of communal sentiment, together with increased feelings of political irrelevance and civic indifference. Although shareholder capitalists insist that such malignancies are the '*inescapable by-product of a free-market economy*', which is the best way to make the macro economy grow, they are

[248] Ibid.
[249] Ibid.
[250] Ibid.
[251] Ibid.
[252] Ibid, pg 8.
[253] Ibid.

not, however, the residues of '*free-market magic*', but the deliberate past made policy choices of lawmakers.[254]

The past promotion of the free-market through the utilization of government in order to serve corporate interests and objectives has eroded many other communal and corporate concerns. While there is so much rent-seeking at play that few markets can really be considered to be truly and absolutely '*free*', a constellation of incentives characterises the current version of the shareholder capitalist system.[255]

The long-standing '*pernicious myth*' that unregulated free-markets would automatically self-correct problems has proven to be totally false. The problem with free-markets is that free-markets for '*widgets*' will only provide a Pareto optimum for the production and sale of more widgets – but not everything in the world is simply a widget or let alone revolves around them. Without assistance and supervision, markets cannot by themselves assure that insurance, healthcare, safety, primary education, common property or large-scale research and development are orientated towards public interest in an equal manner. Even for widgets, nothing lasts forever, as sooner or later markets end up being distorted by monopolies and externalities. The free-market should be both a means and an end – not simply an end state, of or in itself. The free-market is an end state, but one which can only be achieved by way of a very delicate act of balancing.[256]

In view of the decadence of the liberal capitalist system, progressive capitalism aims to break away from the shareholder capitalism of the past forty years in order to restore a proper and equitable societal balance. The conceptual structure of progressive capitalism has been built over the premise of its acid-sharp critique towards shareholder capitalism. It rests upon the assumption that the restoration of societal balance should be based on '*recognising that private enterprise is the core of a broadly successful economy, but that the ideology of supposedly-unfettered markets underpinning shareholder capitalism – abetted, in reality, by subjective public policy choices – is inefficient, destabilizing, and far from inevitable*'.[257]

In complete deviation from rentier capitalism, progressive capitalism has designed a newer and much more refined form of capitalism, which aims to increase both economic growth and well-paid jobs for Americans. Joseph Stiglitz, in his book, '*People, Power, and Profits: Progressive Capitalism for an Age of Discontent*', explains how progressive improvements of capitalism would achieve a much more dynamic economy, with greater shared prosperity and uplifted socio-economic levels. For Stiglitz, the true source of '*the wealth of a nation*', lies in the creativity and productivity of the nation's

[254] Ibid.
[255] Ibid.
[256] Ibid, pg 9.
[257] Ibid, pg 10.

people, as well as in the productive interactions, which they carry out with each other and with the nation's institutions. Progressive capitalism would therefore enable better results for society and families, rather than mere alternatives, such as the command-and-control role of traditional socialism or the concentrating results of today's free-market capitalism, which tends to redirect benefits towards the economic elite, thus marginalizing the economic majority.[258]

The credo of progressive capitalism rests on the following set of basic precepts:

- *That oppressive corporate power can be just as suffocating as oppressive government;*
- *That properly understood, government should be a check on private excess, not its co-conspirator;*
- *That … there is no single formula for distributing the fruits of prosperity, no abstract mechanism that compels it;*
- *That secure and fairly-paid workers are not capitalism's antagonists, but its customers;*
- *That therefore … there is no "big trade-off" between fairness and growth, between equality and efficiency. We don't have to tolerate levels of inequality that offend our moral instincts for our economy to remain prosperous and competitive. If we want to have a bigger pie, it won't hurt to divide the slices more evenly. In fact it is likely to make the supply even bigger.*[259]

Constructed over such precepts, progressive capitalism firmly believes that the state should have an empowering role in the economy, based upon a solid tripartite partnership between the federal government, the private business sector and the academic sector's research universities. It upholds that such a triple alliance would fuel growth, with strategic investments increasing both the demand and supply of well-paid jobs. Consequently, such a partnership would in turn also create and generate new technology, as well as provide launch-pads for new growing businesses.[260]

Progressive capitalism revolves around four main defining tenets:

1. *The central role businesses play in the economy requires for success that they invest in their employees, protect the environment, support their communities, deal fairly and ethically with their suppliers, and increase value for shareholders;*
2. *The important role of institutions providing public goods and services, including: infrastructure, research, schools, health care, social insurance, taxation, labor law and regulation of;*
3. *The need for the state to be involved in their design;*

[258] STIGLITZ, J. *People, Power and Profits: Progressive Capitalism for an Age of Discontent.*

[259] The Bulwark. NORTH PATTERSON, R. *The Case for Progressive Capitalism*, pg 10. https://thebulwark.com/the-case-for-progressive-capitalism/

[260] STIGLITZ, J. *People, Power and Profits: Progressive Capitalism for an Age of Discontent*; and, SAINSBURY, D. *Progressive Capitalism: How to Achieve Economic Growth, Liberty and Social Justice.*

4. *The advocacy of social justice, defined as fairness (the assignment of rights and duties in the institutions of society, which enables all people both to receive the basic benefits of society and to contribute to obligations of society). Further advocacy for stewardship of natural resources and protection of the environment.*[261]

The philosophy of progressive capitalism acknowledges the crucial role of government in the protection of the environment; in investment in infrastructure; in technology; in research and education; in ensuring fair and undistorted competition, as well as in *'preventing corporations from exploiting workers, and guarding against the undue influence of powerful institutions and individuals who believe that their sole societal mission is to liberate themselves from all legal constraints and moral considerations'.*[262]

Progressive capitalists strongly believe that such a '*broader society consciousness*' would assure a secure and proper habitat for capitalism to thrive in an equitable manner, wherein altruism and self-interest would be allies and not enemies. For them, corporations can serve multiple purposes, such as *'rewarding investors; providing secure employment and retirement; developing new products; and paying taxes to the government which makes relatively frictionless commerce possible'.*[263]

The main purpose of progressive capitalism is to enrich America through the expansion of individual opportunity, without fostering a never-ending dependence on an '*overweening government*', as well as by diverging from the shareholder capitalist appropriation of government, which distorts society so much by further embedding inequality.[264]

> *The Progressive political economy … is based on a more realistic model of how the economy works. It doesn't only focus on the allocation of capital and labour in the economy, but also puts firms and entrepreneurs at the centre of the economy and focuses on their accumulation of organisational and technological capabilities. In addition, it recognises that institutions play a large role in the economy, as opposed to the institution-free world of neo-liberalism. For these reasons it is of much greater value to politicians and policy-makers trying to improve the well-being of their societies.*[265]

Progressive capitalism is increasingly gaining more and more recognition and support from active politicians, as well as in world economic fora. On one hand, it is being popularized in the United States by Republican Ro Khanna, who has publicly stated

[261] SAINSBURY, D. *Progressive Capitalism: How to Achieve Economic Growth, Liberty and Social Justice.*
[262] The Bulwark. NORTH PATTERSON, R. *The Case for Progressive Capitalism*, pg 10. https://thebulwark.com/the-case-for-progressive-capitalism/
[263] Ibid.
[264] Ibid, pg 11.
[265] SAINSBURY, D. *Progressive Capitalism: How to Achieve Economic Growth, Liberty and Social Justice*, pg 109.

that *'I call myself a progressive capitalist … I believe in free enterprise but free enterprise that rewards work and innovation, not just those privileged and connected and that I think is the recipe for both economic growth, innovation and for giving people a stake in the economy'.*[266]

On the other hand, both the 2020 and the 2021 World Economic Forum (WEF) held at Davos very clearly revealed the disenchantment felt by most countries with the dominant model of *'shareholder-first, profit-maximizing firms'.* More than fifty years ago, WEF founder and head, Klaus Schwab, argued zealously in favour of stakeholder capitalism, emphasizing that *'enterprises should be accountable for the interests of their customers, workers, communities, and the environment, as well as their shareholders'.*[267] From the 2020 meeting onwards, however, Milton Friedman's shareholder capitalism has been increasingly chided for directly leading to the multiple crises the world faces today.[268]

Summarizing the 2020 WEF, Joseph Stiglitz pointed out: 'In *speech after speech this year, business leaders and academics explained how Milton Friedman's successful advocacy of shareholder capitalism led directly to the crises we face today and the political divisions they have fueled. To be sure, recognition that there is a problem is necessary if we are to change course. But we also have to understand that the causes of societal maladies go beyond maximizing shareholder value. At the root of the problem is neoliberalism's excessive faith in markets and skepticism of government, which underpins a policy agenda focused on deregulation and tax cuts. After a 40-year experiment, we can declare it a failure. Growth has been lower, and most of the gains went to the top. While this should be obvious, there is no consensus among our business leaders … And yet some of the business leaders at Davos this year, especially those from Europe, seemed to have grasped the urgency of responding to climate change and the scope of what is needed. And some have actually taken giant strides, the tide has turned … In short, unfettered capitalism has played a central role in creating the multiple crises confronting our societies today. If capitalism is to work – if it is to address these crises and serve society – it can't do so in its current form. There must be a new kind of capitalism – what I have elsewhere called progressive capitalism, entailing a better balance of government, markets, and civil society.*'[269]

The 2021 WEF continued further rebuking shareholder capitalism, seriously questioning its future, as well as proposing newer, more refined, socialized or

[266] Fox Business. *How Progressive Capitalism Can Be the Recipe for Economic Growth and Innovation.* https://www.foxbusiness.com/politics/progressive-capitalism-is-the-recipe-for-economic-growth-and-innovation-california-rep-ro-khanna

[267] Columbia Business School. STIGLITZ, J. *Has Davos Man Changed?.* https://www8.gsb.columbia.edu/articles/chazen-global-insights/has-davos-man-changed

[268] Ibid.

[269] Ibid.

humanized revised forms of capitalism. Some of the new reformulations include most particularly '*inclusive capitalism*' and '*equitable capitalism*'.[270] Similarly, the 2023 WEF also pressed forward many more new ideas, stewarding other responsible forms of capitalism.[271]

Techno-Feudal Oligopolistic Capitalism

The academic sector's ongoing battle between *'stakeholder capitalism'* and other capitalist reformulations has recently been completely outshone by the bursting onto the international scene of new and very different, in-practice forms of capitalism, such as most particularly, President Trump's *'Techno-feudal oligopolistic capitalism'*, which is ripping across its landscape extremely hard.[272]

President Trump's second mandate, or as it is already been labelled, *'Trumpism 2.0'*, marks a fundamental shift of 'stakeholder capitalism' or global capitalism, as its recently generated 'techno-feudal oligopolistic capitalism' mixes and blends nationalist protectionism, corporate oligarchy and digital feudalism. In just six months, the United States has transitioned from a *'neutral state capitalism'* to a model that utilizes government policies explicitly in order to serve dominant private entities, thus eroding economic democracy and consolidating monopolistic power.[273]

Such a quick and drastic transformation is not only deepening domestic inequality, but has equally become the main driver of international economic fragmentation, trade wars and strategic decoupling. Although the Global South is asserting greater autonomy by way of challenging Western dominance, as well as reshaping economic alliances, if such trends persist, the coming decades may be defined by escalating geopolitical tensions, supply chain disruptions and financial instability. While some critics suggest that the new US political economy may be shifting towards a model resembling that of China under Xi Jinping, others perceive America to be emulating its rival in order to defend its interests, as well as to contain the rise of China.[274]

[270] World Economic Forum. *Chief Economists Outlook 2021.* http://www3.weforum.org/docs/WEF_Chief_Economists_Outlook_2021.pdf

[271] World Economic Forum. DAVOS 2023. *Davos 2023: What You Need to Know about Doing Better Business.* https://www.weforum.org/agenda/2023/01/better-business-stakeholder-capitalism-esg/

[272] European Center for Populism Studies. OZTURK, I. *Trump and the New Capitalism: Old Wine in New Bottle.* https://www.google.es/search?q=trump+old+wine+in+new+bottles&sca_esv=e7c1514da748dd1c&sxsrf=AE3TifOjDfDVfX2pcHwlupz3BUXmWBPogg%3A1756126046143&source=hp&ei=XlusaIn2Bca4hbIPnNqN6Ao&iflsig=AOw8s4IAAAAAaKxpbuN4sNcbTAnp_n_w9wGOqCo8naDi&oq=&gs_lp=Egdnd3Mtd2l6IgAqAggAMgcQIxgnGOoCMgcQIxgnGOoCMgcQIxgnGOoCMg0QIxjwBRgnGMkCGOoCMgcQIxgnGOoCMgcQIxgnGOoCMgcQIxgnGOoCMgcQIxgnGOoCMgcQIxgnGOoCMgcQIxgnGOoCSKkIUABYAHABeACQAQCYAQCgAQCqAQC4AQHIAQCYAgGgAh6oAgqYAx7xBYdKRgrY6z0okgcBMaAHALIHALgHAMIHAzQtMcgHGA&sclient=gws-wiz

[273] Ibid.

[274] Ibid.

The radical swing reflects that the United States has embarked on a very perilous journey, which, however, extends far beyond China. By shifting towards unilateralism, the United States is blatantly disregarding international norms and values, undermining the post-Second World War order it once created and championed, as well as abandoning the institutions and stakeholders that upheld its own system. Whereas it is drifting away from the principles of the rule of law and values, it is instead embracing arbitrariness and raw power – beginning to pose more as a global threat in contradiction of its mere raison d'être.[275]

With the United States' status as world leader in economics, finance, industry and technology being redefined, old certainties are giving way to a new, very uncertain reality. American symbols, which were once synonymous with American greatness, now merely represent the triumphs of a bygone era. The Statue of Liberty, probably the most powerful symbol of democracy of *'the land of freedom and opportunities ... of the fair, the strong and the wise'*, is slowly fading away – and so is the American Dream, with the long-standing promise of *'opportunities, prosperity and success'* becoming nothing but an increasingly unattainable illusion.[276]

The rejection by the Trump administration of the United States' past role as hegemonic leader and other sacrifices, together with its adoption of a unilateral emphasis on rhetoric such as *'America First'* or its new *'Global MAGA'* approach in order to protect the country's *'greatness'*, has already begun reshaping the nature of both capitalism and globalization. The *'new capitalism'*, which the United States has adopted in order to respond to ongoing global power pressures as well as to a very changing environment of competitive conditions, has already much de-stabilized the pre-established stakeholder capitalist order.[277]

Two eminent scholars, Fernand Braudel, an economic historian who focused on long-term structures, and Karl Polanyi, a political economist and anthropologist who analysed economic transformations, have provided fundamental critiques of capitalism concerning the state, power and institutions. While both Braudel and Polanyi converge in their critiques, exposing capitalism's reliance on state power and monopolistic control and its disruptive effects on society, they both view capitalism, when left unchecked, as a grave threat to market economies and open societies. The two thinkers perceive capitalism as often simply operating at the expense of a broader societal well-being and only benefitting elites, while at the same time fostering instability and social resistance.[278]

That is the case, most especially when the economy becomes *'dis-embedded'* from society and socially disruptive, and the adverse effects of non-market processes, such

[275] Ibid.
[276] Ibid.
[277] Ibid.
[278] Ibid.

as externalities and monopolization, begin appearing. With such circumstances always calling for state intervention in order to sustain markets, there are at present three different evolving variants of in-practice active capitalism across the international landscape, based on ownership structures and governance mechanisms: the China-Jinping model, the Turkey-Erdogan model and the US-Trump model. Out of the three active models, the US-Trump model is proving to be the newest, yet most aggressive form of capitalism, seriously ousting 'stakeholder capitalism', which has begun ripping hard across the system.[279]

The China-Jinping Model, *'State Capitalism with Strategic Planning'*, is a hybrid model that blends centralized planning with capitalist dynamics. Within such a model, *'State ownership dominates, yet specific industries operate with market-driven efficiency; despite their semi-independent façade, companies like Huawei and Alibaba align with national economic strategies; the government employs market forces for efficiency while maintaining overarching economic control'.*[280]

The Turkey-Erdogan Model, *'State-Controlled Oligarchic Capitalism'*, is a variant that merges authoritarian populism with capitalist oligarchy. Within such a variant *'the private sector's independence diminishes as the government integrates strategic industries into political control; state-backed business elites thrive through public contracts, incentives, and preferential credit; bureaucrats and politicians hold executive roles in private firms, aligning private enterprise with state agendas'.*[281]

The US-Trump Model, *'techno-feudal oligopolistic capitalism'*, clearly reflects that *'traditional neoliberalism is evolving into a state-elite partnership, with billionaire elites increasingly influence governance, making the state an agent of corporate interests'.*[282]

Whatever hybrid forms of capitalist models evolve, they all, however, underline the rise of *'strategic capitalism'*, diminishing market competition, increasing state-business convergence and greater government control over economic participants. In the United States, *'state capture by entrenched interest-seeking coalitions'* has become increasingly widespread and pervasive, most notably with capital having infiltrated the state through so-called *'legitimate lobbying'*, thereby effectively merging with the government. However and quite understandably, such practices raise many questions. For example, for whom exactly does the state intervene in the market? On whose behalf is the state intervening the market for? Who is the state really siding with or working for?[283]

At present, in the United States *'tech giants like Tesla, SpaceX, Facebook-Meta, and major media conglomerates serve as political tools for mass influence ... Stephen Schwarzman,*

[279] Ibid.
[280] Ibid.
[281] Ibid.
[282] Ibid.
[283] Ibid.

the chairman and CEO of Blackstone, Ana Botín, the executive chair of Banco Santander, Patrick Pouyanné, chairman and CEO of Total Energies, and Brian Moynihan, chair of the board and CEO of Bank of America, participated in a public dialogue with President Trump at the World Economic Forum's 2025 Annual Meeting, indicating a collaborative relationship. Additionally, US business leaders have significantly increased their financial support for President Trump's second inaugural fund, with contributions expected to surpass previous records. Major corporations such as BP, Chevron, Shell, Google, Microsoft, and Apple have adopted the term "Gulf of America" in their communications following President Trump's executive order renaming the Gulf of Mexico. This move signifies corporate alignment with the administration's directives.'[284]

Apart from such domestic political-economy implications of the evolving forms of capitalism, their various configurations are also considered as risky catalysts for conflict, most especially when they attempt to externalize emerging problems and challenges.[285] The main dimensions of problem externalization could take some of the following several forms:

***'Globalization's Externalities and National-Level Risks**: While globalization promotes economic interdependence, it has also resulted in significant negative externalities, such as income inequality, industrial decline, job displacement, and financial volatility.*

***The Shift from National Economic Regulation to External Blame**: Historically, economic nationalism has been used as a policy tool to protect domestic industries. However, the new wave of civilizational nationalism reframes economic struggles as existential conflicts between distinct cultural or civilizational blocs.*

***Civilizational Nationalism Increases the Likelihood of Conflict**: Economic nationalism has historically led to trade wars and economic decoupling. However, civilizational nationalism extends beyond economics, intertwining identity, culture, and geopolitics into economic policy, making conflicts more intense and less negotiable'.*[286]

Through the current trend of replacing domestic policy reform agendas, such as corporate taxation and labor protections, with blame-driven economic nationalism, governments are not only avoiding addressing the root causes of economic discontent, but also fuelling long-term geopolitical instability. If such trend continues, the world could experience an era of intensified trade wars, economic decoupling, and heightened geopolitical tensions (reminiscent of the 1930s), which will in turn increase the risk of larger-scale conflicts.[287]

Although President Trump's populist authoritarian and pragmatist rhetoric lacks a coherent theoretical foundation, his shift towards *'authoritarian capitalism'* is perceived

[284] Ibid.
[285] Ibid.
[286] Ibid.
[287] Ibid.

as *'a contradictory fusion of economic nationalism, protectionism, and populism'*, driven more by emotional appeal than analytical rigor. Drifting away from traditional neoliberalism, which was bred and nurtured in the United States promoting minimal state intervention, Trump's era is witnessing the convergence of state power with elite economic interests. Trump's protectionist policies, such as tariffs, tax cuts, de-regulation and re-industrialization in order to *'Make America Great'* again, or as they are being denominated, *'MAGAnomics'*, clearly reject core tenets of neoclassical economics, like most notably 'free trade and efficiency'. His approach is in perfect alignment with *'techno-feudalism'*, through which large technology firms exert immense economic and social control.[288]

As Nobel Laureate Joseph Stiglitz points out, *'there is already a high degree of market concentration in the US'*. While Trump was elected by appealing to a huge poor socio-economic segment that feels *'left behind and abandoned'*, extremely hypothetically, his policy framework is shaped in order to further enrich giant capital owners. Trump is not only serving the interests of capital, but is equally placing capitalists in key government positions. Although Trump's protectionist trade wars are framed in order to protect American jobs and boost employment and income, *'there is broad consensus among economists that these policies may primarily benefit select corporations at the expense of consumers and citizens'*.[289]

Amid the growing challenges of techno-feudalism, President Trump's rapidly evolving 'techno-feudal oligopolistic capitalism', has emerged as a new hybrid model with transcendental global implications, which combines the following aspects:

***'Nationalist Protectionism**: A more aggressive form of protectionism where the government prioritizes domestic industries and restricts foreign competition. For instance, Trump's decision to block the acquisition of United States Steel by the Japanese company Nippon Steel created tensions with Japan. Prime Minister Ishiba responded by saying that "the president blocking a takeover is a significant 'political interference' and difficult to understand." This could lead to a more insular, self-sufficient economy, with tariffs and trade barriers becoming more prevalent.*

***State capitalism**: A blend of state control and private enterprise, where the government is more active in guiding the economy. This could involve increased government ownership of key industries like energy, finance, or infrastructure.*

***Authoritarian Capitalism**: A system where the government exercises significant control over the economy, often through a combination of state-owned enterprises, regulations, and repression of dissent. This could lead to a more rigid, hierarchical economy with limited opportunities for entrepreneurship and innovation.*

[288] Ibid.
[289] Ibid.

Neoliberalism 2.0: *A revised version of the neoliberal ideology that dominated the 1980s and 1990s. This could involve a renewed emphasis on deregulation, privatization, and free trade but with a more aggressive approach to suppressing labor unions and social welfare programs.*

Corporate-Friendly Populism: *A system where the government prioritizes the interests of large corporations and wealthy elites while using populist rhetoric to appeal to working-class voters. This could lead to a more unequal economy, with greater concentrations of wealth and power.*

Hybrid Capitalism: *A system that combines elements of different economic models, such as state-led development, private enterprise, and social welfare programs. This could involve a more nuanced approach to monetary policy, focusing on balancing competing interests and promoting sustainable growth'.*

Although President Trump's 'trade wars' were initially seen as a simple commercial battle with China, it has become clear that Trump's ambitions go much further and beyond than the Confucian confines. Disregarding the extent of the cost of 'corporate feudalism' to the economy and society's well-being, *'the US will likely turn to asymmetric power, military force, and destructive nationalist and civilizational rhetoric to balance, conceal, legitimize, and make it acceptable. Trump's broad and aggressive stance and his confrontational rhetoric extending beyond trade wars are likely to leave the US deprived mainly of the allies it seeks'.*

In the age of multipolarity, global capitalism is no longer a cohesive system under US hegemony. While there are currently three in-practice active competing forms of capitalism with different norms and values, *'the fact that politicians come to power using right-wing populist rhetoric and then cede substantial control to capital rather than monitoring, directing, and engaging it in government for the benefit of the people underscores the volatile, elusive, and inherently dangerous nature of populist discourse'.*

Under *'Trumpism 2.0.'*, the rising capitalism is not thriving on traditional economic logic, but more on perceptions of cultural and economic displacement. Through President Trump's explicit favouritism towards specific corporations and billionaires, he has blatantly shifted towards oligarchic capitalism (techno-feudalism) or 'techno-feudal oligopolistic capitalism', which signals a transition from *'neutral state capitalism'* to a *'system where the government actively serves dominant private entities'.* While such a brusque shift undermines market competition, as well as reduces economic democracy, it likewise fosters monopolistic tendencies. At the same time, Trump is equally intending to *'export or externalise significant problems of the US economy, such as the ever-rising income inequality, chronic and systemic corruption caused by the rise of "robber barons," and financial risks, to the "rest" of the world via "beggar thy neighbor policies"'.*

In the midst of such a new emerging conflict, the digital economy, technology wars and financial sanctions have become key instruments. However, under Trump's approach, the current global fragmentation and the new Cold War environment have evolved way beyond a simple polarization between the West and the China-Russia axis. The struggle is no longer just between the centre (West) and the periphery (Global South) – it has now equally become a struggle within the Global South and the West. If global fragmentation and its effects persist, *'the global economy may enter an era of trade wars, financial decoupling, and economic fragmentation'*.

The Geo-economic Reconfiguration and Its Geopolitical Realignment

The ongoing clash between the neoliberal model and the neo-national model has in turn and inevitably, produced many strategic displacements within the system, which have instigated a huge geo-economic reconfiguration, as well as generated a big geopolitical tectonic shift and realignment across the international landscape. Together with other exacerbating factors, such as the US-China trade war, the Russia-Ukraine war, increasing tensions in the Middle East, plus the escalating military tension between China and Taiwan, the aspect of the international landscape is changing very rapidly and will regrettably continue doing so in an increasing way.

With the structure of the NLWO having lost the unwavering allegiance and full support of one of its main founding pillars – the United States – it has been left severely destabilized and weakened. Consequently, the destabilization of the NWLO has produced an enormous geo-economic reconfiguration, which has in turn, generated a big geopolitical realigment. The US context clearly reflects that while much of the political focus has been placed upon economic questions and issues, it has been, however, greatly fuelled by culture wars in a world that is changing very rapidly. *'We have entered a new phase in international affairs, leaving behind us the brief moment characterised by untrammelled American dominance'.*[290] The recent centrifugal tendencies of the United States in international and regional economic structures have generated a whole new geopolitical scenario with a number of very distinctive features. With the new geo-economic reality orbiting around the asymmetric bipolarity established by the US and China, new and differing geopolitical strategic alignments are in turn being formed and established, equally assisted by new geopolitical rules of the game.[291]

Ever since the outbreak of the US-China trade war, the geo-economic landscape has been changing very much due to the new patterns of economic integration, which have simultaneously begun rapidly evolving, although it is still not clear whether the

[290] Brookings. JONES, B. *The New Geopolitics*, pg 1. https://www.brookings.edu/blog/order-from-chaos/2017/11/28/the-new-geopolitics/
[291] Ibid, pg 2.

deepening of economic integration truly renders geopolitical competition benign. A few of the new developing patterns are represented by the Canada-EU trade agreement, Japan's efforts to exert free trade leadership in Asia and the expansion of Sino-German economic ties. Although economic integration can raise the stakes in great power relations, it can however do so in both stabilizing ways and in distorting ones, most especially with the rapid ascendance of neo-nationalism. Because of the scale of global economic growth over the past three decades, there are now many more countries whose political and economic internal direction and external relations are impacting very heavily on regional and global dynamics.[292]

With China being widely perceived as the next twenty-first century up and rising world economic hegemon, the ongoing US-China trade war has begun projecting a new geopolitical scenario, which is predominantly defined by the '*Thucydides Trap*'[293] that the two superpowers have fallen into. With many of the world's biggest economies having begun re-evaluating their security relationship with the United States, much geopolitical competition has likewise been instigated. On one hand, several major countries have started deciding whether the United States is still reliable for the proper maintenance of inter-state security in their region, by either balancing China's rise in Asia, containing Iran in the Middle East or curtailing Russian aggression in Europe, and whether or not, they should hence seek the continuation or the deepening of their alignment with it. On the other hand, if such countries were to decide that the United States is no longer reliable, they will undoubtedly resort to either seeking '*self-help*' (in the form of nuclear weapons rearmament) or '*warmer ties with China*'.[294]

Other very prominent examples of the newly reconfigured geopolitical scenario are also exemplified by Russia-Ukraine war; the escalation of the military tension between China and Taiwan; the military tension between the United States and North Korea; the struggle between the European project with a growing neo-nationalist movement; Poland's abandonment of liberalism; Germany's evolving stance in Europe; Britain's endeavours rebalancing national control and regional integration; Saudi Arabia's efforts in shaking up the regional balance of power; the evolving search of Iran and Turkey for partners and patrons, as well as the continuing distrust between Japan and the Republic of Korea shaping and constraining their approaches to China's growing assertive influence. Additional patterns that are more distant from the '*great power muscle movements*', but which will also fundamentally shape the prospects for peace

[292] Ibid, pg 4.

[293] The '*Thucydides Trap*' refers to the tense structural situation created by the rise of a new superpower, such as China, threatening to displace an established one, like the United States. Although in theory, such tension ultimately ends in war, it does not necessarily always have to end that way. (The *Thucydides Trap* is analogous to the clash created between Greece and the rise of Sparta, which led to the Peloponnesian War from 431 to 404 BC). Foreign Policy. ALLISON, G. *The Thucydides Trap.* https://foreignpolicy.com/2017/06/09/the-thucydides-trap/

[294] Brookings. JONES, B. *The New Geopolitics,* pg 3. https://www.brookings.edu/blog/order-from-chaos/2017/11/28/the-new-geopolitics/

and economic development in the Western Hemisphere, are likewise provided by the recent Latin American anti-neoliberal swing, as well as Israel's courtship of Russia.[295]

The new geopolitical setting has correspondingly also introduced new rules of the game. For example, depending on the type of state participating in the renewed landscape of geopolitical competition, differing techniques and instruments are being utilized for the new game in play. Advanced economies are carrying out an '*insidious game of confront and conceal, with cyber intrusions, discreet or disguised financial influence, and disinformation to influence or disrupt an opponent's internal politics*'.[296] In less advanced economies, the new technique chosen by great powers is based on the combination of large-scale infrastructure spending with political pressure and corruption, '*while counter-corruption campaigns are the vehicle for domestic purges*'.[297] In politically unstable countries, such as Syria and Yemen, there has even been a re-emergence of the '*old-fashioned proxy warfare*', largely based on '*the flow of money, weapons, intelligence, and political support to national or sub-national or even trans-national military units fighting for control of politics or territory in an active conflict, with potentially devastating human cost*'.[298]

With every major country feeling its way through the shifting contours of the new geopolitical landscape, together with the Thucydides Trap established between the United States and China, many doubts and queries have begun to abound. Most of the uncertainty mainly rotates around what exact roles the United States and China intend to end up playing in shaping the future of globalization, what exact type of economy will characterise the near-future and many other security issues. Will we carry on along the old free trade dynamics, with goods produced in one country being traded in others, or will we start thriving forwards based much more on the new '*global supply and value chains that repeatedly crisscross national borders?*'.[299] Are we going to try to '*hold back the tides of global economic production, or will we learn to swim in the newly contested waters?*'.[300]

The new contemporary geopolitical scenario equally poses many other new threats and security dilemmas, which affect the future of the international security architecture, through which most new strategies and operations are implemented. With much critique surrounding the existing system of burden sharing, for many, NATO and the overall security architecture, is also in complete misalignment with the changing balance of power and the new threats the world confronts.[301]

295 Ibid, pgs 3–4.
296 Ibid, pg 4.
297 Ibid, pg 5.
298 Ibid.
299 Ibid, pg 6.
300 Ibid.
301 Ibid, pg 7.

The recent huge shift in US-transatlantic relations also implies that the EU will have to be extremely weary as to how it reacts to the new panorama. Europeans should respond in kind, reshape the rules-based order to salvage what they can, fight back against the assault on their democratic model, resist coercion, as well as diversify away from the United States. With the Trumpinian fog having settled in thick, Europeans need to stand their ground and adopt a more confrontational strategy.

Some of the adversarial strategies that the EU could retaliate with that are being pressed forward by the European Council on Foreign Relations include: the need for Europeans to reinvent multilateralism, which have become too reliant on an eighty-year-old order that is being dismantled by Trump; the need for Europeans to work with other states as well – whether they are traditional allies, leaders from the Global South or even China – in order to apply their institutional creativity, such as the multiple formats that have been developed for horizontal cooperation, onto their continent; the need for Europeans to help NATO evolve, given the overarching goal of the Trump administration to renegotiate its terms in the alliance; the need for Europeans to likewise fight back hard against MAGA America's efforts to transform their democracies; the need for the EU to equally open its doors to US and international researchers, activists, NGOs and businesses. Lastly, Europeans are likewise highly recommended to *de-risk* from the United States, in order to be able to resist potential coercive attempts, to diversify their partners, as well as build resilience by rallying countries that belong to the community of liberal democracies.[302]

Caught in the middle of such a new-fangled geopolitical threshold, the choices that the United States is making in relation to its role and interests in such an increasingly competitive world are already reverberating extremely loudly through the new landscape, which is undoubtedly leading us '*either to a situation of tense stability or to a more dramatic, and probably violent, re-ordering of international relations*'.[303]

[302] European Council on Foreign Relations (ECFR). *MAGA Goes Global: Trump's Plan for Europe,* pgs 35–9. https://ecfr.eu/publication/maga-goes-global-trumps-plan-for-europe/

[303] Brookings. JONES, B. *The New Geopolitics,* pg 3. https://www.brookings.edu/blog/order-from-chaos/2017/11/28/the-new-geopolitics/

26

The Intrinsic Flaws of the International Financial Monetary System: *Risks of a Global Liquidity Trap* and a *Great Stagnation*

With such a blurred future looming ahead of us for our time's economic and financial models, the structure of the Neoliberal World Order (NLWO) is being further debilitated and weakened by the second neoliberal scenario, which unfortunately veils more bad omens for the international financial-monetary system (IFMS). The IFMS is being increasingly constrained by deep-rooted defects, which are projecting very negative forecasts for the future of the global economy. The system has developed several deep flaws at its core, which could be leading the global economy into yet another major global financial crisis. With the orthodoxy of monetary policy being threatened by schisms within the system itself, the risks of a potential 'Global Liquidity Trap' are increasing, which would in turn generate an already denominated, 'Great Stagnation'.

Since the 1980s and throughout its years of existence, the IFMS has become increasingly vulnerable due to its development of several deep flaws at its heart. The substitution of the industrial-productive economy for the financial-monetary economy has been gradually creating many rifts and fissures inside the system, which are seriously threatening it from within. It is widely predicted that the global economy could be drifting towards yet another huge financial crisis, due to the orthodoxy of monetary policy being endangered by such schisms within the system itself. The foundations of the IFMS are once again being shaken due to the financialization process having conveyed way too much market liquidity into the system, which has likewise and in turn caused many erratic stock-market ups and downs. With the growth of such a destabilizing asymmetry at the heart of the system, the risks of a potential '*Global Liquidity Trap*' are increasing, which in turn, could trigger yet another huge global crisis or '*Great Stagnation*'.

Ever since the industrial-productive economy was switched for the financial-monetary economy, the IFMS has grown increasingly vulnerable due to its continued development of several deep flaws that are threatening it from within. The globalization process has made the consensus established some forty years ago become untenable. For decades, *'the mainstream view has been that countries can achieve price stability and minimise excessive output variability by adopting flexible inflation targeting and floating exchange rates. The gains from policy coordination were thought to be modest at best, and the prescription was for countries to keep their houses in order'*.[1]

Although globalization has progressively increased the impact of international developments on all economies, at the same time, it has also developed a couple of very negative defects. On one hand, the growing dominant currency pricing (DCP) is reducing *'the shock absorbing properties of flexible exchange rates and altering the inflation-output volatility trade-off facing monetary policy makers'*.[2] On the other hand and most directly related with this chapter's main focusing point – a very destabilizing asymmetry has been growing at the heart of the IFMS. *'While the world economy is being reordered, the US dollar remains as important as when the Bretton Woods collapsed'*.[3]

With such factors having made *'US developments have significant spillovers onto both the trade performance and the financial conditions of countries even with relatively limited direct exposure to the US economy'*,[4] the combination of those dynamics is progressively increasing the risks of a global liquidity trap.[5]

'A liquidity trap is a situation in which interest rates are low and savings rates are high, rendering monetary policy ineffective. In a liquidity trap, consumers choose to avoid bonds and keep their funds in savings because of the prevailing belief that interest rates will soon rise (which would push bond prices down). Because bonds have an inverse relationship to interest rates, most consumers do not want to hold any asset with a price that is expected to decline. In a liquidity trap, should a country's reserve bank, like the Federal Reserve in the USA, try to stimulate the economy by increasing the money supply there would be no effect on interest rates, as people do not need to be encouraged to hold additional cash.

As part of the liquidity trap, consumers continue to hold funds in standard deposit accounts, such as savings and checking accounts, instead of in other investment options, even when the central banking system attempts to stimulate the economy through the injection of additional funds. High consumer savings levels, often spurred by the belief of a negative economic event on the horizon, causes monetary policy to be generally ineffective.

1 Bank of England. Speech by the Governor of the Bank of England, Mark Carney. Jackson Hole Symposium 2019. *The Growing Challenges for Monetary Policy in the Current International Monetary and Financial System,* pg 3. https://www.bankofengland.co.uk/speech/2019/mark-carney-speech-at-jackson-hole-economic-symposium-wyoming

2 Ibid.

3 Ibid.

4 Ibid, pg 4.

5 The History of Economic Thought. The Keynesian Revolution. *The Real Balances Debate.* http://www.hetwebsite.net/het/essays/keynes/realbalances.htm

The belief in a future negative event is key, because as consumers hoard cash and sell bonds, this will drive bond prices down and yields up. Despite rising yields, consumers are not interested in buying bonds as bond prices are falling. They prefer instead to hold cash at a lower yield'.[6]

One of the clearest indicators of the presence of a liquidity trap is low interest rates, which is exactly what the IFMS is considered to be accomplishing, through '*structurally lowering the global equilibrium interest rate, r**',[7] by way of:

- "*Feeding a global savings glut, as Emerging Market Economies (EMEs) defensively accumulate reserves of safe US dollar assets against the backdrop of an inadequate and fragmented global financial safety net;*
- *reducing the scale of sustainable cross border flows, and as a result lowering the rate of global potential growth; and*
- *fattening of the left-hand tail and increasing the downside skew of likely economic outcomes*".[8]

In such an increasingly integrated world, the equilibrium interest rate or '*global r**' exerts a greater influence on the '*domestic r**', which means that with a falling global equilibrium rate, domestic monetary policy makers have a much more difficult task in providing the necessary stimuli to achieve objectives of obtaining equilibrium. Although at present, there are few fundamental imbalances in terms of capacity constraints or indebtedness that would portend a recession, such dynamics are directly relevant to the current risk of a global slow-down, as '*the combination of structural imbalances at the heart of the IMFS itself and protectionism are threatening global momentum*'.[9]

For some time now, the global economy has been put under increasing strain by a growing asymmetry at the heart of the IFMS, mainly due to the fact that despite the transformation of the global economy, huge network effects have maintained the dominance of the dollar as the number one currency in the IFMS. When the Latin American debt crisis broke out, EMEs made up around one third of the global GDP, although since the last tightening cycle of the US Federal Reserve, their share of global activity had risen from about 45 per cent to 60 per cent and it is equally projected that by 2030 such percentage will further rise to about three quarters.[10]

[6] Investopedia. *Liquidity Trap.* https://www.investopedia.com/terms/l/liquiditytrap.asp

[7] Bank of England. Speech by the Governor of the Bank of England, Mark Carney. Jackson Hole Symposium 2019. *The Growing Challenges for Monetary Policy in the Current International Monetary and Financial System,* pg 4. https://www.bankofengland.co.uk/speech/2019/mark-carney-speech-at-jackson-hole-economic-symposium-wyoming

[8] Ibid.

[9] Ibid, pg 4.

[10] Ibid, pg 7.

> *As well as being the dominant currency for the invoicing and settling of international trade, the US dollar is the currency of choice for securities issuance and holdings, and reserves of the official sector. Two-thirds of both global securities issuance and official foreign-exchange reserves are denominated in dollars. The same proportion of EME foreign currency external debt is denominated in dollars and the dollar serves as the monetary anchor in countries accounting for two thirds of global GDP.*[11]

The fact that trade invoicing and globalized financing and banking have strongly based themselves on operating with the US dollar has further reinforced the currency's dominant position within the IFMS. With such huge volumes of trade being invoiced and paid for in dollars, the holding of dollar-denominated assets has thus and in turn become the most common and sensible practice for everyone. While an increased demand for dollar assets lowers their return, firms are that way also incentivized to borrow in dollars, with the liquidity and safety properties encouraging such practice even further. Likewise, companies with dollar-denominated liabilities are also incentivized to invoice in dollars in order to reduce the currency mismatch between their revenues and liabilities. Consequentially, whilst more non-financial companies carry out dollar issuance and more banks perform dollar financing, central banks consider it wise to accumulate more dollar reserves.[12]

Due to the US dollar dominance in cross-border claims, recent developments and changes in the US economy, which have affected the US dollar exchange rate, are creating large spillover effects on the rest of the world through asset markets. Since movements in the US dollar affect significantly the real burden of debt for companies that have borrowed unhedged in dollars (especially in EMEs) and tend to reduce the value of the dollar in companies' collateral, the overall result ends in a tightening of credit conditions, and if taken to extremes, in defaults. In a similar way, while US dollar fluctuations also affect the risk appetite of global investors, such risk spillovers are also significantly impacting receptor economies, especially in EMEs where global risk perceptions closely interact with country-specific risks. '*The global financial cycle is a dollar cycle*',[13] and therefore, changes in the dollar cycle will also affect the overall financial cycle.[14]

In EMEs, such effects translate into volatile capital flows that intensify domestic imbalances and leave them more vulnerable to foreign shocks. Whereas EMEs are about three times more likely to experience financial crises after capital flow upsurges than in normal times, one-fifth of all capital flow upsurges to EMEs have resulted in financial crises. Consequentially, financial crises in EMEs will, in turn, affect the overall balance of the financial system, and that way, the general global equilibrium.[15]

[11] Ibid.
[12] Ibid.
[13] Ibid.
[14] Ibid.
[15] Ibid, pgs 7–8.

At present, whilst financial stability and monetary policy in advanced economies have become more prevalent and more potent, '*push*' factors for driving capital flows have become more important. Since the tightening of the US monetary policy, the spillover to foreign GDP is despite the United States' rapidly declining share of global GDP, twice its 1990–2004 average.[16]

Moreover, when such '*push shocks*' occur, the structure of the financial system or the '*pipes*' increasingly augment capital flows from EMEs, as under stress investment fund flows are particularly '*flighty*'. Ever since the global financial crisis, market-based finance in EMEs has accounted for all the increase in foreign lending, since bank lending has declined and foreign direct investment (FDI) has remained fairly constant. While such a shift has brought diversity to the financial system, it has, however, likewise reduced '*the sustainability of capital flows, as market-based flows are particularly sensitive to changes in global risk appetite and financial conditions*'.[17] In general, the increasing role of '*push factors*', as well as of the '*pipes*' of the system, could soon be bringing fast-reforming EMEs to an abrupt standstill in their quest for sustainable capital flows.[18]

Although such deficiencies of the IFMS affect EMEs more directly than advanced economies, their overall consequences influence all economies as they reduce the '*global r**'. Within the framework of such an inadequate global financial safety net, EMEs have chosen to self-insure against the volatility of capital flows through the accumulation of dollar-denominated safe assets reserves, which has much contributed to a '*global savings glut*'.[19] In turn, such a vast accumulation of safe assets has pushed down the global equilibrium interest rate – '*the rate that central banks must deliver in order to balance demand with supply and so achieve stable inflation*'.[20]

In more fundamental terms, the inherent flaws of the IFMS are not only making the world a riskier place, but are equally exerting much more downward pressure on the '*global r**'. Furthermore, the IFMS is not only increasing the difficulty of achieving price and financial stability, but is equally exacerbating the overall situation by encouraging protectionist and populist policies. All-combined and with the rate of global potential growth being reduced and its downside skew being increased, the likelihood of an extreme downside event (like a fatter left tail) is bolstered.[21]

Whereas in the past '*instances of very low rates have tended to coincide with high risk events such as wars, financial crises, and breaks in the monetary regime*', at present, the lower the global equilibrium interest rate goes, the more reduced the scope of monetary policy makers gets for cutting policy rates in response to demand adverse shocks, which is increasing the risk of a global liquidity trap.[22]

16 Ibid, pg 8.
17 Ibid.
18 Ibid.
19 Ibid, pg 9.
20 Ibid.
21 Ibid.
22 Ibid.

Against the backdrop of the IFMS and its inherent destabilizing asymmetries, much has been inked out about an extremely important and influencing issue. Ever since the global financial crisis or '*Neoliberal Crisis*' and the '*near-death of the global banking system*', not much has changed at all in terms of economic thought and practice. Despite the many readjustments made to the international financial system and the EU financial-banking sector, there has been no real fundamental questioning whatsoever of the basic ideas underpinning contemporary economic thought and financial policy.[23]

The former Governor of the Bank of England, Lord Mervyn King, has criticized the differing ways in which different historical world crises have been dealt with by pointing out an extremely transcendental factor. Following '*the Great Depression of the 1930s there had been new thinking and intellectual change*',[24] which generated big changes in economics. Back then, the Keynesian revolution led to much political rethinking which established a new economic orthodoxy. Similarly, the exact same pattern of change happened after the 1973 Oil Crisis, when the neoliberal counter-revolution provoked the next big swing from Keynesian to Hayekian and Friedmanian economics.[25]

Although after the 2007–15 global financial crisis governments avoided a repetition of the Great Depression's loss of output or rise of unemployment, economies have nonetheless been kept functioning grounded on the exact same monetary orthodoxy. That is, through monetary easing, such as the cutting of interest rates and the injection of more money into the system, as well as by bailing out banks. Most importantly, none of the real fundamental issues underpinning such crises have been tackled at all.[26] We have simply stuck to the '*new orthodoxy of monetary policy ... pretending that we have made the banking system safe*'.[27]

With a weaker recovery from the 2007–15 deep economic slump than recovery from the Great Depression,[28] the synchronized slowdown of the global economy is not just a '*temporary phenomenon*', but a clear '*reflection of how the failure to address the reasons for the financial crisis ... has left the world economy stuck in a permanent low-growth trap*'.[29]

[23] *The Guardian*. ELLIOT, L. *World Economy Is Sleepwalking into a New Financial Crisis, Warns Melvyn King*, pgs 1–2. https://www.theguardian.com/business/2019/oct/20/world-sleepwalking-to-another-financial-crisis-says-mervyn-king

[24] Ibid, pg 2.

[25] *The Guardian*. ELLIOT, L. *The Sluggish Economy Needs to Reform – And Fast*, pg 2. https://www.theguardian.com/business/2019/oct/20/the-sluggish-global-economy-needs-to-reform-and-fast

[26] Ibid.

[27] *The Guardian*. ELLIOT, L. *World Economy Is Sleepwalking into a New Financial Crisis, Warns Melvyn King*, pg 2. https://www.theguardian.com/business/2019/oct/20/world-sleepwalking-to-another-financial-crisis-says-mervyn-king

[28] *The Guardian*. ELLIOT, L. *The Sluggish Economy Needs to Reform – And Fast*, pg 2. https://www.theguardian.com/business/2019/oct/20/the-sluggish-global-economy-needs-to-reform-and-fast

[29] *The Guardian*. ELLIOT, L. *World Economy Is Sleepwalking into a New Financial Crisis, Warns Melvyn King*, pg 2. https://www.theguardian.com/business/2019/oct/20/world-sleepwalking-to-another-financial-crisis-says-mervyn-king

Since the global financial crisis, standard models have been incapable of reforming two key areas of economic policy – *'getting the world economy out of its low-growth trap, and preparing for the next financial crisis'*.[30] Furthermore, the enduring period of low growth and ineffective ultra-low interest rates has reintroduced the *'concept of secular stagnation'*.[31]

The world entered and departed the global financial crisis with a distorted pattern of demand and output, with the only way out of a low growth trap involving the *'reallocation of resources from one component of demand to another, from one sector to another, and from one firm to another'*.[32] Monetary stimulus does not suffice to bring about a shift of resources in both capital and labour. Although there have been excessive investments in some parts of the economy, such as in the export sector in China and Germany and in commercial property in other advanced economies, there have equally been just as many insufficient investments in others, like in the infrastructure sector in many Western countries. *'Without action to deal with the structural weaknesses of the global economy, there is a risk of another financial crisis, emanating this time not from the US banking system but from weak financial systems elsewhere'*.[33]

Monetary policy clearly has its limitations and the risk of a global liquidity trap is becoming more eminent, with rock-bottom interest rates becoming ineffective and people hoarding cash. When banks send out the message that interest rates are going to permanently remain low, individuals and companies are encouraged to load up on debt, and when recessions arrive, individuals lose their jobs and the demand for companies' products collapses. Consequently and as recently experienced, debts become unpayable and the resultant bankruptcies further exacerbate the initial economic shocks.[34]

> *Conventional wisdom attributes the stagnation largely to supply factors as the underlying growth rate of productivity appears to have fallen. But data can be interpreted only within a theory or model. And it is surprising that there has been so much resistance to the hypothesis that, not just the United States, but the world as a whole is suffering from demand-led secular stagnation.*[35]

With high debt levels, governments have to be very cautious about the deployment of fiscal stimuli to improve the situation, although at the end of the day, the global

[30] Ibid.
[31] Ibid.
[32] Ibid, pg 3.
[33] Ibid.
[34] *The Guardian*. ELLIOT, L. *The Sluggish Economy Needs to Reform – And Fast*, pg 2. https://www.theguardian.com/business/2019/oct/20/the-sluggish-global-economy-needs-to-reform-and-fast
[35] *The Guardian*. ELLIOT, L. *World Economy Is Sleepwalking into a New Financial Crisis, Warns Melvyn King*, pg 3. https://www.theguardian.com/business/2019/oct/20/world-sleepwalking-to-another-financial-crisis-says-mervyn-king

demand deficiency is fundamentally a structural problem – and structural problems require structural responses and solutions.[36]

Both Lord King and former Governor of the Bank of England Marc Carney have pointed out that given that the US dollar share of global GDP is shrinking, one of the main structural imperfections of the IFMS is the powerful and dominant position the US dollar holds as the world's number one currency. In accordance with Lord King's forecasts, as far and as much as a '*financial Armageddon*' would be devastating to the legitimacy of the democratic market system, the unfortunate fact remains that having suffered a Great Depression, as well as been recently sucker-punched by the Great Recession, '*the world could be sleepwalking into a new … Great Stagnation*'.[37]

However, there are a couple of very prominent uprising factors that in the years to come might not only bring an end to the US dollar dominance of the IFMS as the number one currency, but also produce big structural changes that would totally redefine the IFMS, if not completely supplant it as a whole. The first factor that might soon take care of such systemic deficiencies is related to the hegemonic rise of other currencies, such as the Chinese Yuan-Renminbi (RMB). The second factor, which is covered and discussed in detail in the following Conclusion, is connected to the eventual taking over of entirely different types of currencies, such as cryptocurrencies, as well as to the consequential gradual phasing out of the financial-monetary economy by the digital-virtual economy. The ongoing transitioning process is gradually eroding such systemic deficiencies, as the current system will eventually completely disappear.

As far and as much as the first factor is concerned, there are many predictions that during the twenty-first century, the Chinese RMB will eventually debunk the US dollar and become the number one international reserve currency. Since the Napoleonic Wars up until more or less 1870, the British Sterling-Pound was the number one international reserve currency, which was then overtaken by the US dollar, whose hegemony has predominated throughout the twentieth century. In much the same way, it is widely predicted that during the twenty-first century, the RMB will overtake the US dollar, and hence, become the number one international reserve currency.[38]

[36] *The Guardian*. ELLIOT, L. *The Sluggish Economy Needs to Reform – And Fast*, pg 3. https://www.theguardian.com/business/2019/oct/20/the-sluggish-global-economy-needs-to-reform-and-fast

[37] *The Guardian*. ELLIOT, L. *World Economy Is Sleepwalking into a New Financial Crisis, Warns Melvyn King*. https://www.theguardian.com/business/2019/oct/20/world-sleepwalking-to-another-financial-crisis-says-mervyn-king

[38] Instituto Español de Estudios Estratégicos. Framework Document. ZURITA, A. *China: The Awakening of the Red Dragon*, pg 6. http://www.ieee.es/en/Galerias/fichero/docs_marco/2016/DIEEEM032016_China_Despertar_DragonRojo_ENGLISH_AlfonsoZurita.pdf

Conclusion

The Industrial Revolution 4.0 and the Digital Age: The Eclipse of the Financial-Monetary Economy by the Digital Virtual Economy

Unfortunately, our extremely convulsed economic epoch projects to continue along the same turbulent flight. The very complex economic hiatus in which the world finds itself has patently turned uncertainty and unpredictability into the most defining nuances holding our economic future still.

The Neoliberal World Order (NLWO) and its two predominating scenarios clearly reflect that despite the still strong predominance of neoliberalism, we find ourselves caught in the threshold of a shifting economic and financial paradigm and orthodoxy. At the same time, the international financial monetary system (IFMS) also finds itself irredeemably flawed, with its increasing monetary disarray projecting an even bigger financial debacle than any of the previously experienced ones.

Notwithstanding, the biggest paradox surrounding our ever-changing economic reality is that, for some time now, we have been experiencing the development, evolution and gradual establishment of a much more transcendental phenomenon of infinite proportions, which is completely transcending it. Such a phenomenon undoubtedly represents the biggest ever, historical economic turning point or game changing phase recorded in either human or economic history.

Since some years ago, the '*Industrial Revolution 4.0*' and its technological-digital transformations have been fusing the physical, digital and biological worlds, with its advanced developments affecting the majority of sectors that surround us, and most especially, transcending the economic and financial realms. The revolution in check is unlocking a completely timeless and limitless virtual reality and metaverse, very strongly characterized by decentralized financial systems and neobanks, down-rooted to an ever-growing solid bedrock of cryptocurrencies, which is dawning a whole new '*Digital Age*'. Whereas the whole process is expected to eventually transcend altogether the established NLWO together with its two predominating scenarios, thus making them part of a totally irrelevant and obsolete past, at the same time, it is predicted that in a not-too-distant future, the current '*Neoliberal Era*' will likewise and in turn be completely eclipsed by the '*Digital Age*'.

The very shaken and stirred NLWO projects a very clear and present shift and displacement of the neoliberal paradigm and orthodoxy, with its future survival having been put into very serious interrogation. The two neoliberal scenarios clearly reflect that while the intellectual collapse of neoliberalism has produced an irreversible shift of neoliberal thought and practice, the IFMS is also on the verge of being monetarily overridden. On the one hand, while neoliberalism has been displaced by 'Neo-nationalism' and 'Modern Monetary Theory' (MMT), 'Stakeholder Capitalism' is also being increasingly challenged and contested by new revised forms of capitalism, such as, most particularly 'Progressive Capitalism', as well as the more recently triggered 'Techno-Feudal and Oligopolistic Capitalism'. On the other hand, the IFMS likewise reveals even more neoliberal fault-lines related to inherent flaws. It can be affirmed that the way both scenarios unravel and the direction they end up taking, will largely determine whether we eventually experience a partial, semi or complete change of economic and financial order in the near future.

Notwithstanding and seen from a much higher perspective, the worst irony about our extremely volatile and ever-changing economic reality is that for some time now, we have been experiencing the biggest ever historical economic turning point or game-changing phase recorded in either human or economic history, which is completely transcending it. Economic history and its groundbreaking revolutions are following the exact same logical progression, leading it to the exact same logical conclusion. After the first industrial revolutions, the rural-agricultural economy was overtaken by the industrial-productive economy. Subsequently and in turn, during the 1980s, the latter industrial-productive economy was replaced by the financial-monetary economy. In much the same way, it is widely expected that the currently established financial-monetary economy will be eventually overridden, as well as eclipsed, by the ongoing '*Fourth Industrial Revolution*' or '*Industrial Revolution 4.0*'. The very rapidly evolving process is progressively leading to a total and complete substitution of the current type of financial-monetary economy for another brand new, much more sophisticated and refined unexplored type of digital-virtual economy.[1]

Since some years ago, the '*Industrial Revolution 4.0*' and its technological-digital transformations have been breaking through our physical and material boundaries, giving way to a whole new timeless and limitless virtual reality and metaverse, very strongly characterized by decentralized finance (DeFi) and neobanks, firmly down-rooted to an ever-growing solid base of cryptocurrencies. Our current economic

[1] World Economic Forum. Agenda. SCHWAB, K. *The Fourth Industrial Revolution: What It Means, How to Respond.* https://www.weforum.org/agenda/2016/01/the-fourth-industrial-revolution-what-it-means-and-how-to-respond/

reality is witnessing how the financial-monetary economy is being steadfastly eclipsed by the digital-virtual economy, neobanks and its ever-growing vast base of attractive cryptocurrencies, as well as progressively replaced by the new services and goods provided by a whole new virtual reality and the metaverse.

While it is widely believed that the whole process will eventually transcend the established NLWO and its two scenarios, thus making them part of a totally irrelevant and obsolete past, it is equally predicted that, in a not-too-distant future, the current '*Neoliberal Era*' will be likewise and in turn, completely eclipsed by the '*Digital Age*'.

Evaluation and Assessment of the NLWO and Its Two Scenarios

The first scenario covers the ongoing intense and virulent clash between the still-standing neoliberal economic and financial models and the new countering models threatening to debunk them. The NLWO has been seriously destabilized and weakened by the revival and growing expansion of mercantilist, protectionist-isolationist models, such as most notably neonationalism. The neonational trend is equally spreading out thicker across the international landscape, with even more neonational conversions, such as in Italy and further expansions like in France.

Although to a lesser degree than neonationalism, MMT is equally gaining much more traction, especially in the United States, where it has become a big part of the Trump administration's economic programme, as well as in Japan. Europe is also becoming increasingly more supportive of MMT, with many calls being made about the need to experiment with '*helicopter money/MMT-type policies*'.

Similarly, at the academic level, stakeholder capitalism is being continuously challenged and contested by revised forms of capitalism, which are gaining more recognition. Progressive capitalism, equitable capitalism and egalitarian capitalism are increasingly defying stakeholder capitalism. Correspondingly, President Trump has recently begun applying his own, homemade capitalist hybrid, Techno-Feudal Oligopolistic Capitalism, which has also burst onto the international scene with a strong sucker punch.

The second scenario surrounds the increasing vulnerability of the IFMS due to its development of deep flaws at its core. Owing to the IFMS having produced such vast amounts of money, there is way too much liquidity flowing through the system, which could end up congesting it at any given moment. For many, the global economy is drifting towards yet another huge crisis, with the orthodoxy of monetary policy being endangered by such schisms within the system itself. While the current financial monetary system is on the verge of being monetarily overridden, the growth of such a destabilizing asymmetry at the heart of the system is simultaneously and steadfastly increasing the risks of a '*Global Liquidity Trap*', which could trigger yet another massive global crisis or as already denominated '*Great Stagnation*'.

In relation to the NLWO and its first scenario, it is evidently clear that despite its prevalence due to its robust architecture and wide-ranging infrastructure, the clash between the old and still prevalent neoliberal model and the new neonational model, is becoming increasingly virulent, with the latter model having produced impressive results in the United States and having lately been re-established, as well as alluring more and more adherents across the world, as most recently observed with the latest neonational conversion in Italy and expansion in France. MMT has equally become more influential than ever by becoming part of President Trump's economic programme, being implemented in Japan, and winning over an increasing number of supporters in the European Union (EU). Likewise, the chastising critique surrounding shareholder capitalism has simultaneously generated new revised capitalist models, such as progressive capitalism, and has lately likewise suffered the irruption onto the international scene of techno-feudal and oligopolistic capitalism.

As regards the second scenario and the inherent flaws of the IFMS, the fact that the orthodoxy of monetary policy is being threatened by schisms deep-rooted within the system itself is projecting risks of a 'Global Liquidity Trap', which, in turn, would ultimately generate a 'Great Stagnation'. As the next subpart will delve into, it is becoming more than evident that regardless of a growing number of neoliberal fault-lines threatening the financial system even more, the digital economy and its wide base of cryptocurrencies are, notwithstanding, equally overriding it at an exponential rate.

Bearing in mind the world's patterns of changes of economic paradigm or order, the same kind of pattern is in a way already repeating itself, with distinct manifestations at both the practice and the theoretical levels – the flaws and failures of the predominant neoliberal model are making newer and more innovative uprising models, revisions or ameliorations, such as neo-nationalism, MMT, progressive capitalism and techno-feudal oligopolistic capitalism become much more attractive and suitable for our time's economic needs.

Although it is still too soon to determine with exactitude whether we are truly facing yet another big change of economic paradigm, the same kind of indicative patterns are very discernibly repeating themselves. Considering the most recent biggest shift of paradigm, which took place between Keynesian economics and Hayekian and Friedmanian economics, although the Bretton Woods system of Keynesian fixed exchange rates and embedded liberalism was in practice for about forty years, they were, however, dismantled and substituted by neoliberal free markets relatively quickly. Back then, Keynes's theories regarding the impossibility of inflation and unemployment rising at the same time were soon debunked by Friedman's predictions and the ensuing stagflation period that followed, which in turn saw the relatively quick crumbling down of the Bretton Woods system. This time round, although the global financial crisis and other examples, like Latin American development, have likewise exposed neoliberalism's defects, they have, however, stood their ground and survived their first '*fundamental crisis*', reasonably well. Not only do the international and EU adjustments project continuity along the same neoliberal dynamics, but most especially over the neoliberal bedrock of the EU, ordoliberalism has been resuscitated, making both currents interact once again, constructively stabilizing the region's financial and banking systems and increasing their resilience. Moreover, the deep imbuement of neoliberalism in institutional frameworks and multilateral economic structures indicates that its complete dismantling would indeed prove to be a very complicated task to carry out in just a few years.

Nevertheless, the failures of the NLWO have, albeit, caused a lot of irreparable damage both at the theoretical and the practical level. The disrepute and unpopularity neoliberalism has gained for itself have generated much more hostile opposition to it than Keynesianism ever did for itself. Although in 1980, Keynesianism was not as deeply embedded in the system as neoliberalism is today, it was then, however, only mainly challenged by one single rival – neoliberalism. At present, despite neoliberalism being imbedded around and within the system much deeper than Keynesianism ever was, it is, however, being shifted and displaced by a bigger and growing number of countering models, some of which have already displaced them being currently in practice and others that are academically boiling up.

On the one hand, at the practice level, the NLWO has already been seriously destabilized by neonationalism, having unexpectedly and ironically experienced the complete abandonment and recent displacement by its staunchest believer and promoter, the United States, and likewise seeing how many other countries across the international landscape are following suit with many more neonational conversions. MMT is similarly beginning to further disrupt the order by influencing President Trump and being successfully implemented in Japan. On the other hand, and at the theoretical level, shareholder capitalism has also become equally bogged down by a very dense academic critique, which has already spawned several capitalist reformulations, such as progressive capitalism. Recently, techno-feudal oligopolistic capitalism has also appeared on the international scene with much thrust.

In evaluation of the whole situation, despite the many cries in the dark about the coming to an end of the neoliberal legacy, it is nonetheless far too soon to work out what direction the clash of economic models will actually take. It is still early to fully assess and determine whether the clash between old and new economic models will truly see the NLWO being superseded by the rising neonational order, or whether another sort of emerging framework – such as an MMT order or techno-feudal oligopolistic capitalist order – might eventually end up developing, taking form and ultimately establishing itself – although the signs of change are already there and increasing on a daily basis. With the neoliberal paradigm and orthodoxy having already been brutally shifted by new progressive thought and practice, it is still hard to conclude whether we are simply caught in the middle of an economic model experimental phase or whether we truly find ourselves at an economic juncture wherein the current neoliberal economic and financial paradigm is being gradually overtaken by another. Notwithstanding, it has already been very displaced, completely abandoned, as well as substituted, in key world regions and countries, as well as continues to be increasingly challenged and contested from several other fronts.

Although at the end of the day, only time will tell, the signs of economic and financial change are already there and spreading out thicker across the international landscape, and while history has indeed proven to unravel that way, history always tends to repeat itself.

The Industrial Revolution 4.0 and the Digital Age

The biggest irony regarding our economic reality, wherein the NLWO and its two scenarios are changing so much, is that it is paradoxically gradually becoming increasingly irrelevant vis-à-vis another huge historical economic turning point or game-changing phase, which has for some time now been manifesting itself. A huge phenomenon has been developing and evolving tremendously quickly, which is completely overriding the NLWO, together with its two scenarios.

The *'Fourth Industrial Revolution'* or *'Industrial Revolution 4.0'* is transcending our physical, material and biological confines and boundaries, conveying a brand new type of digital-virtual reality and metaverse. The phenomenon is widely expected to eventually entirely eclipse the NLWO and its two scenarios, making them totally irrelevant and part of an obsolete past. Bearing in mind the world's historical revolutionary economic turning points or game-changing phases, we find ourselves facing the biggest quantum leap ever taken by mankind or let alone recorded in economic history.

Economic history and its groundbreaking revolutions are following the exact same logical progression as they have across time, which is inexorably leading us to the exact same logical conclusion. The latest developments and advancements are unravelling just like events did after the first agrarian-industrial revolutions. Beginning back then, the rural-agricultural economy was first overtaken by the industrial-productive economy, and subsequently, during the 1980s, the latter industrial-productive economy was in turn likewise replaced by the current financial-monetary economy. At present, the emerging digital-virtual economy is progressively overriding, overtaking and will eventually completely replace the current financial-monetary economy. The changes and transformations that the *'Industrial Revolution 4.0'* is bringing about in everyday life, and most markedly, in the economic and financial realms, are gradually and progressively leading to a total and complete substitution of the current type of financial-monetary economy for another brand new, much more sophisticated and refined, unmapped kind of digital-virtual economy.[2]

In 2015, Klaus Schwab, the founder and executive chairman of the World Economic Forum, coined the term '*Industrial Revolution 4.0*'. In his book, '*The Fourth Industrial Revolution*', Schwab argues that the revolution in check is a completely different revolution from any previously experienced one in terms of scale, scope and complexity, with its impact being much more transcendental and its ramifications much more profound than any prior period of human history. Schwab points out that since some years ago, the '*Industrial Revolution 4.0*', characterized by a range of new technologies, has been fusing together the physical, digital and biological worlds, with myriad developments that are affecting all areas and disciplines, governments, economies and industries. *'Artificial intelligence is already all around us, from supercomputers, drones and virtual assistants to 3D printing, DNA sequencing, smart thermostats, wearable sensors and microchips smaller than a grain of sand. But this is just the beginning: nanomaterials 200 times stronger than steel and a million times thinner than a strand of hair and the first transplant of a 3D printed liver are already in development. Imagine 'smart factories' in which global systems of manufacturing are coordinated virtually, or implantable mobile phones made of biosynthetic materials.'*[3]

Across time and throughout history, different landmarking periods have always been accompanied by key revolutionary economic turning points or game-changing phases. Ever since the Middle Ages and the Early Modern Era, through to the game-changing agricultural and industrial revolutions, differing economic models, systems and structures have intermittently but continuously entered the world economic theatre and staged its developmental, evolutionary and growth path.

The world's economic history provides an excellent record of human economic activities (like the production and distribution and consumption of goods and services), which spans both evidenced pre-history and recorded history. Different landmarking historical periods and phases have progressively introduced more advanced, groundbreaking economic models and systems, together with new accompanying technology. For example, the early Middle Ages saw how the world economy slowly expanded through the increase of population and trade, with the Silk Road trade potential thriving between Europe, Central Asia and China. During the late medieval period, the emergence of rich trading cities in Italy witnessed the creation of the first modern accounting and finance systems. Throughout the ninth century, the Tang Dynasty from China introduced the first-ever banknotes, whose usage expanded

2 World Economic Forum. Agenda. SCHWAB, K. *The Fourth Industrial Revolution: What It Means, How to Respond*. https://www.weforum.org/agenda/2016/01/the-fourth-industrial-revolution-what-it-means-and-how-to-respond/

3 Amazon. SCHWAB, K. *The Fourth Industrial Revolution*. https://www.amazon.com/Fourth-Industrial-Revolution-Klaus-Schwab/dp/1524758868

during the Song Dynasty. Subsequently, the Early Modern Era was very strongly characterized by the epoch of nationalism, mercantilism and international trade, with the progressive waning of feudalism beginning to strengthen new national economic frameworks. After the discovery of America and the opening up of new trade routes with the New World and Asia, newly empowered monarchies sought a new powerful state to boost their status. They thus and therefore developed mercantilism, based on its distinctive triangular trade, which offered both a political doctrine of absolutism and an economic theory advocating the utilization of the state's military power in order to ensure the protection of local markets and supply sources. Later on, in 1661, the '*Stockholms Banco*' issued the first European banknote.[4]

Such historical landmarking periods have been paralleled by equally transcendental economic game-changing revolutions. As Schwab explains in '*The Fourth Industrial Revolution*', when different periods introduce new technologies and ways of perceiving the world, they simultaneously trigger profound changes in economic systems and social structures – even the word '*revolution*' denotes abrupt radical change. For example, the first profound shift in our way of living came about 10,000 years ago with the Agrarian Revolution and the transition from foraging to farming, which was made possible through the domestication of animals. Such a revolution combined the efforts of animals with those of humans, with the main objective of improving production, transportation and communication. Subsequently, the Agrarian Revolution was followed by a series of Industrial Revolutions, which began in the second half of the eighteenth century. On the one hand, the First Industrial Revolution took place between 1760 more or less until around 1840, and it spurred the construction of railroads and the invention of the steam engine, which thus ushered in mechanical production. On the other hand, the Second Industrial Revolution began in the late nineteenth century and lasted until the early twentieth century, making mass production possible, fostered by the advent of electricity and the assembly line. Lastly, the Third Industrial Revolution began in the 1960s and is most commonly named either the technological or the computer revolution, since it was catalysed by the development of semiconductors, mainframe computing in the 1960s, personal computing in the 1970s and 1980s and the internet in the 1990s.[5]

Schwab explicates that since the beginning of the twenty-first century, we have been experiencing a Fourth Industrial Revolution, which has been building on the previous technological revolution, being very largely characterized by even smaller, more powerful and cheaper sensors; a much more ubiquitous and mobile internet, artificial intelligence (AI); and machine learning. The technological-digital advancements of the Third Industrial Revolution, such as digital technologies with core computer hardware, software and networks, have become much more sophisticated and integrated and are,

[4] Economic History – Important Turning Points. https://quizlet.com/185448957/economic-history-important-turning-points-flash-cards/

[5] SCHWAB, K. *The Fourth Industrial Revolution,* pg 11.

as a result, in turn, transforming the global economy and societies in an unprecedented way. The current, *'second machine age'*, has made the world reach an inflection point *'where the effect of these digital technologies will manifest with full force through automation and the making of unprecedented things'*.[6]

The Industrial Revolution 4.0 is not only having tremendous groundbreaking effects in everyday life, as well as on governance and business practices, but most especially in the realms of economics and finance. The revolution in check is opening up a completely timeless and limitless virtual reality and metaverse, very strongly characterized by '*decentralized finance (DeFi)*' and neobanks and very firmly down-rooted to an ever-growing solid bedrock of cryptocurrencies, which is dawning a whole new *'Digital Age'*. While it is largely expected that it will eventually transcend the current NLWO and its two predominating scenarios altogether, thus making them part of an obsolete and totally irrelevant past, it is likewise predicted that in a not-too-distant future, the current '*Neoliberal Era*' will be likewise completely eclipsed by the '*Digital Age*'.

According to Schwab, the scope of the Industrial Revolution 4.0 is much wider than that of any previous revolutions, and it goes much further and beyond smart and connected machines and systems. The ongoing revolution is simultaneously triggering a series of waves of further advanced breakthroughs in areas ranging from gene sequencing to nanotechnology and from renewables to quantum computing. For Schwab, the Fourth Industrial Revolution is fundamentally different from any previous revolutions due to the fusion of such sophisticated technologies and their interaction across the physical, digital and biological domains. At the same time, the changes and transformations of the ongoing revolution are occurring much quicker than those of any previous revolution. The emergence of even more cutting-edge technologies, together with a much faster and wider diffusion of broad-based innovation, is increasing daily. All combined and in general, they are continuing to unfold across the globe astonishingly rapidly, most especially changing our ways of life, governance, business and economics and finance.[7]

> *There are three reasons why today's transformations represent not merely a prolongation of the Third Industrial Revolution but rather the arrival of a Fourth and distinct one: velocity, scope, and systems impact. The speed of current breakthroughs has no historical precedent. When compared with previous industrial revolutions, the Fourth is evolving at an exponential rather than a linear pace. Moreover, it is disrupting almost every industry in every country. And the breadth and depth of these changes herald the transformation of entire systems of production, management, and governance.*[8]

6 Ibid, pg 12.
7 Ibid.
8 World Economic Forum. SCHWAB, K. *The Fourth Industrial Revolution: What It Means, How to Respond to It,* pg 2. https://www.weforum.org/agenda/2016/01/the-fourth-industrial-revolution-what-it-means-and-how-to-respond/

In everyday life, such changes and transformations have been very visible for a long time, with billions of people connected more than ever to mobile gadgets of all kinds, including unlimited processing and storage and access to information capabilities. Likewise, all such unprecedented possibilities are being multiplied daily by more and more technological advances in the fields of AI, robotics, the Internet of Things, autonomous vehicles, 3D printing, nanotechnology, biotechnology, material sciences, energy storage and quantum computing.[9]

> *Already, artificial intelligence is all around us, from self-driving cars and drones to virtual assistants and software that translate or invest. Impressive progress has been made in AI in recent years, driven by exponential increases in computing power and by the availability of vast amounts of data, from software used to discover new drugs to algorithms used to predict our cultural interests. Digital fabrication technologies, meanwhile, are interacting with the biological world on a daily basis. Engineers, designers, and architects are combining computational design, additive manufacturing, materials engineering, and synthetic biology to pioneer a symbiosis between microorganisms, our bodies, the products we consume, and even the buildings we inhabit.*[10]

The Fourth Industrial Revolution has already changed our own personal and collective patterns of behaviour, what we do and who we are, and is likewise even dictating what and how we feel. Today, for example, our identity is greatly affected by it and continues to be so, through the altering of all issues associated with it, such as '*our sense of privacy, our notions of ownership, our consumption patterns, the time we devote to work and leisure, and how we develop our careers, cultivate our skills, meet people, and nurture relationships. It is already changing our health and leading to a 'quantified' self, and sooner than we think it may lead to human augmentation. The list is endless because it is bound only by our imagination.*'[11]

At the same time, the impact and effects of the Industrial Revolution 4.0 are reciprocally also radically changing the way of governance, as well as the way in which business is carried out, but are most especially conferring a whole new technologically and digitally based economic and financial era.

According to Schwab, and as regards government, with the increasing convergence of the physical, digital and biological realms, new technologies and platforms are enabling the citizenship to engage much more proactively with governments and institutions, voice its opinions, coordinate its efforts and even circumvent supervision from public authorities. '*Simultaneously, governments will gain new technological powers to increase their control over populations, based on pervasive surveillance systems and the ability to*

[9] Ibid.
[10] Ibid, pgs 2–3.
[11] Ibid, pg 4.

control digital infrastructure. On the whole, however, governments will increasingly face pressure to change their current approach to public engagement and policymaking, as their central role of conducting policy diminishes owing to new sources of competition and the redistribution and decentralization of power that new technologies make possible.'[12]

The ongoing revolution is likewise impacting very heavily on the nature of national and international security, which is affecting both the probability and the nature of conflicts. '*The history of warfare and international security is the history of technological innovation, and today is no exception. Modern conflicts involving states are increasingly 'hybrid' in nature, combining traditional battlefield techniques with elements previously associated with nonstate actors. The distinction between war and peace, combatant and noncombatant, and even violence and nonviolence (think cyberwarfare) is becoming uncomfortably blurry. As this process takes place and new technologies such as autonomous or biological weapons become easier to use, individuals and small groups will increasingly join states in being capable of causing mass harm. This new vulnerability will lead to new fears. But at the same time, advances in technology will create the potential to reduce the scale or impact of violence, through the development of new modes of protection, for example, or greater precision in targeting.*'[13]

The technologies that underpin the Fourth Industrial Revolution have similarly impacted very heavily on business and industries. On the supply side, new technologies have created new ways of serving existing needs, which have disrupted existing value chains. New global digital platforms for research, development, marketing, sales and distribution are likewise witnessing how much more agile and innovative competitors are ousting well-established incumbents faster than ever through the advanced improvement of the quality, speed and price of the provided values. On the demand side, the growth of transparency, consumer engagement and new patterns of consumer behaviourism (built upon access to mobile networks and data) is forcing companies to change and adapt to the new ways of designing, marketing and delivering products and services.[14]

A key innovative trend has been the emergence of technology-enabled platforms, which combine both demand and supply in order to disrupt existing industry structures, like the ones within the '*sharing*' and '*on demand*' economy. Such technology platforms have created entirely new ways of consuming goods and services, as well as completely altered the business and working environments with a whole new range of platform businesses.[15]

In broad terms, '*there are four main effects that the Fourth Industrial Revolution has on business – on customer expectations, on product enhancement, on collaborative*

[12] Ibid, pg 3.
[13] Ibid, pg 4.
[14] Ibid, pg 3.
[15] Ibid.

innovation, and on organizational forms. Whether consumers or businesses, customers are increasingly at the epicenter of the economy, which is all about improving how customers are served. Physical products and services, moreover, can now be enhanced with digital capabilities that increase their value. New technologies make assets more durable and resilient, while data and analytics are transforming how they are maintained. A world of customer experiences, data-based services, and asset performance through analytics, meanwhile, requires new forms of collaboration, particularly given the speed at which innovation and disruption are taking place. And the emergence of global platforms and other new business models, finally, means that talent, culture, and organizational forms will have to be rethought.'[16]

Decentralized Finance (DeFi), Neobanks and Cryptocurrencies

However, and more specifically towards our main point of focus, the changes and transformations the Industrial Revolution 4.0 is generating in the economic and financial sectors are accelerating at an exponential rate the gradual and progressive overshadowing of the current type of financial-monetary economy by the digital-virtual economy.

Ever since 2009 and the creation of the first decentralized cryptocurrency, '*Bitcoin*', decentralized and autonomous systems – rooted in a huge base of cryptocurrencies – have generated a massive wave of disruption and second-order effects in the financial world. '*Decentralized finance (DeFi)*' together with '*Neobanks*' and their '*Cryptocurrency*' ecosystem, has been developing at an incredibly fast pace, unlocking countless investment possibilities across the global economy and redefining a whole new technological-digital financial age. There are many strong signals being emitted, indicating that the new financial system of tomorrow will indubitably be based on DeFi, neobanks and cryotpcurrencies.[17]

'*DeFi is an emerging alternative financial system that is built on a public blockchain, which enables greater accessibility because anyone has the ability to connect to it.*'[18] Blockchain technology provides the DeFi system with a totally infallible and completely unbreachable security feature, which makes transactions publicly visible and enables greater transparency across the system.

The innovation of distributed ledger technologies has prompted a huge quantum leap in the new possibilities of the functionalities of money, which is giving shape and form

[16] Ibid.

[17] Visual Capitalist. NEUFELD, D. *Cryptocurrency: Redefining the Future of Finance.* https://www.visualcapitalist.com/cryptocurrency-redefining-future-of-finance/

[18] Ibid.

to a brand new global digital financial system that is incredibly fast, secure, available and egalitarian. It is based on DeFi, blockchain technology, *'peer-to-peer (p2p) protocols'* and *'smart contracts'*.[19]

Historically, when central authorities began issuing currencies, they did so in order to be able to underpin our economies, which in turn made the power of monetary systems grow as more and more people began to trust them. However, due to the breaking of trust from time to time, people began questioning the ability of central authorities to manage such money. DeFi was thus and therefore developed, being very strongly based on the idea of creating a financial system, which was both open to everyone and minimized the need to place trust upon any central authority. DeFi began in 2009 with the launching of Bitcoin, which represented the first peer-to-peer digital currency built over the blockchain network. Following the creation of Bitcoin, the idea of transforming the traditional financial system utilizing blockchains was the next big step taken towards the decentralization of legacy financial systems. Such an idea was made possible with the launching of Ethereum, as well as further reinforced with the launching of smart contracts in 2015. The Ethereum network is a second-generation blockchain, which was the first to maximize the potential of such technology within the financial industry. Through its encouragement of businesses and enterprises to build and deploy projects, the Ethereum network came to configure and establish the DeFi ecosystem. Although Bitcoin and other cryptocurrencies were originally developed in order to give individuals complete control over their assets, they were in fact only decentralized when it came to issuance and storage. The provision of access to a much broader set of financial instruments only became possible with the emergence of smart contracts, which enabled DeFi.[20]

DeFi is an umbrella term that covers applications and projects in the public blockchain space, geared towards the disruption of the traditional finance world. The term DeFi, refers to and includes all financial applications that have been built over blockchain technologies, usually through the utilization of smart contracts. Smart contracts are automated, enforceable agreements, which do not need any intermediaries to be executed and that can be accessed by anyone with an internet connection in order to carry out financial transactions or countless other activities. Most smart contracts offer Turing-complete programming languages, which thus permit the interaction of multiple parties, with no need of a centralized intermediary.[21]

DeFi is composed of an ever-growing array of applications and peer-to-peer protocols, developed over decentralized blockchain networks with no access rights required. Most of the current decentralized applications (dApps) are built over the Ethereum network

[19] Hedera. *What Is Decentralized Finance (DeFi).* https://hedera.com/learning/decentralized-finance/what-is-decentralized-finance

[20] Ibid.

[21] Ibid.

and are utilized for easy lending, borrowing or trading of financial tools, although more and more alternative public networks are evolving and delivering superior speed, scalability, security and lower costs. The ability of DeFi to capitalize on smart contracts has turned them into ideal platforms to build financial applications.[22]

DeFi has very successfully developed and evolved into a complete ecosystem of working applications and protocols, which deliver value to millions of users. In April 2022, there were assets worth over $239 billion locked into DeFi ecosystems, which has made it one of the fastest-growing segments in the space of the public blockchain.[23]

Some of the most popular present-day DeFi working applications and protocols include: Blockchain Oracle, which is utilized to connect the blockchain to the outside world; DeFi Lending and Borrowing Platforms that are used for lending and borrowing money; DeFi Insurance, which includes numerous blockchain-based insurance policies; Decentralized Exchanges (DEXs), which allow users to exchange or swap tokens with other assets without a centralized intermediary or custodian; Derivatives, which allow the interaction of users with assets without having to buy them, although they sometimes have a buying option for the underlying asset; Yield Farming, which has become a very popular way among cryptocurrency traders to earn passive income on their tokens; Stablecoins, which are helping DeFi gain much more prominence as they provide a viable solution to volatility issues surrounding cryptocurrencies; MakerDAO, which is an organization-building technology for savings, borrowing, lending, as well as a stable cryptocurrency on the Ethereum blockchain; Prediction Markets, which provide platforms for individuals to make predictions on the realization of future events such as sports betting, politics and predictions on stock prices, as well as Asset Management, which is a class service offered by DeFi that has made investing much faster, far less expensive and more democratized.[24]

Four of those DeFi working applications and protocols, such as the DeFi Lending and Borrowing Platforms, Decentralized Exchanges (DEXs), Stablecoins and Asset Management, are particularly interesting to focus on, as they provide a very good reflection of the new financial reality that is gradually establishing itself.

The DeFi lending and borrowing platforms, allow users to lend cryptocurrencies to others in order to gain annual yields, with the borrowed money set at a specific interest rate. The DeFi protocols remove intermediaries and thus enable peer-to-peer lending. The fact that DeFi lending protocols are based on automated smart contract codes to enable loans means that users do not have to wait to get their funds or pass any credit checks because of their location. Some platforms even offer rare-switching features

[22] Ibid.
[23] Ibid.
[24] Ibid.

that permit borrowers to protect themselves from volatility by switching between variable and stable interest rates.[25]

The top DeFi lending and borrowing platform is Compound Finance, which was launched in 2018. '*The project is a lending protocol developed on the Ethereum blockchain that allows users to gain interest by lending out assets or borrowing against collateral. The Compound protocol makes this possible by creating liquidity for cryptocurrencies through interest rates set using computer algorithms.*'[26]

Decentralized Exchanges (DEXs) represent one of the most essential functions of DeFi. DEXs do not have any centralized intermediaries or custodians, which thus allows users to freely exchange or swap tokens with other assets, without investments being subjected to the wills and costs of traditional exchanges (centralized exchanges).[27]

The top decentralized exchange is Uniswap, which was created in 2018. '*UniSwap is the largest automated token exchange by trading volume deployed on the Ethereum blockchain. The project was launched after receiving support from venture capitalists and the Ethereum Foundation. UniSwap automated transactions between cryptocurrencies through smart contracts. UniSwap today offers three functionalities: Swapping tokens, adding liquidity, and removing liquidity.*'[28]

Stablecoins have become the most viable solution in order to tackle volatility issues surrounding cryptocurrencies, which are at the same time helping DeFi gain much prominence. '*Stablecoin value is tied to a relatively stable asset, like gold or the US dollar, to keep its price consistent. Stablecoins became useful during risky moments in the crypto space, providing a haven for investors and traders. Stability makes them a reliable collateral asset. Stablecoins also play an important role in liquidity pools – an integral part of the DeFi ecosystem.*'[29]

Asset management is another class service offered by DeFi, which has made investing become much faster, cheaper and more democratized. Some aspects of the DeFi ecosystem, such as transparency, composability and trustlessness, play very much in favour of asset management. While transparency is making information more accessible and secure, composability permits users to enjoy '*hyper-customization*' of portfolios, with trustlessness providing access to historically illiquid assets.[30]

Lastly, launched in 2020, Ampleforth provides one of the best non-collateralized digital asset services, which helps traders and investors diversify their crypto portfolios.

[25] Ibid.
[26] Ibid.
[27] Ibid.
[28] Ibid.
[29] Ibid.
[30] Ibid.

'Ampleforth is an asset-management protocol of DeFi designed to be a smart commodity, synthetic money. "Synthetic" because they're created by humans but aren't raw materials like gold. Ampleforth adjusts its tokens' supply daily to match the market demand using a smart contract. These smart contracts use Ampleforth's and Chainlink's price oracle to get real-time data from Bitfinex Exchange and KuCoin Exchange. These decentralized price feeds help determine if the token's price is within the equilibrium range (0.96–1.06 USD). Suppose an $AMPL token price is lower than $0.96 – the supply decreases. If it is greater than $1.06, Ampleforth increases the supply.'[31]

The global financial landscape, most especially the traditional banking institutions sector, is equally being greatly disrupted by the bursting into the fintech scene of '*Neobanks*'. 'Neobanks' are reshaping the financial services industry through increased access to banking as well as by driving innovation. Although traditional financial institutions have long dominated the financial market, 'neobanks', 'fintech banks', 'challenger banks' or 'digital banks' have appeared as innovative digital-only financial institutions that are seriously disrupting the banking industry. Neobanks mainly deliver services entirely online, which thus allows them to offer consumers accesability benefits, as well as reduced fees, faster loan approvals and even early access to their paychecks.[32]

A neobank is a digital-first financial company, which offers banking services, such as checking accounts and debit cards, but does not have a physical location as such. Neobanks are streamlining the banking process by way of delivering financial services in a customer-centric, digital-only format.[33]

In the financial ecosystem, neobanks have become new key elements due to their ease of use lower fees, together with the alternative methods for analysing credit that they offer. '*They often allow formerly unbanked consumers to access credit cards, checking accounts, and tools to improve their financial health. Many neobanks also use technology to provide a streamlined user experience, which reduces customer turnover and friction.*'[34]

Neobanks mostly provide money management and financial services through online platforms or mobile applications. Unlike traditional banks, which provide a wide range of financial services both online and in person, such as checking and savings accounts, car loans, mortgages, credit cards and investment accounts, neobanks often only offer core banking services, such as checking and savings accounts. However, due to the recent increase in the market share of neobanks, the number of services offered by them is increasing.[35]

[31] Ibid.
[32] Plaid.com. ANTOSZ, D. *What Is a Neobank? How Fintech Is Transforming Banking.* https://plaid.com/resources/fintech/what-is-a-neobank/#:~:text=A%20neobank%20is%20a%20digital,challenger%20bank%2C%20or%20digital%20bank.
[33] Ibid.
[34] Ibid.
[35] Ibid.

Diverging from traditional banks, neobanks offer services with low or no fees, as well as provide tools to protect financial health. The wide range of financial services offered by neobanks includes checking accounts; high-yield savings accounts; free peer-to-peer money transfers; early access to paychecks; free overdraft protection; alternative ways to build credit; and financial education tools.[36]

Since neobanks operate without physical locations, they thus have a lower overhead, which allows them to operate more efficiently and rely on interchange fees for the majority of their revenue. While some of the top neobanks are *Revolut, Chime, Varo, N26* and *SoFi,* they generate most of their revenue through interchange fees and charging interest on loans and credit cards. For example, Varo generates 98 per cent of its revenue through interchange fees. Notwithstanding, different neobanks utilize different revenue models, and therefore, fees vary from bank to bank.[37] Other ways neobanks make money include

- *"Transaction fees: While most neobanks don't charge fees for accounts, many do charge a small fee for bank transfers, ATM withdrawals, or money transfers;*
- *Subscription fees: Some neobanks, like Chime and Revolut, offer premium services in exchange for a monthly subscription fee;*
- *Loan interest: Some neobanks offer loans and credit cards. The interest charged on these products contributes to their overall revenue."*[38]

Whereas in 2020 neobanks had 14.4 million US account holders, by 2024, about 40 million Americans had at least one neobank account. It is also expected that by 2030, the industry will have more than doubled, with customers increasingly seeking digital banks. *'In 2021, neobank Chime was named one of the top 10 banks in the US with more than 13 million customers. Today, it has more than 21 million users.'*[39]

Since 2009 and the bursting onto the scene of cryptocurrencies, they have today become a trillion-dollar industry. In 2025, there are over 17,134 cryptocurrencies in circulation (active or not active), such as '*Bitcoin*', '*Ethereum*', '*Namecoin*', '*Peercoin*', '*Litecoin*', '*Dogecoin*', '*NEO*' and '*Ripple XRP*'.[40] Cryptocurrencies have gained much ground on the global stage, increasingly bolstered by new policies and rising adoption by worldwide public and private sector actors.

With the cryptocurrency ecosystem being joined by a growing number of public and private sector actors with very dynamic participation, it is continuing to expand at an exponential rate. In the public sector, in April 2020, China became the first country

[36] Ibid.
[37] Ibid.
[38] Ibid.
[39] Ibid.
[40] Exploding Topics. *How Many Cryptocurrencies Are There in Circulation in 2025?.* https://explodingtopics.com/blog/number-of-cryptocurrencies

to launch and establish an official digital currency – the '*Digital Currency / Electronic Payment (DC/EP)*' – which became fully operational during the 2022 Winter Olympics in Beijing.[41] While the majority of countries have now followed suit and broken into the new crypto space with ongoing pilot research or development programmes for the establishment of official digital currencies, '*Central Bank Digital Currency (CBDC)*' has equally become a very hot topic in the financial realm. Governments, institutions and banks are researching and analysing the economic and technical feasibility of introducing a new form of digital money and what its impact would be on monetary and fiscal policy. As of January 2023, over 80 per cent of the world's central banks were involved in CBDC research programmes.[42] There are also several crypto organizations set up, such as the Crypto Valley Association and Global Digital Finance.[43]

In the private sector, some of the main players in the crypto field include institutional investors, such as Harvard Endowment Fund and crypto hedge funds; cryptocurrency exchanges, such as Coinbase and Bitstamp; big banks and financial institutions, like J.P. Morgan, Fidelity Investments and Swissquote; technological entities, such as IBM and Microsoft; and power and utilities bodies, like RWE.[44]

Interestingly, it is particularly noteworthy to point out, that the currency battle is in check between the US dollar and the Chinese yuan-renminbi, which has already been both elevated and dynamited in the digital dimension. China has already more than proved its great digital financial prowess by overtaking the United States in the new virtual dimension and conquering the new crypto space, as well as by becoming the first country in the world to create and generate its own official digital currency.

*****

In departure, even as the newly reconfigured reality establishes itself and the world economy further stabilizes, our time's rarefied economic atmosphere and the neoliberal two scenarios that it shrouds will unfortunately remain just as agitated, if not much more so. The world will regrettably continue being embroiled in a clash between old and new economic and financial models, and the international financial system will likewise carry on being increasingly jeopardized by its intrinsic defects and flaws. Regardless of the way the two scenarios end up developing and evolving, it will inevitably lead to even more future changes, which will continue further destabilizing

41 Mish Talk. MISH. *Central Bank Digital Currencies on the Way.* https://www.thestreet.com/mishtalk/economics/central-bank-digital-currencies-on-the-way

42 Hedera. *What Is a Central Bank Digital Currency (CBDC)?* https://hedera.com/learning/tokens/what-is-a-central-bank-digital-currency-cbdc

43 Mish Talk. MISH. *Central Bank Digital Currencies on the Way.* https://www.thestreet.com/mishtalk/economics/central-bank-digital-currencies-on-the-way

44 Ibid.

and challenging the established neoliberal paradigm, as well as its economic and financial orthodoxy.

Notwithstanding, at the same time, we are ironically already bearing direct eyewitnesses to the transcendental changes and transformations our established economic reality is experiencing in view of the new emerging digital economic reality. While the signals are becoming stronger, indicating that tomorrow's finance will be based on DeFi, we are observing the dawning of a whole new Digital Age.

We find ourselves on the verge of taking the biggest ever quantum leap taken by mankind, or let alone recorded in economic history. Although we can still consider ourselves to be living in the neoliberal era of Hayekian free markets and Friedmanian monetarism, it is nevertheless an era, which is wading due to countering thought, as well as fading being progressively eclipsed by the Digital Age.

Bibliography

Books

Arestis, P.; Sawyer, M.C. (Eds). *A Handbook of Alternative Monetary Economics*. Edward Elgar Publishing, 2007.

Audier, S. *Aux Origines du Neo-Liberalisme: Le Colloque Walter Lippmann*. Bord de L'Eau, 2008.

Bárcena, A.; Prado, A. (Eds). *Neoestructuralismo y Corrientes Heterodoxas en América Latina y el Caribe a inicios del siglo XXI*. Editorial Cepal, 2015.

Berghahn, V.P. *The Americanisation of West German Industry, 1945–1973*. Cambridge University Press, 1986.

Biebricher, T.; Vogelmann, F. (Eds). *The Birth of Austerity: German Ordoliberalism and Contemporary Neoliberalism*. Rowman and Littlefield Publishers, 2017.

Bockman, J. *Markets in the Name of Socialism: The Left-Wing Origins of Neoliberalism*. Stanford University Press, 2011.

Bonn, M.J. *The Crumbling of Empire: The Disintegration of World Economy*. Hill and Wang, 1993.

Bosenbrook, W.J. *The German Mind*. Detroit Wayne State University Press, 1961.

Cahill, D.; Cooper, M.; Konings, M.; Primrose, D. *The SAGE Handbook of Neoliberalism*. Sage Publications, 2018.

Commun, P. (Dir). *L'Ordolibéralisme Allemande. Aux Sources de l'Économie Sociale de Marché*. Ifaee, 2003.

Crouch, C. *The Strange Non-Death of Neoliberalism*. Polity Press, 2011.

Cuadernos de la Escuela Diplomática. Número 24. *La Comunidad Hispana en Estados Unidos*. Ministerio de la Presidencia, Relaciones con las Cortes y Memoria Democrática, 2004.

Davies, W. *The Limits of Neoliberalism*. Sage Publications, 2016.

Di Nolfo, E. (Ed). *Power in Europe? Great Britain, France, Germany and Italy and the Origins of the EEC 1952–1957*. Walter de Gruyter, 1992.

Dornbusch, R.; Nölling, W.; Layard, R. (Eds). *Post War Economic Reconstruction and Lessons for the East Today*. The Massachussets Institute of Technology Press, 1993.

Eagleton Pierce, P. *Neoliberalism: The Key Concepts*. Routledge, 2015.

Einaudi, G. (Ed). *Rivista di Storia Economica*. Second Series. Volume 1. International Issue, 1994.

Friedman, M. *Capitalism and Freedom*. The University of Chicago Press, 2002.

Gingrich, A.; Banks, M. (Eds). *Neo-Nationalism in Europe and Beyond: Perspectives from Social Anthropology*. Berghahn Books, 2008.

Hardack, K. *The Political Economy of Germany in the Twentieth Century*. University of California Press, 1980.

Harvey, D. *A Brief History of Neoliberalism*. Oxford University Press, 2005.

Hall, P. *The Political Power of Economic Ideas: Keynesianism across Nations*. Princeton University Press, 1989.

Huerta De Soto, J. *La Escuela Austriaca. Mercado y Creatividad Empresarial*. Editorial Síntesis, S.A., 2000.

Kelton, S. *The Deficit Myth: Modern Monetary Theory and the Birth of the People's Economy*. Public Affairs, 2021.

Kingstone, P. *The Political Economy of Latin America: Reflections on Neoliberalism and Development*. Routledge, 2011.

Leiva, F.I. *Latin American Neostructuralism: The Contradictions of Post-Neoliberal Development*. University of Minnesota, 2008.

Locke, R.R. *The Collapse of the American Management Mystique*. Oxford University Press, 1996.

Maier, C.S. *In Search of Stability: Explorations in Political Science*. Harvard-Cambridge University Press, 1987.

Mankiw, N.G. *Macroeconomics* (Second Edition). Worth Publishers, 1994.

Mayer, H.C. *German Recovery and the Marshall Plan, 1948–1952*. Edition Atlantic Forum, 1969.

Ministerio de Defensa. Instituto Español de Estudios Estratégicos. Cuadernos de Estrategia 204. *La Dualidad Económica Estados Unidos-China en el Siglo XXI*. Ministerio de Defensa, 2020.

Mirowski, P.; Plehwe, D. (Eds). *The Road from Mont Pelerin: The Making of the Neoliberal Thought Collective*. Harvard University Press, 2009.

Nicholls, A.J. *Freedom with Responsibility: The Social Market Economy in Germany, 1918–1963*. Clarendon Press, 1994.

Olier, E. *Codicia Financiera*. Pearson Educación S.A. 2013.

Olier, E. *Geoeconomía. Las Claves de la Economía Global*. Prentice Hall, 2011.

Peck, J. *Constructions of Neoliberal Reason*. Oxford University Press, 2010.

Peukert, D.J.K. *The Weimar Republic: The Crisis of Classical Modernity*. Penguin History, 1993.

Robbins, L. *An Essay on the Nature and Significance of Economic Science*. MacMillan, 1932.

Roett, R.; Paz, G. (Eds). *China's Expansion into the Western Hemisphere—Implications for Latin America and the United States*. Brookings Institution Press, 2008.

Sainsbury, D. *Progressive Capitalism: How to Achieve Economic Growth, Liberty and Social Justice*. Biteback Publishing, 2013.

Samuelson, P.A. *Economics*. McGraw-Hill Book, Inc., 1948.

Schumpeter, J.A. *Capitalism, Socialism & Democracy*. Routledge, 1994.

Schwab, K. *The Fourth Industrial Revolution*. Penguin Books, 2017.

Simth, A. *La riqueza de las naciones. Libro IV. De los sistemas de economía política*. Alianza Editorial, 2011.

Springer, S.; Birch, K.; Macleavy, J. (Eds). *The Handbook on Neoliberalism*. Routledge, 2016.

Steger, M.B.; Roy, R.K. *Neoliberalism: A Very Short Introduction*. Oxford University Press, 2010.

Stiglitz, J. *People, Power, and Profits: Progressive Capitalism for an Age of Discontent*. W. W. Norton, 2019.

Temin, P. *Soviet and Nazi Economic Planning in the 1930s*. Economic History Review, XLIV, 4, 1991.
Thomson, D. *Europe since Napoleon*. Penguin Books, 1990.
Zurita, A. *La Sociedad Multiétnica Boliviana: Riesgos de Fragmentación Social y Amenazas a la Formación de la Identidad Nacional*. Thomson Reuters Aranzadi, 2017.
Zurita, A. *Perspectives on China's Role in Global Affairs in the 21st Century* (Second Revised Edition). Difusión Jurídica Editorial, 2017.

Websites, Monographs, Documents and Articles

Bloomberg News. Politics. Economics. *Japan's Kishida Set to Stay on Kuroda Path, Party Official Says*. https://www.bloomberg.com/news/articles/2022-06-05/japan-s-kishida-set-to-stay-on-kuroda-path-party-official-says
Open Edition Journals. Sloman, P. *The Liberal Party and Economic Policy 1918–1964*. https://journals.openedition.org/mimmoc/695
Trading Economics. *Bolivia GDP Annual Growth Rate*. https://tradingeconomics.com/bolivia/gdp-growth-annual
Harris, R.L. *Resistance and Alternatives to Globalization in Latin America and the Caribbean*. https://library.fes.de/libalt/journals/swetsfulltext/16126225.pdf
World Nuclear News. *Nuclear Research and Technology Centre in Bolivia into Pilot Operation*. https://www.world-nuclear-news.org/Articles/Nuclear-research-and-technology-centre-in-Bolivia
Real Instituto Elcano. Elcano Policy Paper. Feás, E.; Martinez Mongay, C.; Otero-Iglesias, M.; Steinberg, F.; Tamames, J. *A Proposal to Reform the EU's Fiscal Rules*. https://www.realinstitutoelcano.org/en/policy-paper/a-proposal-to-reform-the-eus-fiscal-rules/
The Guardian. French Election 2022: Full Second Round Results. https://www.theguardian.com/world/ng-interactive/2022/apr/24/french-election-2022-live-results-projection-second-round-emmanuel-macron-marine-le-pen
BBC News. *Georgia Meloni: Italy's Far Right Wins Election and Vows to Govern All*. https://www.bbc.com/news/world-europe-63029909
Trading Economics.com. *Japan General Government Gross Debt to GDP – 2022 Data*. https://tradingeconomics.com/japan/government-debt-to-gdp
Center for Strategic and Contemporary Policy. Redman, A. *Kishidanomics – The Economic Policies of Fumio Kishida*. https://cscr.pk/explore/themes/politics-governance/kishidanomics-the-economic-policies-of-fumio-kishida/
Foreign Policy. Allison, G. *The Thucydides Trap*. https://foreignpolicy.com/2017/06/09/the-thucydides-trap/
Amazon.com. Schwab, K. *The Fourth Industrial Revolution*. https://www.amazon.com/Fourth-Industrial-Revolution-Klaus-Schwab/dp/1524758868
Exploding Topics. *How Many Cryptocurrencies Are There in Circulation in 2023?* https://explodingtopics.com/blog/number-of-cryptocurrencies
Hedera. *What Is Decentralized Finance (DeFi)*. https://hedera.com/learning/decentralized-finance/what-is-decentralized-finance
Hedera. *What Is a Central Bank Digital Currency (CBDC)?* https://hedera.com/learning/tokens/what-is-a-central-bank-digital-currency-cbdc

International Monetary Fund. *Countering the Cost-of-Living Crisis*. https://www.imf.org/en/Publications/WEO/Issues/2022/10/11/world-economic-outlook-october-2022

Bloomberg News. Politics. Economics. *Japan's Kishida Set to Stay on Kuroda Path, Party Official Says*. https://www.bloomberg.com/news/articles/2022-06-05/japan-s-kishida-set-to-stay-on-kuroda-path-party-official-says

European Council on Foreign Relations (ECFR). *MAGA Goes Global: Trump's Plan for Europe*. https://ecfr.eu/publication/maga-goes-global-trumps-plan-for-europe/

MEDIUM. *TRUMP: The First MMT President*. https://medium.com/@kevin_640/trump-the-first-mmt-president-9df44bd0784d

Economic History. *Important Turning Points*. https://quizlet.com/185448957/economic-history-important-turning-points-flash-cards/

The Library of Economics and Liberty. Henderson, D.R. *German Economic Miracle*. https://www.econlib.org/library/Enc/GermanEconomicMiracle.html

Euro American Forum. *Open Integration: The European Union and the Mercosur and the International System*.

The European Journal of the History of Economic Thought. Volume 1. 1993- Issue 1. https://www.tandfonline.com/action/doSearch?AllField=1993%2C+Volume+1%2C+Issue+1&SeriesKey=rejh20

International Encyclopedia of the First World War. Dietmar, R. *Post-War Economies*. https://encyclopedia.1914-1918-online.net/article/post-war_economies

Treaty of Versailles/Part VIII. Article 231. https://en.wikisource.org/wiki/Treaty_of_Versailles/Part_VIII#Article_232

US Government. US Office of the Historian. *Milestones: 1921–1936. The Dawes Plan, the Young Plan, German Reparations, and Inter-Allied War Debts*. https://history.state.gov/milestones/1921-1936/dawes

Encyclopedia Britannica. *The Great Depression*. https://www.britannica.com/event/Great-Depression

The History of Economic Thought. *The Socialist Calculation Debate*. http://www.hetwebsite.net/het/essays/paretian/socialcalc.htm

Library of Liberty. *Mises on 'Interventionism' as a Third Way between the Free Market and Socialism (1930)*. http://oll.libertyfund.org/quotes/529

Gettysburg College. Gettysburg Economic Review. Volume 5. Article 6. Elliott, C.A. *Friedrich von Hayek: The Socialist-Calculation Debate, Knowledge Arguments, and Modern Economic Development*. https://pdfs.semanticscholar.org/8429/f1327b10c7c389c46f825a46dc52dc8b5a13.pdf

Vanberg, V.J. *Ordoliberalism and Ordnugspolitik: A Brief Explanation*. https://www.eucken.de/wp-content/uploads/Ordoliberalism-and-Ordnungspolitik.pdf

Freiburg. Albert-Ludwigs-Universität. http://www.uni-freiburg.de/

Biografías y Vidas. *Gustav Schmoller*. https://www.biografiasyvidas.com/biografia/s/schmoller.htm

Ordoliberalism and the Austrian School. *Is Ordoliberalism Cyclical?*. https://ordoliberalism.wordpress.com/is-ordoliberalism-cyclical/

Ludwig von Mises Institute. Hülsmann, J.G. *Against the Neoliberals*. https://mises.org/library/against-neoliberals

Butler, E. *A Short History of the Mont Pelerin Society*. http://rybn.org/thegreatoffshore/THE%20GREAT%20OFFSHORE/1.ENCYCLOPEDIA/MONT%20PELERIN%20SOCIETY,%201947/DOCS/A%20SHORT%20HISTORY%20OF%20THE%20MONT%20PELERIN%20SOCIETY%20By%20Eamonn%20Butler.pdf

The Concise Encyclopedia of Economics. *Austrian School of Economics*. http://www.econlib.org/library/Enc/AustrianSchoolofEconomics.html
The Economic Review. *Chicago School vs Austrian School: Battle of Free-Marketeers*. https://theeconomicreview.wordpress.com/2011/09/24/chicago-school-vs-austrian-school-battle-of-the-free-marketeers/
71 Republic. *The Difference between Austrian and Chicago Economics*. https://71republic.com/2018/10/21/difference-austrian-chicago-economics/
The Mont Pelerin Society. *F.A. Hayek*. https://www.montpelerin.org/how-to-join-mps-3/
Exploring Economics. *Austrian Economics*. https://www.exploring-economics.org/en/orientation/austrian-economics/
IESE Business School – Universidad de Navarra. Argandoña, A. *El Pensamiento Económico de Friedman*. www.iese.edu/research/pdfs/di-0193.pdf
Foundation for Economic Education. *Milton Friedman and the Chicago School of Economics*. https://fee.org/articles/milton-friedman-and-the-chicago-school-of-economics/
Investopedia. *Chicago School*. https://www.investopedia.com/terms/c/chicago_school.asp
The London School of Economics and Political Science. LSE Research Online. Venugopal, R. *Neoliberalism as Concept*. http://eprints.lse.ac.uk/60471/1/__lse.ac.uk_storage_LIBRARY_Secondary_libfile_shared_repository_Content_Venugopal%2C%20R_Neoliberalism%20as%20concept_Venugopal_Neoliberalism%20as%20concept_2015.pdf
Kemeny, P.J. *The Decline of Ordoliberal Influence in the Mont Pelerin Collective. Röpke's Occident, the 'Hunold Affair' and the Rise of the Chicago School*. https://ordoliberalism.wordpress.com/2016/02/29/the-decline-of-ordoliberal-influence-in-the-mont-pelerin-collective-ropkes-occident-the-hunold-affair-and-the-rise-of-the-chicago-school/
Sage Journals. Politics and Society. Volume 52. 2024. Laruffa, F. *Making Sense of (Post) Neoliberalism*, pgs 586–629. https://journals.sagepub.com/doi/pdf/10.1177/00323292231193805
The Daily Economy. 11 December, 2018. Magness, P. *The Pejorative Origins of the Term 'Neoliberalism'*. https://thedailyeconomy.org/article/the-pejorative-origins-of-the-term-neoliberalism/
Handelsblatt. *Ordoliberalism and the Alleged Aberration of German Economics*. https://www.handelsblatt.com/today/politics/handelsblatt-explains-ordoliberalism-and-the-alleged-aberration-of-german-economics/23580920.html?ticket=ST-3657522-kxBeT1BaNXhvC07KqeZR-ap5
Social Europe. Wren-Lewis, S. *Ordoliberalism, Neoliberalism and Economics*. https://www.socialeurope.eu/ordoliberalism-neoliberalism-economics
Near Futures. Biebricher, T. *Return or Revival: The Ordoliberal Legacy*. http://nearfuturesonline.org/return-or-revival-the-ordoliberal-legacy/
Bonefeld, W. *Freedom and the Strong State: On German Ordoliberalism*. https://www.tandfonline.com/doi/abs/10.1080/13563467.2012.656082
European Review of International Studies, 2. Bonefeld, W. *Crisis, Free Economy and Strong State: On Ordoliberalism*, pgs 5–14. https://pure.york.ac.uk/portal/en/publications/crisis-free-economy-and-strong-state-on-ordoliberalism
Qeios. Review Article. 21 June 2023. Gabrish, H. *Neoliberalism, Strong State and Democracy*. https://www.qeios.com/read/EEDNVQ.2/pdf
African Journal of Political Science and International Relations. Volume 15. October–December 2021. Gebeyaw Tareke, S. *From the End of History to the End of*

Neo-liberalism: From Fukuyama to Fukuyama, pgs 139–47. https://academicjournals.org/journal/AJPSIR/article-full-text-pdf/15EFAA367996
Nedergaard, P. *The Influence of Ordoliberalism in European Integration Processes – A Framework for Ideational Influence with Competition Policy and the Economic and Monetary Policy as Examples.* https://mpra.ub.uni-muenchen.de/52331/1/MPRA_paper_52331.pdf
Ludwig von Mises Institute. Bagus, P. *Why Austrians Are Not Neoliberals.* https://mises.org/library/why-austrians-are-not-neoliberals
71 Republic. *The Difference between Austrian and Chicago Economics.* https://71republic.com/2018/10/21/difference-austrian-chicago-economics/
The Economic Review. Chicago School vs Austrian School: Battle of Free-Marketeers. https://theeconomicreview.wordpress.com/2011/09/24/chicago-school-vs-austrian-school-battle-of-the-free-marketeers/
Ludwig von Mises Institute. Huerta de Soto, J. *The Difference between Austrians and Everyone Else – In One Easy Chart.* https://mises.org/wire/difference-between-austrians-and-everyone-else-%E2%80%94-one-easy-chart
Reason.com. Sennholz, H. *Chicago Monetary Tradition in the Light of Austrian Theory.* https://reason.com/1971/10/01/chicago-monetary-tradition-in
Tribe, K. *Ordoliberalism and the Social Market Economy.* https://jshet.net/old/annals/het47-50/4901/tribe4901.pdf
Free Market Quotes. Magness, P.W. https://www.goodreads.com/quotes/tag/free-market?page=
George Mason University. Mercatus Center. *Economic Recovery: Lessons from the Post-World War II Period.* https://www.mercatus.org/publication/economic-recovery-lessons-post-world-war-ii-period
Plaid.com. Antosz, D. *What Is a Neobank? How Fintech Is Transforming Banking.* https://plaid.com/resources/fintech/what-is-a-neobank/#:~:text=A%20neobank%20is%20a%20digital,challenger%20bank%2C%20or%20digital%20bank
Pilling, J. *Reactions to the Crisis of Keynesianism.* https://www.marxists.org/archive/pilling/works/keynes/ch01.htm
Toussaint, E. *The Keynesian Revolution and the Neo-Liberal Counter-Revolution.* https://www.globalresearch.ca/the-keynesian-revolution-and-the-neo-liberal-counter-revolution/14376
The Bretton Woods Project. *What Are the Bretton Woods Institutions?* https://www.brettonwoodsproject.org/2019/01/art-320747/
Elsevier. Investigación Económica. Palley, T.I. *Economía y Economía Política de Friedman: Una Critica desde el Viejo Keynesianismo.* https://www.elsevier.es/es-revista-investigacion-economica-122-pdf-S0185166714709178
Forba. Forba Discussion Paper 3/2007. Hermann, C. *Neoliberalism in the European Union.* http://www.forschungsnetzwerk.at/downloadpub/neoliberalism_eu_SR%2003-07.pdf
Journal of Economic Perspectives. Volume 26. Number 3. Lane, P. *The European Sovereign Debt Crisis.* https://pubs.aeaweb.org/doi/pdfplus/10.1257/jep.26.3.49
Investopedia. *European Sovereign Debt Crisis.* https://www.investopedia.com/terms/e/european-sovereign-debt-crisis.asp;
The Balance. *The Eurozone Crisis: Causes and Potential Solutions.* https://www.thebalance.com/the-eurozone-crisis-causes-and-potential-solutions-1978970

The Balance. *What Is the European Debt Crisis?* https://www.thebalance.com/what-is-the-european-debt-crisis-416918

The World Bank. Primo Braga, C.A., Vincelette, G.A. (Eds). *Sovereign Debt and the Financial Crisis. Will This Time Be Different?* http://documents.worldbank.org/curated/en/217391468151502378/pdf/Sovereign-debt-and-the-financial-crisis-will-this-time-be-different.pdf

Scielo. Weber, C. *La Euro Crisis: Causas y Síntomas.* http://www.scielo.org.mx/scielo.php?script=sci_arttext&pid=S0187-69612015000200009

Borrell Fontelles, J. *Euro Crisis Timeline.* https://www.ucm.es/data/cont/docs/518-2015-04-15-TIMELINE%20OCT%202009%20MAYO%202013_ampliado.pdf

The Lisbon Council. Think Tank for the Future. *The 2011 Euro Plus Monitor: Progress amid the Turmoil.* http://www.lisboncouncil.net/publication/publication/68-the-2011-euro-plus-monitor.html

European Voice. *Spain Seeks to Reassure EU Leaders.* https://www.politico.eu/article/spain-seeks-to-reassure-eu-leaders/

Borrell Fontelles, J. *Euro Crisis Timeline.* https://www.ucm.es/data/cont/docs/518-2015-04-15-TIMELINE%20OCT%202009%20MAYO%202013_ampliado.pdf

European Stability Mechanism. https://www.esm.europa.eu/

International Journal of Youth Economy. Akala, I. *The Euro-zone Financial Crisis: Causes, Consequences and Policy Responses.* http://www.naturalspublishing.com/files/published/3zl7oij137v39s.pdf

Rodriguez-Sickert, C. *Homo Economicus.* https://complejidadsocial.udd.cl/wp-content/uploads/2012/05/Homo-economicus-Handbook-E.Elgar_.pdf

European Stability Mechanism. Financial Assistance. *Spain.* https://www.esm.europa.eu/assistance/spain#spain:_a_fast_and_effective_programme

Tatum. *Reestructuración del Mapa Financiero Español.* http://www.gref.org/nuevo/articulos/art_131211.pdf

Nueva Tribuna.es. Barra Galan, C. *Gobierno de Progreso en Tiempos Inciertos.* https://www.nuevatribuna.es/articulo/actualidad/gobierno-progreso-tiempos-inciertos-psoe-pedro-sanchez/20231120105238219729.html

New Statesman. Cliffe, J. *Spain's New Government Could Play an Outsized European Role.* https://www.newstatesman.com/world/europe/2020/01/spain-s-new-government-could-play-outsized-european-role

Statista. Statista Research Department. *Principales Bancos en España tras las Fusiones Bancarias planeadas en 2020.* https://es.statista.com/estadisticas/1188317/ranking-principales-entidades-bancarias-tras-fusiones-bancarias-espana-segun-volumen-activos/

Biblioteca Virtual de Derecho, Economía y Ciencias Sociales. *Consenso de Washington.* http://www.eumed.net/libros-gratis/2007a/252/9.htm

New Voices in Public Policy. Symoniac, J.D. *The Washington Consensus.* http://journals.gmu.edu/newvoices/article/viewFile/14/14

Odio-Ayala, M.M. *Enfoques Principales del Neoestructuralismo como Corriente del Pensamiento Económico Latinoamericano.* www.ojs.uo.edu.cu/index.php/aeco/article/download/674/648

Observatorio de Multinacionales en América Latina. *Neoextractivismo.* http://omal.info/spip.php?article4847

Notimérica.com. *Bolivia, a la cabeza del crecimiento económico en Iberoamérica este 2019.* https://www.notimerica.com/economia/noticia-bolivia-cabeza-crecimiento-economico-iberoamerica-2019-20190410143507.html

Universidad Nacional Siglo XX. Centro de Altos Estudios Nacionales Federico Ahlfeld. *Bolivia Frente al Modelo Neoliberal.* http://cadimavictor.blogspot.com.es/

Estado Plurinacional de Bolivia. Ministerio de Economía y Finanzas Públicas. *El Nuevo Modelo Económico en Bolivia.* http://medios.economiayfinanzas.gob.bo/MH/documentos/DC_interes/Pres._Nuevo_mod_econ_MinEmbBrit_final_vr_%2830.03.10%29.pdf

Estado Plurinacional de Bolivia. Ministerio de Economía y Finanzas Públicas. *El Nuevo Modelo Económico en Bolivia.* http://medios.economiayfinanzas.gob.bo/MH/documentos/DC_interes/Pres._Nuevo_mod_econ_MinEmbBrit_final_vr_%2830.03.10%29.pdf

Senape. *Rendición de Cuentas Parcial. 5 de octubre 2011.* http://www.senape.gob.bo/docs/rendicion-cuentas-pre.pdf

Banco Mundial. *Banco Mundial- Socios de Bolivia- Alianza Estratégica con el País 2012–2015.* http://www-wds.worldbank.org/external/default/WDSContentServer/WDSP/IB/2012/03/09/000386194_20120309024133/Rendered/PDF/651080SPANISH00ianza0print0digital0.pdf

Gobierno de Bolivia. Ministerio de Economía y Finanzas Públicas. *Balance de la Economía Boliviana 2016.* http://www.economiayfinanzas.gob.bo/index.php?opcion=com_contenido&ver=contenido&id=3809&id_item=774&seccion=269&categoria=1576

Notimérica.com. *Bolivia, a la cabeza del crecimiento económico en Iberoamérica este 2019.* https://www.notimerica.com/economia/noticia-bolivia-cabeza-crecimiento-economico-iberoamerica-2019-20190410143507.html

El Español.com. *Las seis grandes 'nacionalizaciones' de empresas españolas en América Latina.* http://www.elespanol.com/economia/empresas/20161115/170983362_0.html

BBC News. Miranda, B. *Arce, nuevo presidente de Bolivia: 4 desafíos del exministro de Evo Morales (y qué papel jugará su antiguo jefe).* https://www.bbc.com/mundo/noticias-america-latina-54831871

Alianza del Pacífico. *Abecé. Alianza del Pacífico.* https://alianzapacifico.net/?wpdmdl=4441

Alianza del Pacifico. *Alianza del Pacífico Visión 2030.* https://alianzapacifico.net/download-category/alianza-del-pacifico-proyeccion-2030/

BBC.com. News Mundo. 18 Agust 2025. Amerise, A.; Oliva, A. *El Senador Rodrigo Paz y el expresidente Quiroga se Disputarán la Presidencia de Bolivia en segunda vuelta, poniendo fin a 20 Años de Gobierno del MAS.* https://www.bbc.com

Cepal. *La Unión Europea y América Latina y el Caribe: Estrategias Convergentes y Sostenibles ante la Coyuntura Global.* https://repositorio.cepal.org/bitstream/handle/11362/43740/6/S1800903_es.pdf

Política Exterior. *Las Inversiones españolas en América Latina en el periodo 2009–2016.* http://www.politicaexterior.com/articulos/economia-exterior/las-inversiones-directas-espanolas-en-america-latina-en-el-periodo-2009-16/

Dirigentesdigital.com. *Aumenta la Inversión Española en América Latina.* https://dirigentesdigital.com/hemeroteca/aumenta_la_inversion_espanola_en_america_latina-DPDD72948

Notimérica. *¿Cuáles son los nuevos acuerdos firmados entre Bolivia y Rusia?.* https://www.notimerica.com/politica/noticia-cuales-son-nuevos-acuerdos-firmados-bolivia-rusia-20190712171021.html

Ryner, M. *Europe's Ordoliberal Iron Cage: Critical Political Economy, the Euro Area Crisis and Its Management.* https://www.semanticscholar.org/paper/Europe%27s-ordoliberal-iron-cage%3A-critical-political-Ryner/db0d9f47d024e4ab13910fd512b10f333615c2cc

EU Law Analysis. Costa, M. *The EU's Financial Supervisory Authorities: Mind the Accountability Gap*. http://eulawanalysis.blogspot.com/2014/01/the-eus-financial-supervisory.html

European Commission. *European System of Financial Supervision*. https://ec.europa.eu/info/business-economy-euro/banking-and-finance/financialsupervision-and-risk-management/european-system-financial-supervision_en

European Commission. *The EU's Economic Governance Explained*. https://ec.europa.eu/info/business-economy-euro/economic-and-fiscal-policy-coordination/eu-economic-governance-monitoring-prevention-correction/european-semester/framework/eus-economic-governance-explained_en

European Parliament. *Review of the 'Six-pack' and 'Two-pack'*. http://www.europarl.europa.eu/EPRS/EPRS-AaG-542182-Review-six-pack-two-pack-FINAL.pdf

Eur-Lex. *European Council Decision of 25 March 2011 Amending Article 136 of the Treaty on the Functioning of the European Union with Regard to a Stability Mechanism for Member States Whose Currency Is the Euro*. https://eur-lex.europa.eu/legal-content/en/ALL/?uri=CELEX%3A32011D0199

Citizens Information. *Summary of the Fiscal Stability Treaty*. https://web.archive.org/web/20120603055020/http://www.citizensinformation.ie/en/government_in_ireland/european_government/fiscal_stability_treaty/fiscal_treaty_summary.html

European Central Bank. Banking Supervision. *Banking Union*. https://www.bankingsupervision.europa.eu/about/bankingunion/html/index.en.html

European Parliament. Fact Sheets of the European Union. *Banking Union*. http://www.europarl.europa.eu/factsheets/en/sheet/88/banking-union

European Central Bank. Banking Supervision. *Single Supervisory Mechanism*. https://www.bankingsupervision.europa.eu/about/thessm/html/index.en.html

European Central Bank. Banking Supervision. *Single Resolution Mechanism*. https://www.bankingsupervision.europa.eu/about/bankingunion/html/index.en.html

White and Case. Financial Regulatory Observer – June 2019. *EU Banking Reforms Imminent*. https://www.whitecase.com/publications/insight/eu-banking-reforms-imminent

Nedergaard, P. *The Influence of Ordoliberalism in European Integration Processes – A Framework for Ideational Influence with Competition Policy and the Economic and Monetary Policy as Examples*. https://mpra.ub.uni-muenchen.de/52331/1/MPRA_paper_52331.pdf

Eui Working Papers. Department of Law. Hien, J.; Joerges, C. *Dead Man Walking: Current Interest in the Ordoliberal Tradition*. https://cadmus.eui.eu/bitstream/handle/1814/51226/LAW_2018_03.pdf?sequence=1

White Rose Research Online. Critical Sociology. Bonefeld, W. *Ordoliberalism, European Monetary Union and State Power*. http://eprints.whiterose.ac.uk/141922/2/_system_appendPDF_proof_hi.pdf

European Central Bank. *Building on the Achievements of Post-Crisis Reforms*. https://www.ecb.europa.eu/press/key/date/2017/html/ecb.sp170921.en.html

Federal Ministry of Finance. *Ten Years after the Financial Crisis: Have Regulatory Reforms Made the Financial Sector More Resilient to Crisis?* https://www.bundesfinanzministerium.de/Content/EN/Standardartikel/Topics/Financial_markets/Articles/2019-04-15-ten-years-financial-crisis.html

EPP Group in the European Parliament. *Banking Reform*. https://www.eppgroup.eu/what-we-stand-for/campaigns/eu-elections-2019/achievements/achievement/banking-reform

European Parliament. *Establishment of a European Monetary Fund (EMF).* http://www.europarl.europa.eu/RegData/etudes/BRIE/2019/635556/EPRS_BRI(2019)635556_EN.pdf

European Commission. Newsroom. *Policy in Focus: European Deposit Insurance Scheme (EDIS).* https://ec.europa.eu/newsroom/fisma/items/27568/en

Alternet.org. Atcheson, J. *Neoliberalism Is Dead – but the Neoliberal Elite still Haven't Gotten the Memo.* https://www.alternet.org/2019/06/neoliberalism-is-dead-but-the-neoliberal-elite-still-havent-gotten-the-memo/

The Guardian. Stiglitz, J. *Neoliberalism Must Be Pronounced Dead and Buried. Where Next?* https://www.theguardian.com/business/2019/may/30/neoliberalism-must-be-pronouced-dead-and-buried-where-next

Monthly Review. Patnaik, U.; Patnaik, P. *Neoliberal Capitalism at a Dead End.* https://monthlyreview.org/2019/07/01/neoliberal-capitalism-at-a-dead-end/

David Harvey.org. Harvey, D. *The Persistence of Neoliberalism Despite Its Loss of Legitimacy.* http://davidharvey.org/2019/07/video-david-harvey-the-persistence-of-neoliberalism-despite-its-loss-of-legitimacy-real-news-network/

Medium.com. *Trump: The First MMT President.* https://medium.com/@kevin_640/trump-the-first-mmt-president-9df44bd0784d

The White House. https://www.whitehouse.gov/administration/donald-j-trump/

The White House. Fact Sheet. 3 July 2025. *President Trump Establishes Make America Beautiful Again Commission.* https://www.whitehouse.gov/fact-sheets/2025/07/fact-sheet-president-donald-j-trump-establishes-make-america-beautiful-again-commission/

Bloomberg Government. Insights. *A Guide to Immigration Policy Changes in 2025.* https://about.bgov.com/insights/federal-policy/a-guide-to-immigration-policy-changes-in-2025/

BBC News. 3 July 2025. *Congress Passes Trump's 'Big, Beautiful Bill' Cutting Taxes and Spending.* https://www.bbc.com/news/articles/cddz3n6vz0go

CNN Business. 4 July 2025. *Here's Who Stands to Gain from the 'Big, Beautiful Bill'. And Who May Struggle.* https://edition.cnn.com/2025/07/03/business/trump-big-beautiful-bill-business-economy

The White House. Fact Sheets. 18 July 2025. *President Donald J. Trump Signs GENIUS Act into Law.* https://www.whitehouse.gov/fact-sheets/2025/07/fact-sheet-president-donald-j-trump-signs-genius-act-into-law/

Investopedia.com. Hyatt, D. *What Has the US Gained from Trump's Trade Wars? It's Still up in the Air.* https://www.investopedia.com/evaluating-trump-s-trade-wars-what-has-the-us-gained-and-what-are-the-economic-costs-11793126

As.com. Martin Sanjuan, L. *Los Aranceles de Trump entran en Vigor: la Lista con los Países que más van a Pagar y los que menos desde el 7 de agosto.* https://as.com/actualidad/politica/los-aranceles-de-trump-entran-en-vigor-la-lista-con-los-paises-que-mas-van-a-pagar-y-los-que-menos-desde-el-7-de-agosto-n/

Cato Institute. Coats, W. *Modern Monetary Theory: A Critique.* https://www.cato.org/publications/cato-journal/modern-monetary-theory-critique

The New York Times. Modern Monetary Theory Finds an Embrace in an Unexpected Place: Wall Street. https://www.nytimes.com/2019/04/05/business/economy/mmt-wall-street.html

Bloomberg News. *Draghi Says ECB Should Examine New Ideas Like MMT*. https://www.bloomberg.com/news/articles/2019-09-23/draghi-says-ecb-should-examine-new-ideas-like-mmt

World Economic Forum. *Does Japan Vindicate Modern Monetary Theory?*. https://www.weforum.org/agenda/2019/07/japans-answer-to-economic-deficit/

Nomura. Economic Research View. Matsumoto, A. *Mr. Shigeru Ishiba Becomes the New Prime Minister*. https://www.google.es/url?sa=t&source=web&rct=j&opi=89978449&url=https://global.nomura-am.co.jp/latestnews/pdf/ecv20240930.pdf&ved=2ahUKEwiu9ZXkt6aPAxWbVqQEHWrNMa8Q FnoECBUQAQ&usg=AOvVaw1I5z8mui1ta6wPvjg1wes5

The Week. Dougherty, M.B. *A New Nationalism Is Rising. Don't Let Donald Trump Destroy It*. https://theweek.com/articles/638440/new-nationalism-rising-dont-let-donald-trump-destroy

Npr.org. Detrow, S. *From Brexit to Trump, Nationalist Movements Gain Momentum around World*. https://www.npr.org/2016/06/25/483400958/from-brexit-to-trump-nationalist-movements-gain-momentum-around-world

Law and Liberty. Movsesian, M. *The New Nationalism*. https://www.lawliberty.org/2016/12/08/the-new-nationalism/

National Review. Brog, D.; Hazony, Y. *The Nationalist Spirit of 2016: A Conservative Spring*. https://www.nationalreview.com/2016/12/conservatives-nationalists-2106-brexit-donald-trump-internationalism/

The Conversation. Postel-Vinay, K. *How Neo-Nationalism Went Global*. https://theconversation.com/how-neo-nationalism-went-global-74095

Global Research. Fotopoupulos, T. *Globalisation, Rise of Neo-Nationalism and the Bankruptcy of the Left*. https://www.globalresearch.ca/globalization-the-massive-rise-of-neo-nationalism-and-the-bankruptcy-of-the-left/5527157

Chron.org. Teeboom, L. *Free Trade vs Protectionism*. https://smallbusiness.chron.com/trade-vs-protectionism-3830.html

Peterson Institute for International Economics. Noland, M. *Protectionism under Trump: Policy, Identity, and Anxiety*. https://www.piie.com/experts/senior-research-staff/marcus-noland

Peterson Institute for International Economics. Noland, M. *Protectionism under Trump: The China Shock, Intolerance, and the First 'White President'*. https://www.piie.com/system/files/documents/wp19-10.pdf

The White House. Economy and Jobs. *Remarks by President Trump at a Signing Ceremony for the United States-Mexico-Canada Trade Agreement*. https://www.whitehouse.gov/briefings-statements/remarks-president-trump-signing-ceremony-united-states-mexico-canada-trade-agreement/

The Tax Foundation. York, E. *Tracking the Economic Impact of U.S. Tariffs and Retaliatory Actions*. https://taxfoundation.org/tariffs-trump-trade-war/

The New York Times. *Trump Signs China Trade Deal, Putting Economic Conflict on Pause*. https://www.nytimes.com/2020/01/15/business/economy/china-trade-deal.html

Politico.com. *Here's What's in the US-China Trade Deal*. https://www.politico.com/news/2020/01/15/what-is-in-us-china-trade-deal-099399

El Economista. Opinión. Olier, E. *COVID-19: Estados Unidos y China*. https://www.eleconomista.es/opinion-blogs/noticias/10483363/04/20/Covid19-Estados-Unidos-y-China.html

Fondo Monetario Internacional. *Perspectivas de la Economía Mundial – Abril 2020. Introducción y Resumen Ejecutivo*. https://www.imf.org/es/Publications/WEO/Issues/2020/04/14/weo-april-2020

FatCheck.org. *Trump's Numbers. January 2020 Update*. https://www.factcheck.org/2020/01/trumps-numbers-january-2020-update/

Brookings. Jones, B. *The New Geopolitics*. https://www.brookings.edu/blog/order-from-chaos/2017/11/28/the-new-geopolitics/

The New York Times. Stiglitz, J. *Progressive Capitalism Is Not an Oxymoron*. https://www.nytimes.com/2019/04/19/opinion/sunday/progressive-capitalism.html

Bresser-Pereira, L.C. *The Two Forms of Capitalism: Developmentalism and Economic Liberalism*. http://www.rep.org.br/PDF/149-2.PDF

The Bulwark. North Paterson, R. *The Case for Progressive Capitalism*. https://thebulwark.com/the-case-for-progressive-capitalism/

The New York Times. Stiglitz, J. *Progressive Capitalism Is Not an Oxymoron*. https://www.nytimes.com/2019/04/19/opinion/sunday/progressive-capitalism.html

The Bulwark. North Paterson, R. *The Case for Progressive Capitalism*. https://thebulwark.com/the-case-for-progressive-capitalism/

The White House. Economy. *Remarks by President Trump at a Signing Ceremony for the United States-Mexico-Canada Trade Agreement*. https://www.whitehouse.gov/briefings-statements/remarks-president-trump-signing-ceremony-united-states-mexico-canada-trade-agreement/

Foreign Policy. Campanellla, E. *Free Trade Is Over*. https://foreignpolicy.com/2020/11/05/protectionism-trump-biden-buy-american-tariffs/

South China Morning Post. US-China Relations. Zhen, L. *US-China Trade War: Joe Biden Hints He Will Keep up Pressure on Beijing with Pledge to Fight 'Unfair Trade Practices'.* https://www.scmp.com/news/china/diplomacy/article/3113726/us-china-trade-war-joe-biden-hints-he-will-keep-pressure

Fox Business. *How Progressive Capitalism Can Be the Recipe for Economic Growth and Innovation*. https://www.foxbusiness.com/politics/progressive-capitalism-is-the-recipe-for-economic-growth-and-innovation-california-rep-ro-khanna

Columbia Business School. Stiglitz, J. *Has Davos Man Changed?* https://www8.gsb.columbia.edu/articles/chazen-global-insights/has-davos-man-changed

World Economic Forum. *Chief Economists Outlook 2021*. http://www3.weforum.org/docs/WEF_Chief_Economists_Outlook_2021.pdf

World Finance. *Modern Monetary Theory Gains Traction in the US*. https://www.worldfinance.com/markets/modern-monetary-theory-continues-to-gain-traction

Bloomberg. *Stephanie Kelton, Modern Monetary Theory Evangelist*. https://www.bloomberg.com/news/articles/2019-12-04/stephanie-kelton-is-the-modern-monetary-theory-mmt-evangelist

Cato Institute. Coats, W. *Modern Monetary Theory: A Critique*. https://www.cato.org/publications/cato-journal/modern-monetary-theory-critique

Nikkei Asian Review. Tasker, P. *Modern Monetary Theory Threatens Revolution in Economic Thinking*. https://asia.nikkei.com/Opinion/Modern-Monetary-Theory-threatens-revolution-in-economic-thinking

Stony Brook University. College of Arts and Sciences. *Dr. Stephanie Kelton Recruited to Work on Biden/Sanders Economy Unity Task Force*. https://www.stonybrook.edu/commcms/cas/news/facultynews/SKeltonTaskForce.php

Fulweiller, S.T. *Modern Monetary Theory – A Primer on the Operational Realities of the Monetary System*. https://ssrn.com/abstract=1723198 or http://dx.doi.org/10.2139/ssrn.1723198

Levy Economics Institute. Tymoigne, E.; Wray, R. *Modern Money Theory 101: A Reply to Critics*. http://www.levyinstitute.org/pubs/wp_778.pdf

Mosler, W. *Soft Currency Economics*. http://moslereconomics.com/wp-content/uploads/2018/04/Soft-Curency-Economics-paper.pdf

Arestis, P.; Sawyer, M.C. (Eds). *A Handbook of Alternative Monetary Economics*. https://econpapers.repec.org/bookchap/elgeechap/3506_5f5.htm

Bloomberg. Kelton, S. *Paul Krugman Asked Me about Modern Monetary Theory. Here Are 4 Answers*. https://www.bloomberg.com/opinion/articles/2019-03-01/paul-krugman-s-four-questions-about-mmt;

Bloomberg. Kelton, S. *The Clock Runs Down on Keynesianism*. https://www.bloomberg.com/opinion/articles/2019-03-04/krugman-s-macroeconomics-is-no-match-for-mmt

The New York Times. Krugman, P. *Deficits and the Printing Press (Somewhat Wonkish)*. https://krugman.blogs.nytimes.com/2011/03/25/deficits-and-the-printing-press-somewhat-wonkish/

Cato Institute. Coats, W. *Modern Monetary Theory: A Critique*. https://www.cato.org/publications/cato-journal/modern-monetary-theory-critique

World Finance. *Modern Monetary Theory Gains Traction in the US*. https://www.worldfinance.com/markets/modern-monetary-theory-continues-to-gain-traction

The New York Times. *Modern Monetary Theory Finds an Embrace in an Unexpected Place: Wall Street*. https://www.nytimes.com/2019/04/05/business/economy/mmt-wall-street.html

World Economic Forum. *Does Japan Vindicate Modern Monetary Theory?*. https://www.weforum.org/agenda/2019/07/japans-answer-to-economic-deficit/

Bloomberg News. *Draghi Says ECB Should Examine New Ideas Like MMT*. https://www.bloomberg.com/news/articles/2019-09-23/draghi-says-ecb-should-examine-new-ideas-like-mmt

Investopedia. Economy. Government and Policy. *Modern Monetary Theory (MMT)*. https://www.investopedia.com/modern-monetary-theory-mmt-4588060

The New York Times. *Modern Monetary Theory Finds an Embrace in an Unexpected Place: Wall Street*. https://www.nytimes.com/2019/04/05/business/economy/mmt-wall-street.html

Nikkei Asian Review. Tasker, P. *Modern Monetary Theory Threatens Revolution in Economic Thinking*. https://asia.nikkei.com/Opinion/Modern-Monetary-Theory-threatens-revolution-in-economic-thinking

Bank of Japan. October 2019. *Outlook for Economic Activity and Prices*. https://www.boj.or.jp/en/mopo/outlook/gor1910b.pdf

Trading Economics.com. *Japan General Government Gross Debt to GDP*. https://tradingeconomics.com/japan/government-debt-togdp#:~:text=In%20the%20long%2Dterm%2C%20the,according%20to%20our%20econometric%20models

Global Risks Insights. Arnold-Parra, S. *Suganomics: What Can We Expect?* https://globalriskinsights.com/2020/10/suganomics-what-can-we-expect/

European Center for Populism Studies. Ozturk, I. *Trump and the New Capitalism: Old Wine in New Bottle*. https://www.google.es/search?q=trump+old+wine+in+new+bottles&sca_esv=e7c1514da748dd1c&sxsrf=AE3TifOjDfDVfX2pcHwlupz3BUXmW

BPogg%3A1756126046143&source=hp&ei=XlusaIn2Bca4hbIPnNqN6Ao&iflsig=AOw8s4IAAAAAaKxpbuN4sNcbTAnp_n_w9wGOqCo8naDi&oq=&gs_lp=Egdnd3Mtd2l6IgAqAggAMgcQIxgnGOoCMgcQ IxgnGOoCMgcQIxgnGOoCMg0QIxjwBRgnGMkCGOoCMgcQIxgnGOoCMgcQI xgnGOoCMgcQIxgnGOoCMgcQIxgnGOoCMgcQIxgnGOoCMgcQIxgnGOoCSKkIUABYAHABeACQAQCYAQCgAQCqAQC4AQHIAQ CYAgGgAh6oAgqYAx7xBYdKRgrY6z0okg cBMaAHALIHALgHAMIHAzQtMcgHGA&sclient=gws-wiz

Bank of England. Speech by the Governor of the Bank of England, Mark Carney. Jackson Hole Symposium 2019. *The Growing Challenges for Monetary Policy in the Current International Monetary and Financial System*. https://www.bankofengland.co.uk/speech/2019/mark-carney-speech-at-jackson-hole-economic-symposium-wyoming

The History of Economic Thought. The Keynesian Revolution. *The Real Balances Debate*. http://www.hetwebsite.net/het/essays/keynes/realbalances.htm

Investopedia. *Liquidity Trap*. https://www.investopedia.com/terms/l/liquiditytrap.asp

The Guardian. Elliot, L. *World Economy Is Sleepwalking into a New Financial Crisis, Warns Melvyn King*. https://www.theguardian.com/business/2019/oct/20/world-sleepwalking-to-another-financial-crisis-says-mervyn-king

The Guardian. Elliot, L. *The Sluggish Economy Needs to Reform – And Fast*. https://www.theguardian.com/business/2019/oct/20/the-sluggish-global-economy-needs-to-reform-and-fast

The Guardian. Elliot, L. *World Economy Is Sleepwalking into a New Financial Crisis, Warns Melvyn King*. https://www.theguardian.com/business/2019/oct/20/world-sleepwalking-to-another-financial-crisis-says-mervyn-king

Instituto Español de Estudios Estratégicos. Framework Document. Zurita, A. *China: The Awakening of the Red Dragon*. http://www.ieee.es/en/Galerias/fichero/docs_marco/2016/DIEEEM032016_China_Despertar_DragonRojo_ENGLISH_AlfonsoZurita.pdf

Visual Capitalist. Neufeld, D. *Cryptocurrency: Redefining the Future of Finance*. https://www.visualcapitalist.com/cryptocurrency-redefining-future-of-finance/

Coindesk. Baker, P. *Thailand Already Using Central Bank's Digital Currency*. https://www.coindesk.com/thailand-central-banks-digital-currency

The Street.com. Mish Talk. Mish. *Central Bank Digital Currencies on the Way*. https://www.thestreet.com/mishtalk/economics/central-bank-digital-currencies-on-the-way

Xataca.com. *China Prepara su Criptomoneda Digital Oficial, llamada DC/EP, y Cuatro de sus Bancos ya están Probándola en Móviles*. https://www.xataka.com/empresas-y-economia/china-prepara-su-criptomoneda-digital-oficial-llamada-dc-ep-cuatro-sus-bancos-estan-probandola-moviles

Exploding Topics.com. *How Many Cryptocurrencies Are There in Circulation in 2024?*. https://explodingtopics.com/blog/number-of-cryptocurrencies

Fintechly.com. *Quotes on the Future of Money – What Experts Are Saying*. https://www.imf.org/es/Publications/WEO/Issues/2020/04/14/weo-april-2020, https://fintechly.com/cryptocurrencies/22-quotes-on-the-future-of-money-what-experts-are-saying/

World Economic Forum. Davos 2023. *Davos 2023: What You Need to Know about Doing Better Business*. https://www.weforum.org/agenda/2023/01/better-business-stakeholder-capitalism-esg/

International Monetary Fund. World Economic Outlook. Update. January 2024. *Moderating Inflation and Steady Growth Open Path to Soft Landing*. https://www.imf.org/en/Publications/WEO/Issues/2024/01/30/world-economic-outlook-update-january-2024

Index

Page numbers in italics refer to figures and tables; page numbers followed by n denote endnotes.

www.ingramcontent.com/pod-product-compliance
Ingram Content Group UK Ltd.
Pitfield, Milton Keynes, MK11 3LW, UK
UKHW021055160926
475466UK00010B/72